THE PROCESS OF MANAGEMENT

Concepts, Behavior, and Practice

THE PROCESS OF

THIRD EDITION

MANAGEMENT

Concepts, Behavior, and Practice

WILLIAM H. NEWMAN   *Samuel Bronfman Professor of Democratic Business Enterprise*
Graduate School of Business, Columbia University

CHARLES E. SUMMER   *Professor of Management and Organization*
Graduate School of Business Administration, University of Washington

E. KIRBY WARREN   *Professor of Management*
Graduate School of Business, Columbia University

Prentice-Hall, Inc., Englewood Cliffs, New Jersey

THIRD EDITION

THE PROCESS OF MANAGEMENT

Concepts, Behavior, and Practice

by William H. Newman, Charles E. Summer, and E. Kirby Warren

ISBN: 0–13–723296–9

This book has been composed in Linotype Optima, a modern sans serif
typeface designed by Hermann Zapf, with headings in Optima Semibold
and italic. The typographical design is by John J. Dunleavy.

Prentice-Hall International, Inc., London
Prentice-Hall of Australia, Pty. Ltd., Sydney
Prentice-Hall of Canada, Ltd., Toronto
Prentice-Hall of India Private Ltd., New Delhi
Prentice-Hall of Japan, Inc., Tokyo

10 9 8 7 6 5 4

Preface

Managerial competence is in short supply. Despite greatly increased management training—in universities and in companies—and a marked improvement in management sophistication, the continuing scarcity of competent managers is caused by three major factors:

1) The pressure for higher productivity is undiminished. Urban renewal, antipollution measures, medical care, housing, space exploration, education, aid to developing countries, and similar activities require careful managing of massive flows of goods and services. Also we need higher productivity to satisfy expectations of a rising living standard for a growing population and to check inflation.

2) At the same time, the task of managing is growing in difficulty. We expect our managers to be more sensitive to social needs, to deal with more obstreperous employees and other contributors, to adjust more quickly to changing technology and world competition, and to direct a variety of newly developed quasi-public institutions.

3) Meanwhile, our improved techniques for managing take longer to learn. Research findings, complex "hardware," and more sophisticated concepts sharpen the judgment of managers, but they also require time for retooling.

Because of these pressures the training of future managers is a primary challenge for professional education.

This book has been revised so that it can continue to contribute to the development of managers to meet this vital social need. New features of the book that can be quickly recognized include the following chapters:

Chapter 2—Design of Operating Units. Treats individual job design, small group structure, and large group association as a related progression of design decisions, even though knowledge about behavior at different levels comes from divergent sources.

Chapter 6—New Approaches to Structural Design. Explores opportunities to use matrix organization, external staff, and a president's office. Also considers interest group representation within a company and the impact of computers on organization.

Chapter 9—Conflict in Organizations. Recognizes the inevitability of conflict in a psychological sense and examines the sources of organizational conflict. Distinguishes between constructive and destructive conflict. Suggests organizational arrangements for dealing with conflict.

Chapter 15—Decision-Making in Organizations. Examines the effect of group, instead of individual, performance of each of the four crucial steps in decision-making: (1) diagnosis, (2) finding creative alternatives, (3) forecasting consequences of a proposed action, and (4) making a final choice. Introduces a new concept of credibility structure.

Chapter 28—Strategy and Management Design. Expands the strategy and structure concept (1) by developing the idea of a total management design and (2) by suggesting a way of matching such a management design to company strategies.

Chapter 29—International Management. Focuses on the problem of transferring United States management practices abroad. Provides a basis for comparative management studies and gives a fresh perspective on United States management practices, one that is particularly pertinent in this period of social change.

All the cases are also new. They deal both with small and large companies engaged in various kinds of endeavor, and two have a foreign setting. Because they are sufficiently descriptive, the cases can be used in several ways: case discussion first, followed by study of concepts; text analysis interwoven with cases; concentration on text and outside readings, with the cases being used for review and application. The optimum arrangement will depend on the educational objectives, the time available, and the background that readers bring to the endeavor.

Most of the questions that follow each chapter have been revised and updated. Bibliographies, also found at the end of each chapter, have brief annotations that will help readers pursue areas in which they are particularly interested. The entire manuscript has been carefully edited and revised to keep the discussion and examples relevant to current issues.

Two other features of the revision are quite important, even though they are less evident at first glance. The adaptation of a *total management design* to the needs of each specific enterprise receives repeated attention. Our conviction is that tomorrow's managers will be dealing with diverse and changing enterprises operating with various kinds of technology. In such circumstances ability to adjust the management design to fit new needs and to keep the phases of management integrated will be of crucial importance. Consequently, as each additional subprocess is discussed, we build this theme of matching management design to its particular task.

Also we feel that new research findings and new theory in the behavioral and quantitative areas should be effectively related to the total management job. The history of management is studded with examples of jumping from a fresh insight into action with inadequate attention to the vital intervening stage of synthesis. The sophisticated manager should be aware of this danger. Our belief, a belief that is confirmed by the experience of many successful managers, is that the total complex process of managing must be thoroughly understood before the full potential of new insights can be effectively harnessed.

Therefore, in this revision we have retained the emphasis on the total process but also provide *bridges* to specialized advanced courses. For instance, Chapters 11 to 15, on decision-making, give a useful operational base for decision theory; Chapters 7 to 10 and 20 to 23 are directly related to behavioral research; Chapter 28 provides a behavioral foundation for systems theory; and so on. New ideas will contribute more potently to management effectiveness when they can be promptly related to the total phenomenon of managing.

To aid readers who have limited background in management, a study guide for this revision is available. And for readers who want recent articles that amplify concepts from the text, a fully revised set of readings will be found in the new edition of *The Progress of Management*.

The general structure of the book has been retained. The sequence of parts—starting with the subject of organizing, moving on to planning and then leading, and closing with controlling–is primarily for convenience in exposition. In real life, the phases of managing are closely interrelated, as we stress time and again. But because all aspects of a complex subject cannot be discussed at the same time, we start with the structure of work assignments and then weave in additional elements. Hopefully, we emerge at the end, not with bits and pieces, but with a single fabric.

A book of this character reflects the efforts of a large number of people. We are especially indebted to Raymond Mullaney of Prentice-Hall, Inc., who skillfully edited the manuscript, and to Camilla Koch of Columbia University, who put together from three authors a manuscript that could be edited.

The Samuel Bronfman Foundation, through its support of management studies at the Columbia Graduate School of Business, made the writing of this book possible. We sincerely hope that Mr. Bronfman and the officers of the Foundation find that this tangible evidence of the work they have sustained is in keeping with their deep interest in a virile, productive business system.

Contents

PART TWO   *page 141*

Human Factors in Organizing

Contents

THE PROCESS OF MANAGEMENT

Concepts, Behavior, and Practice

Chapter One

Introduction: Social Role of Managers

THE MISSION OF MANAGEMENT

Modern man's aims and aspirations call for unprecedented cooperative effort. Our capacity to rebuild the slums, to eliminate pollution, to give individuals an opportunity for self-expression, to raise the standard of living, and to achieve our many other social and personal objectives rests on joint activity. If individuals or even tribes attempt to be self-sufficient—producing their own food, clothing, and shelter—subsistence is meager at best. But when men join together in various enterprises, pooling their resources and exchanging their outputs with many other people or enterprises, they grasp the means to flourish.

The job of management is to make such cooperative endeavors function properly. Managers are needed to convert disorganized resources of men, machines, and money into a useful enterprise. Managers conceive of the service an enterprise can render, mobilize the required means of production, coordinate activities both within the enterprise and with the outside world, and inspire people associated with the enterprise to work toward common objectives. Managers are the activating element.

In the past, management concepts have been vigorously applied in private firms, but the need for effective managers is just as pressing in nonprofit enterprises such as hospitals, training centers, space agencies, urban transport, and wildlife refuges. In today's world of increasing specialization, complexity, size, and multinational dependence, the task of achieving coordinated action has intensified.

To understand the significance of managing, let us take a closer look at the role managers play in our society.

Multiple Integration

One key facet of the management job is integration. The successful firm must be integrated externally with its environment and internally among its departments.

External integration. Every enterprise, be it a university or a steel mill, requires continuing give-and-take relationships with an array of contributors. Consumers provide markets, suppliers provide materials and equipment, investors provide capital, local governments provide functioning communities, and so on. Typically, the relationship with each contributor extends over an indefinite period, and benefits flow both ways—to the contributor and to the firm.

Each of these relationships is dynamic. For instance, the amount, specifications, and delivery schedule that a company desires for its raw materials will change as it adjusts to shifting consumer desires. Likewise, a supplier faces his own shifts in costs, other demands, and capacity. Consequently, continuing mediation is needed to maintain a mutually acceptable flow. While the give-and-take between an enterprise and its community or its financial advisor involves intangibles, nevertheless the need for a sustained exchange of benefits is no less vital.

A nonprofit enterprise such as a university has a comparable set of external relationships. It has consumers of its services, providers of funds, suppliers of materials, local community, and a variety of specialized advisors. For survival, the university must attract and retain a continuing flow of inputs from all these contributors.

Management is concerned with more than maintaining good relations with each contributing group separately. In addition, it must make sure that the "price" for cooperation desired by one contributor is com-

Fig. 1–1 Management must maintain viable external relationships. For a lumber company this poses a question of its obligation to replace timber resources.

patible with the requirements of *all* the others. For example, before a manufacturer can promise a customer goods of a certain quality at a specific price for delivery on a given date, he must be sure that the supplier of raw materials will not insist on conditions which hinder him from keeping his promises. A comparable integration issue arises when the college administrator is trying to induce alumni to support financially the kind of education that is appealing to students, and vice versa.

Employees pose a dual integration problem for management: (1) They, like other contributors, must find the satisfactions derived from their association with the enterprise sufficiently attractive to "take the job." At the same time, the inducements provided by the company to employees (such as steady employment, suitable pay, interesting work) must be compatible with necessary inducements to other contributors. (2) In addition, while they are on the job, employees are a volatile element in internal integration—as we shall see in many parts of this book.

Integrating the enterprise externally with its key contributors is a never-ending task. Much more than price negotiations are involved. Dependability, agreement on timing, numerous intangible benefits and inconveniences, predictability, adaptability to needs of either party—all enter the picture. Fortunately, many aspects of these relationships are covered by custom or even by legal regulation; without some such stability cooperative action of diverse groups of people would be impossible. But change is sure to be occurring somewhere in the total system, and adjustments to meet this change are likely to impinge on existing arrangements with other contributors.

Internal integration. If an enterprise is going to fulfill its side of all the agreements it has made with contributors, internal operations must be astutely managed. Here also integration is vital. The actions of various departments must be synchronized—people must be hired and trained so that they are available when needed, and the like. Balance in the allocation of resources and in setting priorities has to be adjusted in terms of external demands. At the same time that such regulating is being pursued, management also must cultivate enthusiasm for achieving the multifold mission of the enterprise.

A vital part of management's task is the integration of the efforts of employees, each of whom has his own values and aspirations, into a company program—the program itself reflecting the pressures of synchronization and of balancing claims for limited resources (all of which is restrained and shaped by arrangements necessary to keep contributors contributing).

Innovation as Well as Adaptation

For many years a manager was widely regarded as a person who merely adapted to his surrounding situation. If demand for his products fell off, he cut back his production; if a new source of low-cost raw materials opened up, he switched suppliers; if labor became scarce, he raised his wage rates to get the workers he needed. According to this conception, a manager performed an essential function—responding to changed conditions—but his actions were dictated by forces beyond his control. The early economists clearly held this view. Consequently, they gave scant attention to the problems of management; in fact, their attitude still permeates much of the literature of economics.

Although some people say that a businessman, especially a commodity trader or stock investor, simply adapts to the opportunities and pressures around him, this is an inadequate description of a modern manager. An effective manager goes beyond adapting; he exercises a positive influence to make things happen. When he anticipates that the need for his product will drop off, the manager seeks new products or services so as to maintain employment of the resources he has mobilized; he takes the initiative in looking for cheaper sources of raw materials and promotes their development; he sponsors research for more economical methods of production; he tries to anticipate his manpower needs and trains people to fill them. In short, he is a dynamic, innovating force.

Sixty British executives who visited the United States for nine months in search for ways to revive their war-devastated economy reported: "If there is one secret above all of the American achievements in productivity, then it is to be found in the attitude of American management." These executives were impressed with an attitude that "seems to engender an aggressive management which believes that methodical planning, energetic training, and enthusiastic work can solve any problem in business . . ." The visitors attribute this viewpoint to four factors:[1]

1) *The spirit of the frontier* has fostered the sense of opportunity that pervades American industrial and community life.

2) *Faith in business and the individual* reflects the high esteem with which the businessman is regarded in the American national community.

3) *The ideal of competition* leads "even those companies which are not operating in a highly competitive market to run their enterprises as though they were. . . . [American managers] know that their firms must maintain their competitive position if they are to provide their people with a continuing career."

4) *Belief in change* prevents a successful experiment from crystallizing into accepted custom, whereas an unsuccessful experiment is accepted as an occupational risk and is set against the experience to be gained.

This self-confident, aggressive attitude reflects a deep-seated sense of obligation, or mission, in a typical manager. He is not complete master of his activities, of course; indeed, he must be highly sensitive to a wide

[1]See *Advanced Management* (October 1955), p. 30.

range of pressures and restrictions. But a manager does more than simply adjust passively. He *initiates* changes in his operating situation and *follows through* with action that, to some extent, makes dreams come true.

Changing Needs of Society

During the past hundred years management attention has been directed primarily to increasing the output of goods and services desired by a growing population. The unprecedented size of our gross national product attests to the success of these efforts.

National priorities are shifting. Now management must deal with new emphases, including:

1) *Individual self-expression.* The rising generation wants meaningful jobs—as well as the fruits of high productivity.

2) *Race and urban problems.* Society must make racial equality meaningful; interwoven with this is urban renewal.

3) *Pollution control.* Our material achievements are fast overtaking the finite capacity of our natural environment, as is painfully evident in the crises of air and water pollution.

4) *Health, education, and welfare.* An ever-increasing share of our natural resources is being directed into such things as medical care, education, public recreation, pensions.

5) *Guns and butter.* Our combined space and military expenditures are already on a scale that challenges our ability to have both guns and butter.

These new priorities affect the managerial task in various ways. The last two listed, health, education, and welfare and guns and butter, continue the high value attached to increasing the output of goods and services. Their major effect will be a sharp rise in the role of nonprofit enterprises; and this emphasizes the urgency of extending our best managerial practice beyond the business corporation.

The race and political issues pose dual tasks for management. Tremendous allocations of resources will be necessary, so the pressure for high productivity continues. In addition, significant adjustments of internal operating practices must be made to provide job opportunities and to preserve our natural resources.

Individual self-expression, the first point listed, is even more a matter of devising new arrangements for internal operations. Job structure, decentralization, freedom versus regulation, and similar issues, which we examine in later chapters, are involved.

Clearly, these new national priorities, and others that will undoubtedly arise, create additional management problems of internal and external integration. They add to the challenge. The task of maintaining workable balances among all the diverse forces calls for a high order of ingenuity, and in contributing to solutions a manager is dealing with social reform at the level of concrete action.

A single executive rarely performs all the managerial tasks we have been discussing (except in a small "one-man" business). Instead, delegation and use of staff allows the total managerial job to be divided among a variety of people as we shall see in Chapters 3 and 4. Nevertheless, the concepts of external and internal integration are useful in understanding the job of a department manager or a first-line supervisor. Such managers have to integrate "externally" with other departments and service units of their company, and they have an internal integration problem within their own unit.

ORIGINS OF MANAGERIAL CONCEPTS

Modern management has its roots in several different ways of thinking about what a manager does. We are eclectic; we select useful ideas from all these viewpoints. However, a recognition of the different approaches helps us relate ideas encountered elsewhere—in other reading and also in our own practical experience—to the central processes of managing.

Fig. 1–2 Managing is so complicated that separate examination of its sub-processes is necessary for full understanding. But we should never lose sight of the way these processes fit together to form the whole.

Productivity Approach

The oldest theories of management, indeed the main stream of ideas, concern productivity. Attention in this approach centers in learning how to *produce in abundance.*

Two supporting ideas are implied when we speak of productivity: (1) A productive operation yields *results*—results in terms of the goods and services sought by the manager. Here we take a tough and pragmatic stand about whether a specific practice actually produces desired results. (2) A productive operation is *efficient.* The ratio of outputs to inputs is high.

Scientific Management. The first systematic study of management in the United States was made by production engineers. Frederick W. Taylor and his associates shifted an interest in production bonuses to a focus on management, and thus launched what became known in 1910 as *Scientific Management.*

Before bonuses could be set, Taylor insisted that the best conditions and manner of doing a job be determined. To ensure that machines operated properly he insisted on preventive maintenance and on keeping tools properly sharpened in a central toolroom. For these methods to work, raw materials could not vary, and so he set up raw material specifications and quality-control checks. Also, to prevent delays due to time lost in giving workers new assignments, careful production scheduling, dispatching, and internal transport systems were established. Finally, workers suited to the newly designed jobs had to be selected and trained. Only when all of these conditions were met was Taylor ready to use time study to determine a standard day's work.

This sort of approach creates a minor revolution in a shop or hospital that has operated in a haphazard, traditional manner—a revolution in the method of work, in planning and control by management, and in productivity. Nevertheless, these basic concepts, nurtured in a machine shop, have been adapted to all sorts of production operations in plants throughout the world.

The founders of Scientific Management made two great contributions: (1) They invented and developed an array of techniques that vastly improve productivity. The United States could never have developed into the leading industrial nation of the world without their concepts, and developing nations must master these techniques if their output aspirations are to become realities. (2) More important, they fundamentally altered the way we think about management problems. Instead of relying on tradition and personal intuition, we now believe any management problem should be subjected to the same kind of critical analysis, inventive experiment, and objective evaluation that Taylor applied in his machine shop.

Extensions of the productivity approach. The analytical productivity approach soon moved beyond the plant to all divisions of an enterprise. Notable improvements arose, for example, from systematic arrangements for recruiting, training, promoting, compensating, and providing a variety of fringe benefits to *personnel*. Financial *budgeting* and cost analysis, originally control mechanisms but soon used for planning as well, are now applied to all phases of any kind of enterprise. A steady flow of *mechanization* and automation has transferred from men to machines a wide array of tasks that can be standardized.

Best known for their use in industrial firms, all these productivity techniques can easily be adapted to nonprofit enterprises that perform large volumes of similar activities.

Mechanization and automation, especially, bring an old dilemma into the limelight. Productivity, in the sense of a greater flow of goods and services efficiently produced, is aided by standardization, routinization, and stability. This association of stability and efficiency has been true from the inception of Scientific Management to the development of the latest devices for automation. On the other hand, we find pressures for change that upset stability. Changes must be made because the market place demands greater variety, and also because research laboratories are creating new processes and products. The challenge for management, then, is to change deftly while maintaining productivity.

Behavioral Approach

The behavioral approach to management is oriented to *research*, rather than to the successful practice emphasized in the productivity approach. Some research does have practical application, but the behavioral scientist is primarily interested in describing and explaining. Consequently, in seeking guides for management practice, we must select those theories and ideas that relate directly to management and then convert them into operational terms.

From 1927 to 1932, Elton Mayo and Fritz Roethlisberger made a landmark study of the Western Electric Company. In their conclusions they stressed that workers respond to their *total* work situation and that attitudes toward their work and their social relations constitute an important part of this total. A corollary of such conclusions is that the early writers on Scientific Management and many people in personnel management had acted on an inadequate notion of worker motivation; they took a mechanistic or engineering view of man that eventually proved to be much too simple.

Controlled management experiments in real-life settings, such as those at Western Electric, are rare. We do try many new arrangements, but typically these are tests of feasibility; we pick what we think is the best idea and then we see if it works. To experiment with all opportunities —both good and bad—under carefully controlled operating conditions, as is done in a laboratory, is far too complex and expensive for most management problems; often, indeed, it is impossible.

Social psychologists, however, experiment with small bits of human behavior in laboratory conditions, and often their findings throw light on some management issue. For instance, we have learned a lot about small-group behavior from such experiments.

Sociologists rely primarily on field studies. Here the classic is Max Weber's insightful observation of *bureaucracy* in government, churches, and political parties. For him, pure bureaucracy includes (1) a division of labor with each job clearly defined and filled by a technically qualified person, (2) a well-established hierarchy with clear lines of authority and appropriate staffs and salary for those at each level, and (3) a systematic set of aims and regulations so that actions can be impersonal and coordinated.

Even though many of the ideas need more supporting research, managers can learn a great deal from behavioral science, which often supplies solid verification to intuitive judgments. More important, new ways of thinking about a problem are often suggested, and these lead to a clear grasp of what is involved; the psychological reasons for resistance to change illustrate this. Finally, some specific management techniques have been suggested by behavioral research—nondirective interviewing, for instance. But bear in mind that the chief aim of behavioral science is to describe and explain and not to devise tools to increase efficiency.

Rationalistic-model Approach

Modern management concepts are also being enriched by a group of thinkers who use a rationalistic model to analyze the operations of an enterprise. Their opinions are dominated by logical reasoning. Most promising of the rationalistic-model approaches is *operations research*.[2] In current practice operations research is primarily a technique for selecting a course of action. It has three key features that distinguish it from less formal decision-making:

1) Problems are stated in mathematical symbols. Thus the statement is concise and can be manipulated easily by a mathematician.

2) A set of equations, or "model," is designed for each problem. This model shows the various factors that should be taken into account and points out the relationships among them. The model presumably presents an orderly picture of the total problem that otherwise would be dealt with unsystematically in the mind of an executive.

3) Quantitative data must be provided for each of the variables and their weights. To achieve this quantification requires a tremendous amount of digging for facts and the expression of subjective judgments and values in numerical terms. Then a highly rational decision can be made by injecting the data into the model.

Obviously the operations-research technique is particularly well suited to problems that are complex and yet have known characteristics that can be measured in quantitative terms. Prime examples are scheduling in an oil refinery or inventory management in a company having many products in many warehouses. Clearly, the operations-research answers to such problems are highly sophisticated in terms of rationality.

Operations research, then, is a very useful tool for getting answers to particular types of problems. But, like many other management techniques, its indirect contributions may be more valuable than its specific application. Operations research encourages managers to think more sharply about all problems, including those that cannot be quantified or that are not important enough to justify the expense of a complete quantitative analysis. Moreover, we need to keep operations research in perspective. Operations research, like microeconomics, deals with the decision-making aspect of planning, and even here its unique contribution lies more in analysis and choice than in diagnosis and finding alternatives. These are vital aspects of management but by no means the whole picture.

[2]Other rationalistic-model approaches are microeconomics, game theory, and systems engineering.

Naturally, ideas arising from the rationalistic-model, behavioral, and productivity approaches to management often overlap. All three methods deal with the same events, but from different viewpoints. For instance, the rationalist tucks into his equation a single symbol that represents years of research by behavioral scientists; and a production man's new inspection system becomes a "modification in role expectations" to the behavioral scientist. Nevertheless, each approach contributes distinctive insights.

Need for an Operational Framework

All the streams of thought summarized in this section contribute to the emerging profession of management. Each is making a distinctive contribution, and we shall draw freely on their ideas throughout this book. Because the behavioral scientists and the rationalists do not study the total job of a manager, we shall frequently note how the new concepts modify or amplify the how-to-do-it ideas growing out of the productivity approach.

Even in the preceding quick review, three issues kept reappearing. We shall face them frequently in later chapters.

1) What is the proper balance between *stability* and *change?* Stability usually aids short-run efficiency. People know their jobs and what to expect from others; detailed specialization and perhaps automation are feasible; programmed decisions of the operations researchers are more reliable. On the other hand, management must adapt to changing social concepts, take advantage of new technology, and—by no means last—recognize the resource and value of differences in individual personalities.

2) How can we best merge *analysis* and *synthesis?* Breaking management problems down into subproblems and the elements of each is essential for full understanding. But the pieces also have to be fitted together again. We need to grasp the total system and be keenly aware of all the by-product effects of the actions we select. Timing, balance, and human readiness have to be considered, as well as ultimate objectives.

3) What *mental framework,* or way of organizing diverse ideas, is most useful to a manager? As we have noted, behavioral scientists typically are concerned more with description than with action; the productivity approach is work-centered and may give too little weight to human and social consequences; and the builders of rationalist models are enamored with the elegance of their solutions to a segment of the total process. So we face the task of relating valuable ideas into a workable scheme (and of translating special jargon into simple understandable terms). For this purpose, thinking of management as a process has great advantages. The process of management is *operational* because it expresses ideas in terms of operations and actions a manager must take; it is *comprehensive,* em-

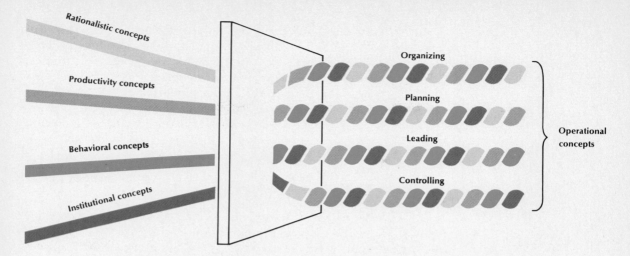

Fig. 1–3 Various valuable but diffuse lines of thought become strong managerial forces when bound together by means of the operational framework used in this book.

bracing the major tasks of managing; and it is *universal*, in that all managers should give some attention to each part of the process. Since conceiving of management as a process serves as a key for harnessing management action to the social purposes we discussed earlier, let us look more closely at the management process.

THE MANAGEMENT PROCESS

Managing is a social process. It is a *process* because it comprises a series of actions that lead to the accomplishment of objectives. It is a *social* process because these actions are principally concerned with relations between people.

We have many social processes in civilized society: We worship together, play group games, stand in line while we wait for buses, negotiate contracts, and try men for murder. In each case, because we have an established pattern of what we should do and what we expect others to do, we can achieve a result that would not otherwise be feasible. The particulars of a process may, of course, be changed from time to time. A major college football game has rituals for spectators and players that are quite different from those of the old-fashioned jousting match, and a modern murder trial has changed considerably from legal procedures in the days of Henry VIII. But to understand what is happening in any social activity—including the management of an enterprise—and, especially, to ensure that what we want to happen does happen, we need a keen appreciation of the social process involved. The aim of this book is to help develop such an understanding about the process of managing.

Management, like education or government, is a *continuing* process. There are always new mouths to feed, fresh minds to stimulate, and more people to govern. And the satisfaction of needs today invites higher aspirations for tomorrow. Thus new problems crop up as old ones are solved. For purposes of analysis, of course, we may focus on a single problem, on just one series of actions that lead to a specific end; but in practice, a manager must learn to deal simultaneously with a wide range of problems, each in a different stage of resolution.

Managing is so complex that our minds cannot consider all its facets at the same moment. We need to divide up the whole activity into parts in order to grasp the full significance of each, just as we get a clear picture of a company by looking separately at its financial statements, its key personnel, its reputation, its facilities, its policies and organization, its traditions and social structure. Then we can fit the different aspects into a total picture.

The total task of management can be divided into four elements: organizing, planning, leading, and controlling. Although all are closely interrelated, each of these elements can be analyzed as a subprocess. Each is vital to the success of managers at all levels—from first-line supervisors to presidents. And these four elements are present in the managing of every kind of enterprise—small and large, manufacturing and selling, partnership and corporation, profit and nonprofit. In looking briefly at these four processes, we shall point out the plan of this book.

Organizing

Once the work of an enterprise grows beyond what a single craftsman can do, organization becomes necessary. We have to assign the various tasks to different people and to coordinate their efforts. As the enterprise expands, this process leads to departments and divisions, each of which has its particular mission. One way to think about the resulting organization is as a complex machine—say, an airplane designed for transatlantic passenger service. Each part of a plane performs a necessary function—supplying power, pressure, heat, steering, communication, and so forth; *and* the different parts are so carefully balanced and fitted together that changing any one of them often calls for an adjustment in several others.

A manager must also view organization as a social arrangement, because it is composed of people rather than physical objects. The men who are assigned tasks are independent, self-respecting individuals with a variety of motives; informal groups influence the way men respond to managerial action; and the attitudes of all these people are continually shifting and evolving. In organizing, then, we have to seek ways of getting the necessary work done at the same time we build a social structure that helps meet the needs of people doing the work. The technical and social aspects of organizing will be examined in Parts One and Two respectively.

Planning

A key activity of all managers is planning the work under their direction. Working with each other and with the people who will carry out the plans, they clarify objectives and set goals for each subdivision; they establish policies and standard methods to guide those who do the work; and they develop programs, strategies, and schedules to keep the work moving toward the objectives. Most of these plans they will have to readjust periodically in the light of new information and changes in operating conditions. And time and again managers will face questions about how detailed the plans should be, who should participate in formulating them, and how much freedom of action should be given to subordinates.

The process of planning can be best understood if we first examine the basic stages in making a specific decision: diagnosing the problem, finding good alternative solutions, projecting the results of each alternative, and, finally, selecting the one course of action to be followed. We shall analyze these elements of decision-making in detail in Part Three.

Decision-making, however, is not the act of an isolated individual; it takes place in the organization we have established. In fact, many different persons may contribute to the formulation and final selection of a major plan. Consequently, since we need to know how the organization can be used most effectively in this decision-making (or planning) process, we explore in Part Four the topic of decision-making in an organization.

Leading

Clear plans and sound organization set the stage, but a manager must also provide leadership if the people in his organization are to work together to achieve its goals. Leadership, which we shall take up in Part Five, involves the way a manager behaves in his man-to-man relationships with his subordinates. In leading, a manager strives to integrate the needs of people with the welfare of his company or department. He recognizes that people have their own desires, but at the same time he knows that cooperation and efficiency are necessary for the survival and growth of the firm. In short, a leader tries to act so as to maintain a good balance between individual motivation *and* cooperative efficiency.

Such behavior is not always easy. But establishing two-way communication, assisting subordinates to perform their duties, and helping them to achieve their personal aspirations are activities that lay a basis for voluntary cooperation. This kind of behavior by a leader also fosters an atmosphere of trust, respect, and confidence between himself and his subordinates.

At the same time, a manager must provide guidance toward a system of order and cooperation. In no complex social system—whether it be national society or a company society—can an individual do as he pleases, without regard for the activities of others. Clear direction, coupled with a spirit of cooperation, typically achieves the necessary coordinated effort. But there are times when a leader must be tough, hold people to high standards of performance, discipline wisely, and occasionally, make use of power.

Measuring and Controlling

For a ship to reach its destination without sailing far off course, the captain regularly "takes his bearings." A manager, likewise, has to measure his progress if he is to obtain his objectives. And when he discovers that operations are not proceeding according to plan, he takes corrective action to get back on course or, if this is not feasible, readjusts his plans. This process of measuring progress, comparing it with plans, and taking corrective action is called control. In practice, as our analysis in Part Six will show, control is not so simple as it sounds. Measuring intangibles, such as customer goodwill or executive morale, poses difficulties, and devising corrective action that both overcomes an immediate difficulty and creates a favorable climate for future performance often calls for ingenuity. Moreover, the dispersal of activities that result from organization creates problems of just who should control what.

Framework Rather Than Procedure

In the following chapters, then, we shall examine each of these four elements—organizing, planning, leading, and controlling—in some detail, and we shall divide these major aspects of the overall management process into even narrower subprocesses. Such a systematic view of management provides a convenient device (1) for diagnosing complex management problems and (2) for working on improvements at one stage without losing sight of other stages.

But a framework that helps us think in an orderly fashion is not necessarily a step-by-step procedure that we must follow. Actually, when we deal with a concrete management problem, the available information is not neatly classified and labeled; instead, a great array of facts hits us at once, while some data remain stubbornly hidden. In response to such confusion our thoughts tend to flit first to one subject and then to another.

So the chief purpose of a conceptual framework, such as the systematic examination of the management process in this book, is to help us quickly to place diverse ideas in a useful order.

The framework is more than a series of pigeonholes to tuck ideas in, however; for among the pigeonholes there is a rational relation that we know in advance. Thus, when we mentally classify a new bit of information as bearing on, say, the long-range objectives of department A, we can immediately relate it to a host of other ideas we have stored in our mind, and, in this relation, the piece of information takes on meaning because it contributes to our comprehension of the total situation. Mankind has advanced from a primitive state largely by developing orderly ways of thinking about problems; in proposing a systematic approach to management, then, we are simply following this time-proved method.

There are, of course, many ways to think about as complicated a subject as management. The approach presented in this book has proved to be very useful for both practical and theoretical analyses of a wide variety of management situations. So while we should be alert for improvements, we can proceed with confidence that this approach has practical value for anyone in a managerial or staff position or for the researcher who is trying to understand how managers get things done.

One further introductory note: Because people with diverse backgrounds talk about management, words are used in different ways. Since this is so, we should clarify our terminology. For ease of discussion, we shall use "manager," "executive," and "administrator" as synonyms. And when we deal with man-to-man relationships, we may use "supervisor" or even "boss" to designate the manager who sits *immediately* above his "subordinate" in the organization hierarchy. For these terms we are simply following common usage. Other words, which have more precise meanings, will be defined as we encounter them in later chapters.

Design of This Book

This book contains two kinds of aid for improving managerial ability: text and cases. The text discussion in chapters assists in analyzing the numerous facets of managing and in finding ways to proceed. It provides help in recognizing problems, seeing their interrelationships, conceiving of possible solutions, and developing sensitivity to the advantages and limitations of alternative solutions. Mastery of the "mental framework" provides a foundation for the development of skill.

The cases offer an opportunity to start applying the general concepts to specific situations, and a discussion of proposed solutions with other persons will give some check on how well the concepts are being applied. At best, these cases can only offer a beginning in the practice that is necessary for the development of proficiency in managing. But this beginning is quite important, because it *builds a bridge* between general concepts and concrete situations; and we hope it will establish a pattern for going on to the use of concepts in real life.

Careful study of the cases serves three other purposes:

1) Cases help us overcome the unreal separations that are inevitable in any analytical treatment of an interdependent phenomenon. For example, we shall discuss organizing, planning, and leading, separately. But in actual problems, the plans and policies of a company (Part Four) are to some extent determined by the organization structure (Parts One and Two), and vice versa. And the leadership pattern of an executive (Part Five) is influenced somewhat by the organization structure. So, in actuality a manager must solve, say, planning and leadership problems *along with* organization problems. Most of the cases in this book present a whole situation, that is, they do not merely illustrate the issues in any one chapter. Instead, the cases provide a way of seeing the interrelated application of various concepts from all chapters in a realistic, whole-problem sense. They provide a sense of the *gestalt* ("whole"), while the chapters enable us to concentrate on the parts.

2) The cases make the ideas in the chapters more *meaningful*. Sometimes we shall find that an idea appears rather simple—even obvious—as explained in the text, but only when we apply it to a real problem will its full and complex meaning begin to unfold. Applying concepts helps to clarify and reinforce their meaning.

3) The cases help show that we do not always have facts and concepts that cover all aspects of a complex management problem. As in medicine, management problems often include variables that theory does not explain; there are unique elements in each specific situation. At times, then, all the answers needed to solve a case *neatly* will not be found in the book. This can be very frustrating. Nevertheless, it is a difficulty faced by men of affairs down through the ages. Actually, it is precisely this need to blend general concepts with the stubborn facts of a practical situation that makes management challenging and fascinating.

CONCLUSION

Two broad developments have made the study of management timely. (1) In a world where hopes and aspirations are mounting, managers play a crucial role in fulfilling these new goals—and we expect it of them. They initiate growth as well as adapt to dynamic forces. (2) Fortunately, we are learning more about how this important task can be performed effectively. The recognition of management as a distinct social process has led to many studies by researchers and by executives themselves. And from this study has emerged a whole array of insights and precepts that can be put to practical use.

Treating management as a *process* puts our ideas about managing into *operational* terms—that is, in terms that directly relate to decisions and actions by an executive. And a further division into the subprocesses of organizing, planning, leading, and controlling provides an analytical framework that has proved useful in all kinds of businesses and nonprofit enterprises.

We can improve our management skill by first learning about these elements of managing, and then by deliberately applying them to concrete situations. Each chapter helps us to learn about managing, and the cases give opportunities to apply the basic concepts.

FOR CLASS DISCUSSION

Questions

1) Many otherwise dissimilar groups find agreement in their common tendency to place the blame for many of our current problems on "the system." The system or systems they criticize, run by "managers," are considered to be impersonal, bureaucratic, inflexible institutions that have not only failed to anticipate or shape change, but have even failed to adapt to it. To what degree do you feel business as part of "the system" is guilty of these charges? How does your response fit with the material concerning the mission of management presented in this chapter?

2) "The primary function of any business is to offer products and/or services to those who can afford them and do so in a way which is profitable to the firm. Thus the basic goal of a business is profit, its source is in the market, and its components are revenue and cost. The science of economics, which has for hundreds of years been devoted to studying these phenomena, is the major school or discipline for a businessman to draw on. Everything else should be viewed in the context of the economics approach." Do you agree? Explain your position.

3) In addition to the factors cited by sixty British executives, what other factors, in your opinion, play an important role in bringing about innovation by American managers rather than mere adaptation?

4) In the section "Changing Needs of Society," five new emphases are presented. All but the first deal with problems and solutions that are probably beyond the scope of any individual corporation. For each of these last four items, discuss what kinds of actions managers of private corporations might take to meet their obligations.

5) One of the scarce resources in many developing nations is trained management. Suppose you were given the responsibility for setting up a "management" course in such a country. Someone else will develop courses in accounting, finance, marketing, and so on. Which of the approaches to management would you draw on in such a course, and why?

6) One of the key elements in the process of management is measurement and control. Before reading about this important part of the process, consider the relationship between it and balance that is sought between stability and change. How may measurement and control systems (1) aid and/or (2) detract from striking this balance effectively?

7) In what ways do you feel the "process of managing" a large private corporation (1) differs and (2) is similar to the process of managing equally large or larger public or nonprofit organizations, such as hospitals, universities, or governmental agencies?

Cases

For cases involving issues covered in this chapter, see especially the following Particularly relevant questions are listed after each case.

Gerald Clark (p. 234), 1, 9, 21
Harrogate Asphalt Products, Ltd.—AR (p. 557), 11
Consolidated Instruments—B (p. 674), 1, 17

FOR FURTHER READING

Andrews, K.R., "Toward Professionalism in Business Management." *Harvard Business Review*, March 1969. *Requirements and necessary steps for professionalization.*

Gross, B.M., *The Managing of Organizations.* New York: The Free Press, 1964. *Comprehensive two-volume synthesis of multidisciplinary writing on management.*

Koontz, H., "The Management Theory Jungle." *Journal of the Academy of Management*, December 1961. *Panorama of approaches to management analysis.*

McFeely, W.M., "The Manager of the Future." *Columbia Journal of World Business*, May 1969. *Knowledge and skill required of future managers.*

Walton, C.C., *Corporate Social Responsibilities.* Belmont, Calif.: Wadsworth Publishing Company, Inc., 1967. *Thoughtful analysis of array of social responsibilities.*

Organizing: Structural Design

Some people take a dilettante view of managing, treating it as an interesting bit of human behavior along with, say, mountain climbing or playing in string quartets. Others are concerned with managing as a means of attaining personal income and status. Both views are valid, and the study of management can be both interesting and rewarding. But the really compelling force that underlies the serious study of management is its profound social value.

If we desire to increase our skill in performing this crucial social process we need to examine each of the subprocesses involved. Managing is too complex to comprehend all at once, and so we shall probe—in separate parts of the book—four essential aspects: organizing, planning, leading, and controlling. All these subprocesses are interrelated; in life they take place concurrently. We turn first to organizing merely because it is easier to perceive.

Organizing helps a manager unite the work of different people in order to achieve goals. Whether the number of people be only two or thousands, their effective cooperation requires organization. Two elements are invariably present in organizing: dividing up the work into jobs and, at the same time, making sure that these separate clusters of work are linked together into a total team effort. We can see these two elements in a football team, in a hospital, or in a government bureau, as well as in business firms. The success of any of these enterprises depends to a significant degree on how skillfully their managers assign tasks so that they combine together into integrated, purposeful action.

This basic process—organizing—will be discussed in the following chapters.

Chapter 2—Design of Operating Units. Here we focus on the merging of operating tasks into jobs, the linking of such jobs into work groups, and the combining of work groups into major operating departments and service divisions of the enterprise. The aim is to find those coalitions that will bring forth the most effective cooperative effort.

Chapter 3—Decentralization. The work of managing also has to be allocated. This involves delegating and redelegating to successively lower levels of supervision. In this chapter, we shall see that the scope and the degree of decentralization are critical features in this dispersing of authority.

Chapter 4—Use of Staff. As enterprises grow, the task of managing them becomes more complex, so in this chapter we explore the ways staff can be employed to lighten the burden of key executives.

Chapter 5—Shaping the Overall Structure. We should then examine the total organization for balance and potentialities for growth. We must make sure that the jobs and departments we have created fit together in a harmonious, effective structure that is well suited to the mission of the enterprise.

Chapter 6—New Approaches to Structural Design. Here we look at five frontiers where social and technological pressures are leading to new organizational forms. The modifications of structure take the form of matrix organizations, external, independent staff, a president's office, provision for special interest groups, and adjustments for use of computers. These are refinements, not replacements, for the basic organizational elements discussed in preceding chapters.

All these chapters deal with "formal" organization, "formal" in the sense that the patterns of division of work and personal relationships are deliberately set up and are clearly recognized and discussed by those concerned. The primary interest is to achieve goals of the enterprise; thus the analysis is based largely on the "productivity approach." The more informal aspects of organization, which arise out of social and personal relationships, will be examined later in Part Two.

Chapter Two

Design of Operating Units

HARNESSING SPECIALIZED EFFORT

Examples of cooperative effort abound in modern society. Schools, government, health care, trade, research, and production, for instance, all require some form of work sharing. One of management's critical functions is to develop effective ways to carry out this division of labor. Throughout Part One we examine various ways to structure cooperative effort. Our focus is on the deliberate design of jobs and on relations between jobs.[1] In this chapter, we explore ways of grouping operating tasks.

Departmentation—the grouping of activities into jobs, sections, and departments—is essential in every joint endeavor. Sailing a tramp ship, running a medical clinic, or administering a bank, for instance, all require a clear understanding of who does what. The way activities are combined into operating units will affect such matters as speed of coordination, cost of performing a service, and which new problems receive serious attention.

The need to allocate work among members of an organization has long been recognized. Aristotle, for example, commented in his treatise *Politics* (Book 2, Chapter 11):

[1]Because the design is deliberately created and explicit, some scholars call it "formal" organization, without any implications about how ceremonial or informal personal relationships may be.

Where the state is large, it is more in accordance with constitutional and with democratic principles that the offices . . . should be distributed among many persons . . . Any action familiarized by repetition is better and sooner performed. . . .

As every Latin student knows, Caesar divided Gaul into three parts for purposes of administration. Adam Smith in his book *The Wealth of Nations* (1776) discussed the importance of division of labor (a pin factory is his example). About a hundred years ago, the choice of territorial versus functional departments became a critical management problem in the early operation of transcontinental railroads.

Despite this long recognition of its value, the question of how or how much to departmentalize continues to be a live issue. The reason the who-does-what question keeps pressing for attention is that neither the "who" nor the "what" stays constant. Rapid and pervasive changes in technology sharply modify the tasks to be done. At the same time, people change. Additional education and new aspirations and values can turn a formerly attractive job into a menial one.

Moreover, when we update one job, misunderstandings are likely to arise during the transition from the old to the new, especially if a new man is put into the revised position. One small firm experienced this problem when its office manager retired after many years of service. The office manager had grown up with the company, and both the scope of his duties and the methods he employed were traditional. The company replaced him with a young man whose sales experience with a business-machine manufacturer had enabled him to observe modern practices in many different firms. It soon became evident that his conception of the duties of an office manager was far different from that of the older employees. He wanted to install new systems that extended his authority to such things as the control of sales expense and the scheduling of production. His efforts led him into disputes with the sales manager and a head-on collision with the plant superintendent. Before the duties of the office manager were finally clarified, so much personal friction had been generated that the young man had to be replaced with an office manager who had more traditional policies.

Organizational design starts with the problem of how the many tasks that must be performed will be assigned to operators and managers.

Initial Emphasis on Operations

In this chapter we shall focus on departmentation of the principal *operations* of an enterprise. By operations we mean the nonmanagerial activities necessary to "get the work out"—the selling, machine-running, bookkeeping, and engineering in a manufacturing plant; the copywriting, art work, media selection, and campaign scheduling in an advertising agency; or the arranging for temporary care of children, locating foster homes, making actual placements, raising funds, and keeping records in a child-placement agency. The organization of a variety of other activities specifically related to managing will be considered later. But operations are basic. Even the most ingenious assignments to senior managers are of value only if they contribute to better operations.[2]

In keeping with this emphasis on first-level operations, our analysis starts with the grouping of operating tasks into individual jobs. Then we treat the combining of jobs into effective work groups. Going further, we consider the consolidation of work groups into departments. By starting with the most simple units and moving to more complex ones, we shall keep the beguiling issues of grand design for an entire enterprise in proper perspective.[3]

A related question, arising in every enterprise of more than a few persons, is which activities should be pulled out of the mainstream of operation and placed in auxiliary, or service, divisions. For example, most people feel that janitorial and maintenance activities should form a separate service division, but the location of purchasing is often a major source of friction.

Throughout this exploration of departmentation at various levels we will be looking for critical factors that can help us in designing all sorts of work. Sensitivity to such factors is a useful aid in structuring any profit or nonprofit organization.

SCOPE OF INDIVIDUAL JOBS

How many different tasks can a single person perform well? In practice we find jobs ranging from the nut-tightener on an assembly line to a cabinetmaker who does everything from selecting his raw wood to polishing his finished product. These are extremes. Let us examine several other examples for keys to how much division of labor is desirable.

How Much Division of Labor?

Flying a small plane in Alaska, a bush pilot fuels, loads, navigates, communicates with the ground, calms his passengers, and makes minor repairs. In the operation of a 747 jet, however, these tasks are divided

---

[2]Similarly, we shall speak of *operators* (often called "workers," a term that seems to imply that executives do not work!) and *managers* (that is, anyone, from first-line foreman to president, who supervises the work of other people).

[3]The departmentation concept can be extended beyond the enterprise into structure of an "industry." The work of the total industry has to be distributed among firms. Although this division is determined by competition, similar issues arise: specialization, coordination, optimum size, maintenance of suitable cost levels, ability to adapt to new kinds of work, and the way firms relate to each other.

among dozens of persons, each of whom has a limited number of clearly specified things to do. Why the difference?

The explanation lies partly in the large volume of work required to operate a 747. But also we want each person to be highly skilled in his particular tasks, and we want to be sure that adequate attention is given to a task when it is needed. Moreover, the larger payload can support the expense of a multiple crew, and so this example suggests that a high division of labor is desirable if it can be afforded.

A more elementary situation is the home delivery of newspapers. In some locations a newsboy has full charge of his route. He solicits new business, delivers the papers, makes collections, and stops delivery during customers' vacations. A major advantage of this arrangement is the ease of coordinating the different tasks; also, control is simplified because one man is clearly accountable for success or failure. Nevertheless, in many other localities one person sells, another delivers, a third collects, and a fourth schedules. The chief benefit of such a split is the ease, and lower cost, of finding people qualified to do the less diversified jobs. The man who gets up every morning at three o'clock and performs physical labor, for instance, does not also have to be a good salesman. The greater use of the mails for collections and selling is pushing the trend in newspaper delivery toward narrower job definitions. The division of labor problem persists, however, for those who must decide the scope of work for industrial salesmen, social caseworkers, and other people who are expected to coordinate all contacts with specific customers or clients.

College teaching is one area where high division of labor along functional lines has been resisted. The tasks of course design, instruction, and testing could be allocated to separate specialists. However, most college professors resent any interference with "their courses." In fact professors are urged to do research and still perform the whole gamut of teaching tasks. The rationale for such a broad job scope includes the ease of coordinating the various phases of teaching and a belief that a man cannot be good at one teaching task without being proficient in all the others. Students themselves undoubtedly have an opinion about the effectiveness of this arrangement!

The question of job scope—how many different tasks a man is expected to carry out—arises in every walk of life. Because of the way jobs are structured, people quit jobs, professions are built, unions call jurisdictional strikes, psychological security is found or lost, and companies prosper or languish.

Striking a Balance

As the preceding examples show, effective job structure requires a careful assessment of what the physical circumstances permit and the primary benefits sought in a specific situation. Some of the factors that usually deserve attention in deciding how many tasks to combine into a single job are described in the following paragraphs.

Benefits of functional specialization. By narrowing the scope of a job, full utilization can be made of any distinctive skill a man possesses. As a man concentrates on a limited range of duties, he can learn these very well and give them full attention. Wage economies may also arise; instead of paying a premium for a versatile "triple-threat man" for all positions, the more routine tasks can often be assigned to less experienced and less expensive employees.[4]

Need for coordination. Often several tasks should be closely synchronized or coordinated—as in labor negotiations—and one person can do this more easily than several. When information about a specific situation has to be pooled in a single spot, the difficulty of communicating bits of information from person to person may more than offset benefits of specialization; dealing with a foreign subsidiary or a student is a case in point. Relevant here is the rule that tasks should be separated only where there is a "clean break," as between lunch and dinner but not during a meal.

Morale of operator. How the operator feels about the scope of his job may be vital. The employee's pride in his work and work suited to professional dignity can be positive factors. On the other hand, monotony is depressing for most people. Sometimes monotony can be partially relieved by rotating people from job to job or by allowing the worker to deviate from his set routine. In fact, if a wide variety of choices must be made, some operators feel that the job is unreasonably complex. This broad area of human response to organization is explored more fully in Part Two.

Rarely will any single design for a job be all good or all bad. Some potential benefits of specialization may have to be sacrificed for better coordination and employee morale, or vice versa. That choice depends primarily on values derived from what we call, in Chapter 16, "master strategy of the enterprise."

Two restraints on designing individual jobs should not be overlooked: (1) The volume of work always places a limit on the division of labor. We do not want a specialist to sit around most of the day waiting to do his thing. Also, it takes effort not only to design a sophisticated system of work but also to have the workers adopt it as a normal way of doing things, and such investment is warranted only when the system will have repeated use. (2) One physical technology may be so superior for some kinds of work that we may have little choice in job design. Operating a taxicab, playing first violin in a symphony orchestra, and removing bark by means of a hydraulic machine in a lumber mill are situations of this type.

---

[4]Whenever a sufficient volume of routine work is isolated, mechanization becomes a possibility; for example, use of computers for office work.

EFFECTIVE WORK GROUPS

Well-designed jobs are not enough. The complexities of modern production require the combined effort of a variety of people, as we have already stressed. After tasks are grouped into jobs, the next level of departmentation is the combining of jobs into work groups. By work groups we mean a set of people who see each other on the job almost daily, whose work is usually interdependent in some respects, and whose output is viewed by outsiders as a single achievement. Of course, it is possible to have a work group that is composed entirely of managers and staff men, but for the present we shall concentrate on people doing *operating* work. Social psychologists and others have devoted a lot of attention to behavior within small groups; here, however, we shall consider a more basic issue: How should the groups be formed?

Whenever several similar jobs exist they can be put in the same section, as suggested in the upper part of Fig. 2–1. Thus, selling can be combined, computing combined, and so on. On the other hand, when several different skills are needed to complete a block of work, jobs can be grouped as indicated in the lower part of the diagram. For example, a salesman, repairman, and bookkeeper could be placed together in a

Fig. 2–1 In functional groups operators perform the same kind of work and their supervisor is a specialist in that field. In compound groups operators perform different but related work and their supervisor is primarily a coordinator.

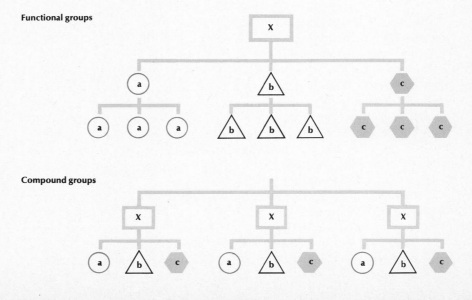

Functional groups

Compound groups

branch office of an office equipment company. The former grouping we call "functional," the latter "compound."

Benefits of Compound Groups

Under some circumstances, the use of compound groups permits us to take advantage of a combination of several benefits that are sought in the design of jobs. Individual members of the group can be specialists in different fields, and coordination is achieved by interaction within the group. Furthermore, close personal relations and a sense of group achievement contribute to morale. Small branches of a bank, a 747 airplane crew, and other geographically separated units often have these characteristics. Compound work groups may also be formed around a product or service, such as a maternity ward in a hospital.

A crew of men operating a highly automated chemical plant or power station is usually a compound group of specialists. In fact the men working on a single assembly line can be viewed as a compound group, although here the design and pace of the equipment carry most of the burden of coordination.

Compound groups should be used especially when local coordination carries a premium. An industrial equipment company, for instance, combines sales, repair service, and parts warehousing in each of its local offices in an effort to provide distinctive customer service. Local coordination is even more vital for a surgical team composed of a surgeon, assisting doctor, anesthetist, and nurses. Here, as in all the previous examples, a clear-cut block of work calls for the efforts of several specialists.

Reasons for Functional Grouping

Attractive though compound groups may be, functional grouping of operations is actually more prevalent. Why so?

Functional grouping usually makes full-time jobs easier to arrange. While a compound group may consist of six salesmen, two repairmen, and one accountant, it cannot readily be made up of six salesmen, one and two-thirds repairmen, and five-sixths of an accountant. With the latter workload usually the spare time of the repairman and the accountant is lost. Also the need for different specialists in any one compound group may be high today and low tomorrow. Functional grouping, with interchangeable people in the same group, allows a manager to balance these partial and irregular workloads more efficiently.

When each specialist requires high-cost equipment, the expenses of idle time are even greater. The operator of a multimillion-dollar wind tunnel used in aircraft engineering is an extreme example, but even the office space and auto of a field investigator can be expensive.

Technical supervision is often desirable. Unless the operators them-

Fig. 2–2 A surgical team illustrates (1) clear division of labor within the group and (2) responsive inter-action of the group to achieve a coordinated result.

selves possess high professional competence, their manager will normally need substantial technical knowledge. Even when plans are made centrally the supervisor must interpret policies, resolve on-the-spot problems, coach new employees, and relay to his bosses information they need. This kind of supervisory work can be done with greater expertise for a functional group. A supervisor need not be the only source of technical guidance, as we shall see in Chapter 4, "Use of Staff," but often his expert under-standing of the work being done is essential.

Compatibility within a group and with the supervisor is more likely to exist in a functional group than in a compound group. Compatibility rests heavily on similar attitudes and values—for example, attitudes toward risk-taking, meeting deadlines, short-run versus long-run achievements, and the importance of people versus things. In these terms we can achieve greater compatibility by putting, say, caseworkers together, researchers together, accountants together, and so forth. It is true that such a group tends to reinforce one another's biases and as a result may be less co-operative with other functional groups, but the social satisfactions they derive from their work will also be enhanced.

The design of work groups, then, involves at least broadly a set of considerations that are similar to those used in the formation of individual jobs. Benefits of specialization, need for coordination, effect on operators' morale, and expense repeatedly claim attention.

As we shall see in Part Two, work groups tend to become close-knit social groups. Once jelled, they tend to resist change. They can be a great source of strength for an enterprise or a seriously retarding influence. So we should compose these groups with care.

SHAPING MAJOR DEPARTMENTS

To achieve unified action, work groups must be combined into de-partments. At this level, we as organization designers shift our attention from an array of very specific operations to broad groupings of these activities that will facilitate central management. The work groups become building blocks. We seek to arrange these blocks so that the major missions of the enterprise receive proper emphasis, while the various operating groups are supported in performing their respective tasks. But as the enterprise adjusts to its changing environment, we may of course have to alter the shape of these major departments.

In one case, growth forced a small manufacturer of instruments to recast his basic organization structure. A resourceful instrument maker and a chemistry instructor had teamed up to make high-quality instruments for laboratories, and the business grew around specially designed equipment. The organization consisted of a production shop, a sales manager, and an office that handled all finance and clerical work. Then the company designed a machine for testing water pollution and found a potential market for hundreds of identical instruments. Sales jumped, and the shop was swamped with work.

The new business called for a major reorganization. Selling a standard item to governments and to utilities differed sharply from selling special designs to laboratories, and repetitive production was a sharp change from making one-of-a-kind instruments. So, instead of merely expanding the three existing departments, the company departmentalized by product line, each of which has its own production and selling subdivisions. A single office department still serves both product departments. Overhead expense is higher in the new setup, but the prospect for preserving the strength of a close-knit, responsive laboratory-instrument business while opening the way for unfettered growth in the pollution-control field offsets this extra cost.

The decline of "central-city" shopping, to cite another reorganization, is causing Schrader's Department Store to scramble for survival. For years Schrader's followed the usual department-store organization and divided itself into product departments—women's wear, jewelry, furniture, and so on—with each doing its own buying, merchandising, and selling. Now Schrader's has pursued its customers to the suburbs by opening four branch stores. Unhappily, the old organization no longer fits. Each branch manager feels responsible for the success of his branch, and at the same time product department heads try to supervise merchandising and selling in the branches as they have been doing in the main store. This conflict has recently been mitigated by placing branch selling clearly under the control of branch managers, but the next logical step of putting a man in charge of all selling at the main store has not yet been taken. If and when this move is made, product department heads will concentrate on buying and merchandising, and selling will be supervised by five "regional" managers. Under the new setup, coordination of buying and selling will be more difficult, but department heads will have more time for product specialization, and selling will receive closer, local supervision.

Note that in this last example the change is away from product grouping toward a functional split, whereas in the instrument company described above the shift was from function to products. The choice of

departmentation depended on where coordination and specialized attention were most needed and on the impact of technology.

Overlapping Patterns

Adjusting major departments to new needs is not always easy. Consider African studies in a university as an example. We accept the premise
that the whole history of black people and their current problems warrant
more attention. Should the added attention be incorporated into existing
courses, or should new African-studies courses be added? Should African-
studies courses be given by a separate department with its own faculty?
Should such a department admit students and set its own degree requirements? Should the department have its own library, scholarship and research funds, and otherwise have the status of a separate school? Instances
of positive and of negative answers to each of these questions can be
found somewhere on the American educational scene. Positive answers
inevitably lead to further questions. If African studies are to be a part of
the university, what will be their relationship with existing departments in
history, sociology, economics, education, law, urban planning, and so on,
and with service departments such as admissions, library, registrar, fund
raising, and the like?

The crux of this problem from an organization point of view is that
the new "product" is unlikely to receive *adequate attention* under the
existing structure, yet organizational separation leads to overlap and
duplication. Comparable departmentation problems often arise when a
new but relatively small product or service is added. Here are some examples: a public library adds phonograph records to its services; a commercial bank begins making small consumer loans; a leading metal ski
manufacturer decides to market ski clothing; a predominantly domestic
company opens an international division.

In all these instances the fledgling activity is too small to justify
revamping the entire organization. But it is also so small, new, and
different that it is apt to be undernourished if it is merely added to the
activities of large existing departments, and so we often give the new
activity independent status. The independence may mean merely that the
new activity is a separate section in one or two existing departments, but
if potentialities for growth are great enough the new venture may warrant
the creation of a new department.

Each time, however, that we grant an activity separate status that
cuts across existing departments we are inviting trouble. The existing departments will resent exceptions to company policy, and jurisdictional
squabbles are likely. We speak here not of new activities having no connection with existing operations but rather of new types of business that
seek to build on some company strengths while enjoying independence
in some other respects. Experience indicates that minor deviations from

the major departmentation can be tolerated but that large overlappings create so much confusion that they need very strong justification.

As the preceding discussion of pressures to create new overlapping departments suggests, the major departmentation of an enterprise is continually open to challenge. Every design embodies preference to some factors—local coordination, functional specialization, and so on—and the reasons for that preference change over time. Growth, new opportunities for service, the occurrence of wars or riots, shifting competition, newly discovered technology, or other shifts may make a formerly good design obsolete. We examine this need for readjustment further in Chapters 5, 6, and 28. This dynamic character of departmentation, however, makes discriminating design even more valuable.

ADDING AUXILIARY UNITS

Designing individual jobs, combining jobs into work groups, and forming major departments of these building blocks establishes the main framework of an organization. But further refining is necessary. One such refinement is creating *auxiliary*, or service, units. The Buildings and Grounds section of a hospital, for example, is clearly a unit serving the basic medical-care departments. The existence of such auxiliary divisions is justified only when operating departments work more economically or effectively as a result.

Potentialities of Service Units

A large variety of such service units is possible. For instance a manufacturing concern may establish a traffic division so that the production and marketing departments will not have to be concerned with moving goods to and from the plant. In financial establishments, the purchasing division typically functions as an auxiliary service for all other departments. Companies may set up a legal division to handle the bulk of corporate legal problems and to work with outside legal counsel on special issues. These are technical matters that the operating departments are rarely qualified to handle.

A market-research unit was established by a computer manufacturer to provide information and advice to district sales managers, to the advertising manager, and to engineers designing new products. In addition to providing better information, separation of the market-research tasks relieved the operating executives of the job of supervising what to them was a minor activity, and they were able to concentrate on their primary responsibilities more effectively.

Among the principal reasons for separating auxiliary activities from primary operating activities, then, are these: to secure adequate attention for all phases of an operation, to ensure that all work is assigned to technically competent employees, and to relieve busy executives of subsidiary duties. But there is another, and perhaps more fundamental, reason for distinguishing between primary and auxiliary divisions. Auxiliary divisions tend to grow uncontrollably like cancer, and it is difficult to tell how much of their service is economically justified. In his zeal for doing a good job, a manager of a service department is likely to magnify its importance. But if in our departmentation we clearly identify service work, we shall be in a good position to maintain a proper balance between services and primary operating units.

Hazards in Separating Services

The reasons for *not* separating service activity from primary operating activity usually center around problems of coordination and of overhead expense. If separated from basic operations, some auxiliary tasks such as janitor service, warehousing, and traffic present no particular difficulties of coordination. However, statistical computations, internal transportation, legal review of activities, and a large part of personnel work typically are closely related to day-to-day operations. The performance of such work by separate divisions generates additional problems. Where there is frequent need for consistent and synchronized action, one may be wiser to sacrifice some skill in performance to secure greater harmony.

In this connection, one danger of functional specialization, such as is found in most auxiliary units, is that it leads to provincial thinking. The functional specialist—for example, lawyer, purchasing agent, or accountant—permits his sophistication in one area to delude him into a misconception of, and lack of interest in, other areas. In his zeal to perform his particular specialty well, he becomes careless about the effect of his action or inaction on related activities.

Service divisions cost money in terms of salaries, office space, and the like. They often produce substantial economies that offset this expense by a comfortable margin, but this is not always the case. The returns from such activities as market research, engineering, and personnel relations are often difficult to measure, and these and similar activities can be expanded to a point where additional savings are not equal to additional expense. A failure to adjust service activities to reduced opportunities for making savings is more likely. The operation of such departments tends to be a fixed-overhead item that is not reduced with a drop in volume of operations. Likewise, a division that originally served a useful purpose may be continued long after its usefulness has passed. This danger of an inflexible expense item should be watched when setting up special auxiliary units of the organization.

Establishment of service units, then, requires careful examination in

A. Organization with no service division; each operating section performs its own auxiliary activities

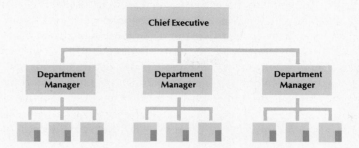

B. Organization with service units in each operating department

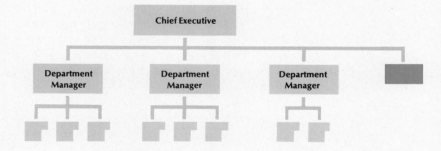

C. Organization with separate service division

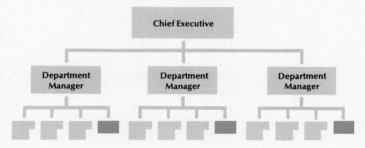

D. Organization with multiple service units

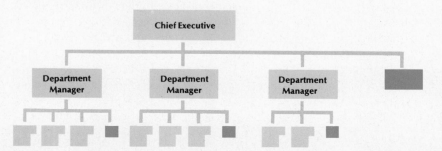

Fig. 2–3 Alternate locations of service activities. In the diagrams, the darker color indicates the service area.

each particular situation. Most enterprises of moderate size have several such units, but the desirability of a particular type of service unit should rarely be taken as a foregone conclusion, and the extent of the service is almost always a topic calling for a considerable amount of judgment. At least one generalization should be borne in mind when dealing with this issue: The burden of proof should always rest on the separation of service from basic operations. Every step in this direction increases to some extent the complexity of the organization; therefore, unless a strong case can be made for separation, an activity should be a basic part of the operation.

CONCLUSION

The designing of jobs or work groups can rarely be done well without also thinking about departments and service units; the scope of departments depends partly on what makes good work groups, and so forth. That is, design choices are interdependent, and so we hold back final decision at one level until we have thought through the impact elsewhere in the structure. Two kinds of considerations are valuable in this more general view of the framework we have constructed—the match with technology and key factors in departmentation.

Think First of Technology

Technology in a very broad sense means the methods used to convert inputs (materials, ideas, labor) into more valuable goods and services. In addition to physical processes for converting raw materials into finished products (crude oil into gasoline), technology includes techniques for the following: converting truckloads of groceries into consumer food purchases; creating medical services in a hospital; providing transportation across the Atlantic; training unemployables to be craftsmen; handling the buy-and-sell transactions on the New York Stock Exchange.

Technology in this general sense is always a consideration when we design an organization. Technology fashions the work to be done; organization merely combines the work into jobs, sections, and so on.[5]

Where physical processes are concerned, the need to match technology and organization is clear. For instance, Hawaiian pineapple is processed in highly mechanized plants by equipment that peels, cores, slices, or crushes the pineapple; the nature of the process largely sets the duties of individual jobs and also the scope of work groups. Similarly,

---

[5]We are treating technology here as an *intervening variable* between strategy (discussed in Chapter 16) and departmentation. That is, selection of a strategy leads to—perhaps even dictates—the technology to be used; then the technology determines the operating work to be done and is a major factor in the way this work is grouped into jobs, small units, and departments. The effect of technology on the total management design is explored in Chapter 28.

modern retail technology has virtually eliminated personal selling in food supermarkets. Even the selling of fresh meats, once the domain of a skilled butcher, is now done by placing packaged meat in showcases. This latter change led many supermarket chains to modify their field organizations significantly. Instead of having separate departments for meats, produce, and groceries, which ran from the main office down to the retail stores, they switched to an area organization in which store and district managers supervised all products, aided by central buying of meat. As the selling technology changed, so did the organization.

Of course, the choice of technology is not always clear-cut. Volume of work, for instance, affects the degree to which standardization and mechanization are feasible; and such mechanization may affect not only departmentation but also other aspects of management (see Chapters 5 and 28). Also, in research laboratories, consulting firms, and to some extent classrooms, operators have wide discretion on how they will do their work; where such freedom exists, technology drops to a minor influence on departmentation. We stress looking at technology early because it so often places limits on the forms of organization that are worthy of careful study and because an ingenious matching of technology and organization can yield outstanding results. Solutions to some of our most pressing urban problems in education, government, and transportation, for instance, undoubtedly require innovation in technology and organization.

Key Factors in Departmentation

Several key factors are found in almost every departmentation problem, regardless of level. So we typically seek an optimum arrangement of the various factors instead of relying on a single consideration. The following paragraphs are a useful summary of factors already noted and add new dimensions to several of them.

Take advantage of specialization. We should always at least consider a division of labor that permits persons to become specialists in certain kinds of work. Such concentration enables people to become experts and, assuming appropriate placement of personnel, allows a company to make full use of the distinctive abilities of its operators.

Usually we think of specialization by functions, but we should not overlook the possibility that an employee may become an expert on a product or on a particular type of customer. In other words, "What is the focus of the man's specialty?" The question forces us to consider whether a particular body of knowledge and skills is important for getting a job done. The more crucial such knowledge and skills are to the success of the enterprise, the stronger will be the pull on us to set up a division or a job built on that specialty.

Aid coordination. Even though certain activities are dissimilar, we may put them under a single executive because they need close coordination. Buying and selling women's hats in a department store, for example, may be the responsibility of only one executive because he can sense style trends and customer reactions and can time changes accordingly.

A clearly recognized *common objective* is important in securing coordination. The type of decentralization stressed by General Motors, General Electric, and many other companies splits up engineering, production, and selling among product divisions. This arrangement enables the management of each division to coordinate these diverse functions because the dominant objective of each unit is to make a success of its particular product line.

Coordination may be a factor when we decide where to place miscellaneous activities, as well as when we group major functions. In any organization, there are a number of "orphan operations"—receptionists, chauffeurs, telephone operators—and no compelling reason may exist for putting them in a particular place. We can decide to assign such employees to the department that makes the *most use* of their work. This solution at least simplifies coordination between a service and its major user.

Facilitate control. The way activities are apportioned has a marked effect on control in an organization. Clearly, if one activity is to serve as *an independent check* on another—as accounting on disbursement of cash or inspection on quality of production—these activities should be separated.

Departmentation, which makes it easier for management to measure performance and to hold people accountable for results, is a real aid to control. Thus it is desirable to make a *clean break* between the duties of one department and those of another. Oil companies, for example, often place all the work done by a refinery under a single manager because the line between what is inside and what is outside the refinery is a fairly clear one and also because all work within the refinery is so interrelated that a neat separation into two or more divisions would be difficult to establish.

Those companies whose volume and technology justify two or more operating units may use the *deadly parallel* as an aid to control. This means that operating units are made as nearly identical as possible so that their respective expenses and productivity can be directly compared. Chain stores, telephone companies, government bureaus, and even schools find that the deadly parallel provides performance standards that bring inefficient operations into sharp focus.

Control of actual operations is always simplified if an immediate *supervisor is on the spot* where he can see what goes on and can talk to workers frequently during the day. For this reason, a firm may place final assembly operations in a branch warehouse under the control of the sales department, even though the work seems logically part of production.

Secure adequate attention. A principal reason for separating auxiliary services from primary operations, as we have already pointed out, is to ensure adequate attention for all phases of work that should be done. Also executives often desire to report high up in an organization structure in order to make sure that their particular operations receive full consideration from top administrators.

"Adequate attention," however, is a difficult guide to use in departmentation. If an executive pays heed to all demands for attention, he may be inclined to break up an otherwise neat pattern that works well most of the time. Therefore an executive must decide not only how important an activity is at a given moment but also how important it will be in the future.

Reduce expenses. The pattern of departmentation may directly affect expenses in two ways. First, a new unit—say, a purchasing department or central training service—may require additional executives. The company must not only pay these executives a salary and traveling expenses, but also must provide them with office space, secretarial assistance, and telephone and other services. In addition to these identifiable costs, the people in a new unit inevitably use up some of the time of other executives by talking with them and writing memoranda that have to be read and answered. Perhaps the addition of a single man will make no marked difference, but if an array of specialists all press for attention from busy line managers the total burden on the line managers can become quite heavy.

A second expense consideration is the rate of pay needed for different kinds of jobs. An industrial sales department, for instance, might require that all salesmen have engineering training plus five years experience with company products, but an alternative organization might reserve such high-paid men only for special assignments, using lower-paid men for routine sales work. Obviously, no company will want to incur additional payroll expense unless by doing so it will benefit significantly by improved effectiveness.

Recognize human considerations. In Part Two we shall give careful attention to the human relations aspects of organization structure. There are a number of reasons why we may have to modify the coldly logical and emotionally detached organization plans we are discussing here in Part One. Among the reasons are availability of personnel, the existence of informal groups, traditions within an enterprise, and prevailing attitudes toward different forms of organization. We mention these points here simply as a reminder that we must bring human factors into consideration before we reach a final decision.

Frequency of Change

Organization structure should contribute to the stability of working relations. It enables each person to know the particular part he is expected to play in the total activities of his company. And from it he also learns what he can expect others to do. For these reasons, we should not shuffle duties among people each time a new idea strikes us. On the other hand, dynamic pressures in society and within a company, which we discussed in the first part of this chapter, require the modern manager to be constantly alert to the need for readjustment of the way he has divided up work among his subordinates. In enterprises generally, *thoughtful* changes in departmentation are made too infrequently rather than too often.

FOR CLASS DISCUSSION

Questions

1) In discussing factors that support greater or lesser degrees of division of labor, we have given examples that lead to different conclusions with regard to the job of a newsboy as compared to the job of a college professor. To the degree that the conclusions are sound, how do you explain this difference? What benefits and drawbacks would you foresee if there were greater division of labor in carrying out the duties of a college professor?

2) Discuss the factors that make it difficult for a modern corporation to adapt to external change that necessitates departmental rearrangement. How did businesses adapt to such changes during the early stages of industrial development?

3) In what ways does the decision on how much division of labor in individual jobs influence the decision on whether to use compound or functional grouping?

4) What factors determine whether it will be easier or more difficult to fix responsibility for success or failure of a functional group than it would be for a compound group?

5) Under what conditions is it advisable to create a separate auxiliary or service unit rather than to enlarge the scope of activities in a major operating unit? How does this relate to the problem of empire building?

6) "We used to have a great safety record in this plant," said a first line foreman. "That is," he went on, "until we set up a separate safety department in the plant personnel office. In the year and a half since this group was set up, accidents have gone up almost 20 percent." How would you explain this phenomenon?

7) In what ways do you suppose the technology available at the time of the building of the pyramids influenced the determination of (1) the grouping of operating tasks into individual tasks, (2) the combining of jobs into work groups, and (3) the combining of work groups into departments? What other factors probably supported these forms of organization design?

8) Which of the seven key factors influencing departmentation do you feel should be given the greatest emphasis when selecting a pattern of departmentation?

Cases

For cases involving issues covered in this chapter, see especially the following. Particularly relevant questions are listed after each case.

General Machinery Corporation (p. 130), 1
Scott-Davis Corporation (p. 227), 2
Bolling Laboratories, Inc. (p. 345), 1
E.W. Ross, Inc. (p. 468), 1
Consolidated Instruments—B (p. 674), 2

FOR FURTHER READING

Anderson, J.W., "The Impact of Technology on Job Enrichment." *Personnel*, September 1970. *Technology and the feasibility of changing job content.*

Filley, A.C., and R.J. House, *Managerial Process and Organizational Behavior.* Glenview, Ill.: Scott, Foresman & Company, 1969, Chaps. 4 and 9. *Digests behavioral research on organization design and division of labor.*

Gulick, L., "Notes on the Theory of Organization," in *Papers on the Science of Administration*, ed. L. Gulick and L. Urwick. New York: Institute of Public Administration, Columbia University, 1937, pp. 3–45. *A classic that is fully applicable today.*

Hunt, R.G., "Technology and Organization." *Academy of Management Journal*, September 1970. *Summarizes recent behavioral science studies relating technology and organization.*

Katzell, R.A., "Contrasting Systems of Work," in *Readings in Organization Theory*, ed. W.A. Hill and D. Egan. Boston: Allyn & Bacon, Inc., 1967, pp. 364–72. *Suggests factors that influence effective organization.*

Learned, E.P., and A.T. Sproat, *Organization Theory and Policy.* Homewood, Ill.: Richard D. Irwin, Inc., 1966, pp. 8–38. *Lucid notes on specialization, departmentation, and coordination.*

Chapter Three

Decentralization

DIVIDING MANAGERIAL WORK

Growth invariably leads to a management hierarchy. As joint action becomes more complicated, we create a hierarchy to assure coordinated planning, direction, and control. Centralization-decentralization concerns the vertical allocation of management action up and down this hierarchy, whereas departmentation involves a horizontal allocation of operating work.

Persistence of the Problem

The question of how much work the chief executive should do himself and how much he should reassign to his subordinates has bothered administrators for centuries. One of the earliest references to the problem is found in the Book of Exodus, where there is a report of Moses' experience with this dilemma:

> Moses sat to judge the people; and the people stood about Moses from the morning unto the evening. And when Moses' father-in-law saw all that he did . . . he said unto him: "The thing that thou doest

is not good. Thou wilt surely wear away, both thou and this people with thee; for the thing is too heavy for thee—thou are not able to perform it thyself alone.

"Hearken now unto my voice . . . Be thou for the people Godward, and bring thou the causes until God. [Then] thou shalt teach [the people] the statutes and the laws, and shalt show them the way wherein they must walk, and the work that they must do.

"Moreover thou shalt provide out of all the people able men, such as fear God, men of truth, hating unjust gain; and place such over them, to be rulers of thousands, rulers of hundreds, rulers of fifties, and rulers of tens; and let them judge the people at all seasons. And it shall be that every great matter they shall bring unto thee, but every small matter they shall judge themselves. So shall it be easier for thyself, and they shall bear the burden with thee."

The fundamental problem Moses faced is still with us. The burden on executives is especially acute in enterprises that are changing and growing. As product lines are diversified and new employees added, executives find that they can no longer give proper attention to all the management problems that cross their desks. Unless they decentralize, they find that they, like Moses, are unable to cope with the job by themselves.

The need for dividing up the administrative work and pushing it down the line, then, is often perfectly clear. What is *not* so clear is just *how* it should be done. Any competent executive feels keenly his obligation to secure top performance in the operations assigned to him. How can he retain adequate control and yet allow his subordinates freedom to act on day-to-day problems? What kinds of decision should be reserved for top executives? Should lower-level executives be assigned responsibility for improving operations in addition to getting results according to established practice?

The allocation of managerial work is one of the most subtle aspects of the organizing process. The degree of decentralization may vary from department to department within a single company. The sales department, for example, may be highly decentralized. But the controller may retain control over a great deal of the planning, organizing, and motivating of the operations under his direction. Even within a department, decentralization may vary. Thus management work in the credit department may be decentralized from the vice-president down to the industry specialists, but then the industry specialists may delegate little authority to the credit analysts.

For insight into this web of relationships we shall first examine the delegation process and then consider factors determining the degree of decentralization that is desirable in a specific situation. The chapter closes with a penetrating look at profit-decentralization—an organizational arrangement well suited to a dynamic society.

THREE INEVITABLE FEATURES OF DELEGATING

Delegation is familiar to anyone in a supervisory position; it simply means entrusting part of the work of operations or management to others. A filling station owner delegates car greasing to Bill and pump tending to Charlie. The president of Republic Aircraft Corporation entrusts financial matters to Mr. MacGregor, the treasurer. Such delegations give rise to what we commonly call a boss-subordinate relationship.

The practice of delegating, along with the resulting chain of command, has persisted as an organizational device through the centuries. Caesar's army, the Roman Catholic church, the East India Company, the Social Security Administration, Students for a Democratic Society, and IBM have all been based on delegation. Although there are numerous supplementary means for coordinating action, the process of delegating provides the skeleton of the formal organization structure. Surprisingly, this familiar and basic aspect of organization continues to be inefficiently handled.

Every time a manager delegates work to a subordinate—say, a president to a foreign manager, or a first-line supervisor to an operator—three actions are either expressed or implied:

1) The manager assigns *duties*. The man who is delegating indicates what work the subordinate is to do.

2) He grants *authority*. Along with permission to proceed with the assigned work, he will probably transfer to the subordinate certain rights, such as the right to spend money, to direct the work of other people, to use raw materials, to represent the company to outsiders, or to take other steps necessary to fulfill the new duties.

3) He creates an *obligation*. In accepting an assignment, a subordinate takes on an obligation to his boss to complete his job.

These attributes of delegation are like a three-legged stool; each depends on the others for support, and no two can stand alone.

Duties

Duties can be described in two ways. First, we can think of them in terms of an activity. For instance, we may say that Tom Turner's duties are either to run a turret lathe, to sell in Oshkosh, to direct an employment office, to discover and analyze facts about the money market and trends in interest rates, or to measure distribution costs. According to this view, delegating is the process by which we assign activities to individuals.

Second, we can describe duties in terms of the results we want to achieve. Following this approach, we would say that in the first two examples Tom Turner's duties are to turn on his lathe a certain number of pieces per day according to engineering specifications, or to build customer goodwill and secure a prescribed number of orders in the Oshkosh territory. Here we are talking about objectives. We define the duties not just in terms of "going through certain motions," but in terms of accomplishment. To express duties in terms of purpose adds vitality to otherwise neutral statements. The description "to measure distribution costs" may be adequate for departmentation, but if we want to avoid aimless activity, we should elaborate our statement and indicate specific purpose—for instance, "to measure distribution costs in order to provide useful information for pricing, controlling costs, and locating warehouses."

Because of differences in jobs, we may state such goals in terms of long-run or short-run results. Our declarations may be general and intangible or specific and readily put into effect. They may represent overoptimism or realistic expectation. Nevertheless, if we phrase the delegation of duties in terms of goals, a subordinate is likely to get psychological satisfaction from his work, and he will have advance notice of the criteria on which his performance will be judged. A man's duties will be clear to him only if he knows what activities he must undertake *and* what missions he must fulfill.

Authority

If we assign a man duties to perform, is it not obvious that we must give him all necessary authority to carry them out? An advertising manager needs authority to buy space, hire a copywriter, and take other necessary steps if he is to gain his assigned objective of building customer demand for company products.

Unfortunately, assigning authority is not simple. In fact, a principal source of the difficulty many executives experience in delegating is their inclination to oversimplify this matter of authority. We should understand exactly what kind of authority is within the power of a manager to grant; in addition, we should recognize the substantial number of restrictions that typically fence in the authority a manager has at his disposal.

Administrative authority consists of certain permissions or rights: the right to act for the company in specified areas (to buy raw material, accept orders from customers, issue press releases, admit people into a plant, for example); the right as spokesman for the company to request other employees to perform activities of various kinds; and the right to impose sanctions and discipline if a subordinate disregards his instructions. These rights are vested in the head of an enterprise by law and custom, and they are supported by the moral approval of society. They stem partly from concepts of private-property rights, partly from acknowledged authority of the political state, and particularly from the long-established human habit of looking to hierarchical leadership in cooperative undertakings. Because of this background, employees and in fact our whole society accept the idea that the head of an enterprise—whoever he may be—has certain rights of authority and that he may reassign these rights.

When an employee takes a job, he expects also to take orders from someone designated by the company, he looks to management for permission to use company property or to act as an official representative of the enterprise, and he expects a superior to review his work and bring pressure on him to improve if it is unsatisfactory. Such socially accepted rights constitute formal authority, and management can assign these rights when it erects a formal organization.

Throughout history men have challenged formal authority from time to time. The drafting of the Magna Charta, the mutiny on the *Bounty*, and the sit-in demonstrations of the 1970s—all represent challenges to constituted authority.[1] But these events are notable as exceptions to the usual willingness of men to recognize formal authority. To be sure, from the time of the medieval serfs to the unionized workers of today, the scope of authority an employer may exercise over an employee has declined. But by and large people expect authority and rely on it.

Modern society can provide a wide range of individual freedoms only if we utilize authority effectively. For instance, high productivity, which makes possible a choice of adventures (travel, communication, artistic expression, recreation, and so forth) and more free time to enjoy these pursuits, requires disciplined collaborative work. Acceptance of authority is particularly necessary when large numbers of people perform specialized services for one another. Such interdependence releases each of us from personally performing a variety of chores, but it also necessitates dependable action. So freedom to participate in our modern style of life has its counterpart in some regulation of behavior.

Authority is an essential element of any modern enterprise, but we must not confuse it with unlimited power. No company president or section manager can grant someone of lower rank the power to change the physical laws of the universe, the power to force customers to sign orders or suppliers to sell raw materials, or the power to compel the *enthusiastic* cooperation of associates and subordinates. The rights that an administrator may transfer are more akin to authorization than they are to power.

In addition to inherent limitations on the authority that an executive can delegate, virtually every company imposes limitations of its own. Typically, an executive is permitted to act strictly "within company policy" and "in accordance with established procedures." A manager may in theory have formal authority to hire and fire people in his division, but in fact he must adhere to a myriad of restrictive procedures that require him, for example, to refer job descriptions to the planning department before he can fill a new position, to satisfy the personnel department that

[1] We refer here only to employee sit-ins. Protests by outsiders do not relate to the delegation process we are discussing here.

Fig. 3–1   A manager's authority must fall within the zone of acceptance created by the attitudes of society and of subordinates. In addition, his authority is bounded by company policies and procedures, and by the specific delegation to him from his boss.

no capable person is available within the company before he can hire an outsider, to set salaries within an established range for each job classification, and to refrain from discharging anyone without two prior warnings at least a month apart. Another department head may have to endure comparable restrictions surrounding purchases of raw materials and, especially, of new equipment.

Because of these various limitations on authority, when we delegate a task we must be sure to specify what rights are associated with it.

Obligation

By obligation, the third inevitable feature of delegation, we mean the moral compulsion felt by a subordinate to accomplish his assigned duties. When duties are delegated to him, a subordinate is not free either to do the work or leave it as may happen to suit his convenience. For instance, a price checker is derelict in his duty if on Friday afternoon he mails out a batch of unaudited bids to customers merely because his "work had piled up and salesmen were anxious to get the bids to their customers." Similarly, a young man assigned to unlock the office in the morning fails in his obligation when he shows up two hours late and gives the excuse that his brother had unexpectedly stopped overnight for a visit.

Although agreement is usually implied rather than expressed, when a subordinate accepts an assignment he in effect gives his promise to do his best in carrying out his duties. Having taken a job, he is morally bound to try to complete it. He can be held accountable for results. A sense of obligation, then, is primarily an attitude of the person to whom duties are delegated. Dependability rests on the sense of obligation, and without personal dependability our cooperative business enterprises would collapse.

In delineating the chief features of delegating, we have avoided using the word "responsibility" because it means different things to different people. Some use it as a synonym for duty, whereas others think its meaning is identical with obligation. To avoid this confusion, we will shy away from the word responsibility. From time to time, however, we shall use accountability as a synonym for obligation.

APPLYING DELEGATION CONCEPTS

Should Duties and Obligations Extend beyond Authority?

A common saying in popular management literature declares that "authority and responsibility should always be equal." Behind this statement lies the conviction that if we assign a man duties, we ought to furnish him with enough authority—no more and no less—to carry them out, and if we give him authority, we certainly expect from him a corresponding obligation to use it wisely. Although there are elements of truth in this contention, it is unfortunately an oversimplification. Let us see why.

The first difficulty is the word "equal." Duties are concerned with objectives and activities, authority with rights, and obligation with attitudes. These three things are of different orders, and it is hard for an executive to find a common denominator for measuring equality among them. They are indeed related—as related as, but no more equal than, a small boy's apples, a spoon, and his fondness for applesauce. As we have seen in our discussion of formal authority, there are only certain kinds of rights that an enterprise can pass along to its managers, and there are usually very substantial restrictions on how even these rights may be used. To permit every man to charge into action without constraints would lead to chaos. Frequently a man must try to achieve objectives with authority far short of his desires.[2]

It is more nearly accurate, though not so pat, to say to the boss, the man doing the delegating, "Duties, authority, and obligation depend on each other and you should therefore correlate them thoughtfully"; and to the subordinate, the man receiving the delegation, "You are obligated to fulfill your duties to the maximum extent that is feasible in the light of your authority and the conditions under which you have to work."

An Obligation Cannot Be Delegated

What happens when duties and authority are redelegated? Does this redelegation relieve the executive who makes it of *his* obligations? Suppose the treasurer of the Omaha Chemical Company, for example, delegates to

[2]*Legal* authority is not dealt with here. It is principally concerned with the enterprise's relationships with outsiders. In business firms men typically have far-ranging legal authority but are restrained by internal limitations on its use.

the chief accountant the task of maintaining an accounts-payable ledger. The chief accountant, being too busy to maintain the records himself, assigns the job to a clerk.

The redelegation of the job by the chief accountant to the clerk does not at all change the initial relationship between the treasurer and the chief accountant. The chief accountant still has the same duties and as much authority, and even though he has turned over the major parts of these to the clerk, he can reclaim them if he wishes. More importantly, the chief accountant still has the same obligations to the treasurer. The additional obligation between the clerk and the chief accountant in no way relieves the chief accountant of his obligation. It is as though the treasurer lent ten dollars to the chief accountant, and the chief accountant in turn lent the money to the clerk; the chief accountant cannot satisfy his obligation to the controller by passing along the clerk's IOU.

If we were to abandon this principle that a man cannot delegate obligation there would be no way of knowing who was accountable for what.

Dual Subordination

An issue we face over and over in delegating is whether each man should have only one boss. On this point, formal organization theory is clear. A worker—operator or manager—may have relations with many people, but he needs one supervisor whose guidance can be regarded as final. What are the reasons supporting this concept of a single chain of command?

All executives and all subordinate employees respond to a variety of influences, not just those emanating from their line bosses. Nevertheless, the evidence indicates that as important as other people may be in influencing the behavior of an employee, the line boss is usually far more significant. Reasons for the overriding influence of the line boss are not hard to find. Normally the boss trains and directs an employee and explains what he should do; the boss authorizes what the subordinate may do; he assists in getting necessary materials and tools and often represents "his" men throughout the organization; he checks results and initiates corrective action when necessary; he praises, blames, disciplines, promotes, recommends changes in pay, and otherwise motivates his subordinates. These activities are closely interrelated, and if they are to have their greatest impact, they should spring, integrated, from one source.

When two bosses try to share the fundamental role of immediate supervisor, their actions are likely to be inconsistent. One may praise, whereas the other may suggest improvements; the first may urge speed and initiative, whereas the second may withhold authority; they may make assignments that conflict. Men can and do get along with two bosses, just as a child adjusts to guidance from two parents; but, as with parents, unless the two bosses have a very close working relationship, they may find many opportunities for maneuvering for advantage and may tend to be unjust to the subordinate. When there is one boss, the likelihood of a consistent pattern of supervision is greatly increased. The experience of managers over the years indicates that we are wise to have one supervisor who resolves conflicting demands and has final say on priorities.

Duties Include Interactions

Clear-cut duties and authorities do not imply that each man should work in his own isolated corner. Instead, in most delegations, managers make it very clear that a subordinate should consult with others and keep them informed as he proceeds with his own duties.

Furthermore, a few assignments are specifically joint undertakings. Some companies emphasize their concern with cooperation by saying that a man is accountable for both work and teamwork, and they are dissatisfied with a man's performance unless he measures up well on both counts. Cooperation is simply a part of a job and should be as clear as other duties.

Relations between supervisors and subordinates are subject to continual adjustment. We should modify delegations as the work to be done and the people who do it change. Nevertheless, the vast bulk of relationships are stable—at least for some period of time. This stability is important. A worker learns what to expect of his boss; the boss learns how much he can depend on each of his subordinates; people doing related work learn how to deal with an established hierarchy. Such patterns of expectations are essential if we are to get day-by-day work done smoothly and quickly. If the delegating has not been done well, and if boss-subordinate relationships are unclear and become sources of friction, then the company unity we seek will be lacking.

HOW MUCH DECENTRALIZATION?

The preceding discussion centered on the process of delegating. Now we turn to the extent and content of such delegations.

Focus on Planning

Experience has shown that *planning*—that is, identifying problems and deciding what action to take—is usually the most crucial element in thinking about decentralization. Organizing, leading, and controlling are also important, but assigning those activities to various executives typically depends on how we have allocated planning duties. When we look more

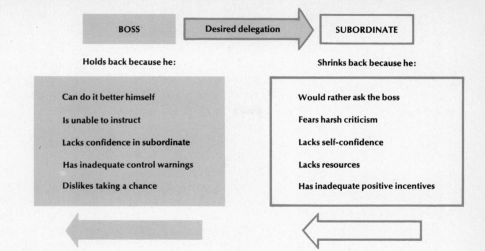

BOSS	Desired delegation →	SUBORDINATE

Holds back because he:

Shrinks back because he:

Can do it better himself	Would rather ask the boss
Is unable to instruct	Fears harsh criticism
Lacks confidence in subordinate	Lacks self-confidence
Has inadequate control warnings	Lacks resources
Dislikes taking a chance	Has inadequate positive incentives

Fig. 3–2 Personal obstacles to effective delegation. Even when organization design calls for delegation, personal factors may obstruct the transfer.

closely later on at leadership and control, we shall trace the interplay of these phases of management with decisions concerning decentralization.

There are several ways to divide the work of planning among executives, and these are important for describing varied degrees of decentralization.

By subject. This is the simplest way to divide planning. An executive normally makes decisions only for the operations that he also directs. In other words, the departmentation of operating work discussed in the previous chapter usually implies a corresponding assignment of planning work among the supervising executives. However, when an operation affects several related departments, as does pricing or inventory control, we may stipulate that certain other persons are to be consulted before binding decisions are made.

Dividing planning by subject is especially useful in situations where there is a senior executive and a lower executive who reports to him. A chief accountant, for example, might say to his office manager: "I'll decide what accounts to keep and where different types of items should be charged—that is, I'll set up the accounting system. But I want you to schedule the flow of work through the office, determine the number and types of people we need, and figure out whether it would pay us to get more automatic equipment." Or the vice-president in charge of sales might select the markets to be cultivated and then assign to his sales manager the detailed planning of direct-mail publicity, personal contacts, and other activities designed to secure orders from the customers within these markets. Note that in each of these examples certain subjects are decided by the senior man and other subjects by his subordinate.

By type of plan. Often a sharp division of administrative work by subject is not feasible. A senior executive may want some say in the way a particular type of situation is handled, and yet lack time to make daily decisions on each individual problem. This partial involvement can be accomplished by the use of *objectives* and *policies*, which set the direction and limits of action. Subordinates can then make decisions on specific cases within this guiding framework. For instance, the president of a telephone company can say, "No employee with more than two years of service is to be discharged as a result of the installation of automatic dialing equipment." The managers of local branches must act within this limit and plan for the transfer or retraining of any displaced workers with a two-year service record.

Sometimes a senior executive wishes to be more specific. If so, he can lay out a step-by-step *procedure* to be followed, or a *schedule* of dates when specific action is to be completed. Thus an advertising manager often sets deadlines for drawings, magazine copy, radio scripts, and other parts of his promotion campaign. His subordinates are free to make detailed schedules for their own work provided the master schedule is met.

In still other situations an executive may announce that certain *premises* are to be adopted when plans are made for the future. For example, he tells the production manager to prepare his budget on the assumption that there will be a 20 percent increase in sales volume during the following year.

From the point of view of decentralization, the questions are to what extent these different types of plan should be used and *who* should set them up. Clearly, the more management circumscribes or regiments work by means of objectives, policies, and so forth, the more highly centralized the organization will be.

By phase of planning. Planning is not typically an isolated activity performed by a single person insulated from his associates. In fact the more important the plan, the more likely it is that several people will participate in formulating it. As we shall see in Part Three, planning consists of several identifiable phases: diagnosing and identifying a problem, finding possible solutions to the problem, gathering facts, and projecting the results of each alternative, and, finally, choosing one alternative as the course of action to be followed. In practice, the work of each of these phases may be performed by different persons.

Except for final decision-making, none of these phases need be regarded as the exclusive domain of some particular person. Anyone who spots a trouble area that needs to be cleaned up or has evidence that will contribute to the sound analysis of a problem should be encouraged to volunteer his ideas. Eliciting such voluntary assistance, however, is not enough in itself. Someone must still be responsible for ensuring that each phase of the planning process is properly performed.

Just how these phases of planning are actually handled depends a great deal on the atmosphere that prevails within each company. In one company it might be presumptuous for a first-line supervisor to suggest a change in personnel policies, whereas in another company the man might get fired if he failed to spot potential trouble and recommend a plan for avoiding it. When a possible change is being studied, some companies expect a lower-level supervisor to provide only the information he is asked for, whereas other firms expect him to speak his mind on anything he believes pertinent and, perhaps, to come up with counterproposals. These are all examples of how the burden of planning may be allocated in terms of phases or steps in the planning process.

Summary. To understand who does what about planning, we need to ask ourselves these questions:

1) What is the subject?

2) Is a single problem being decided, or is a general guide being established—such as an objective, policy, procedure, schedule, or premise?

3) Do several executives participate in the decision? If so, which phase of the decision-making process is each man expected to take on? Decentralization is concerned with how much of this complex planning activity should be assigned to each executive, from the president down to first-line supervisors.

Degrees of Decentralization

How are these concepts put into practice? The following two examples help answer this question. To make it easier to compare the degrees of decentralization, both examples concern sales activities.

Decentralized planning. A company that manufactures materials-handling equipment has a field force of twenty-four men. Six are branch managers, and each has one to four salesmen. The branch managers spend at least half their time in actual selling. Because industrial equipment is purchased at irregular intervals, the salesmen have to follow sales leads; they cannot depend on a regular flow of repeat business from a limited number of customers.

The management of this company thinks it has a highly decentralized sales operation. However, two important subjects are definitely centralized: products and prices.

Product-planning is handled by the engineering department in the main office. A variety of standard equipment is described in a product book, and salesmen are encouraged to sell this equipment whenever it is suited to the customer's needs. If special equipment is required, the salesmen simply gather the operating data and submit these facts to the home office. The engineering department then decides what to recommend to the customer and prepares the necessary sketches. Salesmen's suggestions for new items are always welcome, and one of the branch managers serves on a new-products committee that advises the engineering department. Basically, however, decisions on the products to be sold are highly centralized.

The setting of prices is also centralized. Prices of standard items are set by the sales manager and recorded in a price book. This system enables the salesman to make quotations immediately to the customer, but he has no freedom to modify prices. The sales manager also sets prices on all special orders. In making these decisions, the sales manager draws on salesmen's information regarding customers, cost figures from the estimating department, and his knowledge of the competitive situation. Decisions on the granting of credit are made by the treasurer, and accounting procedures are established by the controller. These, however, are minor matters in the sales activities of the company.

Except for product-planning and price-setting, the men in the field have almost complete freedom. Which customers to call on, what selling methods to use, which conventions and trade association meetings to attend, when a long-distance phone call is worth its cost—all are determined locally. The branch manager is a key man in many of these decisions, but he may require that an experienced, competent salesman do his own planning.

The home office is not indifferent to what goes on in the field. It provides a variety of services to help the salesmen: descriptive circulars, films, prospect lists by type of industry and location, customer leads from magazine advertising, a weekly information bulletin, and technical advice, either by letter or by personal visits from an engineer. Nevertheless, it is up to the branch manager and the salesmen to decide what use, if any, they will make of these services.

Notice that the planning of sales is rather sharply divided by subject. The chief engineer decides what products will be sold, the sales manager sets the prices, the branch managers select the customers. Only a limited use is made of policies and standing procedures. There is considerable cooperation in the planning process, particularly through the exchange

Fig. 3–3 Decentralized versus centralized planning. The intensity of black suggests the degree of regulation, the intensity of color the degree of autonomy.

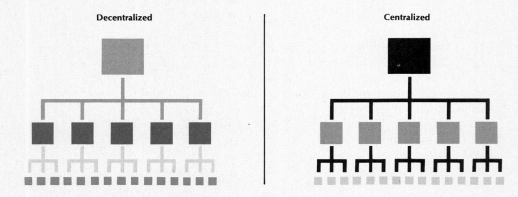

Decentralized   Centralized

of ideas and information. This exchange has not been formalized, however, to a point where the man making the decision feels relieved of any of the preliminary phases of planning (except for the preparation of cost estimates used in pricing).

Not everyone in the company is convinced that the present method of dividing up the sales-planning work is the best. One man advocates much more central planning and direction; he insists that sales quotas should be established, that salesmen should be directed to the industries that seem to have the highest potential in their territory, that direct-mail advertising should be tied in closely with salesmen's calls, and that annual campaigns featuring new products should be instituted. These proposals have not received much support, however. Most of the sales executives believe that the local men can judge what will produce on-the-spot results better than anyone sitting in the home office.

Centralized planning. Now let us turn to a midwestern oil company in which the sales-planning work is divided up in quite a different way. This company sells gasoline, lubricating oil, fuel oil, and related items in ten states. It ranks fifth or sixth in market position in its area. The company has forty-two sales branches, which, for purposes of supervision, are grouped into six districts. Each branch has three main operating executives under a branch manager: A fuel oil and industrial sales manager who contacts independent oil dealers and large customers; a gasoline sales manager who promotes sales of gasoline and associated products through filling stations (both independent and company-owned); and a company station manager who leases, staffs, builds, and exercises financial control over company-owned filling stations.

Most of the planning for all sales activities is done in the main office. An executive committee decides what products are to be sold. The vice-president in charge of sales sets general prices and establishes policies covering any price reduction to meet local competition. Advertising is planned and executed at headquarters. Sales promotion, keyed in with the advertising program, is planned in detail at the home office and includes decisions on the color stations are to be painted and on the design of signs. A variety of training aids for station operators are also planned centrally: instructions for waiting on customers, care of washrooms, methods of car greasing, and the like.

The executives at headquarters prepare similar plans for selling fuel oil, although they are not so elaborate as those for gasoline. The sales vice-president places more reliance on policies and other guides that will help get the right fuel oil dealers to carry the company products and he gives less attention to the particular methods these dealers are to follow.

The district managers devote almost all their time to supervising branch activities and advising the home office on changes that should be made in selling plans. These men perform a necessary and very useful function but make few decisions on how the selling work will be done.

The branch managers, then, are primarily concerned with carrying out plans that have already been made. They hire, train, pay, direct, and motivate the key people in the branch office—all in accordance with company policy and other plans. If a price war breaks out, they adjust local prices in accordance with policy or, if necessary, request the home office to adjust them. They take care of the innumerable little problems that inevitably arise in the sale of a substantial dollar-volume of product. Often they pass new ideas for sales promotion along to the main office. Their principal duty, however, is to carry out the sales program as effectively as possible rather than to generate new ideas. The executives of this oil company would strongly resist any proposal to give branch managers the freedom in planning permitted by the manufacturer described above.

These two examples illustrate not only the general difference between a centralized and decentralized department, but also the need to think specifically about each type of problem (for instance, pricing in the industrial-equipment company) even though a general pattern has been established. In practice, an endless variation in degrees of delegation exists, and properly so. Each company operates in its own unique circumstances of size, reputation, competitive strategy, existing equipment, abilities of key executives, and similar factors. Each manager must figure out what allocation of executive duties best fits his needs. We can, however, identify certain factors that will help a manager make that allocation wisely.

Guides to "How Much Decentralization?"

We should carefully weigh the following seven factors when choosing the best place in the executive hierarchy for each category of decision-making.

1) *Who knows the facts on which the decision will be based, or who can get them together most readily?*

Sometimes a single individual—salesman, caseworker, advertising manager, foreign plant director, purchasing agent—is in constant command, through the normal course of his work, of all the facts needed to make a given type of decision. Such a person is a natural point for decision-making on this issue. Many decisions, however, require information from several different sources—a decision whether or not to buy a new machine, for example, requires data on production methods, plant layout, future volume, availability of capital, workers' attitudes, and so forth. Channels of communication must be established to funnel all this information to a single point; the question, then, is whether it will be easier to pass general information down the line or specific information up the line. This raises considerations of the accuracy, time, and cost of such communication.

2) *Who has the capacity to make sound decisions?*

Clearly, if people at lower levels—salesmen, foremen, office supervisors, branch managers—lack the ability and experience needed to make a wise decision on a given question, there is a compelling reason to withhold decision-making authority from them. Such capacity, however, is usually a relative matter. Perhaps the president can make a very wise decision about granting credit, but the branch manager can make one almost as good. Since we want to save the president's energies for more important matters, and the branch manager's judgment on this subject is satisfactory, we should lodge the planning for extending credit with the branch manager. On another matter, we may find that no one below a vice-president has the ability to make sound decisions.

3) *Must speedy, on-the-spot decisions be made to meet local conditions?*

The repair of railroad breakdowns or the buying of fruit at wholesale auctions obviously requires that someone with authority be on the scene of action. A similar, though less dramatic, need for prompt action occurs in negotiating contracts, employing personnel to meet unexpected work loads, or adjusting the complaints of irate customers.

4) *Must the local activity be carefully coordinated with other activities?*

Sometimes *uniformity* of action is so important that all decisions on a given matter must be made centrally—for example, ensuring that all customers in a given area are charged the same prices or determining the length of vacation for all employees in a given plant. Other decisions, such as determining a weekly production schedule or laying out a national sales promotion program, require that activities in several areas be closely *synchronized*; here at least some central planning is called for.

5) *How significant is the decision?*

A relatively minor decision—one that will increase or decrease profits only by a dollar or two, for example—clearly should be left to a junior executive or operator. The expense of communication up and down the channel of command and of the time required for the senior executive to handle the problem, would be far greater than any savings that might result from his judgment. On the other hand, any decision that will have a major effect on the total operation, be it either a single transaction or a basic policy, should at least be approved by a senior executive.

6) *How busy are the executives who might be assigned planning tasks?*

In dividing up work among executives, overloads must be avoided. A top executive may already have so many duties that he will have to shirk additional responsibility for planning, or a plant superintendent may lack the time for careful analysis and thoughtful decision. If a busy executive has a distinctive contribution that only he can make, perhaps he can be brought in on one phase of the planning, while the rest of the chore is assigned to someone else.

7) *Will initiative and morale be significantly improved by decentralization?*

Decentralization typically builds initiative and good morale in lower-level executives. We should be sure, however, that such feelings will be generated, and that they are desirable, in each specific situation. Companies that are faced with frequent shifts in consumer demand, in technology, or in the competitive situation must actively promote adaptability and initiative among their workers. In other enterprises, such as many public utilities, where the rate of change is slower, too much originality and initiative among junior executives may actually create discontent and lower morale. Similar sharp differences in the need for initiative are also found in various departments of a single company.

In using these factors as guides to the degree of decentralization that is appropriate in a specific situation, we have to determine how much weight to attach to each. Often the factors pull in opposite directions—the need for speed may suggest greater decentralization, while the desire for coordination may dictate greater centralization. Clearly, each factor must be carefully balanced against the others. Allowance must also be made both for traditional behavior and for growth in the abilities of individuals. So we see again that the managerial task of organizing calls for a high order of judgment.

PROFIT DECENTRALIZATION

There is one form of decentralization that is highly important to larger companies: profit decentralization. Under this plan, a company is split up into product or regional divisions, each of which is responsible for its own profit or loss.

Self-sufficient, Semiautonomous Units

Two characteristics lie at the heart of the plan: (1) All the major operations necessary to make a profit are grouped under the manager of a *self-sufficient* unit. This, of course, is a matter of departmentation (discussed in Chapter 2). Typically, several such self-sufficient, self-contained units are established in a company. (2) The management of these units is so highly decentralized that each of them becomes *semiautonomous*. In effect, we have a series of little businesses operating within the parent company. The manager of each unit has virtually the same resources and the freedom of action that he would enjoy if he were president of an independent company, and he is expected to take whatever steps are necessary to ensure that his "little business" will make a profit.

Profit decentralization is the key concept in organizing large concerns such as General Motors Corporation. This company has established

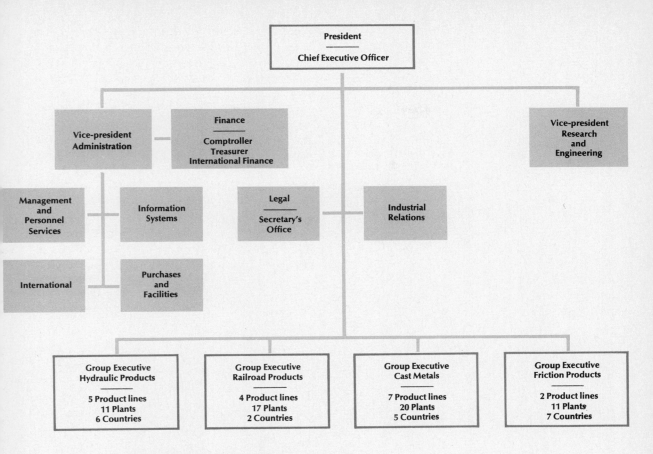

Fig. 3–4   Organization chart of Abex Corporation. Each of the four divisions shown at the bottom of the chart has its own engineering, production, sales, and finance departments and is operated as a self-contained business. The primary task of the corporate services is to aid these operating divisions.

separate divisions for each of its automobile lines—Chevrolet, Pontiac, Oldsmobile, Buick, and Cadillac—and for other products as well, such as Frigidaire, diesel engines, A C spark plugs, and so forth. The General Electric Company has adopted a similar form of organization and now has approximately one hundred separate profit-making units. Profit decentralization is by no means confined to industrial giants, however. Smaller companies such as Johnson & Johnson and Abex Corporation (see Fig. 3–4) have found it admirably suited to their needs.

Ordinarily the operating units are built around product lines, and the engineering, production, and sales of each line are placed within the decentralized division. The same idea, however, has been applied by department store chains, which place all their operations in each *region* on a profit-decentralization basis. In fact this form of organization has become so successful and popular that most diversified companies use it in at least a modified form.

Benefits

A major advantage of profit decentralization is its stimulating effect on the *morale* of the key men in each of these self-sufficient, semiautonomous divisions. Executives are able to see the results of their own methods, to take the action they believe best, and to feel that they are playing an important role. The resulting enthusiasm and devotion to the success of their particular division tend to spread to employees at all levels in the division.

Because operating units established under profit decentralization are of a *manageable size*, fewer people have to exchange information, and they can communicate with one another swiftly and effectively. Executives find it easier to comprehend the information that is funneled to them for it is less diverse and more relevant to their immediate problem than it would be in the complex and unwieldy operations of a large, highly centralized company. The decentralized unit is an operation that the executive can grasp—something that he can "get his arms around."

Situations requiring administrative action are more likely to receive *adequate attention* under profit decentralization. In a large-scale enterprise, it is all too easy to neglect a product or an operation that contributes only a minor part to the total sales volume; to put the operation on a more efficient footing may seem to be more trouble than it is worth. In a smaller division, however, such problems become relatively more important and executives are much more likely to take the necessary corrective action.

The smaller size of the operating units and the heightened ease of communication also lead to improved *coordination*, particularly in the critically important areas of servicing customers, matching production and sales, and keeping costs in line with income. Such integrated action is often hard to achieve in a large enterprise that has been organized functionally, because bureaucratic attitudes are apt to interfere with voluntary cooperation and responsiveness to overall needs.

By making both measurement and accountability more clear-cut, profit decentralization promotes more effective *control*. The profit-and-loss statement of each operating division provides a significant measure of results, for all the relevant activities are under the direction of a division manager. There is less need for top management to make an arbitrary allocation of costs, and to try to decide whether a poor showing was the fault of, say, poor selling or slow delivery. Moreover, because a self-sufficient division is also semiautonomous, its manager can be held accountable for resulting profit or loss. If the results are poor, he can be required to take corrective action; if they are good, he can be, and often is, generously rewarded.

Limitations and Difficulties

If profit decentralization contributes all these impressive advantages, why is it that all large enterprises are not organized in this fashion? Unfortunately, certain distinct limitations and problems are inherent in its use.

For one thing, not all companies can be *divided neatly* into self-contained operating divisions. Technology may make it impossible for a large operation to be broken up into several smaller ones. A steel mill, for example, cannot be split down the middle. General Motors can separate Chevrolets and Buicks; but if the Chevrolet division itself becomes unmanageably large, trying to divide it into two or more self-sufficient units would create serious technical difficulties. On the other hand, in operations such as wholesaling or retailing, which involve a large number of products, sales volume of any one product may be insufficient to support the expense of a separate management and staff of specialists. In still other companies, where a single sales organization is mandatory, it would be disastrous to split up this important activity and place it under the direction of several division managers. One of the limitations of profit decentralization, then, is that the operations of the company must lend themselves to being divided into self-sufficient units of manageable size.

A related problem springs from the auxiliary service activities that the company must perform for the operating divisions. Will a single, central *service unit*, such as purchasing or plant engineering, be really *responsive* to the needs of each of several operating divisions? Will it be able to perform the work more cheaply than outside firms could? Will the operating divisions be required to use the service divisions? If so, what happens to their presumed autonomy and accountability for profits? These are not insurmountable problems, but they do emphasize that profit decentralization brings in its wake a series of potentially troublesome issues.

Although we have referred to this type of organization as profit decentralization, we must remember that profits, though important, may be an *inadequate measure* of the performance of a division, at least in the short-run. A given division may decide, with the full approval of top management, to spend money on advertising and other activities in order to improve its market position; for two or three years it may spend large sums developing a new product. In other words, the division may be achieving its objectives even though it is showing a relatively small profit. Conversely, by keeping down expenses for nonrecurring or deferable items, a division may make a good profit showing even though it is slipping in customer goodwill or development of potential executives. This means that the use of profit for purposes of control is valid only if it is interpreted with a full understanding of what is happening within the division.

Perhaps the greatest difficulty in the use of profit decentralization is to find executives with the *capacity and willingness* to work effectively within the system. Unless administrators, both at headquarters and in the separate divisions, display certain work habits and attitudes, profit decentralization will lead to chaos. The division managers must be prepared to take the initiative on any matter that affects the long-run success of their particular units. They must be aware of the direct and indirect results of their own actions, instead of relying on someone in the home office to keep them out of trouble. In other words, they must act as responsible stewards of the resources put under their direction.

Top administrative officials in the company, in turn, must accept their obligation to maintain a "hands-off" attitude toward the decentralized divisions. As the president of a successfully decentralized company put it, "This calls for confidence in the capabilities of other people, a belief in teaching rather than telling, patience while others are learning—perhaps through their own mistakes—and a willingness to let others stand out in the public eye."

And yet we must remember that many executives of operating divisions have been trained to concentrate on a particular specialty rather than to take an overall view of an integrated business unit and that the top executives of many corporations have achieved their position through positive, aggressive action. It is easy to understand why the attitudes and behavior described in the two preceding paragraphs are difficult to achieve in practice. The key men in a company that adopts profit decentralization must have a realistic understanding of their new roles and must be flexible enough to adjust their behavior accordingly.

Restrictions on Autonomy

There is a great deal of double-talk about decentralization these days. Some companies claim that their operating divisions are semi-autonomous when in fact all major decisions and many minor ones are made by executives in the central office. Everyone agrees that top management should retain some influence over the operating divisions. In consultation with the division managers, top management should (1) set long-range objectives and annual goals, (2) establish the broad policies within which the divisions are to operate, (3) approve the selection of key executives within the division, (4) approve major capital expenditures (which in effect means approving any major expansion), and (5) review any single transaction that might entail a major change in the profit or loss of the division. In addition, the headquarters office might want (6) to establish certain procedures for accounting, personnel, or purchasing in order to assure consistent action throughout the entire company.

Clearly, there are many areas in which the operating divisions are *not* autonomous. Furthermore, top management can interpret all these limitations so broadly that it may retain the right to interfere with the division operations almost anywhere it wants to. Objectives or policies may be made so specific that the division managers are left with little freedom of discretion, or the scrutiny of budgets may extend to such insignificant items that the hands of the local man are effectively tied.

The use of policies, procedures, programs, and other types of plans will be examined later in this book, as will means for securing motivation and control. The point here is that the manner in which these particular processes are performed can either support or vitiate the underlying concept of profit decentralization. Therefore, if we organize along profit-decentralization lines, we must also plan, lead, and control in a manner compatible with profit decentralization.

CONCLUSION

In this chapter, we discussed first the process of delegating and then related this to the allocation of managerial work, especially its assignment to executives at different levels, from first-line supervisors to the president. Planning—that is, making decisions about actions to be taken—stands out as the crucial activity in managerial decentralization; once we decide who should do what planning, then other aspects of managerial work can be adjusted to fit into the pattern. Each manager has to allocate planning work among his subordinates, and we have identified several factors that can help him design a pattern of decentralization suited to the particular conditions he faces.

One special type of allocation, especially appealing to diversified companies, is "profit decentralization." Analysis of profit decentralization highlights the intimate connection between the way we departmentalize a company and the forms of decentralization that are desirable. We shall return to this interrelation in the chapters on overall organization structure. But first we need to consider in the next chapter how staff men can be fitted into the total allocation of managerial work.

FOR CLASS DISCUSSION

Questions

1) In what ways may a manager's experience in lower-level jobs (jobs that now fall under his supervision) positively and negatively affect his decision on how much he should decentralize?

2) Consider the duties of a pitcher on a major league baseball

team in a game in which he is to pitch. (1) How should his duties be stated? (2) Define the nature of his authority. (3) Given your answers to 1 and 2, what is the nature of the pitcher's obligation? (4) How are his duties, authority, and obligation affected by each of the following: his pitching coach, his manager, his teammates, and his opponents?

3) The chief accountant of the Chicago division of a multi-division company reports to the general manager of that division. Accounting forms, regulations, and procedures, however, are designed by the corporate controller and must be followed by the division chief accountant. (1) Who is the chief accountant's boss? (2) What is the nature of his obligation to the division general manager? To the corporate controller? (3) How, by wise delegation, might potential friction be avoided? (4) How does this situation relate to bypassed supervision?

4) A great scholar once observed, "A fundamental pillar of freedom is the willingness of those who seek it to limit its application through the acceptance of just authority." Do you agree? Discuss in the context of the three inevitable features of delegation.

5) To what extent should a manager's authority be based on, and shift with, his competence in any given assignment? Discuss the implications of your answer on: (1) benefits of specialization, (2) coordination, and (3) accountability.

6) In what ways would you expect the degree and type of decentralization that takes place in a conglomerate with sales of $200,000,000 to differ from the degree and type of decentralization practiced in an equally large farm-equipment producer?

7) A significant difficulty in expanding output of developing countries is a failure of senior business executives to delegate (decentralize). What reasons do you think lead to this difficulty? How might these obstacles be overcome other than by limiting delegation?

8) To what extent may the evaluation of decentralized profit-centers affect their ability to balance long-run and short-run company objectives?

Cases

For cases involving issues covered in this chapter, see especially the following. Particularly relevant questions are listed after each case.

Trans-World Mutual Funds, Ltd. (p. 121), 2, 3
General Machinery Corporation (p. 130), 2
Scott-Davis Corporation (p. 227), 3
Dodge Skate Company (p. 337), 1

FOR FURTHER READING

Dubin, R., *Human Relations in Administration*, 3rd ed. Englewood Cliffs, N.J.: Prentice-Hall, Inc., 1968, Chaps. 11–13. *Excellent synthesis of ideas on power, authority, and status.*

Learned, E.P., and A.T. Sproat, *Organization Theory and Policy*. Homewood, Ill.: Richard D. Irwin, Inc., 1966, pp. 38–59. *Lucid notes on decentralization, delegation, and related issues.*

Richards, M.D., and W.A. Nielander, eds., *Readings in Management*, 3rd ed. Cincinnati: South-Western Publishing Co., 1969, Chap. 18. *Articles by E. Dale and R.C. Parsons on practical problems of decentralizing.*

Schleh, E.H., *Management by Results*. New York: McGraw-Hill Book Company, 1961, Chaps. 7–11. *Practical advice for effective delegation.*

Simon, H.A., et al., *Centralization vs. Decentralization in Organizing the Controller's Department*. New York: Controllership Foundation, 1954. *Perceptive study of a difficult function to decentralize.*

Chapter Four

Use of Staff

THE CONCEPT OF STAFF

In our examination of decentralization in the preceding chapter we laid a basis for discussing the important, though somewhat slippery, concept of staff. Use of staff is a special way of dividing up managerial work, and the resulting relationships supplement those created by delegation.

Definition of Staff

Staff work is that part of managerial work that an executive assigns to someone outside the chain of command. If an executive wants to relieve himself of some of his administrative burden, he may assign it to a staff assistant instead of delegating it to subordinates who would also be accountable for operations.

As we explained in Chapter 3, a manager always reserves some of the duties of planning, motivating, and controlling when he delegates operating duties to a line subordinate. If he uses staff help, he simply assigns part of this reserved administration to a third person. The third person is called a "staff man," or often merely "staff."

The head of a large department or a president may use several staff men for different phases of his total management task. Some staff men may even have several subordinates of their own who form a staff section. Whatever the number and size of staff sections, the aim of staff work remains the same—to help an executive manage.

Examples of Staff

Businessmen acquired the concept of staff from military men, who have been developing the idea systematically for nearly a century. The business world, however, has not worked out the role of staff so carefully as the military. Practices vary widely from company to company and from job to job, with the result that we find widespread confusion about what a staff man is supposed to do. Because there is no single pattern, a manager must design each staff position individually, as he does other jobs, deciding what activities he can advantageously assign to each particular position. With three examples, we can indicate the range of possibilities.

Specialized staff. Market research illustrates *specialized* staff work. A typical market-research unit gathers a wide variety of information about consumer habits, economic trends, competitors' actions, and marketing practices. The unit carefully analyzes this information in order to give operating executives advice on marketing problems; for example, market researchers can suggest sales potentials to use in setting quotas for individual salesmen, they can identify locations or types of markets where sales promotion effort is most needed, or they can provide sales forecasts on which to base operating budgets. In addition a market-research unit can make special studies of demand for new products; it can test customer response to changes in product; it can compile data for use in price-setting. In short a market-research department provides specialized information and judgment about it, which executives use principally in planning and to a lesser extent in controlling company operations. Operating executives do not have time to gather such information themselves, and they hesitate to ask their sales force to do the work for several reasons: Specialized skills are required, objectivity is essential, and salesmen should spend their time getting orders from customers.

An industrial engineer is a good illustration of a staff man in the production area. Typically he not only gathers information but goes further than the market researcher in preparing specific plans. Layout of plant equipment, production methods, operating standards based on time studies, incentive plans, systems for production scheduling, quality control techniques, preventive maintenance—these are among the problems an industrial engineer often tackles. Solution of such problems requires concentrated attention and may involve technical knowledge a production manager is not familiar with.

When management asks an industrial engineer to make a study, it expects him to draw on all ideas that operating people can suggest and discuss with them the practicability of any tentative plans. After a production manager has approved the final recommendations, an industrial engineer may be asked to assist in putting them into effect. He interprets the approved plans, assists supervisors to adjust to them, explains their advantages and otherwise helps sell them to operators, and checks on results to determine whether operations are proceeding as he anticipated, or whether he must recommend further adjustments. Throughout all this work, everyone understands that the industrial engineer functions as an agent of the production manager.

An internal auditor is another kind of specialized staff man. He is predominantly concerned with control. He checks the accuracy of accounting records, giving special attention to cash, inventories, securities, accounts payable, and other spots where there is a possibility of fraud. Occasionally the auditor also checks on how well and consistently employees comply with procedures and company regulations. Here again operating executives themselves could conceivably check the records, but companies often feel that it is much more economical to assign the task to a full-time specialist.

General staff. Not all staff men concentrate on a specific type of work. Sometimes a manager will want an assistant to whom he can turn over a wide variety of problems. The assistant's duties can vary all the way from functioning as a first-class secretary to serving as an *alter ego* to the boss in delicate situations. Occasionally he will act as a personal aide, but most of the time he will assist his superior by taking over various administrative tasks. The staff man with such unspecified duties is often called "assistant *to* the —————."

On different days, we might find an assistant to a president gathering information on the national economic outlook, editing a statement for the president to make before a Congressional committee, preparing a speech about company policy on licensing competitors to use company patents, investigating a complaint about company service that an important customer made to the president at lunch at the Union League Club, meeting with a group of long-service employees who urge the company to advance the compulsory retirement age to seventy, attending meetings of the budget committee and the long-range planning committee, or coaching a new office boy on how to please the boss.

Corporate services. Very large companies sometimes attach to the central headquarters staff units that work primarily as consultants to operating divisions. In General Electric Company, for instance, one corporate "service" unit focuses on community relations, another on operations research, and so on. Each "service" is charged with anticipating external developments, advancing the state of the art in its particular field, organizing training courses to pass these advanced techniques on to executives and staff men in the operating departments, and being available as consultants on the invitation of the operating departments. Service is stressed. And to encourage use of the counsel, at General Electric these units are *not* used by senior executives for evaluation and control.

In all these examples of staff and in the many others that will appear from time to time in this book, we find a delegation of managerial work to people who do not supervise operations. These delegations, like all delegations, carry with them duties, authority, and obligation, but the duties are administrative without entailing direct supervision over executives or operators.

SCOPE OF STAFF WORK

Clarifying Assigned Duties

We can define the work of a staff man in terms of both the subjects or problems he covers and what he does about them. Unless a staff man, his boss, and everyone he works with understand the scope of his work, his efforts may cause more trouble than help. It is not enough, for example, for us to say that a personnel director should handle staff services in the field of personnel relations. Rather it is more constructive to list the types of problems in the field and then decide how far we expect a staff man to go in dealing with the problem. Figure 4–1 indicates this general approach.

This chart reveals that the role of a personnel director may be quite different in different areas. In dealing with unions, for example, a personnel director is likely to serve principally as an advisor. On the other hand, when a company selects a man to fill a vacancy, a personnel director will most likely work jointly with operating executives, and it is not an uncommon practice that no appointment can be made without the concurrence of the personnel director.

The chart also suggests that for some activities, such as recruiting employees, handling pension plans, or sponsoring company athletic teams, a firm may grant its personnel director operating authority; in these areas he ceases to be a staff man and becomes a supervisor of auxiliary services. Each check mark on a chart such as this represents careful thought about the functions of a particular staff man in a specific company. The chart is of course only a summary. For many subjects it may be necessary to think through several subtopics. Thus a consideration of training, for instance, would include by implication considerations of what should be done for executive personnel, orientation of new employees, training on the job, personal development plans, and so forth. All this detail cannot be shown on a single chart, but the same kind of analysis applies to each subdivision of a general area like training.

The same approach should be followed when we determine the duties of each staff man. The principal task of the market researcher is to gather and analyze data for his boss and other operating executives—A.3 and B.3 on the chart. The industrial engineer, on the other hand, is likely

Activities	Subjects							
	Recruiting	Selecting Employees	Training	Compensation	Benefit Plans	Health and Recreation	Union Relations	Employee Records
1. OPERATING WORK Supervises service operations	✓				✓	✓		✓
2. STAFF WORK Influences actions outside own department; to do so, he:								
A. Advises boss								
1. Identifies areas that need improvement				✓			✓	
2. Finds likely solutions				✓			✓	
3. Gathers and analyzes data bearing on choice of solution				✓			✓	
4. Gets concurrence or objections of people affected				✓			✓	
5. Recommends tentative solution			✓	✓				
B. Advises associates (mostly operating executives under his boss)								
1. Identifies areas that need improvement			✓				✓	
2. Finds likely solutions		✓	✓				✓	
3. Gathers and analyzes data bearing on choice of solution		✓	✓				✓	
4. Gets concurrence or objections of people affected		✓	✓				✓	
5. Recommends tentative solution		✓	✓				✓	
C. Prepares documents putting plans into effect		✓		✓			✓	
D. Interprets and sells established plans	✓							
E. Reports compliance to associates			✓	✓				
F. Reports compliance to boss			✓					
G. Concurs on specific acts		✓		✓				
H. Sets policies and systems			✓					

Fig. 4–1   Chart for analyzing the duties of a personnel director.

to undertake all duties listed under A to F on the chart. An internal auditor is predominantly concerned simply with reporting compliance to his associates and his boss—items E and F on the chart. If we analyze duties in this manner, we will go a long way toward eliminating misunderstandings about the use of staff.

Completed Staff Work

Some people feel that the ideal staff arrangement results in "completed staff work," a concept that General Archer H. Lerch has described as follows:

> *Completed Staff Work is the study of a problem, and presentation of a solution, by a staff officer, in such form that all that remains to be done on the part of the head of the staff division, or the commander, is to indicate his approval or disapproval of the completed action. The words "completed action" are emphasized because the more difficult the problem is, the more the tendency is to present the problem to the chief in piecemeal fashion. It is your duty as a staff officer to work out the details. You should not consult your chief in the determination of these details, no matter how perplexing they may be. You may and should consult other staff officers. The product, whether it involves the pronouncement of a new policy or affects an established one, should, when presented to the chief for approval or disapproval, be worked out in finished form.*
>
> *. . . It is your job to advise your chief what he ought to do, not to ask him what you ought to do. He needs answers, not questions. Your job is to study, write, restudy and rewrite until you have evolved a single proposed action—the best one of all you have considered. Your chief merely approves or disapproves.*
>
> *Do not worry your chief with long explanations and memoranda. . . . In most instances, completed staff work results in a single document, prepared for the signature of the chief without accompanying comment. If the proper result is reached, the chief will usually recognize it at once. If he wants comment or explanation, he will ask for it.*
>
> *The theory of completed staff work does not preclude a "rough draft" but the rough draft must not be a half-baked idea. It must be complete in every respect except that it lacks the requisite number of copies and need not be neat. . . .*
>
> *The completed staff work theory may result in more work for the staff officer, but it results in more freedom for the chief. This is as it should be. Further, it accomplishes two things:*
>
> *(1) The chief is protected from half-baked ideas, voluminous memoranda, and immature oral presentations.*
>
> *(2) The staff officer who has a real idea to sell is enabled more readily to find a market.*
>
> *When you have finished your "completed staff work" the final test is this: If you were the chief would you be willing to sign the paper you have prepared, and stake your professional reputation on its being right? If the answer is in the negative, take it back and work it over, because it is not yet completed staff work.*

Although there is room for argument about some details of this proposal, such as the heavy use of written documents and the low frequency of personal discussions between a staff man and his boss, the central theme has much to recommend it. All too often, a staff man is willing to toss in ideas or information without thinking a matter through to a practical conclusion. He should put himself in the position of the executive who must carry out a proposal, and try to foresee all its ramifications and repercussions. When a manager discovers a staff man who thinks things through, he will tend to rely increasingly on his assistance.

Useful as completed staff work may be, it is not ideal for all situations. It is expensive in terms of both the quality and the number of staff men needed, and few management posts warrant such extensive assistance. To prepare completed staff work, a staff man must spend a good deal of time gathering facts and discussing problems with many people; he must be cautious in deciding whether a particular problem is serious enough to warrant interfering with the work of busy executives and operators. Interference can become a serious problem if several different staff positions are established.

Still another drawback in some companies is the tendency for a strong staff to undermine decentralization. A staff man may initially emphasize help to managers in lower echelons, but if cooperation is not immediately forthcoming, he then turns to completed staff work and urges the big boss to issue an order. If the boss does so, of course, the center of decision-making moves higher in the chain of command.

In view of these possible objections, we may find ourselves saying, "It's a good idea when used in the right place." To return to our previous examples, we can conclude that completed staff work would fit an industrial engineer very well but would not be well suited to a market research man or an internal auditor.

RELATIONSHIPS BETWEEN STAFF AND MANAGERS

Normal Staff Relationships

The relationship between a staff man and the operating executive with whom he works depends in part on the staff duties we discussed on the preceding pages. A man who only gathers facts or only checks on performance, for instance, will have relations with his superior that are different from those of a man who has concurring authority. Nevertheless, we can identify several features that characterize almost all successful staff relationships:

1) A staff man is primarily a representative of his boss. He does things that the boss would do if the latter had the necessary time and ability. He is an extension of the boss's personality, advising, investigating,

imagining, encouraging, following up on matters in his particular sphere. A staff man's position gives him stature, and it also imposes on him an obligation *not to misrepresent the boss*. If occasionally he declares his own views, which may be at variance with those of his boss, he should be careful to make the distinction clear, for people normally presume that a staff man is sufficiently close to his boss to be able to reflect accurately the thinking of his superior. Let us note in passing that a boss has an obligation to spend enough time with each of his staff men so that they can, in fact, establish a mutual and consistent point of view.

2) A staff man must *rely largely on persuasion* to get his ideas put into effect. Lacking the power of command, he must build confidence in his opinions and he must be sufficiently sensitive to the problems of those he would influence to win their acceptance of his proposals. The staff man who cannot accomplish all, or at least most of, the things he wants done by winning voluntary cooperation had better look for another job.

3) A staff man must be prepared to *submerge his own personality* and his own desire for glory. He must be an ardent teamworker, recognizing that his boss or some other operating executive will get credit for carrying the ball. To achieve improved results, he must be prepared to see others receive recognition for ideas that he may have subtly planted several months earlier.

These three characteristics of staff work, when consistently maintained, go far in overcoming the inevitable friction that arises when a third party is interposed in what is naturally a close, two-person relationship between a line supervisor and his subordinate.

We usually speak of a staff man as though he performed his job by himself. But in larger companies he may in fact have several assistants or even a small division under his direction. Multiplication of staff men does not, however, change the relationship between staff and operating executives. *Within* a staff unit, there are of course the usual subordinate-boss, or "line," relationships. Just as any boss delegates—setting up duties, authority, and obligation—so does the head of a staff unit build a series of line relationships between himself and other people within his group. We call these people "staff" because of their work, not because they are in any way absolved from the customary subordinate-boss relationship.

Staff Influence within the Chain of Command

A staff man charged with bringing about improvements in a particular area has two courses of action open to him: He may make a recommendation to an operating executive who is directly or indirectly his boss and then rely on the executive to issue the necessary orders to put the plan into effect, *or* he may try to secure voluntary acceptance of his ideas from other executives without the support of formal orders transmitted down

72

Part One

Organizing:
Structural Design

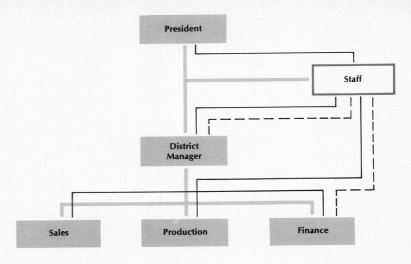

Fig. 4–2 Typical example of relationships of central finance staff with men in the regular line of command. The solid line indicates advice and assistance; the dashed line indicates functional authority.

the chain of command. The second, or voluntary, approach is very common, because a top operating executive is either too busy to bother with an issue or he does not want to upset a pattern of decentralization.

In such circumstances, how does a staff man accomplish his mission? Let us say a senior operating executive—not a staff man—has delegated a task to his West Coast superintendent; he has assigned duties and granted authority, and the superintendent has a sense of obligation to him. Because of the direct relationship with the senior executive, the superintendent is free (except as we will note below) to accept or reject the counsel of a staff man. Why then can a staff man expect to exert any significant influence?

For one reason, people are inclined to accept the advice of a staff man because they regard him as a *technical expert*. Engineer, statistician, repair mechanic, or lawyer, each has a particular field where his word is likely to be taken as authoritative simply because he possesses specialized knowledge. Unless an operating executive feels that he too is an expert in that field, he probably will give careful consideration to the opinion of a man who speaks with the authority of knowledge.

For a second reason, when a staff man has an impressive title, reports high up in the organization hierarchy, and has an office that exhibits the symbols of importance, he enjoys exalted *status*. His views will be taken seriously by reason of his status alone.

Skill in presenting ideas and in winning acceptance for them, as we mentioned earlier, is still another reason why staff men are likely to be influential.

A perhaps more subtle source of influence is *potential backing* by a senior operating executive. If men down the line believe that advice they have rejected is bound to return as a command, they often conclude that it is wiser to take the advice in the first place. Business etiquette usually requires that a staff man present a recommendation turned down by an executive at one level to that man's immediate supervisor before he carries it on up the line. In a large enterprise, several echelons of staff and of operating executives may be involved in a discussion until the matter under consideration finally reaches a top administrator for decision. If it is clear that the staff is going to win an argument sooner or later, resistance is likely to vanish. Conversely, a staff man soon learns when and how far he can push a particular point.

Finally, if a staff man's views may significantly *influence* an employee's salary increases or promotions, that employee will probably accord the staff man's recommendations more than just polite acknowledgment. This inclination is especially potent for employees away from the seat of a company—for example, a branch personnel officer or a branch accountant who aspires to transfer in his functional field, perhaps to the home office.

In summary, then, even though a staff man may have no command authority whatsoever, he may still get his recommendations accepted if he is smart, persuasive, impressive, and influential. Obviously, the potency of influence depends on each man and each situation.

Compulsory Staff Consultation

Despite all the influence he can muster, a staff man may find himself on the sidelines watching the real action taking place without his participation. In a healthy organization, operating executives are strong-minded, vigorous men. Not infrequently, such men welcome staff assistance only on highly technical matters, or when it suits their convenience. To counteract this tendency, some companies follow a practice of compulsory staff consultation. Under this arrangement, a staff man *must* be consulted before action is taken. For example, department heads cannot confront a personnel manager with salary increases already promised or promotions already made; they must instead consult with him before they act. In other cases, a lawyer must have a chance to read a contract before a vice-president signs it, or a public relations man must take a look at a speech before a company representative makes it. Under this plan an operating executive is not blocked from proceeding as he thinks best, but he is required to stop and listen to advice from another point of view.

Compulsory consultation supplements a more general requirement for successful staff work, the requirement that a staff should have access to any information that relates to its field of interest. No mere directive, of course, can insure that a staff man will gain access to underlying motives that are often important for complete understanding of a problem; he can obtain such information only when he shares with others mutual respect and confidence. Nevertheless, it is helpful for management to make clear to employees that they are to keep the staff fully informed.

A related practice that some firms follow is to require each staff unit to make a semiannual or annual report on any weak spots it has uncovered in its particular field. This requirement may put a staff man in the delicate position of revealing a weakness that an operating executive at a low level wants to conceal from senior administrators. The staff man finds himself playing detective and risks not being welcomed back later. On the other hand, the inevitability of the report may prod the operating executive into taking corrective measures, presumably with the help of the staff man, so that the latter can mention constructive steps along with unfavorable conditions. Fundamentally, what each company needs is a climate that nourishes bold statements of fact to anyone concerned, coupled with sympathetic and constructive efforts to help improve deteriorated conditions. Covering up facts because of fear of criticism is not healthy. Managers and staff men can count on a free flow of pertinent information on troublesome situations only if operating men are confident that they will receive constructive help in return.

Concurring Authority

Under some circumstances, a manager may desire to strengthen the hand of his staff. If control over certain operations is very important, a staff may be granted concurring authority so that no action can be taken until a designated staff man agrees to it. Such concurring authority is probably most familiar in connection with quality control where an inspector usually must pass on raw materials or semifinished parts before they move to the next stage of production. But we can also find examples in other departments: An executive may have to seek legal approval before signing a contract; an office manager may have to get the OK of the personnel division before hiring a new employee; or a purchasing agent may have to secure the signature of a budget officer before making commitments for capital expenditures.

Whenever we find a grant of concurring authority to staff, we find a senior administrator who wants to be sure that the staff viewpoint is incorporated into operating decisions. It is a "safe" arrangement, because under it operating executives cannot take heedless action. On the other hand, it slows down action because if the staff and operating people do not agree, someone must appeal up the administrative line, perhaps even to a senior executive who is boss of all operations and staff. In addition, although management can hold both a staff man and an operating man accountable for any actions they *do* take, both have plenty of opportunity for passing the buck when they do *not* take action.

These considerations suggest that we should grant concurring authority only when the point of view represented by a staff man is particularly important, and when possible delay in action, while agreement is being ironed out, will not be serious.

Even when these conditions are met, it is important that we carefully define the grounds on which a staff may withhold its approval of a proposal. For instance, it is one thing for a controller to block a capital expenditure because of lack of funds, and quite another if he blocks it because of his personal disapproval of a plan. An inspector may delay a shipment of goods because they do not come up to standard, but his company should not permit him to take over the engineer's function of deciding how a product should be redesigned. It is especially difficult to define the grounds on which a legal staff may block action; if a lawyer does not believe a certain policy is wise, he can be ingenious in proposing legal objections, and often his position in the organization hierarchy enables him to carry his objections to the top level of management. In government, which so often gives safety priority over speed, we find more frequent use of concurring authority than in business. On an important matter, it is not uncommon for a government worker to have to secure approval, or "clearance," from four or five staff units. Dynamic action is difficult in such a system.

Functional Authority

The most extreme formal technique for extending staff influence is the granting of functional authority. This means that a staff man can give direct orders to operating personnel in his own name instead of making recommendations to his boss or to other operating executives. His instructions then have the same force as those that come down the channel of command. As in direct-line relationships, a staff man probably consults with whomever he gives instructions to, and the man receiving the instructions may point out difficulties in execution to the staff man and to the line boss. But until orders are rescinded or revised, the company expects the worker to carry them out.

Naturally, a staff man would have functional authority only over those areas where his technical competence is recognized and where his opinion would probably be accepted anyway. Thus a chief accountant may have functional authority over accounting forms and systems in use throughout a company, a medical officer over physical examinations, and a legal counsel over responses to any legal suits against the company. On such matters, the word of a staff man will be followed in at least 99 percent of the cases; it is simpler to have it clearly understood that his word is final.

Military organizations, in effect, grant functional authority when they permit staff men to issue orders "in the name of the commanding officer." The wording maintains the fiction that there is a single chain of command. The commanding officer may actually be unaware that an order has been issued, but it would be a rash staff man indeed who issued an order that he believed his commanding officer would not support.

The trouble with functional authority is that it is tempting. It is beguiling in its apparent simplicity. For example, it is too easy merely to say that a personnel director will have functional authority over all personnel matters, a sales promotion director over sales promotion activities, and a controller over all expenses. Such sweeping assignments can wreak havoc in an organization. For if the personnel director can issue instructions that cover the selection, training, and motivation of all employees, he is virtually in a position to dominate all operations. And since expenses are fundamental to nearly every company decision, the controller with functional authority over such matters becomes tantamount to a general manager. When several different staff men have functional authority, even in more narrow areas, there is a possibility that they will overburden operating executives or issue conflicting instructions to them. If a company extensively grants functional authority to staff men, the practice tends to undermine the status of operating executives in the eyes of their subordinates. Not the least of the difficulties is the consequent ambiguity of accountability; when something goes wrong, is it the fault of one or more of the staff planners or is it due to inept supervision? These difficulties arise from the indiscriminate use of a delicate arrangement.

What then are the circumstances in which we may use functional authority? The following three conditions are desirable, and at least two should always be present, before we grant a staff man such authority:

1) *Only a minor aspect of the total operating job is covered.* Accounting forms and Blue Cross contracts, for instance, are only incidental to most operating jobs. Although these matters should receive the thoughtful attention of somebody, the plans adopted do not substantially affect the bulk of operations one way or the other.

2) *Technical or specialized knowledge of a type not possessed by operating executives is needed.* If a sales manager or a production superintendent is going to accept the advice of, say, a tax expert or a medical director anyway, we can simplify decision-making by granting functional authority to such specialists.

3) *Uniformity, or at least consistency, of action in several operating units is essential.* For instance, pension rights of employees who are transferred among several divisions of a company should be treated consistently, as should credit terms extended to customers. A staff unit with functional authority is more likely to deal consistently with such matters than the divisions acting separately.

A Composite Pattern

Of the various means we have considered for strengthening the influence of staff, functional authority moves farthest away from the purely assisting and counseling relationship first described. Compulsory consultation and concurring authority are intermediate positions. For reasons already noted, we should move cautiously from establishing an easy, simply helpful relationship toward insisting that a staff man must be heeded. In fact the guides just outlined for deciding when to employ functional authority indicate that we should carefully restrict its use. Briefly stated, as staff is made more powerful, its scope should be confined.

In practice we often provide a different kind of relationship for different duties of a single man. A company attorney, for instance, might cover the whole range: On most matters he just gives advice, in one or two areas consultation is compulsory, for a limited group of decisions his concurrence is required, and possibly over a few technical matters he has functional authority. But such a composite set of relationships is apt to be confusing. We will court the least trouble by keeping staff men in advisory roles.

PROBLEMS IN USING STAFF

We have implied in the preceding discussion many difficulties that arise in connection with staff. Nevertheless, a summary of four common areas of trouble may be helpful to those who will either use staff or serve in staff positions.

Fig. 4–3 Confrontation over air pollution. The plant manager (left) has line authority over the plant. The staff engineer (center) from headquarters has functional authority regarding anti-pollution equipment. The government inspector (right) has no authority over either man, but he can approve or disapprove the way plant performs.

Vague Definition of Duties and Authority

Time and again, we find friction between operating executives and staff men simply because of a misunderstanding of the role the staff is supposed to play. By now it should be abundantly clear that a staff man may perform any one of a wide variety of administrative roles. The word "staff" provides no magic formula for resolving questions of what these duties should be. Some people within an enterprise may assume that a staff man is merely a fact-gatherer or, at most, an advisor to his own boss. A boss may want a staff man to make suggestions to people throughout the organization; and the staff man himself may be so zealous about his particular areas that he believes he should control as well as plan. With three such disparate views in competition, sooner or later we can expect a clash and perhaps hard feelings. The problem of job definition is frequently complicated by a company's expectation that a staff man will act in one way on one kind of management problem, and in another way on a different problem. We illustrated this problem in the chart that analyzed the duties of a personnel director.

Vague or overly restrictive limits to the authority of a staff man can also lead to trouble. We saw that occasionally companies use compulsory consultation, concurring authority, or even functional authority to strengthen the influence of a staff man. But even when management takes such steps, it typically grants additional authority only over a small part of the total scope a staff man is expected to cover. Perhaps the remarkable thing is that companies using staff do not suffer from more confusion than they actually do.

What we need in order to overcome these problems is mutual understanding by all principal parties of the duties and authority of each staff man and, even more importantly, a working relationship built out of experience that translates the general understanding into smooth work habits and attitudes.

Scarcity of Good Staff Men

All too often, we can trace a staff failure back to a selection of wrong individuals for staff positions. A staff man needs both competence in his specialty and skill in staff work. Without technical competence, of course, he is hardly worth the nuisance he is to other executives. But technical competence alone is not enough. He must be friendly, sensitive, discreet, and honest so that he may earn the confidence of other people; he must be articulate and persuasive so that he may win genuine acceptance of his proposals; rather than resort to commands to produce rapid change, he must be patient but persistent in his efforts to get results; he must find satisfaction in good team results rather than in personal glory; he must have a high sense of loyalty to his boss and obligation to duty, even in the face of the frustration of highly circumscribed authority. Unfortunately, we do not often find a man with this combination of abilities and attitudes coupled with technical competence.

Sometimes a company uses a staff job as a training post for future operating executives, but also occasionally as a dumping ground or pasture for an operating executive who was incompetent. If such a man is a misfit in his staff position, the company creates a new problem in trying to solve an old one. Staff work, by its very nature, creates delicate relationships, and if a company has only unqualified people available, it had better sharply curtail staff jobs in scope or eliminate them entirely.

Mixing Staff and Operating Duties

It is not always practical to separate clearly and completely the staff duties and operating duties in different jobs. We noted, for example, that a personnel director may direct a group of service operations in addition to spending a large portion of his time on staff work. Similarly, a controller typically supervises corporate accounting directly and also has staff duties in connection with budgets and analysis of expenses of other departments.

Small companies that can afford only a limited number of executives may ask a single individual to fill two positions. For instance, a sales promotion manager may supervise selling in one district. Or a company with one large plant and two or three small assembly plants may have its top production man run the main plant and also maintain an undefined staff relationship with the assembly plants.

Still a third type of mixture of staff and operating duties, one which we find in both large and small companies, is to have senior operating executives serve as staff to the president on companywide problems. A large operating department may follow a comparable arrangement by having key executives wear two hats: one when they run their own divisions and another when they act as advisors on whatever problems face the whole department.

Theoretically, such a combination of duties should cause no difficulty so long as an executive and the people he works with understand which role he is playing at any particular time. The practical difficulty is that this distinction is hard to maintain. The executive himself may be unable to shift gears from being a hard-driving operating executive to being a reflective staff counselor. Even when it is clear in his own mind, he may fail to tell others which role he is playing. When we compound this difficulty by failing to define duties and authority clearly in each kind of work, we wind up with a "staff" that has a vague assignment to dabble in other people's problems.

The remedy lies in real understanding of what staff work is, agreement on what each man should do, and care in assigning men who are both technically and temperamentally qualified.

Disregard of Staff by a Boss Himself

A fourth source of staff difficulties may be the very manager who creates staff positions in the first place. He undoubtedly finds his total administrative burdens more than he can carry himself and sets up one or more staff positions to relieve him of part of the load. But if he falsely assumes that he has solved his difficulties and can forget about them, he is certainly sowing seeds for future woe.

A boss must maintain close enough and frequent enough contact with a staff man to enable the latter to serve effectively as an extension of the eyes, ears, and mind of his superior. And if a staff man does not genuinely reflect the general views of a senior administrator, his usefulness throughout an organization is diminished. Moreover, if on some matter he takes a firm position that the boss will not support, he and operating executives have actually lost much time and nervous energy. It is by no means necessary for a specialized staff man to see a boss daily. What is essential is that the two maintain sufficient contact to insure their general accord on approaches and values.[1]

Even more devastating to confidence than lack of contact is the willingness of some executives to make decisions in an area assigned to a staff man without ever consulting him. Let us suppose a manager appoints a budget director and specifically charges him to develop budgets for controlling capital expenditures. But later, when an operating subordinate presses him, the senior executive approves a large expenditure without first talking to the budget director. The next time he needs a capital expenditure, the operating executive will probably turn again directly to the senior administrator. Soon he will regard the budget director as an ineffective and useless adjunct to the business.

In contrast, the budget director will have greater status if the senior administrator insists that his operating executives talk through all matters of capital expenditure with the budget director prior to bringing any request to him. Soon the operating men will learn that to get approval for capital expenditures they must work with the budget director. In short, when an executive creates a staff position, he must be prepared to discipline *himself* to use the staff if he expects others to do so.

[1] In the Army, a Chief of Staff plays an important part in assuring full communication between the commanding officer and the technical staff men. This device has found little application in business; however, occasionally a much more junior "Assistant to the ———" may be sufficiently intimate with the boss to assist in this important communication to the staff.

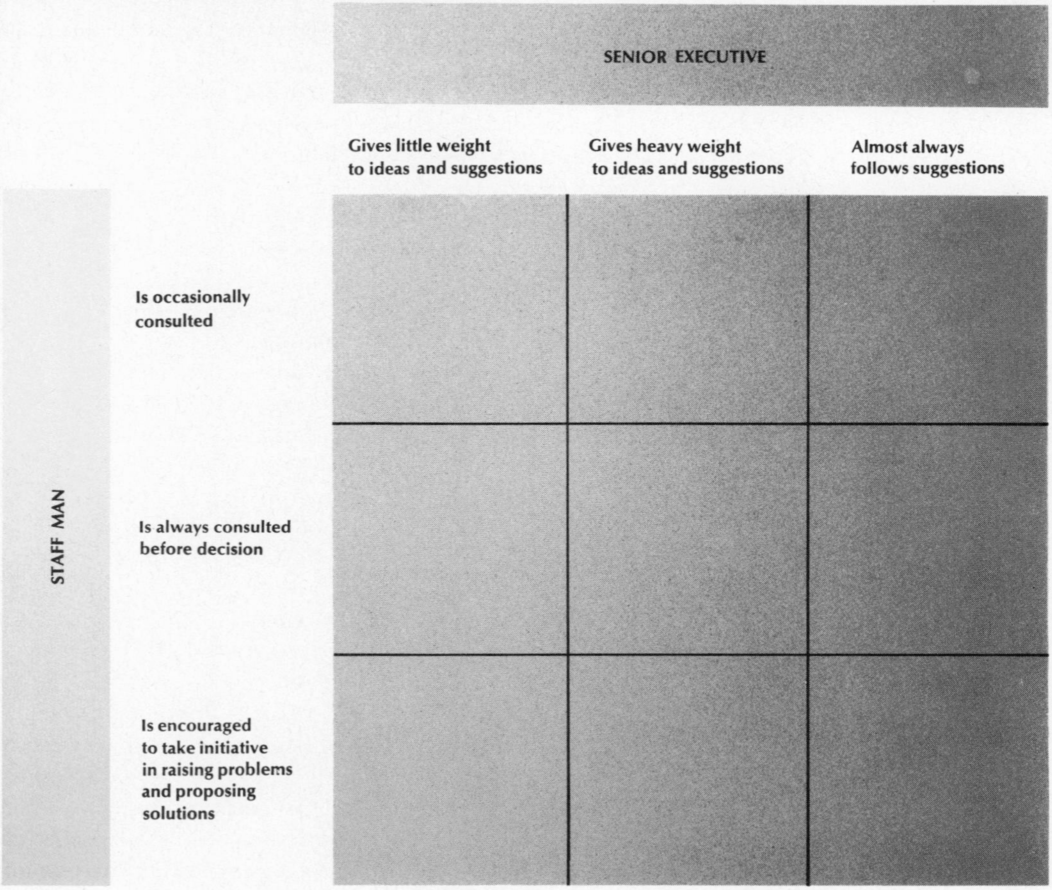

Fig. 4–4   A senior executive, by his treatment of suggestions,
strongly affects the influence of staff throughout an organization.
In this chart the color shading represents degrees of
the staff man's participation; the black shading represents
degrees of the senior executive's response.

CONCLUSION

The concept of staff is appealing, because it permits an executive to extend his capacity. The staff assistant performs managerial work that the executive is too busy to do or perhaps lacks technical competence to do. However, the arrangement is easily abused. Unless mutual understanding exists regarding the subjects covered and the action expected of the staff man, relations between supervisors and subordinates may become confused.

Moreover, anything as delicate as staff relationships rarely continues on an even keel. Somebody will undoubtedly become too aggressive, one man will step on another's toes, people will observe consultations in the letter rather than in the spirit, jealousies will creep in. To keep emotional flare-ups at a minimum and to maintain relationships between staff and operators as he desires, a manager must take time to provide continuing coordination and guidance. He must be sufficiently sensitive to the subtleties of what is really happening to know when to restrain and when to encourage. He must know whether his staff men become autocratic or lazy, whether their assistance is constructive, whether they are persuasive salesmen of their viewpoint, and whether operating men are too submissive or too independent.

In other words, by creating a staff an executive may facilitate his total job, but he also imposes upon himself new burdens: contact with staff men, supervision of relations between staff and operating executives, and self-restraint to the point where he too uses the staff according to his prescription.

FOR CLASS DISCUSSION

Questions

1) In what ways are a staff man's "authority" and "accountability" likely to differ from those of a line manager?

2) A regional sales manager (line position) who has authority to change prices in his region consults with the corporate director of market research (staff position) and is given several "pieces of data" that the market-research manager feels would dictate a price reduction. If the regional manager accepts this advice and later finds his revenue was adversely affected, who should accept the obligation for this loss?

3) If a corporate line officer has staff assistants who perform their functions in the manner prescribed by General Lerch, then what is the line officer's function? How does the functional area in which the staff man works affect his ability to do "completed staff work"?

4) Discuss the pros and cons of rotating staff men to line positions and line men to staff positions every two to three years so that "each may better appreciate the nature of the other's roles."

5) Assume you have been appointed public relations director for a college; your task is not only to issue press releases and other public statements but also to "help the college conduct all its activities so as to create a favorable public image." What kind of authority should the president of the college grant to you so that you could be most effective in your job?

6) Consider the third characteristic of staff work given on page 71. What actions by top management can increase or decrease the likelihood of finding staff men who possess this characteristic?

7) "Staff men are worse than college professors," said an experienced plant manager. "Since they don't have to face the day-to-day problems, they have all kinds of time to develop theories about how we should get our work done but then instead of writing books on their theories like the professors, they write reports to the president and cause us no end of problems. I wish my boss's staff would go to some university. I'd rather deal with the professors." (1) What do you make of this man's comment? (2) Would a good college (business school) professor be a likely candidate for a staff position in industry? Discuss.

8) Assume a staff man takes serious objection to an action recommended by a line manager who reports to the same vice-president as the staff man. Their common boss, the vice-president, hears both parties out and cannot see a clear advantage to either position. (1) What should the vice-president do? (2) If the vice-president supports his line subordinate, what impact has he had on the duties, authority, and obligation of the disagreeing staff subordinate?

Cases

For cases involving issues covered in this chapter, see especially the following. Particularly relevant questions are listed after each case.

General Machinery Corporation (p. 130), 3
Gerald Clark (p. 234), 3, 4
Western Office Equipment Manufacturing Company (p. 457), 2, 3
Consolidated Instruments—A (p. 571), 2
Texas-Northern Pipeline Company (p. 665), 1
Consolidated Instruments—B (p. 674), 3

FOR FURTHER READING

Atchison, T.J., "The Fragmentation of Authority." *Personnel*, July 1970. *Effect of staff expertise on authority and accountability.*

Baker, J.K., and R.H. Schaffer, "Making Staff Consulting More Effective." *Harvard Business Review*, January 1969. *Guides for staff work, based on company experience.*

Dale, E., *Organization*. New York: American Management Association, 1967, Chaps. 3 and 4. *Summary of concepts regarding special staff and general staff.*

Dubin, R., *Human Relations in Administration*, 3rd ed. Englewood Cliffs, N.J.: Prentice-Hall, Inc., 1968, Chap. 9. *Behavioral views of role of staff specialist.*

Litterer, J.A., *The Analysis of Organizations*. New York: John Wiley & Sons, Inc., 1965, Chaps. 17 and 18. *Describes different uses of staff and also covers some line-staff difficulties.*

Schleh, E.H., *Management by Results*. New York: McGraw-Hill Book Company, 1961, Chaps. 15–18. *Suggestions on how staff can share accountability.*

Chapter Five

Shaping the Overall Structure

ORGANIZATION STRUCTURE

To understand the organization of an enterprise we need to look at its total structure. Just as in the design of an airplane the relative size and weight of each component and the way the components are related to one another affect the performance capabilities, so it is with the structure of an enterprise. In preceding chapters we have considered departmentation, decentralization, and staff as separate issues. Now we should think of how decisions on these issues can best be melded together.

Concern for organization structure is all around us. For instance, if the urge to "restructure our universities" is anything more than a general protest, it deals with organization structure. The debate centers around who should approve courses, set entrance requirements, administer discipline, allocate funds, and so on. Typically, little significant restructuring has been done except to establish improved means of communication. At the level of the elementary and secondary school, however, a variety of organizational experiments are being tried. High decentralization to experimental units, replacement of city or statewide staff by local staff, and assignment of teachers to fit a new educational "technology" are all involved. Of course, people and politics and education theories are also key aspects; nevertheless, it is pertinent to note that organizational modification is essential to any substantial change.

Similarly, adjustment to new goals in business is initiated either by a shift in organization or at least by a reorganization that permits new directions of effort to be effective. In such adjustments we have to think in terms of the overall organization.

The following steps represent a constructive approach to recasting an overall organization:

1) Identify *key operating departments* that fit the new mission.

2) Decide on the *level* at which *operating decisions* can be made most effectively.

3) Consider the *nature and location of auxiliary and staff units* which are needed.

4) Adjust the parts to make optimum use of *structural forms*.

We have already examined the major elements, and so we are more concerned here with balancing and designing a workable whole. Also several additional features of total structure—committees, supervision spans, parallel departments, and the like—must be fitted in.

Our discussion will center on the organization structure of an entire business firm, but most of what we say will also be pertinent to a department or a nonprofit enterprise. Whether he is concerned with a division or an independent enterprise, each manager must design an effective structure suited to the specific work within his own unit. The organization of a subsidiary unit should of course be consistent with the general company pattern; nevertheless, divisions may have unique needs of their own.

ACCENTUATE KEY DEPARTMENTS

The way in which activities are grouped into departments was discussed in Chapter 2. Such departmentation is a critical and basic step. As we move on to consideration of overall structure we may wish to do some further combining or to distinguish between major and minor departments.

Balance and Emphasis

The way a total organization works depends in part on the emphasis we give to its various parts. Naturally, we want each department and section to be strong and dependable, but there is also need for balance. An outstanding research division can wreck a company if it creates new products faster than the finance department can find money to pay for both research and product development. Similarly, an overabundance of excellent staff advice on managerial development can create a company with all chiefs and no Indians. As we place departments and managerial work in a total structure, then, we should consider the emphasis and balance that is most needed by a specific company in its current setting.

An enterprise should usually establish as separate, major departments those activities that are most likely to affect its success. The heads of these departments should normally report directly to the chief executive so that he can be in close touch with crucial activities.

What work is emphasized will depend on the nature of the industry and the way a particular firm seeks to be distinctive. Some department stores, for example, believe that advertising is a primary key to success, and so they are likely to set up a separate advertising department that reports directly to the president. On the other hand, a company that sells industrial supplies and raw materials, a business in which advertising is much less important, will probably make the advertising department a service division within its sales department. Developing new and efficient products is vital to the success of any manufacturer of industrial equipment, and so in the organization chart of the Litchfield Corporation, we see that engineering is one of the four major departments (Fig. 5–1). Product development is so important in the chemical and pharmaceutical business that some firms in these industries have both research and engineering departments that report directly to the president. In contrast, a company that is principally concerned with processing established products —such as a dairy or a textile mill—almost always relegates engineering to a subordinate role in the production department.

To discover how much emphasis a department deserves in an organization structure, we cannot simply count the number of its employees or the dollar volume of its transactions. In a commercial bank, for instance, we shall probably find many more employees who maintain the building or sort checks or keep customers' accounts than members of the credit department who analyze the soundness of loans. The former activities, however, are relatively routine, whereas the granting of credit calls for delicate judgment. Consequently, loan experts typically work directly under the bank president, whereas bookkeepers, check-sorters, and janitors are customarily grouped together with other "internal operations" under a cashier.

The strategic importance of a department's function, product, or area may shift with the passage of time. A clear illustration of this point is the changing status of industrial relations. Prior to the recent increase of union power, industrial relations and personnel matters in most firms were handled by a subordinate unit in the department with the largest number of employees. Now more and more companies have a vice-president in charge of personnel and industrial relations who reports directly to the chief executive. Chemical production in the oil industry, variable committees in insurance companies, and family planning in welfare agencies are other examples of activities that have similarly risen in strategic importance and hence in organizational status.

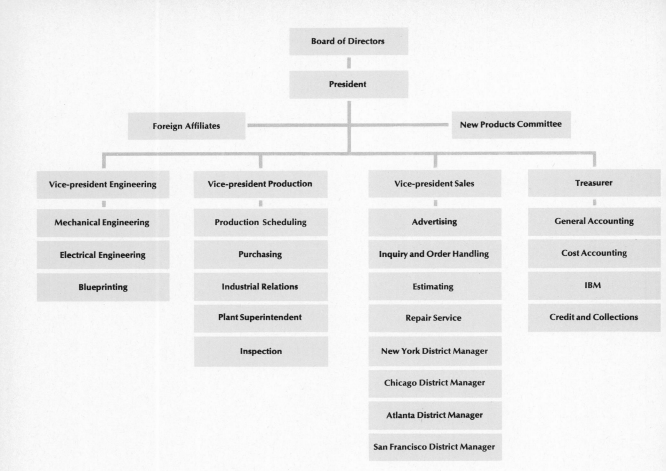

Fig. 5–1   Organization chart of the Litchfield Corporation.

A Consistent Basis

Giving high status to "hot" activities often poses a dilemma. For example, many companies with major departments based on functions—research, marketing, production, and the like—wish to expand their international operations. But establishing a strong international department creates jurisdictional conflicts with all the existing departments. Companies with major product divisions also find that international expansion raises questions of who will adapt products to European standards, which plants will be kept busy, how transfer prices will be set, and a host of similar issues.

Clearly the organization structure will be simpler and clearer if we use a consistent basis for our key departments, basing all on functions, products, or territories. Achieving this consistency probably means sacrificing potential benefits (in international operations in our previous examples), and we may conclude that consistency is not worth its price. One rule to follow in dealing with this recurring dilemma is this: Set up major departments with inherent overlaps only when long-run forecasts indicate that each department will continue to be strategic for a long time. If the high priority for an offbeat department may expire in a couple of years, special attention should be provided by means of staff or some similar mechanism.

LOCUS OF DECISION-MAKING

In designing a total organization structure, we must consider, in addition to key departments, the echelon at which most decision-making is to occur. Should we focus planning high or low in the hierarchy? In other words, the decentralization issues we considered in Chapter 3 must now be reviewed in terms of the overall structure of a company. For example, the president of Corson Wholesale Drugs, Inc. (see organization chart, Fig. 5–2) had to settle this question: Should he himself, with the assistance of home office vice-presidents, make most of the operating decisions? Or should the district vice-presidents? Or division managers? Or

Fig. 5–2 Organization chart of Corson Wholesale Drugs, Inc.

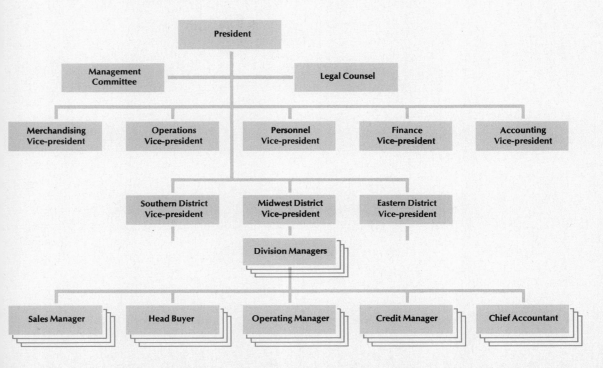

local managers in each division? Because each division is a small-scale wholesale drug company that orders merchandise, warehouses it, sells to retail druggists, extends credit, and makes deliveries, he might have put each one on a profit-decentralization basis. But to take advantage of planning by specialists, he chose to have men at the home office make most of the operating plans.

The use of centralized planning, to cite another example, is a vital element in the strategy of McDonald Hamburgers. However, the continuing desirability of high centralization has become less evident to the Howard Johnson organization as it moves from the operation of restaurants alone into the related fields of restaurant supplies, inns, and the sale of food products through retail stores. In the government field, the organization of the U.S. Internal Revenue Service, which deals with millions of local taxpayers according to national standards, differs sharply from the organization of government programs for training black "unemployables." In the training program, the pressures for local autonomy have been intense and bitter, and our entire thinking about organization structure for this activity is affected by the centralization-decentralization issue.

The choice of level at which decisions are to be made is important to overall structure because it affects the need for services and staff at various levels, the qualities desired for executives in different positions, the design of communication networks, and the form of controls. In other words, we need to know where planning is focused in order to fit other parts of the structure into an integrated pattern.

There are advantages to a *consistent pattern* of decentralization throughout an enterprise. If Corson Drugs permitted some division managers to operate semiautonomously but required others to follow instructions from the home office, it would risk creating many opportunities for confusion. In fact, friction could be generated if home office personnel forgot just how much more or less freedom of action one division manager had than another. Due to personality difference, unusual local conditions, or faulty communication over long distances, exceptions to a general pattern of decentralization may be necessary. Nevertheless we shall find it far easier to think in terms of an exception to a general pattern than to have no pattern at all. Even with its functional setup, the Litchfield Corporation could handle interdepartmental matters more quickly if it maintained a consistent degree of decentralization throughout its organization. But if a section head in one department could agree to a coordinated plan that the boss in another department had to carry to a vice-president, arriving at a decision on a joint course of action would be awkward and slow.

LOCATION OF SERVICE AND STAFF UNITS

After a manager has decided on major departments and has settled on a degree of decentralization, he is ready to consider what service and staff units he wants and where he should place them in the organization structure. Because these units are tributary to the mainstream of management and inevitably complicate an organization structure, a manager should not use them unless there is a clear advantage in doing so. Simplicity is a virtue, at least in organizing a company.

When to Use Auxiliary Service Units

As explained in Chapter 2, we can justify an auxiliary operating unit if it ensures adequate attention to a secondary, yet significant, operation, provides technical competence outside the specialties of operating executives, or relieves busy operating executives from minor chores that otherwise would be a nuisance. For instance, the president of the Litchfield Corporation has defended the separate purchasing division under the vice-president in charge of production, partly because the plant superintendent would not give enough attention to purchasing if he tried to supervise it in addition to his other duties, and partly because the work requires technical knowledge and skill. Another example from the same company is the IBM computer unit, whose personnel, the treasurer explains, have technical skills not possessed by other men in his office. The blueprinting unit under the vice-president for engineering furnishes an excellent illustration of a service provided to operating groups, a service that might be quite a nuisance if operating groups had to supervise the work themselves. These particular service units have fully justified their separate existence.

When to Use Staff Units

The burden of proof is on the advocate of staff units. Generally speaking, a manager can justify assigning duties to staff when he is overburdened with work or lacks a necessary technical skill, *and* when, for any of the following reasons, he hesitates to delegate more of his managerial work to his operating subordinates. We shall draw our examples from the Corson Drugs company.

1) *Operating subordinates would not give an activity adequate attention.* In Corson Drugs, one reason for appointing a strong vice-president in charge of personnel was that many division managers were "old-timers" with limited interest and little faith in modern personnel techniques, and management feared they would slight this activity.

2) *The work requires an expert.* In the office of the vice-president in charge of finance, Corson Drugs has a legal counsel and a staff man to advise on matters concerning real estate.

3) *The company needs coordinated and consistent action among several operating units.* The Corson Drugs vice-president who directs merchandising takes an active part in arranging purchase contracts and monthly sales promotion programs, because he wants a coordinated merchandising program throughout all divisions of the company. Similarly, the vice-president in charge of accounting plans all accounting procedures in order to ensure consistent accounting practice throughout the entire company.

4) *The chief executive wants help in controlling the operating divisions.* In a far-flung operation like Corson Drugs, the president relies heavily on his vice-president in charge of finance to help control capital expenditures by means of a budget and on his vice-president in charge of accounting to provide standards and reports on expenses for each division.

5) *Top management seeks aids in analyzing problems.* The division managers and the district vice-presidents in Corson Drugs are so busy with pressing short-run problems that they do not take time to develop the perspective that might enable them to think through the basic questions.

Placing Service and Staff Units in a Structure

After we have decided to set apart a service or a staff activity, we always reach the question of where to attach the new unit to the organization structure. Let us suppose, for example, that the president of Corson Drugs came to the conclusion that he could ensure adequate attention to public relations in his company only by appointing one or more men to study problems and recommend action. Should he introduce a public-relations man in each division, because division personnel make by far the most contacts with the public? Should he establish a single public-relations office directly under himself so that he could readily give such matters personal attention and could oversee the development of companywide policies and programs? Would a compromise between these two extremes, such as attaching a public-relations man to each district vice-president, be desirable? Or should he try a combination of these plans, perhaps keeping a public-relations man in the headquarters group and also sending one to each division? Each time we create a separate service or staff unit, we must determine where to put it.

All sorts of arrangements are found in practice, and from the experience of many companies we are able to draw the following general guides:

1) Place auxiliary operating and staff units as close as possible to the activities they serve. In the Litchfield Corporation we find an IBM computer unit under the same executive who supervises its primary users—general accounting and cost accounting. The men in charge of production scheduling and inspection are under the same executive as the plant superintendent; blueprinting is tucked in close to mechanical and electrical engineering departments that it serves. This principle would lead us to put a long-range planning unit directly under a president on the grounds that he would make the most use of the aid of this staff. The farther away organizationally—and physically, too—a service is from the person it helps, the greater the chances of poor coordination, unresponsiveness, and unnecessary work.

2) We may have to relax this primary guide when we can obtain substantial economies by combining service work or staff work into single units for the entire company, or when objectivity is essential, as in the case of auditing and other controls. For instance, a division manager in Corson Drugs rarely needs advice on real estate or warehousing problems; for economy, the company provides such specialized services from a central point rather than in each of the operating units. But if the volume of work in the operating units justified competent specialists on such matters, then a good case could be made for locating these services in the operating divisions rather than at headquarters. We must also use discretion when we apply the criterion of objectivity. Whereas an auditor for a bank often reports only to the board of directors, an inspector in a brick factory reports to the plant superintendent. The function of both men is control, but the emphasis we wish to place on control differs widely in the two situations. If management considers the object of control important enough, then it may justify a degree of independence approaching that of a bank auditor. But with such objectivity comes less use of control information by operating men and probably their strong dislike of the system.

When placing staff and service units in an organization structure, we sometimes find the "skip level" concept helpful. For an illustration, let us turn again to Corson Drugs. District vice-presidents have no staff whatever; all staff work is confined to either the operating divisions or the headquarters office. Provision of staff is intentionally skipped at the level of the regional vice-president. This restriction on the regional vice-presidents is a deliberate plan to prevent any of them from building up a duplicate staff of their own. The president conceives of the district vice-presidents as his contacts with the district offices; if they need staff help, they can call on headquarters staff units just as the president does. Under a different decentralization pattern than that of Corson Drugs, of course, each district might be virtually an independent company. In such a case, each district would need a complete staff and headquarters would keep its own staff at a minimum.

We should not hang staff and service units on an organization like tinsel on a Christmas tree, decorating every branch; rather we should place them only where they fill a real gap. And gaps should be identified in terms of the balance and emphasis we want in the overall structure.

Use of Committees for Staff Work

Much that we have said about staff—its role as an aid to management, the need for clear definition of duties and relationships, the caution required in using it unless the task to be done is pressing—applies with equal force to committees. In fact, committees can be regarded as a special form of staff.

A committee is a group of people specifically designated to perform a managerial act. Both its strengths and its weaknesses arise from assigning the task to a *group* rather than to one or more individuals. Typically members devote only part of their time to committee work because they have other major duties.

Where should we use committees—this unique type of staff—in an organization? Two main locations are these: Where group judgment is especially valuable and where voluntary coordination needs encouragement. Group judgment, for example, is the principal reason for the new-products committee in the Litchfield Corporation. On this committee are representatives from the engineering, production, sales, and finance departments. The engineering man reports on new products that look promising, and his marketing colleague predicts the potential demand for such products. When these men agree on an item that seems likely to succeed, the production man gives counsel on manufacturing costs and investment that will be required before the company can get the product on the market. The financial member of the team brings all these figures together and compares the anticipated profit rate with that on alternative uses of the company's capital. All this collective wisdom is used in recommendations by the committee to the president about new products that should be developed. Conceivably, the president himself could get the same information by talking separately to the men who serve on the committee. But the exchange of ideas in committee meetings stimulates new thoughts and uncovers weak points, and thus improves the quality of final recommendations.

The management committee of Corson Drugs, in contrast, is probably more important as a coordinating device than as a source of group judgment, although it does serve the latter purpose to some extent. The president and all vice-presidents are members, and meetings are devoted largely to reports on current problems. In this way, all vice-presidents are kept informed of one another's activities. Often a coordinated plan is agreed to in a meeting—say, a program for dealing with a strike in one of the divisions—and a background is laid for subsequent man-to-man contacts on special issues, because each member of the committee is informed about the total company.

The two preceding illustrations happen to be top-level committees. In other companies, we might find at lower levels a need for group judgment or coordination that would justify setting up committees covering a narrow scope of company operations. Occasionally, committees are also established to provide a safe and/or acceptable decision—for instance, a salary committee to assure that personal bias does not determine who gets a raise or a bonus. (In this last case, the committee probably would be given concurring authority, and would not act, as most committees do, purely as an advisory body.) Another consideration is the motivational effect of a committee on its members.

All these potential uses of committees—to aid in making wise or safe decisions, to promote coordination, to improve motivation—are among the tasks that might be assigned to a single staff man. So the guides we have already considered for adding staff to an organization structure should be applied to committees. *In addition*, we should ask ourselves: Will the use of a group, instead of an individual, be especially helpful in the specific spot under consideration? Are these special benefits great enough to outweigh the inherent disadvantages of committees—notably (1) the expensive man-hours required for committee meetings, (2) the slowness of getting committee members to meet and arrive at a conclusion, and (3) the possibility that committee advice will be cavalier because no one member is accountable?

Committees, then, are a special kind of supplement we use chiefly to knit together parts of a total organization. Where they are needed, if they are needed at all, will depend on other provisions we have made to secure balanced activity.

STRUCTURAL FORMS

A fourth aspect of overall organization design—in addition to accentuating key departments, deciding on the levels of decentralization, and providing service and staff units where needed—involves several structural forms that can add significantly to the effectiveness of the organization.

Parallel Departments

Use of a single pattern for several different parts of the organization eases management. For instance, each of the twenty-five operating divisions of Corson Drugs is organized along approximately the same lines, with a sales manager, head buyer, operations manager, credit manager, and chief accountant. The headquarters office follows a similar pattern with two exceptions: Selling and buying are combined under the vice-president in charge of merchandising, and personnel relations are handled by a separate division instead of by line executives as they are in the divisions. Such repetition of structural design is called "parallel departmentation." A similar scheme is often used by government bureaus, retail chains, or finance companies, if they have several operating units doing like work.

The chief advantages of parallel departmentation are: ease of communication between operating units and headquarters staff; general understanding of who does what and, consequently, a knowledge of whom to contact on specific problems; simplified transfer of personnel from one division to another, because jobs are similar in all divisions; and simplified control, because the output and efficiency of one division are readily comparable with those of another. This latter "deadly parallel" not only helps in measuring performance, but also motivates operating men who do not wish to compare unfavorably with other men doing similar work.

The disadvantages of parallel departmentation, however, may more than offset its benefits. Operating units are likely to vary because of many factors, such as size, local market, competitive conditions, age and design of equipment, and executive abilities. Consequently, a standard pattern may not fit a local unit as one adapted to the unit's particular circumstances. The organization that is appropriate for a large unit may be too elaborate and expensive for a small one.

The degree of decentralization affects the desirability of parallel departmentation. A centralized company like Corson Drugs needs frequent and easy communication between the central staff and men in the operating divisions. On the other hand, a decentralized company like Johnson & Johnson—manufacturer of hospital supplies, pharmaceuticals, baby products, industrial tape, and many other items—finds little advantage in parallel departmentation. Each of its product divisions is self-sufficient, and there is virtually no central staff with which the divisions should keep in touch. Among the divisions, the differences in both manufacturing and marketing are so great that comparisons of the "deadly-parallel" type have little meaning. Consequently, each of the Johnson & Johnson operating divisions is permitted to establish an organization to meet its particular requirements.

Even Strata

As a rule, all people who report to a given manager should have approximately the same organizational status. Under this concept, only key executives would report to a president, and the men who report to, say, a vice-president in charge of marketing would each play a leading role in the marketing department. This arrangement of even strata is not always practical however. To understand why, let us return to the chart of the Litchfield Corporation (Fig. 5–1). We see from the chart that the president directs the work of foreign affiliates despite the minor role that foreign activities play in this particular firm. He undertook this minor assignment simply because each of his vice-presidents had a major task to perform in domestic activities, and foreign duties would have interfered. An even more striking exception to the rule of even strata is the positioning of blueprinting directly under the vice-president in charge of engineering. Litchfield executives simply placed this routine service in the spot most convenient to the operations it benefits. When we deviate from the practice of even strata, we should use titles that distinguish clearly between major and minor divisions in order to avoid possible confusion about balance and emphasis.

Span of Supervision

A final consideration is the workload of each executive. How many immediate subordinates should each executive have? This topic has been the subject of much debate, especially since behavioral scientists discovered what every practical manager knows: no single number is the correct answer in all cases.

We cannot avoid the issue because very real limits do exist on any man's capacity to supervise. His time and energy are limited, and if he has too many subordinates he cannot provide good personal leadership to all. It takes time to assign tasks, to answer questions, to motivate subordinates, to mediate arguments, to coordinate work within a unit and with other departments of an organization, to make sure that necessary supplies and equipment are on hand, and to perform the many other duties of a supervisor.

The question of limits on the span of supervision is important in designing an organization structure because it directly affects the number of executives needed. For example, if we could safely assume that each executive in a company or department with two hundred employees could direct fourteen or fifteen immediate subordinates, we would need only a chief executive and fourteen intermediate-level executives, or a total of fifteen men. But if each executive could supervise only six people, then we would need six men to report to the chief executive and an additional thirty-six supervisors, six of whom would report to each executive at the higher level. And so here we have a total of forty-three people in administrative positions, compared with fifteen in the previous example. Because of the way these two organizations appear on a chart, we call the first a "flat" structure and the second a "tall" structure. The executive payroll in the tall structure will probably exceed that in the flat structure. Another drawback is the additional layer of supervisors who will complicate communications from the chief executive down to operators and back up the line. For these and related reasons, a wide span of supervision is desirable. But should it be five or fifty?

The personal energy of an executive influences to some extent the number of people he can supervise effectively. But other factors go a long

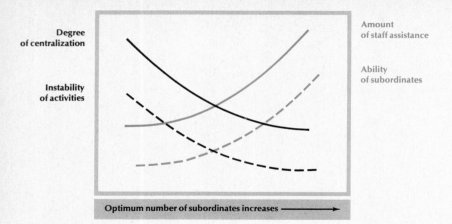

Degree
of centralization

Instability
of activities

Amount
of staff assistance

Ability
of subordinates

Optimum number of subordinates increases ⟶

Fig. 5–3   The optimum span of supervision is not fixed. Rather, it is a variable that is determined through an analysis of several relevant factors in each situation.

way toward determining what spans are feasible in a specific situation. Some of these considerations are the following:

1) *Time devoted to supervision.* Almost all supervisors spend part of their time personally doing operations. Foremen serve as relief men; sales managers call on important customers; research directors work on inventions of their own; company presidents testify before Congressional committees. In addition, nearly all executives spend some time on administrative duties not directly related to guiding their subordinates: participating in company planning, serving on company committees, or pleading for new personnel and equipment. Both types of work reduce the time an executive can devote to supervision.

2) *Variety and importance of activities being supervised.* A manager who is confronted with complex problems that often involve many people needs more time to dispose of them than an executive who deals with simple, one-man problems. Accordingly, a president or a vice-president probably needs to work longer with each of his immediate subordinates than does a first-line supervisor who deals with routine problems.

3) *Repetitiveness of activities.* New and different problems take more time to handle than those that we have faced many times before. Just as we develop skills through practice and physical work, so we can learn also to complete familiar management jobs with increasingly less effort. Some jobs, however, always have an inherently large element of novelty.

4) *Ability of subordinates.* Green, inexperienced help takes more of a supervisor's time than well-trained persons who already know the ropes. Subordinates who have good judgment, initiative, and a sense of obligation need less help from a supervisor than a willing, though none-too-bright, employee.

5) *Degree of decentralization.* An executive who personally makes many decisions is able to supervise fewer people than an executive who must merely provide occasional coaching and encouragement.

6) *Staff assistance provided.* When subordinates get from staff men much of their guidance on methods, schedules, personnel problems, quality standards, and perhaps other aspects of their work, they need less contact with their line supervisor. The line supervisor often becomes involved only when a staff fails to function smoothly. Under such a system, the supervisor can handle more subordinates.

In summary, then, we should tailor the span of supervision for each executive position. If the situation is fixed—that is, duties, people, staff assistance, and decentralization cannot be changed—we should try to adjust the number of subordinates to fit. A more practical approach, however, is to consider modifications in the job and in the surrounding organization at the same time that we decide on an optimum span of supervision. Perhaps adjustments can be made in several directions. We are dealing with interdependent factors, and the important objective is to design a total structure that gives us appropriate emphasis and balance along with reasonable spans of supervision.

CONCLUSION: ADAPTABILITY OF THE STRUCTURE

In this chapter our examination of organization moved from analysis to synthesis. We noted that an effective organization needs balance. Key departments, decentralization, staff units, and committees—aspects of organization we analyzed in preceding chapters—must be fitted together in a viable structure; spans of supervision must be reasonable and possibilities of parallel departmentation considered.

The organization design that emerges from this synthesis, however, is not a final, static structure. As the enterprise continues to develop, so too should the organization be adapted.

Ideally, in designing an organization structure, we should be able to predict changing conditions with reasonable accuracy—for example, a five-year projection of increases in sales volume or a long-range estimate of shifts in production methods. With reliable forecasts of future work, we can prepare an ideal organization plan—a plan that, to be sure, disregards the existing setup and, to a large extent, present executives, but one that would give a company the greatest possible strength for meeting predicted needs. With such a long-range design, when transfers or when opportunities to make organizational changes arise, we can make each move as a step toward our ideal.

Rarely, of course, can we ever fully attain the ideal—partly because actual needs do not conform to a forecast, partly because people qualified to man a new organization may not be available, and partly because of inertia. Nevertheless, most companies that have followed this procedure believe that they have been at least partially prepared for new requirements that confront them. An ideal organization may be a moving target, but it does encourage managers to aim at meeting anticipated needs rather than resolving past problems.

Flexibility can be built into an organization structure, even though future requirements are uncertain. For example, a company that adopts profit decentralization may find that it is in an excellent position to add or drop a product line without upsetting the rest of the organization. Many companies, to increase their adaptability, establish more executive positions than are absolutely essential for getting each day's work done. But executives in these positions, like the extra power of an automobile engine, are available when a need arises. Although it may mean some extra executive payroll, companies who adopt this policy feel that the added flexibility is well worth the expense.

Companies that give little attention to organization planning and simply assign work to their executives on the basis of individual abilities and chance free time, are usually in a poor position to adapt to changing conditions. Such an organization is built around individuals, and when changes become necessary the whole structure has to be modified. These companies are in sharp contrast to those that are able to absorb additional work without seriously interrupting present operations.

Several recent organization developments that are being used by companies to meet changing requirements are discussed in the next chapter.

FOR CLASS DISCUSSION

Questions

1) The text suggests that an enterprise should usually separate those major departments most likely to affect its success and that normally the heads of these departments should report directly to the chief executive. Can you think of reasons for not having such departments report to the chief executive officer?

2) Is it desirable to have one or more major divisions operate as semiautonomous units in a company that is otherwise highly centralized? Why? Under what conditions would such an arrangement be necessary?

3) Other things being equal, does greater diversification of product, technology, or markets lead you to favor more or less decentralization, than you would favor in a more homogeneous company? Discuss.

4) How can tracing the horizontal flow of a complete action—such as buying a new batch of raw material, designing and placing into production a new product, or employing and training a new worker—aid in designing an organization structure?

5) List and discuss several key guidelines which if followed in setting up and using committees would increase their positive effect on decision-making and subsequent evaluation and control.

6) Assume that Joe Archer is promoted from regional manager to national sales manager. His replacement in one of the regions now reports to him. In what ways may Joe's past experience as a regional manager contribute to his ability to decentralize and manage a wider span of supervision? In what ways may it detract from his ability to decentralize and make managing a wide span of control more difficult?

7) Assume the nature of the work to be done made the creation of parallel departments feasible. Standard patterns can fit because local conditions and the size of several divisions are approximately the same. In spite of the potential advantages of such a pattern, what interdivisional problems might crop up?

8) Chester Barnard, in a review of a book by L. Urwick (both men have made major contributions to management thought), says: "Mr. Urwick gives renewed currency to the ancient bromide: 'Authority and responsibility are correlative'. . . . No statement in the whole gamut of twiddle-twaddle about administration seems to me to be so misleading as this. . . . Certainly no one may justly be held responsible for the specific behavior of a particular third party without authority to command that party; but in general most men are held responsible for results as to which no authority can be given." Do you agree with Mr. Barnard? Explain.

Cases

For cases involving issues covered in this chapter, see especially the following. Particularly relevant questions are listed after each case.

Trans-World Mutual Funds, Ltd. (p. 121), 4
General Machinery Corporation (p. 130), 5
Scott-Davis Corporation (p. 227), 1
Gerald Clark (p. 234), 2
Bolling Laboratories, Inc. (p. 345), 1

FOR FURTHER READING

Clee, G.H., and W.M. Sachtjen, "Organizing a Worldwide Business." *Harvard Business Review*, November 1964. *Effect of international expansion on organization structure.*

Kast, F.E., and J.E. Rosenzweig, *Organization and Management.* New York: McGraw-Hill Book Company, 1970, Chap. 7. *Different ways of viewing overall organization structure.*

Litterer, J.A., *The Analysis of Organizations.* New York: John Wiley & Sons, Inc., 1965, Chap. 16. *Analysis of factors affecting overall managerial structure.*

Steiglitz, H., *Corporate Organization Structures.* New York: National Industrial Conference Board, Studies in Personnel Policy, No. 183, 1961. *Corporate organization charts of sixty-one companies with brief analysis. For international companies see Studies in Personnel Policy, No. 198, 1965.*

Steiglitz, H., and A.R. Janger, *Top Management Organization in Divisionalized Companies.* New York: National Industrial Conference Board, Studies in Personnel Policy, No. 195, 1965. *Describes structure and gives position descriptions for central, senior operating, and senior staff executives; based on actual organization of seventy-six companies.*

Wickesberg, A.K., *Management Organization.* New York: Appleton-Century-Crofts, 1966, Chaps. 4 and 5. *Discusses the elements that fuse into the totality of a company structure.*

Chapter Six

New Approaches

to Structural Design

NOVEL NEEDS, NOVEL SOLUTIONS

Organization is an instrument—a powerful tool—designed to fill specific needs. As the needs change, we naturally seek new ways to organize that are suited to the new conditions. In this chapter we look at five frontiers where social and technological pressures are leading to new organizational designs:

1) Rapid technological change and complexity are fostering *matrix organizations*.

2) The magnitude of some corporate commitments is leading to *external, independent staff*.

3) Increasing involvement in social issues accentuates the need for a *president's office*.

4) Current success of organized pressure groups raises the question of how to deal with *interest representation*.

5) Fascination with electronic computers calls for examination of the *impact of computers on organization*.

These five developments, of course, are not the only forces calling for new approaches in design. They illustrate the way environmental change impinges on organization and show how a basic social institution such as managerial organization is adapted rather than scrapped.

MATRIX ORGANIZATION

Landing a man on the moon was largely a scientific achievement. It also required *managing* a huge, highly complex, interrelated and uncertain development and production undertaking. Matrix organization was used in this effort, and part of the "fall-out" of the space program has been more careful analysis of this organizational form. Actually, matrix organization did not originate in the space program, and it has applications in a wide variety of enterprises.

Need for Coordinated, Focused Action

A drawback of the typical organization with functional departments is that unusual, complex projects often get shunted about, progress slowly, and are the cause of endless meetings of key executives representing the various departments. The more unique and complicated the project, the more likely is fumbling to occur.

Matrix organization strives to (1) ensure the coordinated, focused attention that such projects require and (2) at the same time retain the benefits of specialized expertise and capabilities that only functional departments can provide. For example, the production of reactors for nuclear power plants calls for unusual engineering, materials and parts with heat-resistance far beyond any previously fabricated, scientific knowledge concerning reactor design, a special and very large assembly operation, and a whole array of new inspection techniques. Production is complicated by high uncertainty about how to achieve required quality and safety margins, by a desire to keep costs low enough to allow nuclear power to compete with coal and oil generating stations, and by the pressure to complete such units in time to overcome national electric power shortages.

Companies making nuclear reactors do have departments that are expert in science, engineering, purchasing, fabrication and inspection, but each of these departments has twenty to a hundred different orders to work on at one time. Also they do not have standard answers for dealing with nuclear reactors, and they do not know what decisions other departments may make for a specific order, decisions that will affect their own work. Many conferences within and between departments become necessary. Disagreement on design or manufacture is likely to arise. Production falls behind schedule, and costs rise. To overcome these typical difficulties on an important piece of business, some mechanism is needed to channel part of the company's store of talent into the specific project and to ensure open communications on interrelated issues and prompt agreement on action to be taken.

This kind of situation is not peculiar to heavy-equipment manufacturers. An advertising agency, to pick an example far removed from physical hardware, is in the same predicament. It has departments staffed with experts in market research, copywriting, art work, television shows, media selection, and other functions—all useful to various clients. Client A wants a specific advertising mission accomplished, one suited to its particular situation. The organization problem is how to draw on the outstanding capabilities of the functional departments and at the same time get an imaginative, tailored program for client A when he needs it. Comparable situations in management-consulting firms and in large building-construction firms are easy to visualize.

Project Managers of Cross-functional Teams

The matrix organization answer to the problems just posed is to appoint a project manager for each clear-cut mission and then to assign from each of the functional departments the talent needed to complete the mission. Figure 6–1 indicates the arrangement for the nuclear reactor order.

During the time a functional specialist is working on the project he looks to the project manager for direction; he is "out on loan." When the project is finished, or when he is no longer needed, each man returns to his functional department for assignment to other duties. The project manager must rely heavily on these assigned men for counsel and decisions in their respective areas. If the team is small, its members will have frequent contact with one another and will be fully informed of the current status of the project. In these circumstances most of the coordination will be voluntary. From time to time, tough, trade-off decisions may be necessary, and these will be made by the project manager.

The personal relations within a project team are delicate. Although the project manager is the nominal boss, each member of his team is on temporary assignment and will return to his functional department where his long-run career is primarily determined. To draw the best from his group, the project manager must therefore rely on both the challenge of the job and his personal leadership. Because of this heavy reliance on voluntary cooperation, project teams work best on projects for which the quality of the finished product or service, its deadline, and its cost are clearly specified.

Service Role of Functional Departments

Usually a functional department does more than supply the project team with its members. It also provides backup service. The project engineer may want drafting help and advice on technical matters, and perhaps at some stages a whole crew of additional engineers will be

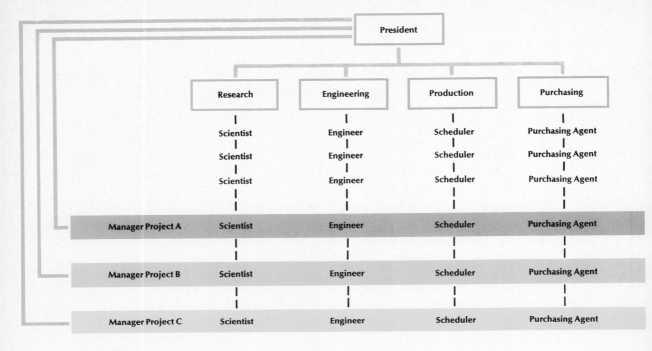

Fig. 6–1 Matrix organization. Each project manager is boss
for his project, borrowing the talent he needs temporarily
from the functional departments. The heads of functional
departments develop capable men—and perhaps other services
—but do not supervise the men while they are assigned to a
project team.

needed. Similarly, the market-research man calls on personnel in his home
department when he needs specialized assistance. When actual production
is begun the work will be done in the company shops (or subcontractors'
shops), which are supervised by the department head. Only in the case of
large projects lasting several years, or when work is performed on a remote site (as in construction), are the people who do this backup work
transferred to the project. Instead, the functional department performs
backup work according to requests from the project team in the same
way an outside subcontractor might take on a specified task.

Thus, with respect to his project, the project manager is the quarterback who calls the plays, watches progress, and decides on the next
moves. His success, however, depends largely on the capabilities that the
functional departments place at his disposal. In the short run, the project
manager supplies the initiative; he and his team provide the coordinated,
positive direction that is hard to obtain in a purely functional setup. How-

ever, in the long run, the quality and training of the specialists and the operating capabilities of the functional departments determine the kind and volume of projects a company can handle effectively.

Obviously this kind of interdependence is hard to keep in balance. Members of the project team, in their push to get specific results, tend to take over line supervision and stir up resentment of men who are being pushed around. Furthermore, the service that a functional department can provide is rarely as much, as good, or as soon as project managers would like. Especially when progress is poor, tension arises over who is failing to do all that he should.

In the construction and space industries and occasionally in other situations suited to matrix organization, the job we have been describing for a functional department may be performed by a subcontractor. For instance an advertising agency may use an outside creator of television commercials rather than maintain a department for this purpose within its own firm. This increases the negotiating aspects of the project manager's job, but basically the respective roles are not altered by the multiplication of legal entities.[1]

Priorities and Trade-offs

The strong position we have given project managers creates difficulties in scheduling work within functional departments. Each project has its own timetable. Wide fluctuations occur in the amount of any one type of service needed by a project. The resulting irregular call for service is likely to conflict with the requirements of other projects, and each project manager will think that his work should have priority. Even when an advanced plan for all products is neatly dovetailed, the inherent uncertainties connected with the kind of projects we are discussing results in some projects being late and others wanting more time of key men or facilities than was originally requested. The manager of a late project naturally feels it is important to catch up, and the manager who has struggled to stay on target strenuously objects to being penalized for another project's tardiness. These conflicting requests for men and facilities cause bottlenecks that will hinder the progress of all projects, and matrix organization must establish some mechanism for overcoming these obstructions.

The head of a functional department is rarely the right man to set priorities. He naturally wants an even flow of work, and what is convenient for him is not necessarily optimum for the overall enterprise. Incidentally, periods of peak demand are often followed by little or no work, and the

[1]Project managers and teams can also be used for special, one-time, across-organization changes, such as moving to a new location, absorbing a small company, or opening a foreign plant. Here the arrangement is clearly temporary and does not create any continuing modifications in organization design.

functional head is then seeking business to justify retaining his trained personnel. Perhaps a bottleneck can be relieved by working overtime, but who decides when the overtime premium is warranted and which project is assessed the additional cost? Priority squabbles are eventually resolved, partly because all the people involved learn to work through peaks (just as we learn to deal with rush-hour traffic congestion), and partly because scheduling methods are improved, as we will note in Chapter 19. But a residual set of priority and trade-off decisions will have to be made by a senior executive who can attach weights in light of total company values.

Because a matrix organization is both delicate and complicated, we should use it only when simpler organization designs are inadequate to cope with the dynamic nature of the work to be done.

Product Managers

Matrix organizations should be distinguished from the use of product managers. Theoretically, a company organized on a functional basis but with several different products could have a manager for each product. Each product manager would work very much like the project managers we have just discussed, and would shepherd his product through the functional departments from research to customer delivery. But there is a difference between projects and products. We expect a product to generate repetitive sales and become "part of the line." Most of the activities relating to it become a normal part of operations. Only occasionally, or in limited areas such as seasonal sales promotions or competitive pricing, does the product need more attention than the functional departments provide.

Therefore, a product manager typically needs less power than a project manager. He serves in a *staff* capacity, making sure that his product does not get lost, calling attention to unexpected opportunities or difficulties, bringing together men from two or more departments when agreement on coordinated action is needed, suggesting ways to improve results, and the like. Usually the final decisions about the product are made by departmental executives, although in the case of highly competitive consumer goods a product manager sometimes decides on pricing, sales promotion, and inventory. Primarily, however, the product manager aids and stimulates the functional departments to do their respective job well, whereas the project manager carries the initiative and accountability while departments act in a service capacity.

Both project and product managers are organizational devices to secure alert, responsive action in a milieu of rapid change. At the same time, both of them rely on the technical competence and efficient operations of functional departments. All sorts of variations are possible. Personal relationships are delicate; conflicts can be sharp. But we have here the possibilities for flexible, sophisticated action.

EXTERNAL, INDEPENDENT STAFF

Sheer magnitude poses new burdens on managers. Our larger enterprises often require staggering commitments of resources—men, materials, capital. Urban renewal, oil from Alaska, new automobile engines, atomic power, and many other developments call for inputs equivalent to the entire gross national product of several United Nations members.

A few large companies use a special type of staff to double-check such major decisions. In contrast to our description of staff in Chapter 4, this external group is not expected to collaborate with operating men in the initial preparation of plans. Instead they provide an independent check.

Seven significant features stand out in this design for staff work as it has been developed by a large computer manufacturer:

1) Each operating division has its own highly competent staff that provides technical and coordinating assistance in the usual fashion. The external staff is not regarded as a substitute for this kind of help. Nevertheless, top management does want assurance that the multimillion-dollar decisions embraced in operating plans are wise, and that no major opportunities for improvement are overlooked. The magnitude of commitments and the uncertainties faced by this company call for extraordinary efforts to ensure that the right action is taken.

2) The external staff is judged on the basis of the success of the operating divisions. If results are good, previous staff work is considered to be good even though the external staff did no more than endorse operating division proposals. However, when divisional results do not come up to par, the external staff man who approved plans of the operating division may be in deep trouble along with executives of the operating division. Clear evidence of bungled execution reduces staff accountability somewhat. But the basic doctrine is: "If the patient is well, the doctor gets a good fee. If the patient gets sick, the doctor may find himself even sicker." This means that both the external staff and the operating divisions are evaluated by the same standard—good results.

To make this accountability stick, the cause of any large difficulty is traced back to major decisions, and the staff man is penalized if he concurred with an error made perhaps two to five years earlier.

3) The external staff reviews the annual and five-year plans of the operating divisions, prior to central management's endorsement. If the staff believes the plans are good it concurs in writing. Concurrence implies that no future hazards or great opportunities have been overlooked. The plan may, and often does, involve substantial risks, but these risks should be fully explored and potential losses minimized.

4) When the staff does not concur, it must develop an alternative proposal. Mere "viewing with alarm" is not enough. The external staff must seek, and the operating division must provide, data that permits the staff to formulate a positive plan to eliminate its objections to the operating division's proposals. The staff has to be realistic and prepared to defend its alternative.

5) Often differences between the proposals of the operating division and the staff are ironed out voluntarily. One group convinces the other, or a third even better plan emerges. Both parties, however, are committed. Pressure from either side is no alibi. When sincere differences in judgment arise, these are presented to one or more senior executives to "umpire" the decision. Such umpiring is necessary to get on with the game—to prevent positive, aggressive action from being stalled.

6) To ensure that staff focuses on major issues and to prevent the entire planning mechanism from being bogged down with nonconcurrences, the size of the external staff is limited. With only a few people to investigate and to prepare alternative plans, the external staff must be very selective in the issues it tackles.

7) In this company, the external staff is organized on a functional basis, whereas the operating divisions are divided essentially on a product or service basis. Separate staff units focus on marketing, production, personnel, and so on, and in its review of operating-division plans each unit considers its specialty. Hence, the major plans are treated in a matrix fashion. The company feels that this feature adds strength to its organization, but it is not an essential feature of the external, independent staff concept.

The external staff concept has strong supporters. The major benefit is an independent check on major planning decisions. Alfred Sloan sought a similar independent judgment throughout General Motors through his "finance" men, but he placed them inside each division; they were internal rather than external staff.

In thinking about when to use external, independent staff, one should recognize these limitations. A comprehensive, explicit, forward-planning procedure must be in use if the external staff is to "tune in" on plans early enough to exercise a constructive influence. The scheme is expensive in terms both of talented manpower and the energies of many executives involved in the duplicate planning effort. The vital accountability concept requires careful postmortems delving back several years and a willingness to censure an executive for his actions that far in the past. Attitudes about external interference with planning have to be modified to tolerate two or more competitive proposals. In addition, but by no means least important, a new type of resilient, farsighted staff man has to be located and trained; unless such men have practical wisdom about the industry they serve the entire procedure is an added burden.

A satisfactory way to carry this external, independent staff concept over to major government decisions has not yet been worked out. Numerous clearances and checks exist in the government, to be sure, but neither the key aspect of continuing accountability nor provision for prompt resolution of differences in judgment are evident in government planning procedures.

OFFICE OF THE PRESIDENT

In today's fast-changing world, the chief executive of every large enterprise is under severe pressure. The demands placed on his time by external and internal problems, by nonbusiness as well as business affairs, by both long-range and short-range planning cannot possibly be met by one human being. Relief must be found.

The intensity of the pressure is growing, but the problem is not new. Chief executives for years have had a few personal assistants to relieve them of minor tasks and to expedite their numerous conferences, public appearances, and problem analyses. In a relatively stable situation, a whole array of corporate staff units may be created. Although these staff units normally provide service to their associates and to others throughout the organization, they are also available to assist the chief executive with problems he deals with personally.

Decentralization, especially profit decentralization, is a second way to relieve the harried chief executive. As we have seen, a variety of factors affect the wisdom of decentralizing, and so this alternative may not be attractive. Furthermore, even after decentralizing the remaining tasks for central management are very heavy.

A third alternative, practiced by a few companies, including du Pont and Standard Oil (New Jersey), is a full-time board of directors. Most board members are full-time employees who have been relieved of supervision of a specific part of the enterprise. They devote their entire energies to central management tasks.[2] Some allocation of work among the board members is made, and channels of communication are established. However, all regular board members are available to give undivided attention to new problems and future opportunities. Two drawbacks make this arrangement unattractive to most enterprises. First, a full-time board of highly successful executives is expensive; few companies can afford it. Second, the benefits of an independent, objective check on company actions by outside directors, who are not judging their own decisions, is lost.

Recently the concept of a "president's office" is becoming more widely used and, as is the case with the office of the President in our

[2]Recently a few outside board members, who devote only part of their time to serving on the board, have been added. The basic pattern of a full-time board continues however.

federal government, the president's office is viewed as a distinct unit of the organization. It has its own internal structure as well as its relations with other separate units and departments. Various staff aides and communication flows are part of the design, but the key feature is a team of two to five senior executives who share the central management tasks.

The division of duties among the senior men depends on their own capabilities and the currently pressing problems. One man might deal with external relations—with customer groups, governmental bodies, industry associations, and the like—while another might concentrate on internal operations. Three other executives might normally handle technological questions, legal matters, and finance, respectively. But the essence of the concept is synthesized action rather than specialization along any line. Regardless of how the work is shared, an intimate and frequent interchange is essential so that the office functions like a close-knit partnership. The office is expected to respond to numerous external and internal integration needs (discussed in Chapter 1) in a way that provides a consistent and unified posture for the company.

The success of this arrangement rests predominantly on the personalities of the executives involved. At the top level they are sure to be strong men, and yet a president's office requires a high degree of sharing and mutual support. Not all strong men are willing to play the game this way. Other features of organization design may depend on the characteristics of persons in key positions, but this dependency is never so great as it is in the case of the president's office.

We should note in passing that the concept of a manager's "office" might be applied to the head of any large, complex unit. Certainly dual executives are not unique. In this case a manager typically has an alter ego who shares with him the duties of the position. For this arrangement to be effective there must be a proper blending of personalities, and the managers must have experience in working together. The senior man must have complete confidence in his associate because, as in a legal partnership, either of the men usually can speak officially for the office. The relationship is so highly personal that if either of the two men is replaced, the scheme may break down. The arrangement is often a useful one, but because of its inherent weaknesses, it should be avoided if some other provision is practical.

REPRESENTATION OF SPECIAL INTERESTS

In reform efforts, requests are repeatedly made for official representation on policy bodies or in management positions. The issue has been pressed in university and local school restructuring, in all sorts of urban renewal projects, and in the management of public utilities, to cite only a few recent examples. The basic proposition is that major "interest groups"—customers or clients, employees, neighborhoods in which these people live, suppliers of materials, investors, or others whose own well-being can be significantly affected by the operation of the enterprise—should participate in the management of the enterprise.

This is a familiar issue to the political scientist who wrestles with questions ranging from the divine right of kings to taxation without representation to recognition of the poor farmer. We do not propose in this book to tackle such broad matters of social and economic structure of society; instead we shall stick to the design of management organization and shall note the kind of response to such pressures from interest groups that we believe is compatible with effective management.

Managers of business firms, hospitals, and other enterprises usually have some experience with interest representation. Labor unions and suppliers of capital have often taken strong positions on how a given enterprise should be run. Interference by a large customer (for example, the Air Force) or a major supplier (auto manufacturers) is not unknown. But too often the reaction has been based solely on traditional "prerogatives." A more constructive approach divides the response to a representation request into two parts.

First, a board of directors composed of "watchdogs" appointed to advocate the views of a particular interest group will rarely perform the essential functions of a board adequately. The board should do all of the following: provide an objective check on the strategy, programs, and management structure devised by the management group; share in the prediction of critical developments; evaluate results; select the top executives; and give personal advice informally. It supplements, stimulates, and checks the judgment of central management. To fill this role each board member should treat the long-run interests of the enterprise as paramount. Even one or two directors who are grinding their own ax will prevent a candid, wholesome review of company problems.

The divided-loyalty objection applies also to the appointment of persons to key jobs because they are selected by an interest group. We do not imply that persons from diverse backgrounds, especially in areas where sticky problems arise, should be unwelcome. The point is that if they are to serve the enterprise—to be on the team—they should not try to serve the conflicting interests of two masters.

This means that neither labor unions nor bankers should be entitled to select directors or executives who represent their interests. It also means that an effective governing body of a university should not be composed of members elected by students, faculty, or employees. To run an enterprise we prefer professional management to politics.

Second, effective two-way communication between the enterprise and each interest group must be maintained. Formalities are not enough. The enterprise needs to know the aspirations, beliefs, values, and alternatives facing each group making inputs into the enterprise system. Also each interest group should be advised in advance of any actions sig-

Fig. 6–2 *Effect of watchdog members on the effectiveness of a board of directors. If the primary interest of some members is directed away from the organization, the area of the board's usefulness shrinks.*

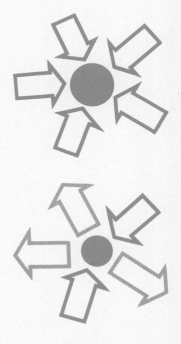

nificantly affecting it so that counterproposals can be made. The interest group should have ample opportunity to recommend action to the enterprise. The aim of such communication is to lay the basis for constructive joint action.

Such a communication arrangement, if conducted in good faith, allows the interest group to influence the decision-making body even though the interest group is not actually represented on the body. The opportunity for mutually beneficial action is retained. No change is made in the underlying bargaining power of the various parties. On the other hand, managing the enterprise as an independent social institution is not hamstrung by ineffective boards or executives, which would be the case if every interest group was permitted to have a member on every decision-making body.

IMPACT OF COMPUTERS ON ORGANIZATION

Dazzling advances in the capabilities of electronic computers have been accompanied by comparable predictions of their effect on managerial organization. Science fiction pictures worlds where managers no longer exist, and learned articles compare machines playing chess with executive decision-making. Actually the serious organization designer needs to consider the impact of computers largely in three areas: (1) mechanization of clerical activities; (2) possibilities of more or less decentralization; and (3) shrinking of middle management.

Mechanization of Clerical Activities

By far the greatest use of computers to date, and their chief effect on organization, has been in performing clerical operations. Millions of man-hours have been saved by machines that sort, calculate, and record. Life insurance companies, banks, internal revenue offices, social security offices, to name just a few, are experiencing a technological revolution in their routine activities. In businesses whose clerical operations are a relatively minor part of the total technology, the payroll, accounting, and billing units are usually affected most.

Note that the change just described does not alter the results; basically the same work is now being done by machines—faster, probably cheaper, and perhaps better. It is mechanization pure and simple. Obviously the units being mechanized are drastically affected, and as with most mechanization a variety of peripheral effort must be devoted to conform the incoming work to the capacity of the machines. The magnitude of the details involved is staggering. Nevertheless, neither the primary functions of the enterprise nor its basic organization have been changed. The effect on overall organization design is minimal.

One familiar problem does appear. The computer-processing unit, because of its large capacity and its high expense, is usually set up as a new auxiliary service. As we noted in Chapters 2 and 5, the organization designer has to decide how many separate service units should be established and where to attach them to the total structure. More than physical processing and hardware are involved. Especially during the introductory stage, learning how to use the computer—the "software"— is an essential part of the service.

The location of computer service units is usually resolved by the "most-use" criterion. If the engineering department is the chief user of the computing center, the center probably will be placed in that department; similar reasoning may lead to a decision to place the center in the finance department. The final resolution of location, however, is very unsettled because of continuing changes in size and capabilities of computers. Perhaps many small computers will meet the needs of an enterprise most economically; if so, small computer units can be located throughout the organization. The dominant consideration, as with any auxiliary service, is providing effective service when and where needed; the second factor is performing the activity at low cost.

Possibilities of More or Less Decentralization

Computers coupled with vastly improved communications equipment can affect decentralization design. Objective data can now be transmitted, analyzed, and retransmitted very rapidly. This new technical capacity changes the answer to questions concerning who can readily get what information, and we know from our examination of decentralization in Chapter 3 that availability of pertinent, current information is one of the considerations in deciding where to center decision-making.

But the effect may be either *more* or *less* decentralization. Background data can be fed to the field, or local data can be fed to headquarters. A few companies are systematically sending information on industry production, competitive prices, and economic indicators to their local sales offices so that these units can move promptly in making contracts with customers. A more common response has been rapid assembly of local information at a centralized point. Commercial banks, for instance, can now centralize both activities and some decision-making formerly done at local branches. Improved air travel permits higher level executives to make more firsthand observation trips. This along with computerized sources of local data contributes to centralization of decision-making.

The impact of computers on decentralization, however, can easily be exaggerated. For instance, the scheduling of the arrival of material at very large construction projects is being carried out more and more by a central purchasing office rather than by the site manager; computers are often used, but the major impetus comes from adoption of new planning and control techniques.[3]

Also computers affect only one of the factors we have to consider when deciding whether to centralize or decentralize. They make objective data available very quickly, but they are not adept at handling subjective impressions, intensity of feelings, shades of values, and other nonquantified information. Computers affect neither the ability and the availability of executives at various points in the organization nor the morale benefits of decentralization (see pp. 54–56). Consequently, in designing organization we should recognize that computers reduce the importance of who has the data but leave untouched the intangible aspects of decentralization.

Shrinking of Middle Management

The elimination of a large number of middle management positions is conceivably the greatest impact of computers on organization. A few conspicuous examples are cited by proponents of this development. Oil refinery output is being scheduled by computers, and engineering specifications for special-purpose transformers are being prepared by electronic means. These achievements have reduced the number of staff planners.

The prediction that a whole layer of middle management can be discarded is based on the premise that most of what these managers do can be automated. In thinking about the validity of this assumption we should first note several requirements for automation. The computer must (1) identify the need for an action decision; (2) possess a suitable array of programmed actions that might be taken; (3) draw upon available data for cues to which alternative is best; and (4) issue instructions in a way that will lead to the desired action. In highly standardized operations where future difficulties can be foreseen and the alternative actions are limited, perhaps the "judgment" of a manager can be duplicated by a computer. Clearly in designing an organization this possibility should be recognized.

A review of the work of virtually all managers will reveal, however, that only a small proportion of managerial decisions can be recast to conform with the four requirements listed above. Furthermore, most middle and first-line managers devote a large part of their energy to mobilizing resources, directing, leading, controlling, and to other tasks beyond decision-making in the narrow sense. Computers have been programmed to play chess, but a chess game is a grossly simplified con-

[3]The most widely used of these new techniques, PERT, is described in Chapter 25.

cept of the role of a manager. Moreover, change is the order of the day. We design organizations to deal with tomorrow's problems, and as fast as some types of problems can be routinized and automated new problems arising from social or technological change will press for attention.

In summary, we should carefully appraise the impact of computers on the operating and managerial work to be done. However, we need not anticipate a new type of social arrangement. The issues and key factors discussed in previous chapters will continue to be the major concern in designing future organizations.

CONCLUSION: INTEGRATING ORGANIZATION WITH OTHER PHASES OF MANAGEMENT

The examples of new emphases in organization discussed in this chapter illustrate again how organization design needs to be adapted to the technological, economic, and social environment in which the enterprise operates. The basic elements of managerial organization have persisted over the centuries, but designing the specific structure is a never-ending task of adjusting to current opportunities.

Before leaving our discussion of formal organization, we should emphasize again the close relationship between organization and other phases of management. Especially when we consider changes in organization structure, we should try to evaluate repercussions in planning, leading and controlling. Rarely can major changes be made in one area without at least some adjustment in others.

The Lerner Shops serve as an example of the need for consistency in management. This operating company sells women's clothes in many small outlets throughout the country. Compared with the apparel industry in general, it does a high-volume business in the low-priced range. To be successful, it must place popular-style dresses on the market quickly and continue to make them available during a season, but the stores must have a minimum inventory on hand at the end of each season because what is left is almost a total loss.

Conceivably, the manager of each shop could be free to buy the dresses that she believed would sell in her locality. If the managers were given such freedom, headquarters in New York would then serve as buying agent and general counsel for the local stores. Instead, the organization is in fact highly centralized. People in headquarters select, purchase, and price the dresses and distribute them to the outlets. Each local store makes daily reports on the style, color, and size of dresses it sells. If a particular style does not move in one locality or the inventory in a store is out of balance, headquarters issues instructions to trade inventory with a store in another town. The chief purpose of a local store is simply to display and sell the dresses. Selecting, training, and supervising salespeople are, of course, largely local matters, and suggestions for new merchandise or advertising are welcome. But virtually all merchandising decisions are made in headquarters.

This manner of operation means that in addition to formulating policies the top-management level of the business must prepare detailed schedules and methods. On the lower level, little initiative is expected. The people selected to manage shops in a company like Lerner's need not be merchants. In fact, a person who bubbles over with new ideas or has highly creative and artistic sensibilities would probably make a poor manager in such a chain. A local manager should be someone who enjoys dealing with people, selling merchandise fast, and keeping a neat and efficient store. Frequent and detailed control reports are required, and regional directors typically insist on close adherence to company procedures and regulations. Thus all aspects of management—the planning process, the organization, the kinds of executives selected, the type of supervision, and the methods of control—fit together into a consistent pattern for this particular business.

When organization changes are not matched by consistent modifications in other phases of management, the move will probably be ineffective or even harmful. To cite a specific case, a steel company, which for years had operated with almost as tight and centralized administration as that of the Lerner Shops, decided to decentralize and made much to-do about pushing authority down the line. But the company did not make corresponding adjustments in other phases of management. For example, heat reports on each open-hearth furnace had to be submitted up the line, and staff assistants in the chief engineer's office insisted on explanations of a heat that varied far from normal. Everyone from the vice-president down continued "to keep right on top of the situation." Because the management did not adjust its planning, supervisory, and control practices to the announced changes in organization, no real change occurred. Staff expenses were higher than they should have been and morale was harmed by building up expectations that failed to materialize.

Organizing must be recognized, then, as only a part of the total management task. We have separated organization issues from the whole maze of management problems for convenience of analysis. The experience of many executives has demonstrated that thinking in terms of formal organization is a practical tool for dealing with tough, live company situations. Nevertheless, organization actually never exists alone, any more than a person's nervous system can exist apart from his whole body. The result of organizing comes to life only in association with other acts of management—planning, leading, and controlling—and in an assembly of real people. Consequently, if our plans for organization are to be carried out, they must be meshed with other forces in the specific situation. We must reverse the act of analysis and reintegrate the total operation. Then, and only then, will our design for an organization bear fruit.

FOR CLASS DISCUSSION

Questions

1) Consider a highly trained group of professionals "working" around a patient during delicate open-heart surgery. (1) In what ways is this group similar and in what ways is it dissimilar to a matrix organization? (2) How does the organizational approach used in the operating room differ from the organizational approach used to care for patients in their rooms or wards? How would you account for these differences and what is their probable effect on patient needs?

2) In what ways does the matrix approach affect the position that "each man should have only one immediate superior," which was discussed in Chapter 3?

3) If external staff does not concur with a division proposal and after much debate no basis for agreement can be found, what elements should be contained in the *review, decision,* and *follow-up* that will be taken by higher level line umpires?

4) In what ways would the technical and temperamental attributes sought in a good "external staff" man differ from those sought for men who fill the more conventional staff roles discussed in Chapter 4?

5) The text suggests the difficulties of bringing representatives of special interest groups to bear on decisions. The potential provincialism of such people may inhibit frank discussions and limit the ability to view company problems with sufficient perspective. If representatives of such groups do come on a board or meet with top management and attempt to share the views of top management, what may happen to their ability to represent their interest groups?

6) What organizational guides can you offer to increase the likelihood that the "service" contribution of computers to line organizations includes the kinds of service most useful to the line organization? Consider, in your answer, the problems raised because line men often fail to understand what the computer can offer, while computer men often fail to understand the kinds of services most needed by line managers.

7) In what ways may the use of computers affect the degree of decentralization possible as a result of the computer's potential contributions to control?

8) As computers mechanize, if not automate, more lower-level jobs, do you see any changes other than shrinkage that may affect middle management jobs? Discuss.

Cases

For cases involving issues covered in this chapter, see especially the following. Particularly relevant questions are listed after each case.

General Machinery Corporation (p. 130), 4
Gerald Clark (p. 234), 2
Bolling Laboratories, Inc. (p. 345), 3
Consolidated Instruments—B (p. 674), 4

FOR FURTHER READING

Brink, V.Z., *Computers and Management*. Englewood Cliffs, N.J.: Prentice-Hall, Inc., 1971. *Organizational and personnel problems associated with computer use.*

Cleland, D.I., and W.R. King, *Systems Analysis and Project Management*. New York: McGraw-Hill Book Company, 1969, Section 7. *Generalized view of project management, primarily in government.*

Daniel, D.R., "The Team at the Top." *Harvard Business Review*, March 1965. *Keen analysis of early examples of office of the president.*

Diebold, J., "Bad Decisions on Computer Use." *Harvard Business Review*, January 1969. *Predicts computer use for strategic decisions by 1985.*

Ernst, M.L., "Computers, Business and Society." *Management Review*, November 1970. *Social problems arising from computer use.*

Juran, J.M., and J.K. Louden, *The Corporate Director*. New York: American Management Association, 1966. *Includes analysis of relations between board and office of the president.*

Myers, C.A., ed., *The Impact of Computers on Management*. Cambridge, Mass.: M.I.T. Press, 1967. *Leading experts discuss effect of computers on organizing, planning, and controlling.*

Newman, W.H., *Administrative Action*, 2nd ed. Englewood Cliffs, N.J.: Prentice-Hall, Inc., 1963, Chap. 18. *Developing effective relationships with interest groups.*

Steiner, G.A., and W.G. Ryan, *Industrial Project Management*. New York: The Macmillan Company, 1968. *Analysis of work of sixteen successful project managers in aerospace industry.*

TRANS-WORLD MUTUAL FUNDS, LTD.

Trans-World Mutual Funds, Ltd., is a diversified financial investing company with headquarters in London. Although legal regulation of such companies in the United Kingdom is somewhat different from that found in the United States, its operation resembles closely that of open-end investment funds in the latter country. Trans-World's sales force sells shares in the fund to the public, and the capital gained from this sale is immediately invested in stock market shares of various operating companies, shares that are held in the fund's name. The assets and portfolio of investments held by the fund can increase as the public buys more stock in Trans-World. At present, the public has already invested over £50,000,000 (about $120,000,000) in stock in the three separate funds owned by Trans-World.

Trans-World was founded by Charles Pitman. He attended the Harvard Business School in the United States and was graduated sixteen years ago. He worked first for a brokerage house in New York and then for a large mutual fund in Boston. Returning to England, he became a securities analyst in one of the large merchant banking houses.

Thirteen years ago, Pitman came to the conclusion that the public in the United Kingdom and Western Europe simply had not had as great an opportunity to invest in mutual funds as had citizens of the United States. In the United States, he had seen small investors buying shares in these funds by either paying for them in lump amounts of $500 and $1,000 or by contracting to invest $50 or $100 a month for ten years. Yet in Europe one generally had to buy individual stocks through brokers. Pitman believed that the success of Bernard Cornfeld, who had founded Investors Overseas Services (IOS) in Geneva, proved that Europeans would be more willing to invest in mutual funds if they could do so according to the same provisions that were followed in the United States. He also believed that he had the ambition and intelligence to build a large fund that would succeed. As Pitman put it:

> The main sources of success are a trained sales force, a force of skilled financial analysts to buy the right stocks for the portfolio, and above all, some kind of control by the top management of Trans-World that will cause those trained men to give their best— every ounce of their energies to sell our funds, every ounce of their brain power to discover, bore in, and analyze, and decide on which stocks are going to produce the highest dividends or capital gains.
>
> There is one more ingredient. That is top management. I knew I had to organize the business—establish jobs and their functions, select and train people, and then establish some kind of controls to ensure that results were actually achieved. I set a growth rate the first five years at 20 percent a year. With these ingredients of success, plus backing by several well-known financial institutions, we had in ten years amassed a portfolio of stocks which had a market value of $240,000,000.[1]
>
> I started out with only a relatively few salesmen and analysts, selling Investor's Fund Ltd. This fund appeals to people who want lower-risk in blue chips, higher current dividends, but not such fast growth and capital gains. My analysts were men who were good general investment men, looking for quality stocks to buy with the public's money. At that time, my organization looked like Exhibit 1. By general investment men, I mean men who were educated as finance and economics specialists, and who spent all of their time reviewing current investment information. They tended to specialize somewhat by industry (for example, petroleum), but not in a clear-cut way. They each simply came up with recommendations across the whole range of securities investments. Their judgment was good at picking successful companies—they just "had a nose for it."
>
> After fast growth during the first years, I started two new funds. One was Growth Industry Fund Ltd., to be sold to people who want fast-growing companies in chemicals, electronics, aerospace, and the like. You see, I could operate two funds almost as cheaply as one— the salesmen could sell both, and my investment analysts could search for growth companies at the same time they were searching for the slower-growing blue chips.
>
> My long-range strategy called for more specialized investment analysts working for each individual fund (instead of for all three funds). But at this stage of development I could not afford so many

---

[1] Throughout, the monetary figures are translated into United States dollars. Mr. Pitman himself freely translated this way when interviewed by the casewriter.

specialists. One year later we began operation of the third fund, Equity Special Fund. Originally, this fund was to specialize in foreign country corporations of the same type as Growth Fund. However, certain foreign exchange regulations have made Equity and Growth practically identical in their goals and investments.

These funds were an immediate success. We grew by leaps and bounds to the point where three years ago we had a total portfolio in Trans-World of $240,000,000—$100,000,000 in Investor's Fund, $80,000,000 in Growth Fund, and $60,000,000 in Equity Special Fund. Our organization chart three years ago reflected these changes, as you can see in Exhibit 2.

You will notice that the central investment analysis department serviced all three firms. By this time, the security analysts had become specialized. As our portfolio became bigger, we had hired eleven analysts. One man, for instance, had done extensive work in office equipment and electronics, investing in Bull G.E., IBM, and Phillips. He could do a much better job of watching markets in both more conservative blue chips and the glamor higher-risk companies such as Computer Laboratories, if he deals only with these industries. I created specialists also in banking, insurance, and real estate, chemicals and petroleum, food and beverages, steel and nonferrous metals, and so on. We had seven men specializing by industry, two general (industrial) men who specialized in "all other" conservative investment grade stocks, and one general industry man who specialized in "all other" growth higher-risk companies. My payroll for the investment department was $110,000 per year, or averaging $10,000 per man (you must remember that executive salaries are lower in England than in the United States). This is slightly higher than the merchant banks pay.

With a growth rate three years ago of 10 percent, funds were coming in at $30,000,000 a year from new accounts and installments on previous accounts which had to be invested during the year. Furthermore, we were switching stocks in the portfolio to sell less attractive issues and buy newly attractive issues at the rate of $5,000,000 a month. Do you see how important it is to have highly motivated investment analysts, who give every ounce of their brainpower to their work?

And yet, I was worried. There was no way to measure the performance of these men. I couldn't supervise them directly. They would do lengthy research on Royal Dutch Shell, then write a security analysis and a recommendation to buy so many thousand shares at a certain price. Every morning the investment committee—myself, two senior analysts, and the investment director—would meet to consider these recommendations. We met all morning every morning but couldn't seem to know enough or study enough to check their work. We spent enormous amounts of time.

A second worry was about the size of their purchases. Three different times we had small companies which suddenly grew very large—British companies with explosive growth like your Syntex birth control pills in the United States, or your Ling-Temco-Vought, which was started by Jimmy Ling as a small electronics firm. These companies were the biggest successes in the securities markets. I asked why it was that Trans-World, with all of its talent, had not invested in these companies when they were small. In all three cases I got the same answer. Since we had to make new investments at $90,000,000 a year, and keep constant vigil on the $240,000,000 in the portfolio, each analyst had an enormous responsibility. The analysts said that when these small companies first started selling stock, the amounts they wanted from the public were $1,500,000 to $3,000,000. They were very small and relatively high risk, and our firm would have purchased perhaps $150,000 to $300,000 at the very most, even if we had spotted them. It would be unwise (and probably impossible, under the underwriters' quota system) to buy more than 10 percent of such a company. The analysts also said that with $240,000,000 in assets to watch, their performance wouldn't look very good if they spent four or five days of their time writing a research report on a $150,000 purchase. It takes just as much time, and sometimes due to lack of information even more time, to consider such an investment as it would take to do research on a $10,000,000 purchase of Imperial Chemicals.

I couldn't agree with them more. If they brought such an amount to the investment committee we would just have to go on to the next large investment.

Reorganization of Trans-World, Ltd.

Fortunately, there were reasons on the sales force side, too, which meant that we should decentralize. And I saw a chance to correct these two deficiencies in the investment side. Three years ago, I created three autonomous subsidiary companies. We already had separate legal companies, with three separate portfolios, but the investment department was actually buying these, for which it charged a .5 percent management fee. This is similar to the practice of some corporations to set a transfer price when one division of the company sells to another. The investment department was selling its services to the funds for $1,200,000 a year, out of which was paid commissions to brokers, salaries, and all overhead. In many instances, a stock would be bought for two or three funds at the same time—the preferred stock of a top chemical company would be placed in Investor's Fund, while its common stock would be placed in the Growth and Equity Special funds.

Under the reorganization, the three directors became managing directors (presidents) of their own companies. We had to duplicate the investment talents in the three divisions. We hired fourteen new industry specialists so that each subsidiary would have its own analyst in, for example, the office equipment and electronics industry. We distributed the two general investment men specializing in investment grade stocks to the Investor's Fund, the two men cutting across industries for growth stocks to the Growth Fund, and hired two more of these for Equity Special. Thus we increased the total staff by sixteen men and our annual salary costs by about $160,000 a year.

Under this plan, the division presidents could make their own decisions, the salesmen and analysts could work directly for their own fund, my top management could be relieved for long-range planning rather than day-to-day investing and selling, and the investment departments could keep an eye on smaller companies for the future, rather than becoming buyers of only big established companies which had passed their growth prime. In addition, we would train three investment committees instead of myself and one committee. I could also have some comparison of performance—I could see which group of analysts in Growth or Equity would earn the most in capital growth, achieve the smallest cost in switching commissions, and so on, and which managing director of all three would achieve the best sales, growth, and investment record.

Results of the Reorganization

Mr. Pitman is convinced that the decentralization move has, in fact, achieved the results he envisioned. He has statistics showing that the number of smaller companies in which Trans-World has invested has increased from almost none to eighty-five in the last three years. Interviews by the casewriter with two subsidiary presidents show that they are, in fact, making investment decisions themselves, that they like this type of function and work longer hours at it, that they believe their investment analysts are working more diligently. Presidents and investment analysts are both very conscious of the fact that Pitman is comparing their performance against that of other subsidiary personnel. The latter are divided on how this affects their "nerves" as one man put it. "The others and I definitely do more work than previously, but I find that I'm a bit more worried at night about how successful I am." Another man disagreed: "I'm a bloody good security analyst when it comes to air transport stocks. I come to work wanting to do better than the Equity Special team and their aviation specialist." The casewriter also noted that members of the investment committees in the subsidiaries were spending long hours studying recommendations and judging them. There were three senior analysts serving on these committees in each company.

Two problems have come to Pitman's attention as of the time this case is written. The first, a business recession in the investment industry, is caused in part by high interest rates ("People are switching from stocks to high yield bonds, to trade acceptances of Ford of England, for example."), and in part by the troubles of Investor's Overseas Services, the leading mutual funds in Europe. Pitman discussed the situation:

Our new sales have declined drastically. We are down to $8,000,000 growth a year in assets, a 3 percent growth rate. Our profits are down from $1,300,000 to $800,000. Of course, this is nothing to get too excited about, but it does spell trouble for the next three or four years.

The second thing I worry about is the relatively high cost of our operation. One factor that came forcefully to my attention is the cost of maintaining decentralized investment departments. In addition to salary, office equipment, and library duplication, we have been paying a fairly high price for diverse investment decisions. Let me give you an example. Last July, the food specialist in Growth Fund recommended to sell a block of Unilever at $165 a share because he thought that the stock had appreciated as much as it is going to for the foreseeable future. The investment committee and president of Growth concurred. It happens that on the same day the food specialist in Equity Special, who had all of the same research information (they often meet or talk on the telephone), judged that we should buy Unilever at $165 because their new acquisition of Findus in Germany would have significant effect to increase the price of the stock.

I had known that this kind of thing would happen when we decentralized, but I'm beginning to wonder how much it is worth to let this go on. I had one of my assistants do a thorough study of what has happened the last three years. As you know, it does not make any difference whether the stock goes up or down after such a dual transaction. You call it "hedging" when a single investor does this on purpose. If the stock goes up $10 a share and we have 10,000 shares, then Growth Fund loses (or misses out on) $100,000 and Equity Special makes $100,000. Obviously both men could not be right. Worse than that, viewing performance of the total firm, we are spinning our wheels. We are wasting valuable time of analysts and investment committees. Also, the administrative cost study found that, over three years, there was a significant number of transactions similar to this one (though they might not have occurred on the same day). We paid out $120,000 on brokerage commissions to buy and sell particular securities. My study also showed that analysts and investment committees put in four and a half man-days on each of these dual hedging operations, thereby costing a total of $10,000.

Pitman's administrative director, F.L. Loring, is "definitely of the opinion that we should bring the investment departments back to headquarters. These kinds of decisions are destructive to the Trans-World group, and we simply cannot afford to have lesser qualified men in the divisions when we could have more specialists at headquarters and a lesser number of total personnel."

A strong dissent to this opinion was made by George Ferguson, managing director of Equity Special Fund. "The cost of the present organization is not the controlling factor. This fund, over the years, will do much better if we do our own analyses. I'm sure that William Jamison who does our food analysis will produce more profits if he is doing it for 'his' fund than if he is doing it for set fee for three funds. I'm sure that my investment committee, and I myself, will do better work."

As of this time, Charles Pitman feels he must decide on this issue. "I've never procrastinated. Whichever way we go, it must be a clear decision with good reasoning and clear-headed judgment."

Exhibit 1 *Original Organization,*
Trans-World Mutual Funds, Ltd.

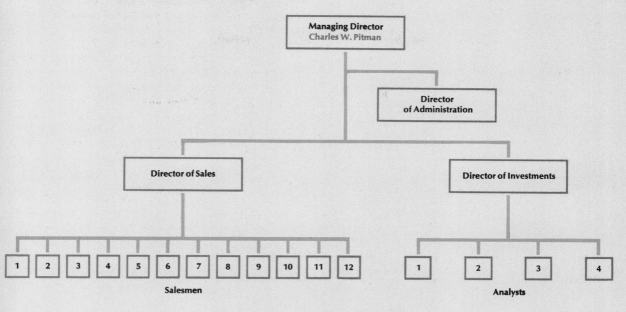

Exhibit 2 *Second Organization,*
Trans-World Mutual Funds, Ltd.

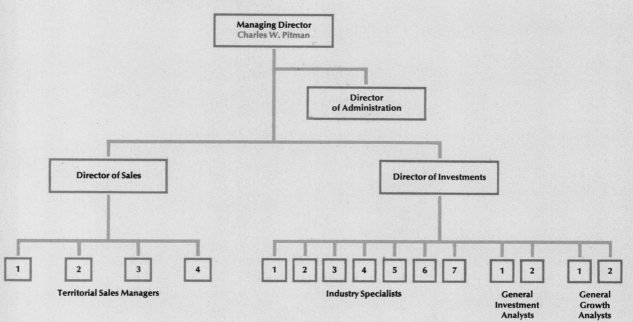

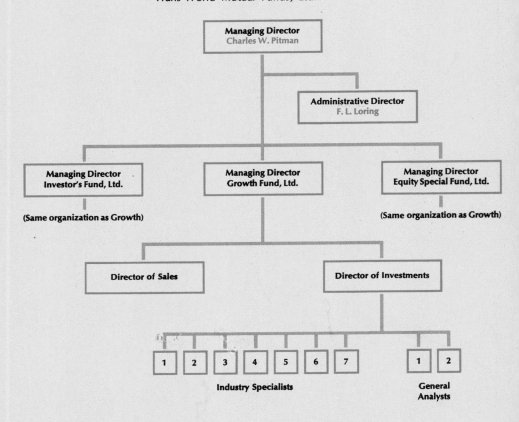

Exhibit 3 *Third (Present) Organization, Trans-World Mutual Funds, Ltd.*

Managing Director
Charles W. Pitman

Administrative Director
F. L. Loring

Managing Director
Investor's Fund, Ltd.

(Same organization as Growth)

Managing Director
Growth Fund, Ltd.

Managing Director
Equity Special Fund, Ltd.

(Same organization as Growth)

Director of Sales

Director of Investments

| 1 | 2 | 3 | 4 | 5 | 6 | 7 |

Industry Specialists

| 1 | 2 |

General
Analysts

FOR DISCUSSION AND REPORT-WRITING

Organizing: Structural Design

1) In deciding on the major operating jobs to be performed at the beginning, when the firm was small, what factors should Pitman have considered when designing the work of a security analyst? How did these factors determine that there would be general analysts rather than specialist analysts?

2) What positive forces caused the move toward decentralization? What advantages did Trans-World gain by decentralizing?

3) What negative results occurred from the change to the decentralized structure? How serious were these?

4) What sequential steps are necessary in shaping the overall structure of a company? Did Pitman seem to follow these? Illustrate with facts from the case.

5) *Summary Report Question, Part One:* After considering the questions 1–4, write a report listing the major problems in formal organization structure faced by Trans-World. For each problem, give the specific case facts to illustrate. Recommend whether Pitman should make a change in the structure at this time and give reasons for this decision.

Human Factors in Organizing

6) The casewriter found that the managing directors and the investment committee members, in the present organization structure, "liked their work." Of what special importance is this to a mutual-fund company? Why *did* they like their work?

7) How do you account for the different reactions of two security analysts to the decentralized structure?

8) On the basis of your knowledge of British culture, should decisions regarding the organization of Trans-World be any different because of its location in London than they would be if it were located in a large city in the United States?

Planning: Elements of Decision-Making

9) The work of finding and analyzing good investments for Trans-World's portfolio is aided in the company by the use of investment committees. Why did Pitman institute these? What kinds of aid to group creativity might you recommend to Pitman and the committees?

Planning: Decision-Making in an Enterprise

10) In what sense is decentralization of the organization structure in Trans-World a form of "participation in decision-making"? Cite specific facts from the case to explain what decentralized managers *do* (what their functions are) when they "participate" in the firm's decisions. Look at the work of both managing directors and investment committees.

11) How do the goals of the Investor's Fund differ from those of the Growth Fund? Explain, using facts from the case, how these goals are forcefully important in the future success or failure of the firm.

12) Explain why the setting of goals for the Investor's Fund and the Growth Fund simplify decision-making *within* those organizations.

Leading

13) Do you think that, as of the end of the case, Pitman had succeeded in getting the voluntary cooperation of the managing directors of his three companies? Of the investment analysts? What is your reasoning, that is, why or why not?

14) Suppose Pitman were to try to change the organization structure a third time to do something about the things that are bothering him. What would he *do* in the way of face-to-face leadership, over the next three months, to gain a maximum of cooperation?

Measuring and Controlling

15) As the organization structure stands at the end of the case, what is the primary quantitative control available to Pitman to see if investment analysts are conforming to his overall objectives? What are the advantages and disadvantages of this measure?

16) Suppose Pitman were to change back to the second organization structure. What would happen to his profit control? What kinds of alternatives might you creatively suggest (for further study) as measures of performance for security analysts?

Summary Question for Solution of the Case as a Whole

17) Considering all factors that bear on the question of the "best" organization structure for Trans-World (including some covered in the questions above), how would you recommend that Pitman solve the organization's structural-design problem? What other recommendations might you give to ensure that the company is well managed in the future? Assume you are a consultant and address your report to Mr. Pitman.

 ## GENERAL MACHINERY CORPORATION

General Machinery Corporation (GMC) was founded fifty-five years ago, initially to produce parts for railroad locomotives. It has grown into a large diversified company with 60,000 employees, sales of $550,000,000, twelve operating (product) divisions, and twenty-three manufacturing plants. According to GMC president, William Schulz, the firm has been successful "because it has pursued certain main goals: lower-than-competitors' prices, economies of mass production, and higher quality than competitors' through superior technology."

An organization chart of the company appears as Exhibit 1. Basic operating divisions (for example, diesel engine, mining equipment) are viewed by Mr. Schulz as "relatively autonomous. We expect that division managers will have the initiative to make GMC the best in their product lines. The electronic equipment division manager, for example, must decide what products to bring out, what kinds of selling talents and methods he needs, and above all, how to manufacture this equipment at the lowest possible cost through mass production."

This case reports on certain problems that the company faces in carrying out its subgoals of scientific research. According to Mr. Schulz, these goals are "to develop new products ahead of competitors, and to develop new mass-manufacturing processes to keep our product quality high and our costs low. We develop these products and processes for our current operating divisions (which we call 'operating research') and for the long-range future changes in our business (we call this 'long-range research' or 'pure research')."

The problems in this case were originally suggested by Dr. Herman Hoffmann, vice-president in charge of the Central Research Laboratories.

The Problem as Seen by Dr. Hoffmann

Dr. Hoffman feels that the present system for operating the Central Research Laboratories (CRL) has some disadvantages for both CRL and for the company as a whole. He views the situation in this way:

There are several problems. I am a bit tired of investigating, with my scientists, which operating projects will be best for the divisions and which long-range projects will be best for the company, and then having many of these turned down by the Executive Committee. We spend great amounts of time writing the technical proposals, getting detailed cost figures, and making judgments about where the money should be spent. It is bad for the morale of the scientists and engineers who do this work, and who judge in their own minds what is good for the company, to see their efforts come to nothing. They feel that their judgment is either being ignored or condemned.

In the case of operating research, I many times know which projects have priority and how much should be spent on them. Yet sometimes the Executive Committee refuses to appropriate enough money for worthy projects. This is caused because division managers, sitting on the Committee, often are afraid that they won't get their fair share of research money. They therefore don't support another division's request. Also, it is very difficult for the two top management members of the Committee to judge when a given technical-research project is necessary and when it is not. They quite naturally must be financially oriented. Since often it is difficult to prove what the payoff for a project will be, they must wonder whether that much money should be spent. I am certainly not criticizing Mr. Seabert, the financial vice-president, since he is responsible for the finances of the company. He votes to turn a project down when he judges that it is not worth the cost to the company. So does Mr. Schulz.

Another kind of error is the opposite of that above. The Committee sometimes will spend too much money on a project—give it more priority than it should have. I remember a project which was proposed to CRL by the mining equipment division. It was budgeted at $80,000 instead of $60,000, which was all that was necessary. I believe that the mining people wanted more research than was necessary, to be on the safe side. You see, they are spending my CRL research budget, and not their own money.

When it comes to long-range (pure) research, I have had a number of projects that certainly would be good for our company's growth, which have been rejected by the Executive Committee. Sometimes it is the division managers who reject the idea, and sometimes the top management managers. Again, I believe that it is unwise (and even dangerous) for such projects to be turned down. The division managers quite naturally have their own businesses to run, and cannot give the time or the expert knowledge required. We have a recent example. We at CRL see a need for increased research in surface and friction physics, and in thermodynamics. I had proposed the addition of two scientists in the first category and seven in the latter. At the Executive Committee meeting this year, six members opposed this addition.

I think that the members of the Executive Committee view CRL as an expensive overhead-cost department, always asking for money but never being able to prove what we are worth. That is what I conclude after going through years of the budget process, with our proposals scrutinized at length. Sometimes I believe that there should be more authority granted to the research vice-president for saying what research will be done. The research in thermodynamics would certainly be carried out.

Research Problems as Seen by the President

Mr. Schulz states that he sees two kinds of problems in management of Research in GMC:

First, I am concerned because we have allocated $7,000,000 for research this year, yet we will spend only $6,500,000. The Board of Directors established a policy that the company should spend 5 percent of sales over the years on research and development if we are to keep ahead of competitors. At current sales, this is $28,000,000. The Board further decided that this should be split between Central Research Laboratories (one-quarter of the total, or 1.25 percent) and the divisions (three-quarters of the total, or 3.75 percent). At current sales, CRL gets $7,000,000 for research on ideas up through the pilot-plant stage and the divisions get $21,000,000 for engineering the successful research projects into actual mass production. It is the budget of the CRL I am worried about. We know we should be spending $7,000,000 for the good of the company. The division managers and Dr. Hoffmann are continuously proposing projects that they think are vital, and which total more than $7,000,000. Why is it, then, that we end up by spending less than both the Board and the divisions judge is best?

CRL employs 550 people, one-fourth (140) of whom are scientists and engineers. CRL is performing an absolutely vital function. We learned long ago that research pays off. We are the lowest-cost manufacturer of certain types of machinery in the world—lower than Caterpillar in the United States, Fiat in Italy, and Volvo in Sweden.

CRL was put there as a central staff department to do this work because we cannot afford to have each division carry out its own research. The work we do in physics, for example, applies to many divisions at once. I expect Dr. Hoffmann and his assistants to be primarily responsible for looking into all of our divisions to get ideas for improvement, and to convince division managers of the need for a specific project.

I have been doing some investigating of the unspent budget gap, trying to find why we can't get projects approved up to our target of $7,000,000. This investigation shows that the Executive Committee approved only eight out of every ten projects submitted to it in the last five years. Dr. Hoffmann tells me that during the same time an average of fifteen projects a year are seriously proposed by CRL, but that they never get to the formal meeting of the Executive Committee because one or more division managers react against them. Budgets for the last five years have been lower than the target (1.25 percent of sales) by from $400,000 to $700,000. The projects proposed over that period, by size, were:

Size of Project	Portion of Total Projects
Less than $25,000	20%
$25,000–$50,000	30
$50,000–$100,000	20
Over $100,000	30

Here are our official procedures. All proposals are drawn up by CRL. About 80 percent of projects are actually "seen" or initiated by CRL, while 20 percent are first mentioned by division people. Dr. Hoffmann and his engineers visit with division managers throughout the year and as the embryo ideas become projects that look to Hoffmann as serious prospects for next year's budget proposal, he contacts the division manager whose products are most likely to benefit from the project to see if he wants the project. The division manager may either want the project badly, be neutral on it, or oppose it. The final decision, though belongs to Hoffman. He and his engineers are the guardians of the state of our products and production processes. Nobody else will have either the interest or expertise to keep us up-to-date. Minutes of the Executive Committee show that 90 percent of the operating research projects have been *sponsored by both Dr. Hoffmann and the division manager in question, but that 10 percent have been proposed by Hoffmann and supported only mildly by others.*

As for pure research projects, Dr. Hoffmann proposes all of these, since they are not applicable to any one division. Those are his, and I must say that neither myself nor other members of the Committee know what he is talking about sometimes.

On October 1 each year, the Executive Committee convenes for the research budget. Members include the four group vice-presidents who represent the divisions under them, Mr. Seabert, financial vice-president, Dr. Hoffmann, and myself. We look at each research project individually to judge whether the project meets the needs of the whole corporation. It must be done this way. No one man can be expert on all the factors necessary. The group vice-presidents cannot simply take their division budgets and add them up—we know from experience that they would always exceed $7,000,000, so somebody somewhere has to establish priorities, to stay within our committed amount. Who is to do this? I cannot do this alone, because I do not know enough about research or about the divisions —I'd have to be a specialist in automobile engines as well as the television business! Dr. Hoffmann has the official responsibility of recommending priorities, but he is a scientist and is not responsible for selling to hospitals or running the production lines for television tubes. Balanced Committee judgment is necessary.

What happens is that the Committee never allocates the full amount for research. I detect the feeling on the part of all of us that we don't think we've done a logical job. The divisions, as well as the CRL people, seem to resent budget sessions and feel a bit badly toward the meetings when they're finished.

The Die Casting Project

One project that generated considerable controversy in the Executive Committee was a project to improve the quality of metal castings made in the diesel engine division. According to the proposal, CRL believed it feasible to develop two new machines to be used in casting, and a new chemical process for certain metals in the casting process.

"I cannot see why they would turn it down," says Julian Hughes, manager of the diesel engine division. "It is absolutely necessary if we are to keep the lead among competitors. The project would only cost $140,000. Also, we worked so hard on this proposal—I'm not inclined to do that again. Finally, we are the leader now, but I know some division managers in competitive companies who are getting a great deal of research support. I was approached informally by one of these companies regarding a job last year, but of course I think GMC is my career. That is why I am concerned that we stay on top."

Herbert Meyer, group vice-president for electronics, commented,

"My position in the Executive Committee was against the Die Casting Project. I have respect for Hughes, Dr. Hoffmann, and Victor Smith (group vice-president for transportation). But we have a large backlog of research projects in the company, many of them in electronics. I know that engine research is a necessary thing, too, and would have voted for the proposal, except that this particular one just did not sound as important as some of the rest."

Peter Rizzuto, head of the division of CRL that did the work on the proposal, says, "I think that failure of this project has set our company back in metal processing technology two years. The project might have been done, in my judgment, for $25,000 less, but Mr. Hughes felt that we needed more certainty in the outcome, and specified a series of experimental checks that I did not think necessary."

The casewriter asked Michael Seabert, financial vice-president, what he thought about the project. He replied:

> First, let me say that GMC is in excellent financial condition. We are growing fast, we have sufficient cash flow to spend $10,000,000 instead of $7,000,000 if we want to, and the banks will lend us more. When the Die Casting Project came up, I listened to the various arguments. We did not need a vote, because it was opposed by three group vice-presidents plus myself. It just seemed to me that the engine group were not too certain of their own argument. I am not blaming them—they must think of their group first, and try to make it the best. Other projects on the agenda seemed much more pressing to me.
>
> And then there was the $140,000 proposed by Dr. Hoffmann to add two scientists in surface physics, and seven in thermodynamics. I supported him in a halfhearted way, but simply did not know enough to express my opinion clearly one way or the other.

Suggestion by Dr. Hoffmann

> I have proposed that Mr. Schulz and the Board should redraw the organization chart, creating a research division from the old CRL. It would no longer be a corporate headquarters staff, but like the other operating divisions, a semiautonomous business in itself. Operating-division managers would be allowed to spend up to $100,000 for research on any one project. As long as their own division profits are to be charged for research, the total expenditure might be considerably in excess of 1.25 percent of sales. The total would vary from year to year depending on how much division managers would each want, knowing full well that (1) they must keep up with the times through research, and yet (2) that it is their budget they are spending, not CRL's.
>
> I would charge them the direct cost of the project—manpower, laboratory materials, and experimental space. I would add 15 per-

cent for overhead costs (our actual ratio of direct costs to general laboratory offices and management), and another 5 percent for "profit." This "price" I charge to divisions would be lower than outside research businesses such as Battelle Institute in Geneva or The Rand Corporation in the United States.

When the demand for research services is great, I would expand my manpower and facilities. When it is less, I would contract. The 5 percent "profit" would be retained by the research division to cover minor periods when business does not support all of our personnel.

Decisions on individual projects would be made by division managers, and the Executive Committee would rule only on projects over $100,000.

As at present, scientists from the research division would suggest projects to our customer divisions, or they can suggest them to us. Whenever the division and I agree on projects less than $100,000, that is final.

For long-range pure research, the procedure would be the same, except that top management, as the customer, would decide what projects they want. There would be a very small percentage of sales, amounting to perhaps $200,000, allocated to the research division

Exhibit 1 *Organization Chart,*
General Machinery Corporation

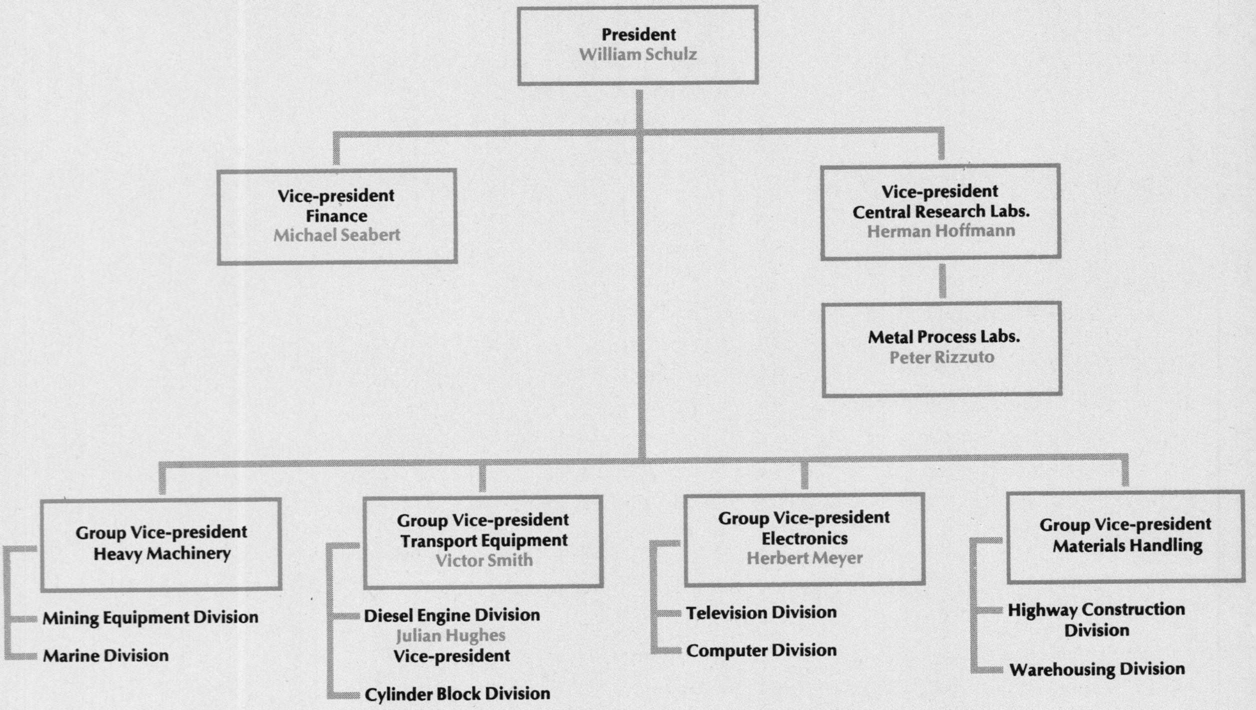

as I see fit. This money would be allocated to scientists to spend at least a portion of their time on any project that interests them in their field—very much as scientists operate in universities.

as I see fit. This money would be allocated to scientists to spend at least a portion of their time on any project that interests them in their field—very much as scientists operate in universities.

Reaction of the President

Mr. Schulz states that he received Dr. Hoffmann's proposal in general form a month ago. Since then, he has been giving it some consideration, and has obtained the thoughts of the financial vice-president. "Frankly, I am having difficulty with it. I am wondering if such a system would work as well as the one we have now."

FOR DISCUSSION AND REPORT-WRITING

Organizing: Structural Design

1) The Central Research Laboratories were set up as an auxiliary unit to the twelve operating divisions of the company. What factors favor separating this unit from the operating departments? What disadvantages might accrue if the laboratory function were placed in the divisions? Use case facts to illustrate your answer.

2) Using the guides to "how much decentralization" from the text, make some judgment as to whether operating division heads in GMC should have authority to authorize research project expenditures, or whether these decisions should be made by others (headquarters managers, or committees). Use case facts to illustrate your argument.

3) In what ways does CRL differ from a conventional staff group? What causes these differences?

4) In what ways might the matrix approach to management discussed in Chapter 6 prove applicable to dealing with the problems of selecting and monitoring research projects?

5) *Summary Report Question, Part One:* Considering the difficulties GMC is having in getting decisions made on research projects, what changes in organization structure would you recommend to Mr. Schulz? Show how these changes might, by means of shifts in, or clarification of, duties, authority, and accountability, lead to a structure more likely to tackle this question in a more effective way. Be certain to note the effect of your recommendations on other aspects of GMC's operation.

Human Factors in Organizing

6) What basic motivations are the following men expressing? Particularly, what motivation do they all have in common:

Hoffmann: *In the case of operating projects, I many times know which have priority and how much should be spent.*
Schulz: *GMC is successful because it has pursued low prices, economies of mass production, and higher quality.*
Rizzuto: *I think that failure of the Die Casting Project has set this company back two years.*
Hughes: *The Die Casting Project is absolutely necessary.*
Meyer: *This project just did not sound as important.*

7) What benefits in the morale of Dr. Hoffmann, as well as of the division managers, would result from Hoffmann's proposal at the end of the case?

Planning: Elements of Decision-Making

8) How might incremental analysis and discounting of future revenues from projects (that is, operating projects, not pure research projects) facilitate the choice between alternative projects?

9) What statistical techniques would help Mr. Seabert and others reduce the uncertainty in their own minds about which projects to undertake? For example, Seabert says that when the Die Casting Project was turned down, "the engine group were not as certain in their argument as they might be."

Planning: Decision-Making in an Enterprise

10) Look at the GMC objectives stated by Mr. Schulz at the beginning of the case. Why are these objectives of key importance in the future success of the company? Think up examples to illustrate your reasons.

11) Show how the goals Schulz states for the scientific research function are related to the hierarchy of goals of GMC and to its master strategy.

12) Illustrate how GMC is experiencing three difficulties (uncertainty absorption, bias, special pressure) often found when an organization must consolidate projections from many different people.

13) What can Mr. Schulz do to overcome the problems mentioned in question 12. Include some reference to the confidence structure as contrasted with the hierarchical positions such as director of CRL, group vice-president for transportation, and so on.

Leading

14) If you were president of GMC, what would you conclude has caused Dr. Hoffmann and his scientists to feel that "their efforts have come to nothing and their judgment is being ignored"? What kind of leadership actions might eliminate these causes and help to develop cooperation?

Measuring and Controlling

15) Let us assume that the company has arrived at a certain return on investment (profit on investment) as a standard for judging all proposed operating (not pure) research projects—18 percent. Would this standard be useful (1) in overcoming the underinvestment problem in the company, and (2) in overcoming the human obstacles in the control system?

16) In the case of pure research, no estimates are available for the revenues that might accrue to the company if a given project is undertaken. Therefore, no standard return on investment can be figured to quantify the value of these projects. What techniques might be used to overcome this obstacle, yet set some kind of useful standard for these projects? (Hint: One technique for dealing with uncertainty from Chapter 14, and one method for devising a control when no direct results are measurable from Chapter 24.)

17) In the case of hiring of two friction physicists, and seven scientists in thermodynamics, no direct estimates of the "payoff," or quantitative control, seem possible. What kind of "symptom" control standards might be devised to control the activities of CRL in these two fields?

18) Toward the beginning of the case, Mr. Schulz states that operating divisions are viewed as being relatively autonomous. Division managers have the initiative to make GMC the best in their product lines. The electronic equipment manager must decide what products to bring out, what kinds of selling talents to use, and so on. Utilizing the concepts of integrating controls with organization structure, how might you help Schulz clear his own mind about how his present control process relates to his model of organization structure?

Summary Question for Solution of the Case as a Whole

19) Write a report for the Board of Directors of GMC that analyzes the various managerial problems faced by the company. Begin with one part that sets down the background situation, then use side headings to state major problems. For each of these, analyze the causes of the problem. Finally, include a section that makes recommendations for future courses of action.

PART TWO

Human Factors in Organizing

Organizing the *work*—both operating and managerial—that is necessary to achieve company objectives was the center of our attention in Part One. Although we often talked about the people who do the work, the focus of our attention was on the problem of how organization could be used to further the *goals* of an enterprise.

In such a "work-focused" study of organization, we made implicit assumptions about the way people would behave in their jobs. We assumed that members of an organization would do what they were told, that higher levels of management could assign goals, that for efficiency management could shift work from one job to another, and that in many other ways managers and operators would adapt their behavior to the needs of an enterprise. The use of simplifying assumptions is a fruitful device, in science and applied arts. It enables us to concentrate our minds on particular aspects of a complex problem. But before we apply a conclusion based on simplifying assumptions to real-life situations, we need to check those assumptions. Often we find that they are only partly valid. If so, then we must take additional factors into account and adjust our conclusion to fit a fuller array of facts.

In Part Two, we shall follow this procedure. We shall examine assumptions about human behavior in light of current concepts in psychology, sociology, and anthropology. Because these sciences, as applied to business management, are "worker-focused," they can provide important insights and qualifications to the ideas set forth in Part One. Our discussion is divided among the following chapters.

Chapter 7—Organization as Social Behavior. Here we consider the pressures of culture and informal groups that may strongly influence what workers do in their jobs.

Chapter 8—Human Needs and Organization Design. This chapter deals both with individual motivation and with adjustment of company organization to help fulfill human needs.

Chapter 9–Conflict in Organizations. Some conflict in organizations, like friction in machines, is unavoidable. In this chapter we explore sources of such clashes of interest, the distinctions between destructive and constructive conflict, and how we can organize to deal with conflict.

Chapter 10—Matching Jobs and Individuals. After pointing out variation in the abilities of specific individuals, we shall consider how far an organization structure should be changed to suit personal strengths and weaknesses.

Many of the ideas about human behavior that we present in this part will be used again later in this book, especially when we examine leadership. We present them this early in our discussion because human considerations are fully as important in designing the structure of work as they are in man-to-man relationships between manager and subordinate. In Part Two, then, we center our attention on the impact of human factors on the process of organizing; we shall be concerned with merging the work-focused and the worker-focused viewpoints.

Chapter Seven

Organization as Social Behavior

THE BEHAVIORAL VIEWPOINT

People are the chief resource of a manager; they are the primary raw material with which he works. Consequently, it is important for him to understand why people behave as they do. Also he should be able to anticipate how they are likely to respond to various organizational designs.

Formal organization that assigns duties and specifies relationships provides only one set of motivations to which people respond. An organization structure that carries "official" approval is a strong influence, but there are many other pressures, and a wise manager will try to design his organization so that these other influences support, rather than detract from, desired results.

One important set of influences arises from a simple and obvious characteristic of human behavior: Men live and work together. Their relationships soon result in patterns of behavior and belief, which social scientists call "cultures." Within the broader national culture, every enterprise develops its own "subculture," that is, the beliefs and patterns of conduct that are associated with living and working together in that company. Two aspects of a business subculture of particular concern to a manager are the following:

1) The customs, habits, and ways of working together that develop *informally* in an expanding enterprise. These customs, which grow up around normal company activities, elaborate and extend, or perhaps modify, formal organization.

2) The informal *social groups* among employees that strongly influence their attitudes, beliefs, and behavior. These informal groups often (though not necessarily) center on personal interests and noncompany objectives.

Research on human relations in established organizations clearly demonstrates that informal social relationships have a direct bearing on effectiveness and efficiency. Formal organization is essential, but we cannot possibly *prescribe* many of the spontaneous relationships that are sure to arise. Prescribed or not, these social patterns influence how people respond to managerial action.

Striking examples of the effect of cultural attitudes and customs arise in international business. American executives have often tried to transplant to a foreign country a formal organization that worked well in the United States. They have attempted, for example, to export the concept of a budget director whose duties are the same as those of the United States model, but the results have often been confusion or sabotage—and an added bit of resentment of Yankee enterprise. Unfamiliarity with the concept of staff guidance, reluctance to mix people from different social strata in informal work groups, reverence for red tape, skepticism of numerical evaluation schemes, and similar reactions have prevented beautifully designed organizations from operating as they were intended.

Similar obstacles may crop up in any domestic company, though probably to a less exaggerated degree. Examples are all around us: a president can start all sorts of rumors by walking hurriedly through the accounting offices in his shirt-sleeves; hotels have begun to use blacks as supervisors only in recent years; a young college graduate is given a rough time in a machine shop because "he doesn't belong here."

Although social traditions and informal relationships can be annoying to an executive, they are also essential for getting a day's work accomplished smoothly. Like fire, the force is destructive when improperly handled; but once a man understands a force and how to work with it, he can employ it for constructive purposes. A manager cannot manipulate social behavior any way he pleases, but he can attempt to design work structures in such a way that social pressures and formal organization tend to support each other.

In the present chapter, then, we shall seek answers to the following questions: How do customs and traditional roles develop in a business enterprise? Can management change worker attitudes on such matters? How do informal social groups affect the behavior of workers? What can we do to encourage group pressure to support company objectives? Are cliques harmful or helpful, and how should a manager deal with them if they arise in the organization?

CUSTOMS AND ROLES

How Customs Develop

Only a small fraction of our behavior is deliberately chosen. During any day, we take part in many activities, and it would be impossible to analyze each separate movement or remark before we act. Because purely intuitive or emotional responses are likely to get us into trouble and deliberate choices are not feasible, we rely heavily on custom and habit to direct our behavior.

Reliance on customary behavior applies to our business activities, as well as to our private lives. When a man buys a car, the dealer has a customary way of recording the sale, arranging for financing, and preparing the car for delivery. Similarly, when a company hires a new employee, it follows customary practices in arranging a medical examination, entering the man's name on the payroll, and introducing him to his new assignment and to his fellow workers. Often a situation will have unique features that call for thought—for instance, the new employee may have a physical handicap—but it is possible to give attention to these unique features because in handling the situation so much can be based on customary ways of doing business.

Once established, a customary way of doing business looks "natural." But many urban renewal projects, for example, have floundered and sometimes failed because social mechanisms for doing unusual tasks were lacking. Often a deep-seated suspicion of procedures used in the white man's establishment has contributed to the problem. It takes time to learn how to work together.

Customs become established, or "learned," principally through personal experience. Some guidance may be provided by company planning—an organization structure assigns duties to various positions, and a company manual formally states policies and procedures. Nevertheless, only when people actually work can a custom become established. Moreover, formal plans almost never cover all aspects of a job. Any employee—be he president or janitor—acts on a problem in a way he hopes will be satisfactory. If the results are poor, he will probably try some other solution the next time he meets a similar problem. Once he finds an acceptable solution, he will probably repeat it each time a similar problem arises. As the same solution is applied over and over again, customary behavior begins to emerge.

Our emphasis on behavior based on experience should be a warning to anyone who thinks of managing purely through formal organization and written plans. Before formal instructions become customary behavior, they have to be accepted in actual use. What an employee considers to be "acceptable" is determined by a variety of factors, such as favorable reaction of other employees, approval by his immediate supervisor, contribution to company goals, and personal satisfaction from doing the work.

If an immediate supervisor does not insist that workers follow official plans, then other considerations are likely to determine the particular work pattern that becomes customary. For example, if employees can disregard a "no smoking" rule without serious consequences, they are liable to adopt smoking on the job as customary conduct. Similarly, if a branch manager finds that he can hire new employees without following instructions in the personnel manual about consulting with the personnel director at headquarters, the formal plan for hiring loses its significance. On the other hand, if a branch manager consistently consults with his vice-president in charge of sales before changing sales territories even though formal organization does not require it, the practice becomes embedded in the company structure as customary behavior. Formal plans can have their full impact only when they become an integral part of custom.

Work customs are especially important when several different people work together. Each person learns to rely on the others to perform their respective parts of the total task in a customary manner. A hospital dietician, for instance, may assume that her order desk will place rush orders on the top of each batch of meal requests she sends to the kitchen; if the clerk overlooks this little custom, a rush order may not get the attention it deserves. To cite an illustration from a Midwestern hardware firm, the production manager normally consulted with the sales manager before authorizing unusually long runs of a product. Once, when the sales manager was away on a trip, the production manager had to decide whether to schedule a long run of chain hoists, so he overlooked the usual crosscheck. Actually, it turned out that the sales manager planned to curtail selling efforts on this model, and only by accident was the prospect of an unusually slow-moving inventory discovered two weeks later and the order cancelled before actual production commenced. These examples show how one person may depend on the customary behavior of another—much as players on a good doubles team in tennis depend on each other to cover different parts of the court. When each person learns what to expect of others with whom his work interlocks, coordinated effort is greatly simplified. And conversely, deviations from usual behavior call for special warnings to other people if we are to avoid confusion that might damage efficiency.

Expected Roles

As we have seen, some customs spring from habitual actions of a particular individual. But, in addition, jobs per se often acquire traditional roles. People have preconceived ideas of how a man appointed as, say,

Fig. 7–1 When a person assumes any given role, his duties and authority, and sometimes even his gestures and clothing, are well defined.

credit manager, foreman, or baseball umpire, should behave. In other words, each established role strongly influences the behavior that is expected of anyone in a given position. Established roles are common throughout society. We expect brides to assume the duties of a housewife, ministers to epitomize virtue, ship captains to be stern disciplinarians, and football coaches to be hard-driving authoritarians whose consuming interest in life is winning games. In each case, the person who fills the established role is expected to have the characteristics of a person in that role.

In business, and especially within a single enterprise, the role for any given position may be firmly established. For instance, what a cost accountant should—and should not—undertake and what his attitude toward traditional accounting should be may be clearly defined in the minds of all people who work with him. The existence of such definite roles gives a stability to relationships in business; at least we predict from them how a man will fill a given position.

We run into difficulty, however, when complete agreement is lacking on all features of a role. Top executives may be inclined to think of a job in terms of a formal organization plan that is embellished with details that contribute to company objectives. An incumbent himself may have a somewhat different point of view based on his own preferences and experiences. His subordinates may attach importance to still other features of the job, and his associates may be concerned with how his position interrelates with their work. One of the best-known examples of such variation in conception of a role is the job of foreman. Top management thinks a foreman is dedicated to getting quality production on schedule at low cost. His subordinates, on the other hand, expect him to be friendly, fair, and helpful, to represent them in dealings with higher management, and to be sympathetic to actual work difficulties. If a foreman himself tries to live up to both sets of expectations, he becomes the proverbial man-in-the-middle. If he accepts either the labor view or the managerial view, he will be subjected to pressure from the other group.

Ideally, the job description that stems from formal organization *and* the other sets of expectations should merge into a single, consistent concept of a job. But, as amplified in Chapter 10, we can accomplish this only if (1) the job description is realistic in terms of both the technological and human resources available, (2) there is full communication and agreement by everyone concerned on what a person in the job is expected to do, and (3) the man actually on the job performs as anticipated. It is when these three conditions are fulfilled that a formal organization becomes a vibrant reality.

An additional reason why managers need to pay attention to socially accepted roles is summed up in the sociologists' concept of "legitimacy." Every complex organization is laced with a maze of contacts between different positions—requests for information, suggestions and counter-suggestions, and inspection of results. Employees regard some of these contacts as entirely legitimate whereas they deeply resent others. Their response to a suggestion or to a request is determined largely by whether it is an accepted, legitimate part of a role. If everyone expects a man occupying a particular position to become involved in the work of other people, then everyone thinks his action is legitimate. On the other hand, if he steps outside the bounds of customary behavior, he is thought to be "poking his nose into other people's affairs," and the result is sure to be friction.

Managerial Change of Customs and Roles

Customary behavior and roles are essential in any complex organization, be it a judicial system, research laboratory, or airport. They provide stable and predictable social relations. But they can also lead to stagnation, to perpetuation of behaviors that an enterprise can no longer tolerate. For this reason, management often desires to change customary practices and prevailing ideas about roles. What does the preceding analysis suggest about this process of change?

First, and probably most important, a manager must recognize that he cannot bring about change in customs and roles by decree alone. Social customs become the normal way of acting, even become, perhaps, deep-seated habits. A person's role is a set of ideas based on experience and personal desires, often reinforced by similar sentiments of his associates. Habits and beliefs cannot be changed simply by a manager's wishing they were different.

But management can take steps that encourage learning new skills and modifying attitudes. Usually the best place to start is with the persons whose actions we wish to modify, hoping that the attitudes and expectations of persons in related positions can be readjusted once key people take on a new pattern of behavior. Among the more important steps management can take to promote a change in habitual behavior are these: (1) communicate fully what change it desires and the reasons behind the change; (2) relieve anxieties regarding future status, job, and usefulness; (3) try to promote in the person whose behavior needs modification a desire to learn; (4) provide opportunities to practice and demonstrate new behavior with real, current problems; (5) reward those who adopt new behavior in place of old; and (6) if possible, devise a measurement and feedback mechanism that tells a person how well he is adjusting to the new concept.

Where customs and roles are strongly supported by group pressures, a manager may have to supplement, or even precede, the *individual* learning process outlined briefly in the preceding paragraph by modifying *group* attitudes.

INFORMAL GROUPS

Social Groups within Organizations

Small social groups significantly affect the way a formal organization actually works. Informal groups of from three to four to perhaps a dozen members spring up naturally whenever people work together. They are common among college students and in large government offices as well as in business firms. Members of such groups see each other frequently on the job, at lunch, or riding home from work. They discover common interests and exchange ideas. A group thus forms spontaneously. If one or two members tend to be leaders, their position arises naturally out of the situation rather than from formal selection.

Most people get many of their day-to-day human satisfactions from such groups. Among the "rewards" for belonging to such a group are sociability, a sense of belonging (which contributes to feelings of inner security and personal worth), a sympathetic ear for troubles, aid on the job (both information and occasional direct assistance), and some protection through a united stand against unreasonable pressure from a boss or outside force. In time, these satisfactions can develop considerable group cohesiveness.

Small-group rewards are especially prized in large organizations where, too often, the work itself provides few satisfactions. If we have fragmented the work and failed to make remote objectives significant to an employee, then the social satisfactions derived from subgroups become a major force in behavior on the job.

A small informal group—whether composed of lathe operators, members of a vice-president's staff, or senior executives in an electrical engineering department—falls into routines for its activities. Members sit together in the lunchroom; Joe stops to chat with Steve before going home in the evening. When the members work near to one another, interchange may take place from time to time throughout the day. Sometimes a pattern of contact is extended to include off-the-job activities, such as bowling, golf, bridge, or union meetings. In addition, a group tends to evolve a pattern of attitudes, at least toward the subjects of common interest. Members frequently discuss their feelings toward their boss, company, rates of output, "young squirts from college," or the accounting office; moreover they all often hold similar views on such subjects.

Each person normally belongs to several small informal groups. One may be founded on physical proximity at work, another on a common interest in baseball, and a third on an interest in a professional society, for example, the Society for Advancement of Management. A political protest group draws together quite a diverse collection of people. Some of these groups may be fairly inactive, and people may drift in and out of them. But those based on daily work relationships are likely to be the strongest and most enduring.

Effect of Social Groups on Worker Behavior

It is typical of social groups to put pressure on members *to conform to group standards* and group routines. This push to conformity is, of course, common throughout life. A schoolboy gets teased by his classmates if his clothing is too fancy. Young couples who move to suburbia match their neighbors by selling the motorcycle and buying a sportscar. Even the nonconformist in college expresses his defiance in ways endorsed by his fellow nonconformists—for instance, new polished shoes

Fig. 7–2 A group may pressure deviants to conform to group standards in ways that are mild or severe. A schoolboy may merely be teased because of his nonconformist clothing, whereas a high performer who upsets group production rates may find that his tires have been slashed in the company parking lot.

must *not* be worn even if the owner has to go to a lot of trouble to get them dirty and scuffed-up. Of course, the particular matters on which to conform vary from group to group.

Restricting output to an accepted group standard is a common practice among production operators. If a group has established a normal output per day, perhaps based on the maximum "the company will let you earn," management will find incentive bonuses of little avail in stimulating higher production. The man who steps beyond the accepted norm will be subjected to severe social censure. On the other hand, if a group endorses high output—which is likely to be true among salesmen—the low performer may find himself an outcast.

The pressure of a group on its members can be substantial, for, as we noted earlier, an individual gets many of his satisfactions in his job through group responses. If he deviates too far from group standards, other members may no longer want to associate with him and may treat him as though he were at least an oddball, if not a traitor. Such treatment is unpleasant even for those people who can move into other social groups. Moreover, a person feels immediately the rewards or punishments of his group, whereas benefits provided by a company for following its plan are usually more remote.

Managers should realize that, in addition to such standards of conduct, groups also *provide many beliefs and values* to the individual. Joe Jones may believe that the personnel director is a "good guy" and that the advertising director is a "screwball," not from any personal observation or conviction, but merely because these are the sentiments passed on to him by his group. He may believe that all senior executives draw fabulous salaries, that only a Stanford man can get ahead in the firm, that his company has the best engineering department in the industry, and many other articles of faith, because they are strongly held by his social group. A group can also influence feelings about such matters as pilfering, accuracy in keeping reports, importance of efficient control of quality, or service to customers.

Even when an individual has direct evidence contrary to group sentiment, he may accept group judgment. In a series of experiments with groups of college students, all persons except one in each group were instructed to give incorrect answers to a simple question about which of several lines was longest. As different sets of lines were flashed on a screen, the exception in each group found his judgment consistently at odds with that of half a dozen other people in the same room; eventually, he began to distrust his own perception and started giving the group answer. At work, when facts are less clear-cut, and group pressure is even greater, the temptation to accept the opinion of a group is strong. Fortunately there continues to be a good sprinkling of rugged individualists who maintain their independence of judgment. Even these people, however, are likely simply to remain silent rather than challenge some cherished bit of lore.

Behavioral research has found one further characteristic of group behavior that is of direct interest to management. A group will probably *resist* any *change* that upsets its normal activities, especially if the change is initiated by an outsider. A new method, a change in office layout, or a reassignment of duties modifies established patterns of social relationships. Social groups may be broken up, and this disruption means loss of known satisfactions in exchange for an unknown future. Consciously or unconsciously, people resist such changes, even when offsetting advantages may accrue to individual members of a group, and new groups may replace old ones. Managers should thus anticipate resistance when they upset social patterns.

HARMONIZING SOCIAL GROUPS AND FORMAL ORGANIZATION

The behavior of small groups has an impact on many facets of management, as we shall note especially in later discussions on motivation, communication, and leadership. In the present chapter, we are particularly interested in the impact on formal organization structure. What can we do to harmonize social groups and formal organization?

Consider Adopting Group Practice

Many times people in a company think up new ways of doing things that are not only more satisfying to their group, but are also better for company efficiency. For example, job descriptions in a plumbing equipment company indicated that the sales department was simply to refer all complaints about product design to the engineering manager, so that the engineering manager or his representative could talk with customers about their specific difficulties. The sales manager, however, had trouble getting minor changes made that he felt were necessary for overcoming the complaints of big customers. So the sales manager developed a habit of obtaining from these customers full information on what they wanted. Then after an engineer had been assigned to investigate the complaint, the sales manager talked at length with the engineer about what changes could be made. Actually, the engineers found that their job was simplified, and in time they began to rely heavily on the sales manager for customer data. Sometimes salesmen would provide information directly to the engineers, and on troublesome cases a meeting of salesmen, sales manager, engineer, and engineering manager would be held.

As new complaints arose, men from the sales department frequently contacted the engineers and pushed hard for changes they wanted made. At this stage, the vice-president in charge of research and engineering protested to the president. He said the sales people were taking up too much engineers' time, interrupting the engineering work schedule, and "high-pressuring" his men to make too many changes. "They are violating the organization structure," he said, "and ought to be stopped."

After thorough investigation, the president decided that product development of the company was being significantly improved by the role the sales people had assumed in modifying products. So the president had the job descriptions rewritten to provide a new duty for the sales manager —that of visiting customers who complained of product design and then holding conferences with the engineering manager. The president worked closely with both men to be sure the new statement of duties was feasible and acceptable. *Now*, even the vice-president in charge of research and engineering says that the new organization is best for the company.

Such cases indicate that our first step in dealing with informal group actions that do not "fit" the formal structure should be at least to entertain the hypothesis that the group standards and behavior are good. We need not accept the group behavior, of course. After investigation, we may decide that the informal action must be changed to meet company requirements. But we should always be alert to the possibility that behavior that develops informally serves the company well and should be incorporated into the formal structure.

Form Integrated Task-teams

A second possibility of harmonizing small-group practice with formal organization lies in the design itself. Formal organization—that is, how workers are grouped together and what the specified relationships are— provides the setting for many informal groups. Can we design a formal organization structure so as to encourage social groups that are inclined to support, rather than conflict with, the aims of an enterprise? James C. Worthy, drawing on his organizational studies of Sears, Roebuck and Company, believes the answer is "Yes." He states:

> *Organization can be set up in such a way as to foster the patterning of personal relations around the task of getting the work done or around the goal of resisting supervisory pressure.... It is a reasonable speculation that where the formal organization is built around technical processes or abstract functions, as in the functional form of organization, informal groups will tend to be oriented in opposition to management, but that this is much less likely to be the case where the formal structure is so arranged as to bring together in close physical proximity and intimate organizational unity all of the*

operations or processes needed to produce a meaningful end product.[1]

Three guides for organization design help foster informal groups sympathetic to company goals:

1) Assign work in terms of "meaningful end-products." First, we should identify blocks of work that have a natural unity, whose end result we can clearly visualize. Such a block may be all activities that pertain to securing a customer's order, or to making a particular product or part. Second, we should place authority for doing such a clear-cut, complete block of work squarely on a small group of men. These men will constitute a team, and it is up to them to carry the ball. One man may be captain, but the assignment belongs to the entire *task-team*.

This proposal is in sharp contrast with the practice, encouraged by scientific management, of dividing work into highly specialized pieces and, when volume permits, of creating a specialized department to perform each narrow task. Under this latter system, detailed, centralized planning is encouraged, and supervisors are primarily concerned with seeing that operators do not deviate from the program. Such a work structure promotes informal groups that are uninterested in company goals.

In contrast, by assigning meaningful jobs to a task-team, we hope that a social group will form that is interested in achieving end results. In fact, there is considerable evidence to indicate that indifference to company goals and restrictions on output will be less under the task-team organization than under a highly functionalized organization.

These behavioral science conclusions relate directly to the forming of work groups (see Chapter 2).

2) Place people with all skills necessary to complete the assigned task as close as possible to the point of action. The best arrangement is to have people with the necessary skills within the task-team itself. Thus a self-contained sales team might include a salesman, a serviceman, a deliveryman, and a secretary-clerk in the office. Each person would understand how the total unit functions and could easily make direct personal contact with any other member of the unit.

Unfortunately, for many tasks such an integrated unit is uneconomical. The need in a single task-team for a particular skill may be insufficient in volume or may occur at such irregular intervals that the inclusion of a qualified full-time worker on the team is unwarranted. An alternative arrangement, then, is to assign a staff man or serviceman to work with *several* operating units and to locate him in close proximity to

---

[1] *Big Business and Free Men* (New York: Harper & Row, 1959), pp. 81, 85. A similar idea has been used by the management consultant B. J. Muller-Thym in a variety of business situations. Many of the ideas in the following paragraphs are based on his unpublished work.

all units. By locating him where he can have frequent face-to-face contacts with people on the various task-teams, we encourage his becoming a member—albeit a part-time one—of their respective social groups.[2]

Still another arrangement is to form a task-team for a specific project. We note here that the behavioral concept of a task-team reinforces the idea of project management explained in the preceding chapter.

In each of these arrangements, men with specialized skills are placed close to the scene of action, where they can form informal groups associated with the end result rather than with their particular specialties.

3) Supply each task-team with full facts on its work. An operating unit, such as we have been describing, should be self-regulating. Of course, being close to its work, a team will readily and immediately have available much control information. For example, if one part of the work falls behind—or gets ahead of—related activities, all members of the team will know it promptly and can adjust their efforts accordingly; or if, say, a customer changes the specifications on his order, the whole team can quickly readjust to the new requirements. In other words, each member of the team, because he has personal contact with what is happening, knows whether all phases of the operation are proceeding as planned. Armed with such information, the team itself regulates its efforts to achieve desired results.

If control information, not obvious to the team members, becomes available elsewhere, this too should be fed back quickly to the operating unit. Data on laboratory tests or costs of materials, for instance, may be first recorded at a point remote from actual operations; this information needs to be communicated immediately to the men who can take corrective action. Because the social group promptly receives data on its efficiency and progress and has full delegation to make changes, the group may become so engrossed with results that it will avoid sparring matches with supervisors. Furthermore, the abundance of available statistical data will allow the group to base its work-related beliefs on fact rather than fiction.

The preceding guides for organizing around task-teams come to us from research on small groups that usually do operating work. Practical application of these guides has been worked out for such tasks as running an open-hearth steel furnace, assembling typewriters, and handling customer orders in an office. Use of the basic ideas, however, need not be confined to operating work. We can also create task-teams to do managerial work. The best-known examples in the managerial area are from companies using profit decentralization. Here, as with task-teams doing

---

[2]The effect of proximity on the ease of joining social groups has long been recognized in the auditing field. But in this instance, to assure independence of an audit, management wishes to *prevent* close friendships, and so it deliberately moves auditors from place to place before loyalties to a social group can become strong.

operating work, tasks are assigned in blocks that have a natural unity, people with the needed skills are placed within the group, and the team is self-regulating to a high degree. Very little research has been done on social-group behavior among executives, and there is great opportunity to discover new ways of applying insights on group action to managerial work. The applicability of the task-team concept to both managerial and operating work illustrates the feasibility of adjusting organization design so as to capture benefits from typical group behavior.

INFLUENCE OF CLIQUES

Another kind of informal group is the clique. We often read of a military clique or of a "tight-money" clique in government. We shall use the term in somewhat the same sense here.

From the point of view of management, the clique differs from most informal groups in that its members are spread throughout several different departments. They may not even have daily, face-to-face contact in the normal course of their work. What unifies them is a common support for some *cause*. The cause may involve helping a popular executive get a promotion or advocating a particular policy (stress on military products or low investment in ghetto areas), social philosophy (planned parenthood or world government), or some other strongly held belief about what the company should or should not do. In government, the cause might be support for a powerful Israeli state. A common background, such as graduation from Podunk College or growing up in Texas, often facilitates the formation of a clique, but rarely is it the common cause that makes a clique significant for management. A clique may be loosely or tightly formed. At one extreme, it may be little more than a group of people with common sympathies on an issue, who occasionally see one another for

Fig. 7–3 Cliques can inter-fere with formal organiza-tion because they cut across departments, as this gen-eralized organization chart shows. Clique members are indicated by the colored boxes.

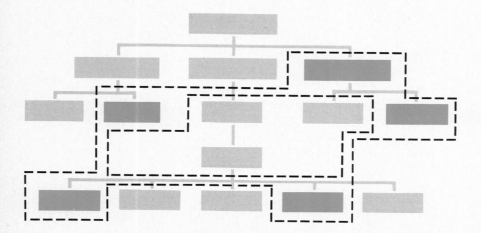

mutual encouragement; such a loose clique lacks a central plan or formal guidance. At the other extreme is a well-defined faction—almost like a Communist cell—that is characterized by clandestine meetings and a central plan of action.

In a business firm, a clique promotes its cause in many ways: by getting its members appointed to influential positions, by proselyting in various departments and in informal groups, by openly advocating its cause whenever it is relevant to the solution of a current problem, by being eager (or reluctant) to carry out plans that make the cause look good (or poor), and perhaps by rewarding the faithful.

A clique may be formed around a worthy cause—for example, improving personnel relations or aggressively pushing new products that will aid company growth. The objectives are not necessarily sinister. From a manager's viewpoint, however, cliques are undesirable if they disrupt programs directed toward company objectives. In fact, a strong clique can seriously interfere with integrated action. Trouble is especially likely to arise if there is a conflict in aims coupled with a high degree of decentralization, because lower-level executives may use their freedom to carry different parts of the company along incompatible courses: One division may seek government subsidy at the same time that a vice-president makes speeches blasting government intervention.

When a manager finds a vigorous clique in his organization, he should first find out what the clique stands for. The cause may be one the company should officially adopt, or at least it may reflect a condition to which the company should adjust in some manner. If, after objective study, the manager decides that the cause is incompatible with desirable aims of the company, he should use influence and power to break the clique up. On the other hand, if he decides the cause is worthy of company support, a manager should adjust company plans to be consistent with the aims of the clique, and then try to let the clique feel that its own aim can be achieved best through "legitimate" company plans and actions. In other words, he seeks to merge the sentiments that support the clique's goal with loyalty to the company program. When he achieves this merger, the clique ceases to be a strong divisive force.

Occasionally, a manager may encourage what is in effect a new clique in order to sponsor a desired change in goals or policies. If there is resistance, for example, to executive development or increasing the proportion of blacks in executive positions, persons sympathetic to the new program will be identified in all sections and divisions affected. These persons will promote and infiltrate the new plan in their respective units. Possibly a central staff office and other outposts will be added to the formal organization. This approach, it is hoped, will gain understanding and support for the new plan more effectively than authoritarian commands; as we noted earlier in this chapter, formal edicts do not necessarily change attitudes and beliefs.

CONCLUSION

When we look at an organization as a social unit rather than as a work-producing machine, three important conclusions emerge:

1) First, the social relationships in an organization are not based on crisp decisions that remain static once they are made, but on a series of continuing personal actions and reactions over a long period. Defining relationships in an organization manual may be useful, but even sharp definitions take on their full meaning only as people learn to work together.

In a business firm, as in a city government or a local P.T.A., we learn a great deal from organization charts, definition of duties, and other formal statements of how the enterprise is expected to work. Nevertheless, to get a full feel of an organization we also need to know which members have the most influence on accepted beliefs, what the prevailing attitude is toward the role of the various officers and executives, what small groups there are and what their influence is, and whether strong cliques are at work.

Moreover, social relationships evolve. For instance, circumstances and individual maturity will change the influence an accountant has over clerks in his section. Likewise, the composition of social groups shifts with time and with changes in personnel. With these shifting social relationships formal job descriptions tend to get out of date.

2) A second major conclusion is that we should view the behavior of people in organizations objectively. When a motor will not run or a fuse blows out, we try to find the cause, correct it, and then proceed with our business. But when we deal with human behavior, our response is much more emotional. If Bob fails to do what the organization manual specifies, we get mad. Having designed a beautiful organization plan, we think *everyone* should behave according to the plan.

In this chapter we have suggested several reasons why people in social groups behave as they do, and research in the behavioral sciences will undoubtedly give us many more useful insights. Instead of simply getting angry when an operation falls behind schedule, a mature manager will try to find out what really happened and why.

3) Finally, if he understands the social forces at work, a manager can be more skillful in designing his formal organization and in his planning, leading, and controlling. Nothing we have said in this chapter diminishes the need for an organization structure to get work done effectively. Our emphasis on social behavior simply indicates that organizing is a more delicate task than it appears when our attention is focused only on the work to be done.

When he includes social dimensions in the total picture, a manager may modify his organization design. Perhaps task-teams or some other arrangement that recognizes social behavior in his group will be introduced; or while thinking about changes in assigned duties, he may give attention to the tugs and pulls in learning new social relationships.

In shaping his organization, a manager should, of course, consider not only social behavior but also individual needs—the subject of the next chapter.

FOR CLASS DISCUSSION

Questions

1) Do you feel there has been any significant change in the last few years with respect to membership of college students in formal or informal campus groups? How do you explain these changes or lack of changes?

2) What effect does a football team, a fraternity, or a campus activist group have on the beliefs, attitudes, and behaviors of its members? How are these beliefs, attitudes, and behaviors inculcated? Do you think social pressures of this sort are stronger or weaker within a business organization?

3) Do you think informal work groups or cliques often strongly influence employees in ways that are in conflict with company objectives? If this should occur what should the company do? Explain.

4) Identify one of your habits. Think of a habitual response you have with regard to some relatively *unimportant* aspect of your behavior. Perhaps it is a speech habit or a tendency to walk from one place to another along a prescribed route. *Do not* select a habit that affects you in a *major* way, such as smoking. Having identified such a habit try to break it. If possible, ask a friend to help by calling it to your attention. How do you feel when this unimportant habit is challenged? How do you explain this feeling?

5) To what extent do you feel you can determine what kind of a person a man *is* based on your observations of him doing his job? How confident are you that you could accurately predict how he would handle a different job (within his technical ability) based on these observations? Relate your answers to the text discussion on habits, customs, and roles.

6) What benefits and drawbacks do you see in using small-group rewards as substitutes for the rewards provided by the work itself?

7) Recently one of New York's most aristocratic banks was merged with a bank that had been very successful in operating many

branches throughout the city. The first bank had considerably fewer customers, but these included many wealthy individuals and large corporations; high prestige was associated with having an account at this bank. The second bank served customers in all walks of life and had aggressively developed over twenty branches during the period when commercial banks generally entered the small-loan and limited-checking-account fields. From an economic viewpoint the strengths of the two banks complemented each other, and the merger was hailed as a sound marriage. Assume you had been assigned to help design the organization of the newly merged institutions. Naturally you would expect to find many duplications of activities and would seek economies by combining departments and eliminating overlap. Also you would seek to use the most capable people in key spots in your new organization. (1) As you design the new organization, to what extent, if any, would you consider the social structure (that is, roles, relationships, and other aspects of group behavior discussed in this chapter) that had existed in each former bank? (2) What, if anything, should the senior officers of the new bank do to develop a social structure in their new institution that will promote the aims and programs of the new bank?

8) How do you account for the fact that the same people may belong to many different kinds of groups?

9) In what ways would the matrix or project form of organization described in Chapter 6 affect the formulation of social groups and the potential for harmonizing them with the formal organization?

Cases

For cases involving issues covered in this chapter, see especially the following. Particularly relevant questions are listed after each case.

Gerald Clark (p. 234), 5
Dodge Skate Company (p. 337), 2
Bolling Laboratories, Inc. (p. 345), 4
E.W. Ross, Inc. (p. 468), 2
Harrogate Asphalt Products, Ltd.—AR (p. 557), 4

FOR FURTHER READING

Davis, K., *Human Relations at Work*, 3rd ed. New York: McGraw-Hill Book Company, 1967, Chap. 13. *Explains informal organization, including the grapevine.*

Hilton, B.L., and H.J. Reitz, eds., *Groups and Organizations.* Belmont, Calif.: Wadsworth Publishing Company, Inc., 1971, Parts 5 and 7. *Group influences on individual behavior and intergroup processes, as viewed by several psychologists and sociologists.*

Katz, D., and R.L. Kahn, *The Social Psychology of Organizations.* New York: John Wiley & Sons, Inc., 1966, Chap. 3. *Delineates the nature of social organization in conceptual terms. Book as a whole provides a framework for thinking about enterprises as social institutions.*

Leighton, A.H., *The Governing of Men.* Princeton, N.J.: Princeton University Press, 1945. *Classic study of United States relocation camp for Japanese; shows crucial need for customs and roles.*

Lippitt, G.L., *Organization Renewal.* New York: Appleton-Century-Crofts, 1969, Chap. 3. *Explains an organization as a social system. Book gives in nontechnical language a lead into psychological literature on people in organizations.*

Strauss, G., "Organizational Behavior and Personnel Relations," in *A Review of Industrial Relations Research,* Vol. I, ed. W.L. Ginzburg *et al.* Madison, Wis.: Industrial Relations Research Association, 1970, pp. 145–206. *Summarizes research findings related to organizations and personnel relations.*

Chapter Eight

Human Needs

and Organization Design

NEEDS SATISFIED THROUGH WORK

Formal organization is one means of guiding the behavior of people. But if we are to understand fully how an organization works, we have to appreciate the full range of influences, formal and otherwise, on the behavior of members of that organization. In the last chapter, we examined the influence of the internal social system. Now we shall focus our attention on the motivations of individuals, since these motivations also have a profound effect on the way a formal structure actually functions.

The purpose of this chapter is threefold:

1) To present a way of thinking about human needs—an approach that will be useful later in the book as well as here.

2) To consider ways an organization design can help meet human needs.

3) To discuss how salaries can be related both to needs and to formal organization.

The term "needs" is sometimes used to refer only to essential requirements for survival. Here, however, we shall follow the practice of psychologists and adopt a much broader meaning. Need includes both what a person must have and what he merely wants. Psychologists say that as long as a man wants something, he has a psychological need for it, regardless of what someone else may think of the justification for this desire. With this usage, we avoid making subjective judgments—for example, whether it is a matter of necessity or desire for a college student to have a car on campus.

Needs vary widely among individuals, but this variation is largely a matter of degree and of different ways of satisfying needs. There is enough similarity in the basic aspirations of most people so that we can talk of general human needs.

Many classifications of needs have been made. We shall confine our attention to those that can be satisfied to a significant degree by working in a business enterprise, for they are the needs a manager may be able to do something about, namely, physical needs, security needs, social needs, and self-expression needs.

Physical Needs

All human beings have needs that pertain to survival and physiological maintenance of the body. The objects of these needs include such things as food, drink, shelter, rest, and exercise. Until such needs are reasonably well satisfied, they are strong, driving forces. Our society is sufficiently prosperous, however, so that the minimum physiological requirements are usually met. Nevertheless, management has devoted a good deal of attention to providing adequate ventilation, heat, and light; in general, management attempts to ensure working conditions that make a work-place physically satisfactory—even attractive.

Security Needs

In an age when our entire Western society seems to have an obsession about security, we all quickly recognize needs in this area. Most of us secretly hope that some omnipotent agent will assure us that all the satisfactions we now enjoy will continue and that no possible misfortune will cross our path. Because such guarantees are impossible in a dynamic society, we should couch our hopes for security in more realistic terms. Both economic security and psychological security are involved.

With respect to work, most attention of social reformers has been focused on *economic security*. Men worry about steady employment, provisions for old age, and insurance against catastrophes that might call for large financial outlays. Private enterprise and government have both sought ways of providing at least minimum financial protection against these risks. Possibly the resulting discussions of pensions, unemployment insurance, health insurance, and similar plans have made all of us even more sensitive about economic security.

But a more subtle matter is the need for *psychological security*. This need relates to a man's confidence that he will be able to deal with the problems that confront him. His ability to meet future job requirements, the fairness of present and future supervisors, the balance of benefits and losses that result from economic and technological changes—all conjure up hopes and fears. Each man needs assurance that he will be able to adjust satisfactorily to such new conditions.

One source of psychological security is knowing the rules of the game. For example, the student who at the beginning of a course wants to know what the final grade will be based on or how long research papers should be is trying to remove an irritating uncertainty. Uneasiness about the effect of a rumored reorganization on one's job can lead to high anxiety because the rules of the game may change. Somehow we have to develop confidence that we shall be able to cope with new situations successfully.

Social Needs

Social needs are satisfied through relations with other people, and the desire for *sociability* is strong in most of us. We need contacts with informal groups as well as with close friends. Such contacts include friendly greetings, casual conversations, and amusing luncheons that a person—whether he is mimeograph operator, foreman, or vice-president—engages in with his associates at the office or plant. Companies have found that when employees have friendly relationships on the job, absenteeism tends to be low. In fact, people often go to their jobs or to a social function despite a headache or a lack of interest in the activity itself just to associate with other people.

Closely related to sociability is a sense of *belonging*. Everyone wants to feel that he is a recognized member of a group; that he will be included in group plans and will share informal information, both gossip and fact; that others will help him in trouble and will expect him to help them. In the Biblical sense, we all desire to love and be loved.

A third social need is desire for *status*. In a business, status depends on the value of a position in the eyes of others. Status always implies a ranking along some kind of scale, and the hierarchy of a formal organization is one of the commonly accepted gauges. In addition, occupations differ in status value in various companies and communities. For example, being an actuary at the Metropolitan Life Insurance Company may command much more respect in "nice" suburbs than being a pier boss at an ocean dock, even though the pier boss is paid more. Within companies, distinctions may be drawn between machinists and pipefitters, between locomotive engineers and firemen, or between sales clerks and cashiers.

Status distinctions are drawn within classes of occupation. Everyone in a company usually knows who is the top salesman, the fastest typist, or the manager of the most profitable branch. Status inevitably implies competition, and competition is especially vigorous in the United States, where most people seek to improve their status. But perhaps even more pronounced than the desire to rise is the desire not to lose status. A lathe operator may refuse to sweep around his machine or an executive may refuse to answer his own telephone—even though to do so might be the simplest way to get work done—merely to maintain his status in the eyes of those about him.

Self-expression Needs

Aside from what others may think, each person is concerned with his private aspirations, and in this matter he measures himself. He asks, "Does this job permit me to do what *I* would like to do, to be what *I* want to be?" In brief, each man needs to express himself. At the nucleus of the cluster of needs for self-expression we find self-assertion, power, personal accomplishment, and personal growth. Let us look more closely at each of these four needs.

Every mature adult wants to assert himself, to be independent at least to some extent. As we grow from childhood to adulthood, we rely less and less on other people to help us survive, to make decisions for us, and to show us how to behave and act. We no longer simply respond when somebody else acts; we begin to take the initiative. We want some control over our own destiny. In short, as we mature we progress from dependence toward independence.

By the time a person reaches maturity, he attains a level of *self-assertion*—we might say independence, or initiative—that he needs to maintain if he is to stay happy. Some people have learned through past experience that the best way for them to face life is to do most of their own thinking and to seize the initiative most of the time. Being independent makes life more pleasant for them than does taking advice from others. Although this drive for self-assertion varies in intensity from person to person, nearly everyone has at least some need to be independent and to exercise initiative.

In some persons, desire for self-assertion slips over into a strong urge for *power*. Like the thrill a boy gets from driving a car for the first time, the ability to make things or men respond to one's own will can be a strong motive.

Men also desire a feeling of personal *accomplishment*. Craftsmen take pride in their work whether it be a neatly typed letter, a difficult surgical operation, or a welded joint that may never be seen by the public eye. Some people feel deeply about educating children, making highways safer, or otherwise contributing to the general welfare. For them, satisfaction comes from knowing that they have done a worthwhile job well; regardless of public acclaim or the size of tasks, they enjoy an inner sense of accomplishment. Few men, in fact, can do their best work unless they feel satisfaction of this sort.

In addition, men normally want an opportunity for *growth*. Satisfaction comes from the *process of achieving* as much as from the accomplishment itself. A college graduate in accounting may be happy while he first learns a small part of the cost accounting of a company, but after he has solved problems there, he wants to move on to something else. He at least wants variety, but he probably also wants a task calling for greater skill. Individuals vary greatly in the kind and amount of growth to which they aspire. Psychologist David McClelland gives us impressive evidence that even the growth of nations is closely tied to their peoples' need for achievement. We can anticipate that with increasing education, travel, and technological change, the desire for growth opportunities will become even more pressing than it has been in the past.

POTENCY OF NEEDS

The total array of human needs seems overpowering. Even those needs related to work—physical, security (economic, psychological), social (sociability, belonging, status), and self-expression (self-assertion, accomplishment, growth)—make us wonder, "Can man ever be satisfied?" Part of the answer lies in the relative potency of these various desires. In this connection, we shall consider marginal values, aspiration levels, and non-rational values.

Marginal Values

How intensely a man wants more of a thing—say, food, social recognition, or job security—depends partly on how much he already has. What is an additional, or *marginal,* unit worth to him? He might sell his birthright for air to breathe if he were suffocating, but when fresh air is in plentiful supply, it loses its marginal value. In times of earthquake or war, starving men have traded diamonds for food; once adequately fed, however, these same men become more interested in security and self-expression.

At a given moment, each person has a hierarchy of needs, ranging from those that seem urgent to those that are faint. As the most basic needs are satisfied, that is, when a person has sufficient water, shelter, and so on, the next most important needs become the real governors of his behavior. After they are met, some needs, such as security of employment, become dormant; but other needs, such as a drive toward personal

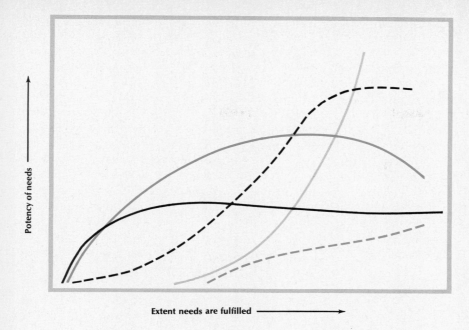

*Fig. 8–1 Marginal potency of needs varies with fulfillment.
Some needs are fully satisfied and level off; others keep
expanding. The shapes of these curves differ among individuals,
and even for the same individual over time.*

achievement or desire for social recognition, tend to keep expanding.
Frederick Herzberg applies the term "hygiene factor" to those needs that
do not expand—they may cause great distress when not met but provide
little drive once they are. The other needs, which keep growing, are the
prime motivators.

Whether a need continues to be potent as a man derives degrees
of satisfaction depends largely on his levels of aspiration and on his ability
to draw qualitative distinctions rationally.

Aspiration Levels

The potency of a need depends on whether a man expects the need
to be met. A desire to become company president, for instance, is not
a strong motive for the man who says to himself, "I know I'll never make
it." On the other hand, a design engineer who expects ample opportunity
for self-expression will be very dissatisfied with his job if he is assigned
routine drafting. To understand human needs, then, we not only have to
identify each need and note how well it is already being met, but we also

167

have to consider how much more satisfaction of each type of need a man really aspires to attain.

A man's self-image strongly influences his aspiration levels, that is, what he believes his abilities are, and what he thinks his role should be. If he regards himself as the best salesman in a company, he will work harder to achieve top ranking than another man who considers himself a plodder, "about as good as the average." Similarly, the executive who views himself as a natural leader will be highly concerned about social approval of his ideas. Of course self-images change over time. Repeated failures to achieve an expected satisfaction normally lead to a downward adjustment in aspiration, whereas successes encourage new dreams of glory, especially if one's friends are experiencing similar failures or successes. A man typically makes adjustments in his self-image quite slowly, however.

Social scientists have observed three things about aspiration levels that are especially pertinent for a business manager:

1) *Change* in the extent of need fulfillment—either up or down— is especially potent. For instance, a drop below a level that has become accepted is felt as a severe deprivation.

2) For many needs, men expect improvement from year to year. Indeed, the improvement is often more important than the absolute standard. (Perhaps this is why our forefathers spoke about "life, liberty, and the *pursuit* of happiness.")

3) Operators and managers recognize that in every firm there is a certain amount of dirty, routine, and otherwise unattractive work to be done. But performing such tasks satisfies few human desires directly; it is simply *necessary work*. Nevertheless, most people realistically expect to do some unattractive but necessary work as part of their jobs. Even though it does not contribute directly to meeting needs, it may be consistent with levels of expectation. Throughout life, every man learns to mix the bitter with the sweet; we are simply seeking to devise a more pleasant mixture.

Uncalculated Values

Rarely does a man calculate marginal values and aspiration levels systematically and logically; the potency of a need is more often based on his feelings. Even the person who wants to act logically is confronted with a formidable task. Our list of work-related needs is already complex, but there are still others, connected with family, religion, and other aspects of life, that all demand satisfaction. There are many ways to satisfy each of these needs, especially when we recognize *degrees* of satisfaction. For instance, we may use numerous foods of varying quality to satisfy the hunger need; we may satisfy social needs by a wide range of activities from going to parties to working in an office together. For any given need, we may select from hundreds of alternative goals to fulfill it. Furthermore, we may adopt any of many alternative actions to attain each goal.

Because of the variety of our needs, the number of alternative goals that might satisfy them, and the number of alternative actions by which we might attain any one goal, we are confronted with almost unbelievably complex decisions about what to do at any one time—or would be if we logically determined each action. Because of this great complexity, we cannot carefully calculate all the pros and cons. Instead we rely chiefly on habits, attitudes, and emotional response.

We may copy unconscious reactions from other people or develop them from our own experience. From trial and error a man learns that some actions make him feel good; others make him feel upset and discouraged. Often, he does not even recognize why he feels the way he does (psychiatrists have clients who spend hours on a couch trying to understand their own feelings). Nevertheless, whether through reason, habit, or emotion, men do take actions; they do attach marginal values to their needs, and they do have aspiration levels, but these feelings arise largely through a nonrational process.

No one can prove that as much as 95 percent of men's actions are uncalculated, but this is a useful approximation for a manager. It warns him that attempts to change people's behavior by logical argument will meet with limited success. Instead he must try to learn which needs have high potency for his subordinates and then try to create a work situation in which each subordinate finds his satisfactions by helping to achieve company goals.

SATISFYING NEEDS ON THE JOB

On-the-Job versus Off-the-Job Satisfactions

In our discussion of human needs, we have concentrated on those desires that can be met, at least to some degree, by working at a job. Such satisfactions, however, may arise either directly or indirectly from the work. This distinction has an important bearing on how a manager seeks to motivate his subordinates.

Work itself can be satisfying. A sense of achievement, for instance, arises from doing a job well. When a man performs an assigned task and at the same time satisfies his basic needs, we say he enjoys "direct," or "on-the-job," satisfactions. In such a case, it is the work itself and the normal relations with other people at work that provide satisfying experiences.

In contrast, there may be rewards for work that are not generated as an aspect of work activity. Familiar forms of this kind of reward are pay, vacations, and pensions. Let us note that the satisfactions that arise from such rewards take place *outside* the management system or work situation, and mostly outside the company. Work is simply a means of obtaining satisfaction at a later time and place. We shall refer to these as "indirect," or "off-the-job," satisfactions.

When these distinctions are applied to human needs discussed early in this chapter, we may be surprised to note how important on-the-job satisfactions are in the total picture (see Table 8–1). Most of the literature in economics and scientific management stresses financial, or off-the-job, compensation. But behavioral scientists have insisted—and this is one of their major contributions—that on-the-job satisfactions are also highly important.

Limitations of Off-the-Job Satisfactions

Off-the-job satisfactions from work depend, in our society, largely on money. We use pay to buy things that satisfy physical needs and contribute toward social status. Economic security during old age or in time of catastrophe is also assured by money. But the lack of direct association between work and such satisfactions has a serious drawback— it too often leads to this familiar attitude: "I don't care about the job as long as the pay keeps rolling in."

Not all off-the-job satisfactions come through money, however. Employment with a well-known company and a good title contribute to social status away from work. Some men would rather be vice-president of a local bank than salesman for Chilean Nitrates at a higher salary, simply because the bank job carries more prestige among their friends.

Companies may provide housing, recreation, and other off-the-job

Table 8–1   Human needs related to work

Needs	Direct, On-the-Job Satisfactions	Indirect, Off-the-Job Satisfactions
Physical needs	"Working conditions"	Money to buy necessities of life
Security needs	Psychological security	Economic security
Social needs	Sociability, belonging, status within company	Money to attain social status, recognized title in recognized company
Self-expression needs	Self-assertion, power, sense of accomplishment, growth possibilities	Improved ability to engage in hobbies, money to seek power

benefits. During recent years, however, most companies have withdrawn such forms of compensation because of worker resistance to "paternalism." Because of a desire for independence, which we already discussed in connection with self-assertion, most employees prefer that their employer keep out of their private affairs. They are likely to resent even a generous program if management clearly expects them to be appreciative of the good things bestowed on them. A company can and should help build a wholesome community, provided it maintains the independence and self-respect of the citizens.

Off-the-job satisfactions, then, are essential in meeting certain types of human needs—notably the needs that can be satisfied through the use of money. But as we shall see later in the chapter, relating pay to an active interest in performing a job well is by no means easy; and many social, self-expression, and security needs must be fulfilled on the job if they are to be satisfied through work.

On-the-Job Satisfaction: A Challenge to Management

Providing on-the-job satisfactions is not a simple matter for two reasons. First, the principal difficulty lies in meeting needs for social contact, self-expression, and psychological security. Fulfilling each of these needs calls for the active participation and often the initiative of a worker himself. A manager cannot *force* a worker to enjoy his associates, be independent, take pride in his work, and be confident of the future; a manager can only create an environment in which such feelings can flourish. For a manager who is accustomed to moving equipment, shaping raw materials, and otherwise achieving goals by positive action, an approach limited to facilitating action by others may seem slow. Yet all he can do is encourage growth and foster independence.

Second, on-the-job satisfactions should arise only *while men do the work that is necessary to meet company goals*. The sequence of events is not that a manager first assures worker satisfaction and then hopes that the happy workers will decide to do the tasks assigned to them; as we observed in our discussion of potency, a satisfied need does not motivate behavior. Nor does a benevolent boss parcel out satisfactions as rewards. Rather, actually doing a task that leads to company success must, at the same time, be what workers derive their satisfactions from. Both parties to the transaction benefit, just as a bee in the process of making honey from a blossom fertilizes the potential fruit.

Because work must be done if an enterprise is to remain in existence, a manager will probably give chief attention to physical requirements and technology. He will undoubtedly use "indirect" incentives to stimulate good worker performance. Nevertheless, if he expects his subordinates to be self-reliant, eager, and dependable instead of apathetic, indifferent, and lazy, he must try to set up the work in ways that offer people substantial, direct, on-the-job satisfactions.

MEETING HUMAN NEEDS THROUGH ORGANIZATION

The structure of a company defines an environment of formal rules, job descriptions, and communication networks in which people live during working hours. This environment can satisfy needs or block them, it can develop good attitudes or bad attitudes, and it can, in part, determine what people think and learn. Therefore, structure—as well as planning, face-to-face leadership, and control—is highly important in getting results.

In the following paragraphs, we shall present a variety of ways in which organization structure may contribute to, or detract from, the satisfaction of human needs. There may, of course, be other, perhaps compelling, considerations in making the final choice of an organization pattern, but our purpose here is merely to point out some ways that organization alone can effect the satisfactions of the people in it.

Small Units

When many workers are required for an operation, the social satisfactions will be greater if we can assign the workers to small groups of, say, three to ten. For instance, an insurance-company typing pool of perhaps sixty girls is too large to serve as a social group. The girls would form small, informal friendship groups, of course, but their socializing would probably be a thing apart from, and not integrated with, their work. On the other hand, if we could organize the work into small units, the girls could, to some extent, serve their sociability needs *while doing assigned work*. Moreover, a sense of *belonging* would probably be stronger in the smaller unit, and if we could measure the group output, we might find that the small groups engendered a sense of personal achievement.

Isolated Jobs

Taking social needs into account in organizing should make us wary of carrying to the extreme the process of cutting down the size of work groups. We should not isolate an individual.

The personal secretary to the president of one of the country's largest corporations once remarked that in many ways she was not as happy as when her boss was a lower executive. "This office is beautifully furnished and has the latest equipment, and I do have prestige as the president's secretary. But it is quiet in here, and the door is always closed. We're so busy I never have a minute to get out and talk with Jean and Betty and Chris like I used to." This girl was isolated by space and walls, but we can produce the same result by breaking down work into such *extremely specialized and independent parts* that a person lacks opportunity to interact with fellow workers while performing his work. We might call this *organizational isolation*.

Consider a roomful of design engineers. We might assign one engineer to a small, specialized project with which no other engineers are concerned. Day in and day out, he designs perhaps only pipelines, whereas all other engineers collaborate in designing chemical-processing units. Because he has little reason to discuss his work with others, he must either sacrifice social satisfaction during his working hours or steal time from the company to have conversations on other matters that are either partly or wholly irrelevant to the job of designing pipelines.

As an alternative, we could include this man in a unit of engineers who design processing-units and pipelines at the same time. Both his enjoyment of his work and the amount he does might increase. He would derive social satisfaction in discussing problems with his colleagues and from talking to construction supervisors who come into the drafting room to seek advice on construction operations. Such "socializing" is inherent in the position and does not involve serious interruption of assigned work. Although off-the-subject conversation can be excessive, behavioral research indicates that management cannot insure peak efficiency by attempting to eliminate it completely.

Narrow Staff Assignments

In order for a man to satisfy his social needs, his relationships with others must be *reciprocal*. We do not enjoy always giving and never receiving any more than we enjoy a one-way conversation. For a high degree of satisfaction, the initiation of contacts and the exchange of information should be roughly equal and reciprocal.

An easy give-and-take is hard to establish when a staff expert on a particular phase of planning simply tells other people what to do. Relationships in such a case tend to run in one direction. Similarly, companies often set up controls so that information flows only upward from the operating level to a staff man who measures and analyzes results. Either arrangement may accomplish its primary purpose, but it would not provide for satisfying social relationships.

The General Hardware Manufacturing Company had an organization that illustrates this point. A staff man who reported to the president was assigned the duty of operating a research department to plan new products and new uses for existing products. After top management approved product innovations, this product-planning director was expected to help the president convey and clarify instructions to the plant and sales managers and to the operating men under them. This one-way flow of decisions did not provide opportunity, especially for the plant manager, to enter into give-and-take discussion with the product-planning director about the work itself. Physical separation and the status of "a man from the head office" contributed to the difficulty of establishing reciprocal relationships. The same company also located in the home office a cost expert who watched over all expenditures—labor, overhead, and manufacture of specific products. His principal duty was to request data and explanations from plant managers and pass an analysis of this information on to the president. Again, the flow was one-way, as indicated in Fig. 8–2. As we might expect, the plant managers did not look forward to their meetings with either the product-planning director or the cost analyst; similarly, dealing with plant managers was just one of the crosses the central staff men had to bear.

If the company had modified the work structure so that the men concerned with product development, plant operation, and cost analysis could come together in frequent discussions of how to operate each plant in order to contribute most to company profits, the feelings and social satisfactions would have been quite different. One organizational change that might have brought this about would have been to combine all three functions under a single executive—a plant manager with expanded duties. Another possibility would have been to locate cost analysts physically in each plant, where they could serve the plant manager as well as prepare reports for the president. Even shifting greater responsibility for product

Fig. 8–2 Relationships in the General Hardware Manufacturing Company. Arrows indicate the main flow of information and the initiation of contacts among selected executives.

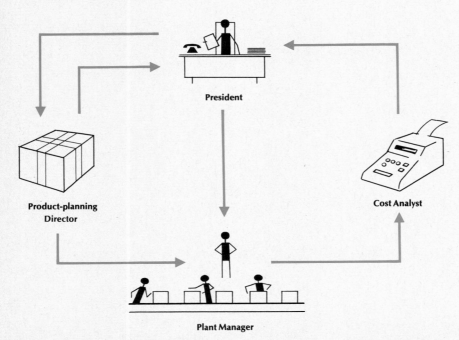

President

Product-planning Director

Cost Analyst

Plant Manager

development to each plant manager, with the result that he would make suggestions and ask for help from the central research group, would have encouraged reciprocal relations. The company would have to make any such modification in view of its total situation, but the alternatives mentioned indicate how the organization could have been restructured to meet social needs more effectively.

When management sets up a committee, either temporary or continuing, it creates a vehicle for satisfying several social needs. In committees, people usually meet as equals; if meetings are properly conducted, they provide a maximum of give-and-take communication; and often, committee membership contributes to prestige within a company.

Clearly, we should not establish committees merely to make members happy. In fact, using committees that contribute little or nothing to company goals may actually have an adverse effect on morale because members feel that the meetings are a waste of time and an interruption of their more important tasks. But if work is potentially suited to handling by a committee, an important consideration in favor of forming one is that social satisfaction will be a probable by-product.

Place in Hierarchy

Most people take pride in reporting to a high-level executive. It enhances their status, even though the executive may be too busy to see them. Indirectly, it may also give independence—if the executive has many people who report to him, he *must* grant considerable freedom of action. Perhaps pride of place in an organization's hierarchy explains why over one hundred important officials report directly to the President of the United States.

Adding a supervisory level in an organization structure cuts into satisfactions from status, especially of those who report to the newly established supervisor. In one advertising agency, for instance, two department managers resigned when they discovered that they would no longer report directly to a vice-president, and the men in their departments felt demoted, even though no one would have suffered a reduction in pay or a change in duties.

Related to the matter of place in the hierarchy is the question of titles. Titles provide significant status satisfactions both within and without a company. Theoretically, titles (or "rank" in military establishments) could be assigned on individual merit, irrespective of job duties or position in an organization hierarchy. But because titles are important in helping people understand a formal organization, they should usually describe where a job fits into a total organization structure. Even within this limit, however, managerial ingenuity in devising attractive titles can make substantial differences in employee satisfaction. "Let's give the guy a title instead of a raise" is not just a wisecrack; the right title may increase a man's satisfaction with his job.

Job Enlargement

Dividing up work into highly specialized jobs takes a toll in worker satisfaction. The assembly-line worker who spends day after day tightening a particular bolt has become a classic example of a man who has a routine, monotonous job. Many workers on such jobs regard their duties as menial, and they enjoy little pride of accomplishment.

Narrow specialization may also affect a person's opportunity for growth. To take a simple example from office work, a large oil company meticulously divided up work in its billing department among four employees: one typist listed in separate columns on an invoice all types and quantities of products from the customer orders; a second clerk entered prices opposite the products typed in the list; a calculator operator multiplied quantity by price and entered the total for each product; finally, a fourth clerk added up product totals, adjusted for special transportation charges, and entered the total amounts customers owed. With each person doing such small tasks, each girl found little room for growth in her job; only by being promoted could she hope for growth. The company in question, however, changed the organization of this operation. Instead of restricting each girl to a specialized task, management divided up the work so that each girl now completes a whole invoice from typing to totaling. Output has gone up and the number of errors down.

Other companies have found that similar job enlargements have improved results. Part of the benefit comes from technical improvements. Coordination is simplified, less time is wasted in moving work from one step to another, and only one person has to give attention to each piece of work—as with the invoice in the preceding example. Another benefit is increased worker satisfaction. A job becomes more challenging than under the former setup; a worker becomes aware of a natural completeness, or wholeness, to his task, and this affords him a greater sense of accomplishment. A worker on an enlarged job also becomes better prepared for other assignments.

Splitting Up Established Roles

Some jobs become firmly entrenched and embrace a fixed range of duties, particularly when a long period of formal training is required and when professional associations are active in the field. In hospitals, for instance, the roles of doctor, graduate nurse, and dietitian are sharply defined by tradition. Similarly, in a manufacturing concern, a first-class machinist or mechanical engineer may have a clear self-image of what he should and should not do. He has a "professional" pride in his job and the way he performs it.

Occasionally efficiency suggests reshaping such a role. Perhaps a draftsman can take over some duties that for years have been done only by engineers; or perhaps—it would be even more devastating to the engineers' pride—some aspects of design work might be transferred to salesmen. Part of the price of any such change will be a loss of self-esteem by the people whose "professional" job is being split up. The probable resistance may be strong enough to cause management to doubt whether a new organization is worth the rumpus. One large electronics firm, for instance, delayed a major reorganization because it would hurt the status and pride of its electrical engineers; at the time, good engineers were hard to recruit and hold, and the firm felt it had to provide a full range of satisfactions to obtain key men.

Degree of Decentralization

By its very definition, decentralization means increasing the freedom of action of subordinates. This freedom naturally affects the fulfillment of self-expression needs. At one extreme a job description for a salesman might simply specify, "Call on all customers in the Norfolk territory at least once a month and present company products that appear to offer most appeal at that time." At the other extreme, the guides and rules defining the same job might spell out exactly how the salesman should approach customers—for instance, by presenting samples first and mentioning price only incidentally, or even by spouting a canned sales talk that he has memorized from the company manual and presents to every customer. In the first case, a man could give his initiative free rein, but in the latter circumstance, he would have much less opportunity for independent self-assertion.

The issue of opportunity for independence is also of concern to managers throughout a company. The supervisor of a cost-accounting department in a factory, for example, may have either a high or low degree of delegation from the plant controller. He may or may not be free to work out his own methods for gathering data from foremen of operating units; he may or may not be allowed to plan the vacation schedule for employees in his department; he may or may not be permitted to determine the schedule for sending summary reports to the controller. The higher the degree of decentralization—that is, the greater freedom allowed—the more satisfaction a subordinate can expect from asserting his own ideas. Moreover, the more a man feels he is "running his own show," the more he will enjoy satisfactions of achievement. With a greater decentralization, a man has more chance to grow in his position and, in so doing, to prepare himself for more complex assignments. Clearly, decentralization ministers to self-expression needs in the sense that it provides opportunity to satisfy them; but, as we noted earlier, fostering opportunity is as far as management can go in satisfying this class of human need.

Organization of self-contained, semiautonomous divisions has already been described in Chapter 3 as a special form of decentralization. The separate divisions of the General Electric Company and the du Pont Company are well-known examples of such profit decentralization. This arrangement offers at least the managers of such divisions unusual chances for self-assertion and for growth. They not only have latitude to exercise their own judgment, but they also control within their orbit most of the activities that must be coordinated to make a profit. Consequently, a division manager and his key men can develop a deep feeling of satisfaction when their division is successful. In fact, a recognized benefit of profit decentralization lies in the strong appeal of challenging experience it offers the managers of each division. Here, indeed, organization structure ministers to human needs.

"Task-teams" also require decentralization as we noted in the preceding chapter. Moreover, they are small units and easy two-way communication becomes normal. In these respects they contribute significantly to personal needs of the members. We may encounter resistance when first establishing them, however, if a technical specialist on the team feels that his established role is being fractured (he may have to leave his office and live where "the shooting is going on") and that his status is downgraded.

In the preceding pages, we have discussed only a few of the ways a manager can creatively apply an understanding of human needs to organization design. Human needs are, of course, only one of the factors that influence the final selection of an organization structure. Nevertheless, as he considers the full range of factors, a manager should keep in mind two important things: the variety of ways a formal organization affects the satisfactions people get from their work, and the possibilities for ingenuity in designing an organization that helps to meet needs while it also provides an efficient framework for company operations.

FREEDOM VERSUS ORDER

A recurring issue in matching personal needs with an organization is how to balance individual freedom against established order. Today nonconformity is fashionable, and many young people regard fitting into any regulated system as a sacrifice. On closer examination, however, we quickly recognize that the issue calls for sensitive balance.

One cluster of basic human needs, already discussed, hinges on security. A known, orderly way of working together is an important source of such security. Established roles, normal procedures, and planned change all help members of an organization to feel psychologically secure. They know what to expect; they have a recognized place in the total activities.

People also want opportunities for self-expression, but for most persons self-expression has an underpinning of security. No person can enjoy freedom in a completely unstructured, unpredictable environment. But, as we have already noted, after a need for such security is fairly well satisfied it drops in importance. The practical questions, then, deal with *marginal increments* of security and of self-expression.

Our reaction to orderliness depends substantially on our feeling about the necessity for it. Musicians, artists, and researchers, for instance, voluntarily submit to all kinds of disciplined behavior—with no sense of loss of freedom—if they regard the drill as necessary to their personal expression. Similarly, when we are committed to an objective, we accept all sorts of necessary guidance in reaching that end.

Needs can be satisfied both on the job and off the job. For centuries most people have looked to their jobs for satisfaction of physical needs, security needs, and some social needs. Jobs have indirectly contributed to the fulfillment of self-expression needs of most men by allowing time for off-the-job activities. In this regard the dramatic reduction in the work week is heralded as a great achievement because of the *freedom* it provides for people to pursue their personal interests. Of course we can design many jobs that provide opportunity for self-expression in their performance, jobs that give extra motivation to the worker, but it is a mistake to assume that all the increments of self-expression must come on the job. Work is only part of a man's life, and it cannot directly satisfy all of his needs.

So we don't face a simple trade-off between the orderliness required by technology or economics on the one hand and individual freedom on the other. Nevertheless, rising living standards, more mass education, and higher aspirations raise the marginal value attached to individual self-expression. Perhaps as a general guide, we should start with the assumption that organization designers tend to overdo systems and formal assignments. This means that we should look for opportunities to leave discretion with individual operators and managers and should be ready to modify existing organization to keep it relevant to current social problems.

INTEGRATING PAY, NEEDS, AND ORGANIZATION

Although to say that "man works for a paycheck" is a gross oversimplification, as our preceding discussion has shown, financial compensation is a vital source of satisfaction. The size of a paycheck *does* matter to virtually every worker, from president to office boy.

The real question is how pay fits into the relationship between jobs and need satisfaction. To be sure, pay enables workers to meet their physical needs and those of their families. If a paycheck is large enough, they may have steak instead of pot roast, two cars instead of one, or even a color television set in the bedroom. But a paycheck means more than just what it buys. It is a symbol of status, a source of self-respect, an avenue to security. These noneconomic aspects of the paycheck often have more impact on how a man behaves in his job than does its purchasing power.

Several of these "indirect" influences of pay on behavior are closely related to organization design. They also intertwine with on-the-job satisfactions. Because an alert manager will want to give attention to such interrelations, we now turn to several key issues in this area: Can we substitute money for other kinds of satisfaction? How should a pay system be related to formal organization? Can we use pay to reinforce the influence of staff and of executives? How should individual raises be related to assigned duties and company objectives? What burdens does the use of incentive pay place on organization structure?

Pay Instead of Other Satisfactions

Can a company pay high salaries and wages and disregard security, social, and self-expression satisfactions? For instance, provided pay is high, will a capable man work as a subordinate for a supervisor who is highly critical, makes even minor decisions, and gives no opportunity for growth in the job? Experience answers, "Money isn't everything." Competent people shift to other jobs where the work is more attractive even if the pay is lower. Those who do stay on an unpleasant job are likely to develop negative attitudes toward their work and the company, to show little initiative, and perhaps even to restrict their output. Even though high pay may attract a worker, it does not win his emotional support if his job is low in direct satisfactions.

However, a job so brimful of direct satisfactions that it is "actually fun" still requires "reasonable" pay. The pay cannot be much below the prevailing rate for comparable work because of the psychological aspect of pay. The amount of compensation reflects the importance a company attaches to the work; it is a symbol recognized by other people inside and outside the company. Even though a man likes a job, he also wants others to think well of him and of it. We can conclude, then, that a wise manager must consider *both* direct and indirect satisfactions. Most people are willing to substitute one for the other only to a limited extent. We can apply the principle of marginal value to both situations: Extra-high pay cannot compensate for the reduction of on-the-job satisfactions below a commonly accepted level, *and* a high degree of job satisfaction will not keep a person working if his pay significantly degrades his self-respect or social standing.

Exceptions to this general proposition can be found, of course. Some jobs, such as preaching or teaching, carry enough social prestige and ego satisfaction to attract people, even though business pays for comparable ability at a significantly higher rate. We can also fill dirty or risky jobs by paying premium rates. In general, however, both fair pay and satisfying work are necessary to attract and motivate good people.

Relating Pay to Formal Organization

This conclusion still leaves us with the question of what compensation is "reasonable" for specific jobs in a specific company. One important guide both for a manager and for those who receive the pay is this: A pay rate should reflect the difficulty of a job. Jobs that require more skill,

Fig. 8–3 A possible salary structure for a small bank. The structure should reflect the difficulty, duties, and status of jobs, the rates paid by other firms, and the possibilities for salary increases in any given position.

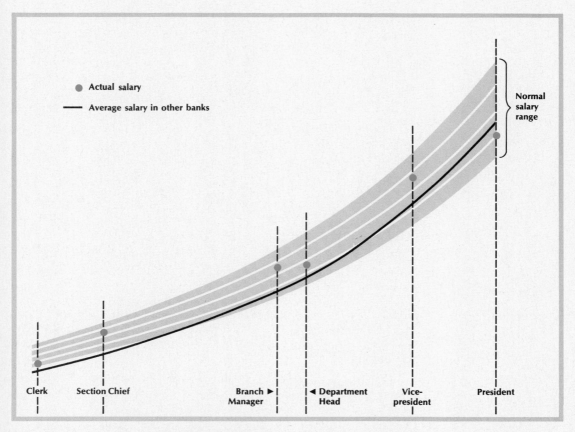

longer training, or more obligation should command higher pay. We should note that this guide is based on formal organization, for job descriptions specify duties, and, at least by implication, the abilities needed to fill each position. Any pay system that is inconsistent with formally assigned duties may lead to discontent. Status is the chief issue. A difficult or important job should have a high status. Because pay level (along with title and place in the official hierarchy) is the most conspicuous evidence of status, we should take great care in matching duties and pay. Employees at all levels are sensitive to this point. Strikes have been called over the amount of differences in wages between, say, electricians and machinists, not because of a few cents per hour, but because of what the difference meant in relative status. On the executive level, a vice-president of a certain department store was quite satisfied with a $35,000 salary until he learned that another vice-president, whose job he considered no more important than his own, was earning $40,000; immediately, he felt insulted, downgraded, and discriminated against.

Management usually dovetails salaries and duties by a procedure called "job evaluation." Steps in an evaluation include: (1) comparing all jobs on many counts—such as scope of duties, skills, and working conditions—and placing the jobs in a series of grades; (2) establishing a general salary level for each grade based on going rates for comparable work among other firms; and (3) creating a salary range for each grade that will permit increases from minimum to maximum as an individual progresses from beginner to expert in any one job.

No matter how elaborate the job-evaluation technique we use for our pay system, it will not be successful unless it is *accepted* by the employees to whom it applies. They must believe that it fairly reflects differences in jobs; the grades assigned must coincide with the relative standing of various roles as the workers conceive of them. Without such acceptance, the status and self-esteem of some workers will suffer, and the pay system will have a negative effect on their eagerness to do their work.

Reinforcing Staff and Executives

Management has a further reason to be concerned about the relative pay level of people in supervisory and staff positions. The feeling is common in American society that we should respect the opinions of persons who earn more money than we do, whereas the opinions of persons earning less are open to challenge. The simple assumption is that earnings are a measure of the soundness of a man's views. We believe that this is an unsound and dangerous assumption, but it does exist whether we like it or not.

Because of this feeling, a low-paid staff man will have more difficulty winning acceptance for his ideas than a high-paid man. An operating executive may say to himself, "Why should I take that fellow's advice? He doesn't earn half as much as I do." Thus if management wants to increase the influence of a particular man, one way to achieve its aim is to give him the prestige of a high salary. Similarly, a supervisor usually should get paid more than his highest–paid subordinate.

Raising a man's salary is not the only way to build a man's influence, but we should not overlook the impact of salary on a man's ability to operate within an organization.

Tying Raises to the Objectives of a Company

How a company grants merit increases has a direct influence on behavior in the organization. To an individual himself, an increase is a sign of his personal progress; he will try to continue behaving the way he thinks led to his raise. His colleagues are likewise alert. They know who gets raises more often, and who gets none at all, and they take their cues accordingly.

If a company grants raises to the man with longest service, the hardest worker, the casual worker who occasionally does something flashy, the man who threatens to quit, the "yes" man, or the best producer, it unwittingly provides a guide for future behavior of other employees. At the same time, workers typically have strong opinions of what they feel is "fair"—that is, who deserves a raise.

Consequently, management should be sure to be careful to grant increases to those who are, in fact, improving their effectiveness and should try to get everyone concerned to agree that a raise is reasonable and fair. In this matter, as with most others, management's actions speak far louder than its words. Playing favorites or being soft and giving everybody a small increase just to avoid arguments will undermine appeals to do a better job. On the other hand, if management consistently matches merit increases with known contributions toward company objectives, it reinforces the whole structure of formal plans and organization.

Incentive Pay and Organization

If merit increases should go to people who perform their assignments well, how about extending the idea to "incentive pay," which varies directly and immediately with performance? Commissions for salesmen and piece-rates for factory workers are common examples of incentive pay; at the managerial level, we find executive bonuses based on profits, on actual results compared with budgets, or on other quantified measures of results. Occasionally, when a whole group of people must cooperate to achieve results, a firm will offer a group bonus.

Desire for security has become so intense that today few employees on any level—president, sales supervisor, or machine operator—subsist entirely on incentive pay. Instead companies assure a degree of security either by guaranteeing minimum earnings regardless of results or by paying a base salary and adding incentive pay as a bonus. Even though incentive pay may be a small percentage of total compensation, it focuses attention on the particular achievements that management uses in determining the amount of a bonus.

Incentive pay introduces several requirements in organization design. We must sharply define the mission—the end result—of a job eligible for a bonus, and the results must be measurable. Many jobs, such as that of chief accountant or personnel director, cannot be defined in this manner. Even the work of a salesman is not simple to describe. His primary task may be to obtain orders, but in addition, he is expected to cultivate new customers, obtain information on new products, deal with complaints, and keep his own expenses low. If his bonus is based solely on new orders, he is likely to slight his other duties.

For an organization, this means one of two things. Either (1) authority should be highly decentralized—for instance, we might authorize the manager of a division to change prices, hire people, and take other action that is necessary to achieve profits, on which his bonus is based—or (2) management should standardize and control the work conditions that affect output—for a production worker who is paid a piece-rate, for example, this means that material should be readily available, machinery in good operating condition, helpers adequately trained, power and light dependable, and so forth. In both instances, the location and adequacy of staff and service work are important to the man who receives incentive pay. Again, we see that an organization pattern and a salary system are closely interrelated. If we use incentive pay, we get into questions of delegating authority, providing service and staff, and defining duties so that they conform to the bases for bonuses.

CONCLUSION

In this chapter, we have focused our attention on the personal needs of managers and operators—especially on their physical, security, social, and self-expression needs, because these can be met to a significant extent through working in an enterprise. A manager should not only identify the specific needs of the people he directs, but he should also be sensitive to the relative potency of these various desires. Such an understanding of his people provides a manager with a foundation for deciding how best to incorporate a high degree of motivation into his actions.

Working at a job satisfies a man's needs in two ways: indirectly through off-the-job satisfactions and directly through satisfactions that arise on the job. Because many off-the-job satisfactions come from the pay a man receives for his work, a manager should try to relate pay to organization design and company aims. By tying the amount of pay to the importance and influence we wish to give various jobs, we increase the chances that the organization will actually work as we want.

A manager should also be alert to the connection between on-the-job satisfactions and organization. Often he can adjust his organization in a way that increases the direct satisfactions of his subordinates. We discussed a variety of such possibilities, and others will occur to a manager who thinks of both work and workers as he organizes. His objective should be to design a structure in which on-the-job satisfactions are enhanced at the same time company aims are furthered.

Satisfying needs through *organization* is, of course, only one approach a manager may follow. As we shall see later, planning, leading, and controlling can also contribute to, or detract from, the fulfillment of needs. We emphasized organization in this chapter simply because we are most concerned in Part Two with the impact of human factors on the process of organizing.

FOR CLASS DISCUSSION

Questions

1) What do you consider the most significant changes in America over the last two or three decades that are likely to influence the attitudes of people toward work as a means of satisfying their potent needs? Consider your answer to the first part of this question in terms of the age of the people you have in mind. Would the changes you consider significant have as much, more, or different kinds of influence on people under twenty-five, say, than they would on those over thirty?

2) A study of various jobs in a large hotel revealed that turnover was much higher in maid service than in the hotel's central laundry. Women of the same general type and qualifications were hired, salaries were comparable, and the work load was actually somewhat greater in the central laundry. What reasons do you think might explain the higher turnover in maid service? How might the hotel management have reduced this turnover?

3) There seems to be much greater concern today than there was fifty years ago with the need to devote more of our resources to dealing with problems such as ecological abuses, racial injustice, war, and so on. How would you explain this concern? How may it affect business?

4) How does a manager identify the needs and aspiration levels of his subordinates? What *problems* could arise (1) from the actions he takes to identify such needs and aspirations, and (2) from his knowledge of them? How may he use this knowledge profitably?

5) If we continue to experience relative abundance, more people will satisfy their lower-order needs earlier and self-expression needs will take on greater potency. Because the greatest opportunity to realize self-expression needs within a large corporation has typically existed at the top management level what problems do you see ahead? How would you deal with these problems?

6) "We cannot hope to know what the specific needs of any group of employees are, and even if we could, the knowledge wouldn't lead to any policy changes on our part. Rather than seek to adapt our operations to individual needs, we make clear what each job offers so as to attract people whose needs are such that they will be satisfied by our work." Discuss this comment by a personnel director.

7) We have suggested that the statement "Let's give the guy a title instead of a raise" is not *just* a wisecrack. Assuming that a man is given a title but little real additional responsibility, what needs are likely to be satisfied? Will the long-run effect of such a reward differ from the short-run effect? Explain.

8) In what ways may incentive pay or rewards for employee suggestions have a negative effect on day-to-day productivity as a result of the implications such systems may have on human needs? Do you feel the benefits are likely to outweigh these negative effects?

Cases

For cases involving issues covered in this chapter, see especially the following. Particularly relevant questions are listed after each case.

Scott-Davis Corporation (p. 227), 4, 6
Gerald Clark (p. 234), 6
E.W. Ross, Inc. (p. 468), 4
Consolidated Instruments—A (p. 571), 4, 5
Texas-Northern Pipeline Company (p. 665), 3
Consolidated Instruments—B (p. 674), 8

FOR FURTHER READING

Blumberg, P., *Industrial Democracy: The Sociology of Participation*. New York: Schocken Books, Inc., 1969. *Useful summary of literature on worker participation.*

Cummings, L.L., and W.E. Scott, *Readings in Organizational Behavior and Human Performance.* Homewood, Ill.: Richard D. Irwin, Inc., 1969, Chap. 4. *Seventeen articles on environmental and structural determinants of behavior in organizations.*

Dubin, R., *Human Relations in Administration,* 3rd ed. Englewood Cliffs, N.J.: Prentice-Hall, Inc., 1968, Chap. 4. *Concise explanation of debate on organization versus individual.*

Hersey, P., and K.H. Blanchard, *Management of Organizational Behavior.* Englewood Cliffs, N.J.: Prentice-Hall, Inc., 1969, Chaps. 2 and 3. *Clear, nontechnical discussion of effect of needs and environment on motivation.*

Herzberg, F., "One More Time: How Do You Motivate Employees?" *Harvard Business Review,* January 1968. *Stresses challenging work, not hygiene factors, as key to positive motivation.*

McClelland, D.C., *The Achieving Society.* Princeton, N.J.: D. Van Nostrand Co., Inc., 1961. *International psychological studies of achievement motivation. For summary of case see "Business Drive and National Achievement,"* Harvard Business Review, *July 1962.*

Chapter Nine

Conflict in Organizations

INEVITABILITY OF CONFLICT

Conflict, in the sense of a clash of interests or incompatible desires, is all around us. We do not want our rustic countryside to be spoiled by civilization, and yet growing population forces us to build suburban homes connected by webs of power and telephone lines. We want full employment and at the same time no inflation. We want neighborhood schools and also integrated schools. We want a higher standard of living and no imports. The list goes on and on.

Similarly, within an organization some people will want assurance of jobs and stability, others the excitement of growth and modernization, and still others more pay for a selected few (including themselves). Life is not a grand harmony. Conflict exists. We have to learn how to live with it, how to use it constructively, and how to minimize its destructive aspects.

In this chapter we shall focus on *intra-organizational* conflict. For instance, when Paul's successful pursuit of his purposes would prevent George from carrying out his plans, management faces a conflict situation. Because both men cannot fully succeed, a lot of jockeying and infighting may arise. In fact, more effort may be devoted to internal competition than to end results. Such intra-organizational conflict often grows out of divergent goals; however, it is through clash in action—or proposed action

—rather than through a difference in motives that conflict becomes apparent.

Psychologists for some time have studied conflict *within* a person—his incompatible desires, the resulting frustration, and responses to such frustration. However, here we are concerned with conflict between persons, not with internal psychological conflict. Of course we should be aware of the possibility that a man may have divergent motives—for instance, a man's personal goals may not match up with those he is presumed to have for the role (job) he accepts. This particular type of conflict relates to matching jobs and people, the topic of Chapter 10.

Intra-organizational conflict poses four broad questions that are particularly significant to a manager:

1) What are the *sources* of such conflict in organizations?

2) What *approach* or viewpoint will help a manager understand the nature of the conflict situations he faces?

3) How can we distinguish *constructive* and *destructive* conflict?

4) How can we *organize to deal with conflict?*

SOURCES OF CONFLICT

To deal constructively with conflict in his organization, a manager has to be sensitive to where the conflict is likely to arise. Let us look at five typical sources.

Competition for Scarce Resources

Committed men want resources with which to achieve their goals. The researcher looking for new products, the regional manager providing service to New England customers, and the guard charged with protecting the plant—all want equipment, men, supplies, and other resources. The total of such requests from all parts of the enterprise usually far exceeds the quantity of resources obtainable, and the resulting scramble is the cause of a lot of action and reaction throughout the organization.

Capital budgeting, the allocation of funds for long-run investment, often becomes a focal point for this kind of conflict. We have sophisticated techniques for making quantitative comparisons of budget requests, but these do not remove the underlying conflict. Too often the kind of rituals that characterize collective bargaining with labor unions are also present: exaggerated requests, one-sided evidence, bluffing, catering to the personal status of the bargainers, preoccupation with precedent, drawn-out negotiations. If we are not careful, this process can degenerate until both motives and honesty are distorted.

Capital is not the only scarce resource. It is often difficult to expand a company's marketing capability. If product A is given more attention, then product B gets less. This generates a tension among those concerned with different products, a tension that is similar to that found among college department chairmen who are agitating for more courses in their respective fields. Although each chairman recognizes that only so many courses can be added, each feels that the expansion of his department should not be fettered.

Manpower is often scarce, and so competition may arise over the allocation of people. In government and other office activities the number of qualified workers sharply affects the ability of a division to expand. So when employment ceilings exist, a scramble to get workers normally ensues.

Competition for scarce resources is such a pervasive feature of organization that managers devote substantial planning and control effort to wise allocations, as we shall see in Parts Four and Six. More than technology and economics are involved. If a company allocates resources to a particular group of employees or to a division, it in effect endorses the group's activities and assures them of their continuing value in the future company program.

Built-in Conflicts

A second normal source of conflict is deliberately created. In the process of organizing, we design jobs that breed conflict. Many staff jobs have this characteristic. An industrial engineer, for instance, may be assigned the task of finding more economical methods of making portable cassettes. His new, efficient methods often are difficult to install; at first, quality will be hard to maintain, and workers may resist change because their previous social relations have been upset. Of course the manager supervising cassette production is not concerned only with the effect of the

Fig. 9–1 Competition for scarce resources is one cause of conflict within organizations. Throughout the enterprise, managers and supervisors vie with one another for a share of available men, equipment, supplies, and funds. If allocations are not made wisely, conflict over resources can be destructive.

new method on costs. He is concerned also with the smooth integration of several aims: employee attitudes, quality, equipment maintenance, and so on. Consequently he tends to be cautious about new methods. We are therefore likely to find the staff man zealously pushing his special assignment while the line manager drags his feet.

This kind of conflict is aggravated when the staff man is a cocky young college graduate and the line manager is a man who has come up from the ranks through long service with the company and who responds intuitively rather than analytically. Furthermore, the two men will be responding to different criteria of success. Then if the change is made successfully, the question of who gets credit for the change is another potential sore point.

Note that we frequently establish staff jobs with the express purpose of assuring adequate attention to an aspect of a total operation that line managers for some reason slight. Moreover, several different staff men often make demands on the same manager—personnel, quality, cost, public relations, safety, to name but a few. By design each of these men has his own ax to grind.

We know in advance that the separation of control from operations will generate occasional conflict. The men concerned with operations are certainly not opposed to dependable quality, fast service, low cost, or other features for which we often establish separate control jobs. But the total operating assignment and the conditions under which the work is done are such that independent checks are necessary. And when an independent control man raises an objection the operating manager is annoyed just like any of us who is handed a ticket by a traffic cop for going through a red light.

Conflict Arising from Differences
in Work Characteristics

The best way to do job A does not necessarily fit together smoothly with the best way to do job B. Each type of work has its own optimum technology, and vigorous pursuit of one specialty may make work more difficult for people in related activities.

Friction between production and marketing is a common illustration of this conflict in optimum technology. Most production benefits from long runs, standardized products, limited variety, and predictable levels of activity. On the other hand, marketing benefits from a variety of products or special adaptations that fit customer desires, fast changes, and prompt delivery. Under these circumstances, the marketing manager may make requests of production that the production manager feels will hinder him from doing his job well, and vice versa.

A research director, to note another common conflict, seeks unique products or processes and insists on high quality. Long lead times are needed for experimentation, and output is limited to the test tube or pilot plant, and so a research director's priorities differ from those of a production chief or marketing manager.

Differences in technology prevail in all kinds of enterprises. In a hospital, for example, a unit treating drug addicts will often want to take action that is not compatible with the smooth operation of inventory control at the dispensary nor with businesslike accounting, billing, and collecting.

Of course, steps are taken to mediate such conflicts. To achieve overall organization goals, some departments must deviate from practices that are optimum when each department is considered separately. Our point here is that people who know that their particular job could be done better if they did not have to cater to an alien activity find it hard to accept these compromises.

Divergent Personal Values and Aims

Paul R. Lawrence and Jay W. Lorsch point to a further reason for conflict between functional departments.[1] The personal values of the type of person who is attracted, say, to research differ sharply from those of a man who moves into production. The usual researcher is intrigued with the unknown, places a high value on scientific "truth," is prepared to wait weeks or months to get an answer, and thinks other people should act as rationally as *he* does. In contrast, the usual production man prefers to deal with known phenomena, has a practical and intuitive sense of what is right, wants prompt and positive action, and is more comfortable with authoritarian relationships. The typical sales executive has still another set of aims, ways of dealing with people, and time span in which he wants to see results. When people with such different orientations try to solve a mutual problem they quickly find that they don't even talk the same language.

Divergence of personal values often comes to the surface in government agencies. One person may advocate a cause (better jobs for blacks or equal rights for women); another may want to follow a strict interpretation of established law; and a third may stress current responsiveness to the electorate or party leaders. These individuals will agree on some matters but sooner or later will find themselves in conflict.

Two persons seeking the same job have a clear conflict in aims. Our system of promotion-from-within on the basis of merit deliberately places people in competition for more attractive jobs. We have traditions about appropriate methods of competition—like the medieval codes of chivalry in combat—but ambitious men sometimes resort to sharp internal politics,

[1] *Organization and Environment: Managing Differentiation and Integration* (Boston: Harvard Graduate School of Business Administration, 1967).

aggressive bids for recognition, and adroit maneuvering. Even when promotion is not at stake, some men compete aggressively for recognition and status.

Ambiguous Organization

Another common source of conflict in organization is lack of agreement on who should do what. For instance, in one company the president thought the controller's job was to establish accurate accounting records, to compare actual expenses with the budget, and to point out deviations to all executives directly concerned. The controller himself thought that he should press executives to avoid budget overruns and that he should report only unresolved deviations to the president. A newly appointed operations-research director thought the controller's task was only to maintain accounting records and to make accounting information available on request from other executives. The ill will that grew out of this role ambiguity lasted far beyond the three months consumed in reaching a formal agreement.

Jurisdictional squabbles can arise anywhere, from the senior level down to the operating level where, for instance, it may not be clear who can commit the company to deliver a special order on Sunday. Job scope is not a trifling matter, as nationwide strikes over jurisdictional lines demonstrate. Many firms prepare written job descriptions only irregularly, and even where more systematic attention is given such descriptions can never be complete and they soon get out of date. The more dynamic the company, the more likely are conflicts to arise from ambiguous organization.

APPROACHES TO CONFLICT SITUATIONS

Conflict, at least in mild forms, occurs frequently in organizations as the preceding review of likely sources indicates. To deal constructively with it, a manager needs some means to categorize, or classify into types, the specific conflict situations he faces. Such categories are especially useful when they suggest a suitable means for dealing with that type of conflict. One analytical scheme is this:

1) Ascertain whether the people in conflict agree or disagree on objectives to be served by proposed courses of action.

2) Determine the degree of uncertainty associated with the outcomes of suggested courses of action.

3) Even though answers to 1 and 2 are rarely completely black or white, try to fit the situation into the matrix in Fig. 9–2.

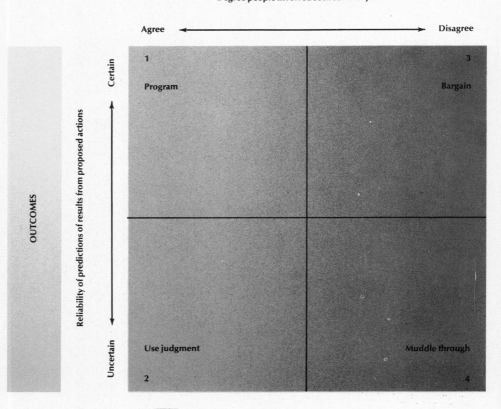

Degree people involved seek same objectives

Agree ←——————————→ Disagree

OUTCOMES

Reliability of predictions of results from proposed actions

Certain

Uncertain

1

Program

3

Bargain

Use judgment

Muddle through

2

4

Fig. 9–2   A matrix for analyzing conflict situations. By determining attitudes toward outcomes and objectives, a
manager can determine a course of action that will deal most
effectively with a given conflict situation.

1. Agree on Objectives, Outcomes Certain

The first type of conflict in this scheme arises merely from misunderstanding the total influences involved. Once the situation is clarified and
the relevant facts assembled, agreement on a desirable course of action is
simple. The alternative that has the best projected outcomes in terms of
agreed-upon objectives is selected. In fact, the choice of action often can
be *programmed*—that is, a particular set of conditions automatically leads

to a predetermined action. This is a world of harmony and light. "Just get the facts out on the table, and intelligent men will have no trouble agreeing on what should be done."

2. Agree on Objectives, Outcomes Uncertain

Here life is more complicated than in the first type of conflict because we aren't sure what will happen if we follow different alternatives. After a clarifying discussion we can agree on the objectives to be sought, but differences of opinion remain concerning the probable results of adopting various alternative means to achieve the objective. For example, we want to cut crime in central cities but are uncertain about the effects of either (1) dispersing underprivileged families, or (2) improving the economic situation through training and jobs for people living in the central cities.

The natural approach to such a situation is to improve our judgment about possible results. Perhaps we can call in an expert, or we can devise experiments that will throw light on likely results. To be sure, people may continue to differ sharply on the action they believe to be best, but the sound approach to a resolution of the conflict is through evidence, reason, and experienced judgment. We are still in a rational, though uncertain, world.

3. Disagree on Objectives, Outcomes Certain

Conflict of the third type differs sharply from the first two. The parties want different results, so more information does not help. Union-management negotiations over wage rates illustrate this type of conflict. No doubt exists about the effect of a 20 percent salary increase on take-home pay and on labor costs (disregarding for the moment the indirect effects on motivation). This conflict gets resolved either by *bargaining* or by appeal to a superior authority.

We lack basic principles for bargaining. Much depends upon power, bluffing, threats, anticipated reprisals, behavior norms set by society, and precedent in resolving other conflicts.[2] Behavioral scientists have observed that intra-organizational bargaining conflicts often move through several stages. (1) The problem is first treated as if it belonged to our first category, "Let's get the facts on the table and act like rational men." In fact, our society is so imbued with the effectiveness of rational analysis that we have to go through the motions of improving our judgment even

[2]For a broad discussion of conflict resolution of major social issues see K. Boulding, *Conflict and Defense: A General Theory* (New York: Harper & Row, 1961). Game theory deals with a narrow subclass of bargaining situations.

when everybody knows it is a sham. (2) Next, various forms of seduction are tried. "George, let's go out for a beer. You and I have been through a lot of tough scrapes together, and I am sure we won't let this matter upset our friendship." Or, "You know, we're really one big family here. . . ." A compromise may emerge at this point. (3) If such overtures are rebuffed, the emotional reaction is likely to shift quickly to anger and attack. At this stage a variety of irrelevant as well as relevant charges and countercharges will be made. (4) Finally, unless some means of arbitrating the dispute is found, the two groups withdraw from bargaining and become conflicting cliques. Of course when more than two parties are involved in the bargaining, the whole process becomes more complicated. Whatever the complexity, a manager benefits from recognizing when he is confronted with a bargaining situation. Formal bargaining procedures, including appeal to higher authority, are designed to resolve bargaining conflicts before they have a chance to move into the third or fourth stage that we have just described.

4. Disagree on Objectives, Outcomes Uncertain

When people fail to agree on what ends are desirable and on where the proposed actions will lead, we face a situation of potential chaos. This situation can occur in the federal government because wide divergence on priorities is often coupled with great difficulty in predicting the consequences of proposed action. In companies the allocation of research funds and proposed movement into new markets often lead to a similar quandary.

Muddling through is a reasonable approach to such a situation. As defined by C.E. Lindbloom,[3] muddling through involves taking one small step at a time. The conflicting persons do not attempt to agree on overall objectives; they are merely asked to support a specific short-run proposal. For example, production and accounting people may agree to the mechanization of inventory records for different reasons—the production department may want fewer shortages while the accounting department looks forward to integrated data processing. The production department probably would not support the move to a totally integrated data processing system, but they do approve of this first step. Following the first move, anyone can propose another step, and so on. Results of earlier steps provide the basis for later moves. Long-run action unfolds as successive decisions are reached.

Note that one or more of the persons participating in the muddling-through process may have his own clear long-run objective. This objective guides him in his response to specific proposals, but he does not

[3]See "The Science of 'Muddling Through,'" *Public Administration Review*, Spring 1959, pp. 79–88.

try to convert others to his view and consequently he cannot be sure that successive decisions will take the direction he desires.

Because specific decisions in the muddling-through process often require a supporting *coalition*, a manager faced with this kind of conflict is well advised to cultivate temporary alliances.[4]

Obviously many conflict situations do not fit neatly into one of our four types. Agreement will exist on some objectives and not on others; some outcomes will be clear while others will be highly uncertain. Nevertheless the proposed categories are very helpful in determining the appropriate approach to a specific situation.

CONSTRUCTIVE AND DESTRUCTIVE CONFLICT

Although conflict can be constructive, destructive conflict captures more attention, and so we tend to overlook the positive influence that can be derived if conflict is constructively channeled.

Constructive conflict increases effort and directs attention toward company goals. For instance, competition for status and promotion and competition for scarce resources stimulate individual effort. If we can focus this competition on activities that contribute to company goals, the overall results should be improved.

Built-in conflict, as we have observed, deliberately seeks the benefits of an additional viewpoint or an extra check. Staff positions frequently are created to ensure that a particular aspect of operations—quality control, product development, personnel training, public relations, and the

[4]The importance of coalitions is stressed in R.M. Cyert and J.G. March, *A Behavioral Theory of the Firm* (Englewood Cliffs, N.J.: Prentice-Hall, 1963). Our view is that the coalition concept is especially relevant to conflict situations of the fourth type.

Fig. 9–3 Conflict over scarce resources, or any other conflict, can be directed toward constructive ends that are designed to benefit not only the disputing parties but the organization as a whole.

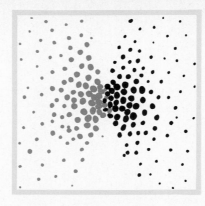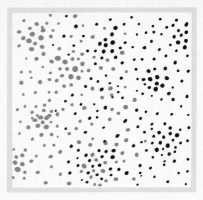

Fig. 9–4 Polarization and depolarization of conflict. At left, lines of conflict are clearly defined, the clash is sharp, and all elements rally on either side of the issue. At right, vague clusters hint at potential issues, but there is some mingling of feelings, and the cluster that is forming in the center at the bottom of the drawing suggests a genuine coalition.

like—gets adequate attention. The external staff described in Chapter 6 improves the quality of major decisions, and the very existence of controls, while sometimes irritating, leads to careful performance of operations that are to be evaluated.

Moreover, the outward expression of conflict, say over the extension of credit to customers, serves as a warning to management that current practice needs reexamination. Some divergence of view is to be expected in a dynamic firm, and if management is to make adjustments to changing situations it needs to know where the old patterns no longer fit.

In contrast to the potential benefits just discussed, conflict inevitably produces emotional stress. We can all stand some stress; research even suggests that a little stress serves as a tonic. But when stress goes beyond the invigorating stage it becomes debilitating, and the point at which this occurs varies from person to person.

Furthermore, conflict pressed too energetically carries some activities beyond a useful service. The hospital clerk is overly concerned with her particular subgoal if she places her need for tidy files above a patient's desire to return home and keeps the patient sitting for several hours until all records are neat. Likewise, an airline ramp service director charged with cleaning planes sometimes insists on completing his task meticulously even when his thorough cleaning of rugs conflicts with getting planes off on schedule. The clerk and the service director are "suboptimizing" from a broad point of view. That is, by pursuing their subgoals to an optimum point they are detracting so much from other desirable results that the overall service is hurt. A similar danger exists for almost all staff services.

The most detrimental effect of conflict is the distortion of goals. Conflict can become so intense that winning the immediate argument becomes more important than the long-range outcome. One way of describing this behavior is to say that people start "playing games"—perhaps bitter personal games—instead of pursuing their assigned mission. In game-playing, as Eric Berne points out, time is often spent pinning the blame for any trouble on the other man, and voluntary cooperation drops to a low level.[5]

Three simple guides emerge from this brief comparison of constructive and destructive conflict:

1) If possible, we obviously want to design measures that will prevent conflict from escalating from a problem-solving debate to a win-lose fight.

2) Where "bargaining" (conflict of the third type) is inevitable, we want to avoid escalation into a local feud in which assigned missions disappear in the cross-fire.

3) We should be especially concerned about conflict between persons whose work closely interlocks. Any lack of cooperation is particularly serious when the quality, quantity, and schedule of the output of one unit affects the operations of adjacent units.

ORGANIZING TO DEAL WITH CONFLICT

Conflict is such a pervasive aspect of modern social action that we have to consider it in all phases of management—planning, organizing, leading, and controlling. At this point in our analysis, however, we are pulling out for special emphasis some of the ways a manager can use organization to create, control, or eliminate conflict.

Create Desired Conflict

To secure adequate, expert, independent attention to a special aspect of an operation a manager can establish a separate staff unit. Recently, for example, some presidents have set up a unit to promote the employment of blacks. In addition to providing counsel and special training facilities, such a unit prods supervisors to put forth extra effort to accommodate the new worker.

Separate control units are also commonly used. In order to permit independent action, such things as inspection, audit, and cost control are set apart from the operations they control. Such independence and divergence of objectives promote conflict, but the net effect on overall results justifies the separation.

[5]See *Games People Play* (New York: Grove Press, 1964).

Competition can be introduced by setting up a series of similar operating units and making regular comparisons of their results—the deadly parallel. Retail outlets, bank branches, national forests, social security offices, and TV stations are only a few of the many activities where this concept can be applied. When units operate at separate locations, conflict among them centers largely on status and allocation of scarce resources, so cooperation is not vital.

These examples indicate that conflict, like fire, can be a useful force when properly directed.

Establish Umpiring System

Virtually all conflicts over allocation of funds and other scarce resources represent the third type of conflict and require bargaining. To prevent such conflicts from escalating we need an agency to settle the matter quickly, an *umpire* who will "call the play" promptly according to a set of known criteria so that we can proceed with the game. Not everyone may like the decision, but the issue ceases to be an open invitation for jockeying and all people concerned can proceed to other more constructive activities. Because the criteria for judging are known, conflicting parties can often anticipate the decisions of the umpire and adjust their behavior accordingly, thus solving the conflict even before it is necessary to bring in the umpire.

The usual umpire is the boss, that is, the executive who directly or through intermediaries supervises the conflicting parties. In small enterprises and within single departments the senior executive normally knows both the local facts and general objectives well enough to make allocations of funds and resources wisely.

For more complex operations, however, the careful evaluation of the alternative uses of resources is a major task in itself. Here we need to designate an individual or committee to make the allocation. Also a procedure specifying the information and opinions supporting a request for resources should be clearly stated. Such a setup is fairly common for capital allocation and for financial budgets, but the mechanisms for resolving other kinds of bargaining conflicts often require special designs.

The use of a committee for allocation purposes creates another organization problem. Who should be on the committee? A committee composed of competing parties merely provides a forum for continuation of the conflict, and its decisions are likely to reflect logrolling rather than company objectives. So if group judgment is desired, a committee of objective members is clearly preferable.

The entire bargaining process can be simplified by formulating policies and other explicit decision guides. As we shall see in Chapter 18, such guides nip some potential conflicts before they arise and expedite the resolution of others that have arisen.

Design Integrated Units

When conflict resolution calls for frequent and varied adjustment in the activities of several people or several units an umpire system becomes slow and unwieldy. In these circumstances, grouping together the interrelated activities may be the best way to localize the conflict. Three examples of this arrangement have already been discussed:

1) In Chapter 2 we noted that compound groups instead of functional groups enable operators to adjust their own efforts so that a completed piece of work is produced. An airplane crew and a surgical team are classic examples. The conflicting pressures are still present, but the evident need for coordination and the face-to-face personal relations submerge the conflict or at least shift it from the third type to the second type.

2) The concept of self-sufficient operating units, which we discussed under "profit decentralization" in Chapter 3, also encourages localized resolution of conflicts. Here again the persons whose work pulls them toward conflicting positions are placed in the same organization unit. Hopefully, the central mission becomes the overriding objective and frequent personal contacts provide the occasions to iron out conflicts. Furthermore, a senior executive is on the spot to umpire when needed.

3) Project teams in matrix organizations, described in Chapter 6, utilize the same principle. The association of specialists needed for the project is temporary, but the hope is that these men will be able to adapt their respective professional orientations to the task at hand. Usually this happens. If conflict arises it typically is not within the project team but between the project team and the service departments and usually concerns the allocation of resources.

Integrated units, such as those just cited, can be very helpful in avoiding destructive conflict. Unfortunately this arrangement is not always practical. The cost of pulling a small piece of a functional unit away from the major department may be high and may result in intense disturbance. Technology may prevent the separation, or the departments may lack people with sufficient competence to exercise the decentralized authority needed in an integrated team. Integrated units are a useful approach but not a panacea.

Separate the Contestants

A design that is the opposite of integrated units may be necessary in some circumstances. If we conclude that the conflicting parties simply cannot work together, then organizational separation *plus* a liaison mechanism can be a useful alternative.

A classic example of this approach is reported in W.F. Whyte's study of restaurant operations. The cooks—the skilled elite in a restaurant—strongly dislike taking orders from waitresses or runners who have less status. The waitresses, under pressure from customers, are persistent in their requests and all too often the conflict about priorities and quality escalates into personal feuds with disastrous results on customer service. In this situation a mechanical system for communicating customer wants to the cooks removes the personal interaction initiated by the waitresses. The status of cooks, the evidence shows, is not hurt by receiving a sequence of inert written requests, and the waitresses learn to wait outside the kitchen until the number of their order is flashed on a screen. The opportunity for cooks and waitresses to get into a hassle is eliminated.

A comparable separation is used by successful plastic companies. In this field, frequent changes in technology and in customer requirements put pressure on relationships between research, production, and marketing. But differences in the attitudes and values of the men in these departments concerning time, costs, quality, personal behavior, and so on are so great that the men have difficulty communicating. Therefore they are kept apart, and an integrating unit serves as liaison. The liaison man can talk the language of each department and so becomes an influential mediator of inherent conflict.

Incidentally a go-between is often used in Eastern cultures. To avoid the embarrassment of an open disagreement or conflict, a third person serves as an intermediary until a mutually acceptable course of action is identified. Not until then do the principals directly discuss the proposition.

Most of us Westerners prefer direct confrontation. But if status differences or other sources of incompatibility are major irritants we may find that separation and use of an intermediary is useful.

Remove Unnecessary Conflict

All the preceding suggestions for dealing with conflict assume that it will continue to be present. However, we do know that some destructive conflict is avoidable. Confusion about the approved organization, for instance, can be cleared up by managerial action. Perhaps formal job definitions have to be interpreted, and the words have to be backed up by action consistent with them. This can be done. More complicated but also desirable is making sure that procedures, information flows, and especially control standards and evaluations match the organization design. Such clear, consistent roles do require some trade-offs, as we noted in Chapter 5, but once understood and accepted they can remove one unnecessary source of conflict.

CONCLUSION: CONFLICT AND GROWTH

In this chapter we have considered conflict that arises in relatively stable situations. Growth or a shift in master strategy further complicates the picture. By upsetting established relationships, by introducing new priorities for allocating resources, and by increasing uncertainty a whole array of latent conflicts flare anew.

The basic sources of conflict, its nature, and its potential usefulness and costs are still the same. But company growth means that a manager must work out a revised set of mechanisms and ground rules. The organizational arrangements that were just discussed probably will have to be adapted to the new situation. Even more demanding of managerial time will be the leading and controlling during the transition. A manager's skill in two-way communication and in gaining acceptance of new objectives will strongly affect the type of conflict that emerges during this unsettled period. We will return to these aspects of the manager's job in Parts Five and Six.

FOR CLASS DISCUSSION

Questions

1) "Conflict is not necessarily a bad thing. In many ways, it is the source of a creative tension which leads an organization to a more balanced, more challenging future." Comment on this statement by the head of a well-known civil rights organization. Could the same statement have been made by a corporation executive?

2) In what ways may decisions on decentralization affect the potential for creating and identifying conflict? Relate your answers to material in Chapters 3 and 6.

3) It is felt that conflict can be reduced among subordinates by writing very detailed and explicit position descriptions and requiring them to follow strict interpretations of these positions. Do you agree? What price is paid by an organization that uses this approach to reducing conflict?

4) Assume that a situation exists where conflict arises from differences in objectives, and where outcomes are relatively certain. How may discussion of higher-level objectives (broader ends for which the conflicting objectives may be seen as means) aid in resolving such conflict?

5) How do we explain the fact that most managers are willing to accept a financial audit of their operations as a necessary fact of business life despite the fact that such an audit implies a lack of complete trust in their honesty? At the same time, these same managers may be greatly upset by a staff audit of, say, a technical recommendation, when the latter audit only implies something less than complete trust in their judgment.

6) How should one deal with conflict that arises when some objectives of the organization are recognized as necessary to realize the purpose of the organization but also seem to be incompatible with the objectives of the larger society to which the organization belongs? Assume that no direct violation of law is involved. Give a specific example of such a potential conflict before discussing possible ways of dealing with it.

7) Discuss the relative merits and drawbacks of using go-betweens to aid in conflict resolution as compared with the direct confrontation approach. Consider criteria that would serve as useful guides in deciding when one approach is more appropriate than the other.

Cases

For cases involving issues covered in this chapter, see especially the following. Particularly relevant questions are listed after each case.

Scott-Davis Corporation (p. 227), 5, 6
Gerald Clark (p. 234), 7
Dodge Skate Company (p. 337), 3
Harrogate Asphalt Products, Ltd.—AR (p. 557), 3, 5, 6
Consolidated Instruments—A (p. 571), 6
Texas-Northern Pipeline Company (p. 665), 4
Consolidated Instruments—B (p. 674), 6

FOR FURTHER READING

Berne, E., *Games People Play.* New York: Grove Press, 1964. *Psychiatric view, in layman's language, of conflict behavior of individuals.*

Dalton, G.W., and P.R. Lawrence, eds., *Organizational Structure and Design.* Homewood, Ill.: Richard D. Irwin, Inc., 1970. *The introduction and readings give convenient summary of Lawrence and Lorsch studies.*

Desi, G.R., "Dealing with Organization Conflict." *Management Review*, October 1965. *Practical suggestions for dealing with conflict.*

Hampton, D.R., C.E. Summer, and R.A. Webber, *Organizational Behavior and the Practice of Management.* Glenview, Ill.: Scott, Foresman & Company, 1968, Chap. 6. *Describes various kinds of conflicts in organizations.*

House, R.J., "Role Conflict and Multiple Authority in Complex Organizations." *California Management Review*, Summer 1970. *Analyzes studies of conflict arising from overlapping authority.*

Sayles, L.R., *Managerial Behavior.* New York: McGraw-Hill Book Company, 1964, Chap. 8. *Impact of external relationships on manager's job.*

Whyte, W.F., *Organizational Behavior.* Homewood, Ill.: The Dorsey Press, 1969, Chap. 8. *Illustrates and analyzes group response to conflict.*

Chapter Ten

Matching Jobs and Individuals

ADJUSTING FOR INDIVIDUAL DIFFERENCES

In the preceding chapters we have considered organization and people *in general*. This approach has been a convenient simplification, but we know that *particular* individuals differ significantly in ability, learning, attitudes, and behavior. Moreover, the same person changes over time as he gains experience and as his personal needs shift.

Each specific job within an organization must be filled by a specific person, and that person may not fit neatly into a job as it has been conceived. If we find ourselves trying to fit a square peg into a round hole, we must fix either the peg or the hole or both.

PREPARING MAN SPECIFICATIONS

The overall process of matching jobs and individuals resolves itself into the following subproblems: What kind of a man do we need for each job? What are the abilities of the men now in the organization? How can we best match men and jobs in the short run? Should we train or replace the man, or should we adjust the job? How can we obtain men to match our long-run needs?

Clarifying Job Specifications

The first step in matching jobs and individuals takes up where organizational analysis left off. If an organization is designed properly, we have a series of *job descriptions*. A job description sets forth objectives, duties, relationships, and results expected of a person in the job. A controller's job description, for instance, might include this duty: "Prepare monthly profit-and-loss statement." A hospital administrator's description might include such diverse statements as, "Coordinate all community relations" and "Promote outpatient services so as to relieve pressure on bed facilities."

In order to match jobs and individuals, job descriptions must frequently be made more explicit and concrete. The declaration that a controller should prepare a monthly profit-and-loss statement, for example, does not tell us whether he personally must compute the state, local, and national taxes, or whether he can delegate this task to an expert. The hospital administrator may be in charge of all community relations, but we do not know whether this duty involves delivering speeches, appearing before medical boards, or conducting health programs for school children.

In addition to specifying duties on the job, we must make explicit the *relationships required* by a position. Does the job require a lot of talking with many different people, or is it independent, calling for only short, terse communications? With what kinds of people must an incumbent deal? Are they sharp traders or indifferent, uneducated operators? Will they interpret "democratic" advice-seeking as a weakness, or have they learned to be independent and to resent orders? Do they want friendship mixed up with their work relationships, or would they prefer to keep their contacts at work matter-of-fact and impersonal?

Perhaps a job description will have to be amplified in other ways, so that it spells out, for instance, how much decentralization is intended, what frequency of innovation is expected, or what managerial techniques are to be used. In clarifying job descriptions, we need not necessarily put our thoughts in writing, but they should be clearly in the minds of everyone involved in the delicate task of matching specific individuals with specific jobs. The central point is to think through the nature of a job completely and carefully.

Translation to Man Specifications

The second major step in matching jobs and individuals is translating the duties in our amplified job description into "man specifications." A statement of duties often does not tell us specifically what to look for in appraising an incumbent or a candidate for a position. Suppose we are seeking a controller for a large company, and one of his duties is to "report any critical developments, as shown by accounting records, to the board of directors." How can we tell whether a man is skilled at this work? If a plant manager must "coordinate sixteen foremen," how do we recognize a man who can do so?

Of course if we are appraising a man already in a position, his past performance, compared with the behavior and results we desire, will be the main evidence used. But when we wish to consider a new man or to change a position, then we want a list of crucial characteristics needed by a person in that job. Clear man specifications are also necessary when we compare a possible replacement with an incumbent. Actually, three quite different ways of stating man specifications are in common use:

1) Certain standardized tasks can be *tested directly*. Candidates for a lifesaving job can be run through a series of tests in a pool; prospective typists can be asked to type a sample passage; often an aspirant can be observed on an actual job for a brief period. Unfortunately, we cannot apply such standards to complicated and unusual tasks (which are typical of many executive jobs), and they tell us little about how a person will fit into a working group. So we need additional specifications, especially for executive positions.

2) Past *work experience and accomplishment* may be useful as an indication of ability to do similar work in the future. For example, a large chemical company specified that its vice-president of finance "should have served as chief financial officer for a medium or large chemical processing company for a period of eight years; should have been responsible for tax accounting in a medium-sized company for at least two years; should have had at least fifty men reporting to him." A water company specified that its plant manager should have demonstrated ability to "reduce costs, develop subordinate personnel, and avoid stoppages and breakdowns."

3) Specifications may include a list of *personality characteristics* that are stated either in the technical jargon of behavioral scientists or in more general terms, such as "friendly temperament" and "apparent energy and ambition." The reason for resorting to personality characteristics is that experience may be an inadequate indication of the qualities needed for a position. A job may be so unusual that few candidates have pertinent experience, and experience may fail to demonstrate clearly all the qualities that might be needed for success in a new situation.

In practice, most statements of man specifications for executive and staff jobs include a combination of desirable experience and personality characteristics stated in lay terms. The use of scientific phrasings of characteristics is limited, expensive, and complex, because such statements require people with formal training to prepare and administer them. Besides, the behavioral sciences have not yet reached a high degree of accuracy, and so a solid record of experience supplemented by intuitive judgments of a person's personality may be just as reliable for predicting managerial ability as the more intricate methods of the social scientists.

Preparing the experience section of a man specification is relatively simple and grows directly from analyzing the duties of a particular job. We fully recognize the value of experience specifications and urge that they be used whenever appropriate. That much of the discussion on the following pages deals with personality characteristics means not that such characteristics are more important than experience, but merely that personality specifications are more difficult to prepare and that the opportunity is greater for managers to improve this aspect of man specifications.

IMPORTANT PERSONALITY CHARACTERISTICS OF MANAGERS

Psychologists, psychiatrists, sociologists, and cultural anthropologists have identified and classified hundreds of human characteristics. None of the classifications is "right" or "wrong." Some are useful in studying individuals in the family, others in dealing with the mentally ill, still others in analyzing small work-groups. In this discussion, we have selected from both science and business practice certain characteristics that, in our opinion, are most *useful to managers* in writing man specifications, in appraising people, and in planning personnel development. For convenience, we shall discuss these under five headings: knowledge, decision-making talent, self-reliance and self-assertion, social sensitivity, and emotional stability.

Knowledge

In matching a man with a job, an inevitable question is, "What does he need to know?" The knowledge an aspirant to an executive position should have can often be specified in terms of specialty, depth, coordination, and management. Every managerial position calls for specialized knowledge of, say, selling methods, water pollution, petroleum economics, or bond discounts. Some jobs require knowledge in depth, whereas others demand only general acquaintance with a field. The president of a company, for instance, may need some general knowledge of public relations, but the public relations manager should have thorough knowledge of sociology, politics, communications media, and kindred subjects.

In addition to identifying the special fields and the amount of depth in each of these fields, we should consider what knowledge a manager will need to tie his activities in with related jobs. Such coordinating knowledge includes an understanding of operations—facts, technology, and problems—as well as the people whose work is related to a particular segment of a company. Managerial knowledge, on the other hand, is a grasp of management principles and techniques that are applicable to a variety of situations. Of course other kinds of knowledge may be necessary for specific decisions, but the divisions mentioned provide a good start in identifying knowledge requirements for a particular position.

Decision-Making Talent

Jobs also differ in the complexity and novelty of problems that must be solved. The president of a large aerospace firm, for instance, needs a different order of decision-making ability from that needed by the head of a motel chain. Let us note several of the personality factors that contribute to decision-making talent.

Analytical ability. This ability enables a person to break a problem into parts, to identify relevant facts, to interpret the meaning of facts, and to project the consequences of a decision. Because so many facts bear on a typical management problem, an executive needs what might be called an intuitive analytical sense in order to select key facts and eliminate the rest.

Conceptual-logical ability. To get meaning from a vast array of facts, we must assemble them under large concepts. For instance, an executive may take a chart that shows declining sales, information from competing companies, and reports on the activities of the company's own salesmen, and pull them all together into one concept—"Poor customer service." Synthesizing facts involves both inventing concepts and using logic to connect the concepts in causal relationships.

Creativity. Really tough problems usually cannot be resolved by known methods. A fresh approach, a new twist, a novel arrangement of recognized parts, or the addition of a different material or system is often necessary to find an acceptable solution. Preferably, an executive should be able to create original ideas himself; at a minimum he needs acumen in spotting good ideas of other people.

Intuitive judgment. This aspect of decision-making ability resembles "hunch." A decision-maker looks at a problem analytically and logically up to a point and then suddenly seems to "know what to do" intuitively. Even though the process is only partially systematic and conscious, a decision does emerge. Intuitive judgment is particularly important when all facts cannot be gathered, when conceptual and logical arguments are fuzzy, or when immediate action is required without waiting for long, rational analysis.

Judgmental courage. Unlike a scientist, an executive must often act without careful research and foolproof logic to back up his decision. Psychologists associate ability to do so with a man's *tolerance of ambiguity* (his capacity to deal with uncertainties without breaking down) and with *frustration tolerance* (his ability to deal continually with difficulties and still push forward in the face of obstacles without becoming discouraged). Courage is needed to go ahead and make decisions when confronted by uncertainties and frustrations.

Open-mindedness. A sixth component of decision-making talent that is particularly important in man specifications is the degree of receptivity to new ideas. Does a person conscientiously listen to others and try to determine the relevance of their ideas in solving current problems?

In summary, we can say that although decision-making talent is difficult to pin down, some of its elements can be identified. An executive who is analytical, logical, creative, open-minded, intuitive, and courageous is more likely to make useful decisions than a man who is weak in these qualities.

Self-reliance and Self-assertion

In satisfying needs and solving problems, people differ in how much they rely on themselves and how much on others. Jobs, too, differ in what they require of a person in the way of taking initiative, asserting his ideas with persistence over those of others, and presenting ideas forcefully and energetically.

Psychologists have studied this trait and describe degrees of self-reliance—or lack of it—in terms of a range between extremes. Some talk of dominant ⟷ submissive characteristics; others speak of independent ⟷ dependent, or of active ⟷ passive behavior. Practical business executives often use the expressions "initiative," "drive," or "self-starting ability" to identify the same quality, at least for the end of the continuum they are most interested in.

This trait is one that is revealed in everyday activities. To check yourself on this quality, observe what you do when you wake up in the small hours of the night because you are cold. Do you try pulling the covers closer around your neck and hope the chilly air will go away? Or do you face the problem, climb out of bed, and get another blanket? Many executive jobs need the type of man who gets another blanket.

Closely allied with a person's self-reliance is his ambition, or his "achievement motivation." Having mastered one problem, most persons set higher goals for themselves and start working toward them. Individuals differ, however, in how much they advance their aspirations. Some aspire to make "big jumps," whereas others are content with modest progress.

Social Sensitivity

Some men react to a managerial problem largely in terms of the feelings of the people involved. Such "other-directed" persons are often contrasted with "inner-directed" individuals, who are predominantly concerned with their own thoughts and matters that seem important to them.

The other-directed person often has a high capacity for *empathy*. This is the ability to project oneself imaginatively into the thoughts, feelings, and probable reactions of another person. We might empathize with an auditor or with a salesman in Alaska without necessarily approving of his feelings and behavior; but because we really sense his reactions, we are likely to be sympathetic with, or at least understanding of, his point of view.

Social sensitivity may be helpful, of course, in almost any job, but it is of critical importance for most selling, staff, and executive positions.

Emotional Stability

Emotional stability indicates a good adjustment to life. People who are emotionally stable tend to act in the following ways: (1) they accept different people, including those they do not like, calmly and objectively; (2) they react to obstacles by calmly increasing their efforts or finding new ways to achieve their desires, rather than by denying that the obstacles exist, becoming overly depressed, lashing out aggressively, or rationalizing their inabilities away; (3) they know when they cannot achieve a given goal, and so they shrug their shoulders and turn their attention to other matters that interest them; (4) they react to moments of success calmly and objectively, without experiencing childlike exhilaration and becoming overly optimistic; (5) they behave simply and naturally without artificiality or straining for effect.

The test of a man's emotional stability comes, of course, when he is subjected to conflict and tension. Some jobs involve more tension than others. For instance, the tension experienced by the sales manager of a newly formed pharmaceutical company is likely to be greater than that felt by the chief accountant in a savings bank. So a higher degree of emotional stability would be needed in the sales job than in the accounting job.

Perceptive Use of Personality Factors

The personality factors we have been talking about will be of greatest usefulness if a custom-made list of specifications is prepared for each job. The following examples suggest how a manager should tailor actual specifications to an actual job.

Frequently we try to provide complementary abilities in an executive and his key subordinates. Thus an executive who has intuition, courage, and a penchant for fast action might want an assistant who has analytical skill and a predisposition for research and fact-finding. If a new supervisor

is to be appointed over a group of subordinates who are highly dependent, he will need considerable self-reliance and self-assertion.

The position of production scheduler presents a different problem.
His work must interlock frequently and closely with that of a wide variety
of people—perhaps a dozen foremen, warehousemen, purchasing agents,
maintenance men, salesmen, and even others. Any man appointed to such
a job should have considerable emotional stability, if he is to remain
problem-centered and get along with everyone.

In contrast, the jobs of research man and development engineer
typically require persons with specialized knowledge and keen decision-
making talent. Social sensitivity and emotional stability, although desirable,
would not be so essential for such jobs as for a production scheduler. The
position of salesman calls for still different abilities, social sensitivity and
self-reliance taking on high relative importance.

Executives need considerable courage and self-assertiveness when a
company is making frequent changes to adapt to new competition or
rapid changes in technology. A high degree of emotional stability is also
desirable, because major changes mean stress on everyone whose job is
affected by new practices.

A final remark about man specifications. All the preceding discussion
has been couched in terms of fixed duties and set working environments
including a stable array of subordinates, associates, and social structure.
This approach implies that a man must adjust to fit a position. But sometimes, of course, adjustment may run in the other direction. A job may be
shaped, at least to some extent, to fit a man. Nevertheless, a manager must
always think closely about both the job—however it may be revised—and
the characteristics of a man who could fill such a job well. Whether we
fit the coat to the cloth, or get cloth for a particular coat, we need to
know the specifications of the coat.

APPRAISING PERSONNEL

Job analysis and man specifications are not ends in themselves. But
they are vital preparations for a third step—appraising specific individuals
to see how well they match the jobs created by an organization design.
Specifications provide standards, and we now have to evaluate people in
terms of those standards.

Appraising Experience

Measuring what a man has done is relatively simple and direct. For
example, if the specifications of a vice-president in charge of production
state that, "He should have ten years of experience as head of manufac-

turing in a medium-sized company," matching his work record to the specification is all that is necessary. The same is true if experience specifications are stated in terms of *results* rather than years; for instance, "He should have increased the sales in his territory significantly during his tenure as branch manager." But when the specified results are intangible —such as having developed good subordinates or maintained goodwill with suppliers—we run into measurement problems. Often, in a complex situation, it is difficult to know how much the man being appraised influenced the outcome, and how much of the outcome was caused by other forces. On such matters it may be desirable to pool the subjective judgments of several individuals.

Appraisal of experience is somewhat analogous to what a statistician does when he predicts the gross national product by fitting a trend line to the experience of the past ten or twenty years. He is not sure of the precise values and weights of all underlying forces, and so, without knowing the forces, he simply projects a line that is the result of all of them. Similarly, we often predict from past achievement a person's likely future success without being sure which personal abilities determined such success. Although such prediction is admittedly risky, it is often the best way to size up a man. In addition, the method has two attractive advantages— it is inexpensive and can be used by executives who lack technical training in psychology.

The reliability of an appraisal based on experience depends partly on the *relevance* of past experience to the new job. If a man is being evaluated in his present position, naturally the pertinent issue is whether current results are satisfactory. But when a man is being considered for transfer or promotion, then we must look to his experience in other jobs. Often, however, a man's background doesn't quite fit the new specifications, and we need to decide whether the fit is close enough. In fact, at this stage past experience is probably used as evidence about personality factors, and our judgment may be improved if we frankly recognize that we have shifted from one kind of criterion to another.

A common safeguard in making promotions in many companies is a policy of testing a man in several different jobs. These assignments are useful *both* for training and for appraisal. If we have any doubt about Pete's ability in, say, getting work out on schedule, we can assign him a task where he can gain experience and where his development can be watched closely.

Personality Appraisal by Executives

A job may be unique or so new that no previous work is like it. If we insist on full experience in this case, we may unduly restrict the number of candidates that can be considered; we may pass over men, both inside and outside the company, who have great ability but are short on experience. For these and related reasons, it is often a desirable practice to make our appraisals of men in terms of their native ability and personality.

Executives rarely are skilled psychologists, yet they must and do appraise personality. For years, managers have depended on their intuitive judgment in selecting men. Because such selection is so crucial, we should obviously adopt any measures that can improve the quality of judgment. Here are three practical rules that are applicable to large and small companies:

1) Make individual judgments on sophisticated grounds. Instead of resorting to vague terms like "personality" or "a good worker," define specifically the qualities needed in a job, as we suggested in our earlier discussion of personality. By doing so, an appraiser can detect his own biases and cultivate objectivity, which will enable him to judge people realistically.

2) Use group judgment. In order to prevent mistakes in perception and judgment, many companies insist that three or four executives appraise a man on each specification.

3) Maintain a file of key incidents in each man's performance. All of us tend to remember and overemphasize recent events. We can make more balanced appraisals if we have before us a systematic record that includes revealing incidents about a man over a period of years. Such a record should denote both strengths and weaknesses, and it may indicate the directions in which a man is developing—perhaps he has overcome earlier knowledge deficiencies, and he may be showing more (or less) self-reliance.

Tests and Clinical Interviews

Personality and aptitude tests provide quite useful information for certain types of well-defined positions, such as salesman, computer programmer, and routine production worker. Clinical interviews by skilled psychologists are also useful when simpler methods do not clearly indicate certain characteristics, for example, emotional stability. As our knowledge about human behavior in work situations increases, the value of such tests should also improve.

Unfortunately, in our present state of knowledge, psychological tests have only limited value as predictors of success in specific jobs. The diversity of job specifications, along with the complexity of individual motivation and behavior, makes the design of a reliable test extremely difficult. Furthermore, only the largest companies can afford the great expense of designing and giving tests that are adapted to specific jobs. Except for preliminary screening of a large number of raw recruits, psychological tests and clinical interviews will probably continue to be used largely as supplements to managerial judgment. For executive posts especially, the chief value of tests lies in corroborating or questioning personal estimates. Assessing people on the basis of experience and observable personality characteristics will endure as an important management duty for a long, long time.

SHORT-RUN MANPOWER PLANNING

Present personnel will seldom match completely the man specifications prepared for existing positions. An appraisal of personnel typically reveals that some people have less ability than desired whereas others have unused talents. What can a manager do to improve this match of human resources and organization needs? Both short-run and long-run adjustments are necessary. In the short run we have to concentrate on present employees and present jobs. The long run gives us much more flexibility, which we shall discuss later.

Fig. 10–1 Short-run manpower planning. Neither subordinates nor available men outside the company are able to effectively fill a gap that has occurred in the company organization. There is a mismatch between the job as now conceived and the qualifications of candidates who are available to fill the position.

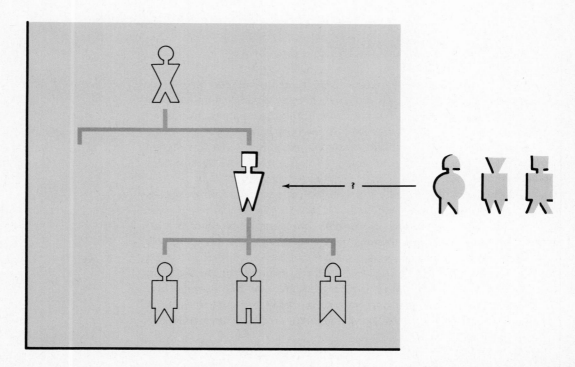

The Weak Incumbent

Probably the most difficult and unpleasant short-run problem arises when a man already in a job fails to measure up. In such cases, we have three alternatives for improving the congruence of man and job:

1) Change the job. This procedure is a matter of "tinkering" with the organization structure. Three examples of such tinkering are withdrawing a duty from one position and assigning it to another position, adjusting the degree of decentralization, and providing additional assistance where a man is weak.

2) Change the incumbent. Perhaps through counseling and training, a man may overcome the gap between his present performance and what the company desires.

3) Remove the incumbent. If a man cannot be expected to become competent in a reasonable time or if the job cannot be changed to fit him, it may be necessary to transfer or dismiss him and fill the position with someone who more nearly fits the man specifications.

Action in such situations is often painful because it upsets expectations and established behavior. But procrastination may undercut the effectiveness of a whole department or company.

Deciding on a Matching Method

In deciding on which of the three methods to follow in matching man and job, we should answer several questions carefully.

How closely does the job interlock with other positions? The degree of interdependence between a given job and other jobs directly affects the ease or difficulty of changing the organization to fit a person. For example, the Montana salesman of a Midwestern paint company may be ineffective without upsetting the work of a lot other people; the company simply has a somewhat reduced volume of business, and we might cut the man's territory or have him concentrate on a limited number of customers, so that his duties match his abilities. But poor performance by a billing clerk may have far-reaching repercussions. Customers may get too many items of one color and not enough of another, the accounts-receivable clerk may spend extra time trying to straighten out invoice difficulties, salesmen may have trouble with customers, inventory records may be snarled up, and so on. To adjust the billing job to fit the capacities of the present clerk would set up a chain reaction that would alter several other positions.

Will training make the man acceptable? Some personal deficiencies can be corrected fairly promptly, whereas others can be altered little, if at all. For instance, product knowledge or specific company knowledge can often be quickly acquired, but conceptual-logical abilities require native capacity plus many years to develop. This distinction is important, because we are always tempted to keep a man in a position because he is familiar with current facts and routines, even when he lacks the imagination and drive to do a really satisfactory job over a period of time.

Is a good replacement available? One small firm had a chief engineer who was cantankerous, uncompromising, and slow. But the company kept the man on because his technical knowledge of the product line was far superior to that of any subordinate or of engineers in other firms who might be attracted by the salary the company could afford to pay. Eventually, it was hoped, one of the younger engineers could take on responsibility for contacts with the sales department, production department, and customers, thereby permitting the current chief to concentrate on developing new products. Pending the event, however, the president took over some of the duties that ideally should have been the chief engineer's, the assistant production superintendent was assigned the task of expediting plans for new products, and a coordinating committee that met weekly was formed. In this instance, the organization was changed to fit a man because a good replacement was unavailable.

In thinking about promotions and transfers, we must be wary of chain reactions. Perhaps our Canadian branch manager is well qualified to replace an ailing vice-president, but how will the present work of the Canadian branch be carried on? Although our analysis starts with matching a particular man and a specific job, we often end up thinking about the best arrangement of the whole structure of jobs and people.

How long will the man remain on the job? If an unsatisfactory incumbent is within a few years of retirement, or can be transferred soon, then temporary and expedient adjustments in work assignments may be warranted.

Is superior performance urgent? The president of a large soap company, which was heavily dependent on advertising to compete with such companies as Lever Brothers and Procter & Gamble, was saddled with "a grand old man" as advertising manager who was not up-to-date on advertising research, use of television, and other new developments in sales promotion. The pressure of competition forced the company to bring in a competent advertising manager in short order, despite what happened to the old man. Urgency, in terms of time and importance, required such a course.

Most cases are not so clear-cut as the preceding example. Just how important is it to have a job filled exactly according to specifications in the organization plan? What obligations does a company owe a man who has given long and perhaps distinguished service? Should any weight be given to long personal friendships? Must the need for change be clearly evident, or can changes be made on the basis of uncertain estimates of the future? Because answers to such questions of value tend to be personal and subjective, an executive should usually check his judgments with two or three associates.

How will removal affect morale? Removing a widely-known, well-liked man may cause other employees to say, "Don't go to work for this company—they fire people at the drop of a hat." Even if everyone else remains in his job, a pervasive feeling of insecurity may be created in a department by removing one popular individual. Negative effects on morale can be lessened by letting it be generally known that the man dismissed was given a fair chance to demonstrate his ability, that he was offered a transfer with dignity to another position, and that he was given a dismissal benefit for early retirement.

Sometimes, on the other hand, morale is improved by removing a man from a position for which he is not qualified. If employees see that a man is kept on a job even though his performance is mediocre, they may develop the general attitude expressed by the question, "Why push yourself?" And many a competent young man has been discouraged to find his advancement blocked by a series of inadequate individuals in key posts. In such situations, removal of a weak man will be a signal that management is prepared to distinguish between good and poor performance, and this will boost morale among the more able employees.

The foregoing list of questions certainly indicates that no universal pat answer can tell a manager whether he should fit his organization to people or find people to fit the organization. Because a manager has an obligation to achieve company objectives, we urge that he give independent and detailed study to the design of an organization that will be well suited to reach these objectives. But in the short run, he must clearly meld this ideal design—as reflected in man specifications—with the abilities of available personnel.

An Unexpected Vacancy

Resignation, death, or unanticipated transfer may create a vacancy with little warning, and the empty position needs to be filled as soon as possible. In such cases, we normally have some choice of people from whom to make the appointment, but rarely will any of the candidates completely match up to the specifications for the vacant position. Again we face the question of how much a job should be modified to fit a man.

Consider the sudden death of your professor or the assassination of a man like Martin Luther King. The issues to be faced in seeking a successor are similar to those already discussed. Must the job be done so that it readily interlocks with other positions? What requirements for the job can be learned after the man is appointed, and what qualities must he already possess? How will the position vacated by the new appointee be filled? Is top performance immediately important, or is gradual learning and adjustment feasible? If duties are to be reassigned, what will be the impact on morale? Does this unanticipated event present an opportunity to correct previous faults in the organization or to move toward a long-range organization plan?

Expedient, compromise steps—such as having one man cover two jobs—may be unavoidable when an unanticipated vacancy first occurs. But these moves should be clearly announced as temporary. Then prompt action should be taken to work out a more satisfactory arrangement. The danger, of course, is that the expedient action may be allowed to continue for so long that later adjustments either will not be made or if they are, people will be upset by what they regard as another reorganization.

The Strong Incumbent

Some people in every organization will have greater, rather than less, ability than their jobs call for. A familiar question arises: Should we adjust the job to fit the man? In fact, such adjustment tends to happen. There are four common situations that call for it. (1) If the work that interlocks with a man's regular duties is poorly performed, a capable man often gives advice and checks on performance that lies beyond his assigned sphere; by doing so, he sets the stage for having duties transferred to him. (2) When a special problem arises, a capable man is often asked to help with its solution. Repeated assignments to special projects may lead to his having additional duties as a regular part of his job. (3) Further, to paraphrase an old rule of science, "Organization abhors a vacuum"; if important activities are not being taken care of at all, the most capable man around often steps into the breach. (4) Finally, quite aside from assigned duties, the "influence" of a strong individual is apt to extend beyond his prescribed area.

Such natural, if unplanned, expansion of a job creates no difficulties until a man becomes so involved in unofficial activities that he neglects his regular duties, or until he gets promoted. The first danger can be avoided if the supervisor insists that the man keep his main assignments in clear perspective. Promotion, however, is likely to cause a more severe jolt. The shock is like that on a football team built around a star backfield man who leaves the game with an injury. Weaknesses formerly covered up suddenly become serious. A wise manager, therefore, should keep abreast of how work is actually getting done and should use his outstanding subordinates for special assignments or in other ways that do not make his organization vulnerable to serious upsets when the exceptional man moves on to another job.

A final observation applies to all shifts of personnel—whether initiated by a manager or by a worker leaving his job. No two men are identical; each has his own strengths and limitations. Consequently, when a man takes a new position, he will—and should—perform the work in ways that are somewhat different from those of his predecessor. At first, he may not be prepared to carry the full load, but later, he will probably take on some duties that were not assigned to his predecessor, whereas other duties may be more fully delegated or initiative for them transferred to staff advisors. Inevitably, then, at least minor adjustments will occur in the assignments of duties and in social structure. During this transition, while people are learning new relationships, a manager has an opportunity to make alterations in organization without treating them as special problems. Such a period is also a natural occasion to introduce features of a long-range organization plan. For all these reasons, *replacing a man should be considered in terms of organization* as well as from a strictly personnel viewpoint.

LONG-RUN MANPOWER PLANNING

Manpower planning for the long run differs from the short-run problems just discussed in several particulars. It is concerned with all jobs and all employees at once, with matching a complete roster of personnel to total job requirements; it is concerned with filling future vacancies rather than existing jobs; and it allows time for long-term learning, especially through rotation of personnel. Three major steps are involved in the process of long-run manpower planning: (1) projecting the organization structure and the manpower that is required to operate that structure, (2) matching the projected manpower requirements with present personnel, and (3) planning for individual development so that men will be qualified when job openings occur.

Projecting Manpower Requirements

The first essential step in long-run manpower planning is to forecast the organization structure that will best meet the future needs of the company. The environment any company operates in is constantly changing—new products are introduced, existing products are modified, production processes alter, automation is introduced, advertising policies shift, and so on. Public service enterprises are changing even more rapidly. The whole job structure should keep pace with such changes. Adding positions because of growth and new activities may be necessary, and existing positions may be assigned quite different duties ten years hence from what they now embrace. We cannot safely assume that a present organization structure will continue to be the best. Instead we must predict as accurately as possible what jobs will be needed three, five, or perhaps ten years hence.

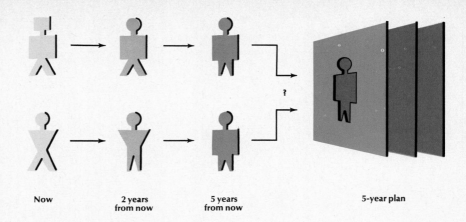

Now	2 years from now	5 years from now	5-year plan

Fig. 10–2 Long-run manpower planning. To prepare for a future anticipated need, the organization guides the development of candidates, so that when the vacancy occurs, one or more individuals will have qualifications that match the requirements of the vacated position.

With this future organization structure as a basis, we can prepare specifications for each position. Naturally, some aspects, such as personality characteristics to complement people in related jobs, cannot be included in these early man specifications, but the main elements of each job should be thought through. The aim is to develop a clear understanding of what our future manpower requirements will be.

Matching People with Requirements

The second step in long-range manpower planning starts with appraising all key personnel, cataloging their characteristics without reference to specifications for a particular position. This *inventory of talent* should include young men who have good potential, even though they are not yet in key spots, as well as present executives, because a good deal of shifting from position to position will undoubtedly occur during the following three to ten years.

With a list of man specifications for jobs and an inventory of talent, we are ready to start matching jobs and individuals. First consideration for any position similar to a present job goes, of course, to the man now filling the existing post. Does he have the abilities we anticipate will be needed in the future? He may be highly qualified; perhaps he needs further development; possibly he should be replaced. We must also consider his age. If he will retire within the period covered by our long-range plan, obviously a replacement should be found. As an analytical device, some companies draw up an organization chart with colored bands around the boxes: red, say, to denote a vacancy within three years, amber for five years, and purple for ten.

From the preceding steps we have spotted the initial set of vacancies—new jobs, jobs where the incumbent should be replaced, and jobs that will be vacated by retirement. Using the man specifications for each of these vacancies, we turn to our inventory of talent to identify the *most probable* candidates to fill the vacancies. Some companies pick a single candidate for each post; others pick two or even three for at least the major positions, because they are not sure which candidate will be best qualified by the time the vacancy opens up.

A second set of probable vacancies is created as soon as men have been identified as candidates for promotion. Do we have men qualified to move into the present positions held by these candidates? Again, a list of most probable candidates can be prepared by comparing man specifications with the inventory of talent. Theoretically, a third set of vacancies could be studied to find replacements for the replacements, and so on. In practice, complete plans for replacements are rarely carried beyond the second set; because so many uncertainties exist, such a projection is unwarranted. Instead, division managers simply recognize that some turnover will undoubtedly occur and they—often with the help of central staff—develop junior men for promotion without knowing just who will probably move where.

The important result of the analysis just described is that management foresees, several years in advance, both its need for men to fulfill certain key vacancies and the most promising men for those jobs.

Planning Individual Development

Few, if any, candidates will have all the essential characteristics for the positions to which they might move. To overcome these deficiencies, management must determine what experience is needed and what personality characteristics should be developed. Some companies call the forms on which this information is listed "gap sheets."

At this stage of planning, any major difficulties in staffing the projected organization will become apparent. It may turn out to be so hard to fill certain positions with satisfactory men that a firm will have to reconsider its organization design, at least at those points. In small firms, whose owners will undoubtedly continue to occupy key posts, adjustments may be necessary because of the owners' particular strengths and limitations. A three-year program, of course, is more likely to require adjustment of organization to personnel than a ten-year program, because there is obviously more opportunity to acquire and develop suitable personnel during the longer period.

Once we have decided on the gaps—the improvement and abilities a man needs to be qualified for promotion—individual development can begin. Management can help in individual development, especially in providing needed experience. For example, a salesman who is a candidate for a job as branch manager might first be placed in a home-office staff position for two years to broaden his perspective and to acquaint him thoroughly with home-office activities and people. Men who need broader perspective can be offered an opportunity to take part in a university executive development program.

Most of the individual development, however, will depend on the man himself. He will have to choose, at several points in his development, a future "career path"—looking toward more intensive specialization, toward overseas assignments, toward managerial tasks, or toward other alternatives. Probably he will not be told exactly what management plans for him, but an ambitious man will guess and will act on any suggestions about where he should try to improve.

Long-run manpower plans, like any other long-range plans, should be revised periodically. With the passage of time, forecasts of operating conditions and concepts of an ideal organization for the company will change. Assessments of people will change too, because some will develop faster and others more slowly than anticipated. In addition, resignations may require a revision of proposals for replacements. Nevertheless, if the whole process of long-range manpower planning successfully serves its purpose, qualified people will be available to fill vacancies as they arise, and short-run organization adjustments made necessary by inadequate personnel will occur less often.

CONCLUSION: ORGANIZING—A CONTINUOUS PROCESS

Matching individuals and jobs, as we have set it forth in this chapter, consists of rather sharply defined steps: clarifying jobs, preparing man specifications, appraising personnel, making short-run adjustments, and planning long-run development of people to fit predicted organization needs. This step-by-step presentation is a fruitful way of thinking about —is a useful approach to—a dynamic problem. But the approach is not intended to provide a blueprint that should remain fixed once it is drawn.

Organizations are never completely finished. Even the best plan soon becomes outdated by changes in work and in personnel. The need for adjustment—often minor, occasionally major—is continual. Instead of being a static machine, an organization is an evolving social system.

In Part One, we were principally concerned with designing a system for getting work done. Clearly, such a plan is essential for efficient operation of any enterprise. But emphasizing work tends to be too mechanistic. An organization will be more effective if we also give attention to the stuff of which it is made—people. So we have tried to point out in Part

Two how we can pay attention to people. We need to conceive of an organization as a social system, not simply as a machine; we need to design jobs that will contribute to the satisfaction of human needs; we need to provide for conflict and conflict resolution; and, by no means least, we need to match individuals and jobs realistically.

The task of a manager, then, is to build a set of roles and relationships of living human beings that is congruent with the structure of work provided by a formal organization.

FOR CLASS DISCUSSION

Questions

1) Often a manager is faced with the following dilemma: He has a job to fill and the man he wants to fill it with lacks many of the specifications for that job. At best, the man will do a barely passable job. The only reason for considering him is that a year or two in that job will add greatly to his breadth, and it is seen as an important step in his career development. What other factors would you consider before assigning the man to the job in question?

2) What should be the role(s) of the following people in preparing a job specification: (1) The immediate supervisor of the man who will fill the job? (2) The superior of the supervisor of the man who will fill the job? (3) The director of personnel or one of his subordinates? How would your answers be affected by the level of the job to be described and whether it was a line or staff position?

3) It has been said, "In our company we tend to promote the man with the best continued performance record in his present job even though he may not have the greatest potential for the new job." What are the advantages and drawbacks of such an approach?

4) What should a company do about public pressure for more blacks and women in key positions?

5) What factors could lead a manager to incorrect judgments when he attempts to make out job and man specifications and then attempts to indicate the personality characteristics required? Assume the position is one of several reporting to him.

6) If personality and aptitude tests provide useful information for selecting people to fill certain well-defined positions, then why not use such tests (given and interpreted by psychologists) again six months or so after selection has been made?

7) A man has been with your company for twenty-seven years; during the last twelve years he has been assistant purchasing agent. With the death of the chief purchasing agent this man is promoted to that job. After several months, it appears that although he was a

good assistant, his former boss had never really developed his initiative, and he is barely adequate in the top purchasing position. As
his supervisor, what action might you take? What factors would
influence your action?

8) As part of long-run manpower planning, what can be done
to enable people to maintain their ability to learn and master new
tasks? Recognize that in the short run it is more efficient to the
organization and less disruptive to the person to have him do what
he does best.

Cases

For cases involving issues covered in this chapter, see especially
the following. Particularly relevant questions are listed after each
case.

Scott-Davis Corporation (p. 227), 7
E.W. Ross, Inc. (p. 468), 3
Consolidated Instruments—A (p. 571), 7
Consolidated Instruments—B (p. 674), 6

FOR FURTHER READING

Finkle, R.B., and W.O. Jones, *Assessing Corporate Talent.* New
York: John Wiley & Sons, Inc., 1970. *Urges businessmen to blend
their own judgment with insights of a psychologist when appraising
personnel.*

Grub, P.D., and N.M. Loeser, eds., *Executive Leadership.* Wayne,
Pa.: MDI Publications, 1969, Chaps. 7, 9, and 10. *Articles from diverse
sources on executive selection, development, and compensation.*

Holden, P.E., C.A. Pederson, and G.E. Germane, *Top Management.* New York: McGraw-Hill Book Company, 1968, Chaps. 11 and
12. *Report on selection and development of executive personnel in
large enterprises; findings are compared with results of similar study
made twenty-five years ago.*

Wickert, F.R., and D.F. McFarland, eds., *Measuring Executive
Effectiveness.* New York: Meredith Publishing Company, 1967. *Review of appraisal practices.*

Wohlking, W., "Attitude Change, Behavior Change." *California
Management Review,* Winter 1970. *Compares structural changes with
sensitivity training as methods for modifying attitudes of managers.*

Case Studies

 SCOTT-DAVIS CORPORATION

Scott-Davis is one of the top five producers of food and household products. Founded more than sixty years ago, it had grown steadily by adding new products and markets until its growth began to slow in the late 1950s. Five years ago, the chairman, Franklyn Davis, son of a co-founder, retired and Norman Hanks stepped down as president. Both Davis and Hanks remain on the twelve-man board of directors but have turned the management of the company over to Martin Richmond. Richmond, who had been group vice-president for household products, became board chairman and chief operating officer. Richmond had served in various sales and marketing posts prior to becoming group vice-president, a post he held for four years.

Under Richmond's leadership, the company has shown considerable growth in the last five years with sales up almost 40 percent in that period and profits up almost 30 percent. Forecasts for this year indicate an increase of 7 percent for sales and of 6 percent for profits over last year's results.

As part of his program to revitalize the company, Richmond sought to "build a fire under the sales organization." When interviewed by a consultant who had been brought in to work with the corporate vice-president of sales, Richmond summed up his ideas about the changes in sales as follows:

Ten years ago, there was a major change in sales organization. Previously, we had one national sales force selling all products. Within a year, we had developed four complete sales organizations. One for each of our major product categories. We also shifted most of our broker business to internal sales. In the next four years we succeeded in building product management teams to parallel our sales organization. Each of the four divisions now has a marketing manager.[1] Reporting to each of these men is (1) a national sales manager who is responsible for field sales and (2) a product group manager who supervises the work of anywhere from three to seven product management teams. Product management teams are charged with developing programs for advertising, promotion, packaging, and pricing which they feel represent sound marketing programs for the one or more specific products to which they are assigned. The division marketing managers also have small market-research and administrative staffs under their control.

This arrangement, while it caused certain problems initially, has worked out very well. Our biggest difficulty, recently, has been to recruit and keep topflight men in the field sales organization. We have always tried to promote from within but in the last five years, we have had increasing difficulty in this respect. I started with this company as a salesman over thirty years ago. During the depression you were glad to find any work and sales was considered a tough but good job. Nowadays the kids coming out of school don't seem interested in sales. Even our company, where sales had always been the center of attention, has had more trouble getting the kind of people we want.

Ever since the end of World War II, our customers, chains, supermarkets, and dry-goods stores have gotten larger and tended to centralize more of their purchasing. This demands that we develop an even more professional field sales organization. Our sales people not only must stock shelves and work with store managers on displays and deals but must understand the structure and politics of buying decisions. In this way we can match our sales efforts with customer buying frameworks and build a proprietary relationship between ourselves and our customers. Thus positions in our sales organization should have infinitely more challenge and respectability than in the old days when we laughingly referred to ourselves as "peddlers."

Richmond went on to describe the company's efforts to attract and develop college and graduate business school students in the following words:

In the last four years, we have hired over two hundred graduates and put them into our sales training program. We overpaid them

[1]See Exhibit 1.

in order to get them and moved them into management positions, even before some were ready, in order to keep them. Yet over this period, we lost almost 80 percent of these kids. We pay as much as our competition and try to move them into challenging jobs as fast as possible. If they move into good district and regional posts, they can earn as much or more, counting commissions and bonuses, as their counterparts in product management posts, but they won't stand still. About one-quarter of the group we "lose" stays with the company in staff or product groups, but we really don't need them there as much as in sales management.

When you talk to them about why they are leaving, you get the same answers: . . . "Too much travel." "I don't like selling." Or things like, "I can't identify with the products." I'm beginning to wonder what kinds of crazy ideas they get in college these days.

The company had expected that this training program would produce more than the normal turnover, but it was unprepared for the magnitude of the difference, which represented a sizable loss of investment. As a result, Richmond requested that the corporate sales vice-president, Richard Stahlings, study the problem and report his findings. As part of this study, Stahlings set up a three-day meeting at a nearby resort and invited all directors of marketing, national sales managers, and regional sales managers. Because Stahlings does not have line authority over these men, he first cleared the meeting with the group vice-presidents and division general managers. They gave him their approval and indicated that they would attend the luncheon and afternoon session of the third day and act as a panel to hear and respond to the issues developed in the first two and one-half days.

Many issues were discussed at this meeting, with high turnover in the sales management training program being but one of five main topics that Stahlings placed on the agenda. The consultant, who attended this meeting as an observer, noted that despite Stahlings' efforts to dig into the causes of the high turnover, there apparently was little real interest or discussion of this topic by the directors of marketing or national sales managers.

One national sales manager commented, "You've got to expect turnover. The kids these days all want the glamour jobs in product management, or they want staff jobs up in the ivory tower, even if they make less money. It's not like the old days when you had to go out and prove yourself in the field before moving up."

A regional sales manager agreed and added, "We start them off with inflated salaries and promise them the moon and then wonder why they are so impatient. If you treat them like prima donnas you have to expect them to act that way."

Each time Stahlings sought to steer the group into a deeper analysis of causes by introducing specific cases, the discussion tended to drift back to generalizations and then to other issues on the agenda.

A second national sales manager, Phil Abel, virtually cut off the discussion by saying:

> *Look, Dick [Stahlings], let's stop worrying about high turnover in the "jet program." Perhaps, if we had a little higher turnover at the district levels, we wouldn't have this problem. We have a certain number of district managers who were promoted as a reward for good sales efforts rather than because they had high management potential. Others did a good job as district managers for a while but may have burned themselves out or become "fat cats." Most of the time, when I suggest we move a man who I feel is in one of these categories, his regional manager leaps to his defense or tells me he hasn't a better man ready. If we get some of this deadwood out of the road, we wouldn't lose so many of our "jets."*

The consultant was surprised at the tense silence that followed this statement. Finally a regional sales manager, Peter Moore, asked, "Are you sure about those 'deadwood' or 'fat-cat' labels, Phil? Have we got people who are not doing a better job than their replacements could do or are we allowing their [district managers] lack of potential for regional management jobs to color our appraisal of how they carry out their district jobs?"

Some discussion followed, and then the meeting broke for cocktails and dinner. The consultant sat with a group of three regional managers, which included Peter Moore. He asked Moore to elaborate on his earlier comment and Moore laughed and said:

> *No thanks! I'm probably already in the doghouse. It's fine for them [national sales managers] to talk about "deadwood" and "fat cats" but I'll be damned if I'm going to sacrifice a lot of good D. M.'s [district managers] just to give their charm school graduates a management position. It takes time for a district or regional manager to get to know the structure and politics of the buying organizations he must deal with. Good sales managers need the charm and drive of the old peddlers plus the instincts of good lobbyists. These are not things you learn in school or practice behind a desk writing reports. Most of these kids lack the background and experience to move as fast as they want whether they realize it or not. Besides, many take a D. M. job merely as a stepping stone either into product management or to another company.*

The others nodded and one changed the subject with a joke about a wrestler who had developed an unbeatable "pretzel hold." The others laughed, and one commented, "If that wrestler ever retires we ought to recruit him for a product management position. He'd fit right in with their ability to tie a guy up in knots."

After dinner, the consultant took a stroll with Peter Moore and tried again to draw him out. After some evasiveness, Moore made the following statement:

> The real problem here is not with regional and district management. It's at division and corporate level. When they created these product management teams, field sales suddenly became a bunch of

Exhibit 1 *Partial Organization Chart (Marketing),*
Scott-Davis Corporation

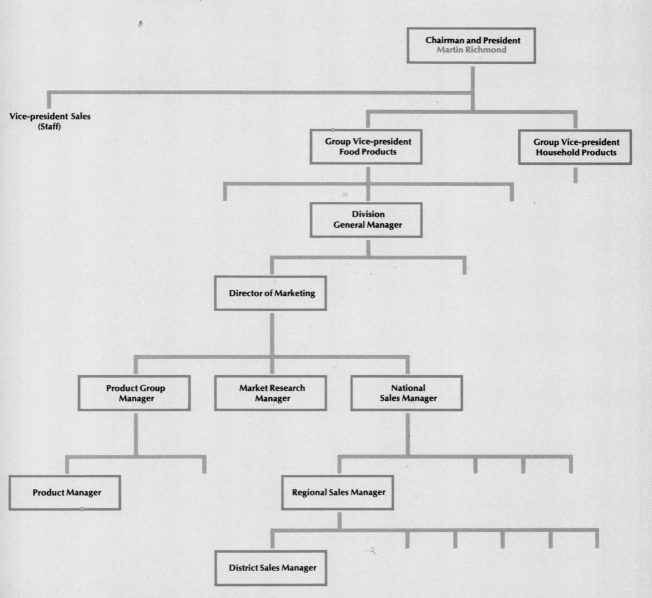

second class citizens. Product management has all the glamour and good money, and like the senator in a book I just read, "unencumbered by responsibility they act with great authority."

We have a lot of good men in district and regional management jobs—and don't be mistaken, when Abel [national sales manager] was sounding off about "deadwood roadblocks," he was talking to us as well as about D. M.'s. Is a man automatically deadwood or a fat cat just because he doesn't want to move up to national sales or higher? There are lots of regional and district managers who have gone as high or higher than they want. I'm not complacent! I have one of the best regions, in terms of results, in the company. I want to make it still better but do I have to aspire to becoming president to convince them I'm not complacent? How can I take good D. M.'s and move them aside or back to smaller districts just because they don't want a regional manager's headache? How can I tell them that they are roadblocks; that merely doing a good job isn't enough; that we need their spot as a stepping stone for some kid who will be gone in less than two years?

Later that evening, at the bar, the consultant found from off-the-record comments that several of the regional sales managers seemed to share Peter Moore's sentiments but most avoided making direct comments on the subject. One regional manager, Gil Green, however, disagreed. "You guys can talk all you want about how unfair it is, but the fact of the matter is we can't afford to keep men in key districts or regions unless they have real upward ambition and potential. Those jobs must be filled by men who use them to train themselves for the top. We can't afford the luxury of filling these positions with people who are content to do a 'good job' there for the next twenty years."

A heated debate between Moore and Green followed. Several regional managers who previously had agreed with Moore either left or remained quiet. At the end, Green chuckled and said, "What are we getting so hot for? I don't know why we're arguing about district and region jobs anyway. Our real problem is to attract and keep more trainees at the lower level, isn't it?"

FOR DISCUSSION AND REPORT-WRITING

Organizing: Structural Design

1) What are the strong points and weak points of the present organization of marketing operations?

2) In what ways might a change in departmentation, within marketing, affect the problems inherent in attracting and holding salesmen with potential for sales management?

3) Discuss the duties, authority, and accountability of a regional sales manager with regard to any potential overlap with the duties, authority, and accountability of a product manager.

Human Factors in Organizing

4) In what ways do the attitudes attributed to college graduates toward sales positions in Scott-Davis reflect a change in "Potency of Needs" as discussed in Chapter 8?

5) To what degree and in what ways do the needs of the "jets" conflict with those of other noncollege salesmen? With the needs of present district or regional sales managers? How would you deal with such conflict?

6) How would you explain the reason for the heated debate between Peter Moore and Gil Green?

7) Why should the new hirees have to spend time as salesmen? Couldn't they be developed into good sales managers without sales experience?

8) *Summary Report Question, Part Two:* How should the management of Scott-Davis deal with district or regional sales managers who are doing a good job but indicate no desire for future advancement? Relate your answer to question 5.

Planning: Elements of Decision-Making

9) Apparently there is more than one "problem" raised by the sales managers' conference. (1) List the major problems you see, stating each as a gap. (2) Attempt to put the problems listed in a means-end relationship. (3) Which of these problems would you tackle first if you were Dick Stahlings?

10) What are the major costs (tangible and intangible) associated with the high turnover and its related problems?

11) At this point what should Stahlings do to refocus the group's attention on the turnover problem?

Planning: Decision-Making in an Enterprise

12) In what ways is this a good or bad problem to present to a group in the hopes of arriving at a better decision through group discussion?

13) How does the trend toward centralization of the buying decisions by large chains affect the way in which sales decisions are made and communicated by Scott-Davis?

14) What changes in Scott-Davis' policies could increase the effectiveness of their college hire program for sales management candidates?

Leading

15) What do you think of Stahlings' use of the law of the situation to deal with the sales turnover problem?

16) In what ways might the company aid national sales managers to increase their potential for leading the new sales management candidates?

17) To what degree was good communication taking place after Phil Abel's comment on the turnover problem? What factors contributed to this status?

Measuring and Controlling

18) In what ways does the current organization of the marketing function contribute to, or detract from, the ease of controlling sales?

19) Given changes in marketing techniques and changing responsibilities for sales management, how should a national sales manager evaluate the performance of his regional sales managers?

Summary Question for Solution of the Case as a Whole

20) What actions should Richmond take with regard to the problems connected with high turnover among college graduates hired for their potential as sales managers?

 GERALD CLARK

Gerald Clark, after less than eighteen months with Tulsa Chemical, has already come to be viewed as an outstanding young man with great potential in the company. Gerry, as he is known in the company, studied chemical engineering as an undergraduate at Tulane where he was graduated first in his class seven years ago. After serving two years in the Army, Gerry enrolled at Cal Tech to begin work on a master's degree but left after his first semester's work. Gerry said:

> I was upset by the turmoil that took place at Cal Tech and at other campuses that term. I don't know what bugged me more, the action of the band of anarchists who were trying to stir up trouble or the reaction of the administration who sought to deal with it. It seemed

to me that the kids had a lot of justifiable gripes about not just the university but about the priorities society seemed to place on the problems of the times. For a few days I joined them in their protests, and they even talked about sit-ins, but it soon became apparent that most of the organizers had absolutely nothing to offer in the way of constructive solutions to the conditions they were so uptight about. Frankly, neither did I and I decided that merely tearing down existing institutions and values was no way of approaching things. The school's administration and the politicians didn't seem to have any answers either and were far more interested in preserving the status quo than really digging in and facing the issues head-on. I figured the best thing for me was to get away from the whole scene for a while and try to think things out. As it turned out, I left just in time because a year later things really got out of hand on campus.

Gerry left the university and spent the next two years in the Peace Corps working for most of that time in Peru.

When I came back, I still didn't have the answers but I figured I had used up about as much time as I could afford to spend on the outside looking in. My work in Peru was as rewarding as anything I had ever done but I felt it was time for me to prepare for a more permanent occupation and perhaps to make some contribution to my own country's problems.

Returning to school in California, he completed work on his master's degree in chemical engineering and went to work for a major oil company. Despite very favorable appraisals, he left the company in less than a year.

I just couldn't live with the conscious irresponsibility towards pollution problems that my superiors took. Not only was the refinery where I worked contributing to both air and water pollution, but the local management actually concealed information which if brought to the attention of top management might have led to changes in company policy. The local managers seemed so concerned about their operating results they covered up things they were doing to air and water in order to look good in terms of production standards.

After leaving this company, Gerry joined Tulsa Chemical, a medium-sized chemical company that has competed successfully on a regional basis with the giants of its industry.[1] Despite national distribution of certain specialty products, 65 percent of Tulsa's sales are in six states— Oklahoma, Texas, Arkansas, Louisiana, Kansas, and Missouri. The company

[1]For additional information on Tulsa Chemical and a related case, see *The Process of Management*, 2nd ed., pp. 161–67. This case may provide an interesting set of issues to consider in conjunction with the Gerald Clark case but in no way is it necessary for full consideration of the issues raised by the Clark case.

has enjoyed considerable growth since the end of World War II at the expense of larger national chemical and petrochemical companies. Tulsa's president, William Lee, attributes this success to Tulsa's ability to offer competitive prices and somewhat faster and more reliable delivery to regional customers.

> It isn't easy [he said] to meet the prices of the giants in our industry, because we enjoy fewer economies of scale. We try to compensate for this with careful supervision of our product lines, selecting products which can be produced competitively on a small scale. In addition, we try to stay on top of the manufacturing, packaging, and shipping technologies to find ways of producing and moving finished products in the most economical way.

The company has three major operating divisions. They are the industrial chemicals division, the plastics division and the agricultural chemicals division. Each division has its own manufacturing, developmental research, and marketing operations, and each is operated as a semiautonomous profit center. The general managers of each division report to the president and are paid a salary plus a bonus based on divisional profits. In good years, their bonuses may amount to 40 or 50 percent of their base salaries.

Under such an organizational arrangement, the president feels he can leave most of the divisional operating decisions to the general managers. To assist him in his review of divisional plans and performance, he has created corporate staff groups in such areas as marketing, production, research, and traffic. With the exception of research, these staff groups are relatively small, having, typically, only one or two technicians assisting each staff vice-president. Lee said:

> I don't want big staff groups who are likely to start masterminding things. Each division has its own staff departments, and they should be able to help their general managers in their functional areas. I've picked my corporate staff people with an eye toward finding the most knowledgeable man around in each functional area. My vice-president of marketing knows as much about the markets for our products and ways of satisfying them as anybody in the company. He and my other staff vice-presidents have three major responsibilities. They are:

> 1. To keep me and my executive committee informed as to the major market and technological factors affecting our business. With this background, we can then develop the broad, longer-range strategies and parameters which we ask the divisions to implement.
> 2. To help the executive committee pass on the one- and five-year plans submitted to us by the divisions and to review their performance. They give us expertise to evaluate the specifics of both where the divisions are headed as well as how they have been doing.

3. Whenever they can be helpful, to assist the division general managers and their divisional staff counterparts to keep on top of fast-moving changes in their fields of specialization.

Clark's first position was in the company's largest plant within the industrial chemicals division.[2] In less than eight months, his contributions came to the attention of the division's general manager, Norman Allison, who gave the following opinion:

Gerry is one of the brightest and most hard-working young men I have ever known. In addition he gets along well with everyone from our hourly production people to the Ph.D.'s in our labs. I pulled Gerry out of the plant and put him on a special project which we have been trying to get off the ground for two years, and in three months he had it in shape to turn it over to the plant. After that, I kept him as my special assistant working as a troubleshooter on critical division problems, and he handled them all like a pro despite his lack of experience. Gerry has the sense and the talent to know when he doesn't have the answers and where and how to go about getting them. With this talent it was no wonder that Harry Young stole him from me.

Harry Young, vice-president of production staff, is viewed throughout the company as the most knowledgeable man in the production and processing area. As a result of this ability William Lee appointed him staff vice-president four years ago. When one of his two subordinates retired, Harry asked Allison if he could have Clark join him for a year or two in order to use his talents and broaden Clark's experience in the work of Tulsa's other two divisions.

"I hated to lose Gerry," said Allison, "but it was too good an opportunity for him for me to stand in the way. That young man will be running one of our divisions in the next ten years if we are lucky enough to keep him."

Gerry felt mixed emotions about accepting the new position:

It was a great chance for me but it posed a real moral problem. For the last few months I have tried unsuccessfully to get George Phillips [plant manager of the division's largest plant] to include money in this year's plan for a pollution-control pilot program. Although Tulsa is far better in its concern for pollution, George is still dumping a great deal of toxic waste into the Arkansas River. Within five years, if it keeps up, either the state or federal government is going to force us to cut the toxicity before dumping and then it will be an expensive crash program.

When I failed to persuade George that we should put $50,000 to $75,000 into a pilot program next year, I took my case to Mr. Allison.

[2]See Exhibit 1.

*He, George, and I have met on several occasions to talk about it,
but Mr. Allison's decision was to wait at least another year or two.
If I had stayed on in the division I might have gotten him to change
his mind without making a big issue of it. As one of Mr. Young's
staff, however, I would have the obligation to call it to his and
perhaps Mr. Lee's attention, if Mr. Allison refused to change his
mind. Somehow I hated to take the new job knowing that one of
my first acts, in my role of reviewing his plan, would be to call attention to a question which no one outside the division, including
Mr. Young, was aware of.*

Despite his misgivings, Gerry took the job and within a few months
was in fact assigned the task of reviewing the industrial chemical division's
production plan. According to past practice, this review was designed to
raise any questions which Young might have so that he could discuss them
with Allison prior to Allison's presentation of the total plan to William
Lee and his advisory committee. The prior review by staff and subsequent
discussions between a staff and division officer often lead to the resolution of controversial issues without taking the time and attention of the
president and other executive committee members.

In his new role as staff reviewer, Clark again attempted to convince
Allison of the importance of beginning the pollution-control program
immediately—but to no avail.

Allison gave his viewpoint as follows:

*Gerry makes a number of good points, but I'm afraid he puts too
much weight on the pollution question. Heck, what we dump is a
mere drop in the bucket compared to what other companies are
doing to that river. Sooner or later we will have to do something
but it may be five or ten years before there is enough pressure put
on the big polluters to get them to take action. In the meantime, our
pilot program will have no significant impact on the river, and it
could add several hundred thousand dollars to our operating expenses over the next three to five years. It's not just the direct
cost of the pilot program but the indirect costs as well. No one really
knows how much it will cost to get and install good devices to
handle volume flows and these untested devices could upset our
whole production process for a week or more if they break down.*

*Gerry is sure that the pilot program will minimize these more
costly problems but he hasn't convinced George Phillips or me.
Maybe he is right, but I can't see spending the money now in any
event.*

Clark, after failing to convince Allison, brought the matter to Harry
Young's attention. Young carefully reviewed Clark's data and came to the
conclusion that the pilot program recommended could, for less than
$75,000, minimize the costs of a full-scale program one to two years
later.

Moreover [said Young], knowing how Bill Lee feels about the growing pollution problem, if I made a big enough fuss I think I could get him to put some pressure on Norm. The trouble is, this is not a good time for me to seek that pressure. I am already involved in a big dispute with Frank Sommers [general manager of the plastics division] and I don't think I can get it settled without bringing it up at the executive committee meeting and trying to get Lee to overrule Frank. The dispute with Plastics involves a lot more money and could have a much greater impact on the company than this pollution question.

In four years, I have only had to go to Lee once with a major objection to a division plan and I'm not about to bring two of them up in the same review conference unless I have to.

Exhibit 1 *Partial Organization Chart, Tulsa Chemical Corporation*

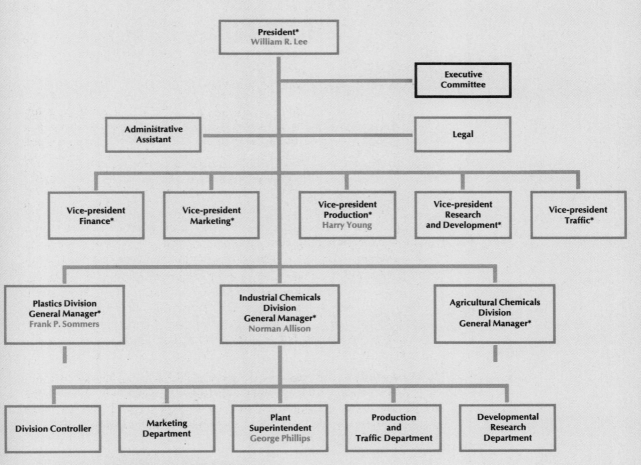

*Member of executive committee. Chairman is William R. Lee.

Young met with Allison, Phillips, and Clark and argued forcefully in favor of Gerry's recommendation but could not change Allison's position. As they left the meeting, Young said to Clark, "I'm sorry, Gerry. I did all I could but as you could see they won't go along with us. I think you are right but it isn't important enough for us to make a big issue out of when Norm presents his plan. I want you to back off and we will try again next year."

Gerry's words reflect his disappointment:

> I didn't say anything to Mr. Young at the time but the more I think about it, the more it bugs me. It's not just the pilot program but the principle of the thing that upsets me. It seems everyone is waiting for someone else to take action on problems that won't wait much longer to be faced. They can always find a dozen reasons why they should not make a big issue out of something which is already big. I just don't know what I ought to do. Obviously, you must compromise on many things. Life is full of seemingly unavoidable compromises. But when do you draw the line?

FOR DISCUSSION AND REPORT-WRITING

Organizing: Structural Design

1) How could a company like Tulsa justify to its stockholders the loss of profits involved in Clark's plan? What is the social responsibility of Tulsa in this case?

2) What are the strong points of the present organization structure? What are its weaknesses? How might the weaknesses be reduced without changing the basic structural design?

3) How well does Lee's definition of the role of staff fit with the existing pattern of decentralization? Would you change, add to, or reduce the three tasks defined for corporate staff?

4) Who is in the best position to estimate the costs of the pollution control project?

Human Factors in Organizing

5) How may Young's decision not to press Allison on this project affect the informal organization and the customs and habits that make up its framework?

6) How would you describe and perhaps rank the potency of Clark's needs and his potential for realizing them on the job? Might he satisfy some of his needs off the job and thereby reduce the pressure to realize them on the job?

7) What further steps might be taken to resolve the conflict without bringing it to Lee's attention?

8) Does it appear that Tulsa has done a good job of matching jobs and individuals in Clark's case?

9) *Summary Report Question, Part Two:* If you found yourself in Gerry Clark's position, what action would you take? Prepare a report that reflects his alternatives and discuss your reasons for selecting the approach you recommend.

Planning: Elements of Decision-Making

10) Develop a means-end chain that puts Clark's "basic problem" in the context of company goals. Put his "basic problem" in a means-end chain that reflects his personal goals.

11) In what ways would Allison's *diagnosis* (not decision) differ from Clark's?

12) How might the concept of subjective probabilities prove useful in this case? Who should develop the probabilistic forecasts?

Planning: Decision-Making in an Enterprise

13) Describe what you see as the process by which basic plans and strategies of Tulsa's three divisions are developed and approved. What are the strengths and weaknesses of this process?

14) In what ways does the present staff-line relationship effectively balance short- and long-range objectives? How might it be improved?

Leading

15) In what ways has Young's decision not to press Allison on this issue affected his (Young's) ability to develop voluntary cooperation within the several divisions?

16) If Clark decides to take the issue over Young's head to Lee, what effect will this have on his future effectiveness in developing good two-way communication with division personnel? With Young?

17) If Clark, over Young's objections, takes the issue to Lee, what action should Young take?

Measuring and Controlling

18) How should Lee measure and control the contribution made by his divisions to longer-run goals? Consider the pollution question as but one case in point. In broader terms, how should he deal with this aspect of evaluation?

19) Under the company's present structure, what role should corporate staff play in evaluating division results?

*Summary Questions for Solution
of the Case as a Whole*

20) If all the issues surrounding the Clark proposal came to your attention, what action would you take if you were in his position? Why?

21) If all the issues came to Lee's attention what action would you recommend he take? Assume Lee subsequently was required to justify this action to his stockholders and a state congressional hearing on water pollution. Prepare statements for Lee's signature for both groups.

PART THREE

Planning: Elements of Decision-Making

Planning is a basic management task, one that has a major place in our overall division of management functions along with organizing, leading, and controlling. In every company, men in managerial positions must decide on a host of issues: what services to provide, what price to charge, how to deal with pressure groups, whom to employ, when to collaborate with the government, what practices to follow on salaries, production schedules, accounting procedures, and many other matters. Planning is not a manager's only task, but it certainly is an essential one. Without planning, an enterprise would soon disintegrate; the pattern of its actions would be as random as that made by leaves scampering before an autumn wind, and its employees would be as confused as ants in an upturned anthill.

A manager can improve his ability to plan—to make decisions—by asking himself two questions about the process: (1) What are the elements, or phases, of making a plan? (2) How are these phases actually carried out in an organization? We shall explore the first of these questions in the next four chapters. Then in Part Four we shall consider planning and decision-making in an organization.

In Part Three, then, our aim is to analyze decision-making as though a single person undertook the whole process alone; at least we set aside for the moment the complications that arise when the process is divided up among many different people. Such a concentration on the elements of decision-making has several advantages. Many plans are, in fact, made largely by a single individual, and if we can discover ways to improve our own decision-making skills, we will be able to make such decisions better. Furthermore, by recognizing all the phases that contribute to wise decisions, we can think more clearly about how a particular organization setup helps or hinders getting good decisions made. Besides, with the elements of decision-making in mind, we can use the planning instruments described in Part Four—objectives, policies, procedures, programs—with discretion and effectiveness.

Each of these basic phases of decision-making is discussed in a separate chapter.

Chapter 11—Diagnosis: A Prerequisite for Sound Decisions. The first, perhaps the most difficult, and often an overlooked phase in decision-making is a careful, thorough diagnosis of the problem or opportunity to be dealt with.

Chapter 12—The Creative Element in Decision-Making. Here we are concerned with finding good alternative solutions to the problems identified by diagnosis. Because no company can be a leader by copying what someone else is already doing, we give considerable attention to how new ideas are born and to what an individual can do to make maximum use of whatever creative ability he possesses.

Chapter 13—Comparing Courses of Action. To choose among alternative courses of action, we must predict for each alternative what would happen if we followed that course. We must then compare the different results. Because a projection and comparison of alternatives can become complex, this chapter includes suggestions for simplification.

Chapter 14—Making the Choice. Finally we shall discuss how to deal with differences in values, and in degrees of uncertainty, when making a firm decision to follow one of the alternatives.

Throughout our discussion of planning and decision-making, we shall often have to skate on thin ice when we deal with the diverse, mysterious workings of the human mind. In Part Two we observed that human responses are based on emotion fully as much as on reason, and that social pressures and experience play a large part in a person's thinking. Although we identified some of the personality characteristics needed for decision-making in Chapter 10, it may be a century before we have reliable scientific knowledge of precisely what happens in a man's mind when he makes a decision. In the meantime, managers must manage. Just as a physician must treat cancer to the best of his present ability without waiting for complete scientific understanding, so too should an administrator take advantage of what is now known about planning. Fortunately, although our knowledge is incomplete, enough is known to make an examination of the planning process very fruitful.

Chapter Eleven

Diagnosis: A Prerequisite

for Sound Decisions

RATIONAL DECISION-MAKING

Wise decisions are crucial to managerial success, but because we make so many small decisions in our lives we often fail to recognize what is involved. This chapter is the first of four that analyze this vital decision-making process.

This careful analysis of the decision-making process is important for three major reasons. The first and most obvious is the desire to improve the quality of crucial decisions by offering guidance to decision-makers. Second, by carefully examining key concepts related to each of the four major elements of individual decision-making, we shall facilitate subsequent consideration in Part Four of how these elements may be carried out separately by different people and ultimately synthesized into a sound company decision.

Finally, because of the great amount of specialized knowledge required for some decision-making, a manager often lacks the time or technical background to assess fully the basis of a decision recommended by his subordinates. In such cases, many managers may have to make indirect assessments based on a review of the *process* by which the recommended decision was developed. They must infer the likely quality of the recommended decision from the quality of the process, and so a conscious awareness of key elements of this process is a necessary first step.

245

Use of Rational Process

Many business decisions, like many personal decisions, are made on the basis of intuition or custom. However, because the business and social setting is changing at an accelerating pace and problems are becoming more complex, modern managers can place less reliance on past experience and hunch. Subjective judgments and personal values will continue to play a major role in most tough decisions, but now intuition is surrounded, enmeshed, and submerged by rational planning.

Fundamentally, rational decision-making is quite simple. In actual practice, however, some part of the process is all too often disregarded or poorly executed. The four essential phases are: (1) diagnosing the problem, (2) finding the most promising alternative solutions, (3) analyzing and comparing these alternatives, and (4) selecting the best alternative as a plan of action. Before we describe these phases in detail, let us note their general applicability.

Problem-solving in medicine. A doctor follows all four parts of this procedure in examining a patient to find out what is wrong and in prescribing a course of action. In practice the diagnosis may not be easy, because the same symptoms can result from a number of quite different causes. Special tests may be necessary to identify the underlying cause. Clearly, if the wrong cause is assumed—say, appendicitis instead of gallstones—treatment will be ineffective, even disastrous. Many of the recent advances in medicine deal with better diagnosis.

Having made a sound diagnosis, the doctor then considers possible remedies—such as changes in diet, medication, or surgery. Some remedies will be standard practice, but if the patient has limitations—a weak heart or allergies, for instance—other possible treatments must be considered. Next the doctor must weigh the advantages and disadvantages of each possible cure in a specific case. How long will the patient be incapacitated? Are the necessary resources—professional aid, equipment, money—available? Finally the doctor uses his judgment in selecting what he believes is the best plan, or "prescription," for each particular case. He considers the probability of success and the risk of complications. He may decide to try a simple remedy before taking more drastic measures. Perhaps he considers it wise to do nothing at present, or he may call for an ambulance to rush his patient to a hospital. Every responsible doctor goes through these steps: diagnosis, review of possible remedies, analysis of probable results, and prescription.

Solving social problems. The decision-making process becomes less clear when we tackle social problems. Objectives, alternatives, and results are all likely to be subject to debate. Take the ownership of guns by private citizens as an example. From one angle, just as the medical doctor saves lives, so too would homicides be reduced if fewer people had guns.

But possible homicide is not the only consideration. Guns are allowed for personal protection and for sport, and so the intervening objective shifts to regulation of ownership and use. The alternatives here are numerous, and nobody can be sure just how any one plan will work out in practice. Nevertheless, as we start to wrestle with a problem our thinking becomes clearer and data can be marshaled more effectively when we resort to rational analysis. What are the objectives? Have we thought of all the good alternatives? What will be the costs, side effects, and contribution to the objectives of each alternative? Which alternative looks best in terms of the values we attach to costs, side effects, and the original objective?

In practice, getting agreement on the diagnosis, defining alternatives, obtaining reliable information on the existing situation, from diverse specialists, forecasting what will happen especially in an uncertain environment, and winning enough support to justify positive action are by no means simple. Conflicting interest groups will deliberately muddy the waters. But these difficulties make a firm grasp of the rational process even more valuable. Experience indicates that only a small percentage of people have the understanding and self-discipline necessary to apply rational decision-making to messy "people" problems.

Basic Phases of Decision-Making

These examples provide a background for a more explicit statement of the four phases of rational decision-making:

1) *Making a diagnosis*. The need for making a decision may arise from diverse sources. Forecasts may suggest opportunities or dangers. Control reports may signal a mismatch of results with plans. Another enterprise may be having unusual success or trouble. At times these stimuli to diagnosis may highlight a specific challenge but often they prompt only vague feelings of uneasiness. Something seems wrong and in need of correction, or some opportunity may be missed if a wise decision is not made. The first aim of a sound diagnosis is to sharpen this feeling, to pinpoint the *gap* between what we want to happen and what is likely to occur if no action is taken. Second, a sound diagnosis should help identify the *cause* of the gap and any obstacles that stand in the way of realizing desired goals. Finally, a sound diagnosis should put the specific problem we are examining in the *context* of more general, higher level goals of the organization. By so doing, we may identify any limits on time, investment, or personnel that must be observed in our subsequent search for ways of dealing with the immediate problem.

2) *Finding alternative solutions*. Next, the executive is concerned with what he *might* do to remove or avoid the basic obstacles identified by his diagnosis. Imagination and originality are needed, because neither market research nor an electronic computer can support a plan until it has been conceived. Alternatives will range from doing nothing, through finding a way around the difficulty or removing it, to modifying the objectives. Unless a good answer nests among the possibilities considered, the final decision is doomed to failure.

3) *Analyzing and comparing alternatives.* To choose among the probable plans, the executive should recognize primary differences, or "crucial factors." All pertinent data—opinions as well as accepted facts—that he can track down in the time available should be assembled and related to these crucial factors. Such an analysis will result not only in a list of pros and cons for each alternative, but also in some evidence of the relative importance of particular advantages and disadvantages.

4) *Selecting the plan to follow.* Only occasionally will the superiority of one alternative be so clear that analysis alone provides the final answer. A manager must balance several different factors (such as morale, cost, consumer acceptance, public reaction), which, in theory, have profit (or "utility") as their common denominator, but in practice may be very difficult to translate into profit implications. Differences in probabilities of failure must be weighed, and the chances of partial success taken into account. In most business situations, time and cost will prevent an exhaustive analysis, and an executive will have to determine when decisiveness is worth more than increased accuracy. By blending such considerations with the results of objective analysis, a manager must form an authoritative decision on action to be taken.

All guides to managerial conduct must be used with discretion; the human animal behaves so variously that we have to adjust even the best generalizations to fit particular circumstances. The four phases of rational decision-making are no exception. When we deal with particular problems, for instance, the phases will vary in difficulty. Sometimes a problem is evident: When your car has a flat tire and your objective is to *fix* the tire and not *prevent* future flats, you do not need to spend much time in diagnosis. Or once in a long while, someone will hatch up such a good solution to a baffling problem that analysis is unnecessary and the final selection is obvious.

But more importantly, few problems yield to a neat step-by-step procedure. New alternatives may pop up at any time; a problem often needs to be redefined as the analysis proceeds and values are formulated; fact-gathering and judgment permeate the entire process. Therefore, we are considering a mental *framework* rather than a procedure. In a general way, we do work through the phases in the sequence listed, but our minds are apt to jump from one phase to another in a continuing effort to refine our previous thinking. We bring clear reasoning and focused attention out of such mental rambling only when we have a framework, such as the four phases just outlined, that aids us in relating facts and thoughts in a rational pattern.

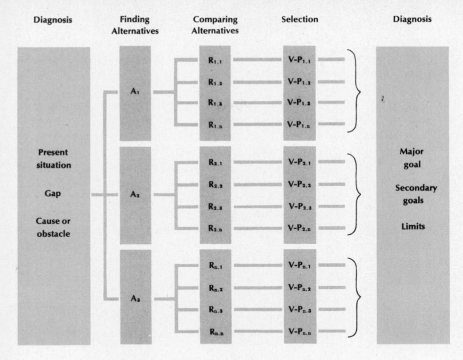

Diagnosis	Finding Alternatives	Comparing Alternatives	Selection	Diagnosis

Fig. 11–1 Elements in decision-making. Key to symbols:
A = alternatives; R = result of following an alternative;
V = value attached to projected result, the values arising from
the goals; P = probability of result occurring. Any diagnosis
should clarify the items shown in the colored boxes.

CRUCIAL ROLE OF DIAGNOSIS

Accurate diagnosis is the essential first phase of sound decision-making. Unless the diagnosis is correct, subsequent planning will be misdirected and wasteful.

Unfortunately, many businessmen pass over diagnosis too lightly. Love of quick action—and perhaps an illusion of omniscience—makes some administrators impatient with detailed planning. Even if they admit a need for planning, they are confident that they know what their problems are. They are so anxious to get moving that they neglect to take time to check the direction in which they are heading. One impetuous president, for example, pushed through extensive plans for sales promotion, brushing aside any question about whether the effort was being directed to the right customers. Later, careful diagnosis showed that he was working with a declining segment of the market; even if the sales promotion had been an outstanding success, the recovery of company sales would have been only temporary. The president might just as well have made the diagnosis earlier and avoided the wasted sales effort.

Sound diagnosis should cover three basic elements, which are high-lighted in the following questions:

1) Just what *gaps* exist between the results we desire and the existing or predicted state of affairs?

2) What are the direct, root *cause* and the intermediate causes of the gaps?

3) Does the broader *context* of the problem place limits within which we must find a satisfactory solution?

We shall first examine the way these three elements can be used in diagnosing a *recognized need*, and then at the end of the chapter we shall consider diagnosing total situations in which attention is not yet focused on a single recognized need.

STATING THE PROBLEM OR OPPORTUNITY
IN TERMS OF A GAP

When a doctor makes a diagnosis he has as a goal a normal, healthy person and he also has a fairly clear concept of what a healthy person is. With this model as the "desired" result, he looks for disparities in the patient's actual state of health or factors which indicate that his future health will fall short of normal.

A manager unfortunately cannot rely on a commonly accepted norm such as a healthy person. The activities he deals with are so diverse that no single set of symptoms can guide him in locating what is wrong. Instead, a manager's diagnosis starts with a "felt difficulty." He may *feel* that something is wrong, or he may vaguely sense that "things could be better." He may compare other companies' accomplishments with those of his own firm, or he may simply desire continuing growth and ever lower costs. Whatever the source, diagnosis starts with sensing an opportunity for improvement. To go further, however, he must sharpen this intuitive feeling as best as he can into more explicit statements of desired and actual or predicted results, so that the felt difficulty or opportunity can be viewed more *precisely* in terms of a gap that must be closed.

If this is easily done, if there is a clear-cut distinction between, say, quality standards and actual or anticipated quality, he can promptly move on to the next element of diagnosis. But many gaps are not so clearly defined. A manager may have only a vague feeling, which he might express as, "Our New England branch should do a lot better," or "I believe Simpson has good potential but is not living up to it." He needs to sharpen up these statements before he can proceed with his diagnosis. He might

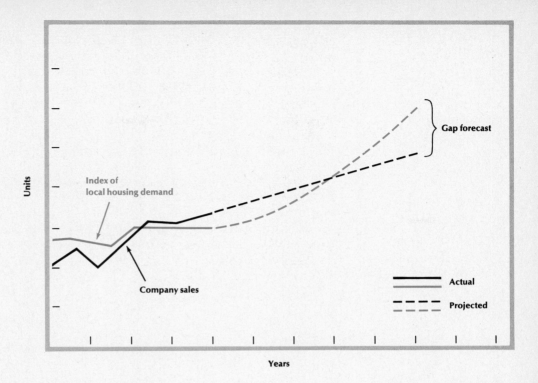

Units

Index of
local housing demand

Company sales

Actual

Projected

Gap forecast

Years

Fig. 11–2 A gap may exist
between forecasts of future
conditions and present company plans, as shown in this
five-year projection of a
mobile housing contractor.

restate his general dissatisfaction with the New England branch thus: "Based on performance of our other branches, and adjusting for differences among branches, New England should get 20 percent more sales without any increase in expenses." This declaration makes the problem a lot clearer. With respect to Simpson it would be more meaningful to say, "Based on aptitude and motivation, Simpson appears to have the capacity to be a regional sales manager in three to five years" (desired). "His failure to keep turnover of salesmen to desired levels and his inability to develop new business has produced less than expected results" (actual).

Likewise, a particular event that provokes our attention may not be the problem. Our company's financial statement, for instance, may show a loss for last month. In common speech we might express the problem this way: "What are we going to do about the loss?" By itself, however, this is an incomplete statement of the problem. For management to proceed, this general statement must be refined by indicating what returns are expected and the premises on which the "desired" financial picture is based.

Once a problem or opportunity is identified in terms of a gap between desired and actual or predicted results, many decision-makers move immediately to seeking alternative means of closing this gap. We should avoid this temptation, though, because seeking alternatives at this stage is premature for two reasons:

251

1) Although the gap between desired and actual or predicted results has been brought into focus, for many situations the root cause of the gap is at this point likely to be at best vague and at worst incorrectly identified. Until that cause has been defined, alternatives designed to close it are likely to fail or to provide only costly relief of symptoms.

2) Unless the gap is defined in terms of very high-level goals, the objective that we have specified is likely to be merely a *means* of accomplishing one or more higher-level *ends* or goals. Before alternatives to closing the gap are sought, then, these higher-level goals should be identified. This exploration of the broader situation often uncovers limits on such matters as time, investment, or personnel—limits which must be observed if the solution to the problem at hand is to be consistent with the higher-level goals of the organization. Also if the stated gap proves tough to overcome, we may want to consider alternative ways of reaching the higher goal.

FINDING THE ROOT CAUSE

Search for Key Obstacle

As the decision-maker seeks alternatives for closing the gap, he usually does so with some notion in mind of the cause of the gap. All too often, however, this intuitive and at times subconscious assumption about causality may turn out to be only symptomatic of the underlying cause or perhaps not even related to the real cause.

For example, in the early days of frozen foods, manufacturers had a difficult time reaching what they believed to be desirable sales levels. Initially, attempts to close this gap between desired and actual sales were made through consumer advertising. Lack of consumer interest in the product seemed a logical cause of low sales. Further, the manufacturers assumed that the source of the indifference was a lack of understanding about the properties and advantages of frozen food. Only after experiencing limited success with advertising designed to educate the consumer did they undertake a more careful quest for the cause of the poor reception of the product.

Studies revealed that, although consumer interest in frozen foods was indeed limited, the major cause of low sales was the reluctance of retailers to stock an adequate supply. The retailers, understandably enough, wished to avoid investing several hundred dollars in refrigerated showcases. Had the manufacturers continued to bombard the consumer, they might have used customer demand to force the retailers to make the investment. This course, however, would have been an expensive way of getting at the now-clearly-seen obstacle of retailers' reluctance to invest in showcases. But having located the basic impediment, the manufacturers could now devise methods for loaning or leasing showcases to hesitant dealers.

At times, then, in searching for a cause or an obstacle, we may have to seek the cause of the apparent cause, to push deeper and deeper until the *root* cause has been identified. Kepner-Tregoe Associates, management consultants who have focused on diagnosis, suggest two key guides for the identification of causes.[1]

First, they stress that in trying to determine why some goal is frustrated, a decision-maker should concentrate on the differences between situations where the desired goal *is* realized and those where *it is not*. For instance, as a simple illustration of the basic concept consider the problem faced by a sales manager who is trying to unearth the cause of late field reports from his salesmen. If some of the salesmen get them in on time while others do not, the explanation may be related to the differences in the men or their work environment. By elaborating on these differences, by spelling them out in terms of *what, where*, and *when*, the manager could formulate a number of hypothetical causes. If he found, for example, that most of the late reports occurred repeatedly in certain district offices, an elaboration on the differences among district offices might lead to the cause. However, if he discovered that all districts had this problem, then he would have to look into differences relating to some other factor to find out why the failure happens when and where it does.

The second Kepner-Tregoe principle stresses the power of *negative* thinking in cause identification. Once a decision-maker has developed hypothetical causes, he should avoid seeking further evidence to support them, endeavoring instead to disprove them or "shoot them down." He should test them against all of the distinctions between where and when the problem exists and where it doesn't, and so on. The logic behind this negative approach is that, whereas a hundred reasons supporting a hypothetical cause as the real culprit may be found, this positive support can never *prove* the suspected cause guilty; however, if only *one* fact demonstrates that a suspected cause *could not* be the real one, the suspect can be eliminated.

Thus if hypothetical causes are tested against all the distinctions of what, when, and where, most proposals can be eliminated. By this process of elimination, the few candidates that remain, and thus *could* account for the differences, can be subjected to more detailed examination and testing.

Moving from Surface to Root Causes

Often in seeking the root cause of a problem we have to move through several levels of causality. Even if the root cause may be found directly, it is well to identify intermediate levels of causality also. In the process, if the root cause cannot be eliminated, symptomatic relief may

[1]C.H. Kepner and B.B. Tregoe, *The Rational Manager* (New York: McGraw-Hill, 1965), Chaps. 5–9. Although dealing with current business problems, the authors make explicit use of canons of logic expounded by John Stuart Mill over a century ago.

be found by dealing with the more direct intermediate cause. For example, consider a situation described by a colleague of ours. A friend of his, who was in his late 60s, complained that late in the day he suffered blurred vision and then headaches and dizzy spells. An optometrist told him that his headaches and dizzy spells stemmed from moderate deterioration of the eyes, which in turn was the result of old age. Stopping the diagnosis here, the optometrist prescribed bifocal eyeglasses to compensate for the change in vision.

As a result of his difficulty in getting used to wearing his new bifocals, the gentleman tripped on a step and bruised his hip. To be certain that it was just a bruise, he visited a doctor and in the course of his examination mentioned his blurred vision and headaches. The doctor then checked his blood pressure, which proved to be too high, and cited this as the primary cause of the vision and headache problems. To put the doctor's diagnosis in our terms, he had compared the patient's actual condition to a desired state of health and saw the announced symptoms as the cause of the difference. He, like the optometrist, did not stop there but asked, "What's causing the blurred vision and headaches?" The optometrist had assumed the basic cause was old age, but the doctor had gone one step further and had pinpointed high blood pressure as the immediate cause. He then asked, "If high blood pressure is causing the eye trouble, what's causing the high blood pressure?"

Here he made the same mistake as the optometrist and assumed that old age was the direct cause of the high blood pressure. As a result, he prescribed medication and change of diet to provide symptomatic relief for high blood pressure. He, in effect, like the optometrist, treated the symptom because he could not deal with what he felt to be the root cause—old age.

Several months later, a routine visit to the dentist revealed that the doctor, like the optometrist, had failed because he had not pushed hard enough in his attempt to correctly identify all the intermediate causes of the problem. The dentist found that the doctor had missed an important link, a molar in which the nerve had died and decay had begun. The impurities introduced into the bloodstream by the decaying tooth were, in fact, the direct cause of the high blood pressure, which in turn was the cause of the eye trouble and headaches and dizziness.

This account illustrates the inadvisability of stopping a diagnosis at a first-level cause. Ask instead, "What's causing the cause?" and then, "What's causing the cause of the cause?" and so on until you have moved to the underlying fundamental cause. In our patient's situation, and the pun is built in, the root cause seems to have been the bad tooth.

The purist may argue that if we follow our own logic we should not settle for the bad tooth as the root cause, but should ask instead, "What caused the bad tooth?" Then, with the optometrist and the medical doctor, we may point to old age. Even so, what we have accomplished by moving in a step-by-step progression to the most basic cause is to identify all the intermediary causes. This sequence is vital because if the real root cause, old age, cannot be removed, we should focus our attention on the next cause in the chain—the bad tooth—for it is at this level that symptomatic relief will hit closest to the root cause and hopefully be most effective.

Strictly speaking, unless we deal with the aging process directly, any treatment will be symptomatic. The closer we can come to the root cause, however, the more satisfactory the symptomatic treatment is likely to be.

Root Causes of a Motivation Problem

Because moving from superficial to ever more basic causes is of such great importance to effective diagnosis and thus to effective decision-making, let us consider one further example.

The BLW Company is experiencing a succession of resignations among black draftsmen in its Chicago plant. A superficial diagnosis indicates that the cause of the resignations is "low motivation." If at this point alternatives (solutions) are sought, we can imagine what they might look like: (1) higher pay (buy them happiness), (2) more office activities (another bowling team), (3) make a few awards for outstanding work (another watch).

Any or all of these alternatives might work, but at this stage of investigation we are not sure whether low motivation is in fact the root cause or whether something else is. As a result, any alternatives based on correcting low motivation are likely to fail or at best provide symptomatic relief. Second, and more important, if low motivation is the direct cause, what is causing the low motivation? If, for example, motivation is low because the men lack proper training or must follow poor directions, none of the solutions just mentioned is sure to work. Even if one does work, it may be much more expensive than alternatives designed to get at the cause of the low motivation itself. The three proposals cited merely surround the basic problem with "human-relations lubricant" in the hope that it may somehow get to the cause of the friction.

If, in this case, the low motivation is traced to poor training, which is in turn chargeable to inadequate staff, we may now tackle the root cause. If, however, budget constraints prevent staff additions, then the root cause, like old age in the previous example, may be taken as an unremovable obstacle, or *limiting factor*, which must be accepted as unchangeable. In that event, symptomatic relief will have to be sought in finding ways of compensating for the staff deficiencies.

Alternatively, it may be useful to reconsider higher-level goals that may be met without a prerequisite of high motivation based on sound supervision. This suggestion brings us to the step which should be taken after defining the problem but prior to searching thoroughly for alternatives.

EXAMINING THE PROBLEM
IN LIGHT OF HIGHER-LEVEL GOALS

Unless a problem is defined in very sweeping terms, the recognized need is a *means* of accomplishing a more basic, higher-level *end* or goal. For instance, the problem of the late sales reports can be stated as follows:

Desired: *Field sales reports for each month should be filed with district sales offices by the fifth working day of the next month.*

Actual: *Salesmen repeatedly submit these reports from one to six days late.*

Although it is necessary to find the cause of the late reports, in many cases it would be wise to ask also, "Why do I want these reports by the fifth working day of the next month?" (see Fig. 11–3).

By asking "Why do I want...," we can put this problem in perspective. Subsequently, when we seek and weigh alternatives, we can do so in light of the higher-order goals. Because getting these reports is only a *means* to an end, we are not interested in ways of reaching the means

Fig. 11–3 Elementary means-end analysis. Diagnosis of a specific problem.

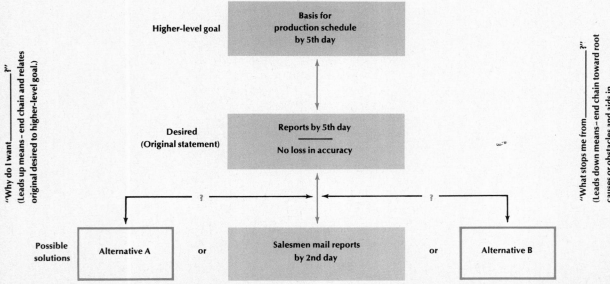

that conflict with the higher-level end. Any limits or constraints imposed by higher-level goals, then, should be stated specifically.

Suppose the answer to the question "Why do I want these reports?" is "to provide the manufacturing department with accurate figures on which to base next month's production." Then we can be careful to seek alternative means of getting the reports in on time that are consistent with the need for accuracy. Moreover, for this purpose we are more concerned with model numbers and delivery dates than with prices and how sales may tie into future business.

A milk company, to cite a similar example, gave the following instruction to a study team: "Do not submit any proposals unless estimated savings are over half a cent a quart." By knowing that the study aimed at finding a major gain, the team could fully understand this limit on acceptable alternatives. Product engineers often have to design not just a better product but one that is, say, faster than competitors' products or capable of being produced within a cost limit. The existence of such limits is often brought to light by extending the diagnosis into higher-level goals far enough to identify the full dimensions of a satisfactory solution.

DIAGNOSIS OF THE WHOLE SITUATION

In the preceding discussion, we focused on diagnosis of a recognized need, either a specific difficulty or a known opportunity for improvement. We urged moving directly to clarifying the gap between the actual and the desired, finding causes, and identifying limits. For most problems, such a diagnosis is all that is necessary.

At other times, though, a broader view may be essential. There are three main reasons why we may need to undertake a "diagnosis of the situation": (1) We may wish to redefine a recognized need because we cannot find an acceptable solution to the problem as originally stated. (2) Several problems may be so interdependent that we have to identify all of them and their interrelations before we can put them into a sequence for study and action. (3) We may feel that potential improvements have not been fully grasped by focusing on recognized problems as they arise.

Broadening the Definition of the Problem

Moving up the means-end chain. The late-report problem discussed in the previous section provides a simple illustration of how diagnosis of the whole situation in terms of a means-end chain can be of great help in paving the way for a subsequent search for alternatives. If we are

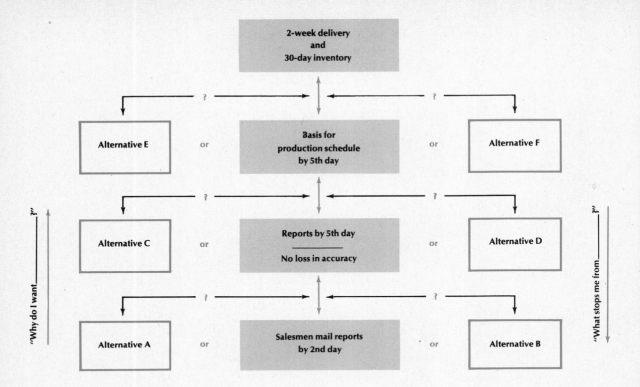

Fig. 11–4 *Broadened means-end analysis. Analysis moves from diagnosis of a specific problem to diagnosis of the situation in which the problem exists.*

stymied in an attempt to speed up reports, we can seek *alternative* ways of meeting the ends towards which field reports are one, but only one, means. Stated another way, if we want these reports primarily to provide accurate information to manufacturing by the fifth day of the month, and if we have trouble getting them on time, perhaps we should examine alternative ways of reaching the higher-level goals, ways that do not require field reports by the fifth day of the month.

Diagrammatically, this step "up" a means-end chain, wherein we move from lower- to higher-level goals, is shown in Fig. 11–4. It illustrates how we have broadened our inquiry from a diagnosis of a *specific problem* —late reports—to a diagnosis of the *situation* in which the problem exists.

Whether it proves desirable to solve our original problem or to seek ways of getting around it can be determined later after examination of the likely costs and benefits associated with various alternatives. By examining the higher-order goals before seeking alternatives to the late-report problem, however, we open up a set of options that might otherwise have been overlooked. We can either continue to solve the "recognized need" within the context of this higher-level goal, or, if this proves difficult, we can bypass the original problem and seek alternatives that satisfy the higher-level goals by means other than field reports.

The possibility of redefining a problem by moving up a means-end chain can also be applied to the problem of low motivation in the drafting

Fig. 11–5 *Extended means-end analysis. By this approach, diagnosis focuses on a specific subpart of a complex problem.*

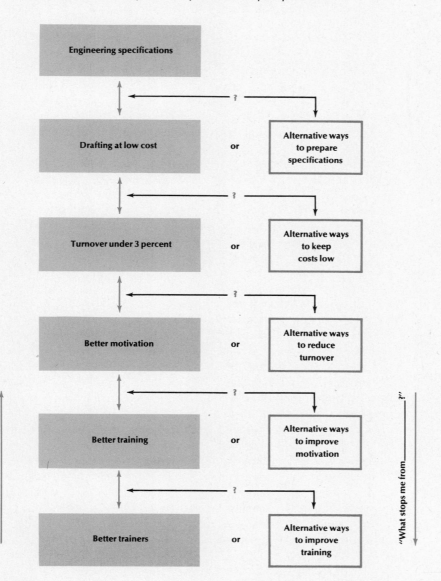

department, which was used in illustrating the search for root causes. Figure 11–5 illustrates how we might add several higher-level goals to the picture. While the personnel department is working on the motivation problem, the engineering department can concentrate on the goal of realizing engineering needs without low-cost drafting. Each can work independently on vastly different types of goals. The key is that some person or persons in responsible positions should attempt to determine how the several pieces relate, how they complement or substitute for one another.

By looking at this diagram, we can see how a more complicated situation might be broken down. This approach permits us to concentrate our analytical talents on each of a number of subparts of a complex problem. We can focus on each part but at the same time be able to see how it fits into the whole scheme. In many problems like the one illustrated here, what originally appears simply as a matter of personnel turnover may in fact lead to a recognition of problems and relationships in many other areas of the business. By moving from a diagnosis of the specific problem to a diagnosis of the broader situation in which the problem exists, we pave the way for recognizing and dealing with these interrelationships.[2]

Determining how far to go in diagnosing the situation. An inevitable question is how far we should go in considering ever-higher goals. Two broad guidelines help to answer this question: (1) the extent of the decision-maker's authority, and (2) the time available for analysis.

Take the first point. A district sales manager, asked to tackle the problem of late reports, may lack the perspective or the organizational authority to look farther than the reason for submitting the field reports— accurate information for scheduling. However, if the vice-president of manufacturing were brought into the decision, he might ask, "Why do I want an accurate basis for making production schedules by the fifth day of the month?"

The answer to this question would reveal the next higher goal in the chain, which might be "to provide for delivery within two weeks of order placement, while maintaining a thirty-day inventory." Perhaps the vice-president of manufacturing will have the authority to search for means of achieving this goal without having an accurate basis for making production schedules by the fifth day of the month.

As a rule, the decision-maker should seek to move as far up the hierarchy of goals as his position and influence in the company permit. If he is in a position to understand and influence goals two levels higher than the "desired" end stated in his problem definition, he should do so.

2Note that a means-end analysis is not sufficient for making a wise choice. All we know is that each means is adequate to meet the higher-level goal; other alternatives may be even more attractive. Moreover, a means-end chain shows only one consequence of a given means; other consequences may sharply affect the desirability of using the means depicted. Therefore, a final action decision should be based on all four steps covered in Part Three. The chief value of means-end analysis lies in diagnosis.

If the nature of the problem warrants going farther, he should seek to involve higher-level decision-makers with the necessary perspective and influence.

When time is pressing, it provides a second guide to how far "up" the means-end chain to go: Go only as far as is necessary to get a soluble problem. In other words, we don't challenge the entire goal structure of our company each time we encounter a tough problem. Instead we push the analysis to a point where we feel confident that one or more acceptable alternatives exist. Then we focus on this redefinition of the problem so that a decision can be made promptly and action started. Obviously judgment is involved in selecting the point where prompt action (and low investigation expense) is more valuable than more exploration.

Dealing with Interrelated Problems

Problems do not remain isolated—especially in enterprises where internal and external integration (discussed in Chapter 1) is a major element in survival. In these situations, as we diagnose one facet of the business we soon realize that any action proposed will have impact on several operations not embraced in our initial analysis. Our diagnosis should grasp all these related facets, even though in the end we may decide to deal with them one at a time. Because they are so intertwined the *sequence* of analysis and action is crucial.[3]

Difficulties faced by the Allegheny Electric Company are clearly of this sort. To serve its growing customer demand, the company must expand its generating capacity substantially. In fact, the company already is vulnerable to customer complaints of brownouts and occasional shutdowns. Any solution to this problem must concern plant size (millions of dollars will be required), timing (five- to eight-year construction cycle), and type of fuel (nuclear, oil, or coal). But along come antipollution campaigns and interest in ecology. The public's strong fear of radiation leaks has all but eliminated the possibility of erecting a nuclear power plant, and ecological protests have forced the company to give up attempts to secure a favorable location for a coal-operated plant. In the face of all this, the company seeks a rate increase to improve its earnings, claiming that it will not be able to borrow money for the construction of new plants unless its earnings are increased. However, the public concern about pollution and about brownouts may pressure the state utility commission to refuse permission for a rate increase.

Obviously, the company has half a dozen major problems each of which should be carefully diagnosed in terms of gaps, causes and obstacles, and constraints. *In addition*, the total configuration must be an-

[3]Here we endorse the concept of a total system and suggest that the diagnosis helps us decide which part of the system we should tinker with first.

alyzed in an attempt to set some kind of sequence for dealing with the related issues.

A well-established pharmaceutical firm recently faced a comparable situation. The research budget was being revised, and one significant project in question dealt with a cheaper method for producing cortisone. This project was challenged because a competitor was reported to have perfected an alternative method. Assuming the report was correct, the company might be successful in obtaining a license to use the method or Congress might pass legislation requiring industrywide licensing. Meanwhile the company was negotiating a merger with a small drug company, which if successful and if approved by the Antitrust Division would shift the direction of new product development for the company. Also two leading researchers of the company had attractive offers from a competitor and would be influenced by the research allotment included in the budget for their projects, even though they were not directly involved in the cortisone study.

Here again the diagnosis is "messy" because several significant problems are interdependent. There is no single answer on how to proceed with such complex diagnoses. If one problem is clearly most important it can be studied first, and its tentative solution sets the limits within which related problems are studied. If preliminary analysis shows that acceptable solutions exist for one or more problems, and the range of solutions will not markedly affect other problems, then these issues can be temporarily deferred. Financing for the power company described earlier falls into this category. Another possible approach is to work on all major needs simultaneously. If this is done, tentative solutions for each need should be provided as quickly as possible to the men who are working on related matters so that the anticipated solutions can be used as planning premises in work on other needs and problems. This process is repeated through a series of successive refinements (assuming all the projects progress at about the same rate).

Clearly some sequencing arrangement must be developed. If each problem is diagnosed and studied separately, the opportunities for incompatibility, wasted effort, and delay are overwhelming.

Exploring for Unrecognized Opportunities

Another characteristic of diagnosing the total situation is an emphasis on *future* conditions. Most diagnosis starts with a recognized need growing out of the existing scene. Obviously the here and now must not be ignored. Nevertheless, a good manager should also deliberately search out opportunities. Even though operations are proceeding well according to present standards, he knows that changes will occur in technology, politics, population, economics, competition, and other aspects of the environment. New opportunities or difficulties are sure to arise.

A shoe company, for instance, predicted a change in employment practice when it opened a plant in the South. Its prediction, which was followed up by a policy of "an equal opportunity employer," has paid off—after a slow start. A more conspicuous example was IBM's prediction about computer needs and competitor offerings, which led the company to introduce its 360 series even though at the time its market position was already very strong. The key is to anticipate the difficulties or opportunities far enough in advance to prepare for them. By thinking in terms of future conditions, the manager can perform his diagnosis before the difficulty or opportunity fully materializes. He can make a decision based on a sound diagnosis, and then, if necessary, he can wait until his guesses about the future can be verified with more certainty before he acts on the decision. By thinking in terms of future conditions, he has time to make a thorough decision in advance of the time when the decision must be implemented.

In terms of the framework of this chapter, we keep a watchful eye on the constantly changing milieu about us, and out of the hurly-burly we select those changes that can be restated in terms of opportunities or difficulties for us. By raising our expectations, or by predicting difficulty in continuing present operations, we identify new problems. Once they are recognized, we can proceed with a diagnosis of each in the manner already outlined on pages 250–57. Such a diagnosis of the total situation does not create problems; rather, it shifts them from an unrecognized to a recognized state.

Such forward-looking diagnosis is difficult. Conscious, rational decision-making takes time and, what is worse, often increases the decision-maker's anxiety about the decision he must make. It forces him to bring questions and causes to a conscious level, doubts and uncertainties that might be less troublesome to his psyche (though not to his company) if left submerged. Dealing with predicted future conditions only adds to the uncertainty and anxiety. We shall return to this stumbling block in Chapter 15 when we discuss planning in organizations. What is needed is reasonable selectivity in the issues that are opened for debate and a planning climate that favors anticipating trouble rather than management by crises.

Planning in terms of the future is a recurring theme in Parts Three and Four. Especially in Chapter 13, on comparing the consequences of alternative courses of action, we shall find that forecasting is a prime consideration. In this chapter on diagnosis, however, we have been concerned with predicting independent variables—that is, those key aspects of an operating situation that are beyond our influence—whereas in Chapter 13 our attention focuses on anticipating the consequences of actions we initiate.

CONCLUSION

The essence of a good diagnosis is discernment and clarity. Usually an executive can achieve these qualities by keeping a diagnosis simple and to the point. But he should be fully aware that a high degree of personal judgment is involved. For example, he may set an unnecessary limit on acceptable solutions and thereby eliminate attractive proposals for solving a problem. Or, in his desire to get to a simple, concrete problem, he may move down a means-end chain too hastily and overlook broader problems that need study. The suggestions we have made should assist him in his diagnosis, but they cannot remove the need for keen discretion.

Discretion is particularly important when diagnosis shifts from a single identified need to diagnosis of the whole situation. Here the executive has to judge whether broadening the definition of a problem is warranted, what sequence should be followed in wrestling with interrelated issues, and the extent to which diagnosis should be based on predictions.

In addition, the definition of a problem should never be regarded as unalterable. Even though a diagnosis has been thorough and the conclusions about situations, gaps, causes, and limits have been put in a clear written statement, new insights may still arise. In searching for alternatives, and in analyzing and projecting alternatives, we may uncover new evidence and new issues. If we do, we should be willing to redefine the problem. It is wise to keep an open mind about this question: "Where do we want to go and what are we up against?"

FOR CLASS DISCUSSION

Questions

1) What is the relationship between custom and habit (as discussed in Chapter 7) and rational decision-making?

2) In what ways may the careful use of a rational methodology for decision-making contribute to effective decentralization?

3) "It is fine to talk about a rational process of decision-making and getting all of the pertinent facts and assumptions, but how often does a businessman have the time for such luxuries? Something happens—a competitor cuts his price or comes out with a new product—and your market is threatened and you have to act fast. This is where an executive earns his salary by making fast, intuitive decisions under pressure." How would you reply to this statement?

4) Using problem-solving in medicine, consider the following situation: A patient comes to a doctor with an injured arm and asks for help. The doctor X-rays the arm and finds a broken bone and no other injuries. Has he reached root cause, or should he inquire "What caused the break?" How does the "gap" statement he might have used to state the problem determine whether he has completed his diagnosis?

5) Often different people fight for the same issue but for very different reasons. In what way may such a situation present real problems when we are seeking group effort to achieve a common objective?

6) How will decisions on (1) departmentation, (2) delegation, and (3) decentralization (Chapters 3, 4, and 5) influence a manager's decision on how far "up" and "down" a means-end chain he should go in diagnosing a problem of his department?

7) Think of a problem you have recently faced or know about that was solved. The specific gap was closed, but subsequently you found that closing that gap (solving that specific problem) gave rise to new and unexpected problems that were at least as serious as the one just solved. How might such situations be avoided? By examining the original problem in the light of higher-level goals?

8) In what ways may advances in application of computers to decision-making aid in the diagnostic aspects of the process?

Cases

For cases involving issues covered in this chapter, see especially the following. Particularly relevant questions are listed after each case.

Scott-Davis Corporation (p. 227), 9, 11
Gerald Clark (p. 234), 10, 11
Dodge Skate Company (p. 337), 4, 5
Bolling Laboratories, Inc. (p. 345), 5, 6, 7, 8, 9, 11
E.W. Ross, Inc. (p. 468), 5
Harrogate Asphalt Products, Ltd.—AR (p. 557), 7
Consolidated Instruments—A (p. 571), 8
Texas-Northern Pipeline Company (p. 665), 5

FOR FURTHER READING

Ackoff, R.L., *A Concept of Corporate Planning.* New York: John Wiley & Sons, Inc., 1970, Chap. 1. *Penetrating comments on the nature of decision-making feasible in an enterprise.*

Braybrooke, D., and C.E. Lindblom, *A Strategy of Decision.* New York: The Free Press, 1963, Chaps. 4–6. *Explains Lindbloom's "muddling-through" process (see also* Public Administration Review, *Spring 1959).*

Emory, C.W., and P. Niland, *Making Management Decisions.* Boston: Houghton Mifflin Company, 1968, Chaps. 2 and 3. *Explains diagnosis in terms of goals and task delineation; theory is presented in terms useful to a manager.*

Etzioni, A., "Mixed-Scanning: A 'Third' Approach to Decision-Making," *Public Administration Review*, December 1967. *Proposal for diagnosing public administration problems in terms of both higher- and lower-level goals.*

Jones, M.H., *Executive Decision Making*, rev. ed. Homewood, Ill.: Richard D. Irwin, Inc., 1962, Chaps. 1 and 3. *Explains use of goals, means-end chains, and premises in decision-making.*

Kepner, C.H., and B.B. Tregoe, *The Rational Manager*. New York: McGraw-Hill Book Company, 1965, Chaps. 3–9. *Clear, concrete instructions for diagnosing operating problems.*

Miller, D.W., and M.K. Starr, *Executive Decisions and Operations Research*, 2nd ed. Englewood Cliffs, N.J.: Prentice-Hall, Inc., 1969, Chap. 13. *Broad discussion of the origin of problems and their significance to managers. This chapter reflects managerial orientation of entire book.*

Chapter Twelve

The Creative Element

in Decision-Making

THE NEED FOR "BRIGHT IDEAS"

A thorough diagnosis defines both a specific problem and the situation in which the problem exists. With this definition in mind, a decision-maker seeks possible solutions. Rarely does he hit upon only one perfect way to solve his problem. Usually several different approaches might work, but none is completely satisfactory, and so he looks for more alternatives hoping to find a better answer. The two most common sources of alternatives are the past experience of an executive himself and the practices followed by other executives or other companies.

Search for Alternatives

Faced with a problem, we naturally review our *past experience* for a similar situation that turned out well. With allowances for obvious differences between the former challenge and the present one, the successful action of the past becomes at least an alternative plan for the future.

Much business planning, as well as individual behavior, is built solely on such past experience. This is the simplest approach to a problem, and it is quite adequate in a majority of instances. As long as all goes well, we are likely to repeat past practice. Before long, it becomes habit or tradition. But the catch is that yesterday's solutions may not be adequate for today's problems, as college administrators discovered during campus revolts. Competitors may have introduced a new product line. Workers may no longer respond to yesterday's incentive plan because their "needs" have shifted. Alternatives suggested by past experience may not be enough.

"How does General Motors handle this problem of dealers' inventory?"

"Pete Jones told me he was having the same kind of trouble in collecting from foreign customers. I wonder what he is doing."

Statements such as these are made every day by executives who scrutinize the practice of other firms or other departments for solutions to their own problems. In fact, a distinctive characteristic of American business, often noted by foreign observers, is the frequency and frankness with which businessmen exchange experiences. Professional papers and trade journals are full of accounts of how the XYZ Company cut its air pollution, boosted sales, or improved quality. Ideas are exchanged at trade association meetings and through intercompany visits. Both the American Management Association and The Conference Board (formerly the National Industrial Conference Board) regularly report business practices of successful firms. In fact, much of what we call "business research" consists in finding out what the man across the street is doing.[1]

Such examinations flush out several alternatives that might not occur to executives within a company, and this practice accelerates improvement in business operations throughout the economy. But as with past experience, we should ensure that operations in one company are enough like those in a second company to make transferring a practice worthwhile. We should also avoid the danger of too quickly falling in step with another company simply because it is a leader in its industry. Relying on past experience and imitating others produce alternatives that at best merely keep us up with the parade. Nevertheless, we should always consider *selective imitation* as a possible source of alternatives.

Although pressures of time and expense may force a company to plug along conservatively as a follower in part of its activities, it should strive to excel in some respects. In our dynamic and competitive society, at least an occasional spark of creativity is needed if a company hopes to endure for long. Shifts in customer demand, new technology, increased government regulation, progressive competition, new attitudes and mores of employees, and similar changes limit the usefulness of past experience. The uniqueness of each company and the rapid rate of change make imitation hazardous. We need fresh, original, distinctive, and independent thinking to develop alternatives that are copied neither from the past nor

---

[1] Students do the same thing. When given a case most of them try to find what a successful company did in a similar situation so that they can follow suit.

from our neighbor but are original and peculiarly adapted to the circumstances in which we happen to find ourselves.

Creativeness

Decisions that add some *new* and useful element are creative. Not all decisions are creative in this sense, of course. Even those that are include much repetition or imitation, but in some important respect a creative decision is different and *original*.

This sort of creativeness is familiar to all of us. Every invention of a product, process, or machine contains some creative element. Sales executives who think up supermarkets, suburban shopping centers, or new packages for their merchandise are being creative. The man who introduced the "first-in-first-out" method of evaluating inventory was creative. Creativeness is perhaps even more familiar outside the business field and is evident in the great advances of medical science, in the development of atomic energy, and in the discovery of new forms in the arts.

It is natural to exemplify creativeness by dramatic discoveries such as Salk vaccine or supersonic planes. But close examination will reveal that even everyday activities are shot through with strains of creativeness. A personnel manager may have a creative idea for dealing with a troublesome problem of closing a plant, or a sales clerk may think of an ingenious way to display Idaho potatoes. Every time an executive faces a problem, large or small, he has an opportunity to be creative.[2]

Surprisingly little systematic study has been given to creativeness, either by social scientists or by business practitioners. Enough is known, however, to give us some useful leads. Scientific discoveries have probably received the greatest attention, so we do have a number of reports on how new and useful ideas were developed in the medical and physical sciences. Essays on creativeness in the arts are also available. In the business world, advertising men have been particularly interested in the subject. From these and similar sources, we can draw up some suggestions on (1) the usual stages in the creative process, (2) on aids to individual creativeness, and (3) aids to group creativeness. Our suggestions lack the comforting assurance of a mathematical formula, but we cannot expect to find fixed rules for developing such an elusive quality. Because creativeness is so important in dynamic planning, we must make the best use of the insights that are available to us.

---

[2]In this discussion, creativeness is stressed as a means of finding alternatives to solve problems. Actually, we can bring creativeness into play throughout the decision-making process—in diagnosis, while looking for underlying causes, in analysis, while thinking of critical factors, and so on. In a strict sense, we could argue that each of these steps in planning is a little problem in itself, and that creativeness enters into finding alternatives for solving these subproblems. This reasoning becomes cumbersome, however, and it is more useful for most people simply to be aware that there may be opportunities for originality *throughout* the planning process.

USUAL STAGES IN THE CREATIVE PROCESS

Although no two persons' minds work exactly alike, the testimony of inventors and great scientists indicates that the creative process has several stages:

1) *Saturation*—becoming thoroughly familiar with a problem, with its setting, and, more broadly, with activities and ideas akin to the problem.

2) *Deliberation*—mulling over these ideas, analyzing them, challenging them, rearranging them, thinking of them from several viewpoints.

3) *Incubation*—relaxing, turning off the conscious and purposeful search, forgetting the frustrations of unproductive labor, letting the subconscious mind work.

4) *Illumination*—hitting upon a bright idea, a bit crazy perhaps, but new and fresh and full of promise, sensing that it might be the answer.

5) *Accommodation*—clarifying the idea, seeing whether it fits the requirements of the problem as it did on first thought, reframing and adapting it, putting it on paper, getting other people's reaction to it.

By recognizing these stages of creative thought we can look for, and more effectively use, techniques that help us at the different stages.

Saturation

There is a common notion that creative ideas fall like manna from the heavens before the chosen few; one of the chosen simply sits around and waits for inspiration to strike. This impression probably arises from stories of inventions, such as Charles Goodyear's discovery of a method of vulcanizing rubber when he accidentally spilled crude rubber on his kitchen stove. We also often read of moments of inspiration in the cultural field, such as Mascagni's waking one morning with the concept of *Cavalleria Rusticana* full-blown and writing it within a few days' time. But these accounts fail to emphasize the many years of study and hard work that precede a flash of insight. Goodyear had been studying and experimenting with rubber for years before his lucky accident, and his work provided both the occasion for the discovery and his ability to recognize what he had found; Mascagni kept his family in poverty while he composed piece after piece of completely dull music. Once in a while, a novice stumbles on a great truth (probably because he is ignorant of what supposedly cannot be done, as we shall note below), but such an event is so uncommon that it offers a poor prescription for developing creative ideas. The sad truth is that the most likely way to get bright ideas is to work on a baffling problem, and work hard.

After careful review of a wide range of reports on creative activity, Brewster Ghiselin concludes: "Even the most energetic and original mind, in order to reorganize or extend human insight in any valuable way, must have attained more than ordinary mastery of the field in which it is to act, a strong sense of what needs to be done, and skill in the appropriate means of expression."[3]

A manager uses creative thinking in solving specific problems; each situation dictates where he should focus attention. For him, the saturation stage normally begins in thorough familiarity with a problem itself, its history, its importance, its relationship to other parts of the business, and its setting. Of course, if an executive has lived with a problem a long while and participates in its diagnosis, he is already intimately acquainted with it. But if he has had only casual contact with a situation, as is often true of a staff man, he is more likely to make a useful contribution if he begins by soaking up background material.

Deliberation

Knowledge alone, no matter how complete, does not produce creative ideas. Information must be mulled over until what we might call mental digestion takes place. Because we do not know just where a breakthrough to an original concept will occur, no one can say exactly how material at hand should be analyzed. In fact, an analysis of how 144 patented ideas were discovered in Standard Oil Company (New Jersey) laboratories revealed five different approaches: (1) finding a *new use* for a product or process, perhaps in another field, (2) *substituting* a better agent or way to accomplish an existing job, (3) pure *theorizing*, or sitting down and thinking, (4) going into the laboratory and *experimenting*, and (5) recognizing the significance of a *lucky accident*. The inventors who came up with the largest number of new ideas were quite adaptable in selecting the particular approach they used at any given time.

Although there is no single and sure path to follow from information to a new and useful idea, deliberation usually includes three steps: (1) analyzing, (2) building relationships and patterns, and (3) seeking useful rearrangements or combinations.

Incubation

If we are lucky, the work we have done in the saturation and deliberation steps has furnished us with as many useful alternatives as we want. Flashes of illumination—or bright ideas—may have occurred while

[3]*The Creative Process* (Berkeley: University of California Press, 1961), p. 29.

Fig. 12–1 As a study at Standard Oil (N.J.) revealed, new ideas have various sources, and the most creative individuals shift freely from one approach to another. Drawing by Richard Erdoes in The Lamp, November 1955, p. 5. Courtesy Standard Oil (N.J.).

we were deliberating. If so, we can omit incubation entirely and move immediately to the accommodation stage.

But not all problems yield so easily. In spite of thorough preparation and much hard thinking, we may not have discovered a really good solution to our problem. In forcing ourselves to think of yet another angle, we may only have added to our mental confusion. This sort of stalemate is so common that some writers list frustration as one stage in the creative process.

Advice at this point is simple and unanimous. Set the whole problem aside: go fishing, go to the theatre, pull weeds in the garden, take a long walk, listen to music, or do whatever else is relaxing. By this time, we are too steeped in a problem to wash our hands of it, but for the present we can turn it over to our subconscious mind. At least we will return to our work refreshed, and *perhaps* a creative idea will pop into our minds.

Illumination

There are numerous accounts of sudden illumination. James Watt is said to have thought of his condenser for a steam engine while walking on a Sunday afternoon. The great mathematician Henri Poincaré reports that he grasped the significance of Fuchsian Functions as he stepped onto a bus one afternoon. The president of a large manufacturing company insists that a plan for financing a merger came to his mind while he was shaving. We could recount many other instances of flashes of insight that occurred to a man while he was not consciously thinking about a problem.

Many of us have had similar, though usually less dramatic, experiences. Often an idea is so simple and obvious that we wonder why we didn't think of it before. We may learn later (if we failed to saturate ourselves thoroughly in background study) that other people have had the idea before us. Nevertheless, for us it was a creative experience; a new and useful idea was born. But we cannot will such moments of illumination. The most we can do is to prepare ourselves along the lines already suggested and hope for inspiration.

So far as we know at present, illumination apparently works in the following way. We all know how speedily a complicated dream can transpire in a short interval of semiconsciousness; this experience gives us some idea of the tremendous rapidity of ideas flashing across our subconscious. It is reasonable to believe that the mind works at least as fast as an electronic computer, and we know that the number of possible relationships between ideas stored in our memory far exceeds the capacity of anything yet designed by the electronics industry. If in the subconscious the restraints of rational thought are relaxed, a myriad of new combinations and new ideas is possible. Using this hypothesis, let us consider what is truly remarkable about illumination: that somehow, utterly wild and useless ideas are screened out. It is as though there were a filter in the subconscious that permits only the more plausible ideas to rise up to the conscious level. In those unusual cases where illumination has unveiled a complete process or financial structure, instead of just the germ of an idea, the subconscious has been able to recognize and select a whole cluster of ideas that fit together into a workable plan.[4]

In the years ahead, science may prove that such speculation about the subconscious mind is naïve fantasy, but our analysis points up two necessary characteristics of creative thinking—somehow, we must swiftly discard a lot of worthless ideas, and at the same time we must learn to recognize a valuable idea when it does occur. Experience shows that there is a real danger that a good idea will pass by unnoticed. Some of the aids to creative thinking suggested later in this chapter are designed to minimize this danger.

Accommodation

Is a bright idea in a finished form when it is first grasped? As James W. Young says, "You have to take your little newborn idea out into the world of reality. And when you do you usually find that it is not quite the marvelous child it seemed when you first gave birth to it."[5]

If the new idea is for a material invention we need to take it to a

[4]Henri Poincaré makes the interesting and distinctly French suggestion that there is true beauty in such configurations and that the subconscious makes something like an emotional response to a thing of beauty; people are likely to be creative, then, only in those fields where they are aesthetically sensitive to the appropriateness of a set of ideas.

[5]*A Technique for Producing Ideas*, 9th ed. (Chicago: Advertising Publications, 1956), p. 52.

laboratory and test whether it will really work. We must write out a new mathematical formula and check it for correctness. A composer needs to commit to paper and actually play a melody that runs through his mind. So too with business ideas. We need to fit a new conception to the actual facts of a problem. Usually a check with cold reality reveals the need for adapting and refining the first conception of an idea. In this creative process, we are seeking practical alternatives for solving a problem, and our search may involve quite a little work to transform an original insight into a concrete proposal for others to examine.

But rounding out an original idea does not necessarily entail a complete plan of action. Perhaps at some future date, as a part of evaluation, tests may be run, pilot plants built, or budgets prepared. The point here is that the man who has had a fascinating daydream is not truly creative unless he can translate and spell out his idea in usable form.

Highly important and elusive, creativeness ordinarily emerges, then, after five stages: (1) saturation, (2) deliberation, (3) incubation, (4) illumination, and (5) accommodation. In administrative situations where we are concerned with achieving given objectives, we assume that a diagnosis of a problem has preceded even the first of these steps. Thus creative search in business typically starts not with unbridled effort but with a defined aim and with background data available. In pursuing his search, the creative worker must be as purposeful and diligent as any other employee.

Unfortunately, knowing about the stages in creative thinking by no means assures us that we can bubble over with new and useful ideas. Our knowledge *may* help us to develop creativeness in ourselves and in our associates, but many of us will still find it hard to generate ideas. Consequently, we now turn to a number of suggestions that, experience indicates, may help individuals or groups to be creative.

AIDS TO INDIVIDUAL CREATIVITY

Two general conclusions emerge from the preceding review of the usual stages in the creative process: (1) Creativity is not an exceptional ability within the grasp only of geniuses—anyone with reasonable intelligence may have an original idea; and (2) a lot of hard mental work is usually required to generate a new idea. Prime requisites for developing creative ability, then, are the Horatio Alger qualities of self-confidence and will to work. The imagination of a creative man is closely related to the intensity and clarity with which he senses the problem to be solved.

Can we suggest anything more about stimulating creativity? Three additional rules that people often turn to in developing new and useful ideas deserve serious attention: Recognize psychological barriers; try to change attributes; and be alert for serendipity.

Recognizing Psychological Barriers

Although psychologists have found no reliable machinery to generate flashes of insight, they have identified a number of common barriers to creative thought. By being alert to these barriers, we can overcome their interference to some extent. The most common obstacles are cultural blocks and perceptual blocks.

Cultural blocks. The push toward social conformity strongly influences our thinking. All of us, consciously or unconsciously, tend to fit in with the modes of living and the attitudes of our associates. Minor exceptions may be acceptable or even desirable, but it is a daring young man who wears pantaloons or goes barefoot to his office.

This same tendency to follow the crowd—this unwillingness to be different—affects our imagination as well as our actions. The current popularity of electronic controls and automation, for example, is so seductive that almost all young process engineers try to include these features in their new designs. Proposals that omit such features are unlikely to be submitted or, perhaps, even conceived.

For many years, credit for personal-consumption items was limited to houses and other goods whose resale value was greater than the debt. In the Puritan tradition of prudence, Americans looked askance at buying any luxury, such as jewelry, on a time-payment plan, and many people felt that the liberal extension of credit by company stores contributed to moral degeneration. In such a social climate, the idea of extending credit to thousands of mail-order customers was unthinkable.

Until we are ready to break with current fashions of thought—in a department, in a company, or in society—truly creative ideas will be scarce. On this point, C. H. Greenewalt, President of E. I. du Pont de Nemours & Company, said in a speech:

> *Behind every advance of the human race is a germ of creation growing in the mind of some lone individual, an individual whose dreams waken him in the night while others lie contentedly asleep.*
>
> *We need those dreams, for today's dreams represent tomorrow's realities. Yet, in the very nature of our mass effort, there lies this grave danger—not that the individual may circumvent the public will, but that he will himself be conformed and shaped to the general pattern, with the loss of his unique, original contributions. The group nature of business enterprise itself will provide adequate safeguards against public affront. The great problem, the great question, is to develop within the framework of the group the creative genius of the individual. . . .*
>
> *I know of no problem so pressing, of no issue so vital. For unless*

*we can guarantee the encouragement and fruitfulness of the un-
common man, the future will lose for all men its virtue, its bright-
ness, and its promise.*

Perceptual blocks. In addition to the barriers that arise from our
social background, we often have difficulty with new ideas simply because
of the way we perceive things. Psychologists have many experiments that
demonstrate the importance of perception. In one of the simplest, they
place six matchsticks before a person and ask him to make four triangles
with the sticks touching each other at the ends. Most people have trouble,
and may even give up, because they think only of arranging the matches
on a flat surface. Once they conceive of the task as a three-dimensional
problem, they quickly form a pyramid.

A dramatic instance of overcoming a perceptual barrier to creative
thinking was the discovery of penicillin. For years bacteriologists had
thought of mold simply as a substance that spoiled pure cultures. Mold
killed all the germs in the cultures so that researchers had to throw them
out and start over again. Then one day, Alexander Fleming had the bright
idea that perhaps the same thing that was spoiling the cultures could
be used as a germ-killer, which was, in fact, one of the objects of research.
A good deal of work remained to be done before the product was refined
and tested, but the original inspiration was the result of dropping a
preconception about mold.

Transferring habits is one cause of perceptual blocks. The men who
built the first automobiles, for instance, were in the habit of thinking of
carriages. It was only natural that their early designs for "horseless carriages" merely substituted a motor for a horse. Similarly, in a company
where engineering has always been physically and organizationally a part
of the plant, executives have a hard time devising a new organization that
ties engineering closely to selling. The transfer of past habits to new situ-

*Fig. 12–2 Our perception of things can be an obstacle to
creativity, preventing us from seeing the wholeness or
diversity of a situation, or even permitting us to see "impossible" objects. In the drawing of the face do you see both
the old woman and the young girl? Does the silhouette show
two profiles or a vase? What do you make of the third
object? New perspectives are often required to enable us to
break through our perceptual blocks.*

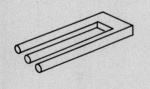

ations may block out the fresh perception of possible alternative courses of action.

An additional source of difficulty is that we too readily approach a problem as an "either-or" dilemma and examine only two courses of action. When one medium-sized manufacturing concern, for example, found its plant running to capacity, its executives wrestled for several weeks with the choice between trying to attract extra capital for building an addition to its plant or giving up plans for further expansion in volume. But these were not the only two courses of action open. A third possibility involved subcontracting some of the work, and a fourth one, which the company actually adopted, was the arranging of a "sale and lease-back" deal whereby the company sold its old plant and the new addition to an investor and then leased them back for a long period.

Change Attributes

The preceding review of psychological barriers to creativity is useful in suggesting attitudes and habits to guard against. But are there any more positive suggestions an individual might follow? Not many, unfortunately— at least not many that appear to have widespread usefulness. But one popular approach—the changing of attributes—may be applied to a variety of problems.

In this approach, we first list the important attributes of the product or problem we are studying. Next, we single out the key attribute for concentrated attention and contemplate all sorts of modifications. Then, if we can identify other attributes, we undertake a similar exploration for each. Small changes in one direction may suggest additional adjustments, and so by mentally moving from one idea to another, something truly new and useful may emerge. Because it emphasizes concentration on one attribute at a time—preferably the key attribute—this approach is really a special form of analysis, which we already discussed under saturation.

Using this approach, we might study a common window screen as shown in Table 12–1.

An industrial concern followed substantially this technique in developing an executive-compensation plan. Among the attributes considered were these: normal amount of compensation, provision for individual incentive, form and time of payment, and method of making changes. For the first attribute—amount of compensation—the company considered many possible guides, including basing pay schedules on a fixed ratio to sales or to profits or following the pattern of neighboring concerns. Finally management decided to set the president's salary arbitrarily but to relate pay for the lowest-ranking executive with comparable salaries in the industry. All other executive positions were then arranged between these high and low points on the basis of what the president believed to be a given position's relative contribution to company profits. Although nothing especially novel developed in this instance, the new plan represented a sharply different approach from the previous practice of the company and dealt with a troublesome problem creatively.

Serendipity

Management's concern is achieving objectives. Consequently it will direct most of its creative effort toward finding ever more effective and efficient ways to reach its ends. Nevertheless, there is always the chance that some useful idea will turn up that is not directly related to an immediate problem.

Serendipity is the art of finding things we are *not* looking for, the knack of making unexpected discoveries. Perhaps a search for a bright idea to solve one problem turns up some interesting sidelights on quite a different issue. The real art is to recognize how we may put these by-product ideas to good use.

Alexander Fleming, as we have noted, turned what at first appeared to be a hindrance to his experiment into the discovery of penicillin. In another instance, Wilhelm Roentgen was experimenting with a cathode tube when he happened to leave a key and an undeveloped photographic plate covered with black paper over a tube. When by mistake a laboratory assistant had the plate developed, it revealed an outline of the key. Roentgen was immediately curious about how the rays from the cathode tube had miraculously passed through the black paper. Out of his investigation came the discovery of X rays.

Probably the most striking example of serendipity in the management field occurred in Elton Mayo's famous experiments at the Western Electric

Table 12–1 *Developing a new product—window screen*

Attribute	Possible Modifications
Stops insects	Repelling odor, electric beam, sonic beam, seductive trap
Passes most, not all, light	Finer strands of tough plastic, fewer heavy strands with light ones in between, fiber glass, tiny mirrors, invisible barrier suggested above
Passes air	Side ducts, small solar-cell fan, baffles
Rigid frame	Adhesive tape, elastic band over corner hooks, roll up like a window shade
Need year after year	Disposable yearly, daily

Company. Mayo and his assistants set out to measure the effect of changes in working conditions on the productivity of workers. They tried changing light and noise and other factors, but with rather indifferent results. Instead, what turned out to be significant—and they were smart enough to recognize the significance—were the social relationships among the workers and the willingness of workers to cooperate with management. In one group the cooperativeness of workers led to increased output, at least temporarily, each time working conditions were changed, even though some of the changes actually made working conditions worse. In another group, differences in output were closely related to the different relationships between operators and supervisors. The researchers then directed experiments more specifically toward testing this new line of thought and thereby laid a basis for the most important advances in industrial psychology during the last quarter century.

Opportunity for insight presents itself in many management fields. For example, James O. McKinsey started his career in accounting and budgetary control. He soon found that he could not work out good budgets for a company without clear company organization. Moreover, he needed clear statements of company objectives and policies before he could put meaningful estimates in budgets. Poking around in the areas of organization and policy proved to be more useful than working out details of a budget and accounting system. It was in these new areas that McKinsey established one of the outstanding top-management consulting firms in the world.

The chance insights on which serendipity rests are so unpredictable that no business dares to rely on them for its continuing development. Still, these opportunities do occur. They are most likely to be recognized in an enterprise that is creative in dealing with its inherent problems. A wise manager should be alert to such unexpected insights and should be hospitable to these little interlopers in his more sharply directed planning activities.

Computers and Creativity

Before leaving aids to individual creativity we should frankly ask ourselves whether computers, the great electronic brains, help or hinder creativity. One point is clear, a computer has no ability for serendipity; it does not know how to catch and evaluate accidental impulses. In fact, computer engineers do their best to avoid anything except programmed impulses. Because all computer output is programmed, novel or original combinations of ideas are off limits.

But computers need not be regarded as a stifling influence. Many have a large memory and an uncanny capacity to recall details. So if we know how to tap into that memory, we can use the computer as a supplement in the saturation stage. Furthermore, with its lightning speed a computer can make a more thorough examination of relationships and exceptions to standard patterns than can the human mind. This capability may help us in the deliberation stage. The computer, then, like libraries and laboratory equipment, is a potential supplement to the human mind in particular stages of the creative process.

Therefore, if we are not overawed by the computer and can use it without losing spontaneity in our thinking and emotions, it need not constrain creative thought. If used alone the computer would give us a dull, automated existence. But, like social conformity and critical analysis, when used as a means to prepare us for the exciting frontiers of human development the computer can be a liberating tool.

AIDS TO GROUP CREATIVITY

Under favorable conditions, a group of people may generate more creative ideas when working together than when working individually. Several different schemes have been devised by business firms to benefit from group stimulation. We shall examine two of the most popular of these schemes, brainstorming and synectics, partly for the techniques themselves but more for the light they throw on the way group activity can contribute to creativity.

Brainstorming

You may have been in a group making up a skit to mimic your professors; but even in a more formal group—perhaps a hospital board thinking about ways to gain public support for a new building—the flow of ideas might be similar. One person tosses in an offbeat idea that someone else quickly tops by another. While chuckling over these suggestions, a third person chimes in with a proposal that is really ridiculous, but can be in part salvaged to improve the earlier ideas. The animated spirit of the group is contagious. No one cares whether each idea is practical; just thinking them up is good fun. Out of such a session, an ingenious plan that no group member would have thought of alone is likely to emerge.

Alex F. Osborn has used many of the characteristics of group interaction in what he calls "brainstorming." When we are confronted with a problem that calls for an original solution, Osborn recommends that we present the problem to a group of people, and ask them to think up as many possible solutions as they can. Important rules for his group procedure are:

1) *Rule out judicial judgment.* Criticism of ideas must be withheld till later.

2) *Welcome freewheeling.* The wilder the idea, the better; it is easier to tame down than to think up.

3) *Solicit quantity.* The greater the number of ideas, the more likelihood of winners.

4) *Seek combinations and improvements.* In addition to contributing ideas of their own, participants should suggest how ideas of others can be sharpened or how two or more ideas can be joined together.

Executives have used this technique on a wide variety of problems, including: how to find new uses for glass in autos, how to improve a company newspaper, how to design a new tire-making machine, how to improve highway signs, and how to cut down absenteeism. An hour session is likely to produce anywhere from 60 to 150 ideas. Most suggestions will be impractical; others will be trite. But a few of the ideas will be worth serious consideration. Note that brainstorming sessions fall under illumination, the fourth stage in the creative process we described earlier in this chapter.

Brainstorming seems to work best when a problem is simple and specific. If an issue has too many facets, discussion lacks focus. If a problem is complicated and excessively time-consuming, and if it requires writing out a possible solution, discussion will lose its spontaneity. To overcome these difficulties, careful diagnosis to identify the "real problem" should precede any brainstorming session. Complex issues should be broken up into parts, and perhaps a separate session should be devoted to each important part.

Brainstorming has other limitations in addition to the requirement that a problem be simple. Both the session itself and later evaluation of ideas, many of them worthless, are time-consuming. It also tends to produce superficial answers. To some extent, we can overcome these restrictions by adjusting the way sessions are handled and by selecting as members of the group people who deeply understand at least one aspect of a problem. Many business executives feel that even though brainstorming sessions do not stir up highly useful ideas every time, the stimulating effect of a session carries over into their other work. This stimulation tends to jar people out of routinized habits of thought and to force them to take a fresh look at all their activities.[6]

Synectics

A more recent and more formalized approach to creativity through group activity is synectics. The word is drawn from a Greek word meaning

---

[6]Controlled experiments by psychologists indicate that during scheduled periods, motivated individuals working independently produce more ideas than when they work in groups. These findings imply that the success of brainstorming may arise largely from ensuring uninterrupted attention, engendering a relaxed and receptive attitude, and stimulating effort. In other words, the conditions surrounding a brainstorming session probably are more significant than the group action per se.

"the fitting together of diverse elements." The approach is largely the product of William J. J. Gordon, chairman and founder of a corporation called Synectics, Inc.[7]

Synectics shares with brainstorming three basic assumptions on creativity: (1) All people possess a greater degree of creativity than they typically are able to tap; (2) in seeking creative ideas, emotional and seemingly irrational elements of thought are as important as the intellectual and rational elements; and (3) the key is to harness the emotional and irrational through methodology and discipline.

Synectics differs from brainstorming in several important respects:

1) As a first step, the problem is thoroughly explored. This step provides a highly analytical treatment both of technical features and of the broad setting. Here the preceding diagnosis is reviewed and questioned. Only after all members of the synectics group are thoroughly oriented to the nature of the problem do they seek novel ideas.

2) Next, the group leader picks a key aspect of the problem and poses this as a general issue or evocative idea.

3) Then explicit devices to "invoke the preconscious mind" are used. These may induce all sorts of fantasies and wild ideas. Typically, all participants are trained in the use of direct and symbolic analogies, impersonations, and other techniques that have proven to be helpful in developing novel viewpoints and ideas. Thus each participant is well aware of the "method in the madness" of a synectics session.

4) Being skilled in the process, the group can move back and forth from an apparently irrelevant discussion to the real problem. A technical expert within the group assists in appraising the novelty and feasibility of various ideas. So instead of producing a large number of superficial and random ideas as in brainstorming, this group screens ideas frequently.

Because of these characteristics, synectics can deal with much more complex and technical problems than brainstorming, and in a sophisticated manner.

Permissive Atmosphere

What general guides to creativity do techniques like brainstorming and synectics suggest? One crucial characteristic is a permissive atmosphere. Probably the cardinal rule of both approaches is this: Postpone the evaluation of ideas. Anyone who says "That won't work" should be quickly squelched, and no one should be afraid to present an idea that is admittedly impractical. Tough, critical, searching analysis is by no means avoided, but it is deferred until a later time. Withholding judgment is sound psychologically. Social barriers, as we already noted, tend to make

[7]See Gordon's book, *Synectics* (New York: Harper & Row, 1961); and "Synectics: Inventing by the Madness Method," *Fortune* (August 1965), pp. 165–94.

all of us conform to conventional ideas, and in many companies a person who makes a novel suggestion is laughed at or considered peculiar. As a result, new ideas are repressed. In such an atmosphere a person thinks about his ideas carefully and assures himself of their practicality before he dares to express them.

In contrast, brainstorming and synectics seek to remove these social barriers for at least a brief period. Because everyone recognizes the distinction between mentioning an idea and recommending it, a man's reputation for sound judgment is not at stake. The influence of social pressure is reversed. Originality is encouraged, and the desirable member of the group is the person who has lots of ideas.

Even when no formal technique like brainstorming is used, a permissive atmosphere can go far in encouraging creativity. New ideas are more likely to emerge when they receive a warm welcome. Specifically, in a permissive atmosphere (1) people are free to express ideas even though they are at variance with past practices, group norms, or the views of the leaders; (2) supervisors and colleagues give positive encouragement to a person who wants to try something new and different; and (3) mutual respect for individuality runs deep enough so that a person expresses his creative ideas without worrying about an unfavorable response. The man who cherishes stability and respects tradition will probably be unhappy in such a permissive atmosphere, but these are the conditions in which creative thinking is most likely to flourish.

Adapting and Borrowing

The encouragement of adaptation and borrowing is a second generally useful feature of both brainstorming and synectics. Each individual may have a perceptual or other mental block that limits the ideas that occur to him. But the reciprocal exchange in brainstorming and the use of analogies in synectics provide ways of hurdling these mental blocks. One member of the group picks up an idea where another leaves off, adds to it, or changes it freely. Still a third individual, not inhibited by the assumptions of the first two, may give the idea a new twist. Thus one idea builds on another.

Such a procedure may open up ideas that would never occur to "the lone wolf" who guards his secret formula until it is in a finished shape and ready to startle the world. Because credit for a creative idea may be hard to assign to a single individual due to extensive adapting and borrowing, such free interchange is likely to work well only when participants are more interested in an end result than in personal glory. To capture the full benefits of adapting and borrowing, then, we need team spirit and dedication to overall objectives.

This analysis suggests, then, that certain kinds of group attitude can help promote creativity. A permissive atmosphere, coupled with a free give-and-take of ideas, is necessary to harness the potential strengths of the group. These attitudes can be encouraged as a general policy even where particular techniques such as brainstorming and synectics do not happen to fit.

RELATING CREATIVITY TO DIAGNOSIS

Having looked at the stages involved in creative thought and at individual and group aids to creativity, we must now consider a criticism of rational diagnosis with respect to its impact on creativity. A few critics contend that the methodical, highly analytical approach suggested for diagnosing a problem by its nature inhibits the decision-maker's creativity. They use the successes produced by brainstorming as evidence to support their position. We strongly believe the opposite to be true.

By clearly and sharply identifying a problem or unrealized opportunity, by clearly homing in on the root cause or obstacle to this problem or opportunity, the decision-maker should be able to utilize his creative talent to the maximum. By looking at the subparts of a complex problem and alternative means of realizing higher-level goals, the decision-maker can focus every ounce of his creative talent on seeking alternative ways of solving more precise subproblems for which no satisfactory solution is known. Further, given the nature of a thorough diagnosis, he can do so without losing sight of the relationships among the parts.

Actually synectics combines both diagnosis and creativity. In a synectics session, the preliminary analysis of a problem is sharply analytical: The entire group's thinking is pushed to root causes and stubborn obstacles. Only then, as in brainstorming, is nonlogical thought encouraged. Moreover, in synectics the group returns to its diagnosis from time to time when someone thinks he sees a possible application of a strange thought to the identified difficulty.

Therefore, when we are faced with tough problems we need keen diagnosis to help channel our creative efforts. The chances that a person who is unaware of a need will think of a novel solution is exceedingly small.

CONCLUSION: IMPACT
OF ORGANIZATION ON CREATIVITY

In concluding our examination of creativity, we might note two points where earlier suggestions for achieving organized effort appear to conflict with proposals for stimulating creative thought:

1) Most conspicuous is the matter of conformity. To achieve harmonious, united effort of workers in an enterprise, we need genuine acceptance of official objectives, policies, and procedures. Yet for creativity we want people to challenge existing beliefs and modes of thought freely. A manager can reconcile these two points of view at least partially by making clear when and where independent thinking is desired and when and where it is not. In our personal life we often draw such distinctions, conforming to many social mores, but defying others. Russian scientists pay homage to communist economic doctrine and still create notable engineering advances. The tough question is whether an individual, by his own volition, and in response to the needs of his enterprise, can conform to, say, a cash-and-carry policy for years and then back off for creative thinking about changes in that policy. We believe many executives—and operators—can make such a switch if they are adjusted to the idea of continual change in at least a few activities at a time in a dynamic system.

2) Organization develops status distinctions. To reinforce the influence of higher-ranking executives and of senior staff we give them titles and other status symbols and place some power in their hands. Does not such status inhibit the free expression of challenging ideas? Will a low-ranking person present an idea that contradicts one proposed by a man of high status? Again we can in part reconcile the apparent conflict by distinguishing where and when novel ideas will be welcomed. Just as an elevator operator may feel free to tell a president about good fishing spots, so can a foreman tell a vice-president in charge of production about possible improvement in manufacturing methods. For such suggestions to fall freely, however, the vice-president must make clear that he welcomes new ideas and recognizes that many of them may not prove to be feasible.

A theme running through our discussion in Parts One, Two, and Four is the degree of freedom of action delegated to managers and operators. One facet of such flexibility is a permissiveness that nourishes creative action. However, more than a favorable management structure is necessary for creativity to flourish. A conducive leadership style is also vital, so we shall return to the freedom-permissiveness-creativity issue in Part Five.

Knowing about creativity will not necessarily make an executive creative, but it should enable him to help build a total work situation where creativeness can thrive.

FOR CLASS DISCUSSION

Questions

1) What do you feel the effects of a clear, complete diagnosis will be in terms of its likely impact on creativity?

2) "One trouble with our younger employees today," said a personnel vice-president, "is that they all want to be 'creative,' to do their 'thing,' and there is only so much room for creativity in a company which also needs enough stability or constancy to permit coordination and economies of scale." Discuss this observation.

3) How does the need for, and likelihood of finding, creativity in business relate to the material on classification and potency of human needs discussed in Chapter 8?

4) Can a computer develop "creative" alternatives to a problem? What similarities may there be between the way a computer operates and the way a human mind may operate in the search for a new idea? What differences may there be?

5) To what extent might one use at least some of the guidelines for brainstorming to carry it out on an *individual* rather than a group basis? What might be the *gains* and *losses* in individual, as opposed to group, brainstorming in terms of their contribution to saturation, deliberation, incubation, illumination, and accommodation?

6) In what ways may explaining a problem to people who lack a detailed understanding of the situation involved aid in developing creative alternatives? Could merely "talking to" a tape recorder and then listening to the tape provide the same help? Different help? Explain.

7) In what ways may a manager's past experiences in a company *improve* his potential for coming up with a creative approach? What factors are likely to determine whether, on balance, his past experience will aid or detract from his natural creativity?

8) A four-story department store, after modernizing its elevators, was still plagued by complaints from women shoppers about the amount of time they had to wait for an elevator. The store owners would like to avoid using any more floor space for escalators or additional elevators. Try to develop at least five creative and feasible alternatives for them. First allow yourself just to "freewheel" and then set the problem up in terms of a means-end chain and see whether this helps.

9) To what extent may "change for the sake of change" contribute to, or detract from, the likelihood of coming up with a creative approach when a creative approach is most necessary?

Cases

For cases involving issues covered in this chapter, see especially the following. Particularly relevant questions are listed after each case.

Trans-World Mutual Funds, Ltd. (p. 121), 9
Dodge Skate Company (p. 337), 6

Bolling Laboratories, Inc. (p. 345), 10, 12
Western Office Equipment Manufacturing Company (p. 457), 7
Consolidated Instruments—B (p. 674), 9

FOR FURTHER READING

Gruber, H.E., ed., *Contemporary Approaches to Creative Thinking*. New York: Atherton Press, 1962. *Symposium by six eminent scholars; stresses distinctive aspects of creativity in the thinking process.*

Parnes, S.J., and H.F. Harding, eds., *A Source Book for Creative Thinking*. New York: Charles Scribner's Sons, 1962. *Comprehensive collection of articles on creativity.*

Schon, D.A., *Invention and the Evolution of Ideas*. London: Associated Book Publishers, Ltd., 1967. *Relates ideas of great thinkers throughout history to specific process of developing new concepts.*

Stein, M.I., and S.J. Heinze, *Creativity and the Individual*. New York: The Free Press, 1960. *Annotated bibliography (actually digests) of psychological studies relating to creativity.*

Steiner, G.A., ed., *The Creative Organization*. Chicago: University of Chicago Press, 1965. *Papers by scientists, scholars, and executives presented at a seminar on creativity in large organizations.*

Comparing Courses of Action

RATIONAL ANALYSIS

Up to this point, we have dealt with diagnosing management problems and finding possible solutions to them. After an executive has his alternative solutions in mind, he must carefully compare them as a basis for finally choosing one.

The scope of this comparative analysis is dictated in part by the preceding phases of decision-making. Ferreting out the root cause or obstacle, for example, may clearly point to a single course of action. Or the search for creative alternatives may uncover a line of action clearly superior to all others. For these situations relatively little projecting of, or choosing among, alternatives is necessary. In other cases, several plausible alternatives may be known but the consequences of adopting any one may be complex and uncertain. In this case, concepts and methods of predicting results aid greatly in putting the alternatives in a form that will permit rational choice.

Of course, not all important choices are made rationally—that is, by deliberate, objective, and logical thought. The selection of a wife, for instance, is occasionally influenced by other than purely logical considerations. Nevertheless, it is a maxim of modern management that executives' decisions will be substantially improved if they rationally analyze the advantages and disadvantages of each alternative.

Defining Alternatives

A rational comparison must rest on a clear understanding of the problem being solved and the alternatives being considered. In this regard, Clarence Day recounts an amusing scene in which his mother returns from a shopping trip feeling very virtuous because the two hats she purchased cost less than the dress she didn't buy. Her husband protests that the family finances cannot stand the extravagance of two new hats, and further observes that he badly needs a new suit. His wife carefully makes a few calculations and proudly advises her husband that the money she saved from buying the hats rather than the dress was large enough so that he could go right ahead and get his new suit.

Obviously, Mr. Day thought of the alternatives as two hats versus cash in the bank, whereas Mrs. Day conceived of them as a new dress versus two hats plus something left over. Until they could agree on which set of alternatives they were discussing (which they never did), there was no hope of agreeing on a desirable course of action.

But we should be charitable in our opinion of Mrs. Day; business executives, who should know better, sometimes let themselves slip into the same kind of thinking. In one firm, for instance, when sales executives met with representatives of their advertising agency to discuss the choice of magazines for ads, the sales manager repeatedly brought up the possibility of spending less money for TV shows and more for salesmen. The meeting got nowhere. The comparison of alternatives foundered because of lack of agreement on the immediate objective being sought.

Restating a problem and adding alternatives are often desirable actions, as we have pointed out, but we should not muddle a comparison of alternatives with such revisions. Orderly, rational decision-making requires that we be aware of which phase of the process we are dealing with at any particular moment. If a revision of a problem appears desirable, we can revert to diagnosis; then, with the new issue in mind, we can concentrate on an analysis of ways of resolving it. Once a problem is clear and alternatives are set forth, a manager can proceed immediately to figuring out the advantages of each.

Tough versus Creative Attitude

In our earlier discussion of the creative process, we emphasized such matters as stimulating imagination, providing a permissive atmosphere, and even nurturing screwball ideas. Our purpose was to propose ways to cultivate fresh and original thought.

The comparison of alternatives requires a different frame of mind. Here we want to be as sure as possible that we are right. Therefore we challenge evidence, stick to issues and rule out irrelevant points, prove points logically, and listen to a man who says "No" in order to discover any valid reasons he might set forth. This is a time for tough, critical thinking.

People are usually adept at either creative thinking or tough-minded analysis, but rarely at both. In fact, a man who excels in one type of thinking is likely to be impatient and scornful of the other. Yet both qualities of mind are needed for decision-making. An executive who is good at both is fortunate indeed. But every manager should at least be aware of the distinction between creative thought and searching analysis in the planning process, and should understand the contributions different people may make so that he can intelligently seek help where he is weak. In the following sections we shall point out ways to apply rigorous thinking to making rational choices.

IDENTIFYING ALL SIGNIFICANT CONSEQUENCES

To appraise an alternative wisely, we must try to foresee its impact on various company goals if we select it as a course of action. Its consequences are likely to be both desirable and undesirable, both immediate and long-range, both tangible and intangible, both certain and only possible, and we should take all possibilities into account.

Failure to think a plan through is easy to spot *after* a decision has been made and trouble develops. For example, the sales promotion manager of a large furniture store once chose a special cut-out circular instead of a customary printed sheet to promote an August sale. He was filled with enthusiasm for the cut-out and offered many reasons why it would attract more attention. But he failed to anticipate a need for special envelopes, extra labor to prepare the cut-outs for mailing, and double postage costs. The resulting delay in getting the circular to consumers offset its attractiveness and the total expense was substantially increased. In this instance, the sales promotion manager's estimate of the added impact of a cut-out was probably right, but by focusing on its merits he failed to see the difficulties involved. Had he forecast these drawbacks, he could then have dealt with each as a subproblem. He could have sought alternative ways of handling each and then added the cost of handling these problems to the total cost of the cut-out alternative. With all costs included in his projections he might well have selected another alternative.

In the early days of scientific management, one-sided emphasis was common. Industrial engineers often devised excellent schemes for simplifying jobs, providing mechanical aids to make work easy, and setting output standards and piece rates that enabled average workers to earn substantial bonuses. But in the application of the schemes, difficulties would crop up. Workers often felt that output standards were so much higher than what they had been accustomed to that they simply refused to try to achieve them. Sometimes women would be assigned to what traditionally was "men's work"; this practice upset status relationships and created passive resistance to a whole plan. In other instances, simplification in one department merely transferred headaches to another department. These difficulties arose because management failed to foresee all significant consequences before selecting a particular course of action.

Predicting Impact of Proposed Action

A manager needs thorough acquaintance with an operation and a realistic imagination to anticipate fully the consequences of each alternative. Often a wide range of factors is involved. For example, the sales manager of a manufacturer of power lawn mowers and related equipment recommended that the company establish an assembly shop on the West Coast. He said that this move would lower costs and improve customer service, thereby enabling the company to meet competition of local West Coast manufacturers. At the time, the company had only a sales office and warehouse for finished products in California. Among the questions to which the company sought answers before making a final decision on the sales manager's proposal were the following:

1) What will be the difference in cost between shipping parts and shipping assembled products?

2) How much will we have to pay for direct labor in the California plant? How much for indirect labor such as maintenance, janitors, and so on? What reduction, if any, in labor costs will there be at the main plant?

3) How much additional overhead will the California shop require? This includes rent (or, if we own the plant, taxes, depreciation, maintenance, and interest), power, heat, and light. How many clerks and supervisors, at what salaries, will we need for assembly work? Will there be any offsetting reduction in overhead at the main plant?

4) How much additional capital will we have to tie up in West Coast operations if the new shop is opened? This includes capital for equipment, office furniture, and other fixed assets; additional inventory; moving and setup costs; and operating losses during the period when the shop is getting under way.

5) Will the new shop be flexible enough to adjust to seasonal changes in volume of business? What minimum staff will have to be retained during low periods? Would there be greater flexibility at the main plant than at the new shop?

6) Will manufacturing in California subject the company to special state taxes or added liability insurance? Will it be advantageous to establish a separate corporation?

7) Just what will be the improvement in service to customers? How will local assembly ensure speedier deliveries than warehousing finished products? Will local repair and troubleshooting be feasible, and how much weight will this carry with customers? Will delivery of repair parts be improved?

8) In addition to actual improvement in customer service, will the "local industry" appeal have a significant effect on sales volume?

9) Will the quality of product be as well controlled in California as in the main plant?

10) Will the union at the main plant object to transferring work to another location? Might jurisdictional problems arise if a different union organizes the West Coast operations?

11) Should the West Coast shop be under the direction of a West Coast sales manager? What responsibility, if any, will the production manager have for West Coast operations? How will accounting and personnel be coordinated with the main plant?

12) How much additional sales volume can be anticipated as a result of establishing a West Coast assembly shop? How much will company profit be increased as a result of this additional volume?

Only after checking into all of these questions was the president of the power mower company prepared to make a decision on the proposed West Coast assembly shop. He had a staff assistant assemble financial information and summarize it as shown in Table 13–1.

In trying to anticipate the impact of an action, executives typically give a lot of attention to the results they wish to achieve—say, a higher sales volume. They tend to overlook the benefits of existing practice that may be lost if the proposed plan is put into effect—perhaps present customers will get poorer service or layoffs may be necessary in an existing plant. One way we can identify the point of impact is to ask each key executive whether he would be glad to follow *any* one of the alternatives being considered. If the answer is "No," then we should ask why he prefers one plan rather than others. His explanation may bring to our attention factors that should be considered.

Thinking through each alternative means not only recognizing where a proposed action will have an impact, but also gathering facts and making judgments about the strength of reaction of each point of impact. Frequently this stage of decision-making entails a great deal of fact-gathering. Once the points of impact have been identified, however, an executive can sift out those facts that really bear on the issue that confronts him.

Weighing "Other Consequences"

No managerial action has a single result. Although an action may make an important contribution to a mission, it will also result in some expense or sacrifice. It may even contribute to two or more recognized objectives—say, immediate sales *and* customer goodwill. In fact, most actions have a full range of consequences, each of which needs to be valued. Sometimes we become so intent on one or two challenging objectives that we brush aside (undervalue) other consequences of a plan to meet the objective. For example, Americans who advocate that the United States give surplus wheat to starving people in other parts of the world

Table 13–1 *Relative income and expenditures if new assembly shop results in doubling West Coast sales.**

	Main Plant (assembles $200,000 worth of mowers for West Coast sales)	West Coast Shop (assembles $400,000 worth of mowers)	Difference (West Coast minus main plant)
Additions to present investment:			
Equipment	0	$ 30,000	
Starting-up costs	0	10,000	
Parts inventory	0	15,000	
Total	0	$ 55,000	$ 55,000
Annual income and expenses affected:			
Income (West Coast sales)	$200,000	$400,000	$200,000
Expenses:			
Cost of parts (increments)	90,000	170,000	
Shipping to West Coast:			
Assembled mowers	15,000		
Parts		22,000	
Assembly labor:			
Direct	12,000	24,000	
Indirect	4,000	12,000	
Overhead:			
Supervision	0	8,000	
Clerical	0	5,000	
Power, heat, light	200	800	
Shop rent	0	7,600	
Depreciation	0	2,000	
Taxes and insurance	0	500	
West Coast sales commissions	10,000	20,000	
Total	$131,200	$271,900	$140,700
Net annual gain (sales difference minus expense difference)			$ 59,300

Rate of return (before income tax):
First year $59,300 ÷ $55,000 = 108%
Average year† $59,300 ÷ $40,000 = 148%

*Only those accounts affected by the choice of one of the two alternatives are listed: the amounts shown in each column are additional expenditures or income that would occur if that alternative were selected.
†Equipment costs presumably will be recovered by depreciation, and so the investment in equipment will drop from $30,000 to zero, or average $15,000. Using the $15,000 figure, the total investment would be $40,000 in an average year.

tend to underestimate the political repercussions in nations whose wheat exports might be curtailed because of our gifts. On a smaller scale, the production manager of a shoe company who wants to cut costs by eliminating low-volume, slow-moving sizes may overlook the interest of a few big retail stores in being able to fit virtually all customers.

The industrial engineering department of a small company proposed a plan for eliminating overtime. By careful scheduling, and by purchasing a few additional machines and hiring operators for them, the company could cut out overtime, which had been averaging four hours per week for all men in the shop. But one consequence the proposal did not consider was the 15 percent cut (four hours at time-and-a-half) in take-home pay that the men now in the shop would suffer. Labor supply at the time was tight, and the industrial relations director felt sure that such a move would indirectly lead to demands for a higher base rate and perhaps to some turnover of experienced personnel. The possibility of these additional consequences was sufficiently serious that only the scheduling part of the proposal was put into effect; this cut overtime only one and a half hours, and no conspicuous event like installing machinery called attention to the change.

"Other consequences" are apt to be overlooked because they do not, at a given moment, prompt managerial action. The spur to decision—what management clearly wants done—gets the limelight. The other consequences are unavoidable extras, whether desirable or undesirable. But as extras, rather than the star attraction, they are only reluctantly included on the bill of what may already be a complex evaluation. The significance of these other consequences reflects additional goals not included in our original statement of the problem. A single objective helps in our diagnosis and in finding alternatives, but we must be prepared to recognize other goals when we project the full range of consequences of a proposed action.

From the preceding discussion, we can see that spelling out the consequences of alternative courses of action is no easy and routine matter. Each managerial situation has its own distinctive characteristics. Because fact-gathering and analysis may become quite elaborate, we need to give special attention to ways of *simplifying the process.* Five useful approaches to simplifying the comparisons are: (1) focusing on differences, (2) stating differences in dollar terms, (3) simplifying the projection of intangibles, (4) narrowing the number of alternatives, and (5) concentrating on crucial factors. Let us examine each of these.

FOCUSING ON DIFFERENCES

Disregard Common Elements

One important means of simplifying the comparison of alternatives is to disregard the common aspects of all proposed plans and to focus on differences in results. This principle is clearly illustrated in the case of the West Coast assembly shop. In choosing between doing *all* assembly in the main plant and doing *part* of it in the West Coast shop, management could ignore the cost of raw materials, which would be purchased by headquarters at uniform costs regardless of the location of final assembly. The company could likewise disregard the West Coast sales organization and sales personnel because no change in them would be anticipated as a consequence of adopting either alternative. Because the president's salary would not be affected, it too could be passed over.

When we suggest disregarding common elements, we do not mean that they are unimportant or that they too may not be improved. The point is simply that we need not clutter up our thinking with them, because they will be unaffected by whatever choice we make. Later, *separate* attention can be given to improving an element that is not involved in our immediate problem—for instance, material costs in the preceding case—but that is an issue apart.

Care is needed in applying this principle, however, for we may be in danger of assuming too many constants. If, for example, further study of the West Coast assembly shop indicates that it would substantially increase sales volume, then management would have to revise its assumption that sales organization and sales personnel would remain unchanged. The cost of shipping finished goods from warehouse to present customers presents a similar problem. If the establishment of the new assembly shop would not alter the pattern of final shipment, then shipping costs could be left out of account. But if, on the other hand, the assembly shop is to be moved to a different city, or if management anticipates that sales will

Chapter Thirteen

Comparing
Courses of Action

Fig. 13–1 One way to reduce the complexity of the task of comparing alternatives is to sort out and ignore any common factors. For example, a comparison of the left- and right-hand groups here reveals only three distinctive elements in each.

jump so much as a result of opening the shop that a more economical method of delivery will be possible, then costs of delivering finished goods should be included as a factor in the decision. In short, there is nothing wrong with disregarding a common element so long as we are positive that the element will, in fact, be unaffected by our choice.

STATING DIFFERENCES IN DOLLAR TERMS

It is hard for any executive to keep in mind all the factors pertinent to a decision and to give each its proper relative weight. One way to reduce the complexity of the job is to translate economic factors into dollars of income, expense, or investment. Usually these dollar figures can then be combined into one or two key *net* amounts, which are concise and relatively easy to handle. But they are dangerous in that they may invite too much consideration because they are easier to grasp than subjective factors and because they seem to be more reliable than is warranted by the assumptions on which they are based. Still, for many decisions the advantages of net dollar figures outweigh the danger that they will be misused.

A choice among alternatives, as we already discussed, depends on the *differences* in their consequences. Insofar as we can compute net income or net expenses for each alternative, it is simple to subtract one from another to determine the difference in income or expense. Similarly, if any alternatives involve a change in investment, we can readily compute the difference in investment. Thus, one or two net dollar figures can summarize a whole series of factors.

We can show more clearly in the following examples both how consolidated dollar figures simplify decision and what the common problems in computation are.

Use of Accounting Data

A first requirement is the ability to use accounting data developed for tax or financial purposes to identify those elements of income, expense, or investment that really change with the alternatives considered. The accounting department in preparing statements for the Internal Revenue Service must follow certain conventions concerning income, expense, and investment. The finance department in preparing reports to stockholders, creditors, and various governmental agencies may be required to follow different reporting conventions. When projected in financial terms, it is entirely possible for the same group of alternatives to look quite different depending on which set of conventions is used. As decision-makers, we should be aware of how a decision will look to a tax collector, a stockholder, or a regulatory agency in Washington, but it is probably more important to know how it will look in terms of the real impact on the elements of profit that the firm can control.

For example, suppose we are trying to decide which of several materials to use in the manufacture of a special product. One type of material is in very short supply, but our company has enough to meet our needs for this product. This material cost the company $5,000 and is carried on the books at this figure. Because the market value of the material has gone up, however, another firm is interested in purchasing it for $8,000. If we use it in making the product, what expense is incurred?

For tax purposes, we would have to enter the cost as $5,000. When reporting the change in inventory for balance-sheet calculations we might consider it as $8,000 (market value) but would probably enter it as $5,000 (original cost). Clearly, though, in projecting the cost of the product, we should consider alternatives—and if we use this material we should for decision-making purposes record the cost as $8,000, for this is what the material is worth today.

The decision-maker must be prepared to take income, expense, or investment figures computed for other purposes and adjust them to reflect the differences among alternatives he is considering. Because this process is so vital, we shall outline below the general concept that guides the decision-maker in carrying out these adjustments.

Incremental Concept

Here is a disarmingly simple principle that seems so logical that you may think it is certainly the way costs and revenues are commonly computed in projections. It is merely a particular form of the "disregard common elements" concept. Unfortunately, we shall find both conceptual and practical difficulties in following the proposed golden rule.

Simply stated, the principle is: In projecting any relevant revenues, expenses, or investments, seek to identify the *difference* between (1) those that will be involved if the projected course of action is adopted and (2) those that would exist even if the proposal were not adopted. We disregard those revenues, expenses, or investments that are "sunk," that is, which would be incurred or realized in any event. Thus we isolate the "incremental" revenues, savings, expenses, or investments that would result from the proposal.

As a first illustration of the incremental concept, consider the case of an international news service that sponsored the design of equipment that would enable the service to use satellite communications. After studying the situation closely, management had decided that the undertaking would be profitable if relatively trouble-free equipment could be developed for less than two million dollars in research and development. Research people and engineers assured central management that there was a good chance of coming up with such equipment for less than two million dollars, and so the project was authorized. Today, after a few years' work, two million dollars has been spent, but satisfactory equipment has not yet been perfected.

The research people have stated that they have made great progress, even though they have been unsuccessful in producing the sought-for results. They are certain that they can now produce the desired equipment with an additional expenditure of under one million dollars, probably about half a million.

What should management do? Even if the new machine were successfully developed with the additional outlay, the project is still doomed to lose money. As much as three million dollars will have been spent to get savings of a little more than two million dollars. It might appear unwise to spend the additional million. The company officials might be accused of throwing good money after bad. If the most recent cost estimates are correct, however, and unless the news service has much more attractive uses for its money, the expenditure should be made. We can quickly see why by applying the marginal concept. At this point in time, if the company does nothing it will recover none of the two million already spent on research. This money represents a sunk cost, one already incurred and not affected by the present decision. Therefore, though it may be painful, we disregard it. The question to be asked is, "What additional, or incremental, costs and savings are involved?"

If the present projections are correct, then the incremental (additional) costs will be less than one million dollars and the incremental (additional) saving received will be something more than two million dollars. Overall, the company will probably still lose money on this venture, but by continuing the project its loss will be reduced by at least a million dollars—the excess of incremental saving over incremental cost.

Pitfalls in Traditional Accounting Concepts

As a further illustration of the incremental concept as applied to cost and revenue, let us take a case in which problems arising out of traditional accounting concepts are encountered.

The Elton Metal Products Company received an invitation to produce a specially designed pipe fitting to be used in warehouse refrigeration. Elton developed and produced 1,000 fittings at a total cost of $2,750. A large portion of this expense was the cost of developing the fitting and of converting a metal-working machine to make it suitable for manufacturing the piece. Now, on completion of this contract, the sales manager of Elton has been offered an additional order from a building contractor for 500 fittings. In setting a price for the second order, the cost statement shown in Table 13–2 has been prepared.

The first question we ask is whether some of these costs would be incurred even if Elton turned down the second order.

Certainly additional costs for labor, materials, and handling would be incurred over and above what Elton will pay out if it does not accept the order. But what of research and development costs, conversion costs, and general overhead? Because the research and development has been done, it is a sunk, or nonavoidable, expense. Turning down the order will not reduce this item by one cent. Therefore, these certainly are not pertinent costs. Let us assume that the same is true for conversion costs. What of "general overhead"? This entry includes the share of general operating expenses charged to this project—such costs as executive salaries, maintaining the factory, and the like. Again ask the incremental question. Will these costs be reduced if Elton does not produce the additional 500 units, and, if so, by how much? These additional overhead dollars are the crucial costs that should be considered in deciding on this order.

After carefully considering each item shown in the cost statement in Table 13–2, the Elton management has isolated certain items that would *really change* if an additional 500 units were produced (Table 13–3).

Many a cry will be raised at such an estimate because the project is not "carrying its fair share of allocated costs." Strictly speaking, this is true. But what will be accomplished if Elton holds out for a price in excess of $1,300 and does not make the sale? Suppose the top offer is $1,100. If Elton holds out for $1,300 they would be passing up $335 ($1,100—$765). Stated in another way, Elton would give up a chance to get incremental revenue of $1,100 while incurring only $765 in incremental costs.

Incremental analysis dictates that unless some alternative use of the facilities represented by $535 in sunk costs added more than $335 in additional revenue, Elton would be foolish to turn down this proposal. It should also be noted that Elton would be wise to turn down the proposal if accepting the $1,100 offer would result in losses of more than $335 in later price negotiations. However, any future loss that will result from taking this order at a low price is really an incremental cost of the decision. The decision-maker can estimate the amount of "opportunity cost" (that is, income lost in other alternatives or future pricing of this fitting) and compare it to the income gained by taking the order.

Table 13–2

	Cost for 500 Units
Labor	$ 350
Material	375
Power and materials handling	25
Research and development	150
Conversion costs	200
General overhead	200
	$1,300

Table 13–3

	Added Cost for 500 Units
Labor	$350
Material	375
Power and materials handling	25
General overhead	15
	$765

Variable versus Incremental Costs

We have just faced the first problem encountered in applying the incremental principle of costs—conventional accounting practice of allocating fixed costs. A second major problem is faced when we attempt to use standard accounting records to estimate costs. A distinction is commonly made between "fixed" and "variable" costs. From our previous observations it would seem that we could get incremental costs by taking only the latter. Unfortunately, the commonly used variable costs are not the same as incremental costs because they are normally computed as average variable costs. In addition, certain costs that are categorized as fixed in accounting terms may be incremental under certain conditions. The following two situations illustrate these problems.

Suppose the Elton company received an order for 5,000 more pipe fittings. Assume that Elton would have to buy a second specialized machine in order to be able to accept this order. The cost of buying the machine, a fixed cost in the usual accounting sense, is an incremental cost in this instance. It is a cost that will be incurred if the proposal is accepted but would not be incurred if the proposal is turned down.

Now you may ask why we cannot merely add such special fixed costs to the normal average variable costs computed by the accountant.

Table 13–4

Volume	Total Variable Cost	Average Variable Cost	Incremental Cost
0	0	0	0
10	$150,000	$15,000	$150,000 (for 10 units)
11	160,000	14,545	10,000
12	168,000	14,000	8,000
13	176,000	13,769	8,000
14	185,000	13,214	9,000
15	200,000	13,333	15,000

To see why not, let us leave the Elton example and examine the lists of costs for Millard Stamping Machines in Table 13–4. This table illustrates why variable costs, computed as averages, differ from incremental costs.

As you can see, the difference between average variable costs and incremental costs can be considerable, because average costs are averages of total variable costs while incremental costs are based only on the variable costs of the additional unit or units being considered.

To illustrate how a wrong decision might be reached if it were based on average variable costs, suppose the best price the twelfth unit could fetch was $11,000. If we were to use average variable costs, we would probably turn the offer down since the incremental revenue of $11,000 does not seem to cover the costs of the twelfth unit. The pertinent cost for the twelfth unit, however, is the incremental cost figure, $8,000; using this measure we see that incremental revenue for the twelfth unit does exceed the increase in costs incurred in producing it.

By the same token, suppose the best price offered for the fifteenth unit was $14,000. Average variable cost ($13,313) reduces the impact of the high cost of producing this fifteenth unit by averaging it in with the lower costs of the first 14 units. As a result, $14,000 of incremental revenue seems to make this price acceptable. Again, however, the significant measure of the cost of the fifteenth unit is the *additional* cost of producing it, the incremental cost of $15,000. In this case, incremental revenue ($14,000) does not exceed incremental costs ($15,000). Unless there are other reasons for taking a $1,000 loss on this sale, the offer should be turned down.

Adjusting for Differences in Time

Alternatives are difficult to compare when one produces large cash income (or requires a substantial outlay) at a much earlier date than do others. If we receive cash early we can use this capital for other purposes; we can lend it at interest if a more attractive use is not available within the company. If on the other hand we have to make large outlays early the capital tied up has a direct or imputed interest cost. To remove this difference caused by *when* cash flows in and out, we can adjust all receipts and disbursements to "present cash value," just as a banker discounts a bond or some other asset that will not turn to cash for several years.

SIMPLIFYING PROJECTION OF INTANGIBLES

This chapter has focused in large part on concepts and techniques for determining the relevant elements of cost and revenue associated with each alternative. In many complex situations, though, alternatives will also produce drawbacks and benefits that are difficult to translate into dollar costs and dollar revenues. Many of these intangible implications, however, can be stated in dollar terms if we avoid the temptation to evaluate them directly. Consider what happened at Millard Stamping Machines when management faced a decision on whether to accept an offer of $11,000 for one of its machines. Assuming that 11 machines had already been produced and sold for $16,000 and that this sale involves a new customer, what should they do?

Based on the tangible and relevant cost and revenue, an incremental outlay of $8,000 will bring in incremental revenue of $11,000. But what about the intangibles? For example, consider just the following two:

1) Possible difficulty in getting the normal $16,000 price from future customers.

2) Possible advantages of getting a foot in the door of the new customer, which may lead to future sales of equipment and parts.

Rather than merely try to weigh apples ($3,000 incremental gain) and oranges (plus and minus of intangibles), we should attempt to put a dollar sign on the intangibles. This is, in effect, what we would do intuitively anyway. So let us identify the elements involved in intangible factors and attempt to express the anticipated effect on these elements in dollar terms. For the first intangible, we should forecast the following:

1) How many future machines are we likely to sell at the $16,000 price if we reject this sale?

2) How many future customers are likely to know what price we charged for the 12 machines?

3) Of those who might know, how many are in a position to demand a price below $16,000?

4) How far below this price will they demand?

Answering any of these questions will indeed involve a great deal of educated guessing. We can make these guesses, however, somewhat easier and more accurately than the global guess about the more global question of "upsetting normal prices."

With respect to the second intangible, the benefits of getting "a foot in the door," the same kind of projections can be attempted:

1) How large a business does this customer do?

2) Is he likely to require additional equipment we make? If so, how much?

3) Will he be willing and able, economically, to pay normal prices for future purchases?

4) How much future parts replacement is required and what is the profit on such replacement?

Again, by taking the elements that determine the nature and magnitude of the intangible and projecting each in dollar terms, we can come closer to developing a dollar projection for the whole intangible factor.

In some cases, to be sure, no matter how hard we try there will be intangible consequences that defy quantification. In the field of operations research, investigators are currently attempting, through forced-choice comparisons, to develop some valid system for translating the implications of intangibles into dollar terms. However, much remains to be done before such "utility models," as they are often called, can be widely used.

In summary, we should seek to forecast and translate into dollar terms as many of the implications of each alternative as possible. Then the remaining, nondollar considerations can be kept to a minimum and presented for final consideration juxtaposed to the dollar projections. This process does not remove the need for some kind of forecasting theory, reduce the desirability of obtaining relevant data, or make the conclusions less subjective. Its purpose is to put projections into a form that will ease comparisons of alternatives.

NARROWING THE NUMBER OF ALTERNATIVES

The energy of managers is limited, and psychologically most of them prefer to work on plans that have a good prospect of being carried out. So the quicker they can hit paydirt, the better. To expedite getting at the main alternatives we can do two things: accept constraint on alternatives, and group similar alternatives during a first screening.

A diagnosis, as described in Chapter 11, often helps develop a list of limits that must be met by a satisfactory solution. We may treat these limits as constraints, that is, we may check proposed alternatives against limits, and if an alternative does not meet them, we can discard it. For instance, one small company seeking an additional product line might decide that a new product must be producible on existing equipment because the company has unused capacity and lacks capital to buy new facilities. Another company might say that a new product must be something its present sales organization could handle; any new product that failed to meet such a basic requirement would be eliminated from further consideration. With alternatives narrowed down by testing them against constraints, we can give closer attention to the eligible ones that remain.

In still other situations we may have such a large number of alternatives that comparing all of them even on one or two crucial factors would be tedious. To deal with this difficulty, we can group the alternatives into classes, pick a representative from each class, and compare these representative proposals. Then, having found the class that shows up best, we can concentrate on alternatives within that class. Such a procedure is often used in plant location studies. First, a region is selected by comparing a typical city from each region; then cities in the most attractive region are compared; finally, specific sites in one or two of the most desirable cities are given detailed study.

In any narrowing process, such as those we have suggested in this section, we risk discarding a course of action that, if completely analyzed, would appear very desirable. Nevertheless, as a practical matter, a complete analysis of all consequences of each alternative is impossible. Using constraints and groupings to narrow down alternatives probably has the least likelihood of error of any method.

CONCENTRATING ON CRUCIAL FACTORS

The burdensome task of projecting the consequences of following each selected alternative can be further simplified by giving primary attention to those factors that help us most in discriminating between good and not-so-good alternatives.

Satisfactory Levels for Some Factors

For some factors, it is possible to simplify by setting a satisfactory level of achievement, that is, a level where an objective is met adequately. Any alternative that achieves this level is acceptable. If all proposed courses of action are satisfactory by this standard, there is little or no difference in incremental values. The factor then becomes a minor consideration in making the choice or may be set aside entirely.

The concept of acceptable achievement ("satisficing") is widely used. Consider production costs. Theoretically, every manager wants to lower his costs continually—at least, so economists assume. But in practice, we find that a manager keeps his eye on critical levels of cost. When competition is sharp, the production costs of other companies set the critical level; or when a product has a popular price—say, one dollar—the important level is the one that permits a company to get the product on the market at the popular price while maintaining adequate margins to distributors in order to sustain sales volume. Production costs higher than such critical levels are unsatisfactory, and executives will press to reduce costs to the acceptable level. Even lower costs are desirable, to be sure, but the pressure to achieve them is not so great. In other words, the importance of increments in cost savings drops markedly after the critical level is achieved.

Establishing satisfactory levels for quality is also often useful. Bringing quality up to a given standard is highly important, but improvements beyond that point, though desirable, are not nearly so valuable. The same may be true for delivery service and water pollution. On the other hand, for such matters as accident prevention or sales volume, there is usually no clear-cut level at which incremental values change sharply.

Where "satisfactory" achievement levels apply, an executive finds that decision-making is simplified. He can reject a proposal if it is unsatisfactory on any count, and thereby narrow the number of alternatives for consideration. If the acceptable standard cuts out all alternatives, he seeks new proposals. As the last resort, he lowers his acceptable levels. If two or more proposals meet all the tests of acceptability, then he is back with the problem of choice between them. Nevertheless, the problem is now simpler because fewer proposals are still in the running, and some factors can be disregarded because differences between proposals are known to be insignificant.

Major Factors Affecting Choice

When we choose among alternatives, one, two, or perhaps three factors almost always are most important in making the decision. If we can single out and study these factors first, we may be able to eliminate the least attractive alternatives promptly.[1]

A paint company, to take an example, was comparing candidates to head up promotional work on a product discovered in its research laboratory. The product was a new plastic that had unusually high resistance to heat and abrasion and could presumably be used for parts in machines and rockets. Because the company's regular sales organization concentrated on paint, a new job was created for this distinctive product. Little supervision would be available, and most of the work would involve developing agreements with other companies for use of the product. Numerous qualifications could be listed for such a job, and so all candidates who met minimum standards or limits could be compared on each qualification. The personnel director of the paint company simplified the comparison, however, by selecting two qualities he considered most important for this particular job—initiative and decision-making talent; on the basis of these criteria he was able to narrow the list of candidates to three men who ranked highest on these qualities. Then, he carefully compared the three men on many other factors, such as knowledge of consumer industries, emotional stability, social sensitivity, salary requirements, and so on. To have attempted to appraise all candidates on all

[1] The advice appears to have run a full circle. In the beginning of the chapter we stressed looking at all consequences, and now we say to focus on the important consequences first. The distinction rests on two factors: (1) Taking a full perspective will ensure that the pressures of the moment, or conventional thinking, do not lead to inadequate coverage; once this perspective is achieved, wise simplification is possible and necessary. (2) A particular sequence for studying factors does not preclude full consideration of all factors for at least a few alternatives. Admittedly, unless the simplifying steps are taken with care, there is some risk of screening out prematurely a good alternative, but the surviving alternatives—the ones being considered at the time of the final choice—should have had the full screening proposed at the opening of the chapter.

factors would have taken more time than the executives of the paint company were able to spend on this selection problem.

The use of major factors can also be illustrated by the power mower company we considered. The firm's analysis of income and costs clearly showed that a move to the West Coast was desirable only if sales would increase substantially thereby. Sales volume was, thus, a crucial factor. So before spending more time in analyzing factors such as quality control, corporation taxes, and labor conditions, management should thoroughly explore the likelihood of achieving a large sales increase.

CONCLUSION

In this chapter, we picked up the decision-making process after a management problem has been discovered and clarified through diagnosis, and possible solutions are already identified. We then have to compare the proposed solutions to develop a basis for finally choosing an action to be taken.

The first guide for rational comparison of alternatives is to identify all significant consequences of each proposed line of action. At this point, we are concerned with anticipating the full ramifications of our decision. Unfortunately this approach may make the comparison tedious and extended, and so we must find ways of simplifying the comparison without doing serious damage to the breadth and perspective we have just urged. Five types of simplification are often helpful: (1) focusing attention on the differences in consequences and disregarding those aspects of a situation that will be unaffected by any alternative; (2) combining all dollar figures into one or two net totals; (3) simplifying the projection of intangibles by assigning "trade-off" dollar amounts to subjective feelings about importance; (4) narrowing the number of alternatives that are projected in detail; and (5) giving primary attention to factors that will most affect the final choice.

But a comparison is not a decision. We still have to decide which set of projected results we want. Value judgment and allowances for uncertainty enter into our final choice. These matters are discussed in the next chapter.

FOR CLASS DISCUSSION

Questions

1) The text suggests that we seldom find people who are adept at both creative thinking *and* tough-minded analysis. What organizational and/or interpersonal problems do you see in asking different

people to apply tough-minded judgment to creative ideas generated by others?

2) Often a manager will develop alternative ways of solving a problem and will find one clearly superior to the others except for one major disadvantage. Before eliminating this alternative, what should the manager do?

3) In what ways will (1) the sharpness with which a gap is stated and (2) the degree to which a specific problem is considered in the light of higher-level goals contribute to the process of comparing courses of action?

4) From the Elton Products example given on pages 298–300, give three specific reasons for turning down an offer to pay $1,100 for the 500 units that have an incremental cost of $765.

5) Assume a company has raw material in its inventory that it purchased months ago for $1,000. This material can be used in the production of a special product which would be made and sold at a marginal price to please a good customer. If the material is not so used it will be sold to another company for $950 in order to make room in the warehouse for other material. The material in question will ultimately be replaced but not for at least one year. It is estimated that the cost of replacing it a year or more from now will be $1,100. What is the relevant cost of material to be added to other costs in deciding whether to produce the special product for the good customer? Explain.

6) What should be the roles of staff groups and of the line manager responsible for a decision in projecting alternatives from which the line manager must choose?

7) In what ways may the generation of new or creative solutions increase the difficulty of comparing courses of action?

8) Often a thorough comparison of alternative courses of action would require a careful analysis of the assumptions and premises on which projected payoffs are based. When such analysis of assumptions and premises is impractical, what steps might be taken to judge the soundness of projected payoffs?

Cases

For cases involving issues covered in this chapter, see especially the following. Particularly relevant questions are listed after each case.

General Machinery Corporation (p. 130), 8, 9
Scott-Davis Corporation (p. 227), 10
Gerald Clark (p. 234), 12
Dodge Skate Company (p. 337), 7
Western Office Equipment Manufacturing Company (p. 457), 6, 8

E.W. Ross, Inc. (p. 468), 6
Consolidated Instruments—A (p. 571), 9

FOR FURTHER READING

Dean, J., *Capital Budgeting*. New York: Columbia University Press, 1951. *Comparison of capital expenditure projects by means of discounted cash flow estimates—a classic on this topic.*

Emory, C.W., and P. Niland, *Making Management Decisions*. Boston: Houghton Mifflin Company, 1968, Chap. 5. *Methods for evaluating alternatives presented in operational terms. Chapters 6–13 give good, nontechnical explanation of quantitative techniques for evaluating alternatives.*

Haynes, W.W., *Managerial Economics*, rev. ed. Austin, Texas: Business Publications, Inc., 1969, Chaps. 2 and 10. *Microeconomic concepts are clearly defined and empirical studies briefly described in this text.*

Shillinglaw, G., *Cost Accounting*, rev. ed. Homewood, Ill.: Richard D. Irwin, Inc., 1967. *The management viewpoint and management problems are stressed throughout this valuable text. Chapter 3 gives introduction to "decisions and costs."*

Tilles, S., "Strategies for Allocating Funds." *Harvard Business Review*, January 1966. *Stresses the need to relate capital allocations to master strategy when comparing alternative uses of capital.*

Chapter Fourteen

Making the Choice

COMPLETING THE ANALYSIS

Decision-making has many facets. Diagnosis defines a difficulty or opportunity in terms of a gap between desired and expected states. It helps pinpoint the obstacles to realizing the desired state and it focuses attention on any limits that must be observed in seeking alternatives. Past experience and creative thought suggest possible ways of achieving the desired goals. Tough, critical analysis enables us to project and compare the consequences of the most promising ways of meeting the problem. And yet there remains the decisive act—picking one of the alternatives and saying, "This is it."

The present chapter is concerned with this final act—settling on the action to be taken. For managers who must make the decisive choice, we shall examine three groups of suggestions: placing values on projected results, adjusting for uncertainty, and testing a choice.

PLACING VALUES ON PROJECTED RESULTS

What emerges from a comparison of alternatives does not constitute a decision. Someone has to decide which set of projected results is best. And to do so, he must apply values.

A college student, in picking an elective course, makes a value judgment. Suppose he has narrowed his choice to either History of the Soviet Union or Corporation Finance. Investigation indicates that the first course would be fun to take—good prof, co-ed, current events; besides, it would be good background for the years ahead. But the Finance course is practical stuff that might really pay off, on the job or in personal investments. The Finance prof is a good egg, but he piles on the work. Tuition and credit towards a degree can be disregarded because they are the same for each course. His projections of the alternatives help him see the implications of each but he still has to make a choice based on the weights his values place on subjective factors. What weight does he assign to enjoyable experience, cultural background, courses that may "pay off"?

Business decisions, although they include more dollar projections, also involve values. For instance, a U.S. manufacturing firm that wished to enter the Toronto market was considering either using an agent or opening its own branch. Table 14–1 summarizes the chief differences in anticipated results.

The firm's choice clearly depended on the relative values placed on investment, expenses, sales volume, and control. If sales volume and control were paramount, then a branch operation would be the better selection. But if the firm wished to avoid risking capital and wanted to be sure that expenses were proportionate to capital, then an agent would be the preferred choice. The fact that not all of the factors to be weighed can be summarized into a single dollar measure of "net benefit" requires a balancing of tangible and intangible payoffs. Some kind of value system, in short, is necessary for most key decisions.

Deriving Values from Objectives

The first place to look for values is in objectives. In the example of the student who was selecting a course, knowing why he was going to college would guide him in putting weights on the advantages and disadvantages of the history and the finance courses. His college objective, in turn, might well be derived from a still broader objective—the kind of person he aspired to be.

In our other example, the firm that wanted to enter the Toronto market found that its objectives indicated where to put the heavier weight. This was a conservative, management-owned company with limited capital, and its executives chiefly sought a stable operation with assured profits. Consequently, they placed high value on the low risk of a sales agency. But if the dominant objective of the company had been growth, it is clear that a different set of values would have prevailed, and a sales branch might have been the final choice.

Subsidiary objectives and values are derived from major objectives

Table 14–1

Considerations	Agent	Company Branch
Investment	0	$30,000
Expenses	5 percent of sales	$12,000 for year
Annual sales range*	$50,000 to $300,000	$100,000 to $500,000
Control	Difficult to specify behavior; agent free to quit	Responsive to specific requests; continuity more assured

*Profits at various sales volumes were not computed. High variable costs plus freight and import taxes indicated that gross profit per unit in Toronto would be virtually constant—and low. Hence the emphasis on sales volume and selling expense.

through a means-end chain. Consider, for example, how the use of an executive-recruiting firm is related to the objective of long-run growth of a plastics company, as shown in Fig. 14–1. Each of the objectives in the right-hand list had high value to the company. The subsidiary objectives, however, had value only by virtue of their relationship to the principal objective through a means-end chain. This particular analysis was helpful to the company's chief engineer when he was confronted with a proposal to install a long-service, versatile mechanic as head of the experimental department. He gave the proposal no value because it was not the best-known means of reaching the ultimate end.

Fig. 14–1   A means-end chain. Each subordinate end must be justified as a good means toward a broader, or more basic, end. Once such ends have been accepted, their fulfillment becomes a desired "value."

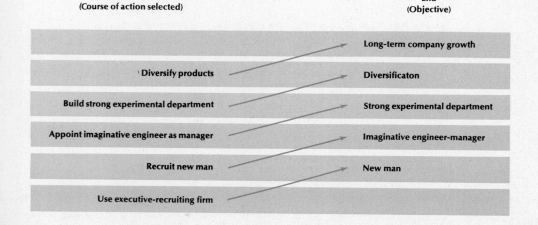

Means (Course of action selected)	End (Objective)
	Long-term company growth
Diversify products	Diversificaton
Build strong experimental department	Strong experimental department
Appoint imaginative engineer as manager	Imaginative engineer-manager
Recruit new man	New man
Use executive-recruiting firm	

Obviously, if any link in such a means-end chain is faulty, the values from that point downward are unsound. Many a passenger agent for a railroad has stressed the value of promoting passenger business because of its contribution to net revenues, whereas some railroad executives contend that passenger business is not a good means of increasing net revenue. If these executives are correct, then the chain between a promotion campaign for passengers and the objective of increased net revenues is faulty; even an ingenious promotional scheme will lack positive value.

Dynamic Social Values

In practice a manager often finds himself working with several means-end chains. He is trying to choose a course of action that will contribute to several different objectives, and there will be a means-end chain for each objective. We have already run up against multiple objectives. Stable employment growth, short-run profit, low risk, ease of control are examples of internal objectives we have frequently mentioned. Theoretically all such objectives could be considered means to some single super objective, but that single goal becomes so abstract and the linkages to it so vague that it serves no practical purpose. Instead, as with our personal goals, we recognize half a dozen or more significant end results to which we would like to contribute, and we appraise a proposed action in terms of all of these objectives.[1]

Multiple goals abound in the external social arena. A quick review of the bills introduced into Congress gives a hint of the diversity of results various groups in society would like to achieve. Enterprises are inevitably caught up in this great swirl of human aspirations because each firm can survive only if it contributes positively to fulfilling some aspirations and if it avoids serious injury to others. Situations similar to that faced by Consolidated Edison Company of New York are common: Responding to growing demand for electricity and customer complaints of brownouts, the company set an expansion goal for its generating capacity. This goal had to be reconciled with environmental objectives; a proposed nuclear plant on Long Island was dropped because of fear of radiation, and expansion of a Hudson River plant ran into thermal pollution obstacles. Moreover, the company could not overlook profit objectives, which were necessary to support the huge loans that would be necessary when an acceptable plant site could be found. In addition to catering to these service, environment, and profit objectives, the com-

[1]The conversion of results directed toward a social or other nonmonetary goal into dollars, as proposed for intangibles in the preceding chapter, does not change the multiple objectives situation. The purpose of the conversion is to simplify comparison of alternatives by expressing as many factors as we can in a single value scale. The objectives remain, as the term "trade-off" implies, and only when an action affects the achievement of an objective do we attach points (dollars) to it. It is important to note that the use of dollars as a convenient common denominator does not mean that we are concerned only with dollar profits.

pany has goals regarding black employment, urban renewal, and other development of the area from which its future business will spring.

Furthermore, these multiple objectives must change because the environment is dynamic. Continuing the preceding example, customer service must respond to the summer peak caused by a dramatic rise in air conditioning, and generating technology must respond to the growing metropolitan air pollution.

The managers of an enterprise, we said in Chapter 1, have to devise a scheme that will effectively integrate the enterprise to its dynamic environment. Whether it be a hospital, an aerospace company, or a public utility, each needs a cluster of objectives that define the particular way it hopes to fit into the current world. As the world changes so too will those objectives. This development of a "master strategy" is examined in Chapter 16.

It is from this set of objectives that the critical value structure of an enterprise is derived.

The stubborn fact is that the integration process results in a *set* of objectives, not just one, which must be modified as the opportunities and requirements of the environment change. Central management selects and modifies the objectives so as to create a unique and unified enterprise. Consequently the task of formulating and reformulating a value system for the enterprise is endless. At any point in time, however, the values on which to base decisions should be tied to the prevailing objectives.

Comparing Incremental Values

When alternative plans contribute to, or detract from, several *different* goals, how does a manager set values on the various results? A simple ranking of goals is likely to be misleading. We cannot say that sales are always more important than expenses, or that investment in equipment always takes priority over labor turnover. Such a ranking may be useful for a particular set of conditions, but we get in trouble if we carry it too far. For a second helping, we might prefer lamb chops over mashed potatoes, but our digestive system (and budget) would get out of whack if we ate all lamb chops and no mashed potatoes.

Actually the importance of any element usually depends on how much of it we have; the more there is, the less value attaches to an additional supply. But this is by no means always true. Under some circumstances, increments continue to be attractive, whereas under other situations, increments are of little significance. Thus a certain amount of good, clear water is a necessity for most factories, but once this supply is ensured, additional water has little value, or utility as it is called by economists.

The idea of concentrating on incremental value applies to all sorts of conditions. Suppose we are setting a purchasing policy and one factor is the number of suppliers of heating oil. The difference between no supplier and one supplier means life or death for the company. Two suppliers are more desirable than one because the competition would free the company from being at the mercy of a single source; even so, a second supplier is by no means so vital as the first. A third supplier is desirable, even though less important than the second. By the time there are five or six firms actively competing for business, each additional contender is of little significance.

It is interesting to speculate how far we can extend this general principle. In considering candidates for an executive position, a manager would normally include honesty as a minimum requirement. But is honesty a black-or-white matter, or are there degrees of honesty? How much more attractive is a fastidious candidate than one who is willing to be "reasonable" as long as everyone gets a "fair deal." High quality of work or of product is always desirable, but what constitutes "quality" varies with the needs of a particular situation. Improvements in quality beyond an accepted standard may be welcome, but the value of successive increments of quality may not keep pace with additional costs.

When an executive makes a choice between action A or action B, he should compare their incremental values. More specifically, he should project the different effects of A and B on, say, employee morale, and then he should consider how valuable this specific difference is to him in his particular circumstances. He similarly evaluates each possible consequence that might be significantly affected by his choice. Finally, he compares all these incremental values and decides whether the balance favors A or B.

For a simple example of this approach, let us take another look at the student who is choosing between two courses: History of the Soviet Union and Corporation Finance. Sam Jones made his decision in the following way.

First factor—enjoyable experience: Sam likes the Finance prof and likes the subject, but because several of his close friends are taking Soviet History, that course has a small advantage. Sam feels that he has been working very hard and assigns a high priority to this small increment of enjoyment.

Second factor—cultural background: Sam admits he is weak on world affairs, and the History course would make a big percentage gain in his understanding of the world; the Finance course would add just a little to his knowledge of world affairs. But, frankly, Sam does not really care about this weakness and gives low value to cultural advance.

Third factor—financial payoff: The Finance course might be of substantially more help than Soviet History. But Sam's grandfather left him a two-million-dollar trust that Sam cannot control until he is forty years old. When he is thirty-five he expects to settle down to five years of studying investments, and he feels he can learn corporation finance then. Hence, he puts small value on the business course for this factor.

Net balance: Sam takes History.

Most students' incremental values for each factor would differ from Sam's (and, we hope, their reasons), but the process underlying their decisions would be much the same.

In our earlier discussion of comparing alternatives, we stressed differences in results—differences in sales income, in customer goodwill, in expenses, in executive enthusiasm, and in any other factor that would be significantly affected by following plan A instead of plan B. Here we are considering how much value to attach to such differences—or increments—and pointing out that their value depends on the urgency of a company's need for a particular increment at a given time. When Northeast Airlines was on the verge of bankruptcy in the 1960s, the incremental value it would assign to a million dollars more capital, for example, was much greater than the incremental values it would attach to a 20 percent improvement in passenger goodwill or two million dollars increase in gross revenues. If Northeast Airlines had been in strong financial shape, the relation between incremental values of capital, goodwill, and gross revenues would have been quite different.

Company versus Individual Values

Making a choice among alternatives clearly involves many subjective judgments, first in projecting the consequences of each alternative, next in placing a value on the differences for each factor, and finally in balancing incremental values to arrive at a decision. Objective data can help, but, especially in the later phases of choosing, an executive must rely heavily on his judgment.

Reliance on subjective judgment unfortunately opens up opportunities for substituting personal desires for company welfare. For example, customer A may get prompt delivery of a scarce product because he is the personal friend of a manager, whereas the company good would have been better served by sending the product to customer B. Although such deliberate mixing of company and personal values does occur, there is surprisingly little of it in American business. Most managers recognize that, in their roles as company employees, their personal preferences are irrelevant. They must view problems in terms of "what is good for the company," and the distinction between business and self is considered a matter of integrity. Ability to make the distinction is an important element in self-respect and is a criterion of central management in selecting men for responsible positions.

Unconscious biases are more critical than deliberate self-serving. A man naturally deals with a problem in terms of his experience and the pressures that weigh on him. A salesman is more sensitive to sales needs, and a production man to plant needs; a man who is fearful of a layoff attaches higher value to stability than a man who feels secure; an executive who recalls with nostalgia the days when his company was small—when he didn't have to fuss with so many reports and when "clearance with staff" was not part of his vocabulary—is likely to place more weight on the difficulties of further expansion than a young, aggressive president. Each of these men is sincere in his evaluation, but we can suspect that personal values have influenced his judgment.

One fact of life is that most of us are good at thinking up logical reasons for doing what we want. We kid ourselves. In making value judgments, it is entirely possible to seek earnestly for the best course for our company and at the same time unconsciously attach values that tend to favor our own personal interests. We must recognize that the danger of confusing personal desires with sound company values is inherent in choosing among alternatives. To avoid this danger is one reason for testing choices along the lines we outline at the end of this chapter. We shall also offer several safeguards when we discuss devices for company planning in Part Four.

ADJUSTING FOR UNCERTAINTY

One other major consideration in choosing among alternatives is *uncertainty*, which is as much a part of business life as breathing is of human life. Business cycles, weather, wars and threats of wars, competition, inventions, new laws, and a host of other dynamic situations and events make the future uncertain. Within a business firm, machine breakdowns, irregularities in human performance, and failures to maintain standard operating conditions increase our quandary. We try to predict what might happen, of course, but no one can fully foresee the future.

A manager must be willing to make a decision even when he is uncertain. The same man who takes a tough, challenging attitude toward proposals that are presented to him must be willing to risk making a decision although he is fully aware that the future may play tricks with his present expectations. Let us take a look, then, at how we may best incorporate the element of uncertainty into a choice of action.

Statistical Probability

For a few types of risks, we have enough statistical evidence to compute the chances that a given event will occur. Life insurance provides the classic example. Life insurance companies know that probably fewer than 1 percent of men age 20 will die during the ensuing five years, whereas about 5 percent of the men age 50 will die in the same period. The companies insure enough lives so that these probabilities fit their business. Thus, if an insurance executive were drawing up five-year contracts for 20-year-olds and 50-year-olds, he knows that he should get over five times

Fire

War

Strike

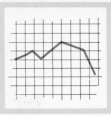
Prices

Timing

Fig. 14–2 Businesses are faced by a variety of uncertainties. Although careful managing can lessen the danger of some of these, managers have little or no control over others.

as much income from the latter to make the two policies comparable.

Similarly, if a manager had an investment opportunity with a 50 percent chance of returning $100,000 profit, a 40 percent chance of only $20,000 profit, and a 10 percent chance of losing $50,000, he could weigh these payoffs by their respective probabilities and develop an "expected value for the alternative"—in this case, $53,000, that is, ($100,000 × .5) + ($20,000 × .4) − ($50,000 × .1).

Statisticians warn us to be cautious about this simple approach to uncertainty. Rarely does a company have enough of the same kinds of risk so that losses and gains work out to the most probable result. Because it is likely that actual results will deviate from the average, we should know something about that deviation. Are the actual results, say, of customer acceptance on bids on special jobs likely to be close to our previous 25 percent average—between 20 and 30 percent, for example— or is there a good chance that they will range anywhere from 5 up to 45 percent? The central figure is the same in both instances, but in the second case we would face much greater uncertainty about future sales than we would in the first.

In only a relatively few decisions can we use statistical probability in a strict sense to adjust for uncertainty. To make precise use of probability techniques, we need data on a large number of similar cases, and we must have a clearly defined sample. Nevertheless, probability theory does give us some useful clues to thinking about uncertain situations, two of which we have mentioned: (1) When the alternatives we are considering have different probabilities, if we multiply the appropriate values in each alternative by their respective probabilities, we arrive at comparable figures; and (2) the width of the range within which results are likely to fall may be as significant as the average or the single result that is most probable.

Inferred Probability

We often infer from limited data the probability of a particular outcome. Such predictions are common in everyday speech. "The Los Angeles Dodgers have one chance in three to win the pennant." "There's only one chance in ten that the UAW will strike at Chrysler this year."

317

"There's a fifty-fifty likelihood we'll land that government order." "The odds are two to one that Smith will turn down the promotion."

Such inferred probabilities help us to deal with uncertainty. They at least offer a rough judgment on how serious a risk is. To say, "There's one chance in twenty our Navy contract will be canceled" is much more helpful than "There's a possibility the contract may be canceled."

Occasionally, management can put these probability guesses to more specific use. For instance, a company with annual earnings before taxes of $750,000 was rapidly approaching a stalemate in its union negotiations. The men wanted a large wage increase that management was not ready to grant. After a long conference with his key executives, the president concluded, "I think there is a 25 percent chance of a serious strike. If it comes, our earnings will probably drop $300,000." The controller responded, "Then in comparing costs of various alternatives, we should figure the risk of a strike as a $75,000 cost [$300,000 × .25]." The comments of the president and the controller can be summarized as in Table 14–2.

After more discussion, the president and controller worked out a

Table 14–2

Situation	Estimated Loss of Earnings	Inferred Probability	Loss × Probability
No strike	0	75%	0
Serious strike	$300,000	25	$75,000
		100%	
	Loss adjusted for probability		$75,000

Table 14–3

Possible Length of Strike	Estimated Loss of Earnings	Inferred Probability	Loss × Probability
0 days	0	35%	0
3-5 days	$ 50,000	40	$ 20,000
3 weeks	200,000	15	30,000
6 weeks	400,000	7	28,000
10 weeks	800,000	3	24,000
		100%	
	Loss adjusted for probability		$102,000

probability chart that is more informative because it shows the likelihood of losses ranging from zero to $800,000 (Table 14–3). It also indicates that when a full range of possible consequences is included, the seriousness of a strike threat is somewhat worse than the company first thought.

A similar analysis would be helpful to the president of the power mower company considering a new West Coast assembly shop. Estimates indicate that $19,000 will be lost if the proposed shop handles only the current volume of business in that territory, whereas a net gain of $59,000 will be realized if a local assembly plant doubles sales, as the sales manager predicts. The chief uncertainty in the picture is sales volume. The president of the company feels the sales manager is overoptimistic. He grants that some increase in volume is likely, but he believes that there is only a small chance to achieve the $400,000 volume within a few years. Table 14–4 sharpens these feelings and relates them to estimates of gain for different sales levels.

The president's informed guess is that sales volume will be between $250,000 and $400,000 per year, with the lower volume much more likely than the higher. When he adjusts the net gain estimates by the inferred probabilities, the final value he assigns to the new shop is about $15,000 per year. Although this figure is not so enticing as what the optimistic sales manager would forecast, it still represents an attractive 28 percent return on added investment in West Coast operations.

Unfortunately, these final figures "adjusted for probability"—the $15,250 in the power mower illustration and the $102,000 in the strike example—are quite synthetic. If we want a single value, they are the best we can do. If the companies in these cases had hundreds of similar (though independent) problems, then the average results might be close

Table 14–4

Possible Sales Volume (Annual)	Estimated Net Gain	Probability Inferred by President	Net Gain × Probability
$200,000	$ —19,000	0	0
250,000	600	50%	$ 300
300,000	20,100	30	6,030
350,000	39,700	15	5,955
400,000	59,300	5	2,965
		100%	
	Net gain adjusted for probability		$15,250

Rate of return on initial investment of $55,000 = 28% (i.e., $15,250 ÷ $55,000)

to the adjusted figures. In a single instance, however, the actual outcome is almost certain to differ from the adjusted total. In deciding whether to open a West Coast branch, the president of the power mower company may be fully as interested in the fact that there is a fifty-fifty chance that the operation will just break even as he is in the synthetic adjusted total. If he had plenty of capital, he might say, "I don't think we'll lose any money, and we might make a handsome profit, so go ahead." On the other hand, if he is short of capital and pressed for earnings, he might decide, "We should allocate our capital and our time to projects where we feel sure of making some profit, even though the potential may not be so high as that in the West Coast operation." In other words, a distribution of probabilities may be as important in making a value judgment as a weighted average.

Similarly, the president of the company confronted with a strike threat may be concerned about the range of chances he is taking. For example, if the company has large payments to make on a bank loan, even a small risk that earnings will be wiped out is serious. But under other circumstances, the company might be quite prepared to take this risk in exchange for other gains. Whenever we face uncertainties, using probabilities—whether by putting them on paper or just estimating them mentally—helps in forming judgments.

Unreliable Data

The vast majority of decisions must be based in part on evidence that is not fully reliable. Trade association figures might not be representative of an entire industry; equipment salesmen present their products in the best possible light; social tradition requires that the published statements by company presidents bristle with confidence; market surveys by advertising agencies usually point to the need for more advertising; Army generals foresee grave dangers if their appropriation requests are not met in full; and so on. Such data are apt to be only part of the whole truth, and the manner of presentation may be slanted to produce a particular impression.

Of course, a manager who must make a decision tries to get data that are as reliable as possible. But usually he cannot get the full story from his sources. He has to pick up grains of truth and new insights whenever or wherever he can find them. He can ill afford to disregard the opinions of well-informed persons, even though they may be tarnished with bias.

We are all familiar with unreliable data in our daily lives. We learn a lot from food advertising without being upset by copywriters' superlatives. When a high school girl pleads, "Everybody is wearing them," parents interpret the remark to mean that three or four of her friends are sporting the style of shoes in question. Such information is not as precise as we might like, but we learn to live with it and even to take effective action on it.

Two simple rules are helpful in using unreliable data: (1) Keep aware of the limitations of the information we are working with; label it "suspect" in our own mind and perhaps adjust it to what we believe is reasonable. (2) Appraise the person supplying the data. What are his interests, ability, judgment, integrity? The more we know of a man, the better able we are to evaluate what he says. We can usually reduce uncertainty by considering unreliable as well as reliable data, provided we use it with discretion.

Incomplete Data

The manager who must choose a course of action is on the horns of a dilemma: more information versus more time and expense.

The expense of planning may be substantial. Boeing Aircraft spent over $4,000,000 in designing its K-135 and 707 jet planes before a single order was on the books; a consulting firm was recently paid $60,000 for advice on locating a suburban shopping center; a new layout for a large industrial plant may require several man-years of effort. Simpler decisions naturally require less effort, but even they entail expense. Selecting a desk calculator for an office, for instance, calls for studying different kinds of equipment, the needs of the particular office, necessary operating skills, maintenance problems, and so on. Although detailed information on all these points might improve the quality of his decision, we cannot expect an office manager to become an expert in calculating equipment just for the purchase of a single machine.

Timely action may also compete for priority with more complete information. When a competitor cuts prices, or an important customer inquires when delivery can be promised, or the still at an oil refinery breaks down, the executive in charge must decide what to do without delay. The costs and risk incurred by delay may be more serious than the probable error inherent in judging on incomplete information.

Overcoming incompleteness of data is a small decision-making problem in itself. Diagnosis, alternatives, projection, and value judgments are needed. Among the ways of increasing the store of information while keeping expenses of obtaining it within bounds are these: bravely singling out one or two crucial factors and concentrating on gathering facts about them; taking just a sample of the total data we might like to have; and, if feasible, postponing decision until good information becomes available.

Reasonably complete information and prompt decision are often hard to combine. The chief hope for conquering this problem is to anticipate the need for such a decision—for instance, guessing that a competitor might cut his prices—and to have pertinent current data already assembled; possibly the military practice of preparing in advance tentative courses of action might even be warranted. Another approach is to split an activity into parts and try to postpone that part where information is the weakest. A multiproduct company, for instance, may plan a weekly television program for months ahead, but may defer writing commercials until market conditions reveal which product will benefit most from advertising at a particular time.

When balancing increased accuracy against expense and time, an executive should think in terms of increments, as with other problems. Will the improved accuracy of a decision that arises from additional data be worth the added expense and added time to obtain it?

To summarize: Uncertainty is inherent in choosing a course of action, and, at best, an executive can only reduce it. Thinking in terms of probabilities; being sensitive to, and adjusting for, the bias in the opinion of others; balancing the cost of more data against likely improvement in judgment—these are all ways of dealing with this troublesome issue. Like levees against floods on the Mississippi River, they are helpful primarily as devices for coping with uncertainty rather than for removing it.

CONTRIBUTIONS OF OPERATIONS RESEARCH

A manager, as we have seen, often must make a choice that involves both a variety of consequences and uncertainty regarding, perhaps, all of these outcomes. So many considerations are involved that devices for summarizing and condensing are very helpful. We shall briefly describe two: operations-research condensations and matrices.

Operations-Research Models

One major contribution of operations research is the concept of a model that summarizes in a few numbers many of the factors involved in a complex choice.[2] Broadly speaking, three features are involved in this method of summarizing:

1) Problems are stated in mathematical symbols. Symbols and equations, which make up a convenient shorthand widely used in science, provide a form of expression that is concise and easy for an expert to manipulate. (It also provides the appeal of a professional jargon. To the

[2]We should note that for some kinds of problems operations-research models also permit us to expand the *number* of alternatives from which a choice is made. When a linear relation exists between *degrees* of input and resulting output, the equations enable us to consider a full spectrum of alternatives involving that relationship. Consequently, by using the equations we can choose the theoretical optimum degree of, say, investment and inventory.

operations researcher, stating a problem in words is clumsy and vague.)

2) A cardinal rule of the operations researcher is: Build a model. The use of physical models is, of course, a common practice in industry. Aircraft engineers use small models to test new designs in wind tunnels; models of new automobile styles are common in the automobile industry; scale models are often used in studying plant layout. Each model is a symbolic picture that represents certain aspects of a real thing. A model of a management problem in mathematical symbols is similar, except that both the thing being pictured and the way of describing it are more abstract. A model of this sort familiar to business students is the balance-sheet equation:

$$A = L + P$$

where A represents total assets, L total liabilities, and P total proprietorship. This can be elaborated:

$$P_n = P_{(n-1)} + \{I_{(n-1) \to n} - E_{(n-1) \to n}\}$$

in which the proprietorship at the end of year n equals the proprietorship at the end of the previous year plus income (I) during the past year minus expenses (E) during the year, and so on.

But instead of using a conventional model like those for financial accounting, the operations-research man is prepared to build a new model for each problem he studies. He seeks a set of equations that will project consequences, attach values to these consequences, and make allowances for uncertainty. The model hopefully presents an orderly picture of the total problem that otherwise would be dealt with unsystematically in the mind of an executive.

3) The third essential feature of operations research is quantitative measurement of the several independent variables and also the dependent variables (predicted results) in the equations. Just as a chemist must measure the temperatures, pressures, and other factors he works with, so must the operations researcher express the elements in a managerial situation in quantitative terms if his model is to be useful in making a choice. This requirement means a tremendous amount of "digging" for facts. It also requires that values be expressed in a uniform scale—usually dollars.

Operations-research models have been applied to a number of complicated management problems. For example, oil companies use them in scheduling refinery runs. Here the problem is determining what proportion of various products to manufacture from a barrel of crude oil. The variables include: different sales prices for gasoline, heating oil, lubricants, asphalt, and other end-products; availability and price of several types of crude oil, each with its own composition and refining characteristics; variations in yields and operating costs of the refinery when a specific crude oil is used to make different proportions of end-products; and costs of storing excess output of specific products during slack seasons. The equations dealing with such refinery-run problems are complex, and electronic computers are necessary to handle the masses of data promptly.

Generally, the situations where operations research has paid off have these characteristics: (1) A problem is so complicated or involves such a sheer mass of data that it cannot be fully grasped by one person's mind, and yet its parts are so interrelated that dividing it into comprehensible units would not necessarily yield the best answer. (2) The relationships are known, clear-cut, and of a type that can be expressed by available mathematical formulas. (3) Statistical data are available for all important variables.

The first of these requirements makes the study worth the trouble, the second is necessary to build a satisfactory model, and the third is a requisite for practical application.

Decision Trees

Some decisions involve a series of steps, the second step depending on the outcome of the first, the third depending on the outcome of the second, and so on. Often uncertainty surrounds each step, so we face uncertainty piled on uncertainty. "Decision trees" are a model to deal with such a problem. Here is an illustration.

Organic Fibers, Inc., exports to Australia have been expanding. The local Australian sales agent is now insisting on a ten-year contract, but Organic Fibers' overseas manager recommends opening a company sales office as a first step toward building a plant three or four years later. Decision A is this choice between the sales agent or a sales office. Decision B, to build a plant, will be made only after sales growth has been demonstrated. An alternative to Organic Fibers' building its own plant is to subcontract. In fact if a sales office is opened and growth is slow, sub-contracting would still be an alternative to exporting from the United States; this would be decision C.

To clarify (1) the decisions to be made, (2) the key uncertainties and probabilities, and (3) the estimated yields, the decision tree shown in Fig. 14–3 was prepared. Laying out on a chart the alternative series of events along with estimates of probabilities and estimated net profit is a very helpful device by itself. However, to sharpen the choice even more we should calculate the "position value" of an established sales office. This can be done by rolling back the expected values as follows:

1) On the basis of our best estimates, *decision B will be to sub-contract.* The difference in expected return from the plant and subcon-

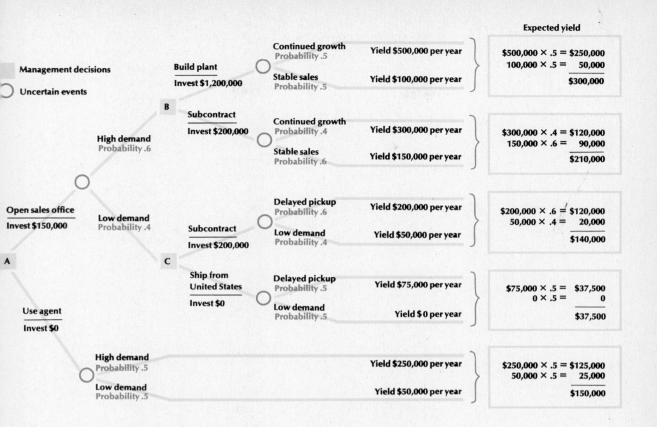

Fig. 14–3   A decision tree for projected Australian expansion.
Probabilities and amounts of investments and yields are
management's best estimates on the basis of present knowledge.

tracting ($300,000 − $210,000 = $90,000) is not large enough to justify the difference in additional investment ($1,200,000 − $200,000 = $1,000,000). So we assume the outcome of decision B will be an expected yield of $210,000 and an investment of $200,000.

2) *Decision C will also be to subcontract.* The difference in expected return between subcontracting and exporting ($140,000 − $37,500 = $102,500) is large enough to justify the additional investment of $200,000. So we assume the otucome of decision C will be an expected yield of $140,000 and an investment of $200,000.

3) Using the probabilities of high and low demand, which dictate whether we will be faced with decision B or C, we can compare the two alternatives at decision point A. If the company opens the sales office, the expected yield from decision B is $126,000 ($210,000 × .6), while the yield from decision C is $56,000 ($140,000 $\times$ .4). The total expected yield from opening the sales office is therefore $182,000 ($126,000 $+$ $56,000) on a total investment of $350,000 ($150,000 to open the sales office and $200,000 to subcontract). On the other hand if the company uses a sales agent, the total yield that can be expected is $150,000, without any initial investment.

4) *Decision A will be to use the agent.* The difference in expected yield of opening a sales office or using the agent ($182,000 $-$ $150,000 $=$ $32,000) is not large enough to justify the initial investment in the sales office plus the investment necessary to subcontract in Australia ($150,000 $+$ $200,000 $=$ $350,000).

Decision trees can be drawn to fit all sorts of situations, and refinements of the preceding illustration—such as more alternatives, more than two levels of risk, discounting for when income and outflows will occur, and risk of losing the investment—suggest themselves as soon as the problem and premises are explicitly stated. But even this relatively simple illustration points up the inherent complexity and difficulty in making precise quantitative projections.

Computer Simulation

In decision trees and most other operations-research models uncertainty is dealt with in terms of "expected value"—the weighting of various possible outcomes by their probability. Such practice enables us to take account of differences in the chances of success, but the resulting figures are only synthetic scores, not a picture of any result we may actually face. One way to get a better sense of what our world might be like *if* this happened or *if* that happened is through simulation.

With this technique a model—admittedly incomplete but the best we can design—is used to project possible results of different alternatives under varying assumptions. Usually the model is programmed into a computer and then we can easily try out all sorts of contingencies—tight money, high demand, and so on—and various actions to deal with such situations. It is like running through football plays on a practice field, knowing that in actual play the situation will be much more complicated. The simulation is helpful in making a choice because it has summarized and condensed at least part of the many considerations.

Unfortunately, in many management situations the factors involved and the relationships between them are not sharp enough for mathematical expression, and if the simulation is oversimplified it loses much of its usefulness.

In conclusion, operations-research models are helpful in making a choice in certain types of complex situations. But even where data are available and a useful model can be constructed, we always face the question, "Is it worth the trouble?" For the myriad of relatively simple problems, use of symbolism and models probably will not improve the quality of decisions.

MATRIX SUMMARIES

Many decision-makers want some means, simpler and more flexible than an operations-research model, for summarizing the projections they must weigh in choosing among alternatives. Especially, they need a way to get the intangibles into the same focus. Matrix summaries are helpful for this purpose.

Here is an example—one of many variations—of how matrices can be used. The president of a large paper company had to choose a new mill location. He had narrowed his choice to four locations and had consolidated as well as he could the dollar benefits of each into an estimated rate of return on incremental investment. He then identified five other factors that, while they were partially reflected in the dollar figures, had additional intangible implications. For each of these intangibles the president faced two questions:

1) What *degree of satisfaction* may I expect for each intangible at each mill site?

2) How *important* is each intangible to me—in the range being considered?

The first question seeks to determine the extent to which a desired intangible need is met by each alternative. The second question recognizes that a favorable position with respect to one intangible may be more important than a favorable position with respect to another.

Because the president could not avoid answering these two questions, at least subjectively, he went one step further and translated his feelings into numbers. He ranked each alternative on a scale from zero to ten for each question, low ranking reflecting low satisfaction or low importance. These evaluations of the intangibles are summarized on the matrix shown in Fig. 14–4.

To arrive at a rough indication of the relative significance of intangibles for each site, in each cell of the matrix the degree of satisfaction (in color) has been multiplied by the relative importance (in black). The resulting numbers are a rough index of the relative degree and importance of each intangible for all four sites.

Then, to summarize, the index numbers have been added to show a combined score for each site. This total score had significance only for comparing the alternative sites. Nevertheless, it did help the president make

Alternative Sites	Predicted Availability of Desired Labor/ Skill Mix	Predicted Favorable Union Relations	Predicted Favorable Local Legislation and Taxes	Predicted Ability to Hold Capable Mill Managers in This Location	Predicted Unlikelihood of Competitors Moving Nearby	Weighted Total Score for Intangibles	Estimated Incremental Return on Investment Compared with Doing Nothing
Site 1	9 × 6 = 54	5 × 8 = 40	9 × 6 = 54	9 × 9 = 81	4 × 3 = 12	241	12.1%
Site 2	5 × 6 = 30	8 × 8 = 64	6 × 9 = 54	9 × 9 = 81	3 × 3 = 9	238	14.7
Site 3	5 × 6 = 30	1 × 8 = 8	8 × 9 = 72	5 × 9 = 45	4 × 3 = 12	167	16.1
Site 4	10 × 6 = 60	6 × 8 = 48	8 × 9 = 72	8 × 9 = 72	5 × 3 = 15	267	10.8

Fig. 14–4   A matrix for choosing mill locations, showing president's subjective evaluation of intangibles. Sites below minimum acceptable level on any factor have already been eliminated. The company can easily finance the dollar investment required at any of these locations with a 6 percent bond issue. Quantity and quality of output will not be affected by the choice of site. Colored numbers = degree factor is achieved at each site. Black numbers = relative importance of a factor. Colored underscore = weighted score.

a choice. By concentrating on the last two columns of the matrix he quickly decided that site 2 was preferable to site 1; the score for the intangibles was about the same and site 2 had a decided edge in rate of return. After a little thought the president decided that site 3 was preferable to site 4; he concluded that the significant intangible advantage of site 4 simply could not offset a 50 percent higher rate of return at site 3. That selection left a final choice between sites 2 and 3.

Were the intangible advantages of site 2 worth sacrificing an estimated 1.4 percent difference in rate of return? Looking at the cells in the matrix, the president could see that the chief difference in intangibles was in the favorability of predicted union relations; after further reflection he decided to sacrifice rate of return rather than build a plant where union relations would probably be quite troublesome.

Although this matrix did not give the president an automatic answer, it did two things. First, it forced him to clarify his judgments about the intangibles. Second, it provided a mechanism to help him balance them out in his mind. Crude though the weightings were, use of the matrix helped integrate the implications of each alternative into a final choice.

All sorts of matrices are possible. Verbal statements instead of numbers may be placed in the cells. Probability estimates may be added. Predictions based on very flimsy evidence may be flagged, weights adjusted for degree of satisfaction, and so on. Basically the matrix is useful because it enables us to summarize a variety of projections in a systematic fashion.[3]

TESTING A CHOICE

Is there any way a manager can tell when he has arrived at a correct choice among alternatives? Unfortunately, there is no sure test. The most he can do is to reduce the chance of serious error. Over the years, several different ways of checking the soundness of a decision have proved useful. Every manager should be familiar with these techniques so that he can pick those that are appropriate for each specific decision. Urgency of action, what is at stake, and degree of doubt will determine how many checks to use and how far to press them.

Reexamining the Analysis and the Evidence

Most people prefer to stick to a line of thinking once it is well drawn in their minds, especially if ideas are familiar, accepted, and attractive. Consequently, a comfortable decision—right or wrong—tends to go unchallenged. To catch errors in such thinking, the following devices are helpful.

Listen to the "devil's advocate." For centuries, the Catholic church has used the institution of the "devil's advocate" as a way of testing decisions, especially those relating to the canonization of new saints. A specific individual is assigned the task of pointing out weaknesses and errors in proposed action. He assembles the best negative arguments he can. If a proposal cannot withstand such an attack, action is postponed.

In business, a decision-maker himself often makes a deliberate effort to stand aside and think of all the reasons why a proposed action won't

[3]Some experienced executives make a tentative decision first and then prepare a matrix with data necessary to justify that decision. Such a practice is not so silly as it first appears, because the executive is testing his intuitive feeling against its logical implications, and if the implications appear unsound when they are clearly exposed, he can revise his intuitive judgment.

work. Before a manager says, "Go ahead," he should take time to calculate everything that may go wrong. But this negative approach may be difficult and unpleasant for an aggressive executive, and if a problem is complicated or involves strong emotions, he should perhaps assign the task to someone else. The role is liable to be unpopular, and so a manager should make sure everyone recognizes that the devil's advocate is not passing judgment on a matter, but simply seeing to it that all adverse points have been carefully considered.

A decision may be challenged on the basis of evidence, logic, values, or other grounds. At the time of the cross-examination by the devil's advocate, all sorts of embarrassing questions are raised. For example, "If officers need the proposed three-week vacation, why not all employees?" Or, "True, our annual reports do show a high correlation of sales volume and advertising expense, but does this mean that more advertising will increase sales? Maybe the causation runs the other way or does not exist. Remember, the United States leads India in heart disease and baths per capita, but it does not follow therefore that baths cause heart trouble." A decision is sound only if it can be defended by good answers to such challenges as these.

Project a decision into detailed plans. Often we can check on the wisdom and practicability of a decision by spelling out its consequences in more detail. A very large manufacturing company, for example, tested its tentative decision to decentralize into product divisions by using this approach of projecting consequences. It allocated customers, outlined a proposed divisional organization, devised a tentative placement of executives, and estimated the administrative cost of the new setup. This analysis uncovered so many weaknesses and difficulties that the original decentralization plan was abandoned. Not until a year later was a substantially modified reorganization put into effect.

Too often a manager incorrectly assumes that once he has made a decision action will automatically follow. Such a disregard of the difficulties of implementation is illustrated in the old anecdote of the arthritic centipede who approached a wise old owl for advice on what to do about his aches and pains. The owl mused, "As I see it, your alternatives are either to go to Arizona where the hot dry climate would help the arthritis, or to turn yourself into a worm. I would recommend the latter." The centipede, delighted with such good advice, asked how to turn himself into a worm. "Oh," replied the owl, "don't bother me with the details. You work them out. I just deal with the high-level decisions."

In an organization we distinguish between broad, high-level decisions and more specific implementation decisions, and we have different people whose job it is to focus on each category. However, just as implementation decisions must be made within the context of higher-level goals and policies, so must top-level decisions be made within a realistic framework of considering whether the decisions can be implemented effectively. Projecting a decision into detailed plans is a good way to test its practicability.

Reconsider planning premises. Every management decision is based on assumptions, or planning premises. They may be assumptions supported by sketchy data about future demands for company products or about the availability of raw materials; assumptions about the attitudes and future behavior of employees, perhaps based on reports of staff men or hearsay evidence; or assumptions about company values that are as much a reflection of personal desires as of company goals. In checking a decision, a manager often finds it useful to ask himself just which assumptions are crucial to the success of a proposed action and to try to obtain further clarification on these pivotal premises.

All premises cannot be verified, of course. There will always remain incomplete data, errors in perception of facts, and distortion in communication to contend with. But an executive should reconsider assumptions so that he at least knows what risks he is taking rather than proceed naïvely. In addition, as the future becomes history, premises can be checked against events and the need for reconsidering the decision may be clearly seen.

Review alternatives discarded abruptly. Too often an otherwise excellent alternative has been discarded because of a single drawback. In such cases, we should ask whether the assumed drawback is insurmountable. Possibly the drawback should be treated as a new subproblem, and attempts should be made to deal with it just as the original problem was dealt with. If it can be removed, a worthwhile alternative may come back in the running for consideration.

Consider the following situation: The plant union of a tool-and-die company complained that seven men in the shipping department had to walk several hundred yards and climb two flights of stairs to reach the main locker rooms and toilet facilities. One alternative for meeting this complaint was to allow the seven workers an extra five minutes for each of two daily breaks. This alternative was quickly discarded, however, because "it will set a precedent" of allowing breaks of different lengths to different employees. The alternatives that remained involved either paying the seven workers for the inconvenience or installing additional facilities nearer the shipping department.

When the assumed drawback of the first alternative was treated as a subproblem, management was challenged to find ways of allowing extra break time that would not set undesirable precedents. In fact, they were able to establish for the entire work force new schedules based on distance from locker facilities. Although designing the new schedule took special effort and break times were extended for more workers than the original seven, the total additional cost was still far less than that of the other alternatives.

Thus, if a critical drawback can be removed, a manager should consider means of doing so, adding their costs to the alternative. He may still reject the alternative, but not until he has reexamined the assumed disadvantage.

Securing Consensus

A director of the Standard Oil Company (New Jersey) has observed, "When a proposal comes before our Board for decision, there is rarely sharp difference of opinion. We try to anticipate problems, and then we discuss possible solutions with everyone directly affected and those who might have useful views. These discussions often seem slow, but by the time we are ready to act a clear consensus backing the proposal has usually developed."

Most of us use this technique, at least occasionally. We make a tentative decision—say, whether or not to accept a job—but before taking action we get the frank opinion of one or two friends. In so doing, we are testing the decision.

Formal arrangements are sometimes made to get consensus on important decisions. The United States Supreme Court is a notable example. Boards of directors and some company committees presumably provide group review and endorsement of key plans. The "independent staff" described in Chapter 6 is specifically designed to provide a second judgment. But the use of consensus to test decisions need not be limited to such bodies. Informal advice from individuals may contribute just as much to the wisdom of a decision.

If the assent or dissent of others is to be meaningful, the advisor should be both well informed about a situation and seriously concerned about the soundness of the decision. Neither polite agreement nor log-rolling politics nor cavalier advice is desirable.

Pilot Runs

The surest way to test a decision is to try it out. A test will not tell us whether some other decision might not work better, but it will tell us whether a proposed plan is at least promising. Sometimes a new product or process can be tried out on a limited scale with custom-made models or equipment. Automobile companies give their new chassis and new engines severe road tests before the products are put into mass production and sold to the public. A chemical company with a new detergent may have its laboratory make up limited quantities for market tests in a restricted area. A large chain-store company experiments with extending credit in only a few of its outlets before modifying its cash-only policy. As these cases show, even if a tentative decision looks good on paper or in the laboratory, a further test under more nearly normal operating conditions is desirable.

Pilot operations have their limitations, of course. They are often costly; they may consume valuable time; and they may not be feasible for some actions (such as floating a bond issue while interest rates are low). Consequently, this test is appropriate for only a few major decisions a manager must make.

Sequential Decisions

Occasionally, we can make a decision one part at a time; when the results of the first part are known, we can use them in deciding the second part; the results of the second part help to shape our decision on the third part; and so on with each succeeding part. Thus we make a series of decisions to solve one main problem.[4]

This form of decision is often used for executive promotions. Suppose a company president has his eye on a salesman named John Pollack as a likely replacement for the sales manager who will retire in three years. The president's first step might be to bring Pollack into the home office as sales promotion director. If Pollack does that job well, he may be put in charge of sales planning. If his work continues to be effective, he may be named assistant sales manager six months before he is moved into the key spot. These successive assignments serve a double purpose. Pollack gets experience and learns about home-office operations, and the company can make a *series* of appraisals of his capability to be sales manager. The results of each move provide data used in deciding what the next move should be.

The sequence of decisions a pharmaceutical company commonly makes in bringing a new product to the market also illustrates the process. A new product typically goes through several stages: laboratory discovery or idea gleaned from nontechnical sources; clinical tests for effectiveness; production-process engineering; market analysis to decide packaging, pricing, and distribution channels; approval by Public Health authorities; sales promotion and quantity production. Each stage provides new evidence for deciding whether to drop the product, proceed to the next stage, or try a new tack.

Sequential decisions are in sharp contrast with bear-by-the-tail decisions familiar in sales promotion campaigns, where it is difficult to discontinue a project after it is launched. Sequential decisions should also be distinguished from the proverbial British habit of "muddling through," whereby one step is taken with simple faith that some way will open up for the next move. In sequential decisions a tentative plan or a new

---

[4]Decision trees, already discussed, also deal with this kind of situation. However, decision trees focus only on the first decision and assume subsequent decisions will follow in the projected fashion. In the sequential decision process we plan to reconsider each step on the basis of newly acquired information. A decision-tree analysis can be used to clarify any one of the steps in a sequential decision, but the two techniques are distinct and may be used separately. As the examples suggest, the sequential decision technique has much wider applicability.

alternative for dealing with a major problem is in mind from the beginning. The plan is then tested against newly acquired evidence and perhaps revised at each stage.

All these proposed devices for testing decisions have their usefulness. Some fit one situation better than others. But in general, they may be applied in the following order: (1) checking our own thinking by the devil's-advocate approach, projecting detailed plans for implementation, reconsidering assumptions, or reviewing discarded alternatives; (2) securing consensus from other competent people; and then, where suitable, (3) making test runs either by pilot operation or by sequential decision.

CONCLUSION

A manager can rarely follow the phases of decision-making in the neat order of our discussion: defining the problem, finding alternatives, projecting and comparing alternatives, choosing a single course of action. Even if our minds tried to follow a disciplined path, the trails through the phases would crisscross. In testing a choice, for instance, we may want to get more data, and the added information might suggest new alternatives; or using a means-end chain to establish values might cause us to revise our diagnosis. Similarly, in discarding alternatives, by setting limits or focusing first on one or two crucial factors, we are in effect making negative choices.

Although we have not discovered a simple procedure for making wise plans, a formal analysis of decision-making, such as we have covered in Part Three, is highly useful as a framework for putting our thoughts and planning efforts into an orderly, understandable arrangement. With this framework, random thoughts can be put in place, and any necessary backtracking need not confuse us.

The more specific suggestions made in the last four chapters about each of the four phases of decision-making apply to all types of management problems, from the daily questions that face a first-line supervisor to the fundamental policy issues that confront central management. Incidentally, these suggestions can be used for intangible problems, for example, how to organize a branch office, as well as for concrete problems, such as, what products to make or what machine to buy. The tough task for each of us is, of course, not merely to be acquainted with an approach to decision-making, but rather to master the concept so well that we use it skillfully and perhaps almost unconsciously.

An understanding of the elements of decision-making will also help us in Part Four, where we explore decision-making in an organization. No one man, single-handed, can follow through all phases of decision-making for a large variety of problems or even for one complex problem. We need the joint effort of many men. A wide range of planning instruments is available to facilitate joint planning effort, as we shall see. But these planning instruments take on full significance only insofar as we understand how they assist in the fundamental decision-making process we have just examined in Part Three.

FOR CLASS DISCUSSION

Questions

1) What are the advantages and limitations of having the same person(s) who gathered data needed for comparing courses of action also make the final choice? Give your answer before and after reading Chapter 15.

2) Relate the discussion "Comparing Incremental Values" to the section in Chapter 8 that deals with the "Potency of Needs." Although Chapter 8 dealt with individual needs, do you see any relationship to choices made in the context of corporate needs?

3) List and discuss the major pitfalls a decision-maker should consider in seeking to develop and use subjective, numerical estimates of probability. How will your answer differ if the probabilities are to be used in decision trees rather than in a matrix summary of a choice that does *not* involve sequential decisions?

4) To what extent may habit and custom, as discussed in Chapter 7, influence the weights we place on different payoffs projected for a given alternative? Is this good or bad?

5) Any decision that can be made by a computer does not require line management attention. Staff technicians who can identify the factors to be processed by the computer are all that is needed. Do you agree? Discuss your answer.

6) To what extent may computers be useful in determining whether to act on incomplete data or to invest more time and cost in seeking more complete data?

7) A small and relatively weak automobile company has sustained losses for four consecutive years. Thorough analysis indicates that the only way to improve performance is to make a sizable investment in new designing and retooling and also in extensive and costly advertising. The investment will, however, bankrupt the company if it does not pay it off in two or three years. Discuss factors relevant to a decision on whether to make this investment.

8) The use of simulation techniques for making a choice requires the combination of knowledge of computer and mathematical techniques with practical experience with the elements of the decision to be made. Because few managers are likely to be strong in both areas, how should the different types of expertise and experience be brought together? What problems do you foresee in this effort?

9) Consider the role of external staff described in Chapter 6. In what ways may such staff personnel aid in making or testing a choice?

Cases

For cases involving issues covered in this chapter, see especially the following. Particularly relevant questions are listed after each case.

Dodge Skate Company (p. 337), 8
E.W. Ross, Inc. (p. 468), 6
Consolidated Instruments—A (p. 571), 9
Consolidated Instruments—B (p. 674), 10

FOR FURTHER READING

Brown, R.V., "Do Managers Find Decision Theory Useful?" *Harvard Business Review*, May 1970. *Survey of the extent of use of, and problems in applying, modern decision theory.*

Magee, J.F., "Decision Trees for Decision Making." *Harvard Business Review*, July 1964. *Clear exposition of basic concept of decision trees.*

Miller, D.W., and M.K. Starr, *Executive Decisions and Operations Research*, 2nd ed. Englewood Cliffs, N.J.: Prentice-Hall, Inc., 1969, Chaps. 4–6. *Cogent summary of decision theory and role of operations research; clearly stated without overlay of mathematical symbolism.*

Shuchman, A., ed., *Scientific Decision Making in Business.* New York: Holt, Rinehart & Winston, 1963, pp. 301–32. *Clear explanation of decision theory. Entire book is useful presentation of operations research concepts for nonmathematicians.*

Walton, C.C., *Ethos and the Executive.* Englewood Cliffs, N.J.: Prentice-Hall, Inc., 1969. *Exploration of personal and company values involved in managerial decision-making.*

Case Studies

 DODGE SKATE COMPANY

General Background

The Dodge Skate Company is a well-established producer of outdoor and indoor roller skates and related products. Located in Ames, Indiana, for more than fifty-six years, Dodge has been the major supplier of skates in the Chicago area and has some scattered sales on both the East and West Coasts.

Five years ago, in a speech before the Ames Chamber of Commerce, Malcolm Dodge, Jr., the company president and son of the founder, summed up his company's basic philosophy as follows:

> *Most companies today think the only way to survive is to grow bigger and bigger and to do so they move into new lines of endeavor. Some succeed but all too many find themselves lost in the complexity of bigness. We at Dodge have set ourselves a different objective. We want to produce the best roller skates and skate accessories possible and sell them at a fair price.*
>
> *We are probably old-fashioned, but we don't really want to grow. We will sell through distributors, anywhere in the world, but our primary concern is with the Chicago market area. I have no intention*

337

of expanding our plant much beyond its present size; and if orders exceed capacity, they will go unfilled, with our old customers getting priority.

Although this may seem strange, it's the kind of business we want to run. I want to know every man in the plant by his first name, and I want to be able to stay on top of all the problems we face. Growing larger might be more profitable but would depersonalize the organization and necessitate all the red tape and bureaucracy that comes with running a large corporation.

Recent Profit Picture

Although this philosophy led Dodge Skate through fifty-three years of profitable operations, four years ago the company showed its first loss since its founding. Total sales declined from $21,700,000 to $15,450,000 and profits fell from $2,628,000 to a loss of $314,000.

In the next year, sales increased to $18,125,000 but the company ended the year showing a small loss. The following year, sales increased again, almost reaching $20,000,000 and the company showed a profit of $220,000. Last year, however, sales fell to $16,800,000, and the company lost almost $250,000.

Douglas Eastman, the general sales manager, blames the decline in sales on increasing competition and the fact that Dodge's prices range from 3 to 18 percent higher than competitive products. Dodge cut prices twice two years ago and made a third cut last year. Commenting on Eastman's request for further price reductions, Mr. Dodge said, "Here we are losing money, and Doug wants me to cut prices. We produce a better product and should receive a higher price. Reducing prices may increase our volume, but I cannot see how it will help with profits."

The company treasurer, Phillip Whistler, agrees with Mr. Dodge that price cuts are not the answer. "Our biggest problem right now is a shortage of cash. We have got to get more cash through sales or from the bank or we will be in real trouble. Our inventory is as low now as we dare let it go; and by offering a 2 percent discount on bills paid within ten days, we have our receivables down to rock bottom. Doug has got to get out there and sell and get every last dollar he can."

Manufacturing

In the midst of the declining sales and profit picture, Max Elton, plant superintendent, states that he has done everything he can to cut costs, but he adds:

One of the company's basic personnel policies has prevented me from reducing plant personnel during the company's slack period.

The company, although its sales are not overly seasonal, through-out the years has experienced a decline in sales following the Christmas season. Production would slack off in late December and early January. During this period the company would catch up on maintenance, and some of the older employees with longer paid vacations would take part of their vacation time. If necessary, a certain amount of production for inventory beyond the normal inventory level would be authorized to prevent layoffs.

While the manufacturing work force has been reduced by attrition, during the slack period there are more men than can be effectively used on maintenance jobs, a situation that has been caused by overall decreases in sales volume. This is complicated by the company's desire not to build up its inventory and also by a lengthening of the slack period.

In a report to the president, Elton noted:

Our slack season used to tail off by January 10; but for the last two years, it's taken us from the post-Christmas sales drop, which starts on or about December 20, until February 1 or 2, for sales to reach a point justifying normal production. Phil [Phillip Whistler, treasurer] is after me to lay off some of the hourly workers during the slack period, but I feel such action would be shortsighted.

At best, we would be able to save about $6,000 on direct labor costs, but consider the impact on morale. Besides, we might lose some of the men we lay off and this means hiring and training new men.

I'm afraid I can't give you a dollar figure to measure morale, and I'd only be guessing on hiring and training costs, but I can't help but feel that these losses would add up to more than $6,000 we might save.

As an alternative use of slack-time, Elton suggested in this report that a more reasonable way of utilizing excess capacity during the six-week slack period would be for Dodge to make some of the oversized metal clamps now produced for Dodge by Ames Metal Products, a subcontractor. The clamps are used on the deluxe outdoor roller skate and have been produced for Dodge by Ames for the last seven years. Although the clamps were developed by Dodge nine years ago, the production of these clamps was subcontracted to Ames because after two years of making the clamps Dodge found that it lacked the capacity to meet its full needs during the peak production months of October through December and March through July.

At this time, Ames supplies Dodge with 30,000 pairs of oversized clamps per month from February through September and 15,000 pairs per month from October through January. For the last three years, Dodge has purchased an average of 300,000 pairs of clamps per year from Ames.

Elton's proposal was that excess capacity be utilized during the six-week slack period to produce 60,000 pairs of oversized clamps. In his request he stated: "We have the equipment and the know-how, and we can retool for less than $2,000. This retooling cost will cover conversion from other processes to clamp production and reconversion when we get back to making other parts. I estimate that during the slack period we can use the services of the nine or ten men that Phil wants me to lay off, and we can produce 60,000 pairs of clamps."

At the president's request, the treasurer prepared an estimate of the costs involved in making the clamps. The costs are summarized in Exhibit 1.

At present, Ames Metal Products charges thirty-eight cents per pair delivered. At this price, 60,000 pairs would cost $22,800. Because Whistler estimates it would cost $27,404 to make this quantity, the difference is $4,604.

Although Whistler doesn't like the idea of laying off hourly workers for six weeks, he points out that he cannot see spending an extra $4,604 to "make work" for them at a time when the company is having real financial problems.

Mr. Dodge, however, is sympathetic to Mr. Elton's position but finds it hard to disagree with Mr. Whistler in the company's current plight.

> It's taken me years to build the kind of work force we have [Mr. Dodge said] and I hate to risk losing good people and making others disgruntled for a few thousand dollars. Business will pick up sooner or later, and I don't want to be shortsighted.
>
> So far we have avoided unionization by paying top wages and by making it clear to the employees that they don't need a union. I hate to throw all that away, but we have to pay our bills.

Relations with Subcontractor

Pursuing the feasibility of Elton's proposal, Mr. Dodge wrote to the president of Ames Metal Products explaining his position on excess capacity and inquired as to the impact of reducing his commitment to Ames from 300,000 pairs of clamps to 240,000. The reply he received from Ames Metal Products is shown in Exhibit 2.

Mr. Dodge is quite concerned about the possibility of having the price of clamps go up because it would add $4,800 ($0.02 × 240,000) to his costs. He feels McCracken may be just bluffing, but he knows of no alternative supplier in that area who can meet his need for clamps at a price approaching forty cents. In addition, McCracken also produces several other parts for Dodge Skate that Dodge cannot make with available equipment and know-how. Up to this point, Mr. Dodge has never worried about an alternative source of supply because of his long and close personal relationship with John McCracken.

Cost Estimates for Manufacturing the Clamp

Max Elton, on reviewing the treasurer's cost projections on the clamp proposal, became quite upset. He stormed into the president's office and stated:

> This is the most ridiculous set of figures I have ever seen, and I've been saddled with Phil's estimates for seventeen years. Here we are talking about a period when we have idle men and machinery, and he has loaded this estimate with everything but the cost of the kitchen sink. Why in the world should we consider factory and general overhead in these costs? No more than 40 percent of the factory overhead and none of the general and administrative overhead will change with this project, so why consider these costs?

When the treasurer heard Elton's position, his comment was:

> Well, here is another good example of mañana thinking. It's a philosophy that says, "Forget the overhead, we will find something else to pay for it tomorrow." If I let Max get away with this in-

Exhibit 1 *Cost of Manufacturing 60,000 Pairs of Oversized Clamps*

Material	$0.12
Direct labor	0.11
Factory overhead	0.15
General and administrative overhead (G & A)	0.04
Unit cost	$0.42
Total normal cost (0.42 × 60,000)	$ 25,200
Retooling costs	2,000
	$ 27,200
Additional carrying cost*	204
Total cost of making clamps	$ 27,404

*The company would normally receive only one 15,000-pair shipment from Ames during this period; if instead the company makes 60,000, they must carry an extra 45,000 pairs in inventory. If the 60,000 pairs represent a cost or cash tie-up of $27,200, the extra 45,000 pairs represent a cash tie-up of $20,400 ($27,200 × .75). The treasurer estimates the cost of clamps tied up at 12 percent a year or 1 percent a month. This makes the carrying cost for one month $20,400 × 1 percent or $204.

cremental nonsense, he would fill the plant with projects that "contribute" something to overhead, but don't cover full cost and don't make a profit. If he spent as much time looking for ways to cut his costs as he does revising my figures, we might get out of this jam. We can't change our approach to estimating cost for every project, or the figures lose their meaning as benchmarks for control purposes.

Elton was equally adamant about his position and replied:

We may go broke if all we can find are projects that contribute something to overhead, but we will go broke a lot sooner if we turn

Exhibit 2 *Letter from John McCracken of Ames Metal Products*

Mr. Malcolm C. Dodge
President
Dodge Skate Company
10 Center Street
Ames, Indiana

Dear Malcolm:

In response to your inquiry regarding the possible reduction in quantity of clamps to be purchased, I have two observations. The first is that we can clearly understand your concern for hourly people and your desire to make fuller use of your capacity. Making some of the clamps yourself seems a most reasonable short-run solution.

However, my second observation is that the reason I can sympathize with your position quite easily is that we are faced with a similar situation. As you know, Malcolm, we have felt the profit squeeze, too. I must, in all honesty, advise you that if you plan on reducing your order by 20 percent, I will be hard pressed to replace the work.

We have always quoted you a rock-bottom price on the clamps and, in spite of rising costs, would like to continue to quote you a unit price of thirty-eight cents. However, if you do reduce your orders from 300,000 to 240,000 pairs per year, we may be forced to quote a price of forty cents per pair.

I want you to know, we will do everything we can to hold the line on prices; but in making your decision, I thought it best to advise you of what seems like a necessary change in our price.

Please advise me at the earliest date of your final decision on this matter.

Sincerely,

(s) John J. McCracken
President

down proposals that make some contribution to fixed overhead. We need figures that show us what something really costs and this varies with the situation as much as with volume.

While Elton was dismayed over the possibility of the price of the remaining 240,000 pairs of clamps going up, he indicated that for an additional $24,000 investment in new equipment, he could produce all 300,000 pairs over the course of the year. The extra equipment would be needed during certain periods of near-capacity production, but would stand idle at other times.

The treasurer's reaction to this proposal was that if Elton recommended a $24,000 expenditure at this time, he obviously didn't realize the seriousness of the company's position.

His comment was:

Even without the retooling and carrying costs, he has a forty-two cent unit cost[1] before considering depreciation on the new equipment. How can we possibly justify an outlay of $24,000 so he can lose us two cents on each unit he produces?[2] This is like the kid selling lemonade who is losing a penny on each cup he sells, but he hopes to make it up on the volume.

FOR DISCUSSION AND REPORT-WRITING

Organizing: Structural Design

1) Who should have the authority for making a final judgment on which costs to use in presenting the alternatives to Mr. Dodge?

Human Factors in Organizing

2) In what ways should Dodge's past practices with regard to layoffs influence his decision on whether to make or buy the clamps?

3) How do you account for the conflict between Whistler and Elton? How might it be reduced?

Planning: Elements of Decision-Making

4) Place the problem of deciding on whether to make or buy clamps in its proper place in a means-end network.

---

[1] See Exhibit 1.

[2] The treasurer figures forty-two cents to make the clamp versus forty cents to buy it—or a loss of two cents per unit.

5) What are the dangers of making the decision on the clamps without placing it in the framework of higher-level goals?

6) In what ways may the conflict between Whistler and Elton influence the likelihood of finding a creative alternative to Dodge Skate's predicament?

7) What are the relevant figures for making the decision on the first 60,000 pairs of clamps if you assume the president is unwilling to invest in the new machine and will continue to buy 240,000 from Ames Metal Products?

8) How might you reflect the uncertainty associated with the possible price increase from thirty-eight to forty cents when deciding on whether to make or buy the 60,000 clamps?

9) *Summary Report Question, Part Three:* Add to the data for question 5 the additional data needed by Mr. Dodge if he were willing at least to consider buying new equipment to make clamps.

10) *Summary Report Question, Part Three:* In addition to these cost and savings estimates, what other factors do you consider important, and how would you recommend that Mr. Dodge weigh them when he prepares to choose?

Planning: Decision-Making in an Enterprise

11) What do you think of the master strategy of Dodge Skate Company?

12) Is the make-or-buy decision on clamps one that, once made, might be dealt with more easily if certain standing plans were written?

13) Prepare a list of steps that you recommend Mr. Dodge follow in his relations with Mr. McCracken of Ames Metal Products.

Leading

14) In what way may the final decision on the clamps affect Elton's potential for developing voluntary cooperation with his men?

Measuring and Controlling

15) How will Mr. Dodge's decision on the clamp question affect his ability to measure and evaluate Elton's performance?

16) How should figures prepared for making a decision on a project like the clamps differ from figures prepared for a budget to be used in planning and control?

*Summary Question for Solution
of the Case as a Whole*

17) Based on the information and weighting developed in questions 9 and 10, what would you do on the clamp question if you were Mr. Dodge? What other actions or plans would you consider as part of the long-run needs of the company?

 BOLLING LABORATORIES, INC.

Bolling Laboratories, Inc., is a large manufacturer of pharmaceuticals with a broad product line covering most segments of a diversified national market. It is known in the industry as a firm with progressive management, good products, and a favorable rate of growth. It sells both ethical drugs (those that may be purchased only with a doctor's prescription) and proprietary items (those sold over the counter in drugstores). The company is also prominent in the sale of veterinary drugs in both ethical and proprietary forms.

At a meeting of the Pharmaceutical Manufacturers Association two years ago, R.M. Gerrard, president of Bolling, had a conversation with executives from another company regarding the future of veterinary pharmaceuticals. One of the others brought up the subject. "At that time," Gerrard says, "I wasn't particularly interested. Bolling has a nice list of veterinary products. In fact, we were one of the first companies in this business."

During the months that followed this conversation, Gerrard

got to thinking about veterinary products. Our brands are well known, but I know that we do not sell as effectively as we could. Our attention has always been rather negligible, because the total market for human pharmaceuticals was so much larger. You see, we have an overall goal of maintaining 15 percent of the total pharmaceutical market in the United States, with gradual increase over ten years to 18 percent. With such a fast growing market, this is not easy. The difficulty of achieving this market share is increasing, especially in the market for human pharmaceuticals. It is getting more and more difficult to clear drugs for sale through federal authorities. We can spend thousands of dollars developing a drug and then not be able to put it on the market for two or three years, even if it is safe. Part of this, of course, is due to the fact that we do not experiment on human beings directly. In addition to this factor, competi-

tion is becoming much stronger in the development of so-called wonder drugs for humans. With these reasons in mind, I instituted a project for the study of our veterinary products and operations. These products are subject to the same difficulties, but to a lesser degree.

Shortly after Gerrard announced this project, M.M. Scanlon, marketing vice-president of Bolling, called a meeting

to discuss the veterinary situation. I wanted to find out from our managers here in headquarters why we are not doing better in this area. Like Gerrard, I don't need a foundation grant to know that Bolling is not a leader. Present at the meeting were myself, Peter Strauss, director of advertising, John Dickenson, director of sales, and Mike Fulton, director of experimental farms.

I started the meeting by saying that it is becoming more and more difficult to maintain Bolling's market share by promoting and selling human pharmaceuticals, that veterinary products represent one avenue for growth, and that we should take a hard look at either (1) what is wrong with our present operations or (2) what might be done to increase our effectiveness. I told them that Mr. Gerrard and I are thinking in terms of increasing our share of the ethical veterinary drug market from 15 to 18 percent.

John Dickenson was first to speak.

The most important key to most market-share problems is always the same. Selling. You cannot move products without salesmen. The key man is the veterinarian. Ethical drugs are the place where the real sales potential exists. Proprietary drugs are strictly secondary. The overwhelming majority of ethicals sold are by the veterinarian. Even when he doesn't carry inventory on his premises (most of them do), he, not the druggist, is the customer. I do not think we have enough men in the field. If we want to increase our market share from 15 to 18 percent, then it may mean hiring 20 percent more salesmen. We now have thirty-two. That would mean an expansion of the sales force to thirty-eight men.

Peter Strauss interrupted and gave his opinion on this issue.

I wouldn't be sure of that. Advertising is important even in the ethical trade. The average veterinarian, like the average physician, reads professional journals constantly. We have a survey of the Advertising Association that shows that in the introduction of new drugs, veterinarians report that in 55 percent of the cases they first became acquainted with the product by seeing a professional advertisement, showing the various technical specifications and treatment results. I believe that we should increase the budget for advertising by an additional $150,000.

"I suppose I agree with you, Peter," Dickenson answered. "But I just don't see that advertising is nearly as important as selling. But I don't know how we'd ever prove that."

Scanlon said at this point that this is the kind of question that has got to be settled, if possible. He also questioned whether the company was selling to the big customers: "I guess it is obvious that one factor is whether we're selling to the big users, or wasting our selling and advertising on small accounts."

Dickenson answered:

> An analysis of our sales shows that 20 percent goes to what we call the "wholesale doctors"—the very large clinics, such as those at Fort Collins, Colorado, and Ithaca, New York (to which animals are sent by veterinarians from all over the country), as well as large private animal hospitals in the suburbs of major cities. We have no trade association statistics on total consumption of ethical products by these institutions.

At this point, Mike Fulton, director of experimental farms, spoke up. Fulton had been invited to the meeting Scanlon said, "because he is a vast repository of information on veterinary products." It was fairly unusual for anyone from "the farms" to attend. These two farms were set up a number of years ago to house experimental rats and guinea pigs used in general research. Today the farms contain several thousand animals of various types and represent a large capital investment. Fulton is an extremely busy man as administrator of the farms. Of course, the actual research there is done by bacteriologists, pharmacologists, and other scientists from the research department. He was originally hired with a degree in veterinary medicine because the animals needed caring for. However, he has continually helped both the sales department people when they have an idea for using a certain drug and the scientists when they have an idea for developing one.

Fulton said:

> I am worried about another thing. There is no one who can be called captain of the team when it comes to veterinary products. Over on the human side, the product managers of antibiotics, reproductive pharmaceuticals, intravenous solutions, and the like are always going to the research laboratories saying, "We must develop a product to compete with Talizene—the competition is killing us," or going to sales and saying, "The research people have just discovered a new and lower cost way to make our standard Thyroxin— get ready with an advertising campaign." I don't see that happening in veterinary products. Sure, we develop and sell them, but they seem to get lost sometimes in the development of all the wonder drugs for humans.

At that point, Scanlon spoke up. He said that in the area of research Bolling seemed to have a good record. "We introduced fourteen products last year which were either completely new or major specification changes in existing products. That kind of record, at today's research costs, is good."

Events of the Next Four Months

At the end of the meeting, Scanlon suggested that this group become a formal task force for improvement of Bolling's veterinary operations, meeting each Monday for four months. At the same time, he obtained permission from the vice-president for research to have Mike Fulton relieved as director of experimental farms for a period of three months, so

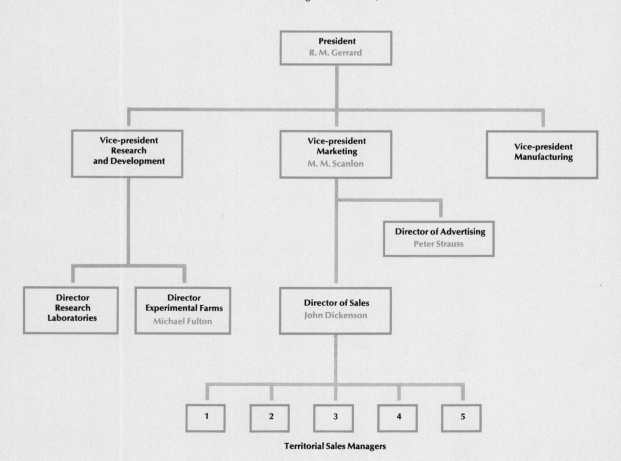

Exhibit 1 *Organization Chart,
Bolling Laboratories, Inc.*

Exhibit 2 *Number of Salesmen Employed, Bolling and Three Similar Competitors**

Bolling	32
Company A	30
Company B	25
Company C	28

*For Exhibits 2 through 6, Mike Fulton selected three competitive companies selling veterinary pharmaceuticals. He selected these three because each company had about the same veterinary sales volume as Bolling ($25,000,000).

Exhibit 3 *Number of New Products Introduced in the Past Two Years*

Bolling	28
Company A	62
Company B	55
Company C	49

Source: Federal Drug Administration Reports; professional veterinary journals.

Exhibit 4 *Where Twenty Wholesale Customers Purchase Their Supplies*

	Portion of Total Purchases
Bolling	26%
Company A	22
Company B	28
Company C	19

Source: Company salesmen interviewed twenty large clinics, nationwide. These were both research clinics at schools of veterinary medicine and large suburban clinics in population centers. In each case, the customer was asked to estimate what percentage of his total use of pharmaceuticals was purchased from each company.

Exhibit 5 *Impact of Advertising on Veterinary Doctors*

Question: Can you cite specific information from advertisements for any of these companies that appeared in the past month?

	Doctors Who Could Cite Information from the Advertisement
Bolling	41%
Company A	45
Company B	32
Company C	38

Source: One hundred veterinary doctors— twenty from the wholesale sample (Exhibit 4) and eighty from the medium-sized sample (Exhibit 6).

Exhibit 6 *How Doctors and Druggists Rate the Sales Effort of Bolling and Three Competitors*

Question: Compared to these three other companies, would you say that Bolling's salesmen spend more time, about the same time, or less time when they call on you? Would you rank the companies from 1 (spends most time) to 4 (spends least time)?

	Doctors	Druggists
Bolling	4	1
Company A	1	4
Company B	3	2
Company C	2	3

Source: Eighty medium-sized clinics nationwide. Ratings indicate average response.

that he could serve as staff investigator for the task force. "Dickenson and I," Scanlon said, "both noticed that he had a flair for selling. He always seemed to be suggesting alternatives that we had not thought of as means for overcoming problems. Often they are unworkable, but he hit on some that are of great benefit."

Over the four months, members of the task force seemed to report solid statistics, but none that could really pinpoint where Bolling had real opportunity for improvement. "It's like my statistics on new products or the question of whether we need more salesmen or more advertising," Scanlon continued. "We all know that the company could probably improve with either, but the question is, which is more important?"

During this time, Fulton reported regularly on certain investigations he was making. Most of these involved getting Bolling salesmen to request information from customers with whom they are personally acquainted. "There was a certain reluctance by the salesmen to take on this added paperwork" Fulton said, "but after clearing with Dickenson and their territorial managers I went straight to the men themselves, spent a lot of time showing them what we're trying to do, and then how it would pay off for them in increased commissions if we could get the information."

At the end of this period, Fulton requested a special meeting of the

Exhibit 7 *Miscellaneous Factors Influencing Sale of Veterinary Pharmaceuticals*

Question: In addition to quality and price of pharmaceuticals, what factors influence you most in the choice of a supplier?*

Factor	Portion of Responses Mentioning This Factor
Helpfulness of the salesman: This item covers such informal actions as "he actually helped me in treating an animal," or "he showed me a new way to prevent spoilage of solutions."	45%
Promptness of delivery: For example, "When my rush shipment was lost, X Company shipping department couldn't even find the order," or "the local salesman traced it right away."	32
Reputation of the company: For example, "my customers are impressed when I use drugs that are well known for treatment of human disease."	31
Ease of packaging and dispensing: For example, "I have noticed that Y Company always has the latest vials, bottles, and plastic dispensers. They look better, too."	30

*This question, asked of the sample of one hundred doctors used in Exhibit 5, did not provide a checklist. The table summarizes answers and gives the percentage of doctors mentioning that item.

task force to explain some of his findings. "This wasn't easy, since they are busy men. But I went to each of their offices and gave them a small part of the total information. When they saw that there were going to be some new statistics, and not just the same we've been over before, they seemed more interested."

At the meeting, Fulton presented large charts on each of the subjects shown in Exhibits 2 through 7. The meeting lasted for the maximum time available. There was not much time for discussion. Scanlon asked each man to study the data and to be prepared to make some recommendations for policy changes at the next meeting. As a final comment, he said that he also wanted the task force to look into several other matters in its coming meetings: (1) the nature of the training given to Bolling salesmen, and (2) the sales incentive compensation system used by the company, particularly with respect to its effect on proprietary and ethical sales.

FOR DISCUSSION AND REPORT-WRITING

Organizing: Structural Design

1) Look carefully at the way various people diagnose either obstacles to, or opportunities for, increasing the sale of veterinary drugs. Which factor indicates an obstacle in the present organization structure of Bolling Laboratories?

2) Does the job of Fulton look like a move toward centralization or decentralization of the decision-making function as it applies to veterinary operations? Using the "Guides to How Much Decentralization" from the text, cite the reason for this move.

3) What might be the activities of a product manager for veterinary drugs? The advantages of such a position?

Human Factors in Organizing

4) It is often said that many formal organizations are codifications, or "charts drawn on paper," that reflect some informal custom that is useful in a group of people. In what sense was this true in Fulton's role when he was first invited? In what sense when the task group became formal? What might be predicted for the future formal organization of veterinary operations?

Planning: Elements of Decision-Making

5) What is the *first* step in the diagnosis of most action-oriented decisions? Quote Gerrard's words and point out his actions to show that he

went through this first step. Quote Scanlon's remarks to show his first step.

6) Gerrard explained at the beginning of the case why he instituted a project on veterinary drugs. Chart this reasoning by looking "up" a means-end chain to the broader context of the problem. Include his "gap" and point out two alternatives he saw for closing this gap. Also indicate the obstacles that can be attributed to these alternatives.

7) Peter Strauss cites a statistic indicating that veterinarians first become acquainted with 55 percent of new drugs by seeing an advertisement in a professional journal. How relevant is this to the real problem of Bolling Laboratories? Answer the same question with regard to (1) Dickenson's feeling that the number of salesmen in the field is a key factor in generating veterinary product sales and (2) his consequent proposal to increase the sales force to thirty-eight men.

8) Scanlon says that the question of whether Strauss or Dickenson is right is one that must be settled quickly. How would the technique of negative thinking help to answer this question?

9) What obstacle worried Fulton? Is this a real obstacle to growth of sales in the veterinary drug line, or is it a "red herring" that merely confuses the rest of the group?

10) Do you see how positive thinking (as opposed to negative thinking) led Scanlon to make one serious error in diagnosing the cause of Bolling Laboratories' veterinary drug problem? (Hint: "That kind of record today is good.") Explain his error.

11) Draw a *preliminary* means-end chain of the whole problem in the case. It will be preliminary in that it raises all possible objectives and obstacles connected with the top problem. It is creative in that you are not yet judging which of the parts are *real* or *root* causes and which are false causes or red herrings. Gather your information from the following sources: (1) various comments of all executives at the meeting; (2) the data gathered by Fulton and included as exhibits; and (3) the instructions at the end, given by Scanlon. As a further understanding of the problem in its broader context, connect this means-end diagram with the one requested in question 6.

12) Look at the preliminary means-end diagram. How does the technique, plus the human interaction at the meeting, illustrate the phenomenon of serendipity? Is the technique valuable for creativity?

13) *Summary Report Question, Part Three:* From your total diagnosis (question 11), draw a circle around the root causes and a box around the superficial "red herrings" raised at the meeting. Then use this chart to write a staff report to Mr. Scanlon, stating (1) the problem and its causes, and (2) recommendations for expansion of veterinary products markets in the Bolling Laboratories.

14) *Summary Report Question, Part Three:* Now look at the finished diagram (question 13). Explain why the diagnosis technique in the book is valuable both for creativity (question 12) *and* for cold, logical analysis.

Planning: Decision-Making in an Enterprise

15) Explain how diagnosis of Bolling Laboratories' problem is an important method of establishing a hierarchy of goals. Do you see why no company can operate logically without such a hierarchy?

16) Give one or two examples of a written policy statement for Bolling Laboratories that might emerge from the diagnosis of this problem.

Leading

17) To what do you attribute Fulton's success in getting the cooperation of the salesmen to do all of the "paperwork" connected with his exhibits? In getting the busy members of the task force to attend a special meeting?

Measuring and Controlling

18) Note the qualifications of all of the information gathered by Fulton. From the diagnosis of root causes, write a hypothetical control standard that would help the company achieve its objectives in the future.

*Summary Question for Solution
of the Case as a Whole*

19) Using a complete diagnosis of the problem (if you did questions 11 and 13, this will already be available), write a report that shows: (1) how diagnosis of problems in this company is linked to design of the organization structure (questions 1 to 3 will help you here); (2) how diagnosis by a "sensor" or "initiator" like Mike Fulton might aid the decision-making process in the entire enterprise; and (3) how group diagnosis of problems is an important aid in the process of leading, as a means to developing voluntary cooperation.

Planning: Decision-Making in an Enterprise

Who should make plans for a company was a major consideration in our examination of formal organization in Part One. We examined de-centralization of planning, the use of staff to assist in planning, and structural arrangements for coordinating planning. In Part Three, we have just explored suggestions on *how* sound decisions could be made. Now in Part Four, we shall integrate the who and the how by studying the way concepts from Parts One and Three can be meshed together.

In this synthesis, we must keep in mind group influences on behavior, personal needs and beliefs, and the existence of conflict and power. These forces, as we noted in Part Two, affect the actual formulation of decisions in an organization as much as a formal assignment of duties.

When a manager shifts his viewpoint on decision-making from individual to enterprise, his task is simplified in some respects and com-plicated in others. The availability of more minds to work on problems is a great advantage. But when several persons take part, we have to introduce ways of securing consistency among decisions, coordination of various planning units, and economy in planning effort. Various types of plans—or planning instruments—are used to obtain such consistency, coordination, and economy; and we shall look carefully at how these instruments aid in the planning process. These issues will be considered in the following chapters.

Chapter 15—Decision-Making in Organizations. Here we shall explore the benefits and difficulties that arise from a division of labor when the elements of decision-making are dispersed throughout an enterprise.

Chapter 16—Master Strategy and Long-range Programming. Central to systematic planning is continuing appraisal of the major services that a firm seeks to provide and of the best way to produce those services. Moreover, the timing of moves to carry out this strategy has to be fitted into long-range programs.

Chapter 17—Operating Objectives. The broad strategy must then be recast in terms of specific goals and subgoals if planning is dispersed to many people. In this chapter, we shall consider how to set up a hierarchy of objectives so that effective action follows.

Chapter 18—Planning for Stabilized Action. Policies, procedures, and standard methods contribute substantially to consistent and economical decisions. But, as we shall see in this chapter, there is serious question about how far to carry this type of planning.

Chapter 19—Adaptive Programming. In every company, a substantial part of its planning deals with nonrepetitive situations. Managers must set up programs and decide on tactics to follow. We shall note how such plans must frequently be adapted to new problems and new opportunities.

Planning in a modern enterprise is becoming more and more complex. Success in the future will depend significantly on how management distributes this increasingly difficult task of planning throughout its organization and *at the same time* maintains a dynamic, integrated operation. The aim of Part Four is to examine the means available to a manager for dealing with this crucial function.

Chapter Fifteen

Decision-Making in Organizations

DIFFUSION AMONG PEOPLE AND THROUGH TIME

In the preceding chapters on decision-making we explored the basic elements in developing creative and wise solutions to management problems. That analysis was simplified by assuming that the process was being carried on within a single man's mind. Most management decisions, in fact, require inputs from numerous members of an organization. So our attention now shifts to how the decision-making process takes place in an enterprise.

Help from Many People

The task of making a particular decision may be assigned to a single executive, but rarely does he make such a decision unaided. The credit manager of a company that sells watches to retail stores, for example, had to decide how to handle a request for long-term credit from a newly organized chain of jewelry stores. The salesman who had the account was eager to work out some arrangement because he believed that granting the request would result in a substantial volume of business over a period of years. The credit manager needed help. First, he asked the accounting department for an analysis of the purchases and payment record of the stores that were being merged together in the new chain; the salesman was asked to prepare a written report on the reasons why the new company needed more time than the credit period extended to other customers; and the assistant credit manager was asked to assemble information from the usual sources—banks, personal references, and credit-rating agencies—and to appraise the new company in terms of standards for normal trade credit.

In addition, the credit manager consulted with the treasurer both about the company policy on using capital in accounts receivable and for general advice. In the course of their conversation, the treasurer suggested several alternatives, one of which was for the company to endorse the customer's note, which could then be used as a basis for a loan by a commercial bank directly to the customer. Next, the sales manager offered his estimates of the likely importance of the new customer in future business and the value of financial help in developing customer goodwill. The company lawyer gave his opinion on several ways of providing financial aid and made specific suggestions for protection should legal action become necessary. Finally, the credit manager decided not to extend credit directly but to help the customer borrow elsewhere, and he asked the treasurer to arrange for a commercial bank to make a loan with his company endorsing the notes.

Such an exchange of ideas and information is the typical and natural way of making decisions within organizations. People at all levels do it, with the degree of interaction depending on the problem. With the increasing complexity of business, skill in such interactions is growing in importance. Most spectacularly in technical research and giant construction projects, the great advances of the last decade reflect coordinated group effort more than the work of some individual.

Two points are of particular significance in this example: (1) Several different people often make a direct contribution to a decision, and (2) previously established policies, procedures, standards, and records also influence decisions.

Succession of Premises

Decision-making in an organization differs from individual decision-making, examined in Part Three, in still another way. The help we get from other people and the guides ("restraints") provided by the enterprise itself rarely come together in a single grand array. Theoretically, if we follow the rationalistic-model approach, we might consolidate all the forecasts and guesses, relate them to selected alternatives, make allowances for time and uncertainty, apply a formally approved value scale, and emerge with *the* decision. Actually, only in small organizations and for relatively simple decisions can we get all the issues and "facts" on the table at the same moment.

Instead, conclusions are reached in *sequence*—often by different individuals—and one conclusion becomes a premise for the next. Thus in diagnosis a district sales manager may conclude that the company's new plastic-base paint is unsuited for the blistering sunshine in his district; the plant engineer, accepting this fact, reports on the technical difficulties of making a special mix for that district; and, on the basis of the engineer's report, the cost accountant prepares some figures on producing two different mixes. These are all preliminary data, but note how one builds on another.

Such interlocking of one conclusion into another is particularly significant in projecting consequences after a problem has been defined and the alternatives identified. Suppose that the difficulty with paint blistering has been diagnosed and we have a proposed second line of "sunproof" paint. The company is now trying to project the results of adding this new line. As general background, the company economist predicts general business conditions and the level of business activity for the next five years. Accepting this forecast, the sales manager predicts sales volume with and without the new line. Then, given these volumes, the chief engineer estimates the new equipment that would be needed and other effects on production; he reports that if the new line is added an automatic grinding mill will be feasible. Now, the purchasing agent, learning from the engineer the kind and quantity of raw materials needed, prepares a cost estimate for raw materials; and the personnel director, using the sales and production forecasts, estimates training and wage costs. With these data, the controller makes a summary estimate of total outlays and receipts.

Note in this illustration that the estimates of each man are built on conclusions of one or more other men. Stated another way, the conclusions of the sales manager become premises for the engineer, the conclusions of the engineer become premises for the purchasing agent, and so forth. Consequently, if we want to be confident that the final decision emerging from this sequence is sound, we must give careful attention to how each premise is set. Personal bias and faulty communication may introduce substantial error in the process. Even officially approved premises need to be reviewed.

Variation in Problems

Problems differ in the number of people who become involved and in the amount of special effort required. The more unique and complex the problem, the more pooling of diverse management talents is necessary. Here are two situations that we shall use as examples throughout the chapter.

The president of Frosty Foods, a successful frozen-food processing company, is aware of the growth in "fast-food" restaurant chains such as McDonald's Hamburgers. These chains use large quantities of frozen food, and variations of basic products especially designed to fit the fashion trends of this market might increase that volume. Possibly Frosty Foods should buy up a chain of outlets. The move of the Howard Johnson chain to sell food products carrying its name through food supermarkets suggests the possibility of synergistic benefits, that is, the combined effect of restaurant and supermarket promotion may be greater than merely the sum of separate promotion of restaurant sales and supermarket sales. In other words, the president of Frosty Foods feels that opportunity for some kind of action in the "fast-food" industry exists, but he is not clear on what action should be taken. This kind of decision-making situation is roughly similar to the opportunity universities face in the area of urban studies. We are concerned here with how a plan of action responding to such an opportunity can best be devised in an organization.

Resolution of the situation just described obviously will involve more people in a manner quite different than would a telephone call from the food buyer of a motel chain requesting information concerning frozen meat dishes suitable for cooking in an infrared oven when the regular kitchen crew is off duty. This latter question is similar to that of a student who has just arrived at Mountainside College and who requests an education that will prepare him to go into international business, "probably in Latin America."

For these and similar problem situations a manager concerned with the decision-making process should know *who* will do the following: (1) sense and diagnose opportunities, (2) come up with creative alternatives, (3) make projections of probable results, and (4) meld separate projections into a component picture and select one alternative for positive action.

SENSING AND DIAGNOSING PROVISIONS

Many management problems come to the surface in normal operations. The control system (Part Six) flags significant deviations from plan. A customer, supplier, or other outsider makes a request, as did the motel food buyer and new student at Mountainside mentioned above. Or a conscientious operator or manager has an idea for improving the work he is doing. Some of these wheels will squeak louder than others, but at least the noise is there to be heard.

Discerning New Opportunities

Anticipating obstacles before they arise and sensing opportunities in the dynamic environment is more difficult. Managers, such as the president of Frosty Foods, certainly watch major developments but they also need the help of a mechanism that is alert to all sorts of developments.

Sensing units. Because employees ordinarily give their chief attention to facts and ideas that directly relate to current problems, they often fail to report other facts and ideas to key executives. Perhaps the unreported information deals with a minor, but nonetheless significant, aspect of the work; perhaps it is an early warning of impending difficulties; perhaps it is a lead to a great opportunity. Somehow, someone in the communication network should recognize the significance of this bit of information and tell the appropriate executive about it.

To search out just such information, we may assign a man—or perhaps a research unit. He may watch consumer behavior, new patents, employee complaints, proposed legislation, or some other special area. Although he will probably be overimpressed with the significance of his particular specialty, his purpose is to call attention to valuable information that might go unnoticed.

Interest-group representatives. Government agencies, especially, often provide a clear avenue for representatives of various interest groups (labor, small business, and so on) to present information and suggestions. These communication devices bypass the points of routine contact; they enable stimuli from the fringe of the complex to reach decision centers with maximum speed and minimum distortion. We indicated earlier that a comparable arrangement seems to serve business enterprises better than does the placement of interest-group representatives on the board of directors (see Chapter 6).

It is hard to keep formal interest-group representation and sensing units alert. After a time they, like managers, tend to accept established institutions and to think in terms of modest changes. Yet we very much need some mechanism to help keep the enterprise relevant to its shifting social, technological, and economic setting. The formal organization is not enough; it must be staffed with perceptive, constructive people.

Communication Barriers

Even with such sensing units, information has to reach someone who perceives its significance, and many bits and pieces of data bear no label as to their relevance. In fact, much information does not flow freely for two reasons:

1) Experience and experiments have shown that man is a poor transmitter of ideas. We know, for example, that people who witness the same automobile accident describe it differently. If these descriptions are later passed on orally from Pete to Bob to Joe, the chances are slim that Joe will have an accurate picture of the accident. As information passes through additional intermediaries, the transmission errors are compounded. Such decay in accuracy is found within businesses as well as outside.

2) Additional distortion occurs when a message passes up or down a channel of command. *Protective screening* tends to intervene between subordinate and superior. A subordinate is apt to tell his boss what the boss likes to hear and will omit or soften what is unpleasant; perhaps too, a subordinate will cover up his own weaknesses. We all adopt this procedure, at least mildly, in ordinary conversation with our friends; we do so even more when we talk to a person in a position of power. After two or three successive screenings of this sort, a report is likely to be considerably distorted. Messages coming down the channel are similarly screened; each supervisor puts his own interpretation on a message, and probably withholds part of the information that he feels his subordinates do not need to know.

The combined result of normal losses in transmission and protective screening is called *organizational distance*. Workers removed by several steps in an organization hierarchy are in serious danger of being isolated from one another. It is difficult for one to know how another really feels and thinks. If they differ in experience, education, and outlook, the inadequacies of communication are further increased.

Initiators

In face of the diffusion of potentially useful information and the normal communication barriers, we dare not assume that unusual and subtle problems will be recognized. Here we have no predetermined controls nor insistent petitioners. Instead, if the opportunity or potential obstacle is to be identified early, we need an "initiator," that is, a person who (1) is exposed to the information cues, often through his own initiative, (2) perceives the significance of the cues to company plans and objectives, and (3) prods or otherwise insists that careful consideration be given to the perceived problem. An initiator may be a manager or a staff

Fig. 15-1   Each time a message passes from one person to the next, filtering and distortion occur. Some of the original meaning is screened out and some new content is added.

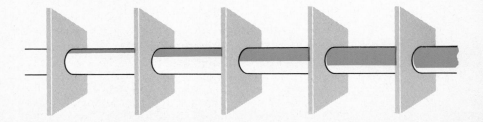

man who has been assigned the duty of discovering problems, or he may be any alert member of the organization with ability to "sense" problems. Rarely is it wise for a manager to rely entirely on himself for this elusive work, and so in his staffing (see Chapter 10) he should seek at least a sprinkling of men with this initiating flair.

Completing the Diagnosis

Spotting a potential problem is only the start of a diagnosis. Defining the problem in terms of a gap, identifying causes and obstacles, and establishing limits within which a solution must fall—all need attention as we saw in Chapter 11. Who in the organization performs this part of the diagnosis?

Complex problems. For complex and unique problems several people should participate in the diagnosis. The initiator, the manager or managers whose sphere of activities will be affected, and perhaps several other experts or investigators all can contribute. For example, the president of Frosty Foods needs more information about the "fast-food" business: critical factors for success, capital requirements, food buying practices, and so on. A staff man can dig up this information. The maximum size of an appropriate merger partner should be discussed with the treasurer; the effect of the merger on company sales to other chains should be gone over with the sales manager; antitrust issues, with the company's attorney; and impact on management motivation, with the chairman. These early discussions are very tentative; the whole idea is still very fluid. Actually the discussion will undoubtedly slide over to specific alternatives and rough projections of results, but the main purpose is to sharpen the concept of what is desired and to identify major obstacles early. The whole idea may be dropped at any stage if the prospects for success look dim.

Participation by a number of people serves several purposes. The initiator is needed for his insights and also to keep the idea alive. The experts consulted help clarify the objective and are the major source of information on obstacles. Starting with the premise that the new objective is compatible with other company objectives, operating executives define acceptable limits. As we noted in Chapter 11, the senior man involved shapes the breadth of the study by stipulating how far it should go up the means-end chain and by deciding which company policies are to be regarded as constraints.

At this stage a manager has an especially responsive opportunity to guide his organization. He can easily encourage or discourage creative planning in areas he selects. Having endorsed a direction in which a search for improvement should move, he can resort to management by objectives. He can generate enthusiasm by having key men participate actively in the formative phases of planning. Because of all these factors, a manager should play an active part in this phase of decision-making and should become as involved here as he does in making the final choice.

Simple problems. Diagnosing the more customary and more simple case concerning the motel buyer who requests information on food for off-hours service involves a very different process. The initiator—the buyer —is an outsider. His request is specific and most if not all of the response comes from established decision guides. If Frosty Foods normally carries products that fit the inquiry, the company has only to convince the buyer that he should deal with Frosty Foods; after this, agreement on price and delivery can be sought. Even if the buyer wants a variation from stock items, the problem can be immediately narrowed by company policy regarding special orders.

Such simple diagnosis is possible because a whole set of policies and procedures have been designed to resolve promptly just this kind of problem. Obviously if Frosty Foods had just opened its doors and had no standard array of products, production specifications, or sales policies, the inquiry would precipitate a great deal of diagnosis and problem-solving. However, the planning structure, which we shall examine in the next four chapters, is formulated for the express purpose of avoiding the need for much diagnosis of single transactions. In advance of the specific request, decisions have been made that cover a whole series of similar situations.

To summarize: The main questions a manager must answer when thinking about how diagnosis occurs in his organization are these: (1) What provision should he make for scanning both the external environment and internal operation to detect future opportunities and problems? (2) How can he minimize the effect of "organizational distance," so that cues once discovered do not get lost? (3) Who should participate in completing the diagnosis and in revising it as the decision-making process evolves? (4) What role should previously established plans play in simplifying and expediting diagnoses?

The two Frosty Foods illustrations make clear that no single set of answers can be given to these questions. Companies vary in the number of unique and complex problems they face, and so do departments within companies. The provisions for diagnosis should reflect this variation. Even in this first stage of decision-making we see the benefits and complexities that arise from having several different people participate.

SOURCES OF FRESH IDEAS

Relying on Operating Personnel

Finding good alternative solutions is the second basic stage in decision-making. Sometimes acceptable alternatives emerge during the diagnosis stage. The men consulted about the problem also know what other firms are doing and they add ideas of their own. In fact, the cue that triggered the recognition of a problem may have been an action taken by someone else, a proposal by a supplier, or a request by a client. Of course someone has to decide that a search for better alternatives is not worth the trouble. This decision not to search further is often made promptly. When at least one satisfactory alternative is at hand, the man who suggests further search has to explain why he thinks a better way might be uncovered.

This tendency to end a search for alternatives too early leads a few wise managers to insist always on serious consideration of at least four alternatives. Such a rule of thumb does not assure a careful search, but it does avoid the tempting simplicity of an *either* A *or* B formulation. Another tack is to invite suggestions from all key people who would be affected by the contemplated change. Too often this is really an early move to prepare men for a change, and proposals submitted are brushed aside as biased or as ploys to avoid some worse fate. Nevertheless, several fairly good alternatives can often be assembled promptly from such sources.

Separate Creative Units

What happens when no acceptable alternative bubbles to the surface? The constraints built into the diagnosis (capital, ownership, time, impact on community, and so on) or a tough obstacle may eliminate all the obvious courses of action. We then turn to creativity.

When the need for creative ideas is predictable and recurs in a known field, we organize to get fresh ideas. Product or process research in a pharmaceutical firm is an example. Men are hired and a laboratory is built to create a flow of new, useful drugs, typically within certain predetermined classes. The results are uncertain, but the approach is straightforward. Advertising agencies similarly hire specialists to generate fresh themes. A variation occurs in new designs for women's dresses. Small firms often buy designs from an independent designer, but the approach still involves a specialist who creates alternatives for a predicted need. The researchers and creative people may share in short-run diagnosis, but they are primarily a separate group of specialists.

One drawback of relying on specialized idea men is the possible generation of friction. In Chapter 9 we noted that sharp differences in attitudes and values of men in sales and production are a source of organizational conflict. The same type of conflict is found very often between "creative guys" and "tough operators." The imaginative man who is ready to entertain all sorts of fanciful notions has an outlook that is very different from that of the operator who carefully distinguishes between fact and fiction, right and wrong, established workability and day-dreaming. Because of this contrast in orientation, we must anticipate friction when two such people are asked to collaborate. To minimize this difficulty, physical separation and relatively few interactions probably are desirable. On the other hand, if we choose to make different types learn to live together, we should use carefully supervised project teams whenever feasible.

Temporary Assignment to Generate Ideas

The use of specialists is unsuitable when the need for creative alternatives is irregular or unpredictable. Frosty Foods, to return to our earlier example, cannot afford to maintain a specialist on mergers with restaurant chains, even if such a man could be located. Instead, men who have other jobs in the company must temporarily become creators of alternatives.

Conditions that foster creativity were discussed in Chapter 11. A permissive atmosphere, for instance, is conducive to a flow of fresh ideas. Note, however, that the need for alternatives to a unique problem is temporary. We may ask three or four men to be creative for a week or only a morning, after which they return to jobs where stress is on analysis and where supervisors tolerate no mistakes. Both the men and their supervisors are asked to shift attitudes and standards for only a brief period. Some men have this flexibility, but a lot of sophistication about different styles of work is required.

Management consultants can be brought in if the problem is large enough to warrant the cost of the special arrangements. Consultants will have ready-made alternatives for only a few fairly standard problems. These men usually work with client personnel on the entire project— diagnosis, alternatives, projection, and choice—and their chief contribution typically is objective, undivided attention to the project and skill in digging out and arranging facts and ideas. Consultants provide ability much more than specific ideas, because the client personnel who work with them supply many of the inputs. Therefore, company personnel work on a strange and temporary assignment as before, but in this case they are under the skillful guidance of the consultants.

Internal generation of creative alternatives for unique problems should therefore be assigned to men who have considerable mental flexibility in addition to the required knowledge concerning the particular situation being studied.[1]

Most significant for successful use of any of these arrangements— relying on operating personnel, using separate creative units, or making temporary assignments—is recognition that the mental attitude and surrounding support needed for creativity differs sharply from that needed for projection and choice.

---

[1] *Synectics* is an exception. With this technique only one or two men have to be qualified to build bridges from fresh ideas to the actual situation.

CONSOLIDATING PROJECTIONS OF RESULTS

What will happen *if* we follow alternative A? If we follow alternative B, what results will follow? Likewise, results should be projected for each alternative.

When such projections are made in an organization, normally many different people help make the forecasts. Also, as we noted at the beginning of this chapter, one forecast often becomes the planning premise of a related forecast; thus a whole succession of estimates may be interdependent. This ability to tap the understanding and judgment of a variety of specialists is a great strength, because it allows organizations to deal intelligently with complex issues that are far beyond the comprehension of a single individual.

The use of different specialists to make projections, however, is not an unmixed blessing. The very fact that each of several individuals contributes a piece of the total picture poses some unique difficulties in consolidating the pieces. We need to appreciate these difficulties and understand what we can do about them in order to grasp fully the potential benefits to be gained from group projections of results.

Uncertainty Absorption

All the estimates used in decision-making deal with the future, and all involve some uncertainty. Future sales, for instance, depend on a host of unknowns—competitors' actions, consumer reaction to our tie-in advertising, health of our sales manager, a Civil Rights boycott, and the like. When our sales manager makes an estimate of sales for the next five years, he might hedge his answer with a lot of "ifs"—*if* competitors cut prices 5 percent, *if* the advertising plan really clicks, *if* everyone is healthy, *then* sales probably will be around four million or maybe five million.

Such an iffy answer is quite unsatisfactory for the engineer. He says, "I don't have time to guess whether your advertising campaign is any good. Just tell me how much you want, because I have plenty of problems of my own." He prefers a single figure, or at most a narrow range. So the sales manager makes the best guess he can, realizing that his figure may not be accurate. If he is a conservative individual (or experience has taught him that he gets into less trouble when his estimates are low than when they are high), he picks a low volume. Or, if he is optimistic, does not mind taking a risk, and wants to impress the boss, then he picks a higher volume. In any event, he "absorbs" a lot of uncertainty when he finally tells the engineer to assume that sales will be, say, four-and-a-half million.

The engineer is in a similar predicament. Will the refrigeration pumps break down in the near future? Can quality be maintained if a new product line is added? How long will it take to make a changeover to new raw material? And so forth. Again, we do not want an answer full of "ifs." Instead, we ask the engineer to use his judgment, which means that he absorbs uncertainty regarding another group of factors. Virtually all the other people who provide estimates used in our projection for expanded production will likewise absorb uncertainty.

Such uncertainty absorption is inevitable and desirable. Without it the analysis of problems becomes hopelessly complex. If we attempted to give attention to all the possibilities as one estimate is built on another, the number of possible outcomes would increase at a geometric rate and would soon become incomprehensible. So we accept uncertainty absorption, but try to minimize its dangers.

Recognizing the Bias of Different Estimates

Whenever we depend upon an estimate prepared by someone else we naturally want to know if it is reliable. We want to know whether it is optimistic or pessimistic. We want to know of any bias especially when we are aware that a particular individual has absorbed a lot of uncertainty in a prediction that is used in other estimates.

Bias of some sort is almost inevitable in a set of projections made by different people. Being separate personalities, each of us has leanings and biases that creep into our respective views of the future. Here are four common reasons why one person's projections of results may not be just what the decision-maker needs:

1) *Differences in perception of objectives.* A man who is making a decision may differ in his objectives from the people who are giving him advice. This situation is especially true when the advisors have strong, professional indoctrination, as in accounting, law, social work, and, to a lesser extent, engineering. The advice and other help such people provide may be strongly influenced by what they believe to be important. If a decision-maker is trying to achieve different objectives, the sympathetic help he would like to receive may turn out to be suggestions leading off on a tangent. The help may still be of some value, but he has to make allowance for its source.

Difference in objectives was found to be an important factor in a study of seventy-four companies' decisions regarding the use of outside contractors for maintenance work. The study showed that senior executives place high values on stable union relations, whereas maintenance superintendents give greater weight to keeping their costs low and to the number of their men who might be laid off. We cannot tell from the information available which objectives deserve priority, but clearly the difference in objectives of the executives affects the way they respond to this problem.

2) *The "persuasive" advisor.* People vary in their persuasive ability, and it is entirely possible that a man who is making a projection will be unduly swayed by the counsel he receives from an impressive individual. A review of the role of business economists in twenty firms revealed that the use made of economic forecasts was significantly influenced by the personal feeling toward the company economist and by how well he "sold" his conclusions.

Status and company politics are factors here, as well as manner of speech. The treasurer of another company served as chairman of a capital expenditures committee, and his views carried heavy weight in decisions on which division received the largest share of capital for expansion. Partly because of this "power," his recommendations on other matters were seldom challenged. Such influence, again, makes it difficult to reach decisions completely objectively.

3) *Special pressure.* Informal groups, as we noted in Chapter 7, have a strong influence on the values, beliefs, and socially acceptable actions of their members. All of us are members of several such groups, and we take part of our counsel from these unofficial sources as well as from the advisors and information centers provided in the formal organization. Informal groups, particularly among executives, may strongly support official company objectives and plans—but not necessarily. When we base our planning on numerous personal interchanges, we must be prepared for this reality: Social relations cannot be prescribed by an organization manual.

4) *Personal needs.* The aspirations and beliefs, as well as the sweet or bitter experience, of a man making a projection affect his response to the array of help provided by an organization. To be sure, supervisory review keeps reminding the advisor of company objectives and other basic "premises." Nevertheless, there is still room for personal bias to affect the predictions the advisor makes. The fallibility of human nature is simply another source of conflict to bear in mind as we contemplate the organization as a machine for making plans.

When several different projections have to be consolidated, as is necessary to appraise expansion alternatives open to Frosty Foods, the cumulative effect of bias can be substantial.

Credibility Structure

Faced with uncertainty absorption and likely bias in the estimates he receives from his expert advisors, what can the man who makes the final choice among alternatives do? He wants to achieve key objectives, and he will be accountable for results, yet he is aware that the projections on which he bases his choice are synthetic and questionable.

Identify reliable projectors. Among the various individuals who analyze alternatives and predict outcomes, a few stand out as persons whose conclusions can be relied upon. "If Oliver says it will work, that's good enough for me." "No one knows for sure, but I'll bet on Philip's estimate." These are highly subjective judgments about specific persons. They are the way the manager who has to make the final decision feels about participants in the decision-making process. The "reliable" person might be disliked or perhaps is ineffective in other kinds of work, but his opinion is respected.

Typically we regard a man as reliable on a particular subject, not on everything. One man has a good feel for labor relations, another for

Fig. 15-2 A circular organization chart. Colored boxes show the president's "credibility chart" for a decision on whether or not to open a new mine in Latin America.

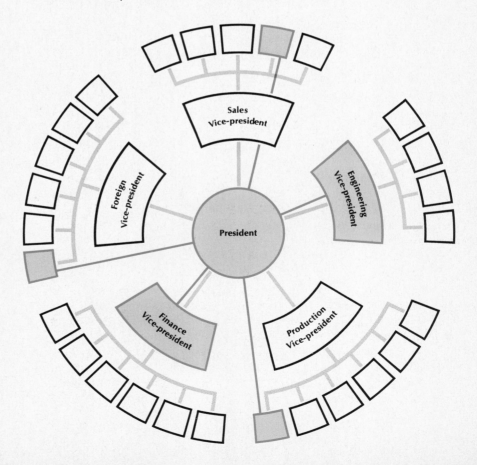

European economic developments, someone else for production feasibility, and so on. One person may possess keen technical insight, whereas another keeps divergent trends in good balance.

Among the qualities that inspire confidence are: knowledge of relevant facts; integrity (not a man who says things to manipulate other people); sensitivity to a broad range of influences; capacity to visualize change, but not be carried away with one possibility; willingness to accept a given premise and use it as a basis for further thought. Capacity to explain why his projections differ from others is helpful but not essential.

No list of personal qualities, however, substitutes for the judgment of the final decision-maker concerning those on whom he can rely for different kinds of inputs. S. L. Andersen of the du Pont Company calls this array of dependable advisors the "credibility structure." It is built on an assessment of persons, not on written job descriptions.

Distinguish credibility structure from formal organization. A widely held role concept is that the administrative head of a unit (1) provides the official opinions regarding activities within scope of the unit or at least (2) reviews, amends, and communicates the business opinions of anyone within his unit. More specifically, the concept holds that the head of the marketing division makes the official market projections, the chief engineer provides the official engineering projections, and so on. Each man normally consults with his subordinates and may authorize them to speak for his unit, but any projection coming from the unit is subject to the approval of its titular head.

The credibility structure may not agree with the concept just stated. In forecasting the results of a set of alternatives a respected staff man may have views that are different from those of the operating executives. Perhaps the opinions of a subordinate carry more weight than those of his boss; or an outsider, such as a former division executive, may have the highest credibility. The reason for such a discrepancy between the credibility structure and the administrative organization is that assisting in making projections is only one, perhaps minor, part of the total job of a line manager. The sales manager, for instance, has to plan an annual campaign, maintain good relations with distributors, build and inspire his own sales force, cultivate key customers, exercise control over sales expense, and so on. The optimism, enthusiasm, and drive needed for these duties may actually interfere with the objectivity and discernment that contribute to reliable projections. Similarly, a first-rate engineering manager may be a wizard at adapting present plants to variation in the product line, but this does not mean that he is necessarily qualified to predict the cost of building a small plant in New Zealand.

Dealing with divergence. Strong operating executives have confidence in their own opinions. They do not relish the thought that another's projections are more highly regarded than their own. So when the credibility structure diverges from the administrative structure, we face a delicate relationship. Among the ways to sidestep this kind of embarrassment are these:

1) Point out not only the importance but also the difficulty of making a reliable projection in the manager's area; it will follow then that this is one area where expert outside judgment is warranted.

2) If necessary to maintain morale, carry forward two sets of projections, one based on the executive's premise and one on the more reliable premise of another person. Rarely will the final choice depend solely on this discrepancy, and the difference will be submerged in the total balance.

The important point is never to lose sight of the confidence that can be attached to the projections that are being consolidated into the final balancing of alternatives.

Approval of premises. Especially when one projection becomes the basis of successive estimates, the manager making the final choice may try to control the premises that are fed into the process at early stages. Unless he has confidence in, say, the sales estimates upon which production forecasts are based or in the engineer's assurance that ecology issues will cause no delay, the entire exercise may have little value. To avoid such fruitless effort, the decision-maker can insist upon his review and approval of conclusions that become premises for the next set of projections.

Control of this sort may also be necessary if a man in the midst of the estimating process finds that he lacks confidence in the premises given to him, and so he privately makes his own corrections. For instance, if a production manager says, "I know those sales estimates are always 25 percent too high" or "The engineers never turn loose a new product when they say they will," and then bases his estimates on a less ambitious assumption, the consolidated projections are not internally consistent. A review and approval of premises at key stages hopefully will reduce this kind of hidden adjustments. Here again, the control of premises seeks to keep the successive projections in line with the credibility structure.

The whole issue of credibility structure relates especially to complex, unique decisions. For simpler, repetitive decisions the future results of various actions are better known, and there is less use of dubious premises for successive estimates. In the case of the Frosty Foods example, this means that the credibility structure is highly significant when projecting different merger alternatives, but for the motel inquiry the projections are more reliable and bias is more easily assessed.

Risk Analysis

The uncertainty surrounding some points in a projection can have a more profound effect than uncertainty at other points. For example, in a massive sewage disposal experiment in western Michigan, the rate of biological decomposition affects the feasibility of the entire scheme, whereas the cost of building a dam can only change the total capital outlay by less than 1 percent. Both points are uncertain but the risk on the technology is critical because (1) the *range* of possible results is wide— from very slow to fast—and (2) the *effect of variations* will determine the capacity of the entire system. In contrast, building costs of the dam are unlikely to deviate more than 25 percent, and even if they do this variation has repercussions on only a few aspects of the total venture.

Risk analysis identifies the critical points of uncertainty in a projection—the decomposition rate in the previous example. These points can be identified by careful thought, as was possible for the multimillion-dollar project just cited. If a mathematical model has been prepared to assist in the projection, the critical risk points can be derived from the model.

Having spotted the critical uncertainties, a manager can: (1) give close personal attention to the forecasts made for these factors and probably can personally approve premises with respect to these factors; (2) provide for later rechecking as better evidence becomes available; and/or (3) make multiple projections using two or more points on the range. By concentrating only on critical uncertainties, multiple projections may become technically feasible.

Stabilizing Projections

Most of the difficulties of making projections in organizations, which we have been analyzing, apply especially to complex, unique problems. To the extent that we can simplify such problems by dividing them into parts and by making the parts less unique, we reduce these difficulties. A company planning structure does just that.

Explicit objectives and subobjectives tend to remove bias arising from bureaucratic maneuvering. Policies, standing operating procedures, and standard methods help establish a customary way of dealing with problems. This customary practice provides a historical basis upon which to base projections and creates a stabilized environment where predictions are more accurate. In addition, consolidation of estimates is easier when each person preparing an estimate visualizes the same consistent manner of operation. Because of these and other benefits of structured planning, we shall carefully examine important planning instruments in the next four chapters.

To summarize: The underlying process of projecting probable results of different alternatives was explored in Chapter 13. In this section, we placed that process in an organizational setting. By using an organization, a wide variety of expert talent can be drawn upon to round out the projections. We inevitably must face uncertainty absorption and biased estimates, but we can reduce the undesirable effects of these factors by recognizing and utilizing the credibility structure, by employing risk analysis, and by creating a stabilized setting for the projected activities.

OFFICIAL CHOICES OF THE ORGANIZATION

The final act in decision-making, which follows diagnosis, identification of alternatives, and projection of results of each alternative, is choice of one alternative to be followed. The formal organization design designates who makes this choice.

Fruitless arguments can be held on who *really* makes the decision. As we have stressed, many people often get in the act. They may sway the way a problem is formulated, decide which alternatives should receive consideration or which consequences should be forecast. They may influence the values used by the decision-maker in his choice and may block effective execution so that a new decision must be made at a later date. But influence is not the official act. In every organized effort, we need a mechanism for decisiveness. If action is to proceed effectively, an official stamp of approval, saying in effect, "This is it," must be provided.

The authority to make decisions, in the sense of selecting one alternative and giving it official sanction, may be delegated, as we saw in Chapter 3. The delegation may be surrounded with limitations on scope or with policy constraints. Perhaps decisions will have to have endorsements of other executives. Nevertheless, we continue to look to the "formal organization" for information on who makes the final choice.[2]

Because the final choice is made in an organizational context rather than by an isolated individual, the decision-maker draws on a quite different set of values in making his choices. He is strongly guided (1) by company objectives, departmental objectives, company traditions and norms, and other institutional values; (2) by the company incentive and control system as related to him; and (3) by company politics growing out of conflict within the organization. Objectives, values, incentives and controls are all explored in following chapters; conflict in organizations is treated in Chapter 9.

MANAGEMENT INFORMATION SYSTEMS

A popular idea is that in the near future information systems will greatly simplify the work of managers; by shrewdly "talking to computers"

[2]Formal organization is not always clear-cut; perhaps it needs clarification, using guidelines already discussed in Part One. Our point here is that with respect to final choice we do not need a lot of description in addition to the formal organization.

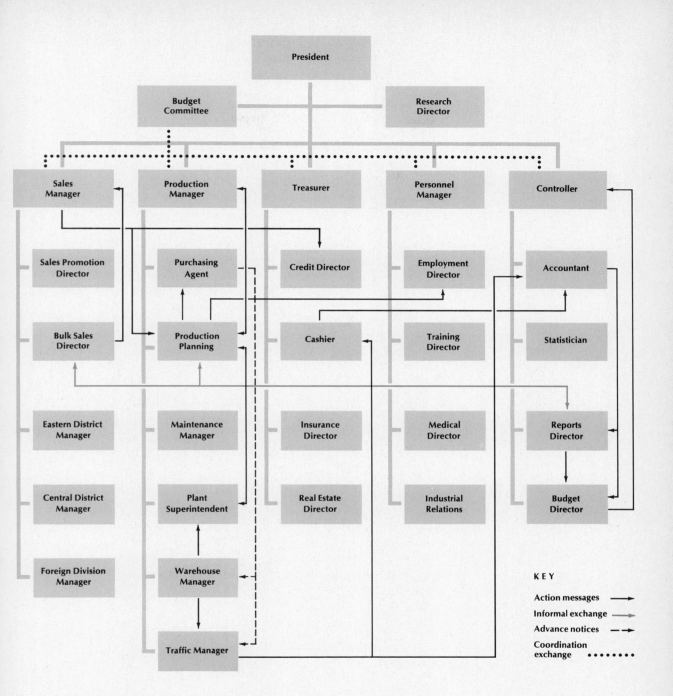

Fig. 15-3 A communication network. The different types of
lines show major communication flows resulting from a large
order received by the Bulk Sales Director. Numerous other
networks exist for other kinds of transactions.

managers will be able to make most of their decisions better and faster. The review of decision-making in this chapter gives us a good perspective on what is and is not likely to occur in this field.

Crucial Flows of Data

Operating data. A vast amount of information flows horizontally through most organizations, that is, instead of going up and down the channels of command, a message passes directly from an operator in one section to a worker in another section. Consider what happens when you arrange an airplane trip from, say, Chicago to Seattle. First you purchase a ticket from an agent, who sends a copy of the ticket along with your cash to the treasurer's office. At the same time, you make a reservation for a specific flight, and for this transaction the agent communicates directly with a central reservation clerk. Later, the reservation clerk prepares a list of all passengers for your plane, copies of which go to the gateman (ground crew) and stewardess (plane crew). At the time of the flight you present your ticket to the gateman who checks your name against the reservation list and, after the plane departs, gives both the list and the collected tickets to an auditor. The audited flight lists are then summarized as traffic information that still other people use in analyzing flight loads, passenger miles, and the like. Additional contacts will occur if the flight is canceled, if it involves two or more airlines, or if the Seattle fog forces your plane to land in Portland.

Similar standard procedures for getting information from one part of an organization to another will be found in all enterprises.

Most horizontal flow of detailed information is carried on standard forms. These forms provide space for essential information, thereby indicating (1) *what* to communicate. They also specify (2) *to whom* and (3) *when* information is to be sent. The forms are quickly *understood* by people who handle them and remain as a record, or (4) *memory*, of what was communicated. Well-designed forms are essential to transmit the specific data that most modern enterprises depend on to operate.

Management summaries and reports. When a large volume of data flows directly among operators and first-line supervisors, senior executives tend to be out of the mainstream of work. Summary reports can offset their remoteness. There are at least two things an executive needs to know: (1) achievements—the volume, quality, and cost of completed work—and (2) exceptional problems that cannot be handled by standard systems. In addition, he may desire reports on key operating conditions—labor morale or customer attitudes, for instance—which he thinks might be a source of future trouble.

Such summary reports are essential features of a management information system. They make possible delegation without loss of control.

Effect of Computers

Great improvements are being made in the processing of information. New electronic computers can store data in "memories," combine new data with what is stored, perform complex mathematical computations, and then print answers, all at speeds undreamed of only a few years ago. When coupled with new devices for transmission, these computers provide business today with dazzling means of handling information.

Where electronic devices are used only to provide more information faster, the basic character of communication networks has not changed. To be sure, executives have more figures to work with and are able to act more promptly. What such improvements do not change, except in minor respects, are the sources, the selection of what to transmit, and the destination of information.

A whole array of sophisticated techniques for aiding managers has been devised—operations-research models, simulation, programmed decisions, risk analysis, and so on. The hang-up is that with rare exceptions these techniques need input data that are not found in the mass of operating statistics described above. We are still a long way from mating the computerized management information flow with the conceptualized decision models. (In fact, we have yet to perfect a system for keeping a magazine mailing list up-to-date!) Except for inventory controls and a few other routinized operations, we have to develop a special set of inputs to utilize the models.

This gap between *standardized* management information and decision-making needs can be narrowed but never removed. Consider the types of data discussed in this chapter: new social and technological developments, causes of unanticipated interruption of plans, forecasts of competitive conditions, creative ideas to overcome obstacles, estimates of all sorts for an array of new alternatives, probabilities based on subjective judgments, adjustments for personal bias, and so on. What is wanted today may be of no value tomorrow. Any system that attempted to have on tap all the information that might be wanted would become hopelessly bogged down.

So we need to be more reasonable in what we expect a management information system to provide. Reports on past operations related to a well-designed control system (see Part Six), reservoirs of operating statistics available for screening and analysis that fit the requirements of the new problem at hand, a very selected array of external data kept on a current basis—all can be very useful indeed. But then we reach a point where competent people accustomed to working together, open personal communication, and systems for developing integrated plans replace any flow of information that we can stipulate in advance.

In our dynamic environment managers need the best data resource we can devise *plus* an "organized capacity" to deal with an endless succession of new opportunities and difficulties. The planning mechanisms discussed in the next four chapters are a vital part of such an organized capacity. These planning mechanisms provide important elements of predictability and stability to which we have frequently referred in this chapter.

FOR CLASS DISCUSSION

Questions

1) The concept of parallel departments was discussed in Chapter 5. In what ways may the existence of parallel departments in a company be an aid or an obstacle to securing help from many people in making decisions?

2) "Group judgment is fiction. If delegation has been carried out properly, one man and not a group has the obligation for making any particular decision. If this one man wants the advice of others, he can get it by conversing with them or through staff and control reports. Forming a committee is a sure way to get men to abrogate their responsibilities and is a costly and time-consuming use of executive time." How would you reply to this statement?

3) What do you see in the way of help offered by computer-based management information systems in sensing and diagnosing? In what ways may such systems inhibit sensing and diagnosing?

4) Given the transmission losses and protective screening that take place as information passes through successive layers of management, why not encourage more direct communication between those who have data and those who need it rather than insist on following the chain of command?

5) Often a subordinate may see a problem or an opportunity to improve operations that would contribute to his boss's effectiveness but his boss does not see it. What factors will encourage the subordinate to bring his ideas to his boss? What factors will discourage this?

6) What suggestions can you offer for reducing the negative impact of differences in perception of objectives or differences in values placed on the same objectives by participants in a decision? To what extent may these differences prove beneficial? Relate your answers to the material in Part Three.

7) The text suggests that one way to minimize friction between "creative guys" and "tough operators" is to create physical separation that permits relatively few interactions. If this approach is followed, what potential negative effects might be expected? How might the negative aspects of this approach be mitigated while still maintaining separation?

8) "One way to increase the soundness of key figures on which I must base decisions is to insist that those who furnish the figures state in writing the assumptions, premises, and techniques used for arriving at them. While I don't have the time and in some cases the background to verify these assumptions, and so on, I keep them on file to help sort out reasons for mistakes." What do you think of this approach as described by a vice-president of marketing?

Cases

For cases involving issues covered in this chapter, see especially the following. Particularly relevant questions are listed after each case.

Trans-World Mutual Funds, Ltd. (p. 121), 10
Scott-Davis Corporation (p. 227), 11, 12
Gerald Clark (p. 234), 13
E.W. Ross, Inc. (p. 468), 7
Harrogate Asphalt Products, Ltd.—AR (p. 557), 8
Consolidated Instruments—B (p. 674), 11

FOR FURTHER READING

Aharoni, Y., *The Foreign Investment Decision Process.* Boston: Harvard Business School, 1966. *Description of how foreign investment decisions are made in United States companies; excellent picture of decision-making in an organization.*

Cotton, D.B., *Company-Wide Planning.* New York: The Macmillan Company, 1970. *An experienced executive discusses the corporate planning process.*

Cyert, R.M., and J.G. March, *A Behavioral Theory of the Firm.* Englewood Cliffs, N.J.: Prentice-Hall, Inc., 1963, Chaps 3, 5, and 6. *Theory of goal-setting and decision-making that stresses internal coalitions, bargains, and avoidance of uncertainty.*

Emery, J.C., *Organizational Planning and Controls Systems.* New York: The Macmillan Company, 1969, Chap. 5. *Good, abstract summary of planning theory.*

Glans, T.B., et al., *Management Systems.* New York: Holt, Rinehart & Winston, Inc., 1968. *Thorough explanation of the design of a management information system.*

Katz, D., and R.L. Kahn, *Social Psychology of Organizations.* New York: John Wiley & Sons, Inc., 1966, Chap. 10. *Decision-making and policy formulation in a social organization.*

Steiner, G.A., *Top Management Planning.* New York: The Macmillan Company, 1969. *Comprehensive treatment of company planning.*

Chapter Sixteen

Master Strategy and Long-range Programming

RELEVANCE AND SURVIVAL

Every enterprise needs a central purpose expressed in terms of the services it will render to society. In addition, it needs a basic concept of how it will create these services. Because it will be competing with other enterprises for resources, it must have some distinctive relevance—in its services or in its method of creating them. Moreover, because it will inevitably cooperate with an array of other firms, it must have the means for maintaining viable coalitions with them. Added to these issues are the elements of change, growth, and adaptation. Master strategy is a company's basic plan for dealing with these factors.

One familiar way of delving into company strategy is to ask, "What business are we in?" or, "What business do we want to be in?" "Why should society tolerate our existence?" Answers to these questions are often difficult. A certain tuberculosis sanitarium almost went bankrupt when antibiotics reduced the need for long rest cure, but it revived by becoming a beautifully located retirement home. Less fortunate was a cooperage firm that defined its business in terms of wooden boxes and barrels and had to shut down when paperboard containers took over the field.

Product line is only part of the picture, however. An ability to supply services economically is also crucial. For example, most local bakeries have closed, not for lack of demand for bread, but because they became technologically inefficient. Many a paper mill has exhausted its sources of pulpwood. The independent motel operator is having difficulty meeting competition from franchised chains. Yet in all these industries some firms have prospered, the ones that have had the foresight and adaptability (and probably some luck, too) to take advantage of their changing environment. These firms pursued a master strategy that enabled them to increase the services rendered and to attract greater resources.

Master strategy is of such cardinal importance, and it so permeates other planning within a firm, that we devote most of this chapter to it. Although our illustrations will be largely from business, the central concept is just as crucial for hospitals, universities, and other nonprofit ventures.

A practical way to develop a master strategy is to (1) pick particular roles or niches for the company that are propitious in view of society's needs and the company's resources, (2) combine various niches and other facets of the company's efforts to obtain synergistic effects, (3) express the plans in terms of targets, and (4) set up sequences and timing of changes that reflect company capabilities and external conditions. Let us look at each of these steps in turn and then see how long-range programming ties into the concept of the company mission.

PICKING PROPITIOUS NICHES

Most enterprises fill more than one niche. Often they provide several lines of products or services. Even when a single line is produced, an enterprise may sell it to several distinct types of customers. Especially as a firm grows, it seeks expansion by tapping new markets or by selling different services to its existing customers. In designing a company strategy we can avoid pitfalls by first examining each of these markets separately.

Because of the long time required to develop new products or services, a wise executive looks beyond modifications of his present line. He focuses on changed conditions in the world that will alter the needs of customers he might serve. Basically we are searching for changing, growing customer needs where adroit use of our unique resources will make our services distinctive and in that sense give us a competitive advantage. In these particular spots, we hope to give the customer an irresistible value at relatively low expense. A bank, for example, may devise a way of financing the purchase of an automobile that is particularly well suited to farmers; it must then consider whether it is in a good position to serve such a market.

Identifying such propitious niches is not easy. Here is one approach that works well in a wide variety of situations. Focus first on the industry—growth prospects, competition, key factors required for success—and then on the strengths and weaknesses of the specific company as matched against these key success factors. As we describe this approach more fully, keep in mind that we are interested in segments of markets as well as entire markets.

Industry Outlook

The sales volume and profits of an industry or one of its segments depend on the demand for its services, the supply of these services, and the competitive conditions. (We use "service" here to include both physical products and intangible values provided by an enterprise.) Predicting future demand, supply, and competition is an exciting endeavor. In the following paragraphs we suggest a few of the important considerations that may vitally affect the strategy of a company.

Demand for industry services. The strength of the *desire* for a service affects its demand. For instance, we keenly want a small amount of dental care, but place little value on additional quantities. Our desire for more and better automobiles does not have this same sort of cut-off level, and our desire for pay-television (no commercials, select programs) or supersonic air travel is highly uncertain, falling in quite a different category from that of dental care.

Possible *substitutes* to satisfy a given desire must be weighed—beef for lamb, motorboats for baseball, gas for coal, Aureomycin for sulfa, weldments for castings, and so forth. The frequency of such substitution is affected, of course, by the relative prices.

Desire has to be backed up by *ability to pay*, and here business cycles enter in. In addition, in some industries large amounts of capital are necessarily tied up in equipment. The relative efficiency, quality of work, and nature of machinery already in place influence the money that will be available for new equipment. Another consideration: If we hope to sell in foreign markets, then foreign-exchange issues arise.

The *structure of markets* also requires analysis. Where, on what terms, and in response to what appeals do people buy, say, jet planes, sulphuric acid, or dental floss? Does a manufacturer deal directly with

Fig. 16-1 Locating a propitious niche is a matter of matching a firm's specific qualities against the outlook of the industry.

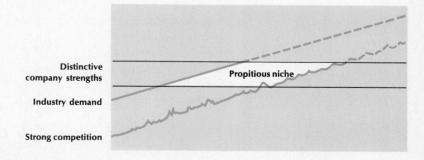

Distinctive
company strengths

Propitious niche

Industry demand

Strong competition

consumers or are intermediaries, such as retailers or brokers, a more effective means of distribution?

Although an entire industry is often affected by these factors—desire, substitutes, ability to pay, structure of markets—a local variation in demand sometimes provides a unique opportunity for a particular firm. Thus most drugstores carry cosmetics, candy, and a wide variety of items besides drugs; but a store located in a medical center might develop a highly profitable business by dealing exclusively with prescriptions and other medical supplies.

All these elements of demand are subject to change—some quite rapidly. Because the kind of strategic plans we are considering here typically extend over a period of years, we need both an identification of the key factors that will affect industry demand and an estimate of how that picture will change over a span of time.

Supply related to demand. The attractiveness of any industry depends on more than potential growth arising from strong demand. In designing a company strategy we also must consider the probable supply of services and the conditions under which they will be offered.

The *capacity* of an industry to fill demand for its services clearly affects profit margins. The importance of overcapacity or undercapacity, however, depends on the ease of entry and withdrawal from the industry. When capital costs are high, as in the hotel or cement business, adjustments to demand tend to lag. Thus overcapacity may depress profits for a long period; even bankruptcies do not remove the capacity if plants are bought up at bargain prices and are operated by new owners. On the other hand, low capital requirements—as in electronic assembly work—permit new firms to enter quickly and shortages of supply tend to be short-lived. Of course more than physical plant is involved; an effective organization of competent people is also necessary. Here again the ease of expansion or contraction should be appraised.

Costs also need to be predicted—labor costs, material costs, and, for some industries, transportation costs or excise taxes. If increases in operating costs affect all members of an industry alike and can be passed on to the consumer in the form of higher prices, this factor becomes less significant in company strategy. However, rarely do both conditions prevail. Sharp rises in labor costs in Hawaii, for example, place its sugar industry at a disadvantage of the world market.

A highly dynamic aspect of supply is *technology*. New methods for producing established products—for example, basic oxygen conversion of steel displacing open-hearth furnaces and mechanical cottonpickers displacing centuries-old handpicking techniques—are part of the picture. Technology may change the availability and price of raw materials; witness the growth of synthetic rubber and industrial diamonds. Similarly, air cargo planes and other new forms of transportation are expanding the sources of supply that may serve a given market.

For an individual producer, anticipating these shifts in the industry supply situation may be a matter of prosperity or bankruptcy.

Competitive conditions in the industry. The way the interplay between demand and supply works out depends partly on the nature of competition in the industry. *Size, strength, and attitude of companies* in one industry—say, the dress industry, where entrance is easy and style is critical—may lead to very sharp competition. On the other hand, oligopolistic competition among the giants of the aluminum industry produces a more stable situation, at least in the short run. The resources and managerial talent needed to enter one industry differ greatly from what it takes to get ahead in another.

A strong *trade association* often helps to create a favorable climate in its industry. The independent oil producers' association, to cite one case, has been unusually effective in restricting imports of crude oil into the United States. Other associations compile valuable industry statistics, help reduce unnecessary variations in size of products, run training conferences, hold trade shows, and aid members in a variety of other ways.

Government regulation also modifies competition. A few industries like banking and insurance are supervised by national or state bodies that place limits on prices, sales promotion, and the variety of services rendered. Airlines are regulated as a utility and subsidized as an infant industry. Farm subsidies affect large segments of agriculture, and tariffs have long protected selected manufacturers. Our patent laws also bear directly on the nature of competition, as is evident in the heated discussion of how pharmaceutical patents may be used. Clearly, future government action is a significant factor in the outlook of many industries.

Key factors for success in the industry. This brief review suggests the dynamic nature of business and uncertainties in the outlook for virtually all industries. A crucial task of every top management is to assess the forces at play in its industry and identify those factors that will be crucial for future success. These we call "key success factors." Leadership in research and development may be very important in one industry, low costs in another, and adaptability to local needs in a third; large financial resources may be a *sine qua non* for mining, whereas creative imagination is the touchstone in advertising.

We stressed earlier the desirability of making such analyses for narrow segments as well as for broad industry categories. The success factors for each segment are likely to differ from those for other segments in at least one or two respects. For example, General Foods Corporation discovered to its sorrow that the key success factors in gourmet foods differ significantly from those for coffee and Jell-O.

Moreover, the analysis of industry outlook should provide a forecast of the *growth potentials* and the *profit prospects* for the various industry segments. These conclusions, along with key success factors, are vital guideposts in setting up a company's master strategy.

Company Strengths and Limitations

The range of opportunities for distinctive service is wide. In picking its particular niche out of this array, a company naturally favors those opportunities that will utilize its strengths and bypass its limitations. This calls for a candid appraisal of the company itself.

Market strengths of a company. A direct measure of *market position* is the percentage that company sales are of (1) industry sales and (2) major competitors' sales. Such figures quickly indicate whether a company is so big that its activities are likely to bring prompt responses from other leading companies. On the other hand, a company may be small enough to enjoy independent maneuverability. Of course, to be most meaningful, these percentages should be computed separately for geographical areas, product lines, and types of customers—if suitable industry data are available.

More intangible, but no less significant, are the relative standing of *company products* and their *reputation* in major markets. Kodak products, for instance, are widely and favorably known; they enjoy a reputation for high quality and dependability. Clearly this reputation will be a factor in Eastman Kodak Company strategy, and any new, unknown firm must overcome this prestige if it seeks even a small share in one segment of the film market. Market reputation is tenacious. Especially when we try to "trade up," our previous low quality, poor service, and sharp dealing will be an obstacle. Any strategy we adopt must have enough persistency and consistency so that our firm is assigned a "role" in the minds of the customers we wish to reach.

The relationship between a company and the *distribution system* is another vital aspect of market position. The big United States automobile companies, for example, are strong partly because each has a set of dealers throughout the country. In contrast, foreign car manufacturers have difficulty selling here until they can arrange with dealers to provide dependable service.

All these aspects of market position—a relative share of the market, comparative quality of product, reputation with consumers, and ties with a distributive system—help define the strengths and limitations of a company.

Supply strengths of a company. To pick propitious niches we also should appraise our company's relative strength in creating goods and services. Such ability to supply services fitted to consumer needs will be built largely on the firm's resources of labor and material, effective productive facilities, and perhaps pioneering research and development.

Labor in the United States is fairly mobile. Men tend to gravitate to good jobs. But the process takes time—a shoe plant in the South needed ten years to build up an adequate number of skilled workers—and it may be expensive. Consequently, immediate availability of competent men at normal industry wages is a source of strength. In addition, the relationships between the company and its work force are important. All too often, both custom and formal agreements freeze inefficient practices. The classic example is New England textiles; here, union-supported work habits give even modern mills high labor costs. Only recently have a few companies been able to match their more flourishing competitors who are located in the South.

Access to *low-cost materials* is often a significant factor in a company's supply position. The development of the paper industry in the South, for example, is keyed to the use of fast-growing forests that can be cut on a rotational basis to provide a continuing supply of pulpwood. Of course, if raw materials can be easily transported, such as iron ore and crude oil by enormous ships, plants need not be located at the original source.

Availability of materials involves more than physical handling. Ownership, or long-term contracts with those who do own, may ensure a continuing source at low cost. Much of the strategy of companies producing basic metals—iron, copper, aluminum, or nickel—includes huge investments in ore properties. But all sorts of companies are concerned with the availability of materials. So whenever supplies are scarce, a potential opportunity exists. Even in retailing, Sears, Roebuck and Company discovered in its Latin American expansion that a continuing flow of merchandise of standard quality was difficult to ensure; but once established, such sources became a great advantage.

Physical facilities—office buildings, plants, oil wells—often tie up a large portion of a company's assets. In the short run, at least, these facilities may be an advantage or a disadvantage. The character of many colleges, for instance, has been shaped by their location, whether in a plush suburb or in a degenerating urban area, and the cost of moving facilities is so great that adaptation to the existing neighborhood becomes an absolute necessity.

Established organizations of high-talented people to perform particular tasks also give a company a distinctive capability. Thus a good research and development department may enable a company to expand in pharmaceuticals, whereas a processing firm without such a technical staff is virtually barred from this profitable field.

Perhaps the company we are analyzing will enjoy other distinctive abilities to produce services. Our central concern at this point is to identify strengths, and see how these compare with strengths of other firms.

Other company resources. The propitious niche for an enterprise also depends on its financial strength and the character of its management.

Some strategies will require large quantities of capital. Any oil company that seeks foreign sources of crude oil, for instance, must be prepared to invest millions of dollars. Few firms maintain cash reserves of this size, so *financial capacity* to enter this kind of business depends either on an ability to attract new capital—through borrowing or sale of stock—or on a flow of profits (and depreciation allowances) from existing operations that can be allocated to the new venture. On the other hand, perhaps a strategy can be devised that calls for relatively small cash advances, and in these fields a company that has low financial strength will still be able to compete with the affluent firms.

A more subtle factor in company capacity is its *management*. The age and vitality of key executives, their willingness to risk profit and capital, their urge to gain personal prestige through company growth, their desire to ensure stable employment for present workers—all affect the suitability of any proposed strategy. For example, the expansion of Hilton Hotels into a worldwide chain certainly reflects the personality of Conrad Hilton; with a different management at the helm, a modification in strategy is most appropriate because Conrad Hilton's successors do not have his particular set of drives and values.

Related to the capabilities of key executives is the organization structure of the company. A decentralized structure, for instance, facilitates movement into new fields of business whereas a functional structure with fine specialization is better suited to expansion in closely related lines.

Matching Company Strengths
with Key Success Factors

Armed with a careful analysis of the strengths and limitations of our company, we are prepared to pick desirable niches for company concentration. Naturally we will look for fields where company strengths correspond with the key factors for success that have been developed in our industry analyses described in the preceding section. In the process, we will set aside possibilities in which company limitations create serious handicaps.

Potential growth and profits in each niche must, of course, be added to the synthesis. Clearly a low potential will make a niche unattractive even though the company strengths and success factors fit neatly, but we may become keenly interested in a niche where the fit is only fair if the potential is great.

Typically several intriguing possibilities emerge. These are all the niches—in terms of market lines, market segments, or combinations of production functions—that the company might pursue. Also typically, a series of positive actions is necessary in order for the company to move into each area. So we need to list not only each niche and its potential, but in addition the limitations that will have to be overcome and other steps necessary for the company to succeed in each area. These are the propitious niches—nestled in anticipated social and economic conditions and tailored to the strengths and limitations of a particular enterprise.

COMBINING EFFORTS FOR SYNERGISTIC EFFECTS

An enterprise always pursues a variety of efforts to serve even a single niche, and typically it tries to fill several related niches. Considerable choice is possible, at least in the degree to which these many efforts are pushed. In other words, management decides how many markets to cover, to what degree to automate production, what stress to place on consumer engineering, and a host of other actions. One vital aspect of master strategy is fitting these numerous efforts together. In fact, our choice of niches will depend, in part, on how well we can combine the total effort they require.

Synergy is a powerful ally for this purpose. Basically, synergy means that the combined effect of two or more cooperative acts is greater than the sum that would result if the actions were taken independently. A simple example in marketing is that widespread dealer stocks *combined with* advertising in one locality will produce much greater sales volume than widespread dealer stocks in, say, Virginia and advertising in Minnesota. Often the possibility of obtaining synergistic effects will shape the master strategy of the company, as the following examples will suggest.

Total Service to Customer

A customer rarely buys merely a physical product. Other attributes of the transaction often include delivery, credit terms, return privileges, repair service, operating instructions, conspicuous consumption, psychological experience of purchasing, and the like. Many services involve no physical product at all. The crucial question is what combination of attributes will have high synergistic value for the customers we serve.

IBM, for instance, has found a winning combination. Its products are well designed and of high quality. But so are the products of several of its competitors. In addition, IBM provides (1) salesmen who understand the customer's problems and how IBM equipment can help solve them and (2) fast, dependable repair service. The synergistic effect of the three attributes is a service of high value to many customers.

Each niche calls for its own combination of services. For example, Chock Full o' Nuts expanded its restaurant chain on the basis of three attributes: good-quality food, cleanliness, and fast service. This combination appealed to a particular group of customers. A very limited selection, crowded space, and lack of frills did not matter. However, if any one of the three characteristics slips at an outlet the synergistic effect is lost.

Fuller Use of Existing Resources

Synergistic effects may be uncovered in any phase of company operations. One possibility is that present activities include a "capability" that can be applied to additional uses. Thus watch companies in the United States undertook the manufacture of tiny gyroscopes and electronic components for spacecraft because they already possessed technical skill in the production of miniature, precision products. They adopted this strategy on the premise that they could make both watches and components for spacecraft with less effort than could separate firms devoted to only one line of products.

The original concept of General Foods Corporation sought a similar synergistic effect in marketing. Here the basic capability was marketing prepared foods. By having the same sales organization handle several product lines, a larger and more effective sales effort could be provided, and/or the selling cost per product line could be reduced. Clearly the combined sales activity was more powerful than separate sales efforts for each product line would have been.

Expansion to Obtain a Resource

Vertical integration may have synergistic effects. This occurred when the Apollo Printing Machine Company bought a foundry. Apollo was unsatisfied with the quality of its castings and with tardy delivery and was looking for a new supplier. In its search, it learned that a nearby foundry could be purchased. The foundry was just breaking even, primarily because the volume of its work fluctuated widely. Following the purchase, Apollo

Fig. 16-2 *The benefits of synergy. Irrigation or fertilizer used alone will increase crop production by a certain amount. If the two are used together, however, the increase in crop production may be more than the total of the two separate increases.*

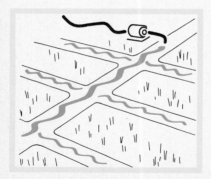  

gave the foundry a more steady backlog of work, and through close technical cooperation the quality of casting received by the new parent firm was improved. The consolidated setup was better for both enterprises than was the previous independent operations.

The results of vertical integration are not always so good however; problems of balance, flexibility, and managerial capacity must be carefully weighed. Nevertheless, control of a critical resource is often a significant part of company strategy.

Expansion to Enhance Market Position

Efforts to improve market position provide many examples of the whole being better than the sum of its parts. The leading can companies, for example, moved from exclusive concentration on metal containers into glass, plastic, and paper containers. They expected their new divisions to be profitable by themselves, but an additional reason for the expansion lay in anticipated synergistic effects of being able to supply a customer's total container requirements. With the entire packaging field changing so rapidly, a company that can quickly shift from one type of container to another offers a distinctive service to its customers.

International Harvester, to cite another case, added a very large tractor to its line a few years ago. The prospects for profit on this line alone were far from certain. However, the new tractor was important to give dealers "a full line"; its availability removed the temptation for dealers to carry some products of competing manufacturers. So when viewed in combination with other International Harvester products, the new tractor looked much more significant than it did as an isolated project.

Compatibility of Efforts

In considering additional niches for a company, we may be confronted with negative synergy, that is, the combined effort is worse than the sum of independent efforts. This occurred when a producer of high-quality television and hi-fi sets introduced a small color television receiver. When first offered, the small unit was as good as most competing sets and probably had an attractive potential market. However, it was definitely inferior in performance to other products of the company and consequently undermined public confidence in the quality of the entire line. Moreover, customers had high expectations for the small set because of the general reputation of the company, and they became very critical when the new product did not live up to their expectations. Both the former products and the new product suffered.

To summarize: We have seen that some combinations of efforts are strongly reinforcing. The combination accelerates the total effect, or reduces the cost for the same effect, or solidifies our supply or market position. On the other hand, we must watch for incompatible efforts that may have a disruptive effect in the same cumulative manner. So when we select niches as a part of our master strategy, one vital aspect is the possibility of such synergistic effects.

CRITERIA OF SUCCESS

Thus far we have discussed strategy in *operational* terms—services to perform, resources to acquire, synergistic benefits to seek. These are the terms that lead directly into managerial action. To say, for example, that a hospital is going to try to cut costs by opening a new wing for ambulatory patients provides positive direction.

Another way to view strategic plans is to look at their potential *results* expressed in terms of selected *criteria*. Here we ask: If we follow a proposed strategy will the results, as measured by our selected criteria, be satisfactory? The key is to pick the criteria, or values, we are concerned about and then translate the proposed action into its effects on these criteria.

Two reasons for making this translation from operational plans to expected results are: (1) The results of the strategy can be compared to general objectives—if the results are not acceptable, a search for a better proposal will be called for. Also (2) assuming approval, the strategy results become targets for the more detailed planning (see Chapters 17, 18, and 19).[1]

Values Sought

The array of values sought by various enterprises is endless. Here are a few: stable employment, filling a specific need of consumers, improving urban slums, assistance to the government of our country, promoting the economic growth of Oshkosh, increasing trade with Central Africa, elimination of the boll weevil, protecting savings of widows and orphans, maximizing short-run profits, improving company position in the industry, having a high percent of graduates in *Who's Who*, optimizing long-run return per share of common stock, perpetuating the enterprise.

Every enterprise, like every individual, pursues several objectives. Theoretically these objectives could all be converted into one common denominator such as profit, but in practice the conversion becomes so abstract it serves no useful purpose. Instead a few objectives are singled out and the predicted results of a strategy are compared against these

[1] This approach to targets *does* imply that, in our view, targets without operational strategy have little value. A statement that the company seeks, say, 15 percent return on capital is not by itself a strategy. Until it is tied into an operational design, it is little more than a pious hope.

values. Thus the Metropole Power Company is primarily giving attention to the following: long-run survival, profits high enough to attract needed capital, minimum government interference, contribution to the economic growth of its geographic area. Hopefully Metropole's strategy will contribute to all four criteria. An important function of central management of each enterprise is developing a widely understood consensus on the primary criteria for values for that firm. These values should be known as strategy is being formulated. Emphasis will undoubtedly shift when the firm's success or environment changes. But at any point in time the chief value criteria should be recognized.

Strategic targets. We should aim not merely in the direction of a target but rather at the bull's-eye within the target. It is ambiguous to say, "More major medical insurance"; "Twenty percent of our policy holders covered for major medical expense by 1975" adds both a quantitative and a time dimension. Similarly, "Sixteen percent return on book value of equity capital" sharpens a loose statement about "increasing profits." So when we convert our operational strategy into targets we should, whenever feasible, express the expected results in *specific degrees of achievement* for each criterion. With such targets as an added dimension, our master strategy sets forth (1) what services to be provided and to whom, (2) the major ways these services will be created or obtained, *and* (3) the primary results expressed as degrees of achievement for selected criteria. The mission is now defined.

SEQUENCE AND TIMING OF EFFORTS

Many actions will be necessary to achieve the mission, and senior executives must decide what to do first, how many activities can be done concurrently, how fast to move, what risks to take, what to postpone. Here we are dealing with major allocations of company efforts; detailed programs for putting plans into action are discussed later in Chapter 19.

Choice of Sequence

A perennial issue when entering a new niche is what to do first—for instance, whether to develop markets before working on production economies or vice versa.

A striking example of strategy involving sequence confronted Boeing Aircraft when it first conceived of a large four-engine jet plane suitable for handling cargo or large passenger loads. At the time Air Force officers saw little need for such a plane, believing that propeller-driven planes provided the most desirable means for carrying cargo. Because this eliminated the military market, most companies would have stopped at this point. However, Boeing executives decided to invest a significant portion of the company's liquid assets to develop the new plane. Over two years later, Boeing was able to present evidence that caused the Air Force officials to change their minds—and the K-135 was born. Only Boeing was prepared to produce the new type of craft, which proved to be both faster and more economical than propeller-driven planes. Moreover, the company was able to convert the design into the Boeing 707 passenger plane, which, within a few years, dominated the airline passenger business. Competing firms were left far behind, and Convair almost went bankrupt in its attempt to catch up. In this instance, a decision to let engineering and production run far ahead of marketing paid off handsomely.

Straining Scarce Resources

Every enterprise has limits—perhaps severe limits—on its resources. The amount of capital, the number and quality of key personnel, the physical production capacity, or the adaptability of its social structure—none of these are ever boundless. The tricky issue is how to use these limited resources to best advantage.

The scarce resource affecting master strategy may be managerial personnel. A management consulting firm, for instance, reluctantly postponed entry into the international arena because only two of its partners had the combination of interest, capacity, and vitality to spend a large amount of time abroad, and these men were also needed to assure continuity of the practice in the United States. The firm felt that a later start would be better than weak action immediately, even though this decision meant losing several desirable clients.

The weight we should attach to scarce resources in the timing of master strategy often requires delicate judgment. Some strain may be endured. But how much, how long? For example, in its switch from purchased to company-produced tires, a European rubber company fell behind on deliveries for six months; but through heroic efforts and pleading with customers the company weathered the squeeze. Now, company executives believe the timing was wise. If the delay had lasted a full year—and this was a real possibility—the consequence would have been a catastrophe.

Forming Coalitions

A cooperative agreement with firms in related fields occasionally provides a way to overcome scarce resources. The early development of frozen foods provides us with two examples of fruitful coalitions. A key element in Birdseye master strategy was to obtain the help of cold-storage warehouses; grocery wholesalers were not equipped to handle frozen foods, and before the demand was clearly established they were slow to move into the new activity. In addition, the Birdseye division of General

Foods lacked both managerial and financial resources to venture into national wholesaling.

Similarly Birdseye had to get freezer cabinets into retail stores, but it lacked the capability to produce them. So it entered into a coalition with a refrigerator manufacturer to make and sell (or lease) the cabinets to retail stores. This mutual agreement enabled Birdseye to move ahead with its marketing program much faster. With the tremendous growth of frozen foods, neither the cold storage warehouse nor the cabinet manufacturer continued to be necessary, but without them in the early days, widespread use of frozen foods would have been delayed three to five years.

Coalitions may be formed for reasons other than "buying time." Nevertheless, when we are trying to round out a workable master strategy, coalitions—or even mergers—may provide the quickest way to overcome a serious deficiency in vital resources.

Receptive Environment

Judging the right time to act is difficult. Thus, one of the contributing factors to the multimillion-dollar Edsel car fiasco was poor timing. The same automobile launched a year or two earlier might have been favorably received. But buyer tastes changed between the time elaborate market research studies were made and when the new car finally appeared in dealer showrooms. By then, preference was swinging away from a big car that "had everything" toward compacts. This mistake in timing, and associated errors in strategy, cost the Ford Motor Company over a hundred million dollars.

The preceding discussion of sequence and timing provides no simple rules for this critical aspect of basic strategy. The factors we have mentioned (1) for deciding which front(s) to push first (where is a head start valuable, early attention to major uncertainties, lead times, significance of secrecy), and (2) for deciding how fast to move (strain on scarce resources, possible coalition to provide resources, and receptivity of the environment) do bear directly on many strategy decisions.

LONG-RANGE PROGRAM

Moving from a master strategy to short-run programs is a grand leap. Many companies prefer to go from strategy first to long-range programs and then to short-range programs.[2] Because the tie between long-

[2]The expression "long-range planning" is loosely used. It may refer merely to carefully considering long-run results of today's decisions. In other contexts it embraces both strategy and long-range programming. Because strategy and programming are quite distinct forms of planning, we prefer to use separate designations.

range programs and strategy is so close, we will take a quick look now at this form of programming.

Strategy, as we have just seen, provides targets and major moves along with general guides for sequence and timing. The long-range program is a comprehensive, companywide plan that spells out more fully the steps to be taken to execute that strategy. It serves as a bridge between current operations and those necessary to pursue the new mission.

For most companies, the results expected in five years provide a reasonable span, but some other period, such as three years or ten years, may be used if it fits better into a cycle of planning. With the strategy set, the actions necessary to achieve it should be laid out for each department or aspect of the business. These actions include not only programs for sales, production, finance, and similar functions, but also plans to provide the necessary resources, such as offices, machinery, plants, executive personnel, trained operators, organization structure, and capital. Typically the progress to be made in each part of the total program is specified for annual intervals. The essential characteristics of such a master plan are that it is *comprehensive*—that is, it covers all major elements of the business—and that it is *integrated* into a balanced and synchronized program for the entire operation.

Many companies use their existing budget machinery to prepare their "five-year plans." Income, expense, assets, and other accounts are simply projected for the period covered by a plan. This practice provides an easy way to express a future plan because existing records and systems for consolidating figures can be followed. But long-range planning, in terms of budgets, involves some risk. The figures for years ahead may be merely financial guesses rather than actual plans of responsible executives; the entire long-range planning effort may be dominated by financial people instead of being a genuine group effort of all the key executives; and planning may be restricted to what shows up directly in accounting records and may omit intangible items like product development, executive personnel, and organization.

To avoid these risks, other companies build their five-year programs around product lines. First, they work out programs that include sales volume in physical units, plant and equipment, key personnel, and specific activities necessary to reach the goal. *Then* they translate these programs into budgetary terms. Cash requirements, of course, must be computed, and the entire program checked for financial soundness. But whatever the sequence of planning, the final result is a set of blueprints that lay out in broad terms the course of action the company hopes to follow over a given period of years.

Such a five-year program can lead to dangers as well as benefits. Inability to forecast feasible action is at the root of the major drawbacks: (1) Commitments may be made too soon for plant, equipment, people, and so on. The existence of a plan naturally encourages an executive to get ready for it, but if a plan has to be modified, an executive may find that he is committed to expansion that no longer fits into the scheme. (2) Most of us are reluctant to change our plans after we have invested time and energy in their preparation. The more elaborate the plans, the more likely will rigidity be serious. (3) Planning entails a good deal of effort and expense, which may be wasted if the plan proves to be inappropriate when the time for action arises.

If a five-year plan is to be used, top management must seek ways to reap the benefits and at the same time minimize the dangers. The purpose is to anticipate difficulties and opportunities, to start tooling up so as to be ready to meet these problems when they arise, and to stimulate the motivation that comes with a feeling of "knowing where you are going and how you are going to get there." Here are three guides for reducing the dangers:

1) Distinguish sharply between plans and commitments; use the plan as a preview of things to come but take action only when there is a distinct advantage in doing so today as against waiting until better information about the future is available.

2) Spell out the long-range program only in such detail as is necessary to test its validity and to provide the basis for sound action today. This practice means that projects with long lead times, such as constructing a dam, will be planned in much greater detail than projects that can be adjusted in a relatively short period, such as an advertising campaign.

3) Provide for at least annual revisions of the long-range program when objectives, steps, and schedules are reconsidered in light of new information and forecasts that were unavailable at the time of the last revision. Unless executives are prepared for this continuing reassessment, they will find long-range programming of little value to them.

Fig. 16-3 Long-range plans for expansion of plant and office space.

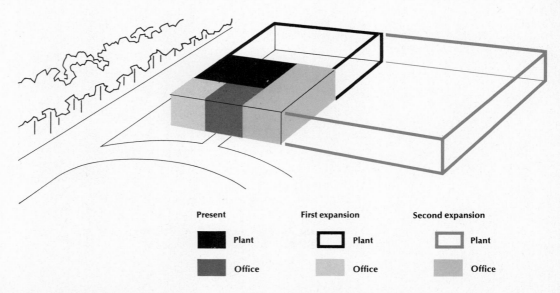

Present	First expansion	Second expansion
■ Plant	☐ Plant	☐ Plant
■ Office	■ Office	▨ Office

These three concepts are illustrated in the planning procedures of electric utility firms. Long-term projections of the demand for electricity are made for fifteen to twenty years in advance. These projections are later revised and broken down by geographic areas for a ten-year advance period; at that time sites are purchased for generating plants and for transmission lines; five years in advance of the anticipated need for service, estimates of capital requirements are prepared and tentative financial plans are laid; later, a formal construction budget based on engineering studies is prepared. Actual orders for equipment and construction are issued as late as possible but still in time to have service available when it is needed. At any of these stages, adjustment is likely in anticipated dates, volume, technology, or other aspects of the program.

To jump immediately into a five-year budget without first thinking through the master strategy will almost surely result in a superficial plan. There is no magic about long-range programming. Unless executives of a company can forecast the future of their industry with considerable reliability, and unless they have time and objectivity to divorce themselves from day-to-day problems, the benefits they derive will probably not warrant the effort long-range programming requires.

CONCLUSION: REAPPRAISAL AND ADAPTATION

Master strategy involves deliberately relating a company's effort to its particular future environment. We recognize, of course, that both the company's capabilities and its environment continually evolve; consequently, strategy should always be based not on existing conditions but on forecasts. Such forecasts, however, are never 100 percent correct; instead strategy often seeks to take advantage of uncertainty about future conditions.

This dynamic aspect of strategy should be underscored. The industry outlook will shift for any of numerous reasons. These forces may accelerate growth in some sectors and spell decline in others, may shift social pressures, may squeeze supply of resources, or may open new possibilities and snuff out others. Meanwhile, the company itself is also changing due to the success or failure of its own efforts, and to actions of competitors and cooperating firms. In addition, with all of these internal and external changes, the combination of thrusts that will provide optimum synergistic effects undoubtedly will be altered. Timing of actions is the most volatile element of all. It should be adjusted to both the new external situation and the degrees of internal progress on various fronts.

Consequently, frequent reappraisal of master strategy is essential. We must build into our planning mechanisms sources of fresh data that will tell us how well we are doing and what new opportunities and obstacles are appearing on the horizon. The feedback features of control—examined in Part Six—will provide some of this data. In addition, senior managers and others who have contact with various parts of the environment must be ever sensitive to new developments that established screening devices might not detect.

Hopefully such reappraisal will not call for sharp reversals in strategy. Typically a master strategy requires several years to execute and some features may endure much longer. The kind of plan we are discussing here sets the direction. In the following chapters we delve into the planning of these more immediate and specific activities.

FOR CLASS DISCUSSION

Questions

1) Much has been made of the statement that the present problems faced by many railroads stem from the tendency of their leaders, years ago, to see themselves as being in the *railroad* business rather than in the *transportation* business. How does this accusation fit with this chapter's advice on selecting propitious niches?

2) In what ways may basic changes in strategy require changes in organization structure, particularly basic departmentation and the nature and degree of decentralization? Illustrate your answer with examples.

3) What can the officers of a company do to increase the objectivity and soundness of its efforts to appraise its strengths and limitations?

4) In the evolution and implementation of a changing corporate strategy, what major internal factors (within the enterprise) should be considered in conjunction with changes in the external environment? How may these internal factors alter a strategy that external conditions seem to dictate as necessary for increased profit?

5) How would you account for the success of conglomerates in terms of the chapter material on synergistic effects?

6) The president of a large and successful cosmetics firm attributes his success to waiting for his competitors to do his innovating, forecasting, and testing for him. "We let them dream up the new products and promotions and we watch the results. If they go over, we copy all of the best features and add a few of our own. Sometimes we get a little less for being second, but considering the number of flops they have which we don't copy and the cost they incur by 'pioneering,' we come off far better than they." What do you think of this approach to developing, forecasting, and testing innovations? Under what conditions will it be most, and least, successful?

7) In what ways may companies fail in their design of a master strategy if they make faulty assumptions about their competitors?

8) Many corporations today have created a position with the title "director of planning." Often the men who have this title report to a top corporate executive and have counterparts at the division level. What should a director of planning do? Explain. How will the nature, rather than the level, of his work differ, depending on whether he is at the corporate or division level? To whom should he report in each case?

Cases

For cases involving issues covered in this chapter, see especially the following. Particularly relevant questions are listed after each case.

Dodge Skate Company (p. 337), 11
Western Office Equipment Manufacturing Company (p. 457), 10, 12
E. W. Ross, Inc. (p. 468), 10
Consolidated Instruments—B (p. 674), 12

FOR FURTHER READING

Ansoff, H.I., *Corporate Strategy*. New York: McGraw-Hill Book Company, 1965. *Practical model for formulating diversification strategy for a company.*

Bower, M., *The Will to Manage*. New York: McGraw-Hill Book Company, 1966, Chap. 3. *Insightful analysis of strategic planning, by a leading management consultant.*

Katz, R.L., *Cases and Concepts in Corporate Strategy*. Englewood Cliffs, N.J.: Prentice-Hall, Inc., 1970, Chaps. 4–7. *Chapter introductions lay out the cycle of strategic analysis, planning, and action in clear, operational terms.*

Miller, E.C., *Advanced Techniques for Strategic Planning*. New York: American Management Association, 1971. *Examines successful applications of "management science" techniques in strategic planning. Essential reading for the operations-research man who wants to tackle strategy problems.*

Newman, W.H., and J.P. Logan, *Strategy, Policy, and Central Management*. Cincinnati: South-Western Publishing Co., 1971. *Strat-*

egy selection (Part 1); policies needed to support strategy (Part 2); organizing and executing strategy (Parts 3 and 4).

Tilles, S., "Making Strategy Explicit," in *Business Strategy*, ed. H.I. Ansoff. Baltimore: Penguin Books Inc., 1970, pp. 180–209. *Stresses elements to be covered in a company strategy.*

Warren, E.K., *Long-Range Planning: The Executive Viewpoint.* Englewood Cliffs, N.J.: Prentice-Hall, Inc., 1963. *Response of managers to different forms of long-range planning.*

Chapter Seventeen

Operating Objectives

FROM STRATEGY TO ACTION

Bridges must be built between broad company strategy (discussed in the previous chapter) and specific objectives that must be carried out next week. Once strategy has been set and long-range programs developed, then operating objectives come into play. Strategy gets translated into effective action only when each member of the organization understands what he is supposed to do about a given situation. For a department or section manager, this setting of sharp local goals is just as vital as establishing master strategy is for the president.

Scope of Operating Objectives

For managerial purposes, it is useful to think of objectives as the results we want to achieve. The words "goal," "aim," and "purpose" also have much the same meaning, because they too imply effort directed toward a preselected result.

In this book, we use the word "objectives" broadly. It covers long-range company aims, more specific department goals, and even individual assignments. Thus objectives may pertain to a wide or narrow part of an enterprise, and they may be either long- or short-range. A salesman may have an immediate objective of clearing up a misunderstanding with a customer, and he may have a five-year objective of cultivating his territory to provide $25,000 in sales each month. Similarly, a company may have a short-term objective of providing stable employment during the next summer and a long-range objective of being a product leader in its industry. These are all results to be achieved.

Often objectives of a particular nature are given a special name. For instance, we may speak of job placement quotas, expense ratios, budgets, absentee rates, or market positions. The use of such descriptive terms does not remove them from the broad category of objectives.

Military and church officials frequently prefer to use the word "mission" instead of objective. A military commander, for instance, may be assigned a mission of protecting a city or a coastline; the mission of a church-worker may be to reduce juvenile delinquency in a given neighborhood. A mission is an objective that has been psychologically accepted by the doer; he is dedicated to its fulfillment. When we speak of a mission, then, we imply moral compulsion to achieve the result. Ideally, in business, all well-thought-out objectives should be accepted as missions, and many are. How to secure such dedication is a recurring issue throughout this book, and we discuss it explicitly in Part Five.

Hierarchy of Objectives

The process of assigning a part of a major mission to a particular department and then further subdividing the assignment among sections and individuals creates a hierarchy of objectives. The goals of each subunit contribute to the aims of the larger unit of which it is a part. We have already used this hierarchy concept, in Chapter 11, to place a problem in a ladder of objectives, but there we did not tie the goal hierarchy to organization units.

The concept of hierarchy was useful to a diversified equipment company. One of the objectives of this firm was to become a leader in the motor scooter business. Toward this end the engineering department was charged with an intermediate goal of designing rugged, easy-to-use, economical, and efficient scooters. Because the test of a scooter's design was whether it continued to work in the hands of users, the engineering department established a small dealer-service section. The objective of this unit, derived from the broader goal of the engineering department, was to keep scooters operating up to the level of their design potential. (The unit also fed back information that was useful in improving designs.) One engineer in the dealer-service section was given the still narrower task of writing clear, useful instructions, both for repairmen in dealers' shops and for owners of scooters. Specifying the audience in this objective was important because it told the engineer to avoid technical jargon, to remember that the reader of his instructions did not have elaborate testing equipment, to anticipate difficulties caused by customer abuse and foolishness, and to keep the instructions from being complex and long. If his instructions had been directed to other engineers, they would probably have been unintelligible to repairmen in the field. As in the means-end chains we examined in Part Three, each of the subgoals in this example derived its worthiness and its character from its contribution to a broader goal.

Meaningful Objectives for Each Job

In the preceding illustration, the aim of being a leader in the industry was too vague to provide a guide to action for most members of the company. What bearing specific decisions have on the objective is often indirect, and particular activities tend to lose their significance when they are merged into a large, total result. Seeing the broad picture, desirable as it is, does not replace the need for more specific goals for each job. In fact, it is entirely possible for an effective worker to be dedicated to doing his particular job well and at the same time to be indifferent to the broad company objectives.

One task of every manager, then, is to help clarify intermediate objectives for each of his subordinates. A subgoal may be a dominant market position in a particular city, leadership in salary administration, keeping abreast of new techniques in the industry, or well-kept grounds around the plant. This is the kind of goal a subordinate executive or operator can "go to work on."

When we stress giving each worker objectives that are specific and meaningful to him, we are still concerned with results. E. C. Schleh has made the following observation in this connection:

> You may say, "Secure $50,000 worth of sales this year from this territory, and in addition, make sure that we get 10 new dealers." You would not say, "Contact the dealers in this territory, set up displays, help train their sales people, and sell, sell more products." Or you might say, "Develop a product which we can produce on the machines in our plant at a (specific) cost and which has sales appeal that would provide a payoff in profit within two years after it gets on the market." You would not say, "Investigate possible products for us, research them, develop various plans, run pilot studies, make analyses of alternative products, and study the design and cost pictures of these products." You will note that in each of these cases there is a distinct difference between specifying what the final outcome would be as against describing the activities or processes by which the man may arrive at the results.[1]

[1] *Management by Results* (New York: McGraw-Hill, 1961), pp. 9–10.

Clarifying objectives and subobjectives is a continuing task. We often like to think that objectives are fixed, but this is only partially true. Shifts in company strategy are made to seize a new opportunity, and because the specific objective assigned to particular individuals are derived from the broad company goals, a change in company strategy is likely to require adjustments in the "missions" of several supervisors and operators. In fact little effective change will occur until assignments down the line are revised. Clearly, selecting objectives is neither static nor automatic.

USEFULNESS OF OBJECTIVES

When properly set forth and accepted, objectives provide the following benefits: individual motivation, unified planning, a basis for decentralizing, voluntary coordination, and standards for control.

Individual Motivation

A common laborer was asked to dig a three-foot hole in the yard beside a plant. When he had finished, his foreman asked him to dig another hole a few feet away. Then the foreman requested a third hole at a different spot, and a fourth. When the foreman asked for a fifth hole, the workman threw down his shovel in disgust and said, "I quit!" Although

Fig. 17-1 Judicious use of objectives. One large company asks these questions to determine how effectively its executives use objectives.

Are objectives for each executive:

Forward looking and courageous?

✓ Do they look to the future with imagination and courage?

✓ Are they high enough to require executives to reach out and stretch themselves?

Sound and comprehensive?

✓ Are they based on objective and sound analysis rather than on rule of thumb or hunch?

✓ Is there balanced emphasis on the long and short range?

✓ Do they cover all important phases of the business (such as profitability, technical and market leadership, growth and devlopment of human as well as material resources)?

Clear and specific?

✓ Are they in writing?

✓ Are goals specific and measurable enough for each executive to know how he is doing?

Known and understood?

✓ If each executive were asked to write his understanding of the division's objectives, would you expect to find a high degree of uniformity?

✓ Is each executive expected to set his own goals?

✓ Do executives refer to these goals as guides to daily decisions?

well paid, he was unwilling to dig three-foot holes aimlessly. The foreman had neglected to tell him that the purpose of digging the holes was to locate a clogged drainage-pipe. Once the man understood the purpose of his work, he continued digging holes willingly until the pipe was finally located.

A sense of accomplishment—of meeting objectives—is desired by men at all levels. The captain of a ship takes pride in keeping his vessel on schedule; a telephone lineman wants to "keep the circuits open"; a chief engineer works overtime to make sure that a newly designed product will not break down under operating conditions; a vice-president in charge of sales spends sleepless nights conceiving of ways to improve the market position of his company. Without a recognized objective, none of these people would put forth such effort.

Each person has a variety of needs that he strives to fulfill, as we explained in Chapter 8. To the extent that an individual accepts business objectives as being desirable, fulfilling them becomes one of his needs. Especially today as a worker's physical and security needs are more fully satisfied and as the desire for self-expression becomes relatively more pressing, the achievement of explicit work goals becomes relevant. So a worker must understand the objectives of his job if he is to work most productively.

Unified Planning

Clear definition of specific objectives encourages unified planning. For example, a manufacturer of automated printing presses promised a customer delivery of a large machine on October 19. With this objective in mind, the purchasing department could obtain parts that were urgently needed, the production department could lay plans for machining and assembly, the personnel department could anticipate some overtime work in September and early October, and the erection department could arrange for transportation and personnel needed to set up the machine in the customer's plant. But the work of these several departments could not have been planned to dovetail closely without a clear identification of the target.

Broad company objectives serve a similar purpose. For years, the Muenster Microscope Company sought to remain privately owned and owner-managed. Because of this objective, the chief engineer concentrated on improving the existing product line rather than on researching completely different products that would have required additional capital and new management. The production superintendent planned his plant improvements within the limits of readily available capital. The treasurer prepared his cash budgets on the basis of retained earnings and borrowed capital, rather than spend time on possible mergers or stock issues. Without an understanding of Muenster's growth objectives, some executives would have probably pushed for rapid expansion while others resisted any change.

Such objectives as these are goals, or "values," which we used in our analysis of decision-making in Part Three. The significant point here is that the same objective is the focus of action for several different individuals. The unifying effect arises when various plans, prepared by several people at, perhaps, different times, are adjusted to achieve a common objective.

Basis for Decentralizing

Decentralizing, as we know, includes assigning decision-making to lower-level personnel. Thereby a subordinate executive or operator is given considerable leeway in deciding how to perform his work. Turning people loose in this way will result in chaos unless the common objectives are well understood.

A few years ago, a large insurance company decided to add accident and health insurance to its line. A regional manager was called to the home office to head up the new department, and half a dozen able men were assigned to assist him. But these assistants could not be used effectively until objectives were clarified. Did the company wish to sell all types of insurance throughout the country as rapidly as possible, or did it wish to experiment in only a few states? Was the new type of insurance to be handled by existing agents, or was a separate selling organization to be established? Once such questions as those were resolved, it was possible to set up fairly specific objectives for each of the assistants. Thus one assistant was expected to develop a training program for company agents, another was to get as many insurance brokers as possible in the Middle Atlantic states to recommend the new line to large company buyers. After the department manager had defined such "missions," the work could be turned over to the assistants with the expectation that they would know what they were supposed to do.[2]

Voluntary Coordination

Detailed plans that completely cover all operations are neither possible nor desirable. Employees must be granted some freedom to adjust

[2]If a person fully accepts and internalizes the objectives of his job, the relationships with his supervisor change. The supervisor takes on the role of an advisor and helper. P.M. Blau and W.R. Scott observed that use of assembly lines and objective performance records create a similar effect. The supervisor is no longer making demands on the subordinate; instead the flow is reversed. This shift in role affects freedom of communication and other aspects of the relationship. Under these circumstances many of the alleged disadvantages of a hierarchical organization disappear. Of course the chances of achieving such a full acceptance of job objectives depend significantly on how the goals are set and who makes the objective measurements.

to immediate circumstances; for highly decentralized operations, the area of freedom is quite wide. Consequently, in every company, for large quantities of interrelated work, people voluntarily coordinate their actions when necessary. Each person, acting within his own area of discretion, adjusts to the needs of other workers.

Such voluntary coordination is more likely to work smoothly if there is common agreement on a set of objectives. A college janitor, for example, who has his mind set on keeping buildings orderly and clean, is apt to work at cross-purposes with a homecoming committee that is thinking only of special events for alumni. If the janitor can be made enthusiastic about the homecoming events, and if the committee will accept the desirability of some cleanliness, a great many adjustments are possible. Through a mutual recognition of objectives, the work of all persons will probably become more effective.

A situation that illustrates this point arose in the training section of an urban renewal center. The training director was pushing hard to maximize the number of people trained and placed in regular jobs. Consequently he encouraged registration and gave first attention to highly competent people who could be placed quickly. Welfare workers in the area, however, reported that as far as they could detect the training center was doing no good in relieving economic distress. The people who needed jobs most were not being trained; welfare workers encouraged their clients to sign up for training, but few stayed more than a couple of days, and most said there was "no use going there." Only after the objective of the training center was redefined and understood did the coordination between the center and the welfare workers improve.

Perhaps only communication is involved. A recent study of companies stressing "management by objectives" reveals that people doing interrelated work voluntarily pass pertinent information back and forth if they are concerned about objectives and results. When the significance of each task is defined in terms of clear-cut objectives, then exchanging information enables each person to fit his actions into a coordinated effort.

Standards for Control

Objectives provide the basis for control. Obviously, meaningful control cannot exist without some conception of what results should be. Control has its own special problems—control points will need to be established, and there may be stubborn questions of measurement; but more fundamental is a clear understanding of what constitutes good performance, and it is objectives that point the way to desired performance.

As soon as the insurance company mentioned above had decided that one of its men should cultivate brokers in the Middle Atlantic states, it had the basis for measuring and controlling that man's performance. Similarly, when the training center shifted its main objective from maximum number of job placements to maximum number of members of families on relief who are trained and placed, the control standards had to be revised. Actually, to avoid too sharp a break with previous operations, a small quota of nonrelief trainees were continued.

Such control standards that are derived from objectives are not used simply to guide corrective action; appraising actual results against such standards is often a guide in paying bonuses and may be a consideration in promotions.

The brief analysis of the usefulness of objectives shows how they interlock with many other aspects of management. The objectives are important to personal motivation, unified planning, effective decentralization, voluntary coordination, and control. It is appropriate, therefore, that we take a closer look at some of the issues involved in setting objectives. The way we frame a person's objectives substantially affects his response to them. Here fumbles are easy.

HOPES VERSUS EXPECTATIONS

An objective may be optimistic, in that the results we hope for will occur if everything works just right—like par on the golf course. Or it may be realistic, a statement of what we actually expect can be accomplished—like par plus our handicap. Both types of goals have their uses, but it is important to distinguish between them.

Advocates of optimistic objectives believe that a man will accomplish more if he sets his sights high. They follow the dictum: "Faint heart never won fair lady." If we have the courage to dream great dreams, then we can bend our efforts to make them come true.

Everyone knows of examples where such determination has paid off. The largest transatlantic air-cargo line would never have been more than a small charter carrier without the high objectives of its president. The company spent years obtaining government permission to operate scheduled flights. In the midst of these negotiations a decision to place a multi-millon-dollar order for new jets was made. In this instance acting on hope, rather than on "sound" expectation, led to significantly better results. A determined, high-flying approach is often used in setting quotas for salesmen. One management consultant achieved considerable success by advising companies to pick the profits they wanted to make and then figure out steps necessary to make them.

In all such cases, the aimed-at results are at least possible, with supreme effort, good luck, and favorable operating conditions. Occasionally objectives known to be unattainable are even used—this, for example: "Give every employee the maximum opportunity to use his highest potential ability." This is an ideal to strive for. It provides direction, as stars do for sailors, but it is never reached.

In contrast, many objectives are stated in realistic terms, and they can be achieved without superhuman effort and uncanny luck. Thus reasonable sales quotas can be filled by most salesmen; with normal diligence, expense ratios can be met by good managers; personnel programs come up with able men, if not geniuses; profit targets bear some resemblance to last year's results. These are goals management expects to be met—or know the reason why. In some areas, performance may surpass the objectives, and these plusses may help offset lagging performance at other spots.

In business planning, emphasis is generally on tough, but achievable, objectives. There are two reasons for this preference: (1) Frustration or indifference is apt to develop if stated goals are rarely, if ever, achieved. (2) Objectives are used for planning and coordination as well as for motivation, and so related activities may get fouled up if management tries to synchronize them with an objective that proves to be more hope than reasonable prediction.

Objectives of the optimistic type do provide inspiration and values for many people throughout an organization. But for the reasons stated in the preceding paragraph, a wise manager will be careful to distinguish between those objectives that are largely hopes and those that are real expectations.

SHORT-RUN OBJECTIVES AS STEPS
TOWARD LONG-RUN GOALS

A major task becomes more manageable when it is divided up into small pieces. This analytical concept is, of course, employed in setting up hierarchies of objectives and in organizing work by departments.

Fig. 17-2 In dealing with so vast an undertaking as an urban renewal project, it is necessary to break down the project into a series of subobjectives—financing, excavation, construction, and selection of tenants. This practice can be useful on a smaller scale as well.

Another manner of breakdown is by steps, or results, to be achieved within a given period of time. This method is commonly used in personal decisions. For instance, suppose John Casey wants to become an executive in a local publishing firm (long-run objective). John may decide that a business education (intermediate objective) will help him achieve this goal. So he takes a course in management as one of several steps toward a formal business education.

A step-by-step breakdown is particularly valuable in complicated business projects. The use of satellites in telephonic and TV communication, for example, is a vast and complex undertaking. Receiving and broadcasting stations have to be located on the basis of technical, economic, and political considerations, equipment has to be designed and built, personnel trained, satellites launched, users of the service educated, rates set, and a staggering amount of capital acquired. A job of this sort becomes manageable only when it is broken down into a series of steps. In fact, each major step will be divided and subdivided.

Even relatively simple assignments, such as making sure that all customers understand a new price schedule, or giving polio shots to all children in a city, may well be divided up into small work units.

The creation of such short-run objectives has several advantages:

1) *It helps make the objective tangible and meaningful.* We all find it easy to project ourselves into the immediate future, whereas the more distant future is filled with uncertainties; besides, we have no compelling reasons to face remote problems now.

2) *Short-run objectives provide a means of bridging the gap between hopes and expectations.* It is entirely possible to have optimistic long-run goals and at the same time be quite realistic about the immediate steps to be taken toward these ends. Working on a tangible, immediate project tends to relieve the frustration that can arise from the magnitude and difficulty of a major objective. This tendency is an asset, provided a manager himself does not become so engrossed with a short-run objective that he loses sight of the existence and nature of the long-run objective.

3) *An outstanding advantage of setting up short-run objectives is that they provide benchmarks for measuring progress.* This advantage is a great aid in motivation and in control. When a person sees that he is making progress, he gets a sense of accomplishment even though a job is not yet finished, and he also builds his confidence to tackle the work still ahead.

PLURAL OBJECTIVES

Never does a job, department, or company have a single objective. It may have one dominant mission, but other goals will also demand recognition.

The manager of an airport, for instance, may be charged with making it easy to move planes, people, and freight in and out of his facility. But, among other things, he will also be expected to keep operating costs low, to use only as much capital for equipment and inventory as is necessary, to maintain an efficient work force, and to develop men for promotion to key jobs. Similarly an advertising manager should not only generate interest in company products, but also coordinate his activities with the sales force, keep costs within budgets, develop capabilities of his staff, and so forth. Just as each of us personally aspires to a variety of goals—for example, good health, challenging work, enjoyable leisure, happy family life, service to our fellow men—so too is a manager confronted with diverse, and perhaps competing, goals.

Multiple Objectives of a Company

The common belief that "the purpose of a business firm is to make a profit" is part of American folklore. It probably got started as an *assumption* made to simplify economic theory. Being a half-truth, it proved to be an easy way for even businessmen to talk about a complex problem. Then when public accounting made the profit-and-loss statement one of the few universal measures of business performance, the notion became ingrained.

But the suggestion that profits are the sole objective of a company is *misleading*. Obviously a company must earn a profit if it is to continue in existence; earnings are necessary to attract additional capital and to provide a cushion for meeting the risks inherent in business activity. But for survival it is also essential that a company produce goods or services customers want, that its conditions of employment continue to attract competent employees, that it be a desirable customer to the people who supply raw materials, and that it be an acceptable corporate citizen in the community in which its operates. Remove any one of these essentials, and the enterprise collapses. To argue that profit is the supreme objective is like saying that blood circulation is more important to human survival than breathing, digestion, or proper functioning of the nervous system.[3]

In discussing strategy in the preceding chapter, we pointed to the need for multiple criteria, in practice if not in abstract theory, for overall company targets. Now, when we are seeking ways to state objectives that have operational relevance, the principle of multiple enterprise objectives

---

[3]Suitable measurement of profit poses an additional drawback. Profit figures reported by existing accounting systems are based on past costs. A new system that attempted to be a common denominator for setting and measuring all company objectives would have to deal with present worths of future values. This would call for estimates about future conditions and the influence of intangibles such as morale and customer goodwill; comparability from year to year and between companies would be desirable. The theoretical and practical difficulties in designing such a system are overwhelming.

takes on added significance. For the manager, no enterprise—public or private—has a single objective.

Instead, the managers of each enterprise should undertake the more difficult task of stating a set of objectives that they can translate into action. Such objectives are shaped, of course, by values and attitudes about society and by strategy decisions on the way the specific enterprise seeks to be relevant to social needs. But in order that decisions about concrete actions will also be relevant, we should be able to relate the objectives to things we see or do.

To assist the managers of the enterprise in setting objectives, the General Electric Company has singled out eight "key result areas":

1) Profitability—in both percent of sales and return on investment.
2) Market position.
3) Productivity—which means improving costs as well as sales.
4) Leadership in technological research.
5) Development of future people, both technical or functional and managerial.
6) Employee attitudes and relations.
7) Public attitudes.
8) Balance of long-range and short-range objectives.

Several other companies use variations of this format. Note that the list identifies only areas; each firm must fill in specific subjects and levels of achievement that fit its circumstance at a particular time.

Service enterprises likewise should determine their key result areas. Here is such a list for a public library: circulation (loans and in library), reference questions answered, cooperation with schools and other libraries, percent of population using the library, contribution to community cohesiveness, collection of books and reference materials, personnel development, operation within financial budget. As soon as we start dealing with objectives that can readily be translated into action we are faced with multiple goals.

Each of the objectives of the enterprise will, of course, call forth an array of more specific operating goals, and this fanning out continues through to the quite detailed objectives for each individual in the organization.

Number of Objectives for Each Man

Too many objectives can be troublesome, especially for one person. When multiple objectives of a company are subdivided and elaborated into an array of specific, short-term objectives, we also split up the work among various people. Nevertheless, one man may be confronted with

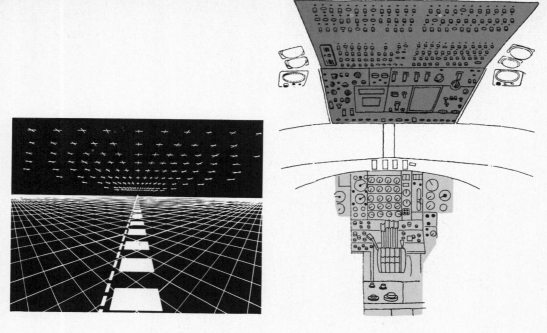

Fig. 17-3 *Too many objectives for one man can be hazardous. In a conventional aircraft, the pilot must contend with a bewildering variety of informational devices. New instruments, such as the contact analog shown at left, condense information concerning the plane's movements and position and present it to the pilot in forms that can be readily grasped. Deviations from the intended course are thus instantly revealed. Matters related to course—speed, position, and so on—can be ignored until deviation is indicated. The contact analog demonstrates two ways of reducing the problem of multiple objectives: (1) Integrating a variety of elements under a few headings and (2) adopting the "exception principle," that is ignoring any given factor as long as every factor related to it is satisfactory.*

thirty or forty identified results he is expected to achieve—quality output, meeting deadlines, overtime pay, self-development, training of others, aid to other departments, plans for next year, budgeted expense, customer service, and many others.

Such a large array of objectives tends to disperse attention and fails to provide clear direction of effort. Consequently, the number of objectives any one man is expected to focus on should be limited. Some executives feel the number should be narrowed to the range of two to five in order to assure concentrated attention; others contend that a man can keep a dozen objectives in mind. In either case, agreement exists that motivation is improved by reducing the number.

Two methods are used to narrow the number of objectives for a single man. First, a distinction is drawn between what Herbert Simon calls satisficing and optimizing. For a variety of results we simply try to achieve a satisfactory standard. Only when results—say, quality, honesty, or maintenance—fail to meet the standard do we give the matter attention. In a sense, these are passive objectives, at least for the time being. Other objectives call for improvement. These are the stimulants to action, and they are fewer in number.

Consolidating several objectives that are means to some higher goal is a second means of limiting the number of key objectives for a particular job. For example, we might say that our Boston salesmen should obtain ten new accounts per month; embraced in this objective are subgoals regarding prospect lists, industry contacts, visits to possible customers, and other means of securing new customers. To be sure, most of the subgoals have to be met if the salesman gets his ten new accounts, but focusing on one net result is easier to deal with mentally, and it encourages delegation of the problem of how to achieve results.

ADJUSTING SHORT-RUN EMPHASIS

Objectives in Competition for Attention

Even half a dozen objectives create difficulties, for emphasis on any one goal tends to reduce attention given to others. Every operating executive, for instance, knows that a strong push for increased output is likely to cause poor quality and increased waste. The welfare worker urged to process more cases gives less consideration to individualized problems. An equipment manufacturer, to cite another example, became concerned about production delays brought about by small shortages of materials or parts. Improvements were made in the scheduling system, and all members of the purchasing department were alerted to the importance of having materials on hand when needed. Within six months, there was scarcely a single production delay due to lack of materials. *But* raw material and parts inventory had increased over 50 percent. In meeting one goal, management had neglected another.

All of us, in planning our own work or in correcting that of others, like to assume that we can give more effort to some goal that is pressing at the moment without slackening off on other work. Sometimes we can. Sooner or later, however, a point is reached where attention and effort are simply diverted from one activity to another. More time on football or campus politics means less with the books, and vice versa.

A technique used in a container plant highlights this issue. A performance-evaluation system was planned that tried to account for 100 percent of the effort of each foreman. Various percentages were assigned to all activities—output, labor costs, material costs, quality, and so on. Then, when the plant superintendent wanted a foreman to give more attention to, say, safety or training, he had to decide what other values could be reduced because the total could never exceed 100 percent. This was a device to keep the requests that superintendents were making of the foremen more realistic.

Problems of Balance

Keeping the emphasis on diverse objectives in balance is no simple task. A common difficulty is that the tangible, measurable ends receive undue attention. It would be easy for a professor to stress the appearance of a report rather than the learning that went into its preparation simply because the paper itself is so much easier to see. Similarly, in business those results that show up directly in accounting reports often command priority; thus, avoiding overtime expense may be preferred over maintaining quality in advertising copy, or a salesman may spend as much time on a $1.38 item in his expense account as on making a $138.00 sale.

Another source of trouble is this: Immediate problems tend to take precedence over long-run issues. The dilemma of choosing crops up time and again in engineering departments. Customers' orders for immediate delivery have a "here and now" quality about them. If he is not careful, an engineer will find himself simply going from one order to the next, always leaving for tomorrow the design of a new product. Similarly, a controller may postpone the transfer of a bright young man to the sales department because personnel development has no fixed due date as does the preparation of an annual financial report.

The case of one's own work versus teamwork may also pose a balancing problem. We all know friendly persons who are so ready to help with another man's problems that they have difficulty getting their own work done on time. But a self-centered view may also cause trouble. A paper-box manufacturer, for instance, had a production superintendent who did an excellent job of maintaining equipment, keeping costs low, and protecting the interests of his men. The sales department, however, had great difficulty getting him to push through rush orders or work with special quality requirements. Early retirement fortunately permitted the company to appoint a new production manager who was much more sympathetic to sales needs, and now a revised scheduling procedure and a technical advisor on specialty printing has enabled the company to make customer service one of its chief selling appeals.

No objective is supreme over all others at all levels of achievement. Nor is any objective inferior at all levels. As we pointed out in Chapter 14 we have to think in terms of incremental values—that is, how important is an added client or a little touch of service or a bit more training? The degree of current achievement relative to acceptable standards affects the stress we should place on any objective.

Fortunately, it is often possible to meet several objectives with the same course of action, at least to an acceptable extent. The preceding examples have all emphasized competition among objectives simply because that is the aspect of the total managerial task we are considering in this section of our discussion.

Periodic Adjustment of Emphasis

Every manager must frequently reappraise the emphasis he gives to his various objectives. This job is like that of a captain of a large ship who is continually changing his speed and direction in relation to his present position, tides, winds, and other conditions.

A regional sales manager of a well-known computer company makes such a reappraisal on a systematic basis. Once every month, he sits down with each of his branch managers to review past performance; together they agree on three, four, or at most five goals that will be emphasized during the following month. This list may include any of several desirable aims: calling on new customers, pushing the sale of a particular product, recruiting additional salesmen, clearing up customer complaints, or reducing expenses. Sometimes the same item appears on the list for several months. It is generally understood that the branch managers will not completely neglect items missing from the list, but special emphasis will be given to only a few goals. This manager contends that he gets better results by *highlighting* a few items than by talking about many. He is able to maintain an overall balance by the frequent reviews and by shifting from one objective to another as necessary.

The details of this particular technique are not important here. But we should note several of its desirable features: (1) Any misunderstanding about the quality, timing, or costs of a specific objective can be cleared up at the monthly discussions. (2) Plans are adjusted in light of progress already being made. This practice permits comparison of incremental values. (3) New information and new pressure from headquarters can be promptly incorporated into the action taken at each branch, thus giving recognition to the problems and needs of the respective branches, instead of blithely following blanket orders from headquarters. (4) Broad objectives are translated into meaningful and immediately applicable terms for each branch manager.

CONCLUSION

Master strategy deals with the company as a whole. It stakes out the role in society that the enterprise wishes to play. But this strategy can be achieved only if it has an impact on the behavior of people working in the company. Consequently we have to give close attention to fashioning objectives and subobjectives that are understandable and significant to the executives and other workers affected by them.

Important steps in making objectives a vital, energizing managerial tool are the following: translating master strategy into meaningful objectives, distinguishing between hopes and expectations, setting short-run objectives as steps toward long-run goals, recognizing the presence of plural objectives, and adjusting the short-run emphasis on various objectives. When we have clarified objectives in this manner, they provide the guiding, unifying core of company planning.

FOR CLASS DISCUSSION

Questions

1) The general manager of a large division of a highly diversified company stated that he was "fed up" with all of the directives he received from headquarters and with the elaborate system by which his plans and results were evaluated. "Let them give me a profit goal, tell me how much capital I can expect, and then leave me alone as long as I get the job done," he said. (1) Even if the general manager in question is an extremely competent executive, why might corporate management want to provide him with more detailed objectives? (2) Why might the general manager and his division be better off with such goals than they would be with a single profit goal and capital constraint?

2) A standard such as a sales or production quota is of little value unless the assumptions and methods of reaching the quota are spelled out and understood both by the man who is to achieve it and by the man who is to evaluate his performance. Comment. Do you agree? Explain.

3) In the text we indicated that as physical and security needs are more fully satisfied, and self-expression becomes relatively a more pressing desire, the achievement of explicit work goals becomes "relevant." Relate this concept to the material on conflict presented in Chapter 9.

4) Should a standard or objective that is given to a man be the most reasonable guess about what can be attained? Or should it always be somewhat higher or beyond what might be considered the most reasonable expectation? Discuss both sides of this question and indicate what the implications are on coordination and subsequent control.

5) In what ways may the demand for clarity and, wherever possible, quantification of objectives lead to difficulties when seeking to balance long- and short-run objectives?

6) Objectives guide decision-making in several ways: They

(1) give direction in the search for alternatives, (2) provide a guide for selecting factors to be used in comparing alternatives, and (3) provide a value system for choosing among alternatives. Give several examples illustrating each of these three effects of objectives.

7) The importance of periodically adjusting objectives is stressed in this chapter. List ways in which a superior may judge whether a subordinate's requests for frequent changes in longer-term objectives are the result of good or poor planning by the subordinate.

8) In what ways may better management information systems (as discussed in Chapter 15) contribute to, or detract from, efforts to develop clear objectives?

Cases

For cases involving issues covered in this chapter, see especially the following. Particularly relevant questions are listed after each case.

General Machinery Corporation (p. 130), 10, 11
Gerald Clark (p. 234), 14
Bolling Laboratories, Inc. (p. 345), 15
E.W. Ross, Inc. (p. 468), 8
Consolidated Instruments—A (p. 571), 10
Consolidated Instruments—B (p. 674), 12

FOR FURTHER READING

Ackoff, R.L., *A Concept of Corporate Planning.* New York: John Wiley & Sons, Inc., 1970, Chap. 2. *Brief, incisive discussion of role of objectives and goals in company planning.*

Granger, C.H., "How to Set Company Objectives." *Management Review*, July 1970. *Suggestions for setting realistic objectives.*

Gross, B.M., "What Are Your Organization's Objectives?" *Human Relations*, August 1965. *Comprehensive, general-systems view of the many kinds of objectives necessary in an organization.*

Miller, E.C., *Objectives and Standards.* New York: American Management Association, 1966. *Describes company practice of translating corporate goals into individual goals.*

Schleh, E.C., *Management by Results.* New York: McGraw-Hill Book Company, 1961, Chaps. 2–5. *Practical discussion of how to set objectives for individual executives and operators that will provide motivation and lead to desired results.*

Chapter Eighteen

Planning for Stabilized Action

CONSISTENT AND ENDURING BEHAVIOR PATTERNS

Objectives, however soundly conceived and clearly communicated, provide only part of the guidance essential to united effort. Even the most highly motivated people need some plan of action, as has become painfully clear in several urban renewal projects where the absence of customary patterns for joint effort has thwarted lofty aims.

Basically, management uses two kinds of plans to direct activities toward established goals: *single-use* plans and *standing* plans. Single-use plans include programs, schedules and special methods designed for a unique set of circumstances. We shall examine these plans in the next chapter. In this chapter, we shall consider standing plans, a group that includes policies, standard methods, and standing operating procedures, all of which are designed to deal with recurring problems. Each time a particular, but familiar, problem arises, a standing plan provides a ready guide to action.

Need for Standing Plans

A leading blanket manufacturer ran into serious difficulty when its sales policies failed to provide consistent guidance to key executives. The company was particularly successful in selling its electric blankets under its own brand name, and for years did not offer them for private-label sale. But finally, at a time when competition was very keen, the Special Account Sales Manager was permitted to solicit some much-needed orders from private-label customers. Because the company was unprepared for this new market, these products were almost identical with those sold under the company brand—except for name. Several of the executives did not regard this as a serious departure from traditional policy because the company already had well-advanced plans for a new temperature-control device for its blankets.

But a major crisis developed a few months later when the Special Account Sales Manager turned up with a tentative order from a very large discount house for electric blankets with the new control device. The Advertising Manager and other executives in the company had assumed that the new device would be used on branded items only and would be, therefore, a major help in building the sales volume of the company line. The Special Account man was upset, believing that if he withdrew his offer of electric blankets, the company would probably lose orders for any kind of blanket from this important customer. Both the Special Account and Advertising managers held a common objective, namely increasing sales. But they lacked the guidance of a *policy* on private-label sales that would have kept them from working at cross-purposes.

Moreover, procedures have to be adjusted to support policies. This became dramatically evident when the City University of New York adopted an "open-admission" policy. The number of entering freshmen jumped 50 percent, and their academic preparation varied drastically. This change had been anticipated—it was the aim of the new admission policy. But the procedures for registering this heterogeneous group and assigning them to appropriate classes were grossly inadequate. For weeks students shifted from class to class, and no one was sure who should report where.

For any group of people to live together or to work together, they must be able to anticipate one another's actions. There must be some

Fig. 18-1 In organizations, there is a continual need for consistent, dependent behavior. If behavior becomes unpredictable and erratic, disaster could follow.

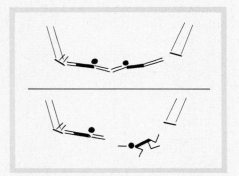

consistency or pattern of behavior. The more interdependent the activities, the more important the ability to anticipate. Without this ability, an individual is at a loss to know what he should do, he is doubtful about what he can depend on from others, and he is unsure whether his own efforts will be helpful or harmful. This is true in a symphony orchestra, football team, diplomatic corps, ship's crew, bank, coffee plantation, and in any other similar situations.

Standing plans are one of the important means for building predictable patterns of behavior in a business firm. If these patterns clearly contribute to the achievement of objectives, they tend to breed confidence and good morale. There is a limit, to be sure. Although every organization requires the stability and aid to coordination afforded by good standing plans, if the plans become too numerous or too rigid, flexibility and initiative are snuffed out.

TYPES OF STANDING PLANS

Within the broad category of standing plans, a manager has a choice of several types, notably policies, standard methods, and standing operating procedures. Like formations for a football team, one type of plan may be more useful in a given situation than another. So a manager needs to know the characteristics of the tools he has to work with if he is to be effective in achieving balanced results. Let us look at the characteristics of the principal types of standing plans.

Policies

A policy is a general guide to action. Typically it does not tell a person exactly what to do, but it does point out the direction to go. Familiar policies are summed up in these statements: "We sell only for cash." "We lease, rather than buy, office space." "We insure all property worth more than $10,000 against fire loss." In each instance, some important aspect of a recurring problem has been singled out, and a guide established for dealing with it.

Although policies are often desirable, the wise way for a manager to use policies is by no means obvious. He has to give considerable attention to these questions: How precise should a policy be? Should it give explicit guidance or merely set limits? How comprehensive should we make it?

Some policies provide only broad guidance. For example, "Our policy is to make college education available to all students graduating from an in-state high school" leaves much leeway as to what is done about availability and about keeping up with standards. Similarly a statement that

"Preference will be given to goods made by union labor" indicates intent but leaves the purchasing agent free to decide whether the preference comes first or whether it should be considered only when all other considerations are equal.

But policies can be much more specific. An investment banking firm makes the following statement on length of vacations:

> Employees shall normally be entitled to vacations according to the following schedule:
> On payroll six to eighteen months prior to March 1—one week.
> On payroll nineteen months to ten years prior to March 1—two weeks.
> On payroll eleven to twenty years prior to March 1—three weeks.
> On payroll over twenty years prior to March 1—four weeks.

What subjects policies should cover and what policies should say about these subjects depend entirely on what will be helpful in solving specific problems. Take customer policies. Many companies believe it is wise to establish lower limits and perhaps upper limits on the size of customer they want; location limits are also common. These guides are useful not only to the selling organization, but to people who must plan production scheduling, warehousing, and shipping. Establishing a useful policy covering the quality characteristics of customers is more difficult. Credit rating, stability of demand, desire for special service, history on cancellation of orders—all contribute to a definition of "a good firm to do business with." Most companies, however, do not attempt to incorporate these considerations into a policy, because most customers are good in some respects and weak in others, and a general guide applicable to many situations is hard to formulate. For guidance on this aspect of selecting customers, a few companies have a policy that simply lists all factors that must be considered in arriving at a decision.

Even when most aspects of a particular problem are unique situations that do not lend themselves to policy guidance, perhaps one or two aspects do. The selection of suppliers of raw materials and parts is a good example. To a large extent, a purchasing agent must make a separate analysis of possible suppliers for each item he buys. Nevertheless, most companies have a few policies about selecting suppliers. A company may have a policy of buying no more than 75 percent of its needs for any one product from a single supplier. The purpose is to avoid being dependent on a single source and so run the risk of a shortage if that firm is shut down because of a strike, flood, or some other difficulty. Another policy may be to secure bids from at least three sources in order to encourage competition for the company's business. Note that such policies deal only with the number of suppliers, leaving open the selection of specific firms.

A policy, then, may (1) be specific or broad in its instruction, (2) deal with one, or many, aspects of a problem, (3) place limits within which action is to be taken, or (4) specify the steps to take in making a decision.

The skill of a manager in using policies lies in how he decides just *what kind of guidance* will be helpful.

For convenience of reference, policies are often classified by subject, such as sales, production, purchasing, personnel, or finance. But at other times, we refer to general policies and departmental policies, depending on the scope of activities to which they apply. Such groupings do not, of course, change the character of policies as a management tool.

Standard Methods

The distinction between a policy and a standard method is chiefly one of degree, because both provide guidance about how a particular kind of problem should be handled. The chief differences relate to viewpoint, completeness, and attempt to control operating conditions.

Viewpoint. A policy is a general guide, whereas a standard method deals with detailed activities. But what is general and what is detailed? The answer depends on our point of view. For example, a vice-president in charge of personnel would probably say that a general rule to pay wages comparable to those prevailing in the local community was a policy, whereas job evaluation was simply a method for carrying out this policy. But the chief of the wage and salary division would look on a decision to use job evaluation in establishing pay rates as a major policy covering his work; he would consider a particular way of relating one job to another— say, factor comparison—a method. How about still a third person, a job analyst who works for the wage and salary chief? He too has his own point of view. He thinks the choice of factor comparison is a policy decision; for him, methods are such things as determining whom to contact and how to conduct interviews in analyzing each job. Clearly, then, whether a particular guide to action is called a policy or a standard method depends on the perspective of the man who is talking.

Still, even such a slippery distinction as this is useful. In planning the work of each job, at whatever level, an executive should think of both the broad framework in which he operates and the more detailed methods he will use. Good planning requires both viewpoints and we need terms that distinguish between them.

Completeness. Standard methods, like policies, never cover every aspect of an activity, although typically they do provide fuller guidance than a policy. Their greater completeness is scarcely surprising, however, because standard methods apply to a narrower scope of activities. Therefore, it is easier to find general guides that fit most cases. Besides, thanks to Frederick W. Taylor's attempt to plan everything in detail, tradition favors developing detailed methods on the assumption that the more completely a method is planned, the more efficient it will be.

Control of environment. The pioneers of Scientific Management— Frank Gilbreth, Taylor, and others—quickly discovered that the conditions surrounding a job often had more influence on output than the performance of the man holding down the job. The successful use of standard methods called for standard conditions.

The scientific managers therefore set about to control raw materials, machine maintenance, work flow, tools, training, and other factors that affect output. After such work conditions were controlled, it became reasonable to expect a man to follow a standard method of work and to achieve a standard output.

Today we can see many applications of this basic idea of controlling conditions so that standard methods will be applicable. An automobile assembly plant is perhaps the most widely known example. In this case, standardized parts reach the assembly line precisely on schedule. Necessary tools are placed within easy reach of the worker. Special instructions for auxiliary equipment are readily available. In fact management has gone to great lengths to make sure that standard methods are applicable to car after car. Although most industries do not go to this extreme, attempts to maintain uniform and effective working conditions are common.

Standard methods are essential in the use of electronic computers to make automated decisions. Several conditions are necessary for a computer to "decide," that is, issue instructions to another machine or to a man regarding action to be taken: (1) The significant variables in the situation must be measured and this information fed into the machine. (The rest of the environment is assumed to be constant.) (2) Any deviation from acceptable performance flashes a specific cue. (3) Each cue trips a "programmed" response—a standard method for dealing with the situation. All three conditions call for intense standardization. It is clear that unless an operating situation lends itself to a very high use of standard methods, automation is not applicable.

One drawback of developing standard methods and standard working conditions is the cost. Industrial engineers may spend months developing "the one best way" to perform a single operation. In a large plant, thousands of similar studies may be needed. Even after all of these studies, the engineers may be unable to discover a feasible way to control one or two factors. All this detailed planning obviously is expensive, and the resulting standard method must apply to a large enough volume of work so that the cost can be recovered by more efficiency in doing the work.

A shortcut is to standardize a method already in use, probably the method of the best workers.[1] This approach enables a company to predict

---

[1] Standing plans are not always consciously and deliberately established. Some are like common law; they are practices that just grow, become accepted behavior, and are then enforced by those in official positions.

There is no sharp line that divides a company's traditions and customs from its standing plans. From a manager's point of view, we might say that a custom becomes a standing plan when (1) it is clearly enough recognized so that those it affects can describe it, and (2) individuals would be subject to criticism if they disregarded it merely on their own initiative. Other customs and traditions undoubtedly influence behavior, but they can scarcely be considered a part of a planning structure, because they are not sharply enough defined to be enforced.

processing costs and delivery times. Careful analysis, however, usually reveals places where methods that have simply evolved over the years can be improved on. If a company is going to adopt a standard method at all, it normally pays to adopt a good one. It is particularly dangerous to introduce incentive pay in order to increase output until a thorough analysis of methods has been completed. Once a production norm has been established, most of us resent an attempt to increase it.

Standard methods are more difficult to apply to sales and other client contact than they are within a plant. The former activities tend to be varied, and the diversity of individual behavior is often an important consideration. Consequently, two approaches already mentioned in connection with policies are often used. First, we can standardize certain parts or aspects of the total activity—for instance, in sales work, the presenting of merchandise and the writing of sales orders, and in a hospital, the handling of admissions, routine tests, and accounting. Second, for some activities, we can specify a series of steps, as in conducting an interview or reconciling a bank statement. An executive or operator can use these standard parts in whatever combination seems appropriate for a particular day's work. This practice permits flexibility while still achieving some of the benefits of standard methods.

Standing Operating Procedures

A procedure details the *sequence of steps* several individuals must take to achieve a specific purpose. When a procedure for dealing with recurring problems becomes formalized, we call it a standing operating procedure.

Company action on even relatively small matters usually requires the work of several individuals. A procedure helps to integrate their bits of work into a meaningful whole. Consider the standing operating procedures set by an insurance company for the employment of exempt personnel (that is, employees not subject to wage-and-hour regulations):

1) A supervisor decides he needs an additional man to help with technical problems.

2) The budget officer must approve the addition unless the supervisor's existing budget has funds available for this purpose (which is unlikely).

3) The supervisor advises the personnel director by phone or in writing of his new need.

4) The personnel director sends a job analyst to the supervisor; the analyst writes a description of job duties and qualifications of a man needed to fill the job, and gets the supervisor's OK.

5) This job description is reviewed by the wage and salary administrator, who classifies the job and thereby sets the salary range for the new job.

6) The employment manager looks for men who have the qualifications stated in the job description. He first checks present employees who might be qualified and interested. If necessary, he turns to outside sources. He then picks the two or three most promising candidates.

7) The supervisor interviews the men sent to him by the employment manager; he selects the man he prefers or asks for more candidates.

8) The employment manager checks the references and tries to uncover other pertinent information about the leading candidate.

9) This man is called back for a second interview with the supervisor. They try to reach a tentative understanding about the job duties, salary range, and other matters.

10) The supervisor's boss interviews the candidate.

11) If everything is in order, the supervisor makes a firm offer.

12) The candidate reports to the office of the employment manager, fills in company forms, retirement instructions, and so on. The employment manager gives the man background information on the company and its personnel policies.

13) The man takes a medical examination from the company doctor.

14) The man reports for duty.

15) The employment manager sends instructions to the payroll clerk about starting date, rate of pay, deductions, and so forth.

Most companies have literally hundreds of such procedures—for grievances, capital expenditures, and arranging to use the company car, to name a few—and most are essential for smooth operation. Picture the confusion if there were no standard procedure for customers' orders. Somehow each order must get immediately from the salesman to the shipping clerk, the credit manager, and the accounts-receivable clerk; later the persons responsible for billing, inventory records, sales analysis, and sales compensation must be advised. Without a regular routine for handling such matters, customer service would be poor, salesmen would be angry, bills would have errors and become troublesome to collect, and inventory controls would collapse.

Most standing operating procedures apply to the flow of business papers—orders, bills, requests, reports, applications, and so forth. The papers are simply vehicles for information and ideas. But there can be standing procedures with no papers at all; for example, when an exception to a normal price is at issue, the three or four people involved may have a well-established understanding about the steps necessary in making a decision.

Although standard forms are not an essential part of a standing operating procedure, they can be very helpful for a large volume of similar transactions. A well-designed form with space for all essential information aids accuracy of communication, permits rapid handling, and serves as a convenient record.

Relation to organization. Formal organization divides the total work of a company into parts, thus permitting concentrated and specialized

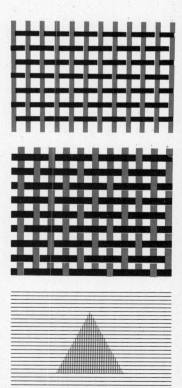

Fig. 18-2 *Standing operating procedures can bind together the many strands of activity that make up an organization. Many patterns are possible in the way activities are drawn to the surface.*

attention where necessary. Procedures help tie all the parts together. Like an automatic shuttle on a loom passing back and forth through the warp threads, the procedures weave woof threads that bind a firm fabric. Some of the weaving must be done by hand, as we shall see in the next chapter, but a large part of it must become routine and standardized. This is the role of the standing operating procedure.

Clearly, the way a company is organized affects the number and sequence of steps in any procedure. For instance, if each supervisor in the life insurance company referred to on page 426 recruited his own technical personnel (as is the case in some companies), at least steps 6, 8 and 10 of the procedure would be changed. Fifty years ago, when there would have been no central personnel department, a supervisor might well have done all the work himself, except for steps 2, 10, and 15. But if the company had more personnel specialists, the procedure might well be more elaborate—as anyone who has been recruited into the Armed Services can testify.

Keeping procedures simple. Standing operating procedures tend to become complex and rigid for several reasons. Each unit takes jurisdictional pride in performing its part accurately. Control points are added to avoid difficulties that are often temporary in duration, and these controls then survive like the proverbial cat with nine lives. Executives habitually look for information at certain spots, not realizing that it might be more simply compiled elsewhere. Standard forms acquire a sanctity that only the brave dare challenge.

To avoid the choking effect of overelaborate procedures is a continuing task for a manager. A variety of techniques is open to him. He may hire a special procedures-analyst for assistance in this area alone. Among the many possibilities for simplification are mechanical devices for communication and duplication. Perhaps a procedure can be revised so that some steps are taken concurrently. One company found that checking all invoices from vendors was unnecessary; by concentrating on those for over $100, 74 percent of the invoices could be handled more promptly with a likely annual loss of only $200; furthermore, the work of two clerks was eliminated.

Job enlargement is receiving increasing emphasis in business organizations. Instead of dividing up work into narrower and narrower specialties, companies are combining a wide variety of duties in a single job, as we noted in Part Two. Job enlargement affects procedures because it reduces the number of stops in a total flow. Typically much more time is used in *moving*, say, customers' orders from desk A to desk B for two tasks in a procedure than is used in doing the actual work at A and B. So merely a reduction in the number of stops is an advantage.

In appraising a standing procedure, a manager wants to ensure that (1) the action each person must take is clear, (2) the information each person requires is provided, (3) the work proceeds promptly, (4) economies are obtained where feasible, (5) control checks are made at strategic points, and (6) necessary records are kept. Meeting these tests and also keeping procedures simple often calls for keen resourcefulness.

HOW STRICT SHOULD PLANS BE?

There is much doubletalk about the flexibility of standing plans. An executive may spend ten minutes emphasizing the need for a policy, standard method, or standing operating procedure, and then finish up saying, "Of course, we want to keep it flexible." In a single breath, he has cast out his whole point. How flexible? Flexible in what way? The catch is that the executive has several courses of action open.

One approach is to change standing plans frequently: A policy, method, or procedure remains in effect until a new guide is established, but such revisions are made promptly whenever operating conditions change. Unfortunately, this approach has serious limitations. Many of the advantages of dependability, habitual behavior, customary social relations, and predictable results are lost. Communication about changes in standing plans is difficult, especially if a large number of people is involved; the reasons for the new plan and its full meaning become confused, and loyalty to informal groups encourages resistance to new alignments. Therefore, using frequent change to secure flexibility in standing plans needs to be confined to a few issues—such as a special procedure to handle a Christmas rush—and preferably applied to a small group that appreciates why the change is necessary.

Another approach to flexibility is to state a standing plan generally, or loosely, in order to permit a wide range of variation within the plan. Or we may list many exceptions to which the plan does not apply. In effect, this simply restricts the scope of the plan; flexibility is achieved by not giving guidance.

Still a third way of obtaining flexibility is to think of standing plans partly as guides and partly as rules. If we can draw this distinction clearly, the usefulness of standing plans can be greatly extended. Let us examine this approach more fully.

Guides versus Rules

Some policies are intended to be definite rules without exceptions. For example, the Cluett, Peabody Company, manufacturer of Arrow shirts and related products, has this policy: "No advertising allowances will be made to our customers." This does not mean that the company prefers not to pay advertising allowances or that only the sales manager may authorize such allowances; it means just what it says. This company wants its products carried by many small stores as well as by large ones. By making no allowances to favored customers, it believes that a greater number of outlets will stock its products. Hence the policy is rigidly enforced. This company also has a policy that no second-quality merchandise will be sold with its Arrow label, and it makes sure that this policy, like the other, is strictly observed.

Contrast these Cluett, Peabody policies with this employment policy of a large consulting firm: "Men added to the professional staff should be between the ages of thirty and thirty-eight." The reason the minimum age was instituted was that clients might object to paying high fees unless all staff men have some maturity and experience. The maximum age was designed to avoid embarrassment if either a man or the firm decided that his employment should be terminated. In the company's experience, it often took three or four years to reach such a conclusion, and if a man was still in his early forties when he left or was let go, he could find another good job with ease. An analysis of this firm after the policy had been in effect for ten years showed that 36 percent of the staff had been employed at ages outside the established limits. What good, then, was the policy? Senior members of the firm insisted that the policy was very helpful. "It is a distillation of our experience. It reminds us that any time we step outside these bounds, we are asking for trouble. However, finding good staff men is so difficult, we do not believe that we should be bound by this single consideration. Because of the policy, we are doubly careful when we stand outside the age limits." In short, this policy served as a guide but not a rule.

Variations in strictness of application will also be found among standard methods. Even the sales pitch of a Fuller Brush man is only suggested, and good salesmen adapt their sales presentation to individual customers. On the other hand, the methods for running a test in a medical laboratory are usually followed precisely so that results will be reliable.

Because standing operating procedures always involve several people, less freedom is possible than with standard methods. Each person relies on the other links in the chain. When exceptions to a usual routine are necessary, everyone affected should be notified, because the very existence

Fig. 18-3 Plans should be clearly plotted out in advance. But they should also be flexible enough to allow for necessary adjustments when put into effect in the field of action.

of the standing procedure creates a presumption that everyone will follow his customary path. Sometimes there is even a standing procedure for making an exception to a standing procedure! Handling rush orders at a plant or registering a special student at a university, for instance, may call for this refinement.

Restrained Use of Rules

Variation in strictness can cause confusion, however. In some cases, the reliability of a standing plan is its virtue. In other instances, rigidity is anything but a virtue. We should recognize the dilemma and deal with it in the following ways.

Making intentions clear. An executive who had built his company from scratch is reported to have had a large rubber stamp that read, "And this time I mean it." When he wanted his orders followed precisely, he used the stamp on any documents involved. Modern executives who are fond of "flexible policies" might well adopt a similar device. Subordinates are often uncertain whether a standing plan is a guide or a rule. Simply making clear how much flexibility is intended will remove much of the confusion.

Establishing rules only for compelling reasons. When we set up a policy, method, or procedure, we often have a strong conviction about the soundness of that plan, and we believe others should follow it to the letter. Our natural tendency is to state it as though it should be strictly observed. But we should remember that a standing plan may remain in effect for a long time. Circumstances may change. The persons who apply the plan later will probably be in a better position to judge its fitness. If they are permitted to treat the policy or method as "recommended practice" they profit by the guidance but are not pushed into action that fails to accomplish major objectives. Consequently we should have compelling reasons for insisting on strict observance.

Strong reasons for strict observance may indeed exist. *Consistency* of action by several people may be necessary, as in pricing to avoid illegal discrimination. Or consistency over time may be desirable; for instance, accounting reports should be comparable from one year to the next. *Dependability* may be crucial if several people must rely on knowing what others will do, as when a plane lands on an aircraft carrier. *Doers may clearly lack judgment* on the subject covered by a standing plan; most operators of electronic computers do not know enough about the inner mechanism to deviate from standard instructions, nor does the boy who is selling magazines to get through college have enough background to adjust subscription rates. In circumstances such as these, standing plans should be strictly observed.

Using the exception principle. The so-called "exception principle" simply refers to an understanding an executive may have with his subordinates that so long as operations are proceeding as planned, the subordinates should not bother him. But when exceptions crop up, they should consult him. The principle applies to standing plans in this way: Subordinates are expected to abide by policies, standard methods, and standing procedures in most instances, but if an unusual condition arises where a standing plan does not seem suitable, they turn the matter over to a higher authority who decides whether an exception should be made. Perhaps the "higher authority" will be the executive who established the standing plan in the first place; at other times, permission to make exceptions may be assigned to lower-level executives. Note that in this latter setup the standing plans are strict rules for operating people, but they are only guides for the executives who handle the exceptional cases. Successful operation of the scheme of course requires that operating people be able to recognize when a situation may merit an exception and therefore demand the attention of the "higher authority."

WHAT TO COVER AND IN HOW MUCH DETAIL?

For what activities should standing plans be established? More specifically: What aspects of such activities? With what type of standing plan—policy, standard method, or standing procedure? In how much detail?

Reasons for Standing Plans

Because the ways of using standing plans and the extent to which they are applied always depend upon specific situations, a manager cannot avoid the continuing task of deciding when to add and when to drop policies, procedures, or standard methods. Here are several potential reasons why a standing plan may be introduced:

1) The need for *consistency* and close *coordination* of work, as we have noted, affects the desirability of detailed planning. Where consistency is crucial, as in accounting, pricing, wages, vacations, and the like, the pressure for detailed plans is strong; where adjustment to local conditions is paramount, detailed plans are liable to get in the way. Similarly if the activities of several persons must interlock (in timing or quality), detailed planning may be necessary; to the extent that work is independent, or coordination is easy to achieve through personal contact, a compelling reason for detailed planning may be lacking.

2) Higher executives may lighten their work load by using standing plans. Once a policy, method, or procedure is developed, an *executive can delegate* to subordinates the job of applying the plan to specific cases. This delegation relieves him of the need to become personally familiar with each case, while at the same time it gives him confidence that work will proceed according to his wishes. One decision—like a pattern in a foundry or a dress shop—can shape the output of many workers.

3) The *quality* of operating decisions may be improved; because a standing plan is followed over and over again, a manager can afford to give careful thought to the formation of the plan. A policy is one means of transmitting the company's heritage of knowledge to many people. The painstaking analysis upon which a standard method is based will benefit many operators when they follow "the one best way."

4) If it uses standing plans extensively, a company may find that it can employ people with less experience or ability to do certain jobs. If so, *payroll economies* should result.

5) Standing plans also lay the *groundwork for control*. By setting up limits within which activities take place, and perhaps by specifying how those activities are to be performed, it is easier to predict results. These predictions can then be translated into control standards as explained in Chapter 24. In fact, establishing detailed plans encourages tight supervision and control, which may or may not be desirable.

6) A manager should also take heed of the people who do the work, as well as of the work itself, in deciding how detailed his plans must be.[2] The greater the dependency of subordinates, the greater the need for detailed plans. Such people want guidance, and they feel ill at ease without it. But if subordinates are highly self-assertive, general rather than detailed plans will be more applicable. Ability also plays a part in deciding on degree of detail. The greater the decision-making talent of most subordinates, and the greater their knowledge about the business, the less detail in planning is necessary.

Drawbacks to Standing Plans

A manager must remember, however, that these possible benefits are offset by several inherent drawbacks, and the more detailed the planning, the greater the drawbacks. Standing plans introduce *rigidity*. Indeed, the purpose of plans is to limit and direct action in a prescribed manner, and such plans become ingrained attitudes and habitual behavior. Especially if the plans are written down, they tend to be followed until new plans are written and approved. Naturally enough, the executives who spend time developing such plans are inclined to defend them. All this means that it will be hard to change standing plans once they are well accepted. In dynamic situations, where frequent change is desirable, such rigidity is a drawback.

[2]Typically a manager is not free to change those already on the job, and their replacements are likely to have about the same attitudes and abilities. Consequently, plans have to be suited to the people, unless a drastic reorganization of the activity, including recruiting new workers, is contemplated.

Planning involves *expense*. Fully as important as direct outlays for industrial engineering and management research is the time that operating executives devote to analysis, discussion, and decision. Teaching people to understand and follow a new plan also takes effort. Unless particular kinds of problems keep recurring, there is no point in even considering standing plans. The more the repetition, either inherent or contrived, the more useful standing plans will be. But as planning is extended to more phases of a business and is increasingly detailed, a point will be reached where the improvements in results do not justify the cost of further planning.

Time taken in preparing and installing standing plans—time for analysis, time to secure approvals, time to develop understanding and skill in their use—may also have strategic value. A customer may want prompt delivery or the board of directors may want a report next week. In such situations, immediate action may be more important than taking time to discover the best possible method.

Clearly, then, the choice of what a standing plan should cover and how detailed it should be is strongly influenced by the particular work and the particular people involved. Essentially, it is the operating situation, not the personal preference of the manager, that dictates a specific structure of planning. The task of a manager is to identify the salient features of each situation.

CONCLUSION

Standing plans are a significant part of a company environment in which workers (managers and operators) make decisions. Policies, standard plans, and standing operating procedures provide decision-makers with limits, alternatives, and other premises. These premises have a double effect: They simplify the task of deciding how a specific problem is to be resolved; and they assure a degree of consistency, dependability, and quality of decision throughout the company.

Nevertheless, the further standing plans are extended the more pressing becomes the dilemma of freedom versus regulation. This is an age-old issue which men have faced as long as they have participated in joint communal activities. But urban living and working together in specialized, purposeful organizations accentuate the problem. How much regulation of individual action is desirable? This question takes many forms and is common in many areas of human activity.

In political philosophy, the problem takes the form of a conflict of authority versus freedom. Every time a law is enacted, it limits someone's freedom. Yet we must have laws when people live together, in order that the actions of one person will not unduly infringe on the actions of others. In psychology and sociology, this is the problem of individual self-expression, initiative, and creativity versus group norms, rules, and customs. Every time a social group derives a customary way of thinking or acting, somebody's decision-making "on his own" is thereby circumscribed. Yet without such customs the group would disintegrate. In ethics, this is the problem of individual dignity versus the common good; and in law, it is a major issue in rendering justice. Finally, in business management, this is the problem of making plans that coordinate the action of people and regulate their activities on the job and their communications, plans that at the same time do not stifle the creativeness and energies of people who are contributing to the group effort.

Unfortunately, no plan is perfect for resolving the conflict between freedom and coordination. In our discussion, we have suggested several key factors a manager should consider in resolving these issues, but his final array of standing plans can be established only on the basis of the specific needs in his particular organization.

Two important aspects of the use of standing plans have not been discussed in this chapter because they are treated in other sections of the book. One is the intimate relation between decentralizing (considered in Chapter 3) and the degree of detailed planning. For instance, if we wish to decentralize, we should do the following: Whenever possible, make the detailed plans *guides* to be followed at a subordinate's discretion; if this is not feasible, provide for quick exceptions to the rule through appeal to some higher executive; and only as a last resort, make the plans a "law" from which no deviations are permitted. Contrariwise, centralization and the wide use of unalterable standing plans go hand in hand.

A second aspect, participation in the preparation of plans, will be explored in Part Five. As we shall see there, the basic conflict between regulation and freedom can be at least relieved by following these guides: In the preparation of a plan, seek the participation of those affected by it; let them help determine the most satisfactory degree of detail; and let them present their views on how various alternatives will work. In addition, allow subordinates continuing freedom to suggest changes in the plan, not only to improve operations, but also to take advantage of their initiative in adjusting details. By such means as these, we must meld the formal planning structure with the interests of the people doing the work.

FOR CLASS DISCUSSION

Questions

1) The president of a large chain of retail stores said, "I estimate that we lose more than $100,000 a year in sales and goodwill by having our store sales personnel follow very specific operating procedures. Though I would like to reduce it, I must regard this loss as a necessary cost of doing business." Explain what you think he meant by this. Do you agree or disagree?

2) "The greatest single limit to creativity and innovation in business is the over-reliance of executives on standing plans. When a problem or opportunity arises, instead of looking at it as it is and seeking to develop a wise course of action, they fall back on a convenient policy or standing operating procedure that at best offers an adequate solution to any of a variety of similar problems or opportunities." Discuss this statement.

3) One solution to the problem of making specific enough plans to offer clear direction, plans that are still broad enough to permit flexibility, was offered by the plant manager of a small electronics firm. "We have very detailed standard plans," he said. "They spell out in very precise terms how certain decisions are to be made and implemented. We get our flexibility, however, by giving department heads and their subordinates great latitude in the interpretation of policies and procedures." What do you think of this approach?

4) What effect, if any, do you think the existence of a headquarters staff unit is likely to have on (1) the type of standing plans used in a company, (2) the scope and detail covered, and (3) the choice between guide and rule? Does the number of people working in the staff unit make any difference? What other features of organization structure will affect the use made of standing plans?

5) Is it possible to develop very detailed standing plans and require them to be strictly interpreted without having those who must follow the plans resent the constraints placed on them?

6) To the degree that standing plans are based on the needs and abilities of personnel who must work with them, might they not need revision with each shift in personnel? How can the need for revision due to shift in personnel be minimized when writing the plans? What factors in matching jobs and individuals, as discussed in Chapter 10, should be reflected in the design and use of standing plans?

7) To what extent may it be wiser to avoid putting policies (not procedures or methods) in written form? Discuss both the pros and cons of avoiding written policies.

8) Consider a fairly significant change in policy that you would like to see implemented in your organization (business, school, class). (1) List other policies affected by this change. (2) List and discuss changes in procedures and methods that would be needed if the change in policy were made and then smoothly integrated.

Cases

For cases involving issues covered in this chapter, see especially the following. Particularly relevant questions are listed after each case.

FOR FURTHER READING

Bower, M., *The Will to Manage*. New York: McGraw-Hill Book Company, 1966, Chap. 4. *Management consultant explains need for policies and procedures to carry out strategy effectively.*

Filley, A.C., and R.J. House, *Managerial Process and Organizational Behavior*. Glenview, Ill.: Scott, Foresman & Company, 1969, Chap. 7. *Excellent discussion on the role of policy and its effect on behavior in organizations.*

Higginson, M.V., *Management Policies I and II*. New York: American Management Association, 1966. *Company practice in formulation and administration of policies; examples of policy statements.*

Neuschel, R.F., *Management by System*. New York: McGraw-Hill Book Company, 1960. *Best book available on analysis and improvement of procedures; relates procedures to total management process.*

Chapter Nineteen

Adaptive Programming

SINGLE-USE PLANS

In the preceding chapters we have examined two broad types of plan—master strategy and objectives, which focus on desired results, and standing plans, which establish a structure of customary behavior for achieving these results. Both types are highly useful devices for managerial decision-making. But they do not exhaust the arsenal of weapons a manager can use in attacking problems.

A third type of managerial plan, as essential as the others for effective management of any group effort, deals with single, rather than repetitive, situations. In such cases, a manager decides in advance what action to take within a given period or what to do to meet a particular problem. Once the time has passed or the problem has been met, a new plan is devised for the next problem. We call these single-use plans.

PROGRAMMING

The basic characteristics of single-use plans can be explained best in terms of programs; other forms, such as schedules and projects, can then be viewed as particular kinds of program. After examining several types of programs, we shall look at timing and implementing strategy, because they are crucial in many programs.

The synchronization of customary, repetitive work is achieved primarily through standing operating procedures and other work habits, as we noted in Chapter 18.

But opening a new office in Harlem, changing organization structure, and countless other executive actions are not routine. They are distinctive, or special, in at least some respects, and their timing calls for specific attention. For such activities, a *program* is needed. A program lays out the principal steps for accomplishing a mission and sets an approximate time for carrying out each step. For an entirely new activity, a program also indicates who should take each step. To cite a very simple example, a program for a branch managers' conference should indicate what topics will be covered, who should lead the discussion on each topic, and when and where each subject will be considered.

Good programming is often crucial to smooth and efficient operations. Consider, for instance, the problem faced by an airline in introducing a new type of plane such as the Boeing 747. Flight crews and ground personnel—literally thousands of people—have to learn new skills. To postpone a reeducation program until the planes are delivered would result in chaos. Instead, a company must anticipate the need for competent maintenance men, experienced flight crews, different weather information, and solutions to other new problems two years ahead of time. Some personnel need classes of only a few hours; others must spend several months learning complex theories and skills. All this training has to be carried on while regular operations with older planes are maintained.

Only through careful programming can an airline (1) anticipate possible crises and make provisions for them, (2) review the subprograms to be sure that they fit together into a consistent whole, (3) avoid hurried decisions that would just get by in favor of taking sound and economical steps, and (4) use its limited (and expensive) training facilities most effectively.

Skill in programming is a major asset for any operating executive. An assistant controller, for instance, needs a program for changing the office layout. A treasurer is concerned with a program for selling new bonds; an executive vice-president works out a program for introducing a new product. Programs, in fact, are useful at all levels in a firm: The president may develop a program for merging two companies, and a first-line supervisor may have a program for training Sally to take over Lorraine's job.

Basic Steps in Programming

Many programming problems can be solved by following six basic steps.[1] In some situations, of course, this approach will not fit exactly.

[1] Adapted from a fuller discussion in W.H. Newman and J.P. Logan, *Strategy, Policy, and Central Management* (Cincinnati: South-Western, 1971), Chap. 21.

But as in learning to ski, it helps to master the fundamentals first; then, we can use variations to meet immediate situations. The basic stages are:

1) *Divide into steps the activities necessary to achieve the objective.* Dividing work into steps is useful for planning, organizing, and controlling. Planning is improved because concentrated attention can be given to one step at a time. Organizing is facilitated because the steps or projects can be assigned to different persons if such a breakdown will give speedier or more efficient action. Controlling is also enhanced because an executive can watch each step and determine whether progress is satisfactory while work is actually being done, instead of waiting for final results. If the division into parts is to be most effective, we should clearly define the purpose of each step, indicating the kind of work, the quality, and the quantity we expect.

2) *Note the relations among each of the steps, especially any necessary sequences.* Usually the parts of a program are closely dependent on one another. The amount of work, the specifications, and the time of action of one step often affect the ease or difficulty of taking the next. Unless these relationships are closely watched, the very process of subdividing the work may cause more inefficiency than it wipes out.

Necessary sequences are particularly significant relationships. In an electric razor sales-promotion program, for example, only after themes and package designs for a national advertising campaign had been settled could displays for windows and counters be prepared, because they were expected to contribute to the impact of the national advertising. Necessary sequences have an important bearing on scheduling because they tend to lengthen the overall time required for an operation; because a shorter cycle gives a company more flexibility, we should carefully check the need for delaying one action until another is completed.

3) *Decide who is to be responsible for doing each step.* If what we are programming is a company's normal operation, the matter of who is to perform each activity will already be settled by the existing organization structure. But if the program covers a new operation, we should give careful attention to deciding who is accountable for each step. These special assignments may create a temporary set of authorizations and obligations. Quite literally, a special team may be formed to carry out the program.

4) *Determine the resources that will be needed for each step.* For realistic programming we must recognize the need for facilities, materials and supplies, and personnel. Next we should appraise the availability of these necessary resources. If any one of them is not available, we should set up another project designed to obtain this resource. For example, if a company is short on qualified personnel, then it should make plans for hiring and training new employees. Many a program breaks down because the executive who prepares it does not realistically understand what resources will be required.

5) *Estimate the time required for each step.* This act really breaks down into two aspects: (1) the date when a step can begin, and (2) the time required to complete an operation once it is started. Starting time, of course, depends on the availability of the necessary resources: How soon key personnel can be transferred to a new assignment, what work is already scheduled for a machine, the likelihood of getting delivery of materials from suppliers, the possibility of subcontracting part of the work— all have an effect on the time any given steps in a particular program may begin.

Processing time, once the activity has begun, is typically estimated on the basis of past experience. In addition, for detailed production operations, time-study data may permit tight scheduling. But for a great many operations, more time is consumed in securing approvals, conveying instructions, and getting people actually to work than is required for doing the work itself. Unless this "nonproductive time" can be eliminated, however, we should include it as part of the estimated time.

6) *Assign definite dates for each part.* An overall schedule is, of course, based on the sequences noted under step 2 and the timing information assembled under step 5. The resulting schedule should show both the starting date and the completion date for each part of the program.

A good deal of adjustment may be necessary to make a final schedule realistic, however. A useful procedure is to try working backward and forward from some fixed controlling date. Availability of materials or facilities may set the time around which the rest of the schedule pivots. In sales, a particular selling season, such as Christmas or Easter, may be the fixed point. We must, of course, dovetail any one program with other company commitments. We must also make some allowance for delay. Allowances all along the line are not desirable, because they would encourage inefficient performance, but a few safety allowances are wise so that an unavoidable delay at one point will not throw off an entire schedule.

In summary, a well-conceived program covers all actions that are necessary to achieve a mission, and it indicates who should do what, and at what time. Note how all the programming elements arise even in this simple example. The controller of a pharmaceutical company decided to install a large Xerox duplicating machine to make multiple copies of the many reports his office issued. The Xerox salesman said, "All you have to do is just plug the machine in." But the controller realized that a shift in the office routine was more complicated than this. After some thought he developed the program that is summarized in the chart shown in Fig. 19–1. With this plan, he was able not only to specify when he wanted the machine delivered but also to prepare both the physical setup and his personnel for the change. He avoided having the office torn up when people were busy with month-end closing, and he had a

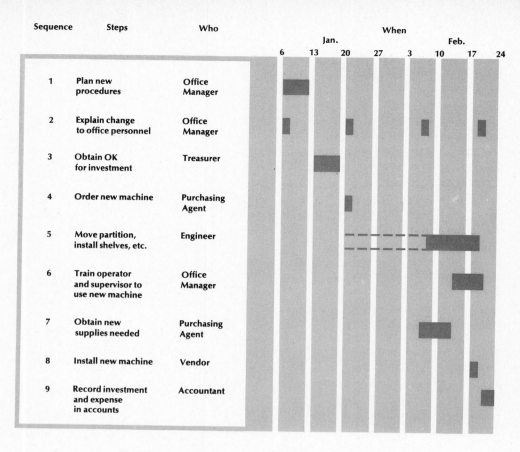

Sequence	Steps	Who	When
			Jan. Feb.
			6 13 20 27 3 10 17 24
1	Plan new procedures	Office Manager	
2	Explain change to office personnel	Office Manager	
3	Obtain OK for investment	Treasurer	
4	Order new machine	Purchasing Agent	
5	Move partition, install shelves, etc.	Engineer	
6	Train operator and supervisor to use new machine	Office Manager	
7	Obtain new supplies needed	Purchasing Agent	
8	Install new machine	Vendor	
9	Record investment and expense in accounts	Accountant	

Fig. 19-1 A program for installing a new duplicating machine in the controller's office. Starting and completion dates for each step are indicated here by the colored bars. The moving of partitions was delayed so that the office would not be torn up at the end of the month. Training included a visit to see a similar machine in operation in another company. Supplies could be obtained quickly from local paper jobbers.

plan that could easily serve as a control as the work progressed. Most programs are more complicated than this, of course, but their essential nature is the same.

Wide Use of Programming

Hierarchy of programs. For some firms, a major program encompasses a large part of company activity. This situation is true in the automobile industry where annual model changes pace the work of all major

442

departments of a manufacturer. Lead times are long, because there is a necessary sequence between market research, styling, engineering, tooling, and actual production and sales. In fact, in any one year a company must do preparatory work for models that will be sold two, three, and four years later.

Such programming of major steps must necessarily lump together large aggregates of work. But each step, in turn, has a program of its own. Thus the stage of providing necessary facilities may be divided into a more detailed schedule showing when building construction and machine purchase must be started and completed. Again, building construction will have its own program, including such steps as defining requirements, selecting a site, getting architectural plans, completing engineering plans, selecting a chief contractor, and so on. The executive charged with, say, finding a site will probably establish an even more detailed program for his own chore.

Detailed programs are not necessarily geared into successively broader programs; any executive may use them by himself if he wishes. Nevertheless, when the programming approach permeates managerial thinking at all levels, it sets a tone and a pace for the entire company.

Projects. Often a single step in a program is set up as a "project." Actually, a project is simply a cluster of activities that is relatively separate and clear-cut. Building a hospital, designing a new package, soliciting gifts of $500,000 for a men's dormitory are examples. A project typically has a distinct mission that it is designed to achieve and a clear termination point, the achievement of the mission.

The task of management is eased when work can be set up in projects. The assignment of duties is sharpened, control is simplified, and the men who do the work can sense their accomplishment. Calling a cluster of work a project does not, of course, change its nature. It may still be part of a broader program, and programming the project itself may be desirable. The chief virtue of a project lies in identifying a nice, neat work package within a bewildering array of objectives, alternatives, and activities.

Schedules. A schedule specifies the time when each of a series of actions should take place. It is one aspect of programs, as we are using that term. When, as a result of standing plans, the tasks to be done and the persons who must do them are clear, then scheduling may be the only element that needs management's attention. This would be the case, for example, in a TV assembly plant where the line is all set to go, as soon as the manager decides when to start and how many of each model to produce. Under some conditions, then, planning is simplified by focusing on scheduling separately. In thinking about management broadly, however, the more inclusive concept of programming has wider usefulness.

Complex schedules are also closely linked to control, as we shall see in Chapter 25 when a special control technique—PERT—is discussed.

444

Part Four

Planning:
Decision-Making
in an Enterprise

STATIC VERSUS ADAPTIVE PROGRAMMING

Our discussion of programming so far has been based on several assumptions that are realistic only part of the time. We have assumed (1) that most of the actions necessary to achieve an objective are subject to direction and manipulation by management, and (2) that management can forecast the time factors—both availability and elapsed time—with considerable accuracy. For a good many problems, notably those that occur chiefly *within* company offices and plants, these assumptions are not far from the mark.

But when the timing of several important steps is outside management's control and is uncertain, the character of programming changes. When we cannot make events conform to a master plan, we need more adaptability, more resourcefulness, and more hedges and retreats. We must still think in terms of major steps, sequences, and timing and duration of each step, but now we must do so creatively rather than perfunctorily as though we were dealing with a routine engineering problem.

Contingency Programs

Typically we draw up a single program; it is the best way we can devise to get from our present position to a stipulated objective. But such a single program requires a lot of uncertainty absorption. We are aware that external events may not occur as predicted and that the results of our actions may not turn out as anticipated. These uncertainties may be serious—perhaps catastrophic. If we stick with our single program we may get into deep trouble.

The most elaborate way to plan for such uncertain events is to prepare contingency programs. Here we prepare in advance a set of programs. Each is ready to use if a particular circumstance arises. In planning flights to the moon, for instance, a whole array of contingency programs are developed in detail. On the Apollo 13 moon shot, such a contingency plan permitted partial completion of the mission and probably saved the lives of the crew. Contingency planning is also common in military operations.

In contrast little contingency planning is done by most enterprises. Aside from limited plans for action in the event of fire, we prefer to focus on making our single program come true. Is this disregard of admitted uncertainty wise?

The reasons for shunning contingency programs are plain. (1) The effort and expense of preparing such programs is large. Contingencies are many, so the number of programs could quickly multiply—as the decision tree on page 325 suggests.[2] To keep the programs viable, necessary preparations have to be put into effect. (2) Contingency programs are disconcerting. A manager tries hard to develop enthusiastic, committed effort behind the preferred program. Discussing and preparing for a lot of "ifs" adds confusion and distraction. (3) Postponement of planning until the contingency arrives (or can be more reliably forecast) *usually* permits us to get by without very serious losses.

The prudent manager, however, should identify those contingencies where the risks are so large that special programs are justified and should make sure that sequential adjustments—discussed in the next section—are made promptly.

Sequential Adjustments

An alternative to setting up contingency programs is making successive modifications in a program as unpredicted (or unassumed) conditions move to the center of the stage.

Anticipating that feedback data will lead to revisions. One way to deal with unpredictable and uncontrollable conditions is to ensure a flow of current information as work progresses and to adjust the program when necessary. A surgeon has a general plan of action before an operation starts; a football coach may have a game-plan in mind before the kickoff. But each of these men expects to be guided more by current developments than by his prediction. An executive development program is similar; a company may have a tentative ten-year plan for the progression of its outstanding young men, but everyone expects that the actual performance of these men and the needs of the company will lead to drastic modifications of the program long before the ten years are up.

On the matter of revising plans, the key distinction between static and adaptive programming lies in executive attitude toward change. When a program is regarded as a blueprint, an executive is heavily motivated to make the plan work; changes, he feels, are a confession of partial defeat. But under the adaptive approach, the manager considers some change normal and actually seeks reasons to modify plans.

Long-range programming, which we have already discussed in Chapter 16 as a device for rounding out a company's master strategy, is always

[2]In theory decision trees differ sharply from contingency programs. A decision tree is designed to help make a single decision now; the spelling out of various courses. results, and probabilities is intended to throw light on a present choice among alternatives. A contingency program, on the other hand, is concerned with future action; it does not weigh probabilities, but says what to do if a given situation occurs. However, in reality the decision-tree estimates lack reliability unless they are based on some kind of programs, and the by-product effect of thinking through how various contingencies will be met is likely to be the chief benefit of decision-tree analysis. So the two concepts do tend to merge.

revised periodically. It is a prime example of anticipating that feedback data will lead to revision of the program. In other programs the feedback and revision cycle occurs more frequently, perhaps monthly or when key steps are completed—for example, after test marketing or when the quantity of available funds is firmly established.

Restricting scheduling to the near future. When a pharmaceutical company put a new tranquilizer on the market, all the executives were confident of a rapid growth in sales, and there was talk of enlarging the plant, opening new branch offices, and using profits for additional research. Until the hoped-for sales volume actually developed, however, specific programming was confined to promoting the new product. Timing and determining the magnitude of other moves were held in abeyance until sales prospects became more certain.

A manufacturer of women's shoes got into trouble for not following a similar course. The firm opened a new plant in the South; it borrowed money and changed executive personnel on the assumption that most of its production could be transferred to the new plant within two years. Actually, the company had great difficulty in securing quality production from its new plant, and training expenses and spoilage made costs even higher than at the old plant. Consequently, the company was forced to postpone the move and found itself in serious financial difficulty. Had this firm merely scheduled the opening of the new plant, while leaving the time of closing the old factory unsettled, it might have avoided the crisis.

These devices for flexibility—anticipating changes and deferring program commitments except for the near future—sacrifice some benefits

Fig. 19-2 When a ship is sailing in uncharted waters, its progress is slow. Its destination is known, but its speed and course depend on current assessment of the path of the channel and underwater obstacles. So it is with sequential adjustment. Although the ultimate goal is known, progress toward the goal is slow because the total situation is reassessed after each step. As our assessment techniques improve, progress in new situations or uncharted waters can be speeded up.

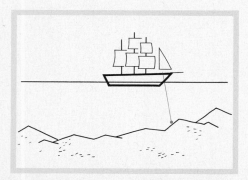 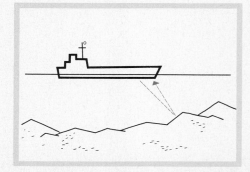

of a clear, positive program. Preparing for the future is more difficult and
some economies may be lost. But these drawbacks are simply the price
paid for a somewhat cautious approach to an unpredictable future.

Adjusting to leads and lags in the flow of goods. A program for a
continuing flow of goods and services differs in important respects from
a program for a single event. Producers and distributors of goods, such
as gasoline or steel, must think in terms of a *rate* of output for a given
week or month. Such companies may be affected by seasonal fluctuations
in consumption and by the buildup or cutback of inventory in the hands
of distributors and perhaps consumers. Any operating program for such
firms must take these fluctuations into account. Thus production must
precede seasonal peaks in demand, and if a stable level of operations is
desired, a firm must build inventories. A manufacturer must also attempt
to distinguish between a temporary flurry to build up stocks and an increase
in demand that will be sustained.

Programs that deal with the flow of goods rarely provide exactly the
rate of activity that proves to be needed. The rates of flow must be
adjusted, a little here and a little there, somewhat as we adjust the hot
and cold water taps in a shower bath. When a variety of products is
involved, this adjusting process becomes complex.[3] Most companies have
operating programs for some months ahead, but revise them at least
monthly on the basis of feedback information. For perishable products,
like bread, adjustments may be more frequent—even daily.

A program, then, must be suited to the operations it covers—building a monument or running a coal mine, for instance—but its essentials
remain the same. By anticipating the what, who, how, and when, it enables
a manager to prepare systematically and carefully for difficulties before
they arise.

TIMING AND IMPLEMENTING STRATEGY

Importance of Timing

Timing deserves special emphasis. Many a plan, sound in all other
respects, has failed in application because action was taken at the wrong
time. Out on the plains of Kansas, one of the early business promoters
built a large brick building to house a university. For a decade the building
stood like a mirage on the horizon, lacking faculty, students, and finances.

---

[3]Programming in terms of flows rather than for specific projects is a source of confusion in government planning. The national income accounts, which reflect flows,
are frequently used to express fiscal policy, but Congress makes appropriations primarily for a particular project or on an annual appropriation basis. Aside from Federal
Reserve actions, we have few good mechanisms (like hot and cold water taps) to
adjust the flows of goods and services.

The building has since been put to excellent use, but the timing of its construction speaks more eloquently of the pioneer's dream than of his good judgment.

More recently, a shipping company built a large dock on Lake Erie anticipating the movement of ocean freight through the St. Lawrence Waterway. The volume of business has been so slow in developing that the dock is now closed down. Perhaps ten years hence the necessary traffic *will* develop, but clearly the construction was premature. On the other hand, many a product has reached its market after the demand has waned—witness the multimillion-dollar loss on the Edsel automobile. Similarly, there are better and poorer times to ask the boss for a raise, to buy raw materials, and to float a bond issue.

Time is an important dimension that must be included before plans are complete. Let us look first at three ways in which this time factor is introduced into the planning process and then briefly at the main factors that may lead a manager to speed up or slow down his actions.

How Timing Enters the Planning Process

A manager can introduce the timing element into his plans in several ways: as a consideration in each operating decision, as an aspect of programming, or as a planning premise. The simplest way is for the manager deliberately to try to pick an *opportune moment* to put each *separate decision* into effect. This works well enough when the action is not closely related to a series of other actions and the decision-maker can be allowed freedom in moving quickly or slowly.

But when a proposed action is a necessary step in a whole chain of events, its timing will be strongly influenced by the *program* covering the entire change. Even here, the repercussions of performing one step at a specified time should be appraised, as we suggested on pages 440 and 441. If a new product, for instance, is scheduled for a pilot run in the plant just at a peak production season, perhaps a delay is called for. Most activities have a time when they can be done most easily; if we schedule them earlier or later than this optimum period, costs will rise. The executive preparing the program, then, has to weigh such added costs against benefits to the entire program if the step is performed sooner or later than the convenient dates. Note that in this kind of a problem we use programs as the managerial tool for adjusting the time action is to take place.

In other circumstances, activities may not be sufficiently interrelated to call for a program, but we still want consistency of action in several areas. Here a *planning premise* can provide guidance on timing. For instance, the president of a refrigerator company may tell his executives to assume that a current steel strike will be settled before the supply of parts is seriously interrupted. That premise will influence the timing of placing purchase orders, scheduling production, and, indirectly perhaps, the delivery dates promised to customers and vacation schedules. Similarly a premise that the research and engineering department will have a new product ready for production by January 1 affects the speed of the production, marketing, and other departments in getting ready for this addition to the line.

But on what basis does a manager set planning premises, alter a program, or modify a separate action to get better timing? Broadly speaking, a manager may act faster or slower than otherwise would be most convenient for him because of two factors: economic conditions and likely responses of key people.

Adjusting to External Conditions

Often the timing of a company's action has to be adjusted to external conditions or, more precisely, to a *forecast* of external conditions. This is no simple task. A United States exporter of motorcycles, for example, expanded his foreign organization just before Japanese products became popular and then faced increasing expenses at a time when he should have been retrenching. Even the most successful companies may misjudge market demand. When Dacron fiber was first being introduced to the market, for instance, du Pont built production facilities that far exceeded the demand. As a result, a new $18,000,000 plant was idle for more than two years. The demand eventually developed, but the mistake lay in judging how fast it would do so.

Improving forecasts. Man's ability to foretell the future has always been limited, and it is unreasonable to hope for more than modest gains in forecasting. To be sure, special methods have been devised to predict broad economic trends and to make market analyses. Still the tempo of business change is accelerating, and new technology requires us to try to look farther into the future. The need for good forecasts keeps growing even more rapidly than our ability to make them.

Many errors in timing can be avoided, however, by following a well-known rule: Take an objective view and get all the facts available. We all usually have a strong bias about what we want a forecast to say—that, for example, demand will go up just when we are ready to produce, or that competitors will not cut prices this year. But somehow, either through talking to outsiders who are not directly concerned or through mental self-discipline, we should make a detached forecast of a situation. Unwillingness to face fairly clear trends in the wallpaper industry, for instance, led one company to postpone closing an old and inefficient plant; this decision prevented the company from taking the necessary steps to pull itself out of serious indebtedness.

Assembling facts to help improve forecasting depends as much on executive attitude as on statistical procedure. The president of a company making steam locomotives, for example, felt he knew from his long experience in the industry that diesel engines were unsuited for long-haul service. He simply did not get all the facts. The chief engineer of another company designed an excellent baking oven suited to the needs of two important customers, only to discover later that most customers wanted a less elaborate product. Competitors obtained more complete market information and stole the lead on this product. Time and again, we find our forecasts are poor because we fail to get and use available data. Even though we lack time and money to make an elaborate study, jumping to conclusions is unnecessary. As a minimum, we should identify the key factors that affect the future success of a specific plan and then think where pertinent information about these factors might be found.

Keeping flexible. When forecasts are not fully reliable—and few are —a wise executive seeks to *avoid making commitments until necessary*. He tries to distinguish between a bear-by-the-tail situation and one that consists of independent steps. For example, in a marketing program one move, such as national advertising, may necessitate a string of accompanying moves. As in passing a car on a crowded two-lane highway, once we start we have to follow through. But in many research projects, a process may be halted at the end of any of several steps and then started up again without major loss. In the latter situation, new timing is possible; in fact, further planning may be deferred until the results of the last step are known.

A related way to retain flexibility is to *keep two or more alternatives open*. At one stage in its development, Boeing Aircraft had a large military contract that would eventually necessitate a new plant. The time arrived when the firm had to acquire a plant site and begin engineering work if the terms of the military contract were to be met, yet there was sharp disagreement among several parties involved about the location of the plant. To avoid being caught later in a time squeeze, the company took options on land in both the Seattle and San Francisco areas and hired engineers to make detailed plans for plants in both localities. More than a year later, but before any building contracts were let, the Seattle location was selected. The company kept two alternatives open until it became clear which one should be followed. Note that substantial costs were involved in obtaining this flexibility. Boeing had to pay for two land options and two sets of engineering plans when it knew that only one would eventually be used. Often, it seems, flexibility can be achieved only at a price.

Anticipating Reactions of Key People

Among the many forecasts needed for good timing of executive action is a prediction of how key people will react to various parts of a program. Temptation is always strong to concentrate on tangible, quantitative elements and slide over the more evasive human factors. Yet the responses of people may make or break a program. Often a proposed action calls for a major effort or readjustment on the part of several individuals or groups, and their behavior patterns, beliefs, and values may be involved. In timing, we have to judge when the situation is ripe for a new move.

For years a leading department store in the Midwest had never used blacks in sales positions. The personnel director believed this tradition should be changed. However, he anticipated resistance from most supervisors and salesclerks. So he waited until there was a shortage of well-qualified salespeople and then hired two blacks, placing them under supervisors who were sympathetic to the change. Actually, these two were noticeably better qualified than most of the white people who could be employed at the time. Word got around that they were unusually competent, and in a few months the idea of black salespeople had become accepted. Soon, several other supervisors were asking for similar help. Had this change been introduced when well-qualified white applicants were in ample supply and were being turned down, the response might have been quite different.

Here is another example. A large bank had just installed a long-needed job evaluation system. Officers and supervisors were pleased with the way the system was working, and the vice-president in charge of personnel was anxious to move on to a training program that was also badly needed. The president turned down the proposal. His explanation was that job evaluation had not yet become normal behavior within the bank. To introduce a second change on the heels of the first "might give us indigestion." This was the president's judgment on how fast his particular group could comfortably adapt to a new personnel practice. Of course, if the need for the training program had been more urgent, perhaps he would have taken a greater risk. But his decision to hold off was apparently sound, for the training program actually was initiated about a year and a half later, and it too has been well accepted.

An executive with a good feel for timing must be socially perceptive. He must know enough about people's needs, hopes, and fears to be able to anticipate their reaction to a proposed plan.

Implementing Strategies

The master strategy of a company, as described in Chapter 16, includes the timing of major moves. Another form of strategy that is less grand in scope involves the directness and speed of implementing a course of action.

Here is a simple, but broad, definition of implementing strategy: It is a matter of adjusting a plan in anticipation of the reactions of those who will be affected. But choice of strategy is based on a variety of factors: urgency of achieving an objective, available resources, temperament of the executive who is making the decision, as well as predictions of external conditions and of responses of key people, which we have just discussed above. Several illustrations of business strategies will demonstrate their nature and importance.[4]

Mass, concentrated offensive. Occasionally, an executive will decide to push through a plan despite opposition and obstacles. Ralph Cordiner did so when he decided to decentralize the management of the General Electric Company. Orders were given, positions were abolished, the gospel was preached, new organization plans were carefully prepared, the most elaborate management education program ever tried in industry was launched, and a few recalcitrants were fired. Within a mere three years, thousands of executives had changed their way of thinking, and the company was prepared to handle the largest volume of business in its history. Rarely has such a large company been changed so drastically so fast.

Fabianism—avoiding decisive engagement. This strategy seeks gradual changes rather than revolutionary ones. The head of an industrial equipment company chose this approach in his engineering department. The engineers, he felt, were too professional in their outlook and not sufficiently oriented to customer needs. Drastic action would have upset morale and probably caused valuable men to resign. So the president made arrangements to have the engineers visit customers' plants; they were invited to sit in with the salesmen when bids on important jobs were being prepared; those engineers who helped meet tough problems posed by a customer were given public commendation; the chief engineer counseled with his men about how they could make their work more valuable to the company. Thus, although management ventured no single dramatic action, the point of view of the engineers changed substantially over a period of time.

Letting someone else pull your chestnuts out of the fire. For years, the thought of variable annuities was shocking to the life insurance industry. But gradually, more companies could see that here was a new form of insurance that would be tied roughly to the general price level. Still, many of the firms that favored variable annuities were happy to let the Prudential Insurance Company carry the brunt of the bitter fight to obtain government permission to sell this new type of coverage. While secretly hoping Prudential would win, they maintained a neutral and respectable position in the industry.

Boring from within. The potency of this strategy in the hands of Communists is well known, but a similar approach may be used in many different situations. One company used it to get its executives to take an active part in community affairs. No general program was announced. Instead, management identified men sympathetic to this cause throughout

---

[4]For additional examples of implementing strategies, see W.H. Newman, *Administrative Action*, 2nd ed. (Englewood Cliffs, N.J.: Prentice-Hall, 1963), pp. 86–98.

the branches of the company, and used them to spread the point of view. Occasionally these men would have dinner with one of the vice-presidents, at which time they talked over progress and problems; more often, however, just two or three would meet together for a discussion. All shared a missionary zeal for "having businessmen live up to civic responsibilities." Although top management let its endorsement of this type of activity be known, the effective ferment really started with these dedicated people— and it took hold in several branches where the local manager was far from enthusiastic.

Things must get worse before they get better. The treasurer of a family-owned company with a five-million-dollar sales volume was convinced that companywide budgets should be installed. Other members of top management were lukewarm to this "big company device." In view of their position, the treasurer might have prepared some estimates simply for his own use. But instead, he waited until the company had a poor six months during which expenses went up while sales went down. There was a good deal of grumbling about who should have done what. At this point, the treasurer again suggested budgetary control. The potential benefits were now clear, and all the executives took an active part in operating the new system.

Striking while the iron is hot. This strategy calls for prompt action while a situation is propitious. Take this example. When the sales manager of a chemical company decided to retire because of ill health three years before the normal retirement age, simply replacing him would have been relatively easy. But because several readjustments in the whole sales management organization were about due, the president seized this opportunity to push through other modifications that would have been resisted if they had been initiated as separate, conspicuous moves.

Keeping one jump ahead. In some circumstances, being the leader is a decided advantage. The management of IBM followed this strategy when that company received orders from the Army for two electronic computers of advanced design. Although the engineering was incomplete and several tough production problems remained to be solved, the company decided

Fig. 19-3 Various ways of moving toward the goal of racial equality. On each front, strategy issues arise concerning methods to be used and the pace with which to proceed.

to go ahead with the production of twenty such machines in order to lead its competitors in marketing this type of computer. The gamble was great for two reasons: (1) several million dollars were poured into the project, and (2) by seeking commercial orders, the company risked damaging its reputation if the machines could not be successfully produced. Fortunately for IBM, this strategy paid off handsomely, although at the time it was by no means clear that the move was a wise one.

Red herring across the trail. With this strategy, a deliberate attempt is made to divert attention. The manager of a European office for a United States manufacturer was a master in the use of this strategy. Whenever he had a sour deal or a messy situation to clean up, he would meet his colleagues in the home office bubbling with enthusiasm about some new proposition with great possibilities. Once the home office executives became intrigued with the new proposal, they had difficulty finding time to examine the trouble spots throughly. The resulting delay gave the foreign representative more time to work out of his difficulties.

These examples of implementing strategy carry us a long way from the rather mechanistic concept of programming discussed in the beginning of this chapter. They strongly suggest the need for some qualitative inputs in the framing of a program. Such implementing strategy need not override or displace a program; rather, it often enters as one of the considerations in making adaptive adjustments.

CONCLUSION

Chapter 15, the opening chapter of Part Four, concerned decision-making in organizations. It dealt primarily with how the problem-solving process described in Part Three is carried out in organizations explored in Parts One and Two. As we examined the ways in which diagnosis occurs, creative ideas are generated, alternatives are compared, and choices are made it became apparent that each decision cannot be treated as an isolated, one-time event. Instead an organization must have a planning structure to expedite decisions, to gain continuity and consistency, and to take advantage of the strengths derived from functioning as an integrated group. So in the last four chapters we analyzed four basic aspects of the planning structure in any enterprise: master strategy, operating objectives, plans for stabilized action, and programming.

This breakdown of the managerial process into parts and subparts enables us to look closely at fundamental elements. But inevitably it makes separations neater than they are in practice. As we have indicated, the master strategy is partly shaped by existing organization, but also it determines the future organization that will be needed. Both operating objectives and standing plans must be drawn in light of departmentation and decentralization, but contrariwise the way such plans can be expressed influences the degree of decentralization and the role of staff. We have just seen that programming may stipulate who is to perform each step, and yet the design of organization strongly influences the way programs are put together. These are only examples of the interrelationships. Organizing and planning are not a one-two punch. Instead they are a kind of reciprocal motion, like the push and pull on a double-handled saw.

A second recurring theme is that of freedom versus regulation of individual behavior. As managers we want unified effort *and* individual initiative, commitment to enterprise objectives *and* fulfillment of personal needs, use of expert judgment *and* creative imagination, coordinated action *and* individual resourcefulness. Fortunately, wise management can provide some of both. In many chapters we have indicated explicitly the factors a manager should weigh in deciding when the benefits of giving individuals discretion counterbalance the advantages of regulation. But the choice is not easy, especially in view of changing values and expectations of the new work force. In this arena the role of leadership is crucial. The process of leading is the subject of Part Five.

FOR CLASS DISCUSSION

Questions

1) Would it be possible to develop standing plans for use in making single-use plans? If so, would such action be desirable?

2) How should a manager determine when to develop a contingency program rather than write a more flexible plan that allows those who must implement it to make on-the-spot adjustments if circumstances require?

3) Is good planning virtually synonymous with good budgeting? How do plans and budgets differ?

4) In what ways will the degree of decentralization influence the way in which the basic steps in programming are taken and coordinated?

5) Develop a fuller set of criteria for determining when contingency planning would prove most desirable.

6) You have been asked by the mayor of your home town, Suburbia, Illinois, population 7,000, to organize and direct a one-day outing for the town's children. The mayor would like to hold the outing in a state park some 25 miles from town and agrees to put up $1,500 to cover the cost of food, transportation, and other expenses. (1) Set up a program for carrying out this assignment indicating where and how you have employed each of the six basic steps in programming. (2) Illustrate how you might reduce the amount of detailed planning you would face by delegating individual projects to townspeople willing to help. (3) What schedules would you have to devise to make the outing run smoothly? (4) How would you provide for the possibility of rain or a larger turnout than estimated?

7) Good planning is based in large part on good forecasting. Yet, areas that are most difficult to forecast are typically most in need of planning. How do you reconcile these statements with the need for, and elements of, good plans?

8) In what ways may plans be tested for completeness and potential soundness?

Cases

For cases involving issues covered in this chapter, see especially the following. Particularly relevant questions are listed after each case.

Scott-Davis Corporation (p. 227), 12
Dodge Skate Company (p. 337), 13
E.W. Ross, Inc. (p. 468), 11

FOR FURTHER READING

Bennis, W.G., "Theory and Method in Applying Behavioral Science to Planned Organizational Change," in *Emerging Concepts in Management*, ed. M.S. Wortman and F. Luthans. New York: The Macmillan Company, 1969, pp. 196–210. *Discusses need for more systematic attention to "planned-change" programs.*

Berg, T.L., and A. Shuchman, eds., *Product Strategy and Management*. New York: Holt, Rinehart & Winston, Inc., 1963, pp. 569–86. *Marketing program for a new product.*

Drucker, P.F., *The Effective Executive*. New York: Harper & Row, Publishers, 1966, Chaps. 1–5. *Programming one's own time.*

Hardwick, C.T., and B.F. Landuyt, *Administrative Strategy and Decision Making*, 2nd ed. Cincinnati: South-Western Publishing Co., 1966. *Full analysis of operating strategies.*

Moore, F.G., and R. Jablonski, *Production Control*, 3rd ed. New York: McGraw-Hill Book Company, 1969, Chaps. 20 and 21. *Techniques of production scheduling, many of which are applicable to general programming.*

Case Studies

FOR PART FOUR

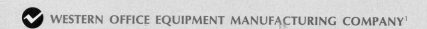 WESTERN OFFICE EQUIPMENT MANUFACTURING COMPANY[1]

Western Office Equipment Manufacturing Company was founded in Salt Lake City, Utah, in 1925, for the purpose of making and selling steel utility shelving used in offices and warehouses. Today it is still a family-owned company, though with the retirement of the founder six years ago, a professional manager, Charles F. Porter, was employed as president. The company still makes its original line of steel shelving but has added a diverse line of medium-priced desks, chairs, bookcases, and other small furniture. Porter says, "We have never tried to compete with high-quality manufacturers—our customers are medium and smaller companies who want serviceable furniture at a good price." Current sales volume is $3,830,000.

Modernization under Mr. Porter's Direction

Since he assumed the presidency, Charles Porter has, in the words of one member of the founding family,

[1]Copyright 1972, Charles E. Summer.

457

*measured up to our expectations. Before he came to our head-
quarters in Salt Lake City, the company was successful mostly by trial
and error. We had developed a good line of products, and our salesmen were good. We were selling in Salt Lake, San Francisco, and
Vancouver. Those places were chosen somewhat by accident. The
founder was originally from Seattle, worked for an eastern competitor and knew those districts well. He had fifteen salesmen when
he retired, all reporting to Mr. Roberts, the marketing vice-president
here in Salt Lake. Several years ago, we entered Los Angeles on a
very modest basis because we hired an excellent salesman who knew
customers and the market there. Today, Porter has organized the
fifteen company salesmen into four district offices, with one of the
senior men serving as district manager. He has also added new products to the line, set up accounting and profit controls, and enabled
us to compete as we never have before with companies that are
much larger than ours. In short, our objective is to grow, and Porter
is the man we depend on for that.*

Allocation of Selling Effort

Among other ways of improving the company, the effective allocation of salesmen to territories has been one of Porter's concerns.

*After I joined the firm [Porter said], there were many things to do.
I did not have time to look into the matter of selling effectiveness.
Sam Roberts, the marketing vice-president, and I looked at the statistics on selling as the company began to grow. We set the policy
that the company should add salesmen to a district as long as the
average sales per salesman in the district did not fall below $250,000.*

The current allocation of salesmen by district, the average sales per
salesman, and the total sales volume are shown in Exhibit 1.
Porter continued:

*We have fifteen salesmen—six in San Francisco, four each in Salt
Lake City and Vancouver, and one in Los Angeles. Several months
ago, we redefined the objectives of the company to include growth
in four districts. Salt Lake City handles Nevada, Wyoming, Colorado,
Idaho, and Montana. San Francisco handles central California; and
Vancouver handles British Columbia, Washington, and Oregon. The
really important decision has been to enter the Los Angeles market
on a full-scale basis.*

*John Olson has been with us as manager of operations analysis
for three years. He specialized in finance and operations research at
Stanford and has done very much to analyze our plant facilities by
using modern quantitative methods. I have asked him to analyze
the selling effort with this objective in mind: How can we allocate
salesmen in districts so that (1) we get the most sales from our total*

sales force, and (2) we employ the least number of salesmen to achieve this volume? In other words, I wanted him to establish some standard that will tell us how many men to hire and where to put them to get the most volume. The company is growing more complex, and we need some guide that can be applied over the years—I do not want rule-of-thumb assignment on the basis of who a particular salesman is. Decisions have to be made for the business as a whole, and over a period of years.

Olson's Analysis and Recommendations

John Olson spent the first month of his analysis visiting with district managers in the four districts. In each case he explained to them that his purpose was to forecast statistics on potential sales in the district under differing manpower assumptions. For example, he would ask the San Francisco manager to study with him market-potential figures from trade associations, statistics on number and types of businesses in the district, and other materials that he had worked up and brought with him. Then he asked the manager to use his own knowledge of territories, distances between customers, severity of competition by other companies, and other information. Finally, he and the manager jointly discussed both the territory characteristics and the market-research data.

Olson described the results:

In each case, we arrived at the estimates in Exhibit 2. Look at San Francisco. You will see that if Western employs only one salesman, we would sell $400,000. If two, $750,000; if five, $1,430,000. The incremental amount sold by each salesman decreases as you add salesmen in a district because the first salesman gets the best customers, the shortest distances to cover, and other advantages. With only one salesman, we would skim the cream off the market. Each time we add another salesman, we either take less desirable customers or raise the cost of reaching customers, or both. In fact, you can see in the column marked "marginal" the incremental amount of sales volume generated by adding one more salesman in each territory.

Notice, too, that the amount that can be sold by each salesman varies by district. The first salesman in San Francisco will sell $400,000, but the first one in Los Angeles will sell only $250,000. These inter-district differences are caused by various factors—there may be more competition in one market than in another, or the distance between cities and customers may be greater and so the result will be fewer calls per day.

Once having determined these figures, the next step was to discover a way of measuring what a salesman is worth to the company. In financial terms, what is his contribution to the company profit picture? It costs the company an average of $40,000 a year to support a salesman. From the records, I found that this does not vary much by districts. At a conference between myself, Sam Roberts, and the district managers, we compared figures on salesmen's performance and agreed that for our company and our line of products there is very little difference in salesmen's capabilities. We have some differences, but salesmen are very similar in output.

Given this $40,000 cost, what does the salesman produce in profit contribution? Well, we very carefully got accounting figures to show that the total cost of delivering products to customers (except the cost of salesmen) was 70 percent of sales. This means that the salesman is adding 30 percent of sales as his part of the contribution to profits. Now here is the important point. We will break even if a salesman sells $133,333 worth of merchandise. Thirty percent of $133,333 is $40,000. If the salesman sells just that, he pays (in revenues) for himself. Anything beyond that is a contribution to profits. Stated in reverse, if his sales fall below $133,333, he is paid more than he contributes.

This is known as incremental analysis. In economics we learn that any resource may be evaluated this way. That is, a company should add additional units of any resource up to the point where marginal cost exceeds marginal revenue.

Now to apply this to Western's sales force, we must look at the marginal column for each district (see Exhibit 2). In the Salt Lake district, the second salesman will add $400,000 to sales, but the third will add only $110,000. Or in Los Angeles, the third salesman will add $210,000.

District	Current Volume (000)	Planned Volume (000)
Salt Lake City	$1,060	$ 850
Los Angeles	250	1,000
San Francisco	1,500	1,300
Vancouver	1,020	900
Totals	$3,830	$4,050

Finally, we can convert all of the analysis to total profits for Western:

	Profit Increase with New Volume (000)
Sales with new allocation	$4,050
Sales volume at present	3,830
Increase in sales volume	$ 220
Profit margin (multiply)	.30
Additional profit	$ 66

The incremental analysis shows that the company should take the following actions, based on the standard of $133,333:

1) *Reduce the sales force in Salt Lake district from the present four salesmen to two.*
2) *Increase the sales force in Los Angeles district from one man to five.*
3) *Decrease the number of salesmen in San Francisco from six to four.*
4) *Decrease the salesmen in Vancouver district from four to three.*

You will also notice that the total sales force comes out to be fourteen, instead of the present fifteen. The reason is that there is nowhere we can put a fifteenth salesman that he will produce the standard sales volume to break even.

Other managerial decisions are also solved by applying this standard. For example, here are the new sales volume quotas compared to the old sales performance figures for each district.

Top Management Approval

John Olson kept Charles Porter informed throughout his analysis, giving reasoning identical with that presented to the casewriter. At the conclusion, using easel charts, he presented the complete report to Porter and the Board of Directors. At that time, one board member said that it looked to him as if one could not draw conclusions about what a salesman could sell until he knew the specific salesman. "Some salesmen simply are better than others." Porter answered that while there will be deviations, a company cannot plan its structure of divisions, including where offices will be located and the size of the sales force, on the basis of one salesman's characteristics. "If he leaves the company, we would have no logical and rational plan."

Porter questioned Olson on how the division managers would receive the new plan and standard. He specifically wanted to know if Olson had obtained their agreement. Olson replied:

I have their complete agreement that our company must plan where to add salesmen on an economic basis. All managers agreed that, for the sake of our competitive position, we must do this. Also, in my meetings with division managers they each helped to draw up the amounts that would be sold by each additional salesman in their regions. In other words, the marginal and total sales figures in Exhibit 2 are their estimates as much as mine.

The board, noting that both the added $66,000 of profits and the expansion into the more profitable market of Los Angeles (from $250,000 sales to $1,000,000) were consistent with the company's growth goal, approved the new plan. On recommendation of Porter, it set a target of three years for transfer of salesmen and buildup to the new district quotas.

Porter then made an implementation plan. He stated that he

> knew that there would be considerable upset among the salesmen and the district managers. In consultation with Sam Roberts, we decided to transfer two men each from Salt Lake and San Francisco to Los Angeles. One of the salesmen in Vancouver will have to be terminated. We decided on him because he only has two years to go until retirement.
>
> Nevertheless, there are times in managing a business when you have to take steps that aren't too popular. It may cause some anxiety in our company temporarily, but five years from now everyone will be operating on the new plan as if it were always that way.

Reactions of Field Personnel

A meeting of district managers was held at the Fairmont Hotel in San Francisco to explain the new financial and selling plan. Porter thought it best not to mail the plan in advance, but simply to explain all of the details on a face-to-face basis. "I thought it necessary to explain the whole thing at once. Only in this way could we get a meaningful understanding of it. If we mailed it in advance, the managers may have focused on only one part or aspect of the whole plan."

Porter opened the meeting by calling attention to the goal of the company to grow, using the most modern management and selling methods available.

> I'm sure that each of you want our company to use our resources to produce the best products at lowest cost to the customer. In this way, we will always be able to stay efficient and come out ahead of competition. For this reason, I know you will want to understand thoroughly a new plan for district realignment—one that is based on the markets "out there"—that takes best advantage of where the customers are who we can serve in the most efficient way. I'm sure, too, that you are interested in the fact that we have set as our goal our company becoming a leading supplier in the Rocky Mountain and West Coast states. We will no longer simply put our efforts into districts as they have grown up, often somewhat by accident, over the years.

Later, John Olson gave a complete summary of the reasoning behind the new moves, as well as a summary of his analytical methods. At the conclusion, Porter stated that there was plenty of time for questions. "I certainly want you district managers to feel free to question John or me, so that you can satisfy yourself that you know what we are doing and why."

Robert Perry, the manager-salesman from Los Angeles, stated that he had been waiting for months for the go-ahead signal to expand sales there. "The market is there just waiting to be sold. Within three years we will show those larger national firms how to sell."

Ralph Hudson asked Olson why it made sense to transfer two of his salesmen, thus decreasing his sales force by 50 percent, when his four salesmen were averaging $265,000 sales each.

> You and I both agree [Hudson said] that salesmen who are doing above $133,000 are making money for the company. The average salesman in the Salt Lake district is not only doing over that, but our average salesman is selling more than that of any other district. It just doesn't seem logical, from the company's viewpoint, to cut down from over $1,000,000 sales to $850,000. Why, I would be giving away customers to competition.

Porter clarified at length the reasoning that Olson had reported in the case. "But I don't think we really got across. Ralph said that he of course would be willing to do what is best for the company, but the tone of his voice and the relative lack of enthusiasm seemed negative."

James Fulmer said that he had just recently started new sales training programs in San Francisco and instituted a new kind of advertising at the same cost as his previous campaigns.

> In this way, I will eventually get those fifth and sixth salesmen up above $133,000 in production. It may take a couple of years, but I can do it. I believe that you should leave the six salesmen in San Francisco. In fact, though your production forecasts are correct, and I helped draw them up, I had no idea you would draw these kinds of conclusions from them.

Exhibit 1 Current Annual Sales Volume*
and Salesmen Distribution by District,
Western Office Equipment Manufacturing Company

District	Number of Salesmen	Total Sales Volume	Average Sales Volume per Salesman
Salt Lake City	4	$1,060	$265
Los Angeles	1	250	250
San Francisco	6	1,500	250
Vancouver	4	1,020	255
Totals†	15	$3,830	

*All amounts given in thousands of dollars.
†Average sales per salesman for the company as a whole:
3,830/15 = 255.3, or $255,300.

Both Hudson and Fulmer questioned how their districts could grow if the company were actually cutting out salesmen and lowering the sales targets, which implied cutting out customers.

Porter explained:

Actually, I see three ways. First you can make better use of sales training and promotion campaigns to raise the marginal sales of each salesman. These are examples of ingenious new methods that can be invented within your own districts. When that contribution level goes above $133,000 you can bet that Olson and I will be quick to add salesmen.

The other method of growth is a little harder to explain. You see, in a complex business, one part actually depends on another part. One of the factors we have used in the standard is the cost of goods sold (excluding cost of supporting a salesman). That is today 70 percent. It is determined by efficiency in our manufacturing plants as well as efficiency in the central office overhead. In short, all of the cost elements in the profit-and-loss statement. Now in the long run, if we strive for efficiency here to the point where, say, our cost of goods sold is 60 percent, and if we keep our price and volume to the customer the same, the salesmen's contribution will go up to 40 percent of sales instead of 30 percent. That would immediately lower our salesmen's break-even point to $100,000 ($40,000 divided by .40). You can see that, right at the present, the two added salesmen in Salt Lake would be justified, as would six in Los Angeles, five in San Francisco, and four in Vancouver.

The same kind of effect would exist if we passed this new efficiency on to the customer in the form of lower price. Our volume would increase, the selling contribution would go up (and the break-even point down). Manufacturing contribution would go down.

Exhibit 2 *Potential Sales Volume* by District,
in Relation to Number of Salesmen,
Western Office Equipment Manufacturing Company*

Number of Salesmen	Salt Lake City			Los Angeles			San Francisco			Vancouver		
	Total Sales	Average Sales	Marginal Increment	Total Sales	Average Sales	Marginal Increment	Total Sales	Average Sales	Marginal Increment	Total Sales	Average Sales	Marginal Increment
1	$ 450	$450	$450	$ 250†	$250	$250	$ 400	$400	$400	$ 350	$350	$350
2	850	425	400	480	240	230	750	375	350	650	325	300
3	960	320	110	690	230	210	1,050	350	300	900	300	250
4	1,060†	265	100	860	215	170	1,300	325	250	1,020†	255	120
5	1,150	230	90	1,000	200	140	1,430	286	130	1,100	220	80
6	1,200	200	50	1,110	185	110	1,500†	250	70	1,140	190	40

*All amounts given in thousands of dollars.
†Denotes current sales volume.

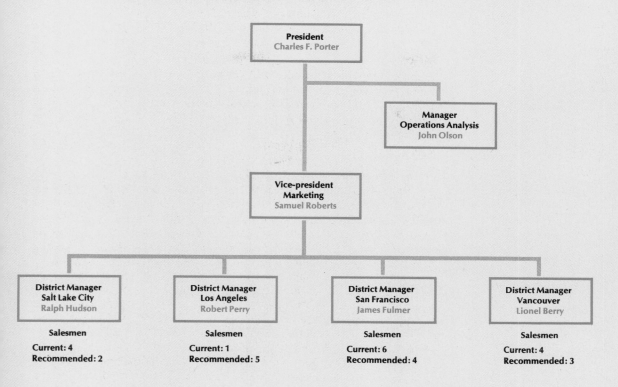

Exhibit 3 *Organization Chart,
Western Office Equipment Manufacturing Company*

President
Charles F. Porter

Manager
Operations Analysis
John Olson

Vice-president
Marketing
Samuel Roberts

| District Manager
Salt Lake City
Ralph Hudson | District Manager
Los Angeles
Robert Perry | District Manager
San Francisco
James Fulmer | District Manager
Vancouver
Lionel Berry |

Salesmen

Current: 4
Recommended: 2

Salesmen

Current: 1
Recommended: 5

Salesmen

Current: 6
Recommended: 4

Salesmen

Current: 4
Recommended: 3

Balancing a complex business like ours is a difficult matter. I'm saying that your contribution depends in part on how efficient our plants and headquarters are. We will work on these other operations as hard as we can. When their efficiency raises the contribution of the salesmen you can bet we will be quick to grow in each and every territory. But in the meantime, it is sometimes necessary to actually hurt one part of the business (for example, the Salt Lake or San Francisco selling branches) to increase overall efficiency. In the long run, it will pay off.

At this point in the meeting, all three managers (with the exception of Robert Perry from Los Angeles) asked a wide variety of questions, most of which, according to Olson, were actually phrased as arguments against the plan. For example, "You don't think you can transfer both Dolan and Franklin to Los Angeles, do you?" Or "Why can't you keep our customers in Vancouver and cut your manufacturing costs now, instead of hurting us in the market place?"

The meeting adjourned at seven in the evening, two hours later than planned. Porter described the results of the meeting:

I told them that in view of their objections, we would declare a temporary suspension of the plan; that we would have another meeting in sixty days to discuss it again. I have a lot of faith in Olson's abilities and am certain in my own mind that the plan is good for the company's growth objectives. Right now, I am wondering what to do, and how to get the plan into effect with the support of the district managers. Their own good work is, of course, vital to a company like ours.

FOR DISCUSSION AND REPORT-WRITING

Organizing: Structural Design

1) After studying the complete system worked out by Olson using incremental cost and revenue analysis, show how the economic aspect of the company has determined organization structure (including whether there will be a Los Angeles office or not, and how much authority the Los Angeles manager will have).

2) What advantage does this company gain by creating the position of "Manager of Operations Analysis" as a staff position?

3) Discuss John Olson's obligations and his methods for meeting them in the light of the text discussion of the use of staff.

Human Factors in Organizing

4) What was the basic cause of Hudson's conflict with Porter over the new sales manpower policy?

5) In what sense are all of the managers expressing basic human needs in their response to the new system?

Planning: Elements of Decision-Making

6) Why did Porter's original use of the *average* performance of salesmen represent faulty reasoning? (Hint: Use the concept of focusing on differences—and incremental analysis—to explain.)

7) Think creatively to see if you can devise a way to make Olson's system more flexible and therefore secure more acceptance of his sales manpower policy.

8) Has Olson projected all of the significant consequences of his approach? What may he have missed by failing to place the specific task assigned him in the context of the total company situation?

Planning: Decision-Making in an Enterprise

9) How strict do you think that the policy on hiring salesmen only if their production is above the break-even point should be? Should it be a rule, or only a guideline? Give reasons.

10) What evidence is there in the case that Western's management has, in its master strategy, picked a propitious niche in its environment? List some of the hypothetical factors in that environment that probably would have been considered in picking this niche.

11) Do you see how the policy on hiring salesmen only if they produce beyond the break-even point can, as a standing plan, enable the president of Western to delegate to the vice-president for marketing authority in a way that he has not been able to before? Do you see the same thing about delegations from Roberts to the district managers?

12) How does the policy referred to in question 11 relate logically, in a master strategy, to manufacturing costs? How do both the sales hiring policy and the manufacturing costs relate in a master strategy to top goals of growth and profitability?

13) *Summary Report Question, Part Four:* Write a report that analyzes the important aspects of Western's decision system. Comment on the organization for decision-making, on difficulties in consolidating projections and opinions, on evidence of a master strategy, and on the potential impact of the company's sales manpower policy on future decisions.

Leading

14) Olson said, "I have the division managers' complete agreement that our company must plan where to add salesmen on an economic basis"? Was this true? If so, how do you account for the reactions of the managers later in the case?

15) What does Porter's statement, "I thought it necessary to explain the whole thing at once, and not to mail the plan in advance," tell you about his leadership?

Measuring and Controlling

16) Utilize the checklist of reasons why people often object to controls (from Chapter 26) to apply to this specific company situation. Why are the district managers objecting to the particular $133,000 standard in this case?

17) If Porter and Olson were to use "fact control" in an attempt to overcome some of the resistance to the new standard, would they likely be successful? Why or why not?

*Summary Question for Solution
of the Case as a Whole*

18) Based on your answer to question 13, write a report to Mr. Porter containing your recommendations on how he might develop an approach to sales manpower planning that is more consistent with what you see as a sound overall organizational design.

 E. W. ROSS, INC.

E. W. Ross, Inc., was founded in 1921 by Edwin Walker Ross. Located in Bloomington, Indiana, it began as a small finance company offering secured loans on cars, trucks, and farm equipment. Mr. Ross, whose family had settled in Bloomington more than fifty years earlier, was highly regarded in the community. His father, Walker Douglas Ross, was an eminent professor of geography at Indiana University. Regard for the family and a willingness to work with customers who were temporarily set back by adverse conditions helped the company survive the worst of the depression, but by 1940 competition from national finance companies and large banks led Mr. Ross to diversify. With the aid of his son, E. W. Ross, Jr., he moved the business into insurance and real estate sales.

Upon the founder's death in 1946, his son assumed the presidency and over the next twenty years built the business into a larger and highly profitable concern.

> I shifted us out of automotive and farm equipment loans [Mr. Ross explained] as it became more apparent that the national finance companies and big banks were seriously eroding profit margins. We concentrated on the returning veterans who needed more than their government loans to start a business or finance their education. We were particularly interested in those men who were headed for professional careers in law, medicine, and dentistry. We sought out the opticians, the pharmacists, and others who would need money to get a business going but who, we felt, would someday become leading members of the community. Our field and credit people used their intuition more often than established procedures of the day, and we expanded rapidly.
>
> Gradually we fanned out from Bloomington and began to cover all of the neighboring communities for about a one-hundred-mile radius. We established small (one or two men) branches in French Lick, Osgood, Clinton, and Evansville. We had another in Valparaiso,

but that one was too far away and didn't work out, and so we closed it.

The branches are run by one man and sometimes he has an assistant. The main function of the branches is to provide the local people with a place to come if they have questions or problems. It makes our company a person to talk to rather than a mailing address or a telephone voice. All of the branches handle local real estate sales and service loan, investment, and insurance accounts.

Actually, the branch people don't make major decisions. They call headquarters for us to handle most requests and they brief the eight full-time people who cover their territories, so that the field people can visit the client with a good understanding of his situation.

Since 1950, we have built our business largely out of contacts established through loans for tuition or through professionals starting a new practice. Our lending rates were higher, and in most cases still are higher, than other sources but we often provided more money and offered more flexible repayment plans than anyone else. At all costs, we tried to avoid the hard-boiled collection practices followed by most of our competitors when accounts became delinquent. Between our field and branch personnel, we select our clients carefully and work with them on a personal basis. We haven't had very many bad debt losses but we have a high number of technically delinquent accounts. Overall, our final collection ratio has been as good or better than that of our competitors though our clients often paid more slowly.

Continued competition for these loans and our high cost of servicing them had greatly reduced our profit from them by 1965. Ten years earlier, however, in 1955, we used our contacts from these loans to launch an investment counseling service. The idea was to capitalize on the relationship we had built up over the years. Most of our former borrowers from the late forties were now successful doctors, lawyers, pharmacists, and so on. As their income increased they paid off their loans and began looking for opportunities to invest their surplus. We had been selling them insurance and so by training our field people in investment counseling we offered a fuller line of services. While we call the field people investment counselors, this job is not the same as counselors in stock brokerage houses. In fact, the title greatly underrates their versatility. They can now go out and set up a loan for a new client, collect from an older one who is a bit too delinquent, or advise another on how to build a balanced investment and insurance program.

These combined services were a natural and we grew in size and profit until five years ago when major banks, insurance companies, and investment houses intensified their selling efforts and broadened their services. The last five years have been tough ones.

Indeed competition has slowed Ross's market growth and last year the company was close to showing a loss for the first time in its more than fifty-year history. Furthermore, because some 75 percent of Ross's capital comes from bank loans, the tight money market that existed had not only severely slowed growth and reduced profits but had resulted in a serious disagreement between the president and his oldest son, E. Walker Ross.

Walker Ross, after completing an M.B.A. degree in California eight years ago, joined a major Chicago bank. Four years later, he left to take a job with a large New York stock brokerage firm. After a brief period in the research department, he took over the management of a number of large individual accounts. Cost-cutting moves by the New York firm led Walker Ross to resign and return to Bloomington two years ago to join the family business.

Edwin Ross, having celebrated his sixtieth birthday, was anxious to have Walker work with him as executive vice-president for a year or two. Then, Edwin would gradually withdraw from active management when Walker was ready to take over. The difficulties of the last two years have made him question this plan.

> I go home some nights [Edwin Ross said] and think I ought to retire immediately and let Walker try his hand the way I did after my father died.
>
> And then the next day Walker will suggest something that makes me hope I live to be ninety and die at my desk. I changed many things when I took over in 1946 but I kept intact the foundation on which the business was built. We stayed local; we kept our flexible, personalized loan service as a base and simply shifted to the kinds of loans and related services people wanted. We have about fifty people on the payroll, including about eleven who work for us part-time, and they average over twenty years service and that includes some of the younger ones in the office. Our eight full-time invest-ment counselors average twenty-three years of service with the most junior man being with us nine years.
>
> These eight men and five part-time counselors (including two women) are the heart of our business. Most started as contact and collection men in the loan business and gradually learned insurance, real estate, and investment counseling. I've invested plenty on each of them, but they have more than returned that investment. There isn't one of them who hasn't tried to help Walker understand what they do and how they do it. They know he will probably take over soon and they are as anxious as I am to get him ready.
>
> Our four branch managers all have at least nine years service and while they haven't the depth of the counselors, they do a great job for us. From the base salary we pay them and from their income from real estate sales in their areas they make a good living.
>
> Walker is a very smart young man. He had excellent grades in college and his experiences in Chicago and New York have helped him and me a great deal, but I'm afraid that the changes he wants to make will destroy the unique character of the business and force us to compete with the major banks and investment services on their terms. Yet every time I think I have convinced him, the banks

squeeze us again and lend new credence to his views. At times I find myself almost forced to accept the fact that he may be right.

Walker Ross made few suggestions in his first year with his father. Although he had worked for the firm throughout high school and during college vacations, he felt the business might have changed in the time he had been away. He traveled with the investment counselors and observed them as they made loan collections or, after lengthy discussions, approved up to six-month extensions on delinquent accounts. He watched as one man spent three hours with a pharmacist's widow helping her understand her late husband's insurance and investment program, which was valued at less than $65,000. He listened as another counselor spent fifteen minutes with a wealthy surgeon recommending changes in the doctor's portfolio, which amounted to more than $800,000. He followed along with another counselor and a branch office manager as they accompanied a young dentist (who was modernizing an office in Rockport) on a 200-mile trip to St. Louis to help him select office equipment and finance the cost. The dentist still owed over four thousand dollars of tuition loans but was in the top third of his class in dental school and was taking over the largest dental practice in Rockport from his uncle.

> I kept quiet the whole time and just watched the field people work [said Walker]. They're absolutely marvelous, but they're about as efficient as coal burning stoves. They spend more time traveling, drinking coffee or bourbon—depending on the client—and discussing trout fishing and politics than they do advising or collecting. I know I could increase their client coverage at least fourfold if I could get them to use the telephone or mails and to follow a few simple procedures of efficient account management.
>
> I spent several weeks with each of the four full-time and five part-time counselors who cover Bloomington, and they are just as good but just as inefficient.
>
> From January of last year, when things began to improve a little, until July, I worked in each of the six home office departments[1] and visited the banks with Dad. The tight money market has been hurting us for over eighteen months. Our tuition loans usually saw us making a loan in, say, 1968 and then not collecting any principle or interest until from 1970 to 1972. Then the premium and interest payments were often staggered to let the recent graduate get started in business before repayment.
>
> We found ourselves refinancing with the banks at rates considerably higher than our average loan income and we still haven't caught up. Not only did we lose money on what we had to borrow but we were unable to borrow enough to finance expansion in our more profitable investment and insurance areas. The banks refuse to increase our total loans until we improve our ratio of delinquent accounts.

[1] See Exhibit 1.

*I've worked with Dad for more than two years now and have
made very few suggestions, because I know how touchy he can be
about the character of the business. But the time has come when
we have to make some fundamental shifts or face, at best, low profit
and little growth or, at worst, bankruptcy.*

Specifically, Walker made the following four recommendations to his
father in November of last year:

1) Instruct the investment counselors to tighten up on collections.
This involved refusing to extend delinquent accounts past thirty days on
equipment loans and taking a much tougher line on collection of tuition
loans.

2) Begin a careful analysis of all accounts to determine the profit
contribution from (1) loan, (2) investment and insurance counseling, and
(3) real estate to Ross, Inc., profits. Also use this study to estimate how
much of the counseling and real estate income was a result of earlier
loans. Based on this study, set up quotas on new business and growth of
existing business and develop expense ratios and budgets to guide the
counselors and branch office managers.

3) If (as Walker felt certain the study would prove) the loan business
was neither profitable nor as vital to other services as Edwin Ross believed,
then the company should not only take a stronger position on collections
and repossessing equipment when necessary, but the home office loan
department should be far more selective in new loans. In addition to approving fewer new loans, those approved would be for people who would
probably be prompt payers.

4) As collection ratios improve and banks make more funds available,
use these new funds to add highly qualified personnel to the research and
insurance service departments; then add more professionally trained investment counselors to the present group.

> *These four steps represent the only way [Walker explained] that
> we can get our accounts in the condition the banks demand before
> lending us the funds we need to grow. They want to see us reduce
> our risks and increase our profits before extending further credit and
> I quite agree. It might be a little tough to get the field people to im-
> plement a new approach, but I'm sure I could show them that it's
> the only way for us to grow, if not survive. At least it's the only way
> unless Dad withdraws his objections to trying to go public and put
> more equity into the business. Even then, to convince potential
> shareholders to put up their money, we would have to make some
> fundamental changes in the business.*

Edwin Ross indicated a general lack of agreement with his son's
recommendations but is prepared to consider them and put them before
the company's Board of Directors. The Board is really more of an advisory
group than a true Board, because of the Ross family's control. It is made

up of Edwin and Walker Ross, Thomas Sewell, who has managed home office administration since 1939, Nelson Flynn, chief accountant since 1947, three of the most senior investment counselors, Edwin's Ross's attorney, and Benjamin Harte, president of Bloomington's largest bank.

Edwin Ross indicated that he felt that few of the Board members other than Harte would favor Walker's proposals.

> Even Harte [Edwin said], as an old friend, may not go along with Walker's notions. If he speaks as our largest source of funds, he would. If he looks at it as one of our competitors then I'm sure he'd like Walker's plan, but as an old friend I'm not so sure.
>
> No, if Walker's thoughts were to be given favorable consideration, I'd have to support them and I just don't think I can get myself to do it. If we get stricter on collections, repossess equipment, and force refinancing at higher rates on the unsecured loans, we may kill the goose that lays the golden eggs. Further, I don't have much hope that any study will sort out profit contributions or clearly show us the sources of our counseling and real estate business. They have been intermingled for too many years to pull apart now.

Walker knows how his father feels and told the casewriter:

> I'm not giving Dad any ultimatums. I love and respect him too much for that but I have to consider my own future too. I really feel that if Dad continues to run the business as it is for another two to five years, it will be too late for me when he retires. I don't want to become president of a stagnant business that is ten years out of

Exhibit 1 *Organization Chart, E. W. Ross, Inc.*

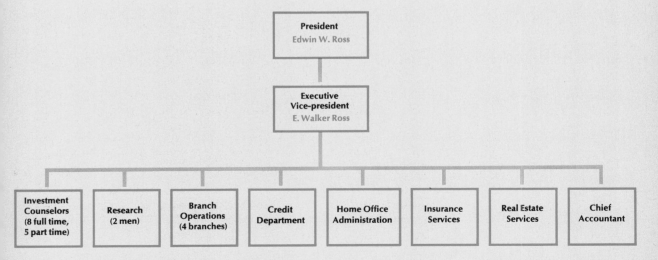

date. I want to leave a positive mark on the business just like Dad did. But time is running out! A serious recession or another rapid increase in bank interest rates, and we could lose everything. If Dad refuses to try some of my ideas in the next six months I may just have to pull out.

FOR DISCUSSION AND REPORT-WRITING

Organizing: Structural Design

1) If Edwin Ross were to accept his son's recommendations, what changes, if any, might be required in the design of the operating units?

Human Factors in Organizing

2) In what ways may the customs and habits of key Ross personnel affect the chances of successfully implementing Walker Ross's recommendations if the Board were to approve them?

3) What changes in personnel may be required if Walker's recommendations were approved?

4) If Edwin Ross refuses to support his son's proposals what action do you feel that Walker should take?

Planning: Elements of Decision-Making

5) Why is it essential to view the problems of delinquent loans and time-consuming collection practices in the context of higher-level goals when seeking solutions to these problems?

6) How might Edwin Ross properly project and weigh the intangible consequences of continuing present practices versus making the changes recommended by his son?

Planning: Decision-Making in an Enterprise

7) From whom should Edwin Ross seek advice in making his decision on whether or not to support Walker's recommendations?

8) If Edwin Ross were to approve Walker's recommendations, what changes in operating objectives would be required? Discuss changes in both short-run and long-run objectives.

9) What changes in standing plans would be required if Walker's recommendations were accepted? Write one new policy, procedure, and method to illustrate your answer.

10) What do you think of the propitiousness of the niche selected by Edwin Ross with respect to meeting competition from larger finance, insurance, and investment counseling firms? What factors will determine whether the company can succeed with its *present* approaches?

11) *Summary Report Question, Part Four:* Assuming Walker's recommendations were accepted, write a detailed plan for the transition period including specific programs for informing key personnel and customers of the changes in the strategy of Ross, Inc.

Leading

12) If Walker is unsuccessful in persuading his father to follow his recommendations, and if he agrees to stay on, how effective do you think he will be in gaining voluntary cooperation from key Ross personnel? Discuss.

13) What changes in planning and review of personnel performance would be required if Walker's recommendations were accepted?

14) What, if any, communication problems do you foresee for Walker and key company personnel if his recommendations are discussed with them? How should they be presented to ensure good communication?

Measuring and Controlling

15) What would be the proper way to measure and control the work of the investment counselors under the present strategy of the business? What changes in measurement and control would be required if Walker's recommendations were approved?

16) Using your answers to the second part of question 15, what responses to new measurement and control instruments might you expect from key Ross personnel? How might the responses of a new man hired after the changes differ from those of a long-time Ross employee?

17) What changes in budgetary controls would be necessitated if the second and third recommendations made by Walker were approved?

Summary Question for Solution of the Case as a Whole

18) Considering all of the changes in process, programs, and personnel that might be involved if Walker's recommendations were approved, what advice would you give to Edwin Ross? Prepare a detailed report of your recommendations, including plans for implementing them and the major reasons for conclusions.

PART FIVE

Leading

If we could assume that managers could plan accurately and in detail all the actions of their departments or companies, that there would be no deviations from plans when the time came for their execution, and that all personnel would be highly motivated and would know just how to carry out plans, we could end this book right here. All that a manager would have to do would be to devise a structure of jobs and plans, find qualified and motivated people to fill the jobs and carry out the plans, and then let the business run itself. But at best these assumptions are only partially true.

Managers have to put the plans and the organization *into action*. They do this by leading and controlling. They must communicate plans to workers, watch results, appraise response and feedback data, make day-to-day interpretations and elaborations of plans, motivate individuals, and make continual changes to fit new conditions. Only when these additional tasks, which we shall discuss in Parts Five and Six, are performed will the process of managing be complete.

Leading, as we shall use the term, is a matter of dynamic *man-to-man relationships* between a manager and his subordinates. It is the process by which a manager directly and personally influences the behavior of those who work with him, and by which his subordinates in turn feed back information—ranging from highly subjective, personal responses to data on operating conditions—that is vital to the manager in his subsequent actions. We shall examine the process in the following chapters.

Chapter 20—Role of Leadership. Here we shall look closely at the functions of leadership as a phase of management, at several attitudes that help an executive fulfill these functions, and at the evolutionary nature of personal relations between an executive and his associates.

Chapter 21—Developing Voluntary Cooperation. An aim of every manager is to create a total work situation that makes cooperation with company plans easy and natural. Eliciting voluntary cooperation involves both building a conducive work structure and considerate behavior by the manager. And, to whatever extent is practicable, the manager has to try to fit the work and his actions to the particular needs of his subordinates.

Chapter 22—Two-way Personal Communication. The kind of relationship proposed in the two previous chapters is possible only when a manager and his subordinates communicate effectively. So in this chapter we shall explore the art of listening and of conveying meaning to others.

Chapter 23—Directing and Disciplining. Occasionally, leading calls for positive—even stern—action, as a moment's reflection on the lives of the great leaders in history will reveal. Voluntary cooperation needs to be buttressed from time to time with direct instructions and elaborations of general plans. In addition, because every executive rewards and disciplines subordinates to some extent, we need to examine ways in which this inevitable use of power can be made compatible with a counseling relationship.

Often in Part Five we shall refer to aspects of individual and group behavior already covered in earlier parts of the book. To some extent, we shall simply be making use of concepts, such as personal needs or informal groups, that are useful in understanding several phases of management. But in addition, we shall see that leading is not sharply separated from organizing, planning, and controlling. The way a manager works in all his capacities with subordinates impinges on the effectiveness of his leadership. Leading is an ever-present element in the process of managing.

Chapter Twenty

Role of Leadership

THE PLACE OF LEADERSHIP IN MANAGEMENT

A manager "leads," in the sense we use the term here, by personally and actively working with his subordinates in order (1) to guide and motivate their behavior to fit the plans and jobs that have been established, and (2) to understand the feelings of his subordinates and the problems they face as they translate plans into completed action. All too often the first of these purposes is stressed at the expense of the second, but as we shall see, both are vital if effective, cooperative action is to take place.

The word "personally" in this definition implies that leading is a close, man-to-man relationship. Leading involves the reactions of individual personalities to each other, and it is rooted in the feelings and attitudes that have grown up between the men over the entire time they have worked together. The word "actively" implies that leading is a dynamic, evolving relationship in which a manager continuously communicates in a way he hopes will induce subordinates to support company plans and objectives.

Such personal, active leadership serves two broad, vital functions in the management process: One stems from the impact of a leader on his subordinates—he guides and motivates them. The other is the result of the impact of the subordinates on the leader—they give him information and responses that modify his behavior and future plans. This is a two-way relationship. Let us look first at the guidance role and then return later in the chapter to the understanding and response aspect.

Guiding and Motivating Behavior

Even the best plans are sterile until someone puts them into action. A construction superintendent has to convert blueprints into, say, a power dam. A football coach has to transform plays that look foolproof on paper into touchdowns on the field. A director has to turn a Gilbert and Sullivan score and libretto into a lively stage production. Such a conversion of ideas into results is an essential element in every manager's job, and how skillfully he does it can profoundly affect the returns from all other phases of management.

Guiding and motivating the behavior of subordinates has many facets. Plans have to be communicated to subordinates meaningfully, for some explanation of the purposes of, and reasons behind, a particular action usually aids an employee in understanding plans and helps develop his motivation. Inevitably, as plans are being executed, questions of interpretation arise and adjustments are needed to overcome minor difficulties. Enthusiasm for doing a job well needs to be generated. Frictions between workers have to be resolved. Adjustments to allow for Joe's wife being sick or Bob's car breaking down have to be considered. A man's disappointment over a failure to get a desired transfer may open the way for friendly counseling. Men on new assignments have to be trained. Carelessness and infractions of rules call for disciplinary action. Work done well should be praised. In all such guiding and motivating, equitable treatment of all subordinates must be reconciled with differences in individual needs.

As we review the preceding examples of the multitudinous small ingredients that make up the broad task of guiding and motivating behavior, we can readily see why this function is both active and personal.

Fig. 20-1 An organization may have excellent plans and the instruments necessary for carrying them out, but without effective leadership to unify the actions of the members of the organization, chaos is likely.

Comparison of Appointed and Informal Leaders

In emphasizing how leadership fits into the total management process, we do not imply that leadership exists only in the service of management. Leaders arise in many situations, and we should appreciate the similarities and differences between informal leaders and appointed leaders.

Even informal social groups have leaders. If we observe a crowd of boys who regularly gather after school to play baseball, we see that certain boys are paid attention to by their comrades. These boys are apt to be the ones who suggest action for the others ("Let's play in the morning instead of the afternoon on Saturday"), and when a minor disagreement arises between two players, most of the boys look to one of the leaders for advice and judgment on settling the matter. Informal leaders also emerge in the social groups, discussed in Chapter 7, that grow up around car pools, coffee klatches, or bowling teams.

When groups endure and become formal, we find them electing leaders officially. Witness unions, civic leagues, and many other nonbusiness organizations. Normally the persons elected to offices are the ones who are natural leaders of the group. Their views would probably get attention even without formal elections, but with elections these natural leaders are consciously acknowledged. It is true that in some organizations the role each officer is expected to play has been established by custom— the Commander of an American Legion Post, for instance; in these cases being an elected officer may increase a man's influence temporarily. But if a man does not provide the initiative and guidance the group wants, he is unlikely to remain an officer for long.

Research on the behavior of small groups indicates (1) that those persons who emerge as informal leaders are perceived by other group members as being the best able to satisfy the group's needs and (2) that the leaders are therefore enabled to influence the actions of other members. The members may not make a rational calculation to establish just who can satisfy their needs best; rather, their feelings about whose lead to follow may be based on experience, on the beliefs of other members of the group, or on positive statements by potential leaders about what ought to be done. Regardless of how valid such a judgment may be, the leader derives his influence from the members' feeling, or intuition, that he can help satisfy their needs; consequently, they are willing to submit, within limits, to his guidance.

Now what happens to these natural leadership relations when a man is *appointed* as supervisor over other workers? The appointed supervisor differs from the informal or elected leader in two important respects. First, with his appointment the supervisor also gets some authority and power from the central administration of the enterprise. This power enables him to increase or decrease the satisfactions of his subordinates in ways not available to informal leaders. Second, he has an obligation not only to help subordinates satisfy their needs but also to achieve the results desired by the enterprise. So, although he has potential strengths for becoming a leader because of his ability to satisfy needs, he also has strong obligations *outside* the group. (Actually, the informal or elected leader often has obligations or personal interests that diverge from those of the group, but these are not inherent in his position as is the case with an appointed leader.)

TYPICAL RECOGNITION OF AUTHORITY

To understand more fully the role of the appointed leader (manager) we need to recall our discussion of delegation in Chapter 3. Authority is granted along with the assignment of duties and creation of obligation. For instance, if Ted Townsend is to open an office in Mobile, he will be authorized to sign contracts, buy supplies, and move equipment. Authority in this sense is *permission*. When an executive delegates authority of this sort, he simply passes on to another member of his organization permission to take certain kinds of action.

Authority to deal with objects is clear-cut. But authority to direct the action of other people is more complicated. A grant of permission to give instructions to workers does not necessarily include an assurance that the workers will obey the instructions. What is crucial—and what complicates the relationship—is whether workers are *willing* to obey. Effective authority over people is possible only when they accept it. Two-way endorsement of the relationship is necessary.

In practice, most instructions are obeyed as a matter of course. A man who takes a job expects to take orders from a manager designated by his company. Such behavior is part of our culture; normal, day-to-day social patterns in an organization include boss-subordinate relationships. Both boss and subordinate believe the boss has a right to request certain actions of the subordinate, and both believe the subordinate has an obligation to act as directed.

Besides obeying because of such beliefs, a subordinate may also submit to authority because direct satisfactions are built into his job (as we suggested in Chapter 8). For example, by following instructions a subordinate may get a sense of contributing to a worthy objective, or an assignment may provide him an opportunity for sociability. Under such circumstances, he usually follows instructions without question.

Nevertheless, a manager dare not rely entirely on custom and direct satisfactions to ensure acceptance of authority throughout an organization. There are many borderline duties that a worker may, or may not, automatically accept. For instance, workers may view disagreeable, risky, or new jobs unenthusiastically. Or a man may accept an assignment but resist guidance on how to perform the job. Furthermore, the attitudes of American workers have changed sharply during the last fifty years. Prevailing ideas today about the length of a working day, assignments suitable for "professional" men, warnings of layoffs, and many other aspects of work have narrowed the range of what workers will readily accept.

For these and similar reasons, we must recognize the need for inducements to secure workers' acceptance of the authority that we have built into a formal organization structure. Among the ways of buttressing the authority of managers is their use of power. In fact, wise use of power is one of the most sensitive aspects of managerial leadership.

USE OF POWER TO SECURE OBEDIENCE

Man has always resorted to power to support authority. By selectively granting rewards or inflicting penalties, he has maintained obedience. This time-honored practice continues to be pervasive in our society—in homes, schools, government, and in business enterprises. A manager should, therefore, thoroughly understand both the use and the limitations of power.

What Power Is

In the broadest sense, we have power over another person when we can supply something he wants and cannot get elsewhere. A small boy with the only football in the neighborhood, for example, has power over other boys who would like to play football. A monoply on salt can be a source of power for a government or a company. Control over the transportation of oil several decades ago gave John D. Rockefeller great power over the petroleum industry. Of course, if there are alternative—even if less convenient—ways of satisfying a need, the degree of power is correspondingly reduced.

Ability to inflict penalties is the negative side of power. In this sense, power results when we can deprive a person of something he has or wants. The "something" can be, say, his freedom, his possessions, or even his head. The political power of dictators rests largely on the use of such penalities, whereas political power in democracies often rests on rewards.

An essential element of a power relationship is fear of punishment. We behave as a wielder of power wishes us to behave because we fear that he will deprive us of important satisfactions. Sometimes we are not sure that deprivation is inevitable, but we simply do not wish to risk the chance. Unfortunately, if a relationship is dominated by fear and uncertainty, it is difficult for the weaker person to be self-reliant and to feel friendly toward the powerful person.

These general concepts can be applied to the internal operations of a business enterprise. The management of a company can design jobs, assign work, transfer, promote, demote, discharge, set pay, provide benefits, select titles, and recognize achievements. If subordinates obey because of fear—fear that rewards will be withheld or punishments inflicted if directions are not carried out—then we can say that a manager is clearly

Fig. 20-2   The degree to which subordinates accept authority determines the type of influence the person exercising authority should use and the amount of commitment that can be expected. (Adapted from M.H. Jones, Executive Decision Making. *Homewood, Ill.: Richard D. Irwin, 1957, p. 130.)*

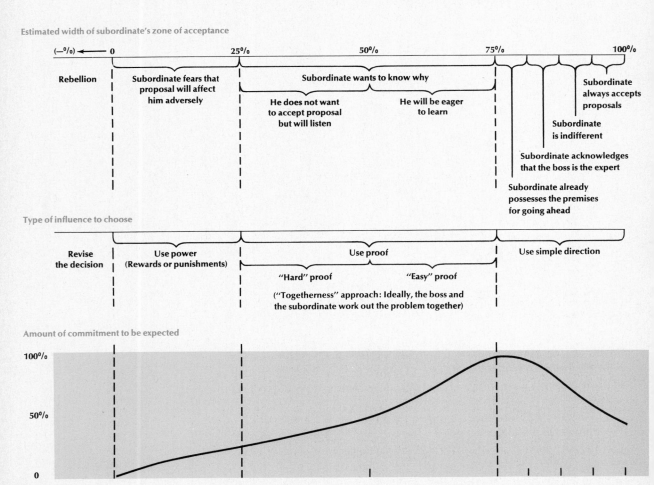

depending on the use of power alone in an attempt to gain compliance with his orders.[1]

Use of Power to Establish Patterns of Behavior

Power has its principal effect in its potential use, rather than in its actual use. We can see this most clearly in the use of penalties. An actual demotion or withdrawal of a challenging assignment, for example, contributes little directly toward meeting an objective of either employee or firm; indeed, the immediate effect may even be a drop in output. What is important is fearful *anticipation* of such a penalty, for it motivates an employee to behave as the company wants.

The actual use of a penalty is, of course, significant—not because it gives a man "what is coming to him"—but because it makes clear what will happen if there are further digressions. A two-week layoff for repeated tardiness, for instance, benefits a company only if the fear of future layoffs leads to punctuality.

Rewards work similarly. Fear of missing a raise in pay or a transfer to a more interesting job—sometime in the future—stimulates effort now. But a policy of making promotions and pay increases routinely on the basis of length of service or seniority provides little power to secure obedience because a person gets his reward even though he fails to obey instructions conscientiously.

The effect of a discharge, transfer, or pay increase is often as great on associates as it is on the man specifically concerned. Everyone in an organization anticipates the consequences of his own actions, and he takes his cues from what has happened to other people. When Joe Doakes, who has been casual about his work, is passed over for a promotion in favor of an ardent supporter of a new company policy, the handwriting is on the wall for all to see: "If you want a promotion, support the new policy." Thus only occasional exercise of power can set a pattern of expectation—and behavior—for a large number of people.

Management naturally hopes that it can induce widespread acceptance of desirable behavior patterns, and that its power can remain latent. But to achieve such a widespread effect on behavior, management must use power consistently. Penalties should regularly follow undesirable be-

---

[1] Power relationships, of course, are not confined to managers and subordinates. A salesman with close ties to key customers, for instance, can wield power over his employer by threatening to go to work for another concern. A plant manager can have power over salesmen if he is free to decide which orders to fill promptly. A vice-president's secretary can even develop some power by regulating the flow of visitors and information to this key executive, and, of course, a labor union with a monopoly of certain skilled technicians has power over industries that require those technicians. The matrix of relationships in a company includes all such sources of power, whether potential or realized, and a manager must often determine how best to channel, reconcile, or curb the interplay among people with different sorts of power.

havior and rewards should follow desired behavior. Moreover, the reasons for penalties and rewards must be made clear to the entire group. Each consistent action reinforces existing beliefs about how management will use its power. But if an executive is capricious—using his power first one way and then another—he will simply stimulate fear without positively influencing behavior patterns.

LIMITS ON THE USE OF POWER

Accounts of early railroading, sailing, mining, and other industries report frequent use of power to get results. But today power plays a lesser role. There are two broad reasons why this is so. First, to avoid its corrupting effect, we have placed sharp restrictions on power. Second, power is ineffective in generating the feelings of personal obligation and initiative that are needed for so many jobs in modern business.

Checks on Executive Power

People of free countries have an ingrained mistrust of putting vast powers in the hands of a single individual or small group. Past experience with sovereign kings and dictators, coupled with a high value on justice for the individual, makes us wary.

This antiauthoritarian sentiment has been carried over into our business practices, especially in recent years. Enterprises have introduced numerous safeguards to prevent any single executive from abusing the power that resides in the firms. Policies often place limits or conditions on permissible actions, and power is often divided up so that two or more executives must concur on an action. Here are some company rules that are typical examples of safeguards:

1) Except for specified causes (for example, smoking in an oil refinery), a worker can be discharged only after one (or two) written warnings and an opportunity to improve.

2) Two levels of supervisor and the personnel director must concur before pay increases or decreases can be made. Increases must fall within established ranges; no one may be paid less than the minimum for the job he holds.

3) A supervisor must secure the agreement of an appropriate staff man before making a promotion.

4) Executives must submit to grievance procedures that provide an opportunity for objective review of any action an employee feels is unfair or malicious.

Inadequacy of Power

A second drawback of relying solely on power to secure obedience to authorized instructions is that power is inadequate to the task. Attempts to use power are in certain circumstances simply ineffective. A threat of discharge, for example, is not serious to the man who can readily obtain as good a job elsewhere. Similarly, the prospect of promotion holds no lure for a man who dislikes added burdens and authority over his associates. Because power rests on ability to deprive a person of a satisfaction, its strength depends on the marginal value the person attaches to that satisfaction. A point is often reached where the satisfactions that an executive controls have little value for his subordinates.

Power is inadequate in other ways. We have already mentioned certain counterpowers that can neutralize managerial power. As noted in Chapter 7, informal groups can, on occasion, enforce standards that are inconsistent with those set by the formal hierarchy in a firm. Labor unions too may have sufficient power to counteract the strength of management in certain areas. Even a large stockholder, an important customer, or a crucial supplier can occasionally use his power to countermand the directives of company management. Such counterpowers, like the safeguards a company voluntarily imposes on its use of power, reduce an executive's ability to enforce his will.

But the most significant drawback of power is that it fails to generate the initiative and enthusiasm that are vital for many jobs in an enterprise. When men respond to power alone, they tend to become yes-men, giving answers they guess a supervisor wants to hear rather than giving their own honest judgment. They are apt to stress superficial accomplishments and neglect hard-to-measure elements of a job, because there will be little payoff for unnoticed quality. Unless tight controls are maintained, men often stall or forget disagreeable work. In short, in a power-centered concern, a worker (manager or operator) focuses his attention on pleasing his boss rather than on achieving results he himself believes worthwhile. Dependency, a psychologist would say, snuffs out self-expression and personal drive.

For most jobs, latent power fosters an acceptance of the legitimacy of formal authority. But power alone is not enough. Dynamic, complex organizations need other means for assuring unified action.[2]

[2]In stressing the *inadequacy* of power we clearly join such writers as Douglas McGregor (*The Human Side of Enterprise*) and Chris Argyris (*Personality and Organization*). However, in a book dealing with the total management process the place of power should be explicitly recognized. Power exists and plays a crucial role in every organized endeavor of men. Pointing out the abuse of power does not, and cannot, imply its elimination. For a manager, the practical questions are (1) when and how he should use the power at his disposal, and (2) as power becomes increasingly ineffective in sophisticated enterprises, what better means are available to supplement it as a motivating and integrating force?

UNDERSTANDING THE FEELINGS
AND PROBLEMS OF SUBORDINATES

The need to build voluntary cooperation, instead of relying on power, calls for a fundamental shift in the way we think about leadership. As we move away from power the nature of the interaction between boss and subordinate changes sharply. Empathetic understanding, ego support, and provision of opportunities become central concepts. So, before we examine various means for engendering cooperation, which we do in the next chapter, several characteristics of a wholesome boss-subordinate relationship should be made clear.

This expanded and more difficult relationship is reflected in the second part of our definition of leading—understanding the feelings and problems of subordinates. Such an upward flow of information is useful to a manager for several reasons.

First, *personal communication is one of the principal ways a manager learns the operational facts he should take into account in making his decisions.* Consider, for example, the communication between Rog Hetzel, the national sales manager of a breakfast-food company, and one of his subordinates, Bill Jones, who is sales supervisor for the Detroit region. If sales are falling off in Detroit, Hetzel, sitting in New York, may receive helpful statistical reports, customer reports, and other official communications from the Detroit region, but in personal conversation with Jones he can find out a wealth of additional facts about the problems in Detroit that he could not learn from formal reports, no matter how complete. He might learn, for instance, that the manager of a local competitor was formerly a trade association executive and is intimate with many members of the food industry in Detroit. We might say, then, that the personal communication of miscellaneous, sometimes intangible, information is an important research tool for a manager to use in decision-making.

A second benefit of finding out the *problems and feelings of subordinates is that they may be as important an element in some decisions as operating facts.* To continue our preceding illustration, suppose Hetzel has decided that the Detroit and Chicago regions should increase their advertising expenditures next year, and that to offset this additional expense they should reduce the number of salesmen engaged in direct selling. But unknown to Hetzel, Jones in Detroit believes that this change is the wrong way to proceed in view of the peculiarities of local competition. Consequently, when Jones hears of the revised selling plan, he develops a feeling that he has been treated unfairly and that the management in New York has hurt his chances of selling a big quota. Regardless of who is *right* in this matter, Jones's feeling will stay with him for some time and will affect his actions both in running his region and in dealing with Hetzel and others in New York management.

If Hetzel had known the full import of Jones's feelings, the decision might have been different. Or perhaps the decision would have stuck, but Hetzel would have tried to convert Jones's feelings from negative to positive ones. Clearly if a manager is going to try to change a subordinate's feelings about a particular decision, he must first find out what those feelings are.

Still another reason why a manager needs to remain in close touch with his subordinates is that the whole structure of management—jobs, plans, authority relationships, influence networks, the matching of individuals with jobs, and the system of control reports—can get out of date. *An executive needs a continuous reappraisal of his management structure.* For example, one way an executive matches people and their jobs—discussed in Chapter 10—is by learning through personal contacts with his subordinates about their progress, problems, likes and dislikes, capabilities, and other characteristics that may indicate when a man's assignment should be changed.

A fourth reason why finding out about the problems and feelings of subordinates is important in leading is that *personal two-way communication has a positive effect on the feelings of subordinates.* Regardless of whether what a subordinate says is valid or whether it actually affects management's decisions, he usually feels better after he "blows off a little steam." Psychologists refer to this phenomenon as catharsis, but in common terms most of us simply say, "He had to get it off his chest." Besides, by freely communicating with his boss, a subordinate at least knows that his boss is aware of his problems and desires.

If Jones, our Detroit sales supervisor, knows that his boss, Hetzel, receives only formal reports on Detroit sales, expenses, competitors' prices, and relative market position, but never talks with Jones about his local problems, then Jones is likely to build up anxieties. He begins to feel that his boss doesn't *understand* his problems, and he is easily annoyed even by factual inquiries from the New York office.

Obtaining a full understanding of the feelings and problems of subordinates, such as we have been describing, is impossible when a manager relies on power. We do not talk freely and frankly with a boss who keeps us aware that he is the one who grants or withholds rewards. We tend to give such a boss only the information that we hope will make us look good to him.

LEADING: A DYNAMIC PERSONAL PROCESS

Leading is an endless process for a manager. Not only do the problems and plans of an enterprise keep changing, thereby creating new issues calling for leadership, but we as individuals also change. Bill Jones on Friday is not the same man he was on Tuesday. Our attitudes, abilities, and feelings are continuously evolving throughout life, with the result that our relations with subordinates, superiors, and co-workers are subject to modification.

This changing, dynamic aspect of managing is illustrated by the way an executive's day-to-day actions modify formal plans, by the interpretations subordinates put on executive responses to their actions, and by the interplay between the successive actions of an executive and his subordinates.

How Actions of a Leader Convey Meaning

By almost everything he does, a manager influences in some way the future actions of his subordinates. When we write job descriptions or make other plans, we obviously intend to tell subordinates what they are expected to do. But—a fact we often overlook—our daily actions probably determine employee behavior more than the written plans and organization charts. We simply cannot understand managerial leadership unless we are aware of the effect that each little action we take during a day may have on the behavior pattern of our subordinates.

Let us note, first, how a manager's seemingly casual action may influence his subordinates' attitudes. The following is an actual case (though names and places have been disguised).

C. T. Crane is the manager of the Buffalo plant of Union Paper Company, the headquarters of which is in New York. His job description states that "the plant manager has authority over all operations and personnel in the plant." M. J. Palmer, the vice-president in charge of production, who is located in New York, drew up this job description for plant managers; he says he is wholeheartedly in favor of decentralizing and of granting autonomy at the plant level. Palmer and Crane have been working together harmoniously in their present positions for about eight years.

Because of a cost-cutting campaign instituted by the president over the past six months, Palmer recently sent one of his staff men to Buffalo "to investigate the production-scheduling system." Although staff men from headquarters had visited Buffalo on other subjects in the past, none had ever delved into the production-scheduling system.

The visit was viewed as a routine, run-of-the-mill activity by both Crane and Palmer. The production-scheduling system was duly modified on the recommendation of the staff man. About four months later, however, Palmer again asked the staff man to "go to Buffalo to see how the scheduling system is working and if there are any further changes that ought to be made."

This time Crane, as he revealed in an interview, felt "a little annoyed that New York was sending a man to make changes." Nevertheless, Crane said that little annoyances came up all the time, and the new procedure did not make very much difference anyway.

Although neither Palmer nor Crane regarded this action as particularly significant, we can note that Crane's attitude about New York headquarters and his feeling toward Palmer were affected to a small degree. A series of such small experiences could, in the course of time, significantly alter the relation between Crane and Palmer. In fact, the production-control staff man continued to visit Buffalo regularly; he worked out the details of the scheduling *procedure*, and also a shipping-invoice procedure, and a system for maintaining employee records.

Regardless of whether the changes in procedure were desirable, we can see that by gradual actions Palmer did change Crane's duties (he no longer decided on these procedures). Crane's job description has not been rewritten, but he, Palmer, and the staff man recognize that the staff man now has the real say-so about the three procedures.

Another series of incidents in this same company further illustrates how a manager's actions communicate meaning to subordinates. Crane had a minor disagreement with the New York sales manager over the level of inventories to be stored at the Buffalo plant warehouse. Theretofore,

Fig. 20-3 *Simplified organization chart of the Union Paper Company, showing principal patterns of communication.*

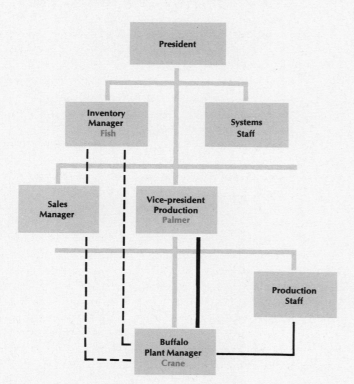

Crane had carried 800,000 sheets of No. 2 grade book stock, but the sales manager requested him to increase this to 900,000 sheets. Both men knew that the sales manager discussed the problem with Palmer in an effort to get him to tell Crane to increase the inventory. About a year passed, and Crane got no word from Palmer on this matter. The sales manager again brought up the subject with Palmer, and once again Palmer failed to take any action.

Interviews with the three men concerned with this inventory question revealed that both the sales manager and Crane *interpreted* Palmer's lack of action to mean that Crane was in charge of deciding the level of plant inventories. All three men also interpreted the sales manager's failure to appeal to the president (again, lack of action) to mean that the sales manager acknowledged the authority of Palmer and Crane over plant inventories. In this instance, we note that neither the sales manager nor Palmer ever said that Crane had authority over the level of inventories. Yet each "sensed" how the others agreed the problem should be resolved. Palmer's action—or lack of action—provided guidance to his subordinate Crane.

Mutual Interaction of Supervisor and Subordinates

Just as the actions of an executive influence his subordinates, so too do their actions affect him. *Perhaps* subordinates do not often try consciously and deliberately to sway their boss, but influences clearly run in both directions. Because leading involves the interaction of two or more personalities, the way subordinates respond to the requests and actions of their boss, as well as the behavior they initiate, are part and parcel of the leadership pattern that emerges in each man-to-man relationship.

In the Union Paper Company case, for instance, Crane's willingness to accept staff guidance on procedures and his disregard of the sales manager's request for a bigger inventory had a marked effect on the kind of leadership his supervisor, Palmer, gave him. Had Crane's responses to any of these situations been different, Palmer also would have behaved differently. Over time, a series of such changes resulting from Crane's behavior and Palmer's reaction to it, might have significantly altered the leadership relation between them.

How a leadership pattern evolves is also illustrated by the experiences of the new president of a large life insurance company. For many years, this company had been run by a man with a dominant personality who was quite conservative about making changes. When the old man retired, the directors replaced him with the president of one of the progressive banks in the city, with a clear understanding that the new president would probably introduce changes in the insurance company.

A few of the vice-presidents were disappointed at being passed over in favor of a man from outside the company, but the new president was a warm, likable person and soon established a friendly relationship with all his key associates. The president announced that his objectives were the growth and modernization of the company, but in developing new plans, being personally unfamiliar with the details of the life insurance business, he used participation extensively. The president hoped that through open and thorough discussions he would be able to lead the vice-presidents to revitalize the company. In fact, not much happened. The vice-presidents always had good reasons for moving slowly.

After two years the president created a new position, that of administrative vice-president "to assist the president on internal affairs." The president explained to the board of directors that he needed a vigorous man to help him get some action, so he selected a young man who had been remarkably successful in operating his own insurance agency. This new vice-president laid out several programs dealing with such matters as reorganization, revised status of the group life department, and automation in issuing premium notices. He pressed for action according to a master schedule, and the president gave strong support to his proposals. Now the atmosphere in the executive offices changed; instead of conservative complacency, there was a general air of uncertainty—everyone wondered, "What's going to happen next?" At the same time, communication between the president and the vice-presidents became guarded, two vice-presidents who opposed certain changes resigned, and other company officers greeted proposals from the administrative vice-president with foot-dragging, if not sabotage. The administrative vice-president's response was to push harder for his reforms. Finally, on two disputes he was called on to arbitrate, the president decided in favor of the older vice-presidents. This lack of support upset the administrative vice-president, who said in a private conversation, "He asked me to get something done in a tough situation, and now he has pulled the rug out from under me."

At the end of three years at the insurance company, the administrative vice-president had an offer of another job, and the president encouraged him to take it. As his replacement, the president selected from within the company a man who was generally respected for his ability to dig out facts and state all sides of a proposal objectively. The new man, who was not highly self-assertive, was more interested in making a complete analysis of a matter than in getting action. With the new man in office, tension was eased, and within six months substantial progress on the modernization programs was clearly evident.

To understand what took place in this company, we should note that (1) in addition to the two resignations several of the older vice presidents had retired during the five years after the new president was first appointed; (2) by the end of the five years no one doubted that the president really meant to make significant changes in company operations—and because in fact there was also general agreement that he was moving in the right direction, his stature had increased in the eyes of key executives; and (3) most of the executives were relieved to have the former administrative vice-president out of the picture. After that man's departure, the president found that his subordinates discussed problems more frankly with him, and that everyone more genuinely accepted the objectives he had stated when he first came to the company. More progress was made toward the goals of growth and modernization during the next two years than had been accomplished during the entire preceding five years.

In this case, we can see how the values and attitudes of the executives evolved in response to different kinds of leadership; how the president had to change his actions because of the response he was getting from subordinates; and how the relations between the president and his subordinates changed, even though the president was, through all the seven years, the same friendly person in search of the same end results. Clearly, leading is a dynamic, personal process.

LEADERSHIP ATTITUDES

Our review of managerial leadership has emphasized the key part personal relations play in this process. As managers, we are dealing with the reactions of individual personalities to one another. To improve our ability to lead, then, we have to be highly perceptive about the people involved in a specific situation. Most of us will never become trained psychologists, but we can develop an awareness of the more obvious factors that might confront us. Even such an awareness, however, requires a set of attitudes that often need cultivating: *empathy, self-awareness, and objectivity*.

Knowing about the importance of these attitudes will not ensure that we develop them, of course—just as knowing we should not get mad and actually controlling our anger are quite different matters. Still, by understanding which attitudes contribute to good leadership, we can diagnose leadership problems better and may discover where we personally should try to improve.

Empathy

Empathy is the ability to look at things from another person's point of view. If a leader is to guide, motivate, and get information from a subordinate, he needs this capacity to project himself into that man's position. How does that fellow feel about the company and his job? What values does he attach to friendships, security, titles, and the many other things affected by his work? How will he interpret the words and actions of his boss, his associates, and his subordinates? What are his hopes and aspirations? What difficulties are bothering him at the moment?

Whom does he trust, and whom does he fear? Note that empathy is not a case of asking, "What would *I* do if I were in your position?" because any one of us might bring to the position quite different knowledge and feelings. We are empathetic only when we can sense and feel, almost intuitively, *how another person reacts* to a given situation.

An executive may set up a new vacation policy or make some other change he intends as an aid to his subordinates, but if he thinks of the change in terms of how *he* would like it rather than how the people affected will like it, the move is likely to misfire. To be empathetic we need *respect* for the other person as an individual. We may disagree sharply with his values and consider his reasoning false, but we should still recognize that his feelings and beliefs seem just as valid to him as ours do to us. A salesman, for instance, often finds he needs such attitudes; if he is a good salesman he has a high degree of empathy for his customer, but he does not necessarily endorse the customer's behavior or beliefs.

Self-awareness

Knowing oneself ranks with empathy as a requisite for leadership. We have already seen in this chapter how an executive's actions influence the behavior of a subordinate. Now we want to stress that each executive needs to be *aware* of the particular impact he makes. He should know his own predilections for, say, taking action hastily, being brusque with people who don't understand instructions the first time, getting so involved in specific problems that he bypasses supervisors in resolving them, and so forth.

Moreover, a leader should know how he appears to other people. Many of us have an image of ourselves that differs from the way others see us. A manager may think of himself as fair and objective, for example, but some of his subordinates may consider him to be biased in favor of young men with college degrees. Regardless of which view is correct, the manager may have difficulty in motivating and communicating with a subordinate who is convinced he is biased unless he knows that the subordinate thinks so. Finally, with an awareness of his own preferences, weaknesses, and habits, and of what others think of him, a manager should learn what impression his actions make on other people. One high-ranking executive, for instance, growled over the telephone at the secretaries and assistants of his immediate subordinates when the latter were "not in." In so doing, he unwittingly created morale problems for his subordinates and virtually cut himself off from any voluntary help from lower-level personnel. But this executive, whose manner with his immediate subordinates was much less gruff, was unaware that by expressing his displeasure to secretaries he was creating minor difficulties.

Objective Attitude toward Behavior

A third quality that is crucial to good leadership is objectivity in man-to-man relations. Something causes everyone to behave as he does. If we can identify the influences on Joe Jones's actions, we have taken an important step toward guiding his behavior. Instead of getting angry with Joe for resisting a new method, for instance, we should recognize his response and try to find out what caused it. Or if one of our salesmen is unusually energetic, we should try to understand what motivates him in the hope of discovering a way to induce similar behavior in our other salesmen.

Such detachment may not be easy to maintain. We commonly react to the behavior of others emotionally instead of coolly and analytically. Besides, a manager is often deeply concerned with the outcome of his subordinate's activities and therefore lets his intense feelings cloud his objectivity.

In addition, empathy fosters sympathy and personal identification with other people; yet a good leader should be both objective and empathetic. The viewpoint of a physician is similar to what a leader needs to reconcile these two attitudes. A good physician understands his patients' feelings—he is empathetic in a high degree; but his *own emotional involvement* with his patients must be limited if he is to make an objective diagnosis and perhaps take action that he knows involves substantial risk. He is well aware of the problems of his patients as individual personalities, and at the same time he deals with such problems in a detached, scientific manner. A good manager, likewise, understands the feelings and problems of his subordinates; yet he keeps enough psychological distance to be fair, just, and constructively concerned with performance.[3]

Many qualities contribute to a manager's ability to lead. We cannot

[3]This point goes back to the statement earlier in the chapter that the appointed leader in a large organization, even more than the informal leader in a small group, is in a tough spot. He has many people under him who have different and perhaps conflicting needs and aspirations. He also has technological processes that must be performed and may conflict with human attitudes, needs, and aspirations. Finally, he has to balance his internal company operations with the norms of society—achieving efficient output, obeying laws and customs, adjusting to economic conditions, and so on. To reconcile these forces, he often needs a dynamic innovation, and yet he must maintain a balance within the enterprise. In the economists' language, there must be some *equilibrium* among people and efficiency, coupled with some *innovation* and growth. Traditional management theorists like Fayol would say the manager must maintain *balance* among the various people and technological processes in a company. Small-group sociologists would say that the leader *satisfies the needs* of people but must also *facilitate change* in group customs. Some psychologists say that the manager must *integrate* the needs and attitudes of people with the economic and technological forces of society. Cultural anthropologists, taking their language from biology, say that the leader facilitates *evolutionary* change of ideas and beliefs of people through mutation or dialectics. Finally, historians would say that the leader must in part influence society (the company) while at the same time letting society (subordinates) influence their careers and leadership. Does the man make the times, or the times make the man? If the leader is objective and empathetic, the answer is, *both*.

make a complete and unassailable list of such qualities, partly because they vary with the people being led and with the circumstances in which the leading takes place. Nevertheless, we can single out three qualities— empathy, self-awareness, and objectivity—that are needed in the vast majority of cases. The importance of these particular attitudes will become increasingly apparent as we analyze leadership activities in the next three chapters.

CONCLUSION

Managerial leadership is primarily concerned with converting plans into action, and in an enterprise this involves highly personal, man-to-man, interaction between each manager and his subordinates. Inevitably power is present. Although a manager can use this power to help shape the social structure within his sphere, power is becoming increasingly ineffective as a motivator of action. Instead a modern manager must try to create a total work situation in which workers find significant fulfillment of personal needs from actions that also contribute to company objectives.

A manager can adopt this latter leadership approach only when he really understands the feelings and problems of his individual subordinates. Such feelings change, partly as a result of the behavior of the manager himself, and problems change with the ebb and flow of events. To keep in tune with these highly personalized "facts," the manager needs empathy, self-awareness, and an objectivity about behavior.

In his role as a leader the manager is in a particularly tight spot. He must act within the constraints imposed by technology and his environment, must fulfill company objectives, and at the same time must be responsive to the individualized needs of his subordinates.

In the following chapters, as we explore several key *activities* of leaders—developing voluntary cooperation, fostering two-way communication, and directing and disciplining—we will not find neat and simple rules. The leadership process is too personalized and too dependent on prior relationships to fit a set of cookbook rules. Nevertheless, we shall find a number of concepts and techniques that any manager may find helpful if he uses them at the appropriate time and place.

FOR CLASS DISCUSSION

Questions

1) What factors may make it (1) difficult and/or (2) undesirable for management to select the informal leader of a group and make him the appointed leader?

2) "For a supervisor to exhibit true leadership over his subordinates is virtually impossible in a business setting. This is so because the needs and values of the subordinates are not only different from, but often conflict with, the needs and values of the organization which the supervisor must seek to satisfy." Do you agree? Discuss.

3) If power, in the broadest sense of the word, is a "moving force," then is not leadership really a form of power? What is the major distinction between leadership and power as these words are used in this chapter?

4) Is it possible for a man to be selected by a group as its leader even though the man, when he is working with other groups, appears to lack empathy? Explain.

5) Is it possible for the appointed leader of a department to enjoy some of the benefits of informal leadership by using a member of the group who is recognized as an informal leader? What are the pros and cons of such an arrangement?

6) What effect does the existence of a strong but fair local union have on the potential leadership of first-line foremen in the plant?

7) Is it possible for a subordinate to exercise leadership over his boss and not run the risk of losing his job if the boss finds out what he is doing?

8) "I'm continually amazed," said a national sales manager of a company selling office equipment," at the failure of many outstanding salesmen to become effective leaders when appointed to branch management posts. A good salesman has very little power over customers. He makes his sales with good products and the attributes of a leader. Why can't he use those same attributes to lead his branch when we put him in charge?" What do you think of this observation?

Cases

For cases involving issues covered in this chapter, see especially the following. Particularly relevant questions are listed after each case.

General Machinery Corporation (p. 130), 14
Scott-Davis Corporation (p. 227), 16
Gerald Clark (p. 234), 15
Harrogate Asphalt Products, Ltd.—AR (p. 557), 10, 12
Consolidated Instruments—A (p. 571), 12
Consolidated Instruments—B (p. 674), 13

FOR FURTHER READING

Dubin, R., *Human Relations in Administration*, 3rd ed. Englewood Cliffs, N.J.: Prentice-Hall, Inc., 1968, Chap. 16. *Especially helpful on interrelations among leadership, power, and democracy in organizations.*

Filley, A.C., and R.J. House, *Managerial Process and Organizational Behavior.* Glenview, Ill.: Scott, Foresman & Company, 1969, Chap. 16. *Good summary and lead into psychological studies of leadership.*

Hersey, P., and K.H. Blanchard, *Management of Organizational Behavior.* Englewood Cliffs, N.J.: Prentice-Hall, Inc., 1969, Chaps. 4–6. *Concise, nontechnical summary of theory about leading and organizational effectiveness.*

Katz, D., and R.L. Kahn, *Social Psychology of Organizations.* New York: John Wiley & Sons, Inc., 1966, Chap. 11. *The functions of leadership in managing an enterprise.*

Martin, N.H., and J.H. Sims, "Power Tactics." *Harvard Business Review*, November 1956. *Advice on the use of power by executives.*

Rush, Harold M.F., *Behavioral Science Concepts and Management Application.* New York: The Conference Board, 1969. *Review of the theories of five influential behavioral scientists.*

Chapter Twenty-one

Developing Voluntary Cooperation

LEADERSHIP AND COOPERATION

The willing, enthusiastic carrying out of plans is essential to a vigorous enterprise. The pace and complexity of modern business force managers to rely heavily on the voluntary cooperation of their subordinates. Especially as work itself becomes less routine and more unique and adaptive, and as all of us move our sights up the need hierarchy to social and self-realizing goals, our dedication to our job becomes crucial. Power alone cannot generate the initiative and resourcefulness needed in many jobs. The best of plans are of little value unless we can develop a genuine *esprit de corps* for executing them. In this chapter we shall explore ways of fostering such voluntary cooperation. In doing so, we shall focus primarily on the behavior of managers in their personal relations with subordinates.

Developing voluntary cooperation, however, is intimately associated with other phases of the management process. A manager can neither turn this activity over to a specialized assistant, nor devote forty minutes a day to it and then forget it. A spirit of cooperation grows principally out of his *manner* of dealing with subordinates as he works with them on specific operating problems; it emerges from the way he treats and responds to other people in *all* his contacts with them. We are considering voluntary cooperation in a separate chapter, not because the job of developing it is a distinct type of work, but in order to emphasize its importance in successful management.

Elements of Managerial Leadership

Before examining ways of encouraging voluntary cooperation, we should see clearly how this task fits into the total leadership process. Figure 21–1 shows the major elements involved. The *purposes* served by managerial leadership—guiding and motivating subordinates toward carrying out company plans and understanding the problems and feelings of subordinates—appear in the right-hand column as results we wish to achieve. The significance of these functions has already been reviewed in the preceding chapter.

The major *activities* a manager undertakes to accomplish these leadership functions are indicated in the center of the chart. These activities are: developing voluntary cooperation, engaging in two-way personal communication, and directing and disciplining. We shall deal with these activities in this and the next two chapters.

But such leadership activities cannot possibly produce the desired results by themselves. They must be backed up by a management structure that is compatible with, and conducive to, good leadership. This structural support is indicated in the left-hand column of the chart, which lists important *prerequisites* for effective leadership. We shall review these prerequisites briefly in the following pages, indicating the way in which many of the suggestions made in earlier parts of the book have a direct bearing on the process of leading.

Fig. 21-1 Elements in managerial leadership that foster active, personal, man-to-man relations between a manager and his subordinates.

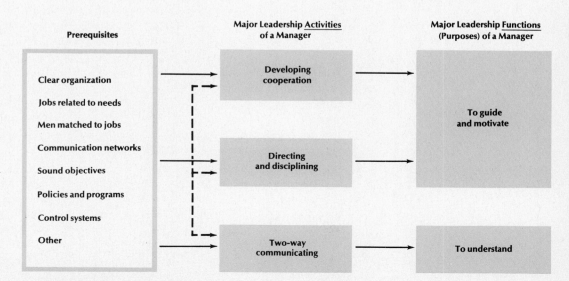

Prerequisites	Major Leadership **Activities** of a Manager	Major Leadership **Functions** (Purposes) of a Manager
Clear organization	Developing cooperation	To guide and motivate
Jobs related to needs		
Men matched to jobs		
Communication networks	Directing and disciplining	
Sound objectives		
Policies and programs		
Control systems		
Other	Two-way communicating	To understand

In the present chapter, then, we shall deal first with the structural prerequisites to voluntary cooperation, next with guides for executive behavior that will foster cooperation, and finally with fitting such behavior to individual subordinates. As a preface to this analysis, two general characteristics of voluntary cooperation should be emphasized: its high emotional content and its need for continuing attention.

Nurturing Cooperative Feelings

Voluntary cooperation is predominantly an *emotional* response. We rarely decide to cooperate with our boss by rationally balancing required effort and possible reward. If we do make a calculated trade, bargaining *power* is likely to be a determining factor. *Voluntary* cooperation between a supervisor and a subordinate is quite a different kind of response. It is based largely on the subordinate's feelings—his attitudes toward the boss, the job, or perhaps the company.

Psychologists tell us that in most situations our emotions dominate our attention, memory, imagination, and energy, and that thinking typically plays a minor part. This means that if we are to obtain the *voluntary* cooperation of our subordinates, the act of cooperation must be emotionally attractive. Ordinarily, a subordinate joins in with our program because he wants to; he doesn't think much about it, but finds cooperation a satisfying way to act.

Consequently, as we examine any measures intended to contribute to voluntary cooperation, the important consideration is how such measures will, in fact, affect the feelings of a subordinate—not how the man logically "should" react. For example, in developing the voluntary cooperation of a particular employee named Bob Bartell, it doesn't make any difference that he *should* consider his bonus payment fair; what is pertinent is whether he does (or does not) *feel* that it is fair. Then there has to be an emotional transfer: When Bob feels he has been treated fairly, he will also feel more like cooperating. Bob's feelings are what matter.

A second general characteristic of voluntary cooperation, in addition to its emotional nature, is its need for continual nurturing. We may have the initial enthusiasm of our subordinates for a program, but interest is hard to sustain over time, especially when other duties, family obligations, or other outside activities compete for a limited supply of energy. H. C. Mansfield and F. M. Marx have stated this problem well:

> *Normally, every individual responds to a wide range of loyalties —some imbedded in his background, some foisted upon him in the school of living, some freely accepted as a matter of deliberate choice. In this agglomeration no single loyalty will dominate all others. . . . Even when there is general accord of loyalties, each loyalty*

separately continues to have some influence upon him. Depending on the circumstances, each may place him in part or for a time in opposition to the organization for which he works.

This is the basic reason why . . . leadership must constantly attempt to magnify individual loyalty toward the institution. Such effort cannot be confined to a single approach—a single "morale program." It must come to the fore in everything the organization undertakes to accomplish. To foster what military language calls "pride of outfit," institutional leadership must be articulate and persuasive on its objectives and policies, adept in developing a general system of internal inducements, resourceful in broadening the base for participation in policy-making, and inventive in distributing credit for collective accomplishment.[1]

Occasionally, for a special program or the introduction of a new policy, we may try to build up an unusual amount of enthusiasm. But such campaigns should be based on an enduring relationship between supervisor and subordinate, for at least two reasons: (1) A sudden burst of energy often expends itself quickly, like the pressure in a bottle of soda pop, and without a continuing source of strength, the first efforts are likely to be followed by indifference. (2) Many of the feelings on which voluntary cooperation is based take *time* to develop; for example, trust and confidence that a supervisor will support his men is often built up only over a period of years. Such feelings cannot be turned on and off to suit temporary requirements.

In a sustained activity like the normal operation of an enterprise, then, we want a spirit of cooperation that is enduring. To achieve this, a manager must continually cultivate and reinforce—by his own behavior—an *esprit de corps* among his subordinates. He develops cooperation by his ordinary actions day by day, year by year.

STRUCTURAL PREREQUISITES
TO VOLUNTARY COOPERATION

Man-to-man leadership can develop voluntary cooperation only under favorable conditions. The total process of managing has to be reasonably well performed for personal leadership to flourish. We cannot do a poor job of organizing, planning, and controlling, and then expect leadership to pull us out of our troubles miraculously.

Managerial leadership operates in a structure—a structure of organization, plans, and controls, and on the basis of this formally designed structure a social structure develops—as we have seen earlier in the book. Many of the habits and persistent feelings of workers (both managers and

[1] F. M. Marx, ed., *Elements of Public Administration*, 2nd ed. (Englewood Cliffs, N.J.: Prentice-Hall, 1959), p. 284.

operators) arise from the formal and social structures we create as a part of managing, and these feelings affect workers' willingness to cooperate. If the structure provides satisfying experiences for workers, the task of leadership is aided; but if the structure fails to satisfy at least the more pressing needs of workers, effective man-to-man leadership becomes very difficult. A good management structure, then, is a prerequisite to a high degree of voluntary cooperation.

Let us very briefly review several major points where our structural design may have a significant bearing on the feelings of workers and on their willingness to cooperate with company plans.

On-the-job satisfactions built into jobs. We can design many jobs so that they provide a man who fills them with direct personal satisfactions. Job enlargement, for example, increases opportunity for self-assertion and a sense of achievement. "Task-teams" provide sociability while allowing considerable self-regulation. Committee assignments open the way for give-and-take communication and often add prestige to individual members. Decentralization too creates major opportunities for self-expression and personal growth. Such direct satisfactions tend to increase a man's willingness to cooperate with his boss.

Men well matched with jobs. A man's feeling about his work also depends on whether his job is suited to his abilities. Through manpower planning we try to make full use of a man's abilities, but at the same time we try not to put him in a spot where he becomes discouraged and defensive because he cannot meet his obligations. Minor modifications in organization structure are often made, either enlarging or contracting an assignment, so that a man and his job are well matched. Such matching fosters a cooperative feeling.

Clear organization. When a man has known duties—and corresponding authority—he can develop pride in his work, recognized status, and a sense of inner security. By making clear the role of staff we avoid a source of confusion and perhaps conflicting obligations.

Effective communications networks. With each man necessarily doing only a piece of the total work in a company, we have to design systems that provide him with the information he needs, promptly and accurately. If he is kept well informed, his work can proceed smoothly and he can take pride in his accomplishment, whereas poor communication leads to confusion, frustration, and negative attitudes toward meeting company goals.

Sound objectives. Company objectives are often accepted as desirable personal goals by company employees. To be most challenging, however, broad goals need to be translated into specific aims that are meaningful to each employee, and then reasonable levels of achievement should be agreed on. Such specific goals can become the basis for a great deal of voluntary cooperation, and achieving them can give a worker a significant sense of accomplishment.

Workable policies, methods, and procedures. A structure of plans for handling repetitive problems creates a necessary stability and a pattern of behavior that make work more satisfying to most employees. For aside from an occasional rebel, most men derive a sense of security from an established, known set of norms. A good body of standing plans also eases the task of performing work. In addition, if we can introduce some flexibility by using many of the plans as guides rather than as fixed rules, employee attitudes are likely to be even more cooperative.

Balanced control systems. In Part Six we shall see that control systems too can be designed in a way that minimizes the usual negative reaction to controls and provides constructive help to individuals in meeting their accepted goals. To achieve this, we must select the right criteria of performance, set reasonable standards, measure output reliably, and provide prompt and direct feedback. A poorly designed control system, in contrast, can give rise to a good deal of discontent and make a manager's job of developing voluntary cooperation difficult.

All the preceding ideas are examined more thoroughly in other parts of the book. The purpose of this quick review is merely to refresh our memories on how often the feelings of employees and the design of plans, organization, and controls are intertwined. In the following discussion of personal actions by a manager that help develop voluntary cooperation, we are assuming that the total management structure is conducive to effective man-to-man leadership. The entire structure may not be completely to everyone's liking, of course, but on balance it must be favorably regarded by our subordinates if through our personal behavior we are to generate enthusiasm in them for carrying out company plans.

GUIDES FOR MANAGERIAL BEHAVIOR

What can a manager do as a leader to encourage voluntary cooperation? We have already set the stage by noting that the manager must have empathy, self-assurance, and objectivity, and that the company structure of organization, plans, and controls must be conducive to voluntary cooperation. But we still have the unanswered question of what a supervisor can do in his man-to-man relations with his subordinates to build a sustained feeling of cooperativeness.

The following pages give a series of *guides* for developing voluntary cooperation. We call them guides, instead of principles or rules, for several reasons: They should be used with discretion, because they do not suit all situations. They have to be followed consistently, often for a long time, because the attitudes and feelings of subordinates may change slowly. Even then, they may not work for all subordinates and for all problems. They overlap to some extent and leave much leeway to anyone who tries to apply them. Nevertheless, they are the best guides we know of. Most of the proposals are supported by some behavioral research findings, and all are based on a substantial body of the practical experience of executives.

Friendliness and Approval

The kind of friendliness we are concerned with here runs deeper than mere cordiality and politeness. A subordinate is dependent on his supervisor for a variety of things—job assignments, information, help in overcoming problems, and the like—and he wants assurance of *approval* from this strategic person. Being friendly is one way a supervisor can convey approval.

There are an infinite number of ways to show friendliness. They range from a cheery "Good morning" or an inquiry about Johnny's measles to entertaining at dinner or lending one's boat for a vacation cruise. How friendliness is shown will depend on the personalities of the supervisor and the subordinate and on local conditions. The significant point is that the subordinate wants to feel that his boss knows him, values him as a person, and approves of him. If such feeling is absent, the chances of getting enthusiastic cooperation are dim.

An essential aspect of friendliness is intent or integrity. A boss who asks about Johnny's measles merely because a personnel director tells him he should do so is only observing a formality. An annual barbecue on an executive's back lawn can be a superficial substitute for closer relations that should have been developed at the office. On the other hand, the barbecue and the inquiry about Johnny may be sincere expressions of genuine friendliness. Usually subordinates can sense the intent that lies back of friendly gestures. If they feel that the actions of their supervisor really reveal his approval, the integrity of the action builds a sense of trust. This kind of friendliness provides a basis for joint endeavors in which voluntary cooperation is a natural way of proceeding.

Consistency and Fairness

Inconsistent treatment by a boss can upset workers to a point where they become disgusted with their entire job. The president of a medium-sized import-export company, for instance, was so unpredictable in his demands that his chief accountant resigned. The accountant explained: "I can't live with a guy like that. One day he's hounding you for figures, 'guesstimates' if necessary. The next day accuracy is all important, right down to the last penny. The Dr. Jekyll–Mr. Hyde act was driving me nuts." Consistent supervision enables subordinates to develop normal patterns of behavior. Knowing what to expect and how to respond, they feel more secure and self-confident.

But trying to be consistent creates some difficulties for a manager. If he is entirely consistent day after day, year after year, his business will stagnate. Actions must be adapted to changing conditions. Perhaps the president of the import-export company just mentioned faced radically different problems from day to day: A deal demanding an urgent decision might call for a quick estimate, whereas another transaction involving a narrow profit margin might require detailed accuracy. To resolve this dilemma between consistency and flexibility, a manager can do three things: (1) Recognize the need for a significant amount of consistency in his relations with subordinates, and be consistent in most facets of his behavior. (2) When he does depart from a customary pattern, let subordinates know that he appreciates their difficulty in adjusting to his shift

Fig. 21-2 How managers treat subordinates and how subordinates judge methods of treatment. Four possible patterns of treatment are shown. Circles indicate which methods three separate groups of subordinates consider to be "fair."

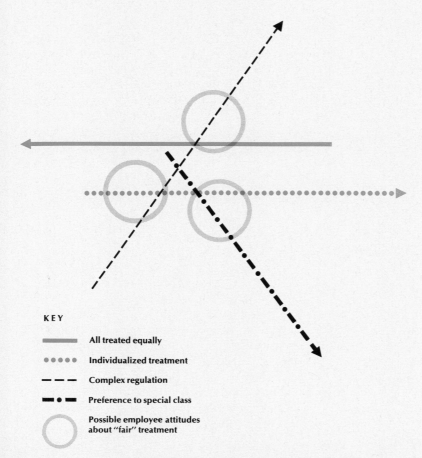

KEY

——— All treated equally

• • • • • Individualized treatment

– – – Complex regulation

— • — Preference to special class

◯ Possible employee attitudes about "fair" treatment

in behavior. (3) Indicate why he alters a familiar pattern so that subordinates will regard his behavior as reasonable rather than capricious.

Even more important to a spirit of cooperation than consistency over time is consistency—or fairness—of treatment among subordinates. A feeling among workers that a boss plays favorites ("Pete gets all the soft assignments." "Sure, he's the fair-haired boy; he can take a day off and nobody kicks.") can quickly reduce voluntary cooperation to zero. In American society we hold a strong belief that people should be treated equally. In fact, one of the major rallying points of labor unions is their assurance of fair treatment for every member. Discrimination on the basis of race or sex are sore points.

Here again we get into difficulty in determining just what is fair. The principle of equal treatment clashes with another strong belief: Every person should be treated as an individual. If Joe has thirty years of service with the company, or his leg is in a cast because of an automobile accident, or he is going to be sent abroad in six months, should he be given special consideration?

To build a spirit of cooperation, we have to give rewards and punishments and perform other supervisory acts in a manner that *subordinates feel* is consistent or at least reasonable. Equal treatment is only a starting point. Many exceptions to strict equality are regarded as fair. Joe can be given special treatment—because of his service, or leg, or future job—if the reason is known and accepted as legitimate and if subordinates believe that future exceptions will be made consistently for other persons in a similar situation. Among many employees, in fact, fairness actually requires that those with long service or in poor health be given special treatment.

Emphasis on Desired Actions

Supervisory actions that call attention to correct behavior are more effective in promoting voluntary cooperation than those that call attention to incorrect behavior. Let us consider the example of the All-American Shirt Company. Sales are down and the president is convinced that substantial cuts in expenses are necessary. One approach the president might take would be to *wait* for one, or more, of his key subordinates to cut expenses on his own initiative; then he could commend the person, even give him a raise. Such treatment would tend to make the subordinate repeat his behavior in the future and would also produce a cooperative attitude. Of course, whether the president can afford to wait would depend on the alertness of his subordinates and the seriousness of the financial position of the company.

The opposite approach would be for the president to call the attention of his subordinates frequently to each high cost-ratio. Always calling attention to a man's deficiencies (even though the charges may be true) tends to generate unfriendliness and to diminish a man's trust that his boss believes in his capabilities. Psychologists would say that this action creates a defensive attitude, and that if the accusations of deficiency are in fact valid the person may distort his thinking by rationalizing the problem away as someone else's fault. He may even become "aggressive" and "hard to get along with."

In any subordinate's performance, we almost always find both results to praise and results that need improvement. All too often in our relations with subordinates, we stress the areas needing improvement and brush over the good points. In view of the typical reactions to praise and criticism, noted in the preceding paragraph, we should be fully as careful to give praise as to criticize, perhaps mixing the two so that defensive reactions do not dominate the feelings of our subordinates. Moreover, in discussing deficiencies we can treat them as problems to be overcome rather than as personal criticisms (a suggestion that we shall examine more fully in Chapter 23). In short, to improve voluntary cooperation we should "accentuate the positive."

Support for Subordinates

A manager can provide a wide range of supports for his subordinates. One is simply to help in getting a job done. For example, machines may need repairing, tough customers may need to be impressed by a man from the home office, letters should be answered while a subordinate is in bed with the flu, and so on. And the supervisor may provide the assistance that is needed. A subordinate will feel more secure and confident if he knows he can get help from his boss *if and when* he asks for it.

A supervisor may also support his men outside the department: He may vigorously seek every salary increase his men deserve; he may try to keep work flowing to his men at a steady pace—that is, avoiding critical demands one week and layoff the next; he may negotiate frictions with related departments—perhaps getting engineers to modify unworkable specifications or answering complaints from customer-service men; and he may push for better offices or equipment. When subordinates know their boss is representing their "needs" with a fair measure of success, they are inclined to follow his lead.

In addition, an effective supervisor supports his men with information. He finds out what is being planned—new products, a big contract for the state, building a branch plant—and keeps his men informed about changes that may affect them. Announced or rumored changes in policy, organization, or key personnel often create anxieties throughout an enterprise—from uncertainty as much as from known consequences. By frankly discussing such matters, using what information is known and admitting what is not known, a supervisor can at least relieve the anxiety.

By supporting his men by actions such as these, a supervisor translates his approval into service. All of us are inclined to cooperate with a supervisor who convincingly demonstrates his loyalty to us.

Use of Participation

Participation in decision-making should be regarded primarily as a means of arriving at better decisions. But if participation is justified as a method for improving decisions, we can also anticipate a strengthening of the motivation of those who participate. A simple case will suggest the difference in the way subordinates feel when participation is and is not used.

Al Harrison, a young man recently graduated from business school, has a job as a trainee in a medium-sized factory that makes automobile wheels for sale to large companies. After a year with this company he has now been in the production control department six months, where he reports to Mr. Baker, the department supervisor. At this point, Baker could treat him in two ways:

High Participation	Low Participation
Almost every day Baker comes over to Al's desk and asks him for some kind of advice. One day it may be whether a large order can be run in between the two small ones on Al's list, the next it may be what Al thinks ought to be done about a bottleneck in the buffing department. Over the six months Al has seen Baker's real interest in his ideas, and has seen him put about 30 percent of them into effect.	*Al thinks that Baker likes him as a person. Baker is always courteous, he shares jokes with Al, and even invited him to dinner a couple of times. When it comes to actual work in the department, Baker is tough but fair. He tells Al what to do, lets him do his job, but expects Al to keep his mind off departmental problems. He does not believe that anyone in the department should take care of problems that are rightly assigned to him as supervisor.*

If we compare these two ways of treating Al, we see that the high-participation approach (left column) gives Al more opportunity for self-expression; he probably enjoys his work more and feels surer of Baker's approval. With such treatment, Al undoubtedly feels more closely identified with results in the entire plant, and will spontaneously cooperate in overcoming plantwide problems.

As a general proposition, the higher the degree of participation (that is, the more the initiative, the wider the scope, and the greater the influence of a subordinate) the stronger will be the resulting inclination to cooperate with company plans.

However, the participation must be genuine. The manager must really desire contributions of knowledge, diverse viewpoints, or decision-making skill from his subordinates and must be prepared to devote the time required to obtain their counsel. If he is merely putting on an act his subordinates will soon detect his insincerity. Then, asking for participation is likely to do more harm than good. As one realistic, autocratic manager put it, "My people already know I am an S.O.B., and I don't want them to think I'm a hypocrite too."

Closeness of Supervision

An operation is closely supervised when a boss frequently observes it and makes suggestions to the worker. The boss in such situations acts much like a backseat driver who calls attention to things the driver has already observed, is free with suggestions about just how the car should be driven, and plays "Monday morning quarterback" for every minor mistake. We often hear men say about this sort of person, "He's a good boss in a way, but he's always needling those who work for him." The most disconcerting action of such a boss is to transfer an assignment before a subordinate has an opportunity to finish it.

Such interruptions of a previously assigned task tend to have adverse effects on a man's cooperative attitude. The boss may well be trying to be helpful, but the subordinate is likely to interpret the boss's actions as a lack of confidence or as a reflection on his ability. Even if the subordinate overcomes his discomfort and impatience with the interruptions, he is apt to feel like an automaton and to become quite indifferent about his work.

In contrast, when assignments are made in terms of results to be achieved and a supervisor becomes involved in the actual performance of the work only on the request of a worker, a feeling of self-reliance is encouraged. The subordinate can rightfully take more pride in his work, and he has clear evidence of his boss's confidence in him. During a training period, close supervision is normally expected, but an experienced worker —from vice-president to janitor—finds close supervision somewhat insulting. If close supervision is continued after reasonable training, a worker develops neither the inclination nor the work habits to take the initiative voluntarily in meeting new problems.

Law of the Situation

Whenever possible, a supervisor should let the fact of a situation tell his subordinates what should be done, rather than say, in effect, "Do this because *I* tell you to." A United States manufacturer of electrical equipment, for example, lost a big order to a foreign competitor who quoted an appreciably lower price, and the domestic firm faced the prospect of losing substantially more business for the same reason. The general manager of the company might well have issued a lot of edicts about cutting costs. Instead, he laid the full facts before his engineers and production men, announcing, "Gentlemen, we have a problem." The situation rather than the general manager issued the order to cut costs.

Similar reliance on the law of the situation can be used for small problems as well as large ones. For instance, a customer's complaint about an error in billing or the illness of a key man in a department obviously requires some kind of action. A manager may in the end decide precisely what is to be done, but the *need* for action is accepted by subordinates not because he says so, but because they recognize an objective to be met. When men respond to a situation rather than to an order, they have a sense of self-expression. Their identification with the result to be achieved fosters a willingness to cooperate with a program of action.

Settlement of Grievances

Over time we can expect subordinates to have occasional grievances related to their work. Most of these will be *minor:* a 50-cent error on a paycheck, a chair that snags stockings, lost telephone messages, failure to announce a new title, and the like. Any minor grievance by itself is not particularly important, but until it is settled, it is a continuing source of personal annoyance. By prompt attention to such matters, a supervisor not only removes the irritation but also shows his concern for the feelings of his subordinate. Even if a grievance cannot be resolved in just the way the subordinate wishes, the boss clearly demonstrates that he considers even the minor needs of his men worthy of respect.

If a supervisor has followed the suggestions already made in this chapter and if the structural prerequisites for voluntary cooperation have been met, we hope that *major* grievances will be eliminated. But perfection is rarely attained. A subordinate may feel that he has been mistreated, and he may place the blame on his boss. Such situations must be aired if we hope to get voluntary cooperation from the aggrieved person in the future. Consequently, we need a channel through which grievances may be appealed around the immediate supervisor. Union members have a formal grievance procedure for this purpose and most other workers all the way up the hierarchy can register complaints, at least informally, with managers above their immediate supervisor. The opportunity of bypassing an immediate boss reduces dependency on a single boss, checks possible abuses of managerial power, and increases the chances of resolving grievances in a way subordinates consider fair.[2]

[2]But what happens to the status of the supervisor who is bypassed? How should he act when one of his subordinates appeals "over his head?" First, let us narrow the issue. The only kind of complaint a senior executive should adjudicate as a grievance is one in which the issue is whether the company has abided by the express and implied conditions of employment. Each employee, in effect, enters into an agreement with the company when he takes a job; if an employee feels his agreement has been violated by his boss, he should have the right of appeal. On all other matters— policies, programs, specific transactions, and the like—the decisions of his boss are binding.

With respect to legitimate grievances, a supervisor can best maintain his status and influence by (1) openly accepting the idea that grievances can be appealed; (2) treating discussions of grievances with objectivity and empathy; and (3) knowing enough about the local situation so that few of his decisions will be reversed if they are

Two-way Communication

In this review of the means for developing voluntary cooperation, two-way personal communication certainly warrants a place. Because we shall explore this process in the next chapter, at this point let us merely note how it helps build cooperation: By giving a supervisor a depth of understanding of his subordinates, two-way communication puts him in an improved position to follow almost all the suggestions made in this section—he will know what support his subordinates want, what they consider fair treatment, what motives underlie grievances, and so forth. Similarly, good two-way communication gives subordinates an understanding of the aims of, and reasons for, their boss's behavior and also a sense of being understood. Both supervisors and subordinates, then, are better prepared for voluntary cooperation when they have achieved good personal communication.

CAUTIONS IN DEALING WITH INDIVIDUALS

In the preceding pages we have examined a wide range of guides a manager can follow in developing voluntary cooperation: approval and friendliness, consistency and fairness, emphasis on desired actions, support to subordinates, use of participation, broad supervision, law of the situation, settlement of grievances, and two-way communication. The actual use of these concepts, however, requires discriminating judgment.

Running through our discussion has been this general premise: As we help satisfy a man's needs, he will be more ready to cooperate with company plans. We do not mean that there is a direct trade on the order of "I'll do this for you if you'll do that for me." Instead we are simply recognizing and adapting to a natural phenomenon—under condition A (favorable treatment), B (cooperation) is likely to happen.

Respect for Private Life

Two criticisms, or possible pitfalls, for a leader who deliberately tries to serve individual needs are: interfering with the private lives of subordinates and creating excessive dependency. J. F. Pfiffner describes the first of these dangers as follows:

---

appealed. In short, instead of becoming upset about an appealed grievance, a supervisor should recognize that he might be wrong and let the subordinate see that he too is concerned about arriving at a fair settlement.

In any relationship with a person who has more power than he, the American views with suspicion any act which might be interpreted as extending that power into the ill-defined realm of personal authority. Any abridgment of a subordinate's personal rights by a superior may be "taken" but will rarely be "liked." Areas included in personal rights are almost all off-the-job activities, and such on-the-job matters as personal dress, those things which give the individual his feeling of individuality. The American will rankle, for example, if his boss forces him, because he is the boss, to adhere to certain patterns of dress if these bear no relation to the necessities of the job. Any feeling that he is subject to the whims of his superior will evoke strong antagonisms. The American resents insistence upon conformity which has no visible reason behind it other than that the superior wishes it. All of this strongly violates the American ideal of personal equality.

Therefore, the American hierarchical leader should be able to recognize those aspects of behavior which might antagonize this American culture trait. Ideally, the skillful manager will interpret his actions, when exercising authority, into a content which emphasizes the functional, impersonal need for such action.

Throughout this book we have focused only on those personal needs that can be satisfied by working in an enterprise. A manager should not become involved in other private problems of his subordinates, except when a subordinate comes to him as a friend for advice; and even in such cases, he should tread lightly because of the risk that his official position will give his views more weight than they deserve.

Dependency

The second pitfall, excessive dependency, we also believe can be avoided. There are, of course, degrees of dependency. At one extreme, a subordinate relies almost completely on his boss for protection and initiative, much as an infant relies on his mother. The whole tenor of our suggestions for managerial leadership is to move away from this kind of dependency. At the opposite extreme are highly individualistic, self-reliant persons who find it to their mutual advantage to act jointly—that is, to cooperate. In a sense, these persons are dependent on one another because they cannot achieve their personal aspirations alone. This latter kind of dependency is inevitable in every complex civilization, and is typical of personal relations in modern business.

When a manager creates a situation in which his subordinates find opportunities for self-expression, security, and self-respect, they become dependent on that situation to get such satisfactions. At the same time they contribute to the aims of the company. Dependency in this sense is good.

MATCHING THE SITUATION,
THE LED, AND THE LEADER

In this chapter we have discussed a variety of ways in which a leader can develop voluntary cooperation, and several of these ways can be varied by degrees. What then is the optimum combination? Is there one best way to lead?

A key to finding the right combination of leadership actions—often called "leadership style"—is to consider carefully (1) the situation in which the leading takes place, (2) the people being led, and (3) the personal characteristics of the leader himself. Because differences occur in all three of these factors, we can expect significant variation in leadership styles that are effective.

Fortunately several leadership concepts fit so many situations that we can regard these concepts as constants. With rare exceptions, *any* manager will be a more effective leader if he utilizes the following precepts discussed in this chapter: friendliness and approval, consistency

Fig. 21-3   *In order to determine the best leadership style, three factors must be considered: (1) the leader; (2) the people who are led; and (3) the situation in which leadership is necessary.*

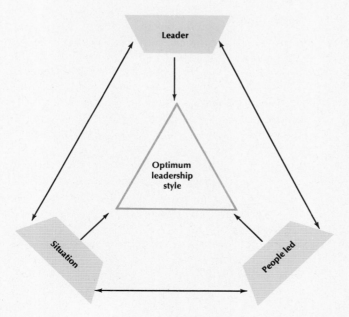

Low Degree of Permissiveness	Determining Factor in Situation	High Degree of Permissiveness
Running a subway train	Degree of discretion technology permits	Running a sightseeing bus
Overcoming a blackout due to power failure	Need for speed	Locating a new power plant
Operating sanitation equipment (garbage truck)	Satisfactions built into job	Finding ways to reduce water pollution
Flying a passenger airplane	Risks involved	Teaching history in college
Operating TV broadcasting equipment	Creativity desired	Producing a TV show

Fig. 21-4 *The impact of the situation on leadership style. Activities that are similar may dictate a high or low degree of permissiveness and participation. Although the activities in the box at left are similar to those at right, permissiveness and participation vary.*

and fairness, emphasis on desired action, support of subordinates,[3] prompt settlement of grievances, and law of the situation. In addition, many of the concepts discussed in the next two chapters on communicating, directing, and disciplining have general applicability.

In contrast, *the degree* to which some other leadership concepts can be wisely employed is a variable. In this category are the following: use of participation, sharing company information, permissiveness in observing company plans and traditions, and closeness of supervision. Leadership style in these respects should be carefully adapted to the leader, the led, and the situation.[4] For example, leading in a research lab differs from leading a crew picking fruit. Of course, closely associated with variations in leadership style are corresponding variations in organization (for example, decentralization), planning (for example, standard methods), and control (for example, frequency of inspection). The whole

[3]A qualification here is that the amount of information provided to subordinates should be treated as a variable.

[4]Many writers in this area advocate a single, "ideal" leadership style. Well-known examples are: R. Likert, *The Human Organization;* D. McGregor, *The Human Side of Enterprise;* and R.R. Blake and J.S. Mouton, *The Managerial Grid.* Actually all these writers are well aware of the total circumstances necessary to make their proposals work. In this respect, we are different from them in that we are more concerned with the total management job. The manager has to deal with external and internal integration and in doing so he becomes involved with organizing, planning, and controlling, as well as with leading. He is forced to balance diverse pressures. Some of his most difficult decisions concern how far he should push a particular form of planning, or organizing, or controlling. We feel that it is more useful if a manager views participative leadership in the same light.

management design should match the mission to be accomplished, as we shall see in Chapter 28.

Adjusting to the Situation

The situation in which a manager is striving to get action often constrains or encourages the leadership style he uses—that is, the extent to which he uses participation, shares information, is permissive, and supervises only in general terms.

In the examples shown in Fig. 21-4, we see the desirability of matching a leader's permissiveness to such factors as need for fast action, risks involved, creativity desired, and amount of discretion permitted by the technology employed. Theoretically congruence between leadership style and a situation can be achieved either by the leader's adjusting his style to suit the situation or by our changing the situation to fit the leader (or by a little of both). In the examples given in the first column, changing the situation would be difficult, so, at least in these instances, most of the adaptation should come in the behavior of the leader.

Adjusting to the People Led

Participative, permissive leadership affects the behavior of some kinds of subordinates more than others. One simple distinction is the rate of turnover. On some jobs employees are not around long enough to grasp, and have an interest in, the ramifications of their job. Similarly routine work often attracts workers who do not expect or want their jobs to be too demanding; they get their kicks off the job. In terms of our discussion in Chapter 8, such employees do not look to their job for fulfillment of self-expression needs. We are not suggesting that these employees will have a negative response to, say, minor participation. Rather the point is that we cannot assume that such people welcome deep involvement, nor do they relish the self-discipline that is entailed under a permissive leader who expects subordinates to set their own high goals and regulate their behavior to achieve the goals. On the other hand, if the group to be led consists of energetic, ambitious persons who expect to be with the company a long time and hope to find personal challenge and self-expression in their work, participative, permissive leadership is called for.[5]

[5]Different types of work naturally attract different types of people. College professors differ from maintenance men; locomotive engineers differ from security analysts; and so forth. The differences in values and orientation of production, research, and marketing men reported by Paul Lawrence and Jay Lorsch have already been noted in Chapter 9 as a potential source of conflict. This suggests a different leadership style for various departments partly because the work situation calls for different kinds of behavior and partly because the people to be led differ. In other words, from the viewpoint of leadership, the situation and the type of people to be led may be mutually reinforcing factors.

Adjusting to the Leader

A third factor to be considered in picking an effective leadership style is the leader himself. From our experience and under many other influences, each of us develops a set of attitudes, values, beliefs, and habitual ways of coping with our environment. This set of personal characteristics may make it easy for some managers to be highly permissive and participative. Such managers have a strong respect for other people, believe that virtually everyone has high potential, take a keen interest in helping people reach their potential, and are willing to take personal risks on the success of other people. They are said to be *people-oriented*.

Other managers are less sure of the capacity of their fellowmen. They prefer to put their trust in system, law and order, and checks and balances. These men are not antisocial, but when they have heavy obligations and want to be sure to accomplish a mission, they tend to rely on facts and figures, regulations, cross-checks, and their own direct involvement. Let us say that they are *system-oriented*. These managers have difficulty when there is a high degree of permissiveness, participation, and sharing; they tend to supervise closely.

In the hurly-burly of running an enterprise mismatches occur. A situation plus the people to be led may call for a people-oriented leader but the actual manager may be system-oriented—or vice versa. Behavioral scientists have given much attention to this predicament. They are especially concerned about a shortage of people-oriented managers.[6]

When we face a mismatch we can (1) try to adjust the situation and subordinates to fit the leadership style suited to the present manager, (2) replace the manager, or (3) convert the manager. The first alternative is unattractive because we shall then lose potential performance due to less-than-optimum leadership. (Actually in similar situations Sears, Roebuck did just this because good overall store managers were scarce, and the loss due to less-than-optimum leadership style was smaller than the cost of trying to force the managers to use a style unsuited to them.) The

---

[6]This preoccupation with making managers more people-oriented reflects (1) higher expectations of workers regarding job satisfactions, (2) a high degree of voluntary cooperation required by more jobs, and (3) the personal values of many behavioral scientists. The emphasis is in tune with the times, but we should not overlook the possibility that some managers need conversion in the other direction—toward a systems orientation. (R.R. Blake, in *The Managerial Grid*, contends that managers can be both people- and systems-oriented, that is, 9–9 on his grid, but he joins others in emphasizing people orientation in his training.) For effective leading, attitudes and beliefs are indeed critical because subordinates quickly detect insincere actions. A manager can do more damage than good if he tries to act out a leadership style that he does not believe in.

alternative of replacing managers is rarely used because an equally effective replacement in all managerial functions is hard to find. Therefore, most effort goes to converting systems-oriented managers to people-oriented managers.

Conversion of mature managers is tricky. Intellectual reasoning is not enough; a man's beliefs and attitudes have a deep emotional basis. The most popular technique used for this purpose, called sensitivity training—or T-group training—ranges from mild shock to group psychotherapy coupled with small doses of more conventional learning. Unfortunately the effectiveness of sensitivity training (and available alternatives) varies widely among individuals, and the impact wears off unless a man returns to a situation that reinforces his new outlook on human relations.

The net effect, then, is that we may have to go slow in striving for the fullest degree of voluntary cooperation. Only when we can achieve a propitious match of the situation, the led, and the leader will the more extreme forms of participation and permissiveness be feasible. Many managers may conclude that some lesser degree of participation and/or permissiveness is more suitable in the particular circumstance they face. Such a choice does not, of course, preclude the substantial amount of cooperation attainable through the other leadership concepts outlined in this and the next two chapters of Part Five.

CONCLUSION

A manager is concerned with both productivity and personal satisfactions of his associates. To argue, as some people do, that one of these aims must be sacrificed to achieve the other is to pose a false dilemma. Instead, under favorable conditions productive work can be the source of, or at least associated with, high personal satisfactions. In fact, securing voluntary cooperation—the subject of this chapter—rests on a merging of personally satisfying experiences with the relationships arising out of tough and demanding productive activity.

Such a merger is not easily accomplished. We have noted that it is built upon a wisely designed managerial structure, a prerequisite for effective leadership. Then an objective, empathetic manager can work with his subordinates in a manner that gives each individual the continuing support and encouragement he needs. The various guides that we have suggested give no formula, but they do point to the quality of relationship that builds sustained cooperative attitudes.

One important skill needed in developing these constructive relationships is two-way communication, a process we consider in the next chapter.

FOR CLASS DISCUSSION

Questions

1) In general, do you feel it is more or less important to develop voluntary cooperation at high management levels rather than, say, between first-line managers and hourly workers?

2) What is the distinction between *paternalism* (which is strongly criticized by both unions and human relations experts) and measures for securing voluntary cooperation discussed in this chapter? Is paternalism wise in other countries such as Japan or India, but not in the United States? Why?

3) In what ways may changes in priorities placed on human needs influence the degree of voluntary cooperation likely within corporations?

4) "My door is always open. Any employee who has a complaint or suggestion can always see me," said Mr. Lincoln, president of the company. Except for a few old-timers who had known Mr. Lincoln for years, few employees accepted the invitation. Those who did usually had a complaint about their pay, work assignment, or days off for special reasons. To show his sincerity, Mr. Lincoln took a personal interest in adjudicating all such cases. Do you believe this is a good leadership practice? Explain.

5) "There is only one real ingredient to leadership," said the president of a large union, "and that's fairness. A man will do anything you ask of him if he knows you will treat him fairly." What do you think of this comment in terms of voluntary cooperation?

6) The supervisor of maintenance in an ink and dye factory has to get two of his men to repair the inside of one of the plant's large mixing vats. This is a most unpleasant job and the supervisor sees no way of making his men *want* to do this job or associate their needs with this particular project. Of course, he can order them to climb into the vat and make repairs. Is there any chance of getting voluntary cooperation in this instance? If not, what would you do?

7) It is suggested that trust is an essential ingredient in developing voluntary cooperation. Assume a manager asks a subordinate to do an important job and gives him wide latitude in determining *how* that job should be done. Is the superior then supposed to ask no questions of the subordinate until after the results are in? If he does anything but this would it indicate a lack of trust?

8) Think of a situation in your past experience in which you were required to carry out a request and resented having to do it but where the person requiring this action might have produced more voluntary cooperation on your part had he used the law of the situation.

9) Think of a situation in which you succeeded in producing voluntary cooperation on the part of one or more people. Try to recall what you did to make this happen. To what degree might the things you did have failed if you were working with people *other* than those actually involved?

Cases

For cases involving issues covered in this chapter, see especially the following. Particularly relevant questions are listed after each case.

Trans-World Mutual Funds, Ltd. (p. 121), 13
Scott-Davis Corporation (p. 227), 15
Gerald Clark (p. 234), 15
Bolling Laboratories, Inc. (p. 345), 17
Western Office Equipment Manufacturing Company (p. 457), 15
E.W. Ross, Inc. (p. 468), 12
Texas-Northern Pipeline Company (p. 665), 7

FOR FURTHER READING

Blake, R.R., and J.S. Mouton, *The Managerial Grid.* Houston: Gulf Publishing Company, 1964. *Explains the development and use of Blake's 9 x 9 grid to identify leadership styles.*

Likert, R., *The Human Organization.* New York: McGraw-Hill Book Company, 1967. *Summarizes findings of many leadership studies by the Institute for Social Research.*

Lippitt, G.L., and W.H. Schmidt, "Crises in a Developing Organization." *Harvard Business Review*, November 1967. *Lists knowledge, skills, and attitudes needed in different stages of growth.*

McGregor, D., *The Human Side of Enterprise.* New York: McGraw-Hill Book Company, 1960. *Sets forth his classic Theory X and Theory Y.*

Myers, M.S., "Every Employee a Manager." *California Management Review*, Spring 1968. *Successful application of democratic leadership at Texas Instruments.*

Tannenbaum, R., and W.H. Schmidt, "How to Choose a Leadership Pattern." *Harvard Business Review*, March 1958. *Leadership style related to forces in local situation.*

Chapter Twenty-two

Two-way Personal Communication

Leading is impossible without communication between persons. The leader in man-to-man relationships exerts his influence only by conveying ideas, feelings, and decisions to his followers. The followers, in turn, have to communicate with the leader in order for him to be able to appreciate their responses to his actions as well as their personal feelings and problems.

In this chapter we shall focus on the transmission of personal feelings and nonstandardized information, because this is the intangible area where managers encounter their chief difficulties in working with subordinates. Of course, a great deal of standardized, factual information is passed throughout an organization, as we noted in Chapter 15. Such flows of data are vital. But here we are assuming that necessary procedures and reports are in existence.

In the leadership process, we are more concerned that, say, Peter and his boss, Paul, develop a mutual understanding of each other's attitudes toward, interpretations of, and intentions about, the problems they face in getting their work done. The raw data that flow through a formal communication network have to be translated into meaningful knowledge and proposals for action; yet many important facts about problems never get expressed in a form that can be transmitted over a formal network. If such messages get transmitted at all, they are conveyed by two-way personal communication.

What Is Communicated?

In a managerial situation, most man-to-man communication includes some *facts* or objective ideas. One (or perhaps each) of the two men is confronted with a problem, and he needs information and suggestions to help him solve it: engineering facts, tardiness records, customer reactions, possible sources of cash, ideas about business trends, and so on. Such facts are an important part of most messages.

But in addition, the enthusiasms, the fears, the prejudices, the likes, the trusts, or other *feelings* of the communicator relative to the problem are a second aspect of many messages. These feelings are not ordinarily stated; a man may not even be able to define them clearly to himself. Nevertheless, they color what he presents and may in themselves be information a manager needs to know. A message may also convey *inferred intentions*. That is, the receiver may read into the words certain motives of the sender. For instance, a "reexamination of our organization" may be interpreted in a particular situation to mean that two product planners who have been in difficulty are soon to be fired.

Full communication occurs only when one person receives *both* the same intellectual message *and* the same emotion that the other person sent and felt. In order for the second person to receive the message, it is not necessary for him to agree with the content of the message or to have the same emotional response to it as the first person. But he should understand the other person's meaning and feeling.

Differences in Personal Viewpoints

One reason why communicating is not easy lies in the differences in point of view of receiver and sender. Let us take an example. Bob Brown is sales manager for one of the leading United States manufacturers of men's shirts and related apparel; his salesman in the Atlanta territory is Al Williams. Brown has always gotten along with Williams, enjoys talking to him, and likes to help Williams when he can. Recently Brown has been looking at figures on population and buying power that indicate that the Atlanta district has greatly increased in both categories. So on a visit to the Atlanta office, Brown says to Williams, "I've been wondering if the Atlanta territory is about the right size for one man to cover."

In making this apparently simple observation about the Atlanta territory, Brown means to imply that the work load in Atlanta has apparently increased, and that some arrangement must be made to keep the company growing and profitable in relation to its competitors. He is also trying to convey a feeling towards Williams—that he likes Williams and is concerned about his satisfaction with his job.

Al Williams, however, has just returned from 300 miles of travel on a July day with temperatures over 90 degrees, a trip that included 60 miles of a dusty, unpaved road. Before his boss came in, he read his mail and found a routine communication from New York asking him to fill out a complete set of forms on forecasting purchases by each customer and to "get these back to us next week if possible." Williams knows that he will have to work a couple of nights in order to finish the forms in time. So when Brown says, "I've been wondering if the Atlanta territory is about the right size for one man to cover," this series of thoughts runs through Williams' mind: "Brown has never been over the back part of the territory; he doesn't know what the territory is really like; he thinks of it as a big smooth map; now he thinks I'm not working hard enough so he's asking why I'm not producing more sales."

Situations like this occur in industry every day. An executive makes a seemingly simple statement, and a responsible subordinate who gets along well with his boss receives quite a different communication. Why was Brown's communication ineffective?

First, we should note that to Brown and Williams the word "territory" means different things, as a factual, intellectual matter. Williams has seen 30 towns in the back part of the territory, known 45 customers in those towns, traversed 30 roads connecting those towns, and experienced how much time it took to talk to Al Jackson in Marietta compared with the time it took to talk to Jack Freeman in Valdosta. These 107 facts he has lumped together in his head with many hundreds of other facts into a construct called the "territory." From literally thousands of things he has felt and seen, Williams has abstracted a "territory." It has *meaning* to him. Brown, on the other hand, has looked at many maps, reviewed statistics on the number and names of customers, measured distances,

Fig. 22-1 *A person's perception of a situation—here a power failure—depends on his particular point of view. A different attitude toward the same situation can lead to a breakdown in communication.*

looked at population and buying power statistics, and has lumped all these facts together into something he calls a "territory," and the word has *another* meaning to him.

In addition to such differences in intellectual content, the feelings a person wants to transmit may not correspond to those that are received. Bob Brown, for instance, when he spoke, actually felt friendly toward Al Williams but Al did not, at least in this particular communication, receive that impression. He may generally feel that Brown likes him, but this one statement on Brown's part did not convey or reinforce that feeling. Thus at this point in time, just as each man is thinking of different intellectual abstractions, so each one is feeling different emotions.

If Al Williams is to understand Bob Brown, the latter must find some way to overcome this semantic barrier, a barrier created by the difference between his own factual experience and that of Williams.

Incidentally, Brown will gain very little by asking Williams, "You know what I mean by the Atlanta territory, don't you?" Williams can really only answer, "Yes." If he says anything else, his boss is likely to think he is not too bright. Furthermore, if by saying "Yes" Williams really believes that he does understand, he can only mean, "I understand what *I* heard," not "I understand what you heard yourself say."

Obstacles to Clear Understanding

As a basis for our examination of ways to improve two-way communication, let us briefly summarize the obstacles to clear understanding that appear in the preceding case, along with the obstacles we have already noted in Chapter 20. Man-to-man communication may break down for several reasons.

Semantic difficulties. Words mean different things to different people. We have just seen how the word "territory" meant something quite different to Bob Brown from what it meant to Al Williams because their jobs and their experiences led them to think about territories in different ways. Similarly, "a hard day's work," "good schools," and "active reporting" may convey quite different things to a longshoreman and a certified public accountant—because of the dissimilarity of their personal experiences.

Some words also acquire symbolic meanings that are more potent than their literal meanings. For example, so much shoddy work has been done by so-called efficiency experts that many of us find the word "efficiency" repugnant. We may be quite willing to increase the ratio of output to effort expended, but if this is called efficiency we have a negative feeling about it. To some persons, concern about the "welfare" of workers implies a distasteful paternalism; and some people object to anything done for their welfare because they feel that the word means that they are unable to take care of themselves. "Management prerogatives" may have good connotations to some people and bad connotations to others. We must overcome, or at least avoid, such semantic difficulties if we are to transmit meaning accurately to other people.

Organizational distance. Any subordinate naturally wants to look good in his boss's eyes. Consequently he protectively screens the information he passes up the line. A boss, likewise, may feel that, because of his position, he should not be completely candid with his subordinate. Men differ, of course, in the extent to which they permit a status discrepancy to interfere with a free exchange of ideas and feelings, and in extreme instances organizational distance blocks all except formal communication.

Perfunctory attention. Often in our conversations with other persons, we only half-listen to what they say. We are so busy with our own thoughts that we tend to give attention only to those ideas we expect to hear. When an accountant talks to the controller, for instance, the controller may pay attention only to how work is progressing and may disregard clues on the state of morale or friction with staff men. In fact, psychological studies show that many of us ignore information that conflicts with our established patterns of thought; we simply do not believe, say, that Steve is serious about quitting or that a key customer would buy foreign-made equipment, because such thoughts do not conform with the ideas we already hold. Especially if we are deeply committed to, or emotionally involved in, some matter, we prefer to pay no more attention to bad news than Hitler did to reports of inadequate supplies during the latter part of his regime. We tend to retain our private concept of the world by saying to ourselves, "I just don't believe————is so."

A manager is especially likely to give perfunctory attention to incoming communications when he is very busy with other matters. He simply has so many other distractions that he selects those parts of a total communication that can be readily used. Novel and irreconcilable bits of information or unexpected feelings get brushed aside. Under some circumstances, an executive may be justified in such cursory treatment of messages, but he pays a price in being superficially informed.

Inferred meanings. Still another difficulty we face in developing a clear, mutual understanding with our boss and with our subordinates is the meaning—or interpretation—that we make out of a message. We do—and should—consider the source of a message: The sender may be biased, he may draw his ideas from an unrepresentative sample, or he may deliberately twist the evidence. But we get into trouble by lumping everyone in broad classes—say, assuming that all salesmen exaggerate. True, the typical salesman tends to be overoptimistic, but we should not assume from that trait that everything he says is unreliable. Moreover, our hopes may lead us to infer a meaning that was never intended; for example, a friendly talk with the boss does not necessarily mean we are in line for a promotion.

Then, too, the particular situation at the time a message is received may *accidentally* affect the meaning we attach to it. In our earlier example, if Al Williams had been working over his prospect list instead of just returning from a hot, dusty trip, the meaning he drew from Bob Brown's comment about the size of the Atlanta territory might have been quite other than it was. To take an example of the same point from another company, a plant superintendent happened to talk to one of his foremen about the high cost of particular products on the same day that the company controller distributed a bulletin on keeping time cards posted accurately. The foreman inferred that the superintendent thought he was faking his time reports. Actually, the superintendent had no such idea in mind; the arrival of the two messages on the same day was a pure accident.

There are other obstacles to good man-to-man communication, of course. But these four—semantic difficulties, organizational distance, perfunctory attention, and inferred meanings—indicate how easily a leader can misunderstand others or be misunderstood by them. We need real skill if we are to develop a mutual exchange of ideas and feelings with our subordinates.

EMPATHETIC LISTENING

The kind of two-way communication we are considering in this chapter is the mutual exchange of ideas and feeling between manager and subordinate. The manager must *listen* and he must also *impart* facts and feelings. But for the interchange to be most effective, he should emphasize listening. If he starts by telling his views to a subordinate, as many managers are inclined to do, he is likely to stifle upward communication because of his status and latent power. Of course, a manager does give directions, as we shall note in the next chapter, but the form of communication we are examining here builds understandings and relationships that underlie and greatly simplify his task of directing.

What Empathetic Listening Involves

When listening empathetically, an executive opens the way for a subordinate to talk freely about his ideas and feelings without worrying about justifying each statement he makes. The executive reserves his own views and preconceived ideas, while giving close attention to the sentiments the other man is trying to express. The executive is simply trying to gain an insight into what is "on the other fellow's mind" from the other man's point of view.

Empathetic listening makes use of certain techniques employed in psychiatry whereby, ideally, a patient first expresses his feelings, then recognizes the facts of his problem, and finally develops a workable adjustment of these facts. A manager, of course, should not undertake psychotherapy of deep-seated personal problems, but he can use some of the elementary concepts to nurture a mutual understanding of day-to-day problems at work. The manager can listen sympathetically, without injecting his own views, to a subordinate's expressed attitudes and emotions about his job, and in so doing the manager may help the other man gain a more objective appreciation of the total situation.

For a manager, this kind of nondirected interview may be the only way he can learn the full feelings and operating problems of his subordinates. Without such an understanding, a manager is in a poor position to give constructive advice; he has an insufficient basis for making his own decisions; and he has difficulty in giving subordinates a sense of personal worth and integrity.

Example of Free Response

An illustration of empathetic listening will give concreteness to the free-response technique we have been discussing in general terms. Let us compare the way two different executives approached the same situation. The following facts were presented to executives at a management development program; then members of the group interviewed a man who knew the full story and responded as Tony Flynn probably would have reacted.[1]

> Tony Flynn works in the assembly department of a company that manufactures television broadcasting equipment. The operation requires that men work in teams. Tony has been employed by the company six years. During the first two years he showed aptitude for the job, but his attendance record was so irregular he was warned twice that he would be dismissed unless he got to work regularly. For the past four years he has a good attendance record and he is a competent, experienced workman. Although Tony gets along well with his fellow workers, he has always been very quiet and reserved, and company records do not contain any explanation of his early absences. Three days ago (Monday) Tony did not show up for work, nor did he phone that he was sick—which company rules require a man to do when he is ill. Tuesday the same thing happened, and the employment manager got no answer when he tried to call Tony's home. Again, on Wednesday, no Tony. This morning Tony appeared on time, but looking a bit disheveled and glum. The superintendent

[1] Professor Alex Bavelas assumed the role of Tony in both of the "role-playing" views digested here. The men who took the position of superintendent were given only the facts known to management prior to the interview; they were free to conduct the interview as they chose and did not listen to anyone else before their turn. The two interviews selected represent contrasting approaches. The conversations have been condensed to conserve space.

of the assembly department asked the lead-man under whom Tony works to send him to his office.

One interview with Tony developed as follows:

Supt.: *Hello, Tony, it's good to see you. Sit down a minute.*
Tony: (Taking a chair beside desk) *Thanks.*
Supt.: *Tony, we've missed you the last few days.*
Tony: (Half to himself) *Yeah, been out all week, until this morning.*
Supt.: *That's right, I'm sorry to say, and you know how one man out upsets your crew. We didn't have a substitute most of the time.*
Tony: (Pause) *Yeah, afraid I caused some trouble.*
Supt.: *And not calling in, Tony, that made matters worse because we didn't know what to plan on. You've been here long enough to know how important it is to keep full crews in assembly.*
Tony: (Again, half to himself) *Should have called in, that's right.*
Supt.: *Tell me, when you realize how important it is, how could you just disappear for three days? We couldn't even get an answer at your home.*
Tony: *I just couldn't make it, and been too messed up to call in. Sorry I caused so much trouble.*
Supt.: *Tony, I've looked over your record. The last four years have been fine. We need good men like you. A few years back the absences were pretty serious, and I sure hope we're not going to slide back to that trouble again. Yet, the recent record looks real good. (Pause) What do you think, Tony, can you keep that record as clean as it has been the last couple of years?*
Tony: *I'd sure like to. I've been trying. (Pause)*
Supt.: *We need good men like you. You know the work, and you pitch in when we have to get work out in a rush. But we have to be able to depend on the men we keep in your spot. If you think this won't happen again, we're mighty glad to have you back.*
Tony: *Well, I need my job, and I'll do the best I can.*

Another executive took a different tack with Tony:

Supt.: *Hello, Tony, we've been missing you. Sit down and let's talk about it.*
Tony: (Taking chair beside desk) *Thanks.*
Supt.: *You been under the weather, Tony?*
Tony: *I'm all right, I guess.*
Supt.: *Gee, Tony, the way you say that you don't sound very sure.*
Tony: (Half to himself) *Well, I've got to feel all right.*
Supt.: *Hmm?*
Tony: (Pause) *I just gotta keep going somehow.*

Supt.: *It takes some real push, sometimes.*

Tony: *Lost three days' pay already. Not sure I can stay awake today.*

Supt.: *Been losing sleep?*

Tony: *Can't sleep even when I get to bed. (Pause) Took Mary to the hospital Sunday—no, that would be Monday—about 2 a.m. She darned near died that morning. Went home to see about Patsy that evening. She was bawling to see her mother, but I left her with the neighbors anyway. Spent most of the night at the hospital. Tuesday, Mary at least knew who I was. Tuesday night I took Patsy home—the neighbors got kids of their own—and she cried and fussed most of the night. Last night I tried to give her supper. It was awful. Mary's getting better, they say, but she still looks like a ghost. Well, I figured I had to get back to work this morning.*

Supt.: *No wonder you look bushed. Think you can keep going?*

Tony: *Guess I can get through to the weekend. The neighbors will keep Patsy in the day and a high school girl is coming to sit with her in the evening so I can go see Mary. But we can't keep this up forever, and I don't know how to pay the doctor's bills and blood transfusions and all that. (Pause) Guess I'd better take Patsy down to Mary's sister's. Could do that Sunday without losing any more pay.*

Supt.: *Tony, you don't have to settle everything right away. You say your wife is getting better, and that's most important. If you can get Patsy taken care of for a couple of weeks, maybe the public nursing service can help your wife get back on her feet. The personnel department could tell you about that.*

Tony: *Sure, we might make out that way for a while.*

Supt.: *I'll phone Joe [Tony's lead-man] to find a few minutes you can talk with the personnel people today. And if you do have to take time off, be sure to phone us, Tony. You know how important it is to make up a full crew.*

Tony: *(Leaving) Yeah, thanks. I'll call in if I have to be out any more, but I don't think it will be necessary.*

In the first conversation the superintendent was not unfriendly, but he was so preoccupied with the problems of manning his department that he failed to get information from Tony that was needed in dealing with the situation constructively. In the second interview, the superintendent said very little until Tony had talked about *his* problems. Then the superintendent was in a much better position to take action that would avoid future absences.

Guides for Listening

From studies in clinical psychology and psychiatry, and from over twenty-five years of experience with nondirected interviewing in industry, have come a series of guides for empathetic listening. For a manager the most useful of these guides are:

1) Listen patiently to what the other person has to say, even though you may believe it is wrong or irrelevant. Indicate simple acceptance (not necessarily agreement) by nodding, lighting your pipe, or perhaps interjecting an occasional "Um-hm," or "I see."

2) Try to understand the feeling the person is expressing, as well as the intellectual content. Most of us have difficulty talking clearly about our feelings, and so careful attention is required.

3) Restate the person's feeling, briefly but accurately. At this stage, you simply serve as a mirror and encourage the other person to continue talking. Occasionally, make summary responses such as, "You think you're in a dead-end job," or, "You feel the manager is playing favorites"; but in doing so, keep your tone neutral and try not to lead the person to your pet conclusions.

4) Allow time for the discussion to continue without interruption and try to separate the conversation from more official communication of company plans. That is, do not make the conversation any more "authoritative" than it already is by virtue of your position in the organization.

5) Avoid direct questions and arguments about facts; refrain from saying, "That just is not so," "Hold on a minute, let's look at the facts," or "Prove it." You may want to review evidence later, but a review is irrelevant to how the person feels now.

6) When the other person touches on a point you do want to know more about, simply repeat his statement as a question. For instance, if he remarks, "Nobody can break even on his expense account," you can probe by replying, "You say no one breaks even on expenses?" With this encouragement he will probably expand on his previous statement.

7) Listen for what is *not* said—evasions of pertinent points or perhaps too-ready agreement with common clichés. Such an omission may be a clue to a bothersome fact the person wishes were not true.

8) If the other person appears genuinely to want your viewpoint, be honest in your reply. But in the listening stage, try to limit the expression of your views because these may condition or repress what the other person says.

9) Do not get emotionally involved yourself. Try simply to understand first, and defer evaluation until later.

A great deal of practice and self-awareness is needed by most managers before they can follow these guides for listening. Much of the time a manager has to assume a positive, self-confident role, making decisions and giving orders. Clearly, empathetic listening calls for a sharp change in pace. But unless he can develop the self-discipline and humility to listen respectfully, a manager is likely to lose touch with reality.

Essential Requirements

The process of listening we have just described will be effective only under several necessary conditions. One requirement is *time*. The kind of conversation we have considered takes more than a minute or two. An executive must be willing and able to give his subordinate uninterrupted attention in private for fifteen minutes, half an hour, or perhaps longer—just for listening. With other demands on his time, an executive must value highly the benefits of listening before he will take such a block of time out of his busy day. Moreover, he must be willing to listen when a subordinate wants to talk. Some flexibility in timing is usually possible; unless a subordinate is emotionally upset, tomorrow may be as good as today, provided "tomorrow" is not an indefinite postponement.

Another requirement is recognizing the unique qualities of each subordinate. We cannot understand the feelings and problems of another person unless we *respect his individuality*. R. L. Katz has pointed out that each person has his own values, which

> *stem from his previous experiences (his expectations of how other people behave), his sentiments (the loyalties, prejudices, likes and dislikes which he has built up over a long period of time), his attitudes about himself (what kind of a person he is—or would like to be), the obligations he feels towards others (what he thinks others expect of him), his ideals (the ways he thinks people should behave and how things ought to be done), his objectives and goals (what he is trying to achieve in a given situation), and perhaps many other things.*

For empathetic listening to be successful, we do not have to know everything about an individual but we must be prepared to respect individual differences in personalities.

Personal discipline on the part of the executive is a third requirement. All of us are inclined to respond emotionally to what others say. We normally approve, challenge, get angry, or react in other ways. Yet for empathetic listening, we have to remain objective, and objectivity calls for practiced self-discipline.

Finally, a passive, nondirective approach by a manager presumes that his *subordinate has feelings or problems he wants to talk about*. Perhaps the subordinate is disturbed by something that has happened, or he may have a strong response to a proposal his boss or some other executive has made. But if the man is contented—or indifferent—about his work, then "Um-hm" tactics by his boss will result in a dull conversation indeed. Empathetic listening is a valuable leadership process, but as with so many other phases of management, we have to exercise a good deal of discretion in applying it.

CONVEYING MEANING TO OTHERS

Listening deals with one direction in two-way communication. A manager also has to *transmit* his ideas to subordinates. Here again, the aim is to develop a mutual understanding of ideas, problems, and feelings; and again, the difficulty is that each party—the manager and his subordinate—may assume the other assigns the same meaning to a message that he does.

Technical Communication Model

A simple model, used in analyzing electronic communications such as television or bouncing messages off satellites, may help us identify the reasons why B does not always understand just what A meant to say. Figure 22-2 shows the basic elements.

In electronic communication, the message usually consists of words or physical forms; encoding and decoding involve converting the message to and from electric impulses; and major difficulties of distortion and noise may arise in the channel. In face-to-face communication, we have fewer channel difficulties, but in encoding and decoding we run into many subtle, psychological problems.

Many of the concepts we have used to analyze listening apply equally well to the job of imparting ideas. The meaning of words, for instance, enters directly into encoding and decoding, and the effect of emotions on what we give attention to can garble the meaning of a message as it flows in either direction. In the following suggestions for improving the transmission of ideas from supervisor to subordinate, then, we shall review insights about the kind of behavior that should permeate a leadership relation.

The World of the Receiver

Once an executive has conceived of a message he wants to get across to a subordinate, he should take time to reflect on the attitudes and in-

Fig. 22-2   A simple technical communication model.

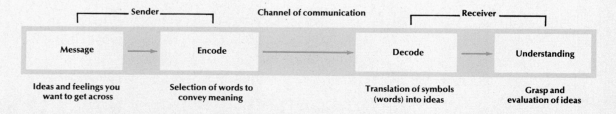

Sender		Channel of communication	Receiver	
Message	**Encode**		**Decode**	**Understanding**
Ideas and feelings you want to get across	Selection of words to convey meaning		Translation of symbols (words) into ideas	Grasp and evaluation of ideas

terests of that man. The subordinate will probably be preoccupied with other matters that seem important to him, and in the modern world, which bombards him at every turn with advertising and reading matter, his initial response to still another communication may be negative. Most likely, he will be inclined to pay attention primarily to those ideas that are related to his personal needs. Moreover, his emotional state will affect his receptiveness to new messages.

Consequently, if we want to get across an important idea, a new meaning—not just routine information—we must be sensitive to the world of the person who will receive the message. How he perceives it will depend as much on what is already in him as on the content of the message. If we have a close relationship with him, based on previous empathetic listening, we will know something of his world and how he is likely to interpret our new message. Of one point we can be sure: "Logical" arguments will not get us far if our message requires him to alter his values. Therefore, as a sound starting point, we should carefully consider the personality of the man to whom we wish to convey a meaningful message. In addition, we should ask ourselves: How will the idea look to him? Is there anything we can do to prepare him for the point we wish to transmit?

Meaningful Language

As we have seen, words—even ordinary terms like "territory"— may mean different things to the sender and the receiver of a message. To get our meaning across, we must try to use words in the sense that the receiver will take them. Long words and technical words, although perhaps more precise to *us*, often have to be discarded in favor of short terms that are easily grasped. Maybe the other man *should* be smart enough to understand our language, but our aim is to reach a mutual understanding with him—not to test his literacy.

Some repetition helps in most learning—assuming that the learner is trying to understand. So we may want to repeat a message, preferably in different words or with new examples. It is even more effective to draw attention to the idea we wish to get across when it is related to a current experience of the subordinate; he then sees the meaning of the words in terms of his personal behavior.

Free, Face-to-Face Interchange

It takes a while for us to assimilate an important idea, to get used to it. We have to roll it around in our minds and savor its implications.

When we are trying to communicate a significant message to a subordinate, we should provide him the time for such assimilation. One way to do so is simply to exchange thoughts with him about the message, to talk it over. The subordinate may think out loud, "Wow, that new product would louse up our production schedule.... We could promote a couple of those young engineers who are getting restive.... How would the shipping department handle it?...," and so forth. The executive may also express his thoughts—both pro and con—about the proposition. This interchange is highly informal, and neither person states firm conclusions.

During such a give-and-take discussion, many doubts and misunderstandings come into the open. If the executive is skillful at listening, he can probe long enough to uncover misunderstandings and then restate his meaning or intention. Frequently the executive himself has not thought through all aspects of an idea, and a discussion of this sort may result in clarification—and perhaps modification—in his own mind.

Note that during this assimilation stage, authoritarian relationships are set aside while both persons seek a mutual understanding. Mutual respect and trust are necessary, because each person is exposing his tentative, speculative, unconsidered reactions. If the conversation has rambled, the executive may well summarize the message as it has been redefined at the end, but the free, face-to-face interchange should have clarified the meaning substantially.

Communicating through Behavior

One of the best ways an executive can give meaning to a message is to behave himself as he asks others to do. The new president of a sugar refinery wanted to break a tradition that pay increases and promotions for executives depended primarily on long, loyal service. He stated on several occasions that raises would be made only on the basis of demonstrated improvements in performance. Most executives let the statement slip by as just another part of a pep talk. But at the end of the year, a good many executives (including the president's son) did not get raises even though they had worked hard; a few men who could show significant improvement in results received good bonuses. The grapevine spread the word, and at this point the president's message took on meaning.

In contrast, the vice-president in charge of sales of another company became worried about low gross-profit volumes and told each of his district managers not to grant special discounts to large—or tough—customers. Within a few weeks, however, the vice-president himself made several concessions to two customers he handled personally. This action changed the meaning of his "no special discount" statement to "no special discounts except by the vice-president." It also created resentment on the part of the district managers because they felt the vice-president was inconsistent in what he said and did.

Subordinates sense quickly the presence, or lack, of consistency in their boss's words, spirit, and action. In fact, subtle feelings and values may be conveyed better by example than by words, although there is no reason for not using both. The poet Emerson put it this way: "What you are [do] thunders so loud I cannot hear what you say."

Feedback Confirmation

These general guides—recognizing the interests and attitudes of the person receiving a message, expressing the message in terms that are meaningful to him, having a face-to-face discussion of the idea, and accompanying the words with consistent action—aid us in conveying meaning to our subordinates. But how can we be sure they actually receive a message as we intend it? We have already noted that merely asking a man whether he understands provides scant assurance.

To confirm that our communication has resulted in mutual understanding, we need to keep alert to any feedback that is available. The simplest check is to observe whether the subordinate behaves in accordance with the message. When direct observation is not practical, as is often true of executive behavior, we can watch various reports and results for cues. And for more intangible or subtle messages, the listening process described earlier in this chapter may be the most reliable feedback we have. If we have developed a close leadership relation with a subordinate—the kind we are exploring throughout Part Five of this book—we should have enough frank interchange of ideas and feelings to provide indications of how well we have communicated.

CONCLUSION

In this chapter we have been examining communication, not as a routine or a procedure, but as one of the essential elements in leading. Both facts and feelings need to be transmitted between a leader and each of his subordinates. For this purpose, we have explored what is necessary for an executive to listen empathetically to his subordinates and to convey real meaning by his own words and actions. In a superficial sense, these are techniques. Far more significant than techniques, however, is the kind of relationship developed. Mutual understanding, mutual respect, confidence and trust that permit frank discussion of personal feelings and problems, integrity in matching actions with words—all these reflect leadership at it best. We may not achieve such two-way personal communication with all our subordinates all the time, but our effectiveness as leaders will be enhanced to the extent that we succeed in doing so.

FOR CLASS DISCUSSION

Questions

1) Does a well-developed communication network at lower levels in an organization undermine the influence or the obligation of higher-level executives? What effect might it have on the optimum span of supervision of, say, a plant manager?

2) The president of a large midwestern bakery chain, in going over a number of reports sent to him by the personnel director, noticed that during the last two years only eight of the seventeen men placed in supervisory and executive positions were college graduates. The president wants to increase the number of college graduates working for the company but does not want to instruct the personnel director to do so. The personnel director, not a college graduate himself, is an extremely capable man and tends to view degrees as being just so much window-dressing. As a means of making the personnel director aware of his feelings, the president commented quite casually, while having lunch with the personnel director and other top executives, that he thought a college education was one important criterion for screening men for executive positions. "Look at our competitors and you'll find that they really put emphasis on formal education," he concluded. Nothing further was said on the subject. Do you see any chance for misunderstanding in this situation? Explain.

3) One expert on communication has suggested that the term "co-perception" would be a better word to describe what is needed to bring about true communication. What do you feel he means by this? Relate your answer to material in Part Two concerning human needs.

4) "Management's most important job is communication. If a superior can clearly communicate what is expected and explain the facts that make the expectations valid, no reasonable man will fail to accept the expectations and seek to achieve them." Do you agree? What several key assumptions are implicit, if not explicit, in this statement? Discuss the validity of each.

5) In what ways may the guides for listening given in this chapter be applied when the communication that is sought takes place in written, not oral, form and distance makes face-to-face feedback impossible?

6) As an experiment in empathetic listening, try the following. Have one participant play the role of a top-notch young executive who has just informed his boss that he is thinking about taking another position. Have a second participant play the role of the man's supervisor. The young executive, while being honest with his boss, should be somewhat reticent about revealing his real reasons for quitting. With the man who is to take the role of the boss out of the room, agree on the real reasons for quitting; for example, you might select any of the following: fear that nepotism will block his advancement; his feeling that the company president is stubborn and not very bright; desire to move away from his mother-in-law who is a close friend of the boss's wife; belief—based on grapevine information from a source that cannot be revealed—that the company will be sold to a much larger firm; or you might think up some other reasons. Then have a role-playing talk between the boss and his subordinate. See if the boss can uncover his subordinate's reasons for leaving by using the guides for empathetic listening. Following the role play, write down illustrations of (1) where the superior succeeded in employing these guides, (2) where he failed, and (3) how a different approach might have been more successful.

7) How may the concept of using the law of the situation described in Chapter 21 aid in improving two-way communication? What pitfalls should one be aware of when using the law of the situation as an aid to communication?

8) In what ways may custom and tradition as discussed in Chapter 7 (1) aid, and (2) interfere with good two-way communication?

Cases

For cases involving issues covered in this chapter, see especially the following. Particularly relevant questions are listed after each case.

Scott-Davis Corporation (p. 227), 17
Gerald Clark (p. 234), 16
Western Office Equipment Manufacturing Company (p. 457), 14
E.W. Ross, Inc. (p. 468), 14
Consolidated Instruments—A (p. 571), 13, 16

FOR FURTHER READING

Davis, K., *Human Relations at Work*, 3rd ed. New York: McGraw-Hill Book Company, 1967, Chaps. 19–21. *Communication and counseling in company setting.*

Dubin, R., *Human Relations in Administration*, 3rd ed. Englewood Cliffs, N.J.: Prentice-Hall, Inc., 1968, Chap. 14. *Explores personal communication in an organizational setting.*

Gelfand, L.I., "Communicate Through Your Supervisors." *Harvard Business Review*, November 1970. *Formal communications program of the Pillsbury Company.*

Geneen, H.S., "The Human Element in Communications." *California Management Review*, Winter 1966. *The president of ITT comments on communication in a multinational giant.*

McMurry, R.N., "Clear Communications for Chief Executives." *Harvard Business Review*, March 1965. *Barriers to good two-way communication with top executives and suggested ways to overcome these difficulties.*

Strauss, G., and L.R. Sayles, *Personnel*, 2nd ed. Englewood Cliffs, N.J.: Prentice-Hall, Inc., 1967, Chaps. 10 and 11. *Clear discussion of barriers to communication and of nondirective listening; good blend of theory and practice.*

Chapter Twenty-three

Directing and Disciplining

GIVING INSTRUCTIONS

Every supervisor-subordinate relationship must include a series of activating steps: issuing instructions, elaborating decisions, reviewing performance, and rewarding or disciplining. These steps are an inseparable part of managerial leadership.

How can we assure that these tasks are well done without undermining the friendly trust and mutual understanding we have discussed in the preceding three chapters? Is it possible that the kind of leadership behavior we have outlined will facilitate the activating steps? Contrariwise, can the steps be taken in a way that will enhance the personal, man-to-man relations between a leader and his subordinates? Let us look first at the task of giving instructions.

Need for Official Instructions

Managerial plans must be communicated. We have already discussed the question of who in an organization structure should make decisions, and we have considered how an executive uses information and ideas from many people in making decisions. From such organizing and planning emerge the official decisions—or plans—of an enterprise. In the process of directing, these plans are passed on to line executives or operators in the form of *official instructions*, or "orders." Whether written or oral, brusk or diplomatically stated, welcomed or resented—official instructions are necessary. We call them "orders" without implying that an executive has to act like a proverbial Marine sergeant.

Among all the communications that flow back and forth and up and down in an enterprise, orders constitute a small but highly important part. Coordinated action directed toward a set of objectives requires plans that everyone recognizes as official, and the actions of different persons must be synchronized whenever their work interlocks. Consistency and compatibility are necessary even in relatively more independent activities. Therefore, to achieve this unity of behavior, managers first decide on particular plans and give them official approval; the approved plan, or order, must then be transmitted by executives to any of their subordinates who will be guided by that decision. Clear transmission of official instructions is one leadership function of every executive.

The use of official orders does not imply dictatorship, however, for they are essential even when a manager relies heavily on participation in the preparation of plans, two-way communication, or other joint activities. But the point is that, whatever the preceding relationships, sooner or later a moment is reached when the appropriate manager says, "This is it; this is what we will do." Under normal conditions workers expect official plans and, in fact, feel uncertain and confused if they are not given official instructions.

Necessary Components of a Good Order

An order should always be (1) complete, (2) clear, and (3) doable. Yet in a surprising number of instances, managers fail to fulfill these simple requirements.

Often a manager states in general what a subordinate should do, but he omits specific information about desired *quantity, quality,* or *time limit* for completion.[1] The sales manager of an air-conditioning equipment company, for instance, told his branch managers, "We have decided to push the sale of repair parts. They represent a good source of profits, and we expect the full cooperation of every branch manager in this new campaign." Two branch managers appointed a special representative to concentrate on repair parts and planned visits to all distributors and large dealers in their areas. Other branch managers simply relayed the message to their salesmen: "Push sales of spare parts." Within a month, the failure of the sales manager to specify how much effort he expected, and how rapidly action should be taken, resulted in wide variation in practice among the different branches.

[1] The concept of a complete order is compatible with "management by results." A complete order often stipulates fully the desired results but leaves the *how* to the receiver.

The matter of completeness can be critical even in minor instructions. A research director in a small electronics firm said to one of his section chiefs, "Here is our proposed budget. I'd like your comments on it." He intended that the subordinate merely look over the expenses for his own section and return the budget the same day. The section chief, however, assumed he had been asked to appraise the plans and projected expenses for the entire research department. Unfortunately the section chief had devoted three full days of work to the project before the misunderstanding was discovered.

A manager should also consider the feasibility of an order before issuing it. This problem occurred in a company that makes flour-milling machinery. The firm had received complaints from several important customers, and the cause was finally traced back to parts that had not been machined according to specifications. The general manager wrote a note to the plant superintendent stressing the seriousness of the problem and concluding that "parts *must* be kept within standard tolerances." He asked that a copy of his letter be sent to the foreman concerned and to the men in his shop. The men were highly indignant because the machinery they operated was so old it would not produce the quality desired. The foreman also felt that the order was unreasonable and feared that already poor morale would become even worse if some of the work were sent to an outside shop with more modern equipment. The net effect of the general manager's order, then, was bad morale and little improvement in quality.

Manner of Communication

In stressing that every order should be clear and complete, we do not mean that each instruction has to be long and elaborate. Two features of an established organization greatly simplify the issuing of *routine* directions.

First, standing operating procedures and methods may already have established a whole framework for action. In most companies, for instance, we could simply tell the personnel office to "transfer Ralph Alexander to a sales trainee spot in the El Paso office at $600 per month," and the order would be sufficiently complete. Existing procedures in payroll, accounting, and personnel would spell out the specific actions to be taken.

In addition, customs and habits help round out the meaning of many orders. After two persons have worked together on similar problems several times, they develop customary ways of cooperating. A manager with a good secretary need only say, "I'd like to go to Atlanta Tuesday afternoon," and his secretary will be able to arrange a plane flight in accordance with his usual wishes. Or when a credit manager asks his assistant to make a collection call on the Triple-A Corporation, the latter will understand what to do and how much pressure to exert on the customer. A subordinate's knowledge of what his boss wants may come partly from conscious training, but a large part of his behavior will be the result of previous informal guidance and "decision-elaboration" by his superior.

So much for routine situations. But some orders deal with new problems or have unique aspects that require special treatment. A manager must not assume that terse instructions, which work so well for repetitive actions, will adequately convey what is wanted in an unusual situation. He should instead explain more fully what is desired, perhaps using *two-way communication* to check his subordinate's understanding of, and response to, the new direction. And if *participation* in at least the detailed planning is feasible, the chances of adequate communication will be substantially improved. As a minimum, for novel situations an executive can at least *explain why* he specifies a particular result—quantity, quality, or time; such an explanation both aids the man who receives the order in interpreting it intelligently and also tends to increase his interest in the assignment.

One danger in using participation, two-way communication, or even thorough explanation, is that an extended discussion may not leave a subordinate with a sharp, crisp idea of what is expected of him. So many aspects of a problem have probably been examined, and the pros and cons of so many possible solutions considered, that he and his boss may not have a clear meeting of the minds when the conversation ends. If several people are involved in a discussion, the possibility is even greater that at least one man comes away from the meeting with understandings and impressions that are far different from those of others who attended the meeting. To avoid this pitfall, someone—normally the senior man—should summarize everyone's agreement on what action is to be taken. This summary, then, is the order.

Consistent Follow-up

A valuable check on the appropriateness and adequacy of instructions is consistent follow-up: Once an order is issued, a manager should either see that it is carried out or he should rescind it.

This simple practice has a salutary effect on both the manager who issues instructions and the man who receives them. Perhaps the more obvious effect is on the subordinate. He knows for sure that an unpleasant task cannot be postponed in the hope that the boss will forget it: Reports due on Monday cannot be slipped in on Thursday; parts that almost fit are not acceptable. When a supervisor consistently means what he says, a subordinate soon learns to discipline himself—and he tries to be sure he understands his instructions.

More significant to our present discussion of leadership, however, is the effect of consistent follow-up on the manager issuing the instructions. He must avoid giving vague and impossible orders, hoping that his subordinates will decide what really should be done. He must draw a distinction between rules and guides, which we discussed in Chapter 18. These requirements mean, of course, that he must carefully think through the impact of each order before he issues it; if so, he will very likely do more suggesting and guiding and less ordering.

The practice of consistent follow-up also imposes on a manager the necessity of admitting that some of his decisions may need to be changed. If he issues an unwise instruction and then tries to disregard it—or bury it in a bustle of other activity—he will only confuse subordinates. For they, in fact, then have to decide when the unwise instruction can be forgotten. But by rescinding an order—because it was poorly conceived, because events did not turn out as he anticipated, or for some other reason—a manager admits that he too is fallible.

Of course, some managers are reluctant to rescind an order because they fear that admitting a mistake will detract from the confidence and enthusiasm of their subordinates. But such stubbornness is shortsighted. If a mistake has been made, subordinates will probably know of it—whether their boss admits it or not. Clearly the way to engender respect and confidence is to issue lucid and carefully thought-out instructions in the first place. Any calculated risk that might be involved can be recognized from the start. Later, if a change in an order is necessary, an executive can admit that the best way to reach objectives *now* appears to be along a modified or new course. In subjecting his own actions to objective review and constructive, impersonal modification, he sets an example for examining his subordinates' performance in terms of recognized goals.

Issuing orders, then, can be a natural part of a wholesome leadership relation. There are pitfalls a manager should avoid, to be sure. If instructions are vague and incomplete, if they are passed down arbitrarily without thought of their practicability and consistency, and if there is wide variation in the carefulness with which orders are observed, a supervisor-subordinate relationship will be strained. But assuming we skirt such pitfalls, formal instructions simply become one aspect of cooperative effort in an enterprise. The use of orders need not be autocratic; rather, orders represent officially endorsed plans of action that are an accepted necessity in any joint endeavor. One of the tasks of managerial leadership is to communicate orders well.

DECISION-ELABORATION

Managers must nearly always elaborate their decisions when they put plans into action. For example, the president of a company may set forth a policy that all employees are to be paid salaries slightly higher than the competitive market rate, but a lot of additional decision-making is necessary to translate this broad statement into the reality of action. Part of his translation is accomplished by establishing detailed methods and procedures. The vice-president in charge of sales, for instance, may establish a procedure for determining the competitive rates of salesmen's pay. Yet, when we come down to the specific question of how much of a raise to give Bob Davies, a salesman in Los Angeles, and at what time to give it, the decision involves many unique aspects that are not covered by any advance planning. Supervisors fill in the gaps by their specific day-to-day decisions.

In "decision-elaboration" supervisors or operators make successively more detailed plans for their work. This is a continuing day-by-day process. Two vital purposes are served: (1) The planning structure is completed by *filling in the gaps* between broad plans and more detailed decisions. (2) *On-the-spot exceptions* to advanced plans are made to deal with unforeseen circumstances.

The need for decision-elaboration applies at all levels of an enterprise. Even in an assembly line—say, for automobile headlights—that has a detailed manual of methods, an unforeseen event may occur. Suppose the machine that fastens the reflectors to the lamp socket breaks a bearing, and can be run, even at part capacity, only by risking a worse breakdown. The standby machine, an older model, cannot meet the output standard of six hundred units per day. The foreman of the assembly line personally observes the difficulty and talks with operators about what might be done. Obviously, he has to modify former plans either about daily output or production methods, and so he makes an *exceptional* decision that fits the actual operating situation.

On-the-spot decisions call for diagnosing the problem, conceiving of alternatives, projecting results, and making a final choice—all the phases of decision-making described in Part Three. The distinguishing considerations in decision-elaboration, however, are *time, importance*, and *personal involvement*. Seldom is there time for lengthy research; normally, no single elaborative decision will have a major influence on company profits; and a manager is involved personally through direct observation and communication in the event that calls for his judgment.

Beyond being concerned about getting an immediate task done, in making elaborative decisions a manager should give consideration to two important matters. He should recognize, first, that if he repeats a particular decision over and over, he is building a custom that can become just as binding on departmental behavior as official plans. The work habits that result from his decision-elaboration will probably become a part of the informal social system that never gets written into instruction manuals. As we have already noted, detailed work habits and customary behavior patterns have a significant effect on the whole task of coordinating the efforts of a group of people toward efficient output.

Second, decision-elaboration gives an executive many occasions to foster voluntary cooperation. In his frequent day-to-day resolutions of operating problems, he can often do several things: provide direct aid to subordinates in getting work done, use participation in reaching decisions, show consistency and fairness, acknowledge effective performance as well as troublesome results, vary the closeness of his supervision according to the ability of individual subordinates, encourage a "law of the situation" viewpoint, and otherwise conduct himself along the lines suggested in Chapter 21. Decision-elaboration entails numerous personal contacts on unprogrammed aspects of company activities; in this respect, it offers unique opportunities for personal leadership.

A competent manager, then, sees decision-elaboration as a process that presents him with an opportunity to blend several leadership aims: overcoming immediate problems, developing effective work habits and customs, and eliciting voluntary cooperation.

PLANNING AND REVIEW
OF PERSONAL PERFORMANCE

Official plans and their elaboration are inherently geared to company goals. Personal relations have a vital part in the process of transmitting these decisions, as we have just seen, but the initiating impulse arises from *company* needs. Even so, quite naturally, the persons who do the work wish to take a different personal perspective, at least occasionally, and ask, "How am *I* doing? What about *my* particular contribution to the whole operation?" Because answering these personalized inquires is an important facet of every manager's man-to-man relationships, we now turn our attention to evaluation of individual performance.

Appraisals for Different Purposes

Actually, we evaluate executives and operators for several different reasons. For example, three important purposes are manpower planning (as explained in Chapter 10), setting rates of pay, and helping a man improve his performance in his present job. We need *different* appraisals for each purpose. In manpower planning, for instance, we are chiefly concerned with a man's potential ability, whereas in paying a man we appraise primarily his past performance. Here in this chapter we are focusing on how a manager can assist his subordinates to improve their results in their present positions.

Joint Planning and Review of Performance

One particularly effective method of personal appraisal aimed at helping a man improve his performance has the following features:

1) Both a subordinate and his supervisor draw up statements of the actions the subordinate should perform and the results he should achieve in some given period, say, the next three months. The two men then meet to try to arrive at a common list of job goals. These are the short-range performance *objectives* we considered in Chapter 17. They should be as specific as possible and should be couched in concrete operational terms. For example, a dairy superintendent might set these goals: Train a replacement for the chemist who will retire, get output of the new packaging machine up to 80 percent of its rated capacity, develop and install improved irradiation methods, and reduce absenteeism rate to company average.

2) After the period is over, the two men sit down to review results. On most matters, what has been accomplished is clear to both men. So their discussion can focus on results that were outstanding—and why they were achieved—and on goals that were not accomplished—and why they were not. Together the men can then proceed to devise ways to overcome the unsatisfactory results. After this review, another set of goals is established for the next period, again with the subordinate taking the initiative in proposing what he thinks he can do.

3) Each time a new set of short-run goals is set up, the supervisor finds out what *he* can do to help the subordinate achieve the goals.

This kind of joint planning and review of individual performance has several advantages in man-to-man leadership. It centers the conversation on meaningful problems that the subordinate recognizes, and the supervisor has an opportunity to offer his help on these problems. The "how am I doing" question gets answered by objective results, rather than by the boss's subjective judgments. A joint review of results provides an excellent opportunity for the supervisor to "listen"—in the manner we outlined in the last chapter—if the subordinate has feelings he wants to express. If the subordinate seeks advice on his personal development, the superior can provide it by counseling. Finally, the approach provides new grist for each planning and review session, so it is applicable to men who have no promotion possibilities as well as to "comers."

Many variations in this personal review procedure are possible, of course. But whatever the specific steps, we will further managerial leadership (1) by directing primary attention, not on personality traits, but on individual goals and performance, and (2) by casting the supervisor in the role of helper to his subordinate.

Counseling

Personal counseling is more informal and irregular than performance appraisal. A supervisor typically counsels a new subordinate on the spot as he is learning his new duties. Likewise, assistance to a man preparing for promotion is mostly *ad hoc*, as suggested in Chapter 10. It includes special assignments, more than normal information about reasons for actions taken, and suggestions for improving skills that the trainee recognizes he will need on future assignments. The relationship is normally like that of a coach to a younger person wanting to learn. Of course, this kind of counseling is not confined to a person's supervisor.

Counseling may also arise directly from a performance review. If improved performance clearly depends on changed attitudes or improved skill of a subordinate, a natural follow-up to recognition of the need is a discussion on how to make the change. Important here is that (1) the subordinate wants help, and (2) the supervisor gives advice not orders. If either of these elements is missing, the chances of constructive change are low.

DISCIPLINING AND REWARDING

Typically, the predominant leadership activities of an executive consist of listening to, guiding, encouraging, and helping his subordinates. Our attention throughout Part Five has been on such activities. Yet although they are his principal concerns, occasionally a manager has to discipline a subordinate. Disciplining is an inescapable part of his role. Just as any free society uses police forces to repress antisocial behavior, so in the operation of an enterprise we insist that certain minimum behavior standards be observed. The task of maintaining this discipline is assigned to managers along with their other duties. A supervisor knows most about his people and local conditions, and so normally he is the best-qualified agent to perform what is inevitably an unpleasant task. *How* he disciplines his subordinates can have a profound effect on both group attitudes and his personal relations with individual workers.

Fig. 23-1 *Personal counseling. Supervisors often provide on-the-job counseling to new subordinates. An analogous situation exists in the realm of sport; when a beginner is trying to learn new skills, he is often coached by an expert.*

Role of Disciplinary Action

For any cooperative enterprise to function effectively, certain kinds of behavior are necessary. These necessary behaviors may be dictated by technology, law, social relations, or economics. For example, a company may have minimum standards on safety, the operation of equipment, honesty, divided interest, hitting people in the nose, showing up for work, accepting official orders, maintaining acceptable output, carelessness, personal morality, and so on. The enterprise is able to operate because most employees meet, or exceed, these basic requirements most of the time, and through positive incentives and leadership action, many minor transgressions can be corrected. But what should we do about the persistent failures and the major violations?

Reprimands, demotions, temporary layoffs, withheld promotions or bonuses, and discharges are penalties a manager can impose for failure to behave according to requirements. Note, however, that none of these penalties produces desired behavior directly; in fact, layoffs and discharges may temporarily increase the difficulty of achieving goals. The purpose of disciplinary action is solely to improve *future* behavior—the future behavior, it is hoped, of the man being disciplined, and even more importantly, the future behavior of other people in the enterprise. We may be indignant about a subordinate's behavior and feel that he deserves punishment; but loss in output because of tardiness or the careless destruction of valuable papers are sunk costs. Our leadership problem is to discover how to avoid a recurrence of similar difficulties, and our disciplinary action should be taken with this aim in mind.

Guides for Disciplining

Disciplining will have its greatest impact on subsequent behavior if we observe a few basic guides: prompt, objective attention to digressions; forewarning of rules and penalties; and consistent and fair application of rules. Let us see what each of these guides entails.

Prompt, objective attention. The best time to correct an error is soon after it occurs, while facts and feelings are fresh in mind. If a man refuses to follow instructions, for instance, a review of the matter a month later is likely to find everyone's memory clouded, and the influence of any disciplinary action will have lost some of its potency because the association between the act and the consequence will be blurred. But there are two important qualifications to the principle of promptness: (1) We should not act when we are angry and emotionally upset. If possible, everyone concerned should take time to cool off so that disciplinary action is objective and wise. (2) We may need time to get the full story. If a prolonged investigation is necessary, then we must usually make sure that the persons involved know the event has not been overlooked or considered unimportant, because we don't want them to assume that they can get away with a similar action without serious consequences.

Forewarning. Men should know in advance what they are expected to do and what not to do. The burden of such forewarning rests on the supervisor. Nearly everyone anticipates discipline for violations of common social norms of honesty (stealing, and the like), but most workers feel that punishing a man for an act he did not realize was wrong is unfair. Consequently, for many transgressions a supervisor should first formally warn a man; only when he repeats the action is more severe discipline warranted. Or if a certain action is especially serious—smoking in an oil refinery is the classic example—then the standards that apply and the consequences of violating them should be explicitly stated in advance. Then the facts of the situation, not the caprice of a manager, determine the need for disciplining. Note that the forewarning itself tends to promote the desired action—and that is really the result we are seeking.

Consistent and fair treatment. Consistent discipline has several implications. One is automatic, impersonal justice—if a purchasing agent accepts a bribe he is immediately fired, no matter how important he has been; or if an airplane pilot flies low over his home town he is grounded. The discipline is as sure and impersonal as the result of holding a lighted match over the opening of a gasoline tank to see how full it is.

But as we saw in Chapter 21, strict consistency may not be entirely fair. Court judges and public administrators, who have to strive for consistency in administering laws, use the term "strategic leniency" in circumstances where some bending of the rule is wise. Intent, provocation, inexperience, temporary disability, and other related matters may justify more favorable treatment of one person than another. Of course, once an exception is made, the door is open to further appeals and abuse. Here

Fig. 23-2   One guide for discipline is the so-called "hot stove rule." When you touch a hot stove your discipline is immediate, forewarned, consistent, and impersonal.

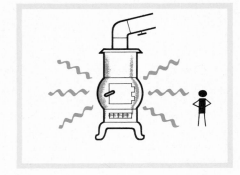

again we need to recall the purpose of disciplining. If the subsequent behavior of the people who know of the case will be improved by making an exception, then consistency should be sacrificed. In such cases, we should be prepared to make further exceptions to any person in similar circumstances, and we should let the reasons for the exception be known so it will not appear to be arbitrary favoritism. When handled in a way that is generally regarded as fair, adjusting discipline to individual circumstances actually can improve the effect that it has on future behavior.

Use of Rewards

Disciplining is a response to undesirable behavior and is a matter of imposing penalties. Rewarding is just the opposite; it is a response to unusually desirable behavior and is a way of bestowing approval.

The rewards we mean are in addition to satisfactions that arise directly from the job and commitments for salaries, pensions, and the like. We are thinking of extra benefits: special commendations, transfers to more attractive work, bonuses, salary increases, and so on. Granting such special consideration is much more pleasant than imposing penalties, of course, and generally is not subjected to quite such close scrutiny by workers as is disciplining.

But from a leader's viewpoint, many of the same concepts apply to rewarding as to disciplining. He must make rewards partly with an eye on the probable future behavior of the recipient and his associates. This means that the executive must not act like an unpredictable Santa Claus or respond only to flashy behavior. Instead, he should take time to find out which subordinates contributed most to the exceptional results, and he should relate the reward to the kind of behavior (performance) he wants to encourage. If Chris has done an unusual engineering job that enables Dick to sell a big order, giving Dick the major credit is not the best way to promote similar activity.

When rewards—bonuses, for instance—can be given to all who deserve them, the need for consistency can be easily met. A tougher problem arises when only one, or a few, subordinates must be selected for, say, a desirable transfer. The hopes and status of those passed by are hurt by giving the reward to someone else. In such situations, we can mitigate the disappointment by calling attention to the necessity of choice, by stressing the compelling reasons for the choice (a promotion, for example, should be based more on a person's capacity for a new job than on his performance in the present one), and by trying to devise offsetting compensations where they are warranted—perhaps a change in title or readjustment of both jobs. Even so, making discriminating rewards remains a ticklish task for the leader fortunate enough to have several deserving subordinates.

LEADERSHIP AND THE USE OF POWER

Throughout our analysis of leadership in Part Five, we have focused on developing voluntary cooperation, listening to the other man's problems, and getting him to exercise self-motivation and self-discipline. But in disciplining and rewarding, we find that managers use power, power that prompts the employee's fear of being punished or of losing something desired. And we know from our discussion of power in Chapter 20 that its use tends to stifle initiative and enthusiasm. Resort to power, then, tends to undermine the friendly man-to-man relationships we have nurtured so carefully.

Undoubtedly, some of the most painful decisions a manager must make deal with the use of power. He must decide, for instance, when his efforts at generating enthusiasm and self-motivation have yielded such meager results that a subordinate should be reprimanded and perhaps threatened with dismissal. The manager need not abandon his other leadership approaches when he decides that a firm—even tough—position is necessary, but he should know that his appeals to a positive response are likely to be less effective after he has "waved a big stick."

There are, however, some broad guides that can help alleviate this lack of harmony between positive leadership and the use of power:

1) A leader should not flaunt his power. Certain powers may be his, but he holds them in reserve and never presents them boastfully. We accept the existence of power in many areas of life (in the home and in the law courts, for instance), but we resent continuous reminders of it and, even more the brandishing of power. A good leader accepts his power with humility and with a sense of obligation to use it carefully and discreetly.

2) A manager should try to use his power objectively. He can accomplish this by making known when he will use it, and by following his rules consistently. The use of power then becomes part of a system, or framework, within which work is performed. Once such a system is accepted, a manager can work with individuals to help them function effectively in the system. When he does exercise power, it may be unpleasant, but it is not a personal, capricious act on his part.

3) A manager should employ power in a way that contributes to building a desirable pattern of behavior. Each discipline case requires his close attention to its particular circumstances, to be sure, and exceptions or qualifications may be wise. But the effect of a decision on group attitudes and group norms must also be carefully weighed. Many leadership activities contribute to the development of a little social structure in the section or department, as we have already noted, and "justice" in the exercise of power is part of that social structure.[2] Leniency may be accepted, even demanded, by workers in special circumstances, but any exception should be clearly recognized as such so that the normal, expected pattern of behavior is not jeopardized.

By following these guides—not flaunting power, preserving objectivity in the use of power, and employing power to reinforce patterns of desired behavior—we can use power when necessary, and at the same time devote our major attention in leading to the development of constructive, positive understandings and feelings.

CONCLUSION

A drawback of concluding our examination of the process of leading with a chapter on directing and disciplining is the inevitable emphasis that such a discussion places on action that flows from an executive to his subordinates. Perhaps we should look back over all of Part Five and remind ourselves that the upward flow of information and responses is also an integral aspect of the process of leading. Putting plans into action involves a man-to-man interchange—it is a two-way mutual adjustment. The able leader realizes that he, as well as his subordinate, learns and adjusts his behavior.

We must also remember that talking about leading and doing it are quite different matters. Actually leading along the lines we have discussed is difficult for many men because: (1) It calls for a great deal of self-control and for genuine respect for others. You cannot merely go through the motions superficially. Perhaps some deep changes in your own attitudes may be necessary. (2) Even when you can control yourself your interaction with *each* subordinate is distinct, changing, and somewhat unpredictable. The kind of leadership action you should take depends on him as well as on yourself.

The analysis of leading in Part Five can help each of us become better leaders by pointing out what is involved in managerial leadership and by suggesting some guides for dealing with several basic problems. But we have no handbook filled with tested formulas for solving leadership problems in a routine fashion. Yet it is precisely the intangible, personalized characteristics of leading that probably explain why being a good leader is one of the most challenging and satisfying aspects of managing.

[2]The question of desired social structure is especially pertinent in a conflict situation. If a manager finds himself an arbitrator of conflict, he should be sensitive to the impact of his decision on desirable and undesirable conflict and on the possibilities of escalation (see Chapter 9).

FOR CLASS DISCUSSION

Questions

1) An officer of a large insurance company who read Chapter 23 commented, "You suggest that a good order should always be (1) complete, (2) clear, and (3) doable. How can I possibly limit my orders to ones which satisfy these criteria? I always try to make them clear but I often do not know whether they are 'complete' or 'doable' until after my subordinates work on trying to carry them out. In order to give them an opportunity to stretch themselves I may ask for something which may not be *doable* but we won't know till we try. Further, if I want them to show initiative and feel they can influence *how* they carry it out, my requests may not be *complete*." Discuss this observation.

2) *Comment A:* "I always give my men directions in a few words, telling them clearly what is expected of them. When possible, I do this in writing to give them a permanent statement of what is required. If they have questions on what is expected they may raise them, but I don't encourage questions dealing with why a decision was made as it was. This way they are clear as to precisely what I want."

Comment B: "I usually talk over my decisions with the men who carry them out so as to be sure they not only understand what is expected of them but why, and how what they do fits into the total picture. This way they see the reasons for my requests and they can carry them out with higher motivation and greater perspective."

Under what conditions might *A* be better? When would *B* be better? If you were receiving the orders, which of the two practices would you prefer?

3) A national sales manager requested all field salesmen to file a lengthy sales report at the end of each month. Most of his salesmen's reports were late and/or incomplete for the first six months after the request. Subsequent analysis showed that with slight modification of the company's computerized marketing information system all of the vital information could be obtained without this sales report. Upon learning of this, the sales manager decided to abandon the field sales report but did not inform his salesmen of his intentions and delayed the abandonment for six months longer than necessary. During that time he put great pressure on the field salesmen to get the report in on time and in complete form. What positive and negative results of this action can you foresee? Why do you think the sales manager put off the change in policy?

4) Because a supervisor may find it difficult to evaluate and counsel his subordinates for fear of upsetting a good relationship, would it be advisable to have a staff personnel specialist evaluate each man after discussing his strengths and weaknesses with the man's supervisor and fellow workers? Then the staff man, who would be expert in counseling, could sit down and discuss the man's strengths and weaknesses with him. Discuss this proposal and relate your answer to the material in Chapter 4 concerning the use of staff.

5) A personnel director of a large and successful company made the following observation: "All too often I find that managers tend to do a much better job of counseling, directing, and disciplining their good subordinates than their weaker people." What might account for this phenomenon and what effect is it likely to have where it occurs?

6) Often a supervisor may feel he is being consistent in his disciplinary action, but his subordinates may not see his action in the same way. What causes this to happen and what may managers do to minimize such feelings of inconsistency?

7) In what ways do the leadership practices proposed in the last four chapters fit the relationships between the following: (1) a football coach and members of his team; (2) the supervisor of a group of transient agricultural workers, say grape pickers, and the workers; (3) the art director in an advertising agency and his artists; (4) the manager of an atomic energy research laboratory and his engineers? How do you explain any difference?

8) Many people feel that the elements of leadership discussed in Part Five are not able to be taught. In other words, "Leaders are born not made." To what degree do you believe managers can develop in their subordinates the elements of leadership discussed in the last four chapters? How should they go about increasing the leadership skills of subordinates who show little innate talent in these areas?

Cases

For cases involving issues covered in this chapter, see especially the following. Particularly relevant questions are listed after each case.

Gerald Clark (p. 234), 17
E.W. Ross, Inc. (p. 468), 13
Consolidated Instruments—A (p. 571), 14, 15
Consolidated Instruments—B (p. 674), 14

FOR FURTHER READING

Coleman, C.J., "Avoiding Pitfalls in Results Oriented Appraisals." *Personnel*, November 1965. *Realistic article with emphasis on personnel development.*

Huberman, J., "Discipline Without Punishment." *Harvard Business Review*, July 1964. *A plywood mill finds a way to avoid minor punishments.*

Sloan, S., and A.C. Johnson, "New Context of Personnel Appraisal." *Harvard Business Review*, November 1968. *Recent changes in purposes and methods of appraising employees.*

Strauss, G., and L.R. Sayles, *Personnel*, 2nd ed. Englewood Cliffs, N.J.: Prentice-Hall, Inc., 1967, Chap. 14. *Clear, practical discussion of disciplining.*

Case Studies

FOR PART FIVE

 HARROGATE ASPHALT PRODUCTS, LTD.—AR[1]

Company Background

This case concerns the financial and managerial relationships between two companies: British Commercial Investments, Ltd. (BCI), an industrial holding company located in London, and Harrogate Asphalt Products, Ltd., located in Frampton, a small town in Yorkshire near Harrogate.

BCI, Ltd., started life as the Pentiling Rubber Plantations, Ltd., a Malayan rubber company. The directors decided to diversify out of the politically risky area of their operations, and acquired a number of small- to medium-sized private companies, mainly in the United Kingdom. Twelve years ago, the last of Pentiling's rubber plantations was disposed of and the company was renamed British Commercial Investments, Ltd. The BCI group now comprises some sixteen subsidiary companies, with operations ranging from the manufacture of oil drilling equipment to electrical components and from special steel fabrication to the construction of agricultural buildings.

[1]Copyright 1968, l'Institut pour l'Etude des Méthodes de Direction de l'Enterprise (IMEDE), Lausanne, Switzerland, reproduced with permission. The original version of this case has been revised and edited for use in this book.

Mr. Henry Lampton, the managing director of BCI, described the group's progress as follows:

Our subsequent growth, due partly to the acquisition of new sub-sidiaries and partly to internal expansion has been pretty satisfactory. Our gross tangible assets have increased in the last seven years from £9,000,000 to £31,000,000, and our pre-tax profits from £900,000 to £3,400,000. This large growth has caused us to institute increasingly elaborate systems for forecasting financial requirements and planning to meet them. We have instituted what we call the BCI Three-Year-Forecast, which involves much forward thinking-in-detail. This kind of planning is accepted as essential in modern company planning, but even if it wasn't, something very similar would be needed to ensure the continued strength of BCI.

Furthermore, our present investment effort is directed mainly toward internal expansion by existing subsidiaries, and the acquisi-tion of no new subsidiaries, unless they complement technologically those we already have. These two efforts—growth from within and acquisition of related companies, are what will produce the kind of profit we are interested in.

We have been trying recently to provide additional help to our subsidiary companies. In today's world, we do not think that they can expand to their full potential, without some help from central advisory services provided by BCI central staffs. Until very recently, however, we were rather diffident about providing these services to give specialized advice in particular fields; it would be fatal to try to force them on unwilling subsidiary managements. But recently, the success of our operations-research group, the welcome accorded to the monthly economic bulletins of our chief economist, and the de-mand for the services of our BCI Marketing Adviser, all attest the need felt by subsidiary managers. Only in the last three weeks, Mr. J.F. Roberts has joined our staff as Computer Adviser and has begun to familiarize himself with existing EDP installations and projects. We have been too slow in recognizing the part that EDP techniques will play in the future. We hope to provide companies individually too small to justify their own EDP units with access to facilities, and to reduce costs for all by organizing a coordinated net-work available on a BCI-wide basis.

It is, however, a part of our philosophy that our subsidiaries should be of a size that they can support their own local functional staff of a high caliber. We are not suffering under the delusion that we can operate a large central-services team capable of resolving the local problems of such a diverse organization. Our advisory staff is used as catalysts.

Finally, I would like to say something about the services rendered to subsidiary operating companies by our BCI nominee director. We like to think that the personalities, experience and sometimes wider contacts that our directors have, are an important source of help to managements of BCI subsidiary companies.

In an interview with Mr. E. M. Jackson, another executive of BCI, the casewriter was told that

> BCI maintains a [nonexecutive] director on the Board of each of its subsidiaries, and he usually serves as chairman. Although he has no formal line authority over the managers of the subsidiaries, the BCI nominee normally visits each of his two or three companies about once a week, or twice every three weeks. The BCI nominee typically has had considerable industrial experience before joining our organization, either with a firm of accountants or management consultants, or with some other industrial corporation in an executive capacity. Many of them have university education, and have also attended advanced management programs such as the Administrative Staff College at Henley, Harvard Business School, Stanford Business School, or IMEDE in Lausanne.

After this statement by Jackson, Lampton continued:

> The position of a BCI nominee director involves a rather heavy responsibility. We are not bankers, interested only in the financial aspects of the business. We are not there to take a normal dividend and let it go at that. In some financial holding companies, the local managements have the idea that they are entirely self-sufficient, except for dividends. At the same time, the directors nominated by the parent company to the boards of those subsidiaries create the impression that they are banker types—somewhat superior to getting into real operating problems. I personally believe that, in some such holding companies, the headquarters managers are being supine— they sit there with talent that could add to operations, but they make no contribution. Specifically, I am certain that in this day of complex technology and society, the director has a moral responsibility to help his managers in subsidiary companies—to encourage them to do planning for the future, to aid them in selecting and staffing their operations, and to give advice in areas where the director has talent or knowledge.
>
> I can give you one example. In June, one year ago, BCI acquired the L.M. Trowbridge Company from the Trowbridge family. This company specializes in construction projects using asphalt products —parking lots, tennis courts, large industrial asphalt areas. It is to the benefit of everyone—BCI, Harrogate (which produces asphalt materials) and Trowbridge managers, and employees of both companies—to merge the operations of the two companies [Harrogate and Trowbridge]. In this way, both will be more profitable, enjoy more growth, and stand a much better chance of survival in the British economy. This autumn we are going to form a company to hold both Harrogate and Trowbridge, in the interest of better all round operations. The move was, inevitably, initiated by the BCI nominee chairman; the managers of Harrogate and Trowbridge don't have the same chance of standing back and taking an overall view

of their operations. Without our BCI man, the merger would never have come about.

This shows how far we have moved from our position when BCI was still mainly involved in Malayan plantations and when our United Kingdom subsidiaries were regarded merely as diversified investments to be bought and sold; managerial responsibilities rested wholly with the underlying unit. Gradually we have come to acknowledge that this is an untenable position, and have taken on full responsibility for the underlying units, while allowing them a very wide degree of local autonomy in the main areas of their businesses.

The Acquisition of Harrogate

Seven years ago, Mr. Jack Stanley, a man of eighty-two, approached a member of BCI management in London, with the idea that BCI might be interested in acquiring Harrogate Asphalt Products, Ltd., as part of the BCI group. Lampton, now managing director of BCI, was then thirty-one years old, lived in Birmingham, and was the BCI Midlands representative. He was assigned the job of doing a management evaluation of the Harrogate Company for possible acquisition.

Excerpts from Lampton's management and operating appraisal appear as Exhibit 1. It will be seen from that exhibit that his general conclusion was that Harrogate represented an excellent investment. He based this on a thorough analysis of finances, management, marketing, production, and raw material procurement. He also found that the Harrogate management had sold the less profitable coal business fourteen years ago, concentrated on the more profitable asphalt operations, introduced a revolutionary technological process eleven years ago, and expanded production and sales.

The First Five Years of Operation

As of the time this case is written, BCI has owned Harrogate Asphalt for seven years. During the first year, the Board of Directors of Harrogate consisted of Jack Stanley, Paul Denham, and Gerald Kemp, a full-time executive in BCI who was assigned as the parent company representative. More information on these men appears in Exhibit 1.

During those years, Henry Lampton was serving as BCI representative in the Midlands and as nominee director of two BCI subsidiaries located near Birmingham. Nevertheless, Lampton recalls certain things which he knew went on during the first five years:

In that period, the new equipment installed from Mason and Grant gave Harrogate an overwhelming competitive advantage in a business mainly served by fairly small companies, with the result that profits, sales, and return on new capital increased dramatically. Here is a company whose return on net worth was among the highest of any BCI company. Nevertheless, in my judgement, there were definite signs of trouble. Stanley died at the end of the second year. This left the BCI director and Paul Denham. About a year later, these two directors recommended as the third director Roger Sample, a young man who was hired by Denham six years ago (in the second year of our ownership). I'll have more to say about him later, but I acknowledged Roger from the first time I met him to be a capable chap, though his experience in Harrogate was limited.

The Board meetings of those days consisted of a rather formal, cut-and-dried reporting of figures, once a month.

The casewriter, at this point, asked, "Was Paul Denham making the policy decisions?" Mr. Lampton responded:

If there were any policy decisions being made—though I doubt there were.

Also, in about the second year, Harrogate suddenly found itself with a strike on its hands. Denham was at loggerheads with the union[2] and he was at a loss as to what to do. The BCI director had to go up there and deal with the union, and a settlement was reached. As I recall, Denham simply gave up and said that he could not deal with them.

Also, Denham operated by turning up at eight in the morning, opening the mail, then sitting in the sales (internal) office for two hours, returning to his own office where he would incarcerate himself and merely look at figures of past performance. He rarely went to see customers off site, or saw customers when they came in.

Operations in the Past Two Years

About two and a half years ago, while some other changes were being made in BCI organization, Lampton, at age thirty-five, returned from Birmingham to the BCI London head office as a director of BCI; at the same time he was also assigned to the Board of Harrogate subsidiary. The remainder of this case covers the past two years of his relationships with the latter company. Incidentally, Lampton, just recently, was named managing director of BCI Industries. Lampton described his experience with Harrogate:

I arrived on the scene of this highly successful company (60 percent on net worth is remarkable by any criteria) full of youthful bounce, and asking why they don't look at the situation in the

---

[2]In Lampton's appraisal report (Exhibit 1) it is shown that there was no union at the time of acquisition of Harrogate.

building-products industries for growth. I knew that the company was doing no real forward planning, and that with the addition of a lot of hard work along this line the company could do much better. I also had a certain amount of goodwill and ambition—and the knowledge that I would have a delicate time with Paul Denham.

But I soon found that it was an unusual company. I saw a managing director making £15,000 a year, but no other men of responsibility. His four top men, including Roger Sample, were making £3,000 or under. This came as a surprise—here was an outstandingly successful company, profit wise (£600,000), with no staff in depth. In fact, in addition to Roger Sample, the only talent I could see was a good production assistant who had just given notice of his termination.

I'm going to give you a number of facts about what happened during those two years, but first let me say that I am not adverse to local autonomy—I believe it is best—but not for one local autocrat. Let me also say that my relationship with Denham was a good relationship, personally speaking, but when I tried to bring some things up for improvement, around the Board table (I had instituted more frequent Board meetings, and insisted that we discuss company policy problems, rather than just review figures of past performance), he did not want to discuss them. Instead, he would say, "This is not a matter for formal Board—why don't you come around to my office and let's talk about it informally." Nevertheless, I thought that all three Board members (including Sample) should be in on important matters, and that there should be formal Board meetings where responsible action could be taken.

Let me give you an example. Our operators in the plant were getting very high piece-rates, but it was physically very hard work, fifty-eight hours a week, and two one-and-a-half week holidays that had to be split, one and a half weeks in summer and one and a half in winter: anyone absent without a doctor's note got instant dismissal. When Denham asked me not to bring this up in the Board, but to come to his office, I said, "No! This is a Board matter." I could see that these conditions would mean trouble, and Roger Sample was telling me—not as a moral issue at all, but as a practical issue—we couldn't keep things this way. For my own part, I regarded it as a practical issue and a moral issue. In a way, we were blackmailing the workers with high pay and not providing opportunity for recreation. They were spending money in considerable amounts in gambling and drinking (this seemed to be a problem in the town). So I proposed that we allow them to take their two one-and-a-half-week holidays together, thus affording more of a real holiday and rest away from the job.

As I persisted in placing this matter before the Board, Denham finally said, "I don't want any part of this dsicussion. If you want to make Board policy, do it." Notice that he wasn't saying, "I am the managing director, I will think and be responsible about this." Instead, he was abdicating the managing directorship to us.

I mentioned Roger Sample. Denham had hired him five years ago from a local construction firm, and he subsequently became production manager. Although he had rather narrow experience working locally up there in Yorkshire, he is a man of talent. He knew I thought highly of him, but he was reticent with me at first, because he didn't know what kind of game I was playing. He did not have much confidence in pushing his ideas, because when Denham resisted, he did not know if I would back him. Gradually, however, we established a relationship of trust. It came about through situations like the following. On my side, I could see great need for looking beyond the narrow confines of present products and processes. The company needed market research and research on new technology. On Roger's side, he had been reading magazines of the industry and had become aware of some new processes that were being developed in Sweden. He wanted to go there to investigate, but had been forbidden by the managing director. Later, I raised this at the Board table, but Denham's reaction was, "Don't let's meddle outside the company now. We have a system that is producing high profit." Why he took this attitude I don't know. I suspect that the real trouble lay in the fact that Denham had been outgrown by the company he managed, and he was afraid that anything new might put him still further out of his depth. Harrogate's very success was against him.

Some time later, the accountant for the plant quit. I think it was because he was mistreated by Denham. At this point, I tried to get Denham to go out and find a really topflight managerial accountant —one who could think and plan rather than simply be an audit clerk. As things proceeded, I could see that Denham just wasn't capable of doing this, so I persuaded him that we should go out and hire an outside firm of consultants to do the recruiting. The consultants presented four candidates for our approval. I was party to interviewing them. We rejected two immediately, and there were two left in my opinion, who were suitable. About this time, I left to attend a thirteen-week advanced management program then being offered in the United States. When I returned, I found to my amazement that he had rejected both of them and instead hired a local accountant at £1,800 a year, rather than the £4,000-man I had envisaged.

About this time I recognized that Paul Denham was a man who was going to reject any sort of idea, and any sort of talent, that he was not familiar with. I was utterly disenchanted with what he was doing. When I got back from America, Paul Denham also recognized that I was a chap who was going to stick to his guns. I could see trouble ahead and was determined to do something about it, even though the company's profit record continued to be outstanding.

This last remark reminded the casewriter of something said by E. M. Jackson, another BCI executive, who read the first draft of this case at the request of Mr. Lampton. Mr. Jackson said that, during the Harrogate affair,

> Lampton knew that Denham must go and yet he was very conscious that the company's success was in some measure due to the tremendous pace that Denham set for the company in earlier years. Indeed, the competitive edge that Harrogate had gained came largely from the fact that the company utilized its machines so intensively— the credit for which, at any rate initially, was Denham's.

Mr. Lampton continued:

> At the second Board meeting after I returned, Roger Sample brought up a subject that I had encouraged him to study (I had encouraged him to look at all facets of the business). Our office staff had very high turnover. The staff was working on Saturday mornings, but there was no need, no work, for this. When Roger proposed that Saturday morning hours be eliminated, Paul again said he wanted no part of it. He wasn't even fighting it. I suspect it was because he knew it was going to be put into effect anyway.
>
> At any rate, I was intent on pursuing this to some sort of conclusion. The meeting became heated and intense. Denham said, "Hell, why do we waste our time on these matters—go out and find out what the order position is and let's get down to work." At this point, and in front of Roger, I blew my top. "This is real business," I said, "and if we don't pursue it we have a real crisis."

After this incident, which took place about a year ago, Lampton came back to London and wrote to Denham the letter that appears as Exhibit 3, and that requests Denham to come to London for a meeting. "I felt that it was stupid to keep this up," Lampton said, "and that we must resolve it somehow. Anyway, Denham had not once been to London in the six years we owned the company. I always invited him to the annual dinner we hold for subsidiary managing directors, but he always accepted and then sent a last minute excuse. The night before the meeting was to take place here at head office, Paul Denham telephoned to say that he was not feeling well."

Exhibit 1 Excerpts from a Financial and Managerial Appraisal of Harrogate Asphalt Products, Ltd., by Henry Lampton

This appraisal was written by Henry Lampton seven years ago, shortly before the acquisition of Harrogate. All quoted material in this exhibit is from the Lampton appraisal; all other comments are those of the casewriter.

DIRECTORS AND PERSONNEL

P. Denham: Age 48, Managing Director and Secretary, Salary £4,000-plus

Mr. Denham has spent the last twenty-five years with Mr. Stanley and has grown up with the business. Originally, he was responsible for the coal distribution concern (sold eight years ago, but has been the prime mover in the expansion of Harrogate materials over the past ten years.

As will be appreciated later in the report, despite the rapid growth of this company, it is still relatively easy to administer and Denham has a tight personal control over it.

He has a very pleasant personality. He is a strict disciplinarian and is respected for it. As the company is in a rural area and there is a very low labor turnover, Denham regards the employees with Edwardian paternalism.

He has three sons at public school, the eldest (at sixteen) works in the company during vacations. Denham hopes one of the three will join him in the business later.

His remuneration has risen rapidly and it is intended that in future he should have a basic salary of £4,000 per annum and a commission of two and one-half percent on all net profits over £100,000 per annum.

P. Jenkins: Age 35, Works Manager, Salary £1,600

He has spent all his life in the asphalt product industry and joined Harrogate eighteen months ago from Dackman Products of Nottingham. Denham has a high regard for his technical ability, but believes he is rather weak and immature in his handling of employees (this may well be because Denham himself is "ever present").

He appeared to be rather shy, but showed great enthusiasm when explaining production methods and new developments.

K. Warren: Age 32, Transport Manager, Salary £1,600

Most of the day-to-day problems in this company are not concerned with production, but rather with transport of finished goods. Until recently this has been done entirely with hired vehicles, and Warren has been responsible for handling this. To deal with sixty or seventy hired vehicles requires considerable tact, patience, humor, planning ability, and downright strength. Warren appears to have these qualities in full. He was in the Royal Navy prior to joining Harrogate some five years ago.

J. Nixon: Age 45, Sales and Production Planning Manager, Salary £1,700

Nixon was not met, but from the way Denham referred to him he was a weak member of the management team. He evidently does his work well enough in a pedestrian way, but has not much strength of personality or many ideas.

. . . . .

"Jenkins, Warren, and Nixon are regarded by Stanley and Denham as future board members, but it would appear that Warren is the only one who is likely to grow to sufficient stature."

OUTSIDE STAFF

In this section, Mr. Lampton pointed out that the workers in the plant earn very good wages compared to general conditions in British industry. The wages are exceptionally high in relation to the surrounding agricultural area. Wages of between £30 and £40 per week were due to the fact that when the new revolutionary production machinery was purchased eleven years ago, neither the manufacturer of the machinery nor the Harrogate management knew that it would be so productive. Piece-rates were established based on what the machines were estimated to produce, but these were "grossly wrong."

The Company (in the event wisely) did not change these rates, but reserved the undisputed right to trim all production units to a bare minimum of labor. As the company has constantly expanded, no surplus labor has been laid off, but merely transferred to new units.

Needless to say, at these rates competition for jobs at Harrogate is very high. There was an intensely "brisk" air about the whole place. It is nonunion labour. There is no pension scheme. Hours worked are long (normally 07:30 to 18:30) and annual holidays are split, a week in the summer and another in the winter. The work is arduous, and in the winter, conditions are not good by the very nature of the business. As the rates are all fixed by team output there is no room for individual slacking. Relations with management appear to be good. Total labour force has risen rapidly in the past year to around one hundred.

FINANCE AND OPERATIONS

After presenting a profit and sales summary (Exhibit 2), Mr. Lampton, among others, made the following points:

1) The increase in gross profits has been due primarily to the introduction of new manufacturing equipment.

2) The productivity of labor could be still further reduced if one operation were not necessary. "Through the engineering firm of Mason and Grant, secret experiments are taking place with a mechanism that must be changed only once daily, instead of once with each batch of product. This would mean that each large machine could be filled automatically, cutting out one man's work on each of the five lines (at £1,500-plus per annum per line)." Mr. Lampton also made the point that "the finished product is a very strong and high quality job. Harrogate's products withstood the British Standard tests to a very satisfactory degree."

3) In the area of purchasing and supply logistics, Harrogate has a favorable location for securing raw materials economically. Because production is increasing very rapidly (75 percent in the past year), one of the company's principal raw material suppliers suggested to Denham that a subsidiary transport company could be set up to pick up raw materials, rather than have them shipped by the vendor. This subsidiary company has been set up with Stanley and Denham as directors. A significant cost saving in raw materials has been achieved. The company has its own electricity substation. "Overall, there is no problem with regard to raw materials."

4) In storage, and in distribution, Harrogate is regarded "as an excellent call" because large amounts of finished product can be handled and loaded in a short time. Use of modern materials handling equipment (the company owns, for example, 40 fork lift trucks and 20,000 pallets) has made this possible. Also, the Company has bought five flat lorries and intends over the years to build up its own fleet. However, management

Exhibit 2 *Selected Financial and Operating Results, Harrogate Asphalt Products, Ltd.*

Years Ago	Sales*	Profits before Taxes*
14	£ 31,000	n.a.
13	55,000	£ 22,000
12	83,000	28,000
11	110,000	39,000
10	178,000	62,000
9	224,000	87,000
8	361,000	136,000
7	520,000	150,000
6	867,000	260,000
5	1,053,000	310,000
4	1,096,000	300,000
3	1,638,000	450,000
2	1,922,000	595,000
1	2,050,000	600,000
Present	2,500,000	750,000 (estimated)

*Figures are rounded to nearest £1,000.

indicates that they will still use contractors for uneconomic trips and in emergency.

CURRENT PROGRESS AND FUTURE PROSPECTS

In this section, Mr. Lampton pointed out that productive capacity has increased significantly. He cites the month of June in each of the last four years, showing that production, in tons, had progressed from 5,600 in the first year, to 8,000, 10,100, and 17,700 in the successive three years. A new production line, together with machines, has been set up in the last three months (adding 950 tons to usage of raw materials). Sales for the last ten months have increased to £452,000 compared with £301,900 in the same period last year.

> The reason for the company's success is probably due to its geographical position (both for raw materials and markets), the fact that it invested early in revolutionary production machinery (outside engineers reckon that Harrogate has more of this machinery than anyone else, but Denham has no proof of this), very efficient management (mainly by Denham) and because it is supplying a material in increasing demand over the past decade.
> The future looks good. This is a first-class company and should prove an excellent investment for BCI.

Exhibit 3 *Letter from Lampton to Denham*

Mr. Paul Denham, Managing Director
Harrogate Asphalt Products, Ltd.
Frampton, Yorkshire

Dear Paul,

I have given myself some cooling time since our last meeting to consider its implications. I believe that it is most important that you and I meet away from Harrogate to discuss both the future of the business and the way in which you and I can operate together constructively for its good.

Could you come to see me and have lunch on Tuesday 2nd August, Thursday 4th or Friday 5th? At the moment I have these days free from outside appointments.

Yours,

(s) Henry Lampton

FOR DISCUSSION AND REPORT-WRITING

Organizing: Structural Design

1) What do you think Lampton meant when he said that the BCI headquarters staff "are to be used as catalysts"? Apply this term to how the market research director in BCI should act with the president of a BCI subsidiary. If you are a chemist or chemical engineer, use the technical meaning of "catalyst."

2) In what sense did the original BCI merchant banking system of dealing with its subsidiaries represent a very high degree of decentralization? What advantages would this have had? What disadvantages did it have according to Lampton?

Human Factors in Organizing

3) Look at the beginning of the conflict between Lampton and Denham, two years after BCI took over. What do you think Lampton *really* wanted Denham to do at that point? Why did he want this?

4) Does the fact that Lampton became president of BCI about the time the case was written throw any light on why he believed in the "moral obligation" of BCI officers to "help subsidiary managers"?

5) To what do you attribute Denham's lack of cooperation with Lampton when Lampton instituted more frequent Board meetings?

6) What do you predict will happen in the future between Lampton and Denham? Who will do what?

Planning: Elements of Decision-Making

7) To what extent may Lampton's recommendations on employee vacations and no Saturday work be attempts to deal with symptoms rather than causes of a problem? Define the problem these recommendations were designed to deal with and place it in the context of higher-level company objectives.

Planning: Decision-Making in an Enterprise

8) Look at the two examples of policies that Lampton wanted the Harrogate Board to make (vacations for employees and no Saturday work). Suppose that Denham had readily agreed to them. How would this have facilitated decision-making within the whole (BCI-Harrogate) organization?

9) At the beginning of the case, Lampton states that one of BCI's objectives is to acquire new companies, but only companies that are *related to* the existing technology of other BCI companies. Later, he gives an example of the L.M. Trowbridge Company. How does this *objective* benefit the future decision-making process in BCI?

Leading

10) Toward the beginning of the case, Lampton states, "until very recently we were reluctant to provide corporate staff advice to subsidiary companies. It would be fatal to try to force them on unwilling managements." Explain further what he meant. Do you agree or disagree?

11) Do you agree with Lampton that BCI headquarters managers have a "moral obligation to help subsidiary managers"? Clarify what he meant before stating your views.

12) In terms of Lampton's own part in the relationship with Denham, do you view him as an effective leader? Why or why not?

13) What effect, if any, do you think the location of Harrogate Asphalt Products, Ltd., in a small town in Northern England and BCI in London might have on the personal relations between Lampton and Denham? To what extent should Lampton consider local mores in the standards he sets for Harrogate managers? If the company were located in Malaya how would you have answered the previous question?

14) *Summary Report Question, Part Five:* Suppose that you are in Lampton's shoes as of the end of the case, just after the telephone call from Denham. Suppose further that you went up to Yorkshire to see Denham the next week. What kinds of leadership actions would you hope to carry out?

15) *Summary Simulation, Part Five:* After thoughtfully studying the case, and with some insights from the questions above, take the part of Lampton. With another student playing as realistic a Denham as possible, conduct a conversation as of the end of the case.

Measuring and Controlling

16) In what sense was the merchant banking system of BCI a deficient system for a modern conglomerate to use to try to control the operations of a subsidiary?

Summary Question for Solution of the Case as a Whole

17) Look at the entire management process for integrating Harrogate as a successful subsidiary of BCI. Assume the role of a BCI staff analyst

who is assigned the same type of project as Lampton was assigned a number of years ago. Diagnose the present situation of the company and make recommendations for future growth.

✔ CONSOLIDATED INSTRUMENTS—A

Donald Robinson was born in August, 1942, in Kershaw, South Carolina. His father was highly regarded by the black community of Kershaw, served as minister of their rural Baptist church, and managed, with his four sons and three daughters, to scratch out a living from a small farm.

Although Donald's father preached on many subjects on Sunday, during the week he sought to impress his children with one goal— *education.*

"Knowledge is the equalizer," he would say. "If you study and learn, soon you will have the power of knowledge. Some men may never get used to the color of your skin, but if you really educate and discipline your mind they'll listen because you can help them." Although Don felt that many of his father's views were old-fashioned and not totally realistic, he had followed his father's advice on education and hard work.

At the age of thirteen, Donald and a younger sister, Rose, were sent to live with their aunt in Brooklyn, New York. As the brightest of the Robinson children, it was hoped that by going to high school in New York they might go on to a university. Despite rather poor elementary school training, Donald passed a citywide examination that qualified him to go to one of three select New York high schools and from there he was graduated third in his class and received a scholarship to Rensselaer Polytechnic Institute. As an electrical engineering major, Donald—or Robby, as he was now called—did B+ work as a freshman and sophomore but slipped slightly in the first semester of his junior year, as he got more heavily involved in extracurricular activities. In addition to being elected vice-president of the junior class, he also enjoyed the rare honor of being chosen captain of the wrestling team as a junior.

In March of that year, a fire swept the Robinson house in Kershaw, killing Donald's father and youngest sister and badly burning his mother and two other children. Although there was a rumor that the fire was set as a result of Reverend Robinson's efforts to bring about integrated schooling no evidence was found to support charges. Donald left school and returned home to care for the family. Working as a laborer in nearby Camden, he cared for his mother and younger brothers until his mother died in October. The brothers were then sent to live with relatives and Robby requested early induction into the Army and was accepted.

During a year in Vietnam as a Signal Corps "advisor" Robby was wounded twice and received a Bronze Star for his leadership under fire. Working under the command of a Vietnamese lieutenant, he and one other advisor and a squad of eight Vietnamese were caught in a Vietcong ambush. The lieutenant and three men were killed; Robby, despite serious wounds, kept the remaining men from fleeing and returned fire until darkness, when he led them back to their base.

Upon return from Vietnam, Robby was stationed at Fort Ord where he taught until his discharge. Returning to New York, he accepted a technician's job with a small electronics firm, Norbert Precision Controls, located on Long Island and attended evening classes at Brooklyn Polytechnical Institute. Three years later, Robby completed the requirements for his B.S. in electrical engineering.

Earlier that year, Norbert was acquired by Consolidated Instruments (CI), a large diversified electronics firm with major facilities in Houston, Texas, San Diego, California, and Salem, Massachusetts. Upon receiving his degree, Robby was offered an opportunity with the parent company, as a member of a special projects task force. Even though this meant moving to Houston, Robby accepted.

"At first I was a little leery about a move to Houston," Robby told the task force supervisor. "Things have changed a great deal in the last few years, but I wasn't at all sure how I would be received. You and the other CI people have made it easier for me, and I want you to know how much I appreciate it. When people treat me fairly and give me a chance to show what I can do, I give 110 percent."

His supervisor was pleased with his work and despite some friction that developed between Robby and two others on the team, the project was completed on schedule. Robby was offered a job at CI's headquarters in Salem as a senior technician in the corporate engineering department. This was considered an important move for a young engineer because men working in this department were exposed, through project review work, to a wide range of company products and technologies. Success in this work was seen as a way to move into any of the major divisional engineering departments and increased the opportunities for rapid movement up the engineering management hierarchy.

Eager to accept the job, Robby was upset by the fact that a girl he had met in Houston and become engaged to a month later did not want to move to Salem. In discussing the problem with his superior in Houston, Robby said, "I love Laura and she says she loves me but she doesn't want to move. I explained what a great chance this was for me and that if I want to make it, I've got to be prepared to move."

After several weeks Robby accepted the transfer and said:

> I've got to take the job. If I'm going to advance I've got to be prepared to sacrifice. Maybe Laura will change her mind; maybe I'll end up back here in a year or two but I've got to take the opportunity. Someday I hope to be a vice-president of this company and I'll never make it if I let this kind of chance go by.
>
> I owe CI a lot already and I'm grateful to you for backing me after my run-in with Sprague. I won't let you down!

The run-in Robby referred to stemmed from his insistence that one of the six men with whom he worked on the Houston project "was just not pulling his share of the load."

> Robinson maintained [the project supervisor said] that Joe Sprague was goofing off and doing sloppy work. Joe and his friend Ed Montez resented Robinson's comments and told him that he wasn't their boss and should mind his business.
>
> Frankly, Sprague was not strong technically and had a tendency to loaf and was a bad influence on Montez. I would have replaced him if a better man was available but was prepared to make do. Robinson brought the issue to a head, however, and left me no choice but ultimately to let Sprague go. Unable to replace Sprague for six weeks, we all had to work harder and Robinson put in all kinds of off-the-clock overtime to help. He's a bit stubborn but he drives himself harder than any man I've ever known.

Robby began work in Salem and six months later was made a project supervisor. His immediate superior, Paul Horn, was a highly qualified man who had served in several key operating jobs before being placed in charge of this corporate review department. Speaking to Robinson, Horn said:

> They told me this was a promotion when they sent me here. But as far as I'm concerned they needed someone expendable to do their dirty work. With the dip in sales, they needed a hard-nosed, experienced man to help sort out which areas to put more money into and which ones to cut back on or eliminate. If I do this job right, I won't have many friends left at the division level. My boss, Shel Thayler [vice-president of engineering] wants results and I intend to keep him happy.

As one of six project supervisors reporting to Horn, Robby was the youngest and least qualified in terms of experience and formal education. Frank Lindemer, another project supervisor and friend of Robby's, irritated him greatly once at lunch by suggesting in a joking tone that Robby might be receiving a little "reverse discrimination."

In reply, Robby snapped:

> I don't want any favors! I'll earn what I get. There are so darn few people these days who are willing to give you an honest day's work that I'd make out fine even if I was spotted.
>
> To get anywhere you have to be willing to make sacrifices. Most men reach a certain level of accomplishment and then spend the rest of their life trying to live on past successes and protecting themselves from people they regard as a threat to the status quo. Someday, I'll be sitting in Mr. Thayler's office and it won't be because I'm black. At that level, it's technical know-how and drive—not color—that counts.

Paul Horn liked Robby's work.

> Robby has a good technical instinct [Horn said]. He works hard; is tough-minded and takes orders. He hasn't got as much schooling as the others, but he is enrolled in night school and is working on his master's degree already. If he has one fault it's that he tends to be impatient with people who don't work as hard as he does. He tells them how he feels about them and needles them, and naturally they resent it. He'll be okay though. He reminds me very much of myself when I was his age. The only difference was in 1939 you had enough people around who wanted to work so that you didn't have to put up with some of the stuff you do today.

Horn's reputation as a demanding manager was well known and in a one-year period, he lost or replaced three project supervisors. At the end of this period Horn was sent to a six-week management seminar offered by a leading business school. Much to the other project managers' surprise, he recommended that Robinson be given temporary responsibility for coordinating projects while he, Horn, was away. Shel Thayler, vice-president of engineering, did not concur and brought in an experienced plant engineering manager, Lee Bradley, as Horn's "temporary replacement."

Thayler explained:

> Horn was to be at school for six weeks and then had four weeks vacation coming. This was a good chance to see how Bradley worked out. We are bringing in a lot of highly trained younger men to work in these project groups and we need someone who will develop project managers and will handle them effectively.
>
> If Bradley hadn't impressed me as being ready, then I would have kept Paul Horn here and hoped that the time he spent in that program might have helped him develop his interpersonal skills.

Apparently Bradley impressed Thayler for Horn was assigned as engineering manager of a new CI acquisition immediately upon returning from vacation, and Bradley was appointed to Horn's old job.

Horn was somewhat bitter about the move and told Robinson, "Be careful, son, they're going through a human relations phase now that we have carried them through the worst of the recession. I told you this was a thankless job."

Robby liked Paul Horn, though he had felt uneasy when Horn spoke harshly about "management." He once commented to Lindemer, "I wonder how high you have to get in this company before you stop talking about 'management' as if you weren't part of it. Mr. Horn is a great guy but he never really seemed as loyal to the company as a man at his level should be."

Robby had mixed emotions about Bradley. He told Lindemer that he was relieved when Bradley took over as temporary department manager.

> I knew I wasn't ready for even caretaker duty [Robby said], and although I was pleased that Mr. Horn thought that highly of me, I knew the other project supervisors would resent it. More important, I hope to get back into division work as a department manager. We both know that to move up in management you need that kind of operating experience. If I had taken Mr. Horn's job before I was ready I might have ruined my chances of getting into one of the divisions.

"That all depends," Lindemer said. "If you had the coordinator's job for a few months you might have done a division manager a favor or two and improved your chances."

Robby laughed at Lindemer's cynicism at the time but in recent months has begun to wonder about Frank's observation. Bradley, although initially impressed by Robinson's hard work, has become increasingly more critical of his way of running his eleven-man group and has told Robby this.

After six months as Robby's superior, Bradley told Thayler:

> Robby's just too much of a driver. I'm afraid that he is following Paul Horn's approach and trying to do it all on drive, energy, and technical competence. He just isn't building a team, and several of his people have requested transfers. I've tried to convince him that he must spend more time working on his human relations skills but he doesn't seem to understand what that involves.
>
> I have signed him up for next quarter's course on the "Grid" [a popular development seminar designed to increase interpersonal skills and run four times a year by CI]. Until then, I think I'll just leave him alone. He knows that Paul Horn recommended him as the temporary department head and although I think he's smart enough to know he wasn't ready for the job, he just might resent me trying to help him too soon. Let's see how he makes out after the course.

Thayler admitted he was surprised at Bradley's assessment of Robinson. "I thought we had a real comer in that young man," he said. "I hope you can work with him because I planned to send him to a division for an operating job in the next year but I wouldn't dare if he is too hard-nosed. He has enough problems as a young black man who worked in the pruning department." (The divisions had referred to Horn's review groups as "Paul's Pruners".)

During the next three months, Robinson sensed that Bradley was dissatisfied with his work and he became more upset when Bradley refused to permit him to dismiss two of his group.

"Work with them, Robby," Bradley said. "A good manager doesn't transfer or fire his problems—he works with them."

Two weeks after this exchange, Robinson spent one week at the "Grid" course but came back unimpressed.

"Maybe I had a poor teacher," he told Frank Lindemer, "but I couldn't get a straight answer out of him. He had lots of labels but no answers. Lots of theories about people but no hard data. If an engineer tried to sell a proposal based on the data these 'joy boys' use to sell their human relations stuff, he'd be thrown out on his ear."

Robinson communicated his reaction to the course to Bradley in much the same manner and was angered by Bradley's reply.

"I'm sorry you feel that way," Bradley said. "We were hoping you'd get more out of the course to help you in the people-area."

Robinson wondered who "we" was but didn't ask. He later commented on this to Lindemer, saying that he found Bradley a difficult man to talk to. "For some reason, I always feel guilty of something when I talk to Bradley. He tells me to call him 'Lee.' He's always telling me to level with him, but when I do he seems to get irritated."

Over the next several months the relationship between Robinson and Bradley became more strained. Although Robby's group met agreed-upon targets, Bradley felt that morale was becoming critical and so he advised Thayler of the situation.

> If we don't see marked improvement in Robby's skills in developing and dealing with his people in the next four to six months [Bradley said], we will have to seriously consider taking him out of his job. I'm afraid Robby may be a classic case of a technical man who doesn't develop as a manager. I now have four requests for transfers out of his group. He's driving his people, not leading them, and is doing much more of the work himself than he should just to stay on schedule. In my opinion, it's just a matter of time before he has a real blow-up in his group.

Thayler has had little direct contact with Robinson and what little he knew of him had been good and so he questioned Bradley.

"Look, Lee, normally I wouldn't get involved in this at all; I'd leave it entirely in your hands. But Robinson is an unusual case and I'd hate to lose him. You have had him for almost a year now and that should be long enough to make a judgment, but have you really sat down and told him exactly what you want in the way of change?"

Bradley said, "I've tried, but this is a difficult area to lay out in clear terms, particularly to a man with a strong technical background who doesn't really have a feel for people-problems. I had hoped the 'Grid' course would help but it hasn't. Suppose I have a real man-to-man talk with him and then report back to you? He is about due for his annual performance appraisal anyway."

"That's fine," said Thayler. "Then we'll see what we have to do next."

FOR DISCUSSION AND REPORT-WRITING

Organizing: Structural Design

1) Should Robinson be required to obtain Bradley's permission to fire the two men he feels are holding his group back? How do you reconcile his "duties" and "obligations" with his lack of authority to dismiss his subordinates without Bradley's approval?

2) Would it be helpful to have Bradley bring an experienced man from the personnel department in with him during his upcoming "man-to-man" talk with Robinson? What should guide the staff man's actions if he were invited to sit in?

Human Factors in Organizing

3) What factors other than his personality may have contributed to Robinson's concept of how he should perform as a successful manager?

4) How might Robinson go about getting a better feel for the needs and values of his subordinates?

5) In what ways might Robinson's approach to his job lead to a different appraisal by his immediate supervisor if he worked in a similar position in a facility located in India?

6) What factors other than personality or differences in background might account for the conflict that appears to exist between Robinson and Bradley?

7) To what degree may Robinson be experiencing some of his difficulties with Bradley as a result of poor matching of jobs and individuals?

Planning: Elements of Decision-Making

8) What is Bradley's basic problem with Robinson? Or is there more than one problem? Develop a causal chain for at least one of these problems.

9) How should intangibles be balanced with more quantifiable factors when attempting to make a choice in what action to take with Robinson?

Planning: Decision-Making in an Enterprise

10) In what ways do Bradley's efforts to shift Robinson's attention to the development of "people-skills" as well as technical skills illustrate the difficulties in setting useful objectives?

11) What kinds of standing plans would be helpful in making an earlier diagnosis and in providing more effective treatment of problems faced by a new manager? How might these standing plans help men in Bradley's or Thayler's position in selecting and developing new managers?

Leading

12) Bradley seems to be having trouble explaining to Robinson the difference between "driving" and "leading" his people. What do you feel the real differences are?

13) What difficulties would you anticipate in trying to explain the meaning of such terms as "leadership," "voluntary cooperation," and "two-way personal communication" to Robinson?

14) Even if Bradley does an excellent job in counseling Robinson, do you feel that Robinson can learn what Bradley wants him to learn?

15) Would Bradley's task in talking to Robinson be easier or more difficult if after he puts his feeling on paper as part of the company's formal performance review procedure, he gives the written document to Robinson a day or two before their "man-to-man" talk?

16) What effect might your answer to question 15 have on good two-way communication during the "man-to-man" talk?

17) *Summary Report Question, Part Five* Based on your answers to questions 3, 4, 13, 14, 15, and 16, prepare notes for, and conduct, a role-play in which you take the role of Bradley. Seek a volunteer from class to play the role of Robinson. Ask the class to make notes during the role-play on what they feel is taking place and compare their reactions after the role-play to your own. How well were you able to follow the plan you worked out in your notes before the role-play?

Measuring and Controlling

18) How should Bradley measure Robinson's performance, before and after counseling, in areas involving leadership and team-building?

19) What kinds of responses might you predict on the part of Robinson to the measures of performance suggested in your answer to question 18?

Summary Question for Solution
of the Case as a Whole

20) Based on your experience in answering question 17, what action would you recommend be taken with Robinson? How would you implement this action in terms of a specific program? What kinds of responses would you anticipate from Robinson and other managers at his level as a result of your recommendations?

PART SIX

Measuring and Controlling

Managerial control is akin to the thermostat system of a furnace. The thermostat keeps track of the actual temperature in the house, compares it with the desired temperature, and switches the heat off or on, according to whether the house is too warm or too cool. Many activities of business need to be similarly controlled—actual results should be measured and compared against plans, and then corrective action should be taken to bring results more nearly in line with what is desired.

Controlling business operations cannot be reduced to a mechanistic process, however, as in the thermostat analogy. People are involved and they complicate the process. Human behavior is especially important in the corrective-action phase. For example, both managers and operators *anticipate* measurement of their work and also the consequences—good or bad—of these measurements. Accordingly, they may make special efforts to produce desirable results. But if they feel that the measuring is unwarranted or unfair, the control system may produce negative responses.

Measuring and controlling depend on, and contribute to, the other management processes—organizing, planning, and leading. Without plans to set objectives and specify activities, control would serve no purpose. Without organization, guidance would be lacking about who should make evaluations and who should take corrective action. Without effective leading, a whole carload of measurement reports would have no impact on actual performance. Consequently, we must carefully fit together executive action in all these phases of management.

In Part Six we shall first examine the basic elements of a control system, and then explore ways of integrating controls with the behavioral and formal management structures of a company. This will be done in the following chapters.

Chapter 24—Basic Elements of Controlling. Here we shall discuss selecting strategic control points, setting levels of desired performance, evaluating results on the basis of various kinds of evidence, and making reports that lead to timely corrective action.

Chapter 25—PERT and Budgetary Control. These two control mechanisms are of special interest to us because they are companywide in their scope. Budgets give a comprehensive view of financial plans and results. PERT provides a coordinated control of the timing of diverse actions involved in major programs. Both concepts can be used in many circumstances, but we need to understand their limitations as well as their advantages.

Chapter 26—Responses of People to Controls. The idea of being controlled is repugnant to most people, even though they readily accept controls as a normal part of civilized living. In this chapter we shall explore why people react as they do to controlling and shall consider ways we can design and administer controls in order to engender a positive feeling about them.

Chapter 27—Integrating Controls with Other Managerial Processes. This chapter deals with the interrelations between controlling on the one hand and planning, organizing, and leading on the other. We shall examine a series of special problems that arise in keeping the various aspects of managerial action coordinated and integrated.

Under Utopian conditions control would be unnecessary. Plans would include realistic provisions for overcoming any obstacles in the way of achieving objectives; organization structure would be clear and men would be qualified to perform their respective duties; and managerial leadership would assure the impetus to carry plans to completion. But in real life there is many a slip between the plan and the result. Black customers stage a boycott; lack of rain lowers crop yields; Sally falls in love and makes a lot of errors on her invoices; the Federal Reserve Bank raises its discount rate. For these reasons, and for a myriad of other possible ones, actual operations deviate from a laid-out course. Clearly, control is needed to detect these deviations and to prompt the necessary adjustments.

Chapter Twenty-four

Basic Elements of Controlling

THE CONTROL PROCESS

The primary aim of control is to assure that the results of operations conform as closely as possible to established goals. A secondary aim is to provide timely information that may prompt revision of goals. The following three elements, or phases, are always present in the control process:

1) *Standards that represent desired performance.* These standards may be tangible or intangible, vague or specific, but until everyone concerned understands what results are desired, control will create confusion.

2) *A comparison of actual results against the standards.* This evaluation must be reported to the people who can do something about it.

3) *Corrective action.* Control measurements and reports serve little purpose unless corrective action is taken when it is discovered that current activities are not leading to desired results.

Regardless of what is being controlled, these elements are always involved. Expense control, from the use of electric lights to the total cost of goods; quality control, from the appearance of a typed letter to the dependability of an airplane engine; investment control, from the number of spare parts in a repairman's kit to the capital investment in a fleet of tankers—all involve standards, evaluation, and corrective action. We may have serious difficulty in designing the controls for a particular activity, but knowing that the three basic elements are always present provides us with a useful approach for resolving the difficulty.

Although the basic control process may be simple, its application poses many questions. When and where should a review of performance take place? Who should make the appraisals? What standard should be used for evaluation? To whom should the results of evaluation be reported? How may the entire process be completed promptly, fairly, and at reasonable expense? Our answers to questions such as these will determine the effectiveness of any control system we design.

SETTING CONTROL STANDARDS

The first step in setting standards for purposes of control is to be clear about the results we desire. What shall we accept as satisfactory performance? Usually we must answer this question in terms of (1) the outcome characteristics that are important in a particular situation and (2) the level of achievement, or "par," for each characteristic.

Characteristics That Determine Good Performance

An executive who wishes to control a particular part of the operation under his supervision often finds that the work in question has several characteristics, and he must conceive of good performance in terms of these characteristics. A furniture store, for instance, found that it had to think about the following factors in appraising its credit department: the attitude of customers who had dealings with the department, the total credit extended, the operating profit earned on goods sold on credit, credit losses, department operating expenses, gross income from credit charges, net expense of running the department, and departmental cooperation with the treasurer, sales manager, and other executives of the company. It was decided that the credit manager of this company had to look good on all these counts if his work was to be rated as satisfactory.

In an earlier discussion of objectives (Chapter 17), we noted that companies with decentralized operating divisions have found that profits are an inadequate measure of success. In addition to profits, a number of companies are now considering market position, productivity, leadership, personnel development, employee attitudes, and public responsibility. It is, of course, possible to focus controls on one aspect of a job, such as current profits or market position. But to do so without first thinking through *all* the characteristics that contribute to good performance and without making provision for these characteristics in the control system is to court trouble.

Each time a manager designs some new control he faces this question of what characteristics to consider. An approach that is suggestive for some, though not all, jobs is to give thought to the following three matters:

1) *Output.* What services or functions are expected to be performed? Perhaps each of these services can be defined in terms of quantity, quality, and time.

2) *Expense.* What direct dollar expenses are reasonable to secure such an output? What should be normal indirect expenses in terms of supervision, staff assistance, interference with the work of other people, and opportunities foregone to perform other kinds of work?

3) *Resources.* Does the operation require capital investment in inventories, equipment, or other assets?[1] Are scarce human resources or company reputation being committed? If so, effective use of resources should also be considered.

---

[1]Although the cost of developing a well-trained corps of workers, a smooth-running organization, or a good reputation with outside groups does not appear on a company balance sheet, such assets do require investment in the same way that machinery does; such investment is essential if future "output" is to be achieved within desired future "expenses."

Fig. 24-1 *The control process. Although this is the basic process, questions must be asked concerning each stage— when and where should the sensing take place, who should carry it out, and so on—in order to arrive at the most effective control system for a given organization.*

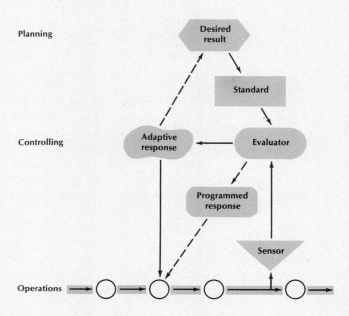

Par for Each Characteristic

Having identified the characteristics of good performance, we must then determine how high a level of achievement for each characteristic we desire. More precisely, what is a reasonable expectation, or par, for good performance? For example, pars for the credit department in the furniture store mentioned earlier might be as shown in Table 24–1.

For most performance characteristics, par is simply an ordinarily feasible achievement level. Variations beyond this level are usually desirable —such as output above par or expenses below par. But in special circumstances, such as the rate of production on an assembly line, there may be only narrow tolerance limits for deviation above or below the established par.

On highways, the speed limit is a single standard that is applicable to all drivers. Similarly in business, a single standard may be applicable to such things as quality of delivery service, but for many other characteristics we may adjust the standard for a particular individual and local circumstances. A branch manager of a national sales organization who tried this individualistic approach reports as follows:

> *Don't compare an individual to the group average, but rather to a "standard" set for him. I have tried this on quotas for both gross and coverage requirements during the current canvass, and the results are interesting. The salesmen are more quota conscious than I have ever before known them to be. I find they will work much harder to*

Table 24–1

Characteristic	Standard
Attitude of customers	90 percent of furniture purchased on time, financed by the store
Total credit extended	Outstanding loans approximately equal to last 90 days' sales
Operating profit earned on goods sold on credit	$250,000
Credit losses	0.5 percent of credit extended ($3,500 in normal year)
Department operating expenses	$12,000 per year
Gross income from credit charges (above interest paid to bank)	$14,000 per year
Net expense of running department	$1,500 per year

make their own *standards* than they will to "beat the high man" or surpass crew average. Also—each man is much more aware of his own quota (through interest) and the total book standing than previously.

Securing flexibility through adjustment of par. In control, as in other phases of management, we have a legitimate need for flexibility. For instance, a firm may increase inventories if there is reason to anticipate a shortage of raw materials; it may cut its price to meet competition knowing that dollar sales figures will be thrown out of line; during a depression it may decide not to cut employment in proportion to the drop in production; and so forth.

Unfortunately, "flexibility" is sometimes used as an excuse to disregard control entirely. Because the previous standards are no longer reasonable, there is a temptation to say that no control is feasible. A more sensible way of dealing with unforeseen conditions is to adjust par. The performance characteristics being watched, the measurements, and the reports continue to be useful; we only need to change the levels of expectation. As we shall note in Chapter 26, this is precisely the result of "flexible" budgets, and the concept may be adapted to many other control standards.[2]

Relating Results to Individual Accountability

Control standards are most effective when they are related to the performance of a specific individual. Thus both a man himself and his supervisors can know if he should be praised or blamed when actual results are compared against the control standards. In addition, fixing accountability for a deviation helps focus the search for causes of that deviation and thereby sharpens corrective action. We can see this principle in the example of the furniture store credit manager discussed earlier. In many other situations, too, where we naturally think of desired results in terms of the work of a particular operator or manager, it is easy to tie control standards to that one man.

But at other times, accountability for a desired result is not so simply assigned. A company's investment in inventory, for example, is affected by purchases, rate of production, and sales. The man to whom each of these three activities is assigned looks on inventory from his own point of view, as does the treasurer, who is concerned with the financial strength of the

[2]Both automatic and semiautomatic adjustments of par are usually based on variation of a key external variable (that is, external to the domain of the man being controlled) such as volume, price, or wage rates. The original pars are based on a set of *planning premises*, and so when these premises shift through no fault of the controllee, some offsetting revision of pars is called for. In a broader scope, this kind of adjustment suggests that when control is used for personal evaluation the key planning premises should be identified and then their accuracy observed along with the results of a person's efforts.

company. In some companies, only one person, who has the task of coordinating these different viewpoints, is accountable for the level of inventories. In other companies, the task is divided: For instance, the sales manager estimates sales, the plant manager schedules production and indicates the quantities of raw materials he will need each month, and the purchasing agent decides when it will be advantageous to buy the materials specified by the plant manager. In such a situation, where no one person is accountable for the level of inventories, standards may be set for each step that is performed by a different man. Then if there is trouble with inventories, we can ascertain where the system broke down.

The establishment of standards for control purposes is heavily dependent on the previous decisions of management on plans and organization. Specifically, objectives (discussed in Chapter 17) are the direct counterpart of "desired results." Similarly, the assignment of duties (discussed in Chapters 2 and 3) is the key to the assignment of accountability for achieving control standards. Theoretically, then, setting objectives and defining job duties make unnecessary the first two steps we have suggested for setting control standards. But in practice, this is rarely so. The needs of workable control almost always call for refining and clarifying objectives and duties. Without fail, though, we should start with the plans that have already been developed. Then the process of developing standards from these plans for purposes of control is really a matter of refinement.

Picking Strategic Points to Watch

"Desired results" have been urged as a good starting point for designing managerial controls. We now want to turn to a qualification, or refinement, of this principle. Two types of difficulty arise in the sweeping use of desired results as control standards:

1) To attempt to evaluate all the results of everyone's work would be very burdensome. Instead we typically measure results only at various stages in the total process. For instance, a dairy farmer may measure his output by the number of pounds of butterfat produced per week. Moreover, as we shall discuss in the section on evaluation, sometimes only samples of the output are measured. The aim is to watch enough to keep track of what is happening without going to the expense of watching everything. That is, the aim is to pick *strategic points* that will, at least indirectly, reflect the total operation. If results at these points are off standard, a more detailed check can be made of intermediate stages to find the reasons for the deviation.

2) Evaluating results necessarily takes place after work is completed —it is postmortem. To be sure, such evaluations are highly useful in planning for repetition of the same operation, in planning for the next step, and in rewarding, disciplining, training, or promoting the persons con-

cerned. Nevertheless, the evaluations are in the nature of scorecards after the game is over.

To supplement the final evaluations—the scorecards—it is often desirable to keep watch on an operation while it is progressing. If we can detect or predict trouble early, we may be able to make adjustments before the final results are in. For this purpose, we seek out points to watch that serve as warning posts. The purpose of these strategic points is principally to *direct attention* rather than to evaluate.

The president of an automobile-parts manufacturing company, for example, keeps his eye on four key items that reflect operations in the plant: total output, efficiency, back orders, and inventory. This company has figured out the number of man-hours of direct labor that are required to produce each type of product, and as a normal practice it computes the ratio of standard hours to actual hours. By watching this ratio every month, the president believes he can detect any major difficulties with equipment or with operating personnel and so keep track of overall efficiency. The back orders indicate whether the plant is meeting sales requirements. The inventory figures show whether good deliveries and efficiency of the plant are being achieved by accumulating a very large inventory. There are, of course, many other aspects of good planning and operation, such as quality of output, overhead expense, spoilage, community relations, and capital expenditures. But in this particular instance, the president believes that these other features are unlikely to cause difficulty and can be controlled intermittently. The four points are what he watches closely.

Control Points at Early Stages

When the purpose of control is to catch trouble while it is forming, strategic control points are necessarily different from those used in evaluation. The Hilton Hotels, to cite an example, keep close tab on

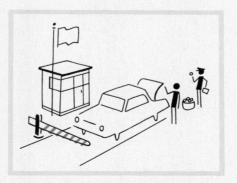

Fig. 24-2 Where international highways cross national borders, checkpoints help prevent the spread of contaminated plants and animals. Likewise in an organization, strategic control points ensure that one defective operation does not upset future steps.

advance bookings of conventions—one, two, or even three years ahead. With this warning of the ups and downs of business volume, they can undertake special promotions to fill in valleys. On a month-to-month basis, when it is too late to change volume, advance bookings are used to expand or contract staff to fit the expected level of operations.

In safety work, control is achieved largely through training in safety methods and through maintaining safe operating conditions. In other words, management locates strategic control points in the formative stages, and inspections are made to try to prevent trouble from ever arising.

Where control is exercised is important to smooth and harmonious administration. In many companies, requests for capital expenditures for such things as new buildings, equipment, and sources of raw materials have to be presented in writing with an explanation of why each particular investment will be advantageous to the company. By controlling approval of the projects at this formative stage, the president or financial officer can exercise an influence that would be futile after orders are placed and contracts let. Note that the control goes clear back to the planning period before any action has really begun.

Checking on How Work Is Performed

In the preceding discussion of control standards, we have emphasized the results of work rather than the method for accomplishing the work. Even strategic control points at early stages are basically devices for anticipating results. This emphasis is consistent with our stress on objectives in the earlier discussions of planning and decentralizing. Nevertheless, there are times when control over method is more expeditious than control over results.

Sometimes we set controls on work methods simply because it is more economical to watch the methods than the results. In addition, an executive may feel that the outcome is of such great importance that he must exercise control wherever he can: Diamond-cutting and quality control in the manufacture of spacecraft or parachutes are undertakings in which control will probably be exercised over methods as well as results.

Then there are baffling situations wherein it is extremely difficult to know just how good results should be. Research work on cancer or negotiating with a group that is protesting ecological abuses are examples. In these situations we may resort to evaluating the method by which work was done.

A great deal of staff work has to be appraised chiefly in terms of how work is done. What kinds of standards can we set, for example, for the output of a legal counsel? If he makes a terrible boner, we can probably discover it in the results, but such clear mistakes are unlikely to happen. Tough cases are highly individual in their characteristics, and many factors of judgment are involved. About the most we can do is to see whether he commands the respect of other lawyers and conducts himself intelligently and impressively.

Whenever control is undertaken, then, from the entire company down to the work of one man, we need to consider what kind of results and the level of par to incorporate into our standards. And since busy executives cannot give regular attention to a complete array of standards, we should identify strategic points to watch: summaries of overall results, results of key activities, warnings of impending trouble, and—for some jobs—how the work is done. One of the arts of good management is setting the right standards at the right control points.

THE TASK OF MEASURING

Once standards are set, the second basic step in control is the evaluation of performance. This step involves measuring the work that is done in terms of the control standards and communicating the appraisal to persons who search for reasons for deviations and take corrective action. Broadly speaking, control measurements seek to answer the question, "How are we doing?"

The specific methods of measuring results are almost as diverse as the activities of business. Because at best we could give only a few suggestive examples here, it will be more useful to examine some of the common difficulties in measuring for control and to note several promising ways of dealing with these difficulties.

Need for Ingenuity

Engineers are far ahead of managers in their ability to measure what is going on. We have for one thing tended to rely on accounting far beyond its intended purpose and inherent capacity. To be sure, surveys of employee attitudes and morale, and Nielsen reports (which provide current data on the sale of goods in the grocery and drug fields by brand, region, and type of outlet) are steps in overcoming this deficiency. But great opportunity remains for improvement.

Actually many companies have information they do not fully utilize. For example, an employment office may be able to provide a lead on labor costs long before these figures show up in accounting reports. A market-research department may be able to provide control data as well as planning. The information necessary for production scheduling can be used to measure productivity. These illustrations indicate that facts for use in control may be found in a variety of places around a company.[3]

Leadership in product design was set as a major control point for the engineering department of one company. Because product leadership is very difficult to measure, this company decided to try at least to summarize personal opinion systematically. Each year a committee composed of the general manager, sales manager, chief engineer, and two outside experts try to agree on the following points:

1) The number of the company's significant "firsts" introduced each year versus competitors' "firsts."

2) A comparison of company products with competitors' products in terms of market requirements for performance, special features, attractiveness, and price.

3) The respective percentages of sales of products that are appraised to be superior to competition, equal to competition, or inferior to competition, together with corresponding market position and gross margin ratios of each category.

4) The percentage of company products in the total machines used in the plants of the twenty most efficient customers in the country.

In spite of the high degree of personal judgment involved in several of these criteria, this company has substantially better control over its product development than it did before it undertook such measurement. As this example shows, the design of managerial controls can benefit greatly from ingenuity.

Considering Qualitative as Well as Quantitative Results

Because measurement is often difficult, it is only natural to use any figures that are available. This is to be commended. There is danger, however, that those characteristics of an operation that can be easily measured will receive far greater attention than their importance warrants.

An office-equipment manufacturer relied heavily on dollar sales figures to control its ten regional salesmen. As the sales manager was

---

[3]Auditing is concerned with control, but not the type of managerial control we are discussing in this chapter. A manager focuses on achieving certain results. Financial auditing, on the other hand, is designed chiefly to ensure that no skullduggery has taken place. An auditor deals with the accuracy of financial reports—be they bearers of good tidings or bad—and especially with making sure that there has been no pilfering of cash or valuable inventory and no fraud or embezzlement.

Occasionally the concept of auditing is broadened beyond the financial matters just discussed. If an auditor is asked to verify "proper execution of policies and programs," then the auditor moves into the area of managerial control. Rarely is this a desirable arrangement. Measuring for managerial control is far from exact; it tends to be intimately associated with operations themselves; and its usefulness is enhanced by a cooperative relation between those who are making the measurements and those who are doing the work. Auditing, on the other hand, needs to be specific and objective, and independence from operating personnel is to be encouraged. In a well-run company, action for managerial control should have taken place long before an audit is completed.

fond of saying, "The signed order tells who's on the ball." The salesman in the southern territory was an older man, and for two years before his retirement, he and the company had a clear understanding that he planned to settle down in Florida when he reached sixty-five. The man's sales held up reasonably well. But when he was replaced, it was discovered that he had neglected to cultivate new customers. He had called only on his old accounts, and even with them he had glossed over troublesome service problems and had failed to cultivate the younger men in the customers' organizations. Several years of hard work were required before the territory again produced the volume it should. This unsatisfactory condition developed because the firm relied only on the easy measurement of results. If other, more intangible, factors had been watched, the deficiency in the old salesman's performance would have been noted before too much damage was done.

The danger that ease of measurement will dictate what gets attention is even more serious in operations where quantitative results are hard to pin down. The public-relations department of a pharmaceutical company, for instance, kept close track of the number of letters received as a result of the news releases it issued. "Letters received" became one of the department's few quantitative measures of performance, and soon public relations was issuing news releases written expressly for the purpose of creating a flow of mail. Unfortunately, although controversial subjects and hints that a remedy for some widespread malady was being developed did produce a lot of letters, publicity on these topics did not provide the best public relations for the company.

Besides public relations, another place where quantitative and qualitative considerations may get out of balance is in expense control. Zealousness in controlling travel or telephone expenses occasionally causes people to pay as much attention to these minor aspects as to the results of the work. Probably the best-known example of this tendency is in the federal government, where the General Accounting Office is likely to deduct $2.83 from a travel voucher because a man failed to discover the cheapest route; yet, because there is no readily available quantitative data, no question is raised whether the entire trip was necessary. Expense control is necessary in every enterprise, but it should be administered to avoid being "penny wise and pound foolish."

Use of Symptoms for Control

Just as the smell of smoke is an indication of fire, or bloodshot eyes and a haggard look at examination time are an indication of cramming, so in business we may use symptoms as indications of what is going on.

Employee attitudes, for example, are hard to measure directly and economically. Consequently, several companies have used such criteria as turnover, the number of absences and tardinesses, the number and content of grievances, and the number of suggestions submitted in a formal suggestion system. Under normal conditions, such factors probably do reflect employee attitudes. But we must exercise care in using symptoms as measuring devices because (1) outside factors may cause a symptom to vary, and (2) when it becomes known that a symptom is being used as a measure, it may be possible to manipulate the measuring stick—for instance, tardiness in one office may be low because the office manager is a tyrant and not because employee attitudes are good.

Use of Predictions in Control

Sometimes we can use predictions as a basis for corrective action. As with the use of symptoms, we do not measure actual results. But here the reason for using less reliable criteria is our desire for prompt action. Customer inquiries may be used to predict a rise or fall in sales; a machine's vibration may be used to predict a breakdown; or grievances may be used to predict a strike. The prediction in such a case initiates corrective action; we don't wait for the predicted event to occur.

One of the large can companies has a control procedure that encourages corrective action based on predictions. A monthly profit-and-loss budget is prepared for each operating division and plant. Then, ten days before the start of the month, the respective managers are asked to estimate how close they will come to the budget. Each prepares a revised estimate about ten days after the beginning of the month. A major advantage of preparing these two estimates lies in forcing the manager to predict what is likely to happen and to adjust his operations to current conditions. Because local demands for vegetable cans vary with the weather, short-run expansion or contraction of operations—and of expenses—is very important. Top executives do compare the performance of each division and branch against the original budget, but they give more emphasis to the ability of their managers to predict results accurately and take prompt corrective action.

Sampling

A familiar way of simplifying the measurement task is to consider only a sample, which is presumably typical of the whole of whatever we are measuring. For example, the quality of most food products, from kippered herring to corn meal, is tested by sampling. And students are well aware that an examination is only a sample of what they know, just as office workers realize that in his periodic visits their supervisor samples their behavior.

Sampling is better suited to some activities than others. If a machine set to perform a particular operation turns out good-quality products both when the run is started and at the end, we can usually assume that the intervening production has also been satisfactory in quality. In a check of routine sales correspondence, if a random sample indicates that letter-writers are using good judgment and diplomacy, a supervisor will probably assume that all the work is satisfactory. On the other hand, a 100 percent check is desirable for some operations. A manufacturer of hearing aids, for instance, may sample at the early stages of production, but will undoubtedly insist on a careful inspection of every finished product for performance before it is shipped.

Broadly speaking, to determine what portion of an operation should be measured, we try to balance the cost of incremental measurements against the increased value that might accrue from catching more errors. "Statistical quality control" is a special application of this general idea. When products are produced in large quantities, we can use statistical probabilities to decide when the number of errors is large enough to warrant stopping production and finding the cause; in addition, probabilities can be used to decide how large a sample should be tested. Substantial economies in inspection costs may result in situations where this technique applies. Unfortunately, the vast majority of managerial control situations do not involve the large number of similar actions that are needed for this refined statistical technique.

Personal Observations and Conferences

Even with all the various kinds of measurement that we have suggested in the preceding paragraphs, a supervising executive still needs to hold informal discussions with the persons whose work is being controlled, and, at least occasionally, he should visit the actual operations. Anyone who has corresponded over a period of time with another person whom he knows only by letter, and then has an opportunity to meet and talk with him, knows that there are certain kinds of impression and information that can be conveyed only in face-to-face contact, personal observation, and conversation.

More importantly, personal observations permit an executive to keep track of different items at different times. Ability to make prompt delivery to customers may be crucial at one moment and the number of executives worthy of promotion at another. When a man is new in a job, a supervising executive will want to watch his work more closely than he would that of an experienced operator. Personal observation has a flexibility that permits an executive to keep his eye on what is "hot" at the moment. Even if we could incorporate these factors into a formalized, continuing flow of information, to do so would probably be undesirable because of the cost and the added burden.

Earlier discussions in this book dealing with organization, planning, and leading have already presented compelling reasons for close personal contact between an executive and those who work with him. To those reasons we should now add this: effective measurement of results.

CONTROL REPORTS

Measurement of performance is of little value until we get the resulting appraisals communicated to executives who can take corrective action. Such reporting is a vital phase of useful evaluation.

The smaller the operating unit, the simpler the control reports need to be. In fact, in a small company or within a small unit of a large company, a supervising executive often evaluates results himself, and the only report is an oral discussion with the man who is doing the work that is being evaluated. A great many controls, perhaps the most effective ones, have this informal character. The basic steps of control are present— setting standards, evaluating results, taking corrective action—but the formal recording of results and of comparisons with standards is simple and rudimentary. Few people are involved, the facts are known to everyone, and the main purpose of control is simply to draw attention to how well performance matches acknowledged standards so that corrective adjustments may be initiated.

As more people are involved, the task of reporting evaluation becomes more important. Common knowledge of the facts is no longer possible because people work in different places, and are concerned with different parts of a total task, and because there are more detailed facts than any one person can keep in his mind. A need arises, therefore, for control reports that summarize and communicate the conclusions of the measurements that have been undertaken.

Who Should Receive Control Reports?

Control information should be sent immediately to the man whose work is being controlled. He is the one who is most likely to be able to do something about it. Not that the information should go to a machine operator or a clerk who is merely carrying out specific instructions. Rather it should go to the purchasing agent who decides how much to buy, to the foreman who decides when overtime work is necessary, to the salesman who may be able to secure additional orders for slow-moving products, or to the foreign manager who might decide to withdraw from a particular market. In other words, information should reach the person who, by his own actions, can have a strong influence on final results.

Prompt feedback to the point of action encourages use of the "law of the situation," one of the means for obtaining voluntary cooperation discussed in Chapter 21. In most instances, the man on the firing line will start corrective action as soon as he knows the results are falling short of the established norm.

In addition, control information should flow, perhaps as a summary at a later date, to the man's boss. The man on the firing line may need help or he may need prodding; it is the duty of the supervisor to see that he gets either or both as the situation warrants.

These elementary observations about the flow of control reports are meant to emphasize that action which results from control measurements should be taken by the people who have primary responsibility for an activity being measured. Only in rare circumstances is it desirable to separate the action, or dynamic, phase of control from the duties of the man who initiates and supervises performance of the activity. But other people are often interested in these reports, to be sure: (1) executives who will use the control information to help formulate new plans, and (2) staff personnel who are expected to be familiar with, and give advice about, the particular activity under control. These people should be provided with such reports as they find helpful. But their claim is secondary to that of operators and immediate supervisors.

Timeliness versus Accuracy

Promptness is a great virtue in control reports. If some job is being mishandled, the sooner it is reported and corrected, the less damage will be done. Moreover, if the cause of a difficulty is not obvious, a prompt investigation is more likely to turn up true causes than one conducted when events are no longer fresh in the memories of the people con-

*Fig. 24-3 Alternative flows
of control reports.*

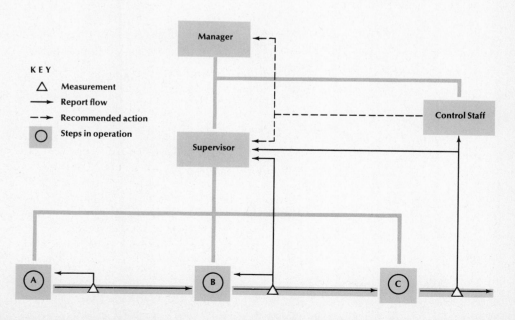

cerned. If a student turns in a report late, he can explain the reasons for the delay immediately far better than he will be able to do later at the end of the semester.

The distinction between the controls for overall evaluation and those intended primarily to direct attention affects the importance of promptness. Timeliness is especially urgent with the latter group, because they lose most of their potency if they are tardy.

Unfortunately, it is often difficult to be both prompt and accurate. An accurate evaluation may require a certain amount of investigation and double-checking. The person making an evaluation naturally wants to be sure he can justify his conclusions, especially if they draw attention to inadequacies in someone's work. In addition, delay is likely to be compounded if a report is prepared by someone who is trained to balance accounts to the last penny. A hospital administrator, for example, was having great difficulty in keeping down expenses partly because expense reports—laboriously compiled at the end of each month—did not become available until six to eight weeks following the events presumably being controlled.

Executives who use control reports should be fully aware of what kind of information they are getting. If they insist on prompt reports, they must learn to disregard insignificant variations and to expect some false alarms. On the other hand, if we are interested in having the full facts and being deliberate in taking action, then we need a different kind of report. Because most companies need both accurate and timely reports, managerial skill is required to ensure that the control reports are really suited to their purposes.

Form and Content of Reports

Most control reports can be kept simple and present only key comparisons. They are not intended to present a full analysis; furthermore the people using them are intimately familiar with the operations they reflect. These reports are not designed to impress the public; they are valuable if they give the operating people the facts they need quickly and understandably.

A relatively few postmortem reports may contain a great many details, especially if they are directed to an executive who is located some distance from the actual locale of the work. Even such reports, however, usually have a brief summary statement, and the mass of the detail is simply made readily available so that a reader can check a detail if he cares to.[4]

---

[4]As we learn to put our management information systems on computers, the detail need not accompany the summary report. Instead, the detail will be stored in the memory bank and retrieved on request.

In addition to offering a comparison of performance against standard, control reports often reveal whether a situation is getting better or worse. They do so by comparing present performance with that in the recent past and with that during the same period a year ago. Such "trend" information is a helpful guide to a manager in deciding what kind of corrective action is appropriate.

CORRECTIVE ACTION

Control reports call attention to deviations of performance from plans, but they only signal trouble. The payoff comes when corrective action is taken. The control information should lead to investigating difficulties, promptly deciding how to overcome the difficulties, and then adjusting operations.

Sometimes a control report will start a new management cycle; new planning and organizing, more leading, and another set of measurements and reports. But often, the original objectives and program are retained, and we simply make minor adjustments at one point and push a little harder at another. These adjustments may be necessary anywhere along the line—needling a supplier, pinch-hitting for Joe Zilch who is ill, running department A overtime, and so on. In such situations a manager is like a captain who gets information on the location and bearing of his ship, and then adjusts his course in order to arrive at his planned destination.

The distinction between replanning and corrective adjustments is not sharp. For convenience, we speak of "corrective action" if plans remain substantially unchanged and we continue to strive for the same final result. If our appraisal of current difficulties indicates that major changes in plans or goals are in order, then we should "replan." In both kinds of action, data from measuring are fed back to executives who modify their operation.

Finding Reasons for Deviation

That actual operations do not always turn out just as planned is not surprising when we think back over the planning process described in Parts Three and Four. To proceed with planning, we often have to adopt predictions as premises—predictions of sales, competitive prices, availability of capital, research results, productivity of new machines, and a host of other things. Such premises are our best estimate at the time, although we recognize they may not be accurate. Also, many plans involve a calculated risk; for we may know that there is, say, about one chance in five that an assumed event may not occur.

So, when our control measurements indicate that all is not well, we have to investigate many possible causes to discover the one that is creating the difficulty. Perhaps some person is at fault, but, what is even more likely, one of our premises may be wrong or perhaps we have unluckily run into the one chance that we hoped could be avoided. At this stage, we are more interested in identifying the cause than the culprit, so that necessary adjustments in operations can be made promptly.

Moreover, the control measurements themselves may lead us astray. We may deliberately watch symptoms or estimates for early warnings of trouble—sales inquiries or employee absences, for instance. But we know from our discussion of diagnosis that symptoms can mislead us (see especially pages 252–57). Here again, prompt investigation is called for; the conditions may, or may not, require a change in plans. A similar situation is possible if we use the "exception principle," that is, watch only for exceptionally high or low performance. An exception may flag serious trouble, or it may be a unique instance that probably will not recur.

Even when control measurements are comprehensive—total output, total expenses, net profit—corrective action starts with identifying the reason for a deviation from standard. The comprehensive measures embrace so many factors that we do not know where to make adjustments until we have narrowed down a source of difficulty.

In some highly routinized operations, we can act like a servo-mechanism on a machine, automatically making a given adjustment when certain conditions are detected. Automatic pilots on airplanes and thermostats on furnaces work this way. But most managerial situations are not so simple; we have to identify which of many possible causes is creating difficulty before proceeding with corrective action.

Corrective Adjustments

Once a difficulty is spotted, as a result of an investigation prompted by an unfavorable control report, we move quickly to corrective adjustments. If the operating situation has shifted from what was planned—perhaps raw materials are delayed by a dock strike or our computer breaks down—we will take steps to get the working conditions back to normal. If our subordinates are ineffective, we will clarify our directions to them, provide additional training where necessary, consider motivational lacks, and perhaps reassign work. Or, if it is not within our power to overcome the difficulties—say, customers simply will not buy our product—we must then recast goals and programs. From a managerial point of view, a control is not effective until such corrective action as may be necessary has been undertaken.

CONCLUSION

Controlling, like many other aspects of management, is simple in its basic elements but calls for ingenuity and deftness in its application. Setting control standards at strategic points, sampling and measuring qualitative results, balancing timeliness and accuracy in reports, translating reports into corrective action—all are examples of the many issues we have to resolve adroitly for a control system to be potent.

Although we have seen in this chapter a range of points a manager should consider in the controlling phase of his work, other vital factors remain to be considered. The design of comprehensive control systems will be illustrated in the following chapter. Next, the responses of people to controls will be examined, and finally, the integration of controls to other phases of management will be reviewed. These further considerations are important in making control an integral and consistent part of our total management structure and behavior.

FOR CLASS DISCUSSION

Questions

1) "If a standard or goal is to be useful in the control process it should be accepted as par and met. All this talk about the need for flexibility is largely an excuse for sloppy forecasting before the standard was set or poor performance in attempting to seek it." What do you think of this observation by the works manager of a large steel mill?

2) Accept the proposition that federal officials can control to some extent the level of business activity and price levels through rediscount rates, open market operations, tax rates, deficit spending, and the like. Explain how ideas in this chapter—such as (1) the setting of control standards, (2) the picking of strategic control points, (3) the use of symptoms and predictions, and (4) timeliness versus accuracy—apply to government control of business activity and price levels.

3) Frederick Taylor is often cited as the father of Scientific Management. In what ways do the basic concepts that shaped Taylor's approach to organizing and planning influence the nature of controlling?

4) In most foreign countries, the Pepsi-Cola Company grants a franchise to a local bottling and distributing firm. The franchised firm must use Pepsi's secret extract shipped from the United States. Otherwise, all activities are performed within the country by local nationals. The United States company provides advice on production and distribution and permits the use of the well-known Pepsi-Cola trade mark. The company in the United States naturally is concerned about both short- and long-run profits in the foreign country and about the worldwide reputation of Pepsi-Cola. What controls should the company establish over the activities of a franchised dealer in a foreign country?

5) "The essential difference between *freedom* and *license* is that freedom carries with it the obligation to provide the grantor with sufficient control to determine how the freedom granted has been used." (1) What historical figure might have made this statement? (2) How do you feel about it? (3) Relate your answer particularly to the section "Relating Results to Individual Accountability."

6) The president of a chain of fourteen dry-cleaning stores stated that the only control information he wants from his branch stores is their monthly profit figures. (Each store is charged at standard rates for work sent to the company's central cleaning plant.) Only if results are below expectations does he request supplementary information. (1) What are the advantages and disadvantages of this approach to control? (2) As president of this chain, what control information would you request and how often would you request it? Discuss the factors you would consider in making this decision.

7) List and discuss several key factors in determining *who* should be assigned the task of comparing measurements of results to standards for the purpose of determining the cause of deviations.

8) "In our division we have an excellent control system. When things get off the track, we not only learn of it quickly but typically have the data necessary for intelligent analysis designed to find out why we missed a standard. Analyzing that data, however, may take some time, and my boss (division manager) will often jump in and start suggesting corrective action before we really know what caused the deviation." What do you think of this statement made by a young department manager?

Cases

For cases involving issues covered in this chapter, see especially the following. Particularly relevant questions are listed after each case.

General Machinery Corporation (p. 130), 15, 16
Scott-Davis Corporation (p. 227), 19

FOR FURTHER READING

Bonini, C.P., R.K. Jaedick, and H.M. Wagner, eds., *Management Controls*. New York: McGraw-Hill Book Company, 1964. *Research papers on regulation, influence, and control.*

Litterer, J.A., *The Analysis of Organizations*. New York: John Wiley & Sons, Inc., 1965, Chap. 13. *Basic elements in the design of a management control system.*

Richards, M.D., and W.A. Nielander, eds., *Readings in Management*, 3rd ed. Cincinnati: South-Western Publishing Co., 1969, Chaps. X and XI. *Useful articles on application of control and control standards.*

Schleh, E.C., *Management by Results*. New York: McGraw-Hill Book Company, 1961, Chaps. 12–14. *Practical suggestions for achieving balanced results.*

Shillinglaw, G., *Cost Accounting*, rev. ed. Homewood, Ill.: Richard D. Irwin, Inc., 1967, Parts III and VI. *Thorough explanation of accounting systems for expense and profit control; emphasis is on management use of data.*

Strong, E.P., and R.D. Smith, *Management Control Models*. New York: Holt, Rinehart & Winston, Inc., 1968. *Basic control instruments explained in nontechnical language.*

Chapter Twenty-five

PERT and Budgetary Control

TOOLS FOR INTEGRATING PLANNING AND CONTROL

Two mechanisms of control are examined in this chapter. We pick them out for special attention because each can be applied to a wide variety of situations, and each aids planning and coordination as well as control. By discussing them here in Part Six we underscore the interdependence between planning and control.

Financial budgeting is widely accepted, whereas PERT (Program Evaluation and Review Technique) is relatively new and its potentialities are not yet fully understood. Let us look first at budgeting.

Elements in Budgetary Control

Basically, financial budgeting involves these three steps:

1) *Expressing in dollars the results of plans anticipated in a future period.* These dollar figures are typically set up in the same way as the accounts in a company's accounting system. The budget shows how the accounts should look if present plans are carried out.

2) *Coordinating these estimates into a well-balanced program.* The figures for sales, production, advertising, and other divisions must be matched to be sure that they are mutually consistent; the financial feasibility of all plans added together must be assured; and the combined results must be examined in terms of overall objectives. Some adjustments will probably be necessary to obtain such a balanced program.

3) *Comparing actual results with the program estimates that emerge from step 2.* Any significant differences point to the need for corrective action. In short, the budget becomes a standard for appraising operating results.

These steps will be illustrated first by an extended example of a small company. Then we shall discuss the implication of the budgeting concept for larger firms and for special situations. Finally, we shall look into ways of securing flexibility and also into some of the dangers and limitations of budgetary control. Our aim is to see how financial budgeting fits into the management processes; we are not concerned here with the details of budgetary procedure.

BUDGETING IN A NEW ENTERPRISE

Examining budgets for a new, small company enables us to see readily how operating plans can be translated into financial figures and how budgets provide an opportunity for overall coordination. For this purpose, we shall use Belafonte Fashions, Inc., as an illustration.

General Plans of Belafonte Fashions, Inc.

After working as a stock boy, presser, and, more recently, foreman in several apparel plants, Paul Bailey went into business for himself. He had an opportunity to buy the total equipment of a defunct ski-suit plant and to take over a lease on the space it occupied. The $40,000 price was attractive, especially since the equipment was already installed and experienced labor was available in the area. Bailey, a black himself, had a strong desire to establish an all-black enterprise in a depressed area on the Near-West side of Chicago. His new venture was made possible by an investment by High Horizons, a private urban-renewal corporation. High Horizons matched Bailey's capital contribution of $30,000, arranged for an equipment mortgage with a bank, and made a temporary working capital loan of $23,000. Because Bailey had little background in finance and accounting, High Horizons stipulated that he use the "MBA Consultants" from Northwestern University for help in this area; Morris Barkin is the student assigned to this client.

Bailey decided to concentrate on a limited line of women's pants, which are relatively simple to manufacture and use existing skills of the work force. Purchased fabric of polyester and cotton or wool is cut, sewed, and pressed; permanent press finishing is subcontracted to a nearby company. Bailey started in business in the autumn, a season when the demand for pants is brisk, and by the end of the year he had a going concern. The balance sheet at that time was as shown in Table 25–1.

Morris Barkin, after a careful industry survey, urged Bailey to prepare a profit-and-loss budget for his new company. At the beginning of the new year, Bailey had the following plans in mind:

1) The company would first establish itself by making four fairly standard pants at low cost. With this operation as a base, more highly styled and novelty numbers could be added later to provide wider profit margins. But to attempt to operate a business on novelty items alone was too risky.

2) The four types of pants Bailey had in mind typically sold to retailers at an average price of $45.50 per dozen. Even with allowances and markdowns, Bailey hoped his average selling price would be at least $42.00 per dozen.

3) Selling would be done through manufacturers' agents, one in New York, covering the territory east of the Mississippi, except for Illinois and Wisconsin, and one in Chicago covering the remainder of the United States. In the plant, Bailey figured, he needed an experienced cutter and a sewing foreman, each of whom would be paid $250 a week. He expected to take care of designing, buying, marketing, and general administrative work himself. However, he had hired a man to act as bookkeeper and general office assistant at $10,000 per year. All other employees were to be paid on an hourly or piece-rate basis. While the business was getting on its feet, Bailey planned to pay himself only $700 per month.

Table 25–1

BELAFONTE FASHIONS, INC.

Balance Sheet—January 1

Cash		$ 8,700	Accounts payable		$ 17,200
Accounts receivable		33,600	Accrued taxes, etc.		2,700
Inventories:			Current liabilities		19,900
Raw material	$20,500		Mortgage on equipment		16,000
Finished goods	16,800	37,300	Loan from High Horizons		23,000
Current assets		79,600	Total liabilities		58,900
			Equity		
Equipment	40,000		Common stock	$60,000	
Less depreciation	1,500	38,500	Loss for first three months	800	59,200
Total assets		$118,100	Total liabilities and equity		$118,100

4) Experience during the fall had indicated that fabric, zippers, and other materials would cost about $21.50 per dozen finished pants. Provided the work was well planned, direct labor amounted to $10.00 per dozen.

5) Every apparel company is torn between being able to make prompt deliveries and avoiding a large obsolete inventory. Bailey sought to meet this problem (1) by keeping well stocked with fabric (each month he would purchase the fabric needed for producing the pants he expected to sell during the next thirty to sixty days) and (2) by restricting his stock of finished goods to expected shipments during the following two weeks. This plan was intended to permit him to adapt the sizes and styles of pants being produced to the orders being received (assuming the right kinds of fabric were on hand).

Profit-and-Loss Budget for the New Year

After talking with his sales agents, Bailey estimated he could sell 10,000 dozen pants during his first full year of operations. In fact, the New York agent talked of large sales to chain store buyers, but this would have involved making price concessions and maintaining a large inventory that Bailey wanted to avoid at this time.

By translating his plans and estimates into dollar results, Bailey and Barkin came up with an estimated profit-and-loss statement, which is shown in Table 25–2. The young proprietor was pleased about two features of this budget: It indicated that he should be able to earn a modest profit, and it showed that a large part of total expenses could be adjusted downward if sales volume did not develop. This meant that through close control of "variable expenses" he should be able to avoid large losses, even if sales were smaller than anticipated. He now saw more clearly the financial results he might expect, and he had a standard to guide him while he was attempting to achieve these results.

Monthly Cash Budget

Morris Barkin was dubious. He did not challenge the annual profit budget, but he was worried that the company might go bankrupt before the end of the year arrived. He pointed out (1) that wide seasonal fluctuations in sales would cause temporary demands for larger inventory and accounts receivable; (2) that High Horizons hoped to get back $10,000 of its loan by the middle of the year; and (3) that the company might have to make additional investments in equipment. An examination of this last point revealed that Bailey was using his personal car for company business and that a station wagon ($4,000) would be needed before the end of the year; besides, a different kind of fabric was needed for

Table 25–2

BELAFONTE FASHIONS, INC.

Profit-and-Loss Budget for the Year

Net Sales (10,000 dozen @ $42)	$420,000
Expenses:	
Materials ($21.50 per dozen)	215,000
Labor ($10.00 per dozen)	100,000
Plant supervisors' salaries	26,000
Repairs	7,200
Heat, light, janitor	7,200
Rent	8,200
Depreciation	6,000
Office salaries	18,400
Travel expenses	2,000
Office miscellaneous	1,200
Sales commissions (2.5 percent)	10,500
Shipping (1 percent)	4,200
Interest and financing charges	4,720
Total expenses	410,620
Operating profit	9,380
Income tax	1,380
Net profit	$ 8,000

the autumn lines, and this would require the purchase of secondhand sewing machines for a total of $4,800.

Faced with these facts, Bailey and Barkin undertook to prepare a monthly budget of cash receipts and disbursements. For this purpose Bailey assumed that customers would pay for merchandise within thirty days after shipment and that he would pay for his purchases within a similar period. But it was more difficult to estimate how his annual sales volume would be distributed by months throughout the year. Industry figures supplied by the local sales agent indicated that the distribution would probably be as shown in Table 25–3.

With the data he already had and with his inventory policy, Bailey was now able to budget his monthly flow of cash. This analysis indicated that he might just squeeze by the March sales peak and that cash would accumulate rapidly in April and May as he collected from customers and reduced his inventories. May and June, then, appeared to be the best time to buy the new equipment and reduce the loan to High Horizons.

Serious trouble would arise in August and September, however, as inventories and accounts receivable would rise to an autumn peak. Without financial aid Belafonte Fashions, Inc., could not possibly meet its budgeted annual sales.

The crucial assistance was found in a finance company. An agreement was made for Belafonte Fashions, Inc., to borrow whatever it needed up to 80 percent of its accounts receivable. The accounts were pledged as collateral, and special records and collection procedures were established. For its services, the finance company would be paid both a flat annual fee of $1,000 to set up the arrangement and also interest on any money borrowed at the rate of 10 percent per annum. With this assistance, the estimates indicated, Paul Bailey would be able to weather the financial crisis forecast for the autumn.

The budget that reflects all these plans is shown in Table 25–4. Note that the preparation of this budget required some adjustment in financial plans in order to arrive at a feasible balanced program.

Comparison of Actual Results with the Budget

During the first six months of the year, the operating results of Belafonte Fashions, Inc., were surprisingly close to the budgets. Sales during March, April, and May were 400 dozen below the budget, but the comfortable accumulation of cash tended to obscure the influence of this drop. More serious trouble arose in November and December when business did not hold up to expectations. Mild weather in the fall left retailers well stocked with the type of pants Belafonte made, so reorders did not come in as anticipated. This in turn left Bailey with a high inventory of raw materials; also Bailey could not pay off the finance company in December because of inadequate receipts. Price-cutting was

Table 25–3

BELAFONTE FASHIONS, INC.

Estimated Monthly Sales

Month	Sales (dozens)	Month	Sales (dozens)
January	800	July	400
February	800	August	500
March	1,100	September	1,200
April	900	October	1,300
May	600	November	1,200
June	400	December	800

necessary in order to move the finished stock, and even with this action sales were 800 dozen below the budget forecast for the last two months. The final profit-and-loss figures for the year compared with the budget are shown in Table 25–5.

A first glance at actual results compared with the budget indicates that virtually all the unsatisfactory showing can be ascribed to the drop in sales. This is somewhat misleading. Price-cutting to an average of $41.50 accounts for over $4,000 loss in revenue even on the 8,800-dozen volume. In addition, the direction labor cost was $.74 per dozen higher than the

Table 25–4

BELAFONTE FASHIONS, INC.

Budget of Monthly Cash Receipts and Disbursements

	Jan.	Feb.	Mar.	Apr.	May	June
Sales (dollars)	33,600	33,600	46,200	37,800	25,200	16,800
Sales (dozens)	800	800	1,100	900	600	400
Goods produced (dozens)	800	950	1,000	750	500	400
Cash received from sales	$33,600	$33,600	$33,600	$46,200	$37,800	$25,200
Disbursements:						
Materials	17,200	20,425	21,500	16,125	10,750	8,600
Direct labor	8,000	9,500	10,000	7,500	5,000	4,000
Plant supervision						
Repairs	4,050	4,050	4,050	4,050	4,050	4,050
Heat, light, janitor						
Rent						
Depreciation	0	0	0	0	0	0
Office salaries						
Travel expenses	1,800	1,800	1,800	1,800	1,800	1,800
Office miscellaneous						
Sales commissions	1,170	1,170	1,620	1,325	880	590
Shipping						
Interest and financing charges	0	0	780	0	0	780
Disbursements for operations	32,220	36,945	39,750	30,800	22,480	19,820
Cash gain or loss from operations	1,380	−3,345	−6,150	15,400	15,320	5,380
Loans received or paid						−10,000
Investment in equipment					−4,000	− 4,800
Cash balance at end of month	10,080	6,735	585	15,985	27,305	17,885

budget, which points to inefficiency in this area; the total labor cost went down, but not as much as it should have. Fortunately, material costs dropped even more than might be expected from the shrinkage in volume. Variations in other expenses were minor; sales commissions and shipping naturally went down and tighter control of other expenses would have made only a minor difference in the final outcome. In short, this comparison points directly to sales volume, price, and direct labor costs as the areas where improvement must be made if the company is to become profitable.

July	Aug.	Sept.	Oct.	Nov.	Dec.
16,800	21,000	50,400	54,600	50,400	33,600
400	500	1,200	1,300	1,200	800
450	850	1,250	1,250	1,000	800
$16,800	$16,800	$21,000	$50,400	$54,600	$50,400
9,675	18,275	26,875	26,875	21,500	17,200
4,500	8,500	12,500	12,500	10,000	8,000
4,050	4,050	4,050	4,050	4,050	4,050
0	0	0	0	0	0
1,800	1,800	1,800	1,800	1,800	1,800
590	735	1,770	1,910	1,770	1,170
0	1,000	580	0	0	1,580
20,615	34,360	47,575	47,135	39,120	33,800
−3,815	−17,560	−26,575	3,265	15,480	16,600
	10,000	30,000		−10,000	−30,000
14,070	6,510	9,935	13,200	18,680	5,280

The budgets that happen to be suitable for the first year of operation of Belafonte Fashions, Inc., provide a simple example of the three basic steps in budgeting. Plans were translated into accounting results, plans were adjusted where the combined picture proved to be unworkable, and the resulting budgets served as a useful standard in highlighting places that need corrective action. Clearly, budgets need not be elaborate to be a useful management tool.

BUDGETING IN A LARGE FIRM

Company size does not affect the essentials of budgeting, but it does influence the complexity of the budgetary system. As a company grows, several things are likely to happen to the budgeting process:

Table 25–5

BELAFONTE FASHIONS, INC.

Comparison of Actual Profit and Loss with Budget for Year

	Budget	Actual	Difference
Net sales	$420,000	$365,200	$ − 54,800
Expenses:			
Materials	215,000	185,800	− 29,200
Direct labor	100,000	94,500	− 5,500
Plant supervisors' salaries	26,000	26,000	0
Repairs	7,200	5,900	− 1,300
Heat, light, janitor	7,200	7,300	100
Rent	8,200	8,200	0
Depreciation	6,000	6,400	400
Office salaries	18,400	18,400	0
Travel expenses	2,000	2,500	500
Office miscellaneous	1,200	1,600	400
Sales commissions	10,500	9,130	− 1,370
Shipping	4,200	3,700	− 500
Interest and financing charges	4,720	4,720	0
Total expenses	410,620	374,150	− 36,470
Operating profit	9,380	−8,950	−18,330
Income tax	1,380	0	− 1,380
Net profit	$ 8,000	$−8,950	$ − 16,950

1) Separate budgets are prepared for each department or division of the company. Because each operating unit is somewhat independent, standards to measure its particular performance are needed. Moreover, detailed budget information is often helpful for control within the division. In a large company there may be literally hundreds of subsidiary budgets dealing with the sales, expenses, or other appropriate items of many different operating centers.

2) Communication of "planning premises" is important if these numerous subsidiary budgets are to be prepared consistently. Each person who prepares or interprets a budget needs to know what assumptions to make about, for instance, wage increases during the budgeting period. The plant manager is dependent on the sales department for information on volume of activity. Are prices and the availability of raw materials going to change? How soon will a certain new product be ready for the market? Such matters as these will affect the budgets of several departments. Therefore, someone must provide a forecast or guess that can be used consistently in all the subsidiary budgets.

3) Coordinating the many subsidiary budgets into a balanced program becomes complicated. A big company tends to have a large number of specialized units, and a good deal of effort is needed to synchronize their activities. Even in highly decentralized companies, the total activities of the various units, as reflected in their budgets, must not exceed the company's resources. In other words, preparing a consolidated budget for a large company entails more than merely adding the budgets of the various divisions; the budget should represent a feasible program that is in the best interest of the company as a whole.

4) A special unit that concentrates only on budgeting may be desirable. Such a unit can help design the budgetary system that is best adapted to the particular needs of its company—emphases and procedures do vary considerably among companies. A budgeting unit may provide routine clerical services in processing figures and in compiling and circulating reports; perhaps it will also make substantive analyses of both proposed budgets and actual experience, with recommendations for action. This staff unit, however, should neither prepare the budgets nor try to enforce them; budgeting is a tool for operating executives to use and not a device for usurping their duties.

APPROPRIATION BUDGETS

The budgets we have discussed thus far are concerned mainly with managerial actions that produce observable results within a given accounting period—a month, a quarter, or at most a year. Other managerial actions are taken that are not expected to yield results for two years, five years, and often longer. Such actions pose special control problems;

appropriation budgets help meet this need. These budgets cover expenditures for items such as:[1]

1) Land, building and equipment.
2) Research for new products and new processes.
3) Institutional advertising.
4) Personnel development.
5) New market development.

Expenditures of the type just listed deserve management attention for several reasons. When wisely made, they are often crucial to the long-run success of the company. But on these items management has a wider latitude of discretion—it can expand, contract, or even discontinue them—than it has for most current expenses, which must be met in order for the company to continue operations.

Appropriation budgets provide some help in their planning and control. Typically, all large requests for new buildings and equipment are submitted once a year to top management, which examines the justifications for each project, compares prospective yields, considers the relation of each to long-term objectives, matches the total requests against available financial resources, and finally makes an overall appropriation. This appropriation, which usually includes an allowance for small and emergency requests, becomes the approved budget for the year. A similar procedure is often followed for research and advertising appropriations. Budgets for development expenses, however, are apt to be less formally established.

A great deal of work is devoted to preparing these appropriation budgets, and in large companies we find elaborate procedures for review and approval—especially for new equipment and buildings. In essence, these procedures focus control on authority to proceed with—or hold back on—proposed expenditures *before* any money is spent or contracts signed.

Usually, purchasing or hiring commitments are not permitted unless they are covered by an appropriation. But note that this provides a one-sided check. It does not even attempt to measure the results—which is the original purpose of making the investment.

Unfortunately, a useful check on the results of long-term investment is extremely difficult to devise. The period from initial decision to fruition is long—extending far beyond the time when corrective action during the formative stages would be possible. During this long interval, many other events occur, thus making a clear chain of cause and effect difficult to establish. Such efforts as we can make to match a particular appropria-

[1] Conventional accounting spreads the costs of buildings, equipment, and inventions over their presumed useful life, whereas the other items listed are treated as an expense at the time they are incurred. From the viewpoint of management planning and control, however, all expenses of this type present similar problems.

tion with specific results are more for "learning from our experience" than for control. (One company, however, does check results of capital expenditures two years after installation "just so operating executives won't forecast all sorts of benefits they can't deliver.")

Nevertheless, appropriation budgets have some clear benefits: (1) They keep disbursements for the purposes they cover within known limits. (2) They provide an opportunity for key executives to review and compare alternative uses of limited funds. (3) They provide important information for cash budgets and permit coordination of investment and financing plans.

BENEFITS AND DANGERS OF BUDGETARY CONTROL

Budgeting is no panacea. We need to understand its strengths and weaknesses so that we may fit it into the total control structure we design for a particular company or subdivision.

Unique Advantages

First, perhaps the greatest strength of budgeting is its use of a single common denominator—dollars—for many diverse actions and things. TV advertising, tons of coal, and liability insurance can all be reflected in a budget in terms of dollar cost and dollar result. Dollar language has its limitations, as we shall see, but it does lend itself to summaries and comparisons. The dollar, more than any other measuring device in business, government, or even military and church administration, can be applied to a wide range of work, and financial budgets capitalize on this unique feature of a monetary unit.

Second, budgeting uses records and systems that are already in existence. We must keep elaborate accounting records for tax returns, financial reporting, and internal management. In budgeting we utilize this system, rather than a new set of records. Figures on past experience are likely to be already prepared. Some new accounts or reports may have to be added, but the basic information system is available and easy to use.

Finally, budgeting deals *directly* with one of the central objectives of a business enterprise—making a profit. What shows up in budgets is what affects recorded profit or loss. Thus the relevance of items being controlled by a budget can be easily traced to the profit objective.

Stimulant to Good Management Practices

Budgeting often makes its greatest contribution as a stimulant to other good management practices. These are practices an executive might wisely use without budgets, but the adoption of budgetary control may bring them to life. For instance, here are several critical management requirements, with suggestions of how budgeting can help vitalize them:

1) Formal organization should be clear. An understanding of who is assigned to make each type of plan should be a prerequisite to the translation of such plans into budget form. Similarly, accountability for execution has to be clear if comparisons of actual performance with a budget are to have their full impact.

2) Financial accounts need to be set up for each department or other unit of administration. When expenses, investments, and income are readily traceable to specific managers, they are more easily controlled. Such correspondence between accounts and departments is especially important in both the preparation and the evaluation phases of budgeting.

3) Planning must be done well in advance and should be highly specific. Without such plans, a budget for, say, a year ahead would be little more than a guess. Precision in planning, in turn, calls for clarifying objectives and for coordinating the plans of interrelated departments.

4) Once annual budgets are well established, tentative budgets for three or five years become feasible. In Chapter 19 we noted that this was one form of long-range planning. Experience with budgeting is also very useful in what some companies call "profit planning"—setting targets for profits and related matters and then working back through financial accounts to determine the actions that will be necessary to achieve these targets.

5) When line managers use budgets as a key management tool, they at least provide an opportunity for clear directing and constructive counseling. Because budget figures are objective and tangible everyone can avoid misunderstandings and all parties can focus on improving results.[2]

When we dream about a "turkey dinner and all the fixin's" it is hard to tell whether the turkey itself or what goes with it is the most attractive. And so with budgeting. Budgets are useful merely as a financial control,

[2]A major drawback of budgets when used to evaluate personal performance is their tie to a single forecast of external conditions. When external conditions (volume, prices, strikes, and so on) deviate from the forecast, a new standard is needed if a budget is to be fair. Two ways of obtaining flexibility are (1) a "flexible budget" that permits the calculation of expense standards based on the actual volume of work (an interpolation between high- and low-volume budgets) and (2) "standard costs" that permit calculation of expense standards based on the actual product-mix. The greatest flexibility, however, is obtained through periodic budget revisions. For example, each month a twelve-month budget can be drawn up, including a revision of previous estimates for the period immediately ahead. This modified budget can take account of any external change and thus become a realistic standard. An added advantage is that if the man who will be evaluated participates in the budget revision he is motivated to adjust his operations to the new external conditions. The realistic standard plus the improved motivation both lead toward changed behavior—the aim of controls. Incidentally, while "expected values" and "decision trees" are useful devices for dealing with uncertainty in *planning*, they tend to confuse the setting of reasonable standards for control.

but when they are accompanied by other elements of good management they can be an even more cogent force.[3]

Dangers in Using Budgets for Control

The most serious risk in using budgets is an *unbalanced emphasis* on factors that happen to be the easiest to observe. For example, the operating expenses of the engineering or personnel department stand out clearly in budget reports, and the supervising executives are under pressure to keep expenses within prescribed limits. But the services such departments perform are of even greater importance. Inadequate service, unfortunately, is reflected only indirectly in the profit-and-loss figures—perhaps in costs or in low sales—and is difficult to trace back to the service division. In terms of budget controls, a service department can look good by keeping expenses in line even though it performs its major mission poorly.

At the same time a budget highlights the orders received by the sales department and low cost in the production department. Executives of these departments make a good budget showing by demanding more, rather than less, help from related operating and service divisions. Consequently, a budget tends to create *internal conflict* and pressures. Intangible results may not be measured at all, or they may not be properly associated with the units that produce them.

A related danger of budgetary control is that we may *treat symptoms* as though they were basic problems. We may become involved in a numbers game rather than probe the reality that lies behind the numbers. If total office salaries look high, for example, a manager may withhold merit increases and fill vacancies with low-salaried, inexperienced help. This remedy may make a bad situation worse. Perhaps the salary figure is a symptom of poor office organization, and a realignment of jobs is what is really needed.

To cite another example, high material costs do not necessarily mean that the foreman in the processing department is ineffective. High material costs may be a symptom of any of the following weaknesses: unnecessarily rigid specifications, competition for limited supply of raw stock, inept purchasing, inadequate inspection of materials put into the production process, poor process engineering, or old or poorly maintained equipment. A financial budget cannot and should not be expected to reveal which is the real cause of difficulty.

For another drawback, a budget system opens the way for *dictatorial* action. The terse objective figures of a budget make it easy for an execu-

[3]A similar effect arises from other management tools. The introduction of organization planning, operations research, and output standards, for instance, all stimulate a lot of associated improvements. Consequently, we can pick a tool that is appealing at the moment and use it to overcome inertia on an array of improvements.

tive to say, "Cut that expense 30 percent." If the executive is pressed for time or does not know what else to do, he may order a change in the budget without thinking through the ramifications of such action.

Finally, there is the danger that a company will go through the *form* of budgetary control *without the substance*. All too often some staff man in the controller's office merely predicts what the accounts will look like several months in the future, with little or no actual planning by operating managers. In other instances, budgets are prepared routinely and mechanically, with no thought given to how operations might be improved. Later the managers simply make excuses if performance compares unfavorably with the budget. In such circumstances, budgeting is a nuisance rather than an aid to management; it simply adds paper work and red tape to an already complex task. Budgetary control can be helpful only if key executives incorporate it as a dynamic part of their way of managing.

PERT

Dollar incomes and dollar expenses are the grist of financial budgeting. Although the timing of action from budget period to budget period is considered, synchronization of work is a secondary aspect of budgeting. With PERT, the emphasis is reversed. Timing is primary, expense control is an accessory. Consequently, PERT serves quite a different role in a total control system.

Time is crucial in many management situations. Quick results are often important. In addition, by synchronizing activities we can utilize resources more fully and maintain a steady pace of work. The control of when events occur is especially important in complex, interdependent ventures like launching a new product or erecting a bridge. For these reasons, a manager often needs a control device that focuses on the timing of each step necessary to arrive at an established goal.

A recently developed means to analyze and control the timing aspects of a major project is PERT (Program Evaluation and Review Technique). Originally developed for the highly complex task of producing Polaris missiles, PERT has been adapted to a wide variety of undertakings. Let us take a brief look at its basic features.

Recording the Network

As with any control, we start with a plan of action. Suppose our goal is to launch a new product or place a communications satellite in orbit, and we arrive at the stage where we know the actions that will be necessary to achieve our goal. The first phase of a PERT analysis is to note carefully each of these steps, the sequence in which they must be performed, and the time required for each. This information is recorded in the form of a network—usually on a chart such as those shown in Figs. 25–1 and 25–2.

The chart in Fig. 25–1 is highly simplified so that we can easily grasp the main features. It shows the main steps that a United States auto equipment manufacturer would have to follow to market a new antismog muffler. The manufacturer has purchased a tested European patent so that engineering to United States requirements is simple, and he already has a well-organized plant and distribution setup. Arrows on the chart indicate the sequence of events he must follow to get his new product on the market, and the numbers on the arrows show the required time for each step.

Note that the network is really one way of recording a "program"— a concept we examined on pages 439–43. This list of events, the sequences, and the elapsed times are all the data necessary for program planning. The network does not show resources needed for each step, but an understanding regarding men, machines, and money underlies the estimated time for each step. The chief advantage of expressing a program as a network is its emphasis on sequences and interrelationships.

The Critical Path

Because we are focusing here on time, we wish to know where delay will be most serious. The network is very helpful for this purpose. By tracing each necessary sequence and adding the time estimates for each step, we can identify which sequence will require the maximum time. This is the "critical path." Other sequences will take less time and hence are less critical.

Fig. 25-1 A simplified PERT chart. Events—that is, the start or completion of a step—are indicated by circles. Arrows show the sequence between events. The time (in days) required to move from one event to another appears on each arrow. The critical path—the longest sequence—is shown in color.

EVENTS

- (A) Decision to add product
- (B) Engineering work completed
- (C) Financing arranged
- (D) Material purchase orders placed
- (E) Production started
- (F) Sales campaign arranged
- (G) Initial orders received
- (H) Initial orders shipped

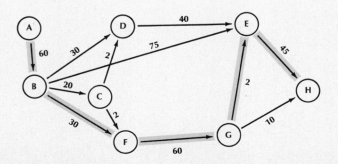

The critical path is especially important in planning and control. Any delay along this path will postpone the completion date of the entire project. On the other hand, knowing in advance which series of steps are critical, we may be able to replan (allocate more resources, perform part of the work simultaneously, and so on) in order to shorten the total time. In other words (1) we focus control where it is most essential, (2) we are in a good position to spot potential trouble early, and (3) we can avoid putting pressure on activities that will not speed up final completion.

Moreover, as work progresses reports on activities that are ahead or behind schedule will enable us to reexamine the timing. Perhaps an unexpected delay has created a new critical path. (For example, if tooling up— B to E in Fig. 25–1—required an additional thirty days, a new critical path would be created.) Then corrective action can be shifted to the new sequence where no slack time exists.

Control of Major Projects

PERT is typically applied to a much more complicated network than the illustration we have used. Even this new product example was oversimplified; in practice, each of the major steps would be programmed in more detail. The preparation of the sales campaign, for instance, would involve packaging, pricing, sales brochures, installation manuals, training of salesmen, placing of advertisements, and the like; and each of these activities should be shown separately in the network. Such delineation improves our chances of catching delays early, and it also spells out the need for coordination at numerous points.

For a complex project, such as the construction of a large plant, the network becomes complicated indeed. One network with 137 events is shown in Fig. 25–2. PERT is especially suited to large "single-use" programs having clear-cut steps and measurable output.

PERT/COST

PERT's forte is control of time. However, as we noted in the preceding chapter, control over one aspect of performance tends to diminish attention to other aspects. So, if timing is stressed, costs are likely to get out of line. To counteract this tendency the original PERT concept has been expanded to include both time and cost.

To put it in a nutshell, most PERT/COST systems merely add an estimated—or budgeted—cost for each step in the network. Then, as work progresses the actual cost to date is compared with the estimate, just as actual time is compared with estimated time. Basically, the cost-control mechanism is the same as the normal budgetary control of costs.

The distinctive aspect of PERT/COST is its direct association with each separate step in the total operation. PERT provides a unique way to measure how much progress has been made, and if we have a standard for costs for each step, we can also tell whether costs are running ahead of accomplishment. Normal accounting does not keep track of costs in this way, and so we have a new potential cost control.

The unique features of PERT/COST are also its drawbacks. Costs for each step in a network are both hard to budget and hard to keep track of. Even when several minor steps are combined together, companies have difficulties setting standards and making measurements. PERT frequently deals with activities that are new, and this fact makes estimating of costs difficult; also, it often stresses joint contributions of different departments, which makes the allocating of overhead difficult. Consequently, we still have much to learn about making a PERT/COST system work smoothly.

Uses of PERT

Currently, PERT controls are fashionable. They are associated with spacecraft and other scientific achievements; they often, though not necessarily, use computers for tabulations and reports; and they are described in terms of "systems," "networks," and other management science lingo. Naturally, this source of popularity will pass. From a basic management viewpoint, we need to know where PERT will fit as a continuing instrument of control.

Lasting applications will probably be of two sorts. First, we will use PERT to plan and control the progress of highly complex projects. Here, the design, engineering, purchase or production, testing, and assembly

Fig. 25-2 PERT in an actual situation.

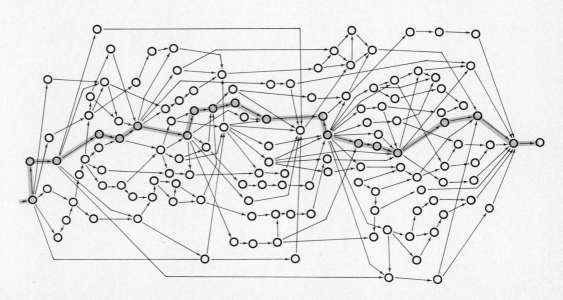

of hundreds of parts must be synchronized.[4] The task of controlling such work differs sharply from control of repetitive operations. Second, we will use a simplified version of PERT for all sorts of single-use programs such as a sales promotion or floating a bond issue. The concepts of a network of events and of the critical path can be applied to many kinds of situations where we are interested in getting a job done on time.

CONCLUSION

One striking aspect of both PERT and budgetary control is the need for careful planning before the control feature can be effective. In fact, the pressure to refine and clarify plans when setting up these controls may be a major contribution in itself. Also, although neither device assures corrective action at early stages, both permit prompt identification of trouble and both provide us with a framework for making adjustments that recognize the ramifications of the actions taken.

In this review of budgeting and PERT we have made only passing reference to the way people respond to the controls. Actually, the effects of both instruments depend greatly on getting executives and operators to accept and use the data provided. We shall explore this subject in the next chapter.

FOR CLASS DISCUSSION

Questions

1) To what degree does the existence of a detailed budget indicate that good planning has taken place?

2) A number of companies now present forecasts on key variables not as single-point estimates but in terms of "best, worst, and most likely" estimates. How should these multiple point estimates be handled when they must be recorded as budget targets?

3) In many companies a twelve-month budget is prepared in December for the following year, and then each month of the budget

[4]The Department of Defense requires its contractors for major projects—supersonic planes, submarines, and the like—to develop a Cost/Schedule Planning and Control System. Such a system normally includes a network of steps such as we have described with the added features of (1) "milestone" events to be used as control points, (2) dates related to each step, (3) cost estimates broken down by material, labor, and overhead for each step, (4) regular reviews and reports of actual time and cost versus the plan, and (5) revised "estimated-to-complete" costs and time. Such systems are the most elaborate planning and control mechanisms used in non-Communist countries.

for the next month is revised on the basis of more up-to-date estimates. At the end of the year, for comparing actual expenses and income to the budget, which set of budget figures for any one month should be used—the figures prepared the previous December for the entire year or the revised monthly budgets? Support your answer.

4) If Paul Bailey had not had the kinds of budgets he developed with Morris Barkin, what would have been the differences in first-year results? How will the budgets help him in his second year's operations?

5) What should be the roles of, and relationships between, the line manager who must follow a budget and the accountants who aid in its preparation? What potential dangers should be considered in this "participative" process? How may they be minimized?

6) In what ways has computer technology contributed to budgetary control? Has it created any problems with regard to using budgets for control?

7) In what ways is PERT like, or unlike, quality control?

8) "The trouble with systems like PERT," said the experienced director of a key federal agency, "is that the man responsible for planning and controlling results becomes unduly dependent on the technicians who have to put all of the plans into these networks and then interpret them." How do you feel about this criticism?

Cases

For cases involving issues covered in this chapter, see especially the following. Particularly relevant questions are listed after each case.

Trans-World Mutual Funds, Ltd. (p. 121), 15, 16
Dodge Skate Company (p. 337), 16
E.W. Ross, Inc. (p. 468), 16

FOR FURTHER READING

Bacon, J., *Managing the Budget Function*. New York: National Industrial Conference Board, 1970. *Clear summary of the use of budgets for management purposes, based on survey of company practice.*

Hofstede, G.H., *The Game of Budget Control*. London: Tavistock Publications Limited, 1968 (U.S. distributor, Barnes & Noble, Inc., New York), Chaps. 2 and 4. *Summary of concept of budgeting in accounting theory and in systems theory. Parts III and IV are best report in existence on actual responses to budgets.*

Koontz, H., and C. O'Donnell, *Principles of Management*, 4th ed. New York: McGraw-Hill Book Company, 1968, Chaps. 29 and 30. *Review of newer control techniques and control of overall performance.*

Novick, D., "The Origin and History of Program Budgeting." *California Management Review*, Fall 1968. *Explains the concept of "program budgeting" as developed for government and business use.*

Schoderbek, P.P., ed., *Management Systems*. New York: John Wiley & Sons, Inc., 1967, Parts XII and XIII. *Well-selected articles on PERT, PERT/COST, and real-time systems.*

Vatter, W.J., *Operating Budgets*. Belmont, Calif.: Wadsworth Publishing Co., 1969. *Lucid, condensed description of the budgeting process as a managerial tool.*

Chapter Twenty-six

Responses of People to Controls

BEHAVIORAL VIEW OF CONTROLLING

Managerial controls will be a waste of effort—unless they cause people to alter their behavior. In the two preceding chapters, we have considered controls primarily from an engineering, or mechanistic, point of view. Control standards derived from company objectives, control points selected in the light of technology and administrative organization, financial budgeting made attractive by the existence of an accounting system—these are valid considerations, but they are not enough. The payoff comes only when somebody—manager or operator—does his work better because the controls are in operation.

Effective Controls

This chapter takes a look at how people respond to controls. We have already seen that the effectiveness of organizing, planning, and leading can be substantially enhanced if we take the time for an explicit examination of how these managerial devices actually affect people. This same human behavior approach is vital in understanding how controls really work. First, we shall look at reasons why people object to controls. Then, in the second part of the chapter, we shall examine ways of getting them to respond positively to controls.

WHY MEN OBJECT TO CONTROLS

The responses of people to standards, measurements, reports, and other control devices depend, of course, on each total situation. The way a man feels toward his boss, whether he likes his work, his opportunities for self-expression, and similar factors influence his responses to controls as well as to other managerial actions. In the following discussion we are concerned with a narrower issue. What is there about controls per se that makes them objectionable to so many people? Why do we so often hear people say, "This is a good place to work. But I sure don't like those damn controls."

Controls—at least those we are aware of—are usually disliked. It is certainly common to hear students groan about examinations, executives complain about expense budgets, and clerks give snippy answers to anyone who audits their books. But such reactions are not inevitable, and if we can discover ways of avoiding negative responses, the chances that a control will be effective will be greatly enhanced.

A review of the reasons why people dislike controls may present a discouraging picture. Fortunately, only one or two of these reasons are likely to apply in any single situation. The following list, then, is intended only to suggest *possible* sources of difficulty. It points to pitfalls that should be avoided if possible.

Failure to Accept Objectives

One reason why people may not like a control is that they have no genuine interest in accomplishing the objective behind the control. A movie cameraman simply may not care about reducing waste; he is likely to think, "The company's rich." Or the branch manager may not be interested in pushing a new line of low-priced products because he feels "They are junk. They don't belong with products that made this company famous." Perhaps another person believes that customers do not really need the service they ask for. It should not be surprising that controls designed to keep costs down, to promote the sales of a new line, or to provide prompt delivery are unpopular with such persons.

Each of us has only a limited amount of energy, but many things he would like to do. A control, by its very nature, prods us to expend more energy in particular directions. If those directions are not so appealing to us as other things we might do, we resent the prod.

For a variety of reasons, a man may accept a given objective as worthwhile, and those he accepts he will endorse with varying degrees of intensity. Consequently, Tom Berg's feeling about a particular control may range all the way from hostility to acceptance as a valuable aid. Diversity of objectives has a further complication. Tom Berg may feel that the objectives are vague; that his boss wants first one thing and then another; that, in fact, some objectives are incompatible with one another (for instance, low cost and fast service). In such a situation, if controls are placed on particular parts of a job—say on costs but not on service—even acceptance of the objectives leaves an employee feeling uneasy about the uncontrolled portions. The control will probably be blamed for this feeling of uneasiness because it keeps raising the unresolved question of what emphasis he should give to competing objectives.

To put this matter in terms of personal "needs" (as the term was defined in Chapter 8), if a person fails to accept certain objectives and does not include them among his needs, he is likely to find any control mechanism that pushes him toward those objectives a distinct annoyance.

Feeling That Par Is Unreasonable

Often a person may agree with an objective but dislike a control because he thinks the standard of performance is set too high. "Unreasonable!" may be the verbal reaction of a salesman to his quota, or of a purchasing agent to a schedule for reducing inventories.

Especially annoying to anyone subject to control is a shifting target. A person is likely to say, "The boss is never satisfied. No matter how good a job I do, he always wants more." Under these circumstances, a control is a device to stimulate ever greater effort, even though a person is already doing what formerly was considered an outstanding job. One reason for the early opposition to scientific management was the short-sighted practice of some managements to change an output standard as soon as an operator earned more than what was considered appropriate for his job.

Whether a standard is considered reasonable also depends on how it is administered. Circumstances beyond the influence of a person who is

Fig. 26-1 Even if a person wants to achieve a given goal, he may resent a standard of performance that seems extremely demanding.

being controlled may affect his actual results. Or a standard may be so tight that it can be met only half the time. If a supervisor recognizes these facts and uses good judgment in dealing with his men when standards are not met, there may be no cause for serious complaint. But if standards are rigidly applied, just one or two instances of "unfair" treatment may create a persistently sour attitude toward controls.

A person's feeling about the unreasonableness of controls is also influenced by the total number of different controls that bear on him. Most people expect, and even welcome, some control over their activities, but as more and more aspects of their work become subject to standards, inspection, and reports, a feeling of being pressed on arises. What has been an acceptable standard for, say, the number of customer calls per week now becomes irritating because it is combined with other controls.

Belief That Measurements Are Inappropriate

"We've no kick about the goals you set; the trouble with the controls is that we don't get credit for the work we do." So said the manager of a repair-parts department when his record of the number of days taken to fill orders was being reviewed. His chief point was that slow shipments were usually of parts for old machines or special parts that had to be approved by the engineering department. Similarly—and not uncommonly —a man in a maintenance department might say, "You can't measure the breakdowns that didn't happen." And what of a man who puts forth a lot of effort with only mediocre results and, when the control report comes through, feels like a student who spends all spring vacation on a paper that gets only a "C." In all these examples, the man believes— rightly or wrongly—that the measurement does not appropriately gauge his work, and consequently he dislikes the control process.

Controls may increase the squabbles between departments when the people involved lack confidence in the measurements. For example, when a job-order firm installed a control over the length of time elapsed between receipt of an order and shipment, the arguments among the sales, engineering, and manufacturing departments rose sharply. Each department promptly sought to speed up its part of the process. But the engineering department complained that sales sent along orders with incomplete requirements, and the production department accused engineering of sloppy specifications that necessitated extra work by the men in the shop. It was easy enough to measure the time it took an order to move from one department to the other, but exceedingly difficult to measure the quality of work that involved so many details. In this particular instance, the company decided to discontinue the control over the flow from one department to the other because of its deleterious effect on the spirit of cooperation. In fact, the control was so intensely disliked that several key men wanted to throw out both the keeping of any records and the standard for the overall time to process orders.

Manuals for supervisors often advise, "Before you criticize a man, be sure of your facts." This warning applies to control systems as well.

Dislike of Unpleasant Facts

Another fundamental reason why controls are unpopular is that from time to time control reports bear bad news. A person who is loath to face unpleasant facts almost always wishes the control system would vanish.

Each of us has his own personal aspirations about his work. These include both hopes and expectations. They reflect the kind of person and the quality of worker each of us thinks he is—our "self-image." Control reports are one means of learning whether we have lived up to our own expectations. Often we fail, and a realist accordingly adjusts the balance between expectations and facts; he may even readjust his hopes. Other persons, however, find it difficult to accept the facts of life, and so develop a sense of frustration. Because a frustrated person needs some relief, it is only natural for him to transfer part of the blame to the mechanism that tells him he is not as good as he thinks he ought to be.

Furthermore, control reports may put us in an unfavorable light before our associates. To the extent that control systems measure desirable action, reports can make us appear strong or weak. A batting average in baseball, the number of booked orders in a sales department, grades in college—these are usually thought to be measures of a man. Here again, if those measures make us look inept and stupid, we probably will not like the measuring system.

The fear of unpleasant consequences can add to our aversion to controls. If an unfavorable report may lead to demotion, a cut in pay, or a bawling-out, we are not going to feel very kindly toward the control system.

Fortunately, all is not dark. As we shall see later in this chapter, it is possible to make the controls bearers of good news as well as bad, and for at least some things, a control system may be regarded as dispassionately as the scorekeeper at a football game.

Pressure to Adjust from "Illegitimate" Sources

The response to controls depends, in part, on who tries to do the controlling. A plant foreman, for example, may accept control action by his superintendent as part of the normal way of life, but he may become highly annoyed if some "stuffed shirt" comes into his shop and asks a lot of questions about why expenses were so high last month. Certainly if the company accountant asks the foreman to come over to the accounting office and makes suggestions about what should be done, the latter's reaction will probably be, "Who does he think he is?" We can note a like relationship in a family, where young Johnny takes checking up by, and suggestions from, his parents as a matter of course, but starts a family row if his sister tries to do the same thing.

Once the social structure of an enterprise has been established, people become sensitive about what kind of action is "legitimate." The pattern varies. A college instructor, for example, expects colleagues in his own field to suggest content and teaching methods for a new course. In contrast, attempts at guidance from administrators or professors outside his department are often regarded as infringement on his academic freedom. The exercise of control runs into similar attitudes. Fairly strong opposition can be generated if the control pressure comes from sources employees believe are illegitimate.

Feelings of legitimacy apply to subjects as well as to persons. Thus if a high degree of decentralization has become traditional in a company, many workers will regard certain problems as theirs to decide. A West Coast manager of a firm based in the East, for instance, may feel that he is the one to select local employees and set their pay. If anyone—even his boss—back in headquarters tries to appraise the quality of his employees or the appropriateness of their pay, he will probably resent this new control. Such an executive often has intense pride in a particular job that he considers his own, and he is likely to react to any new control from outside as though it is an interference with his private life.

Social Pressure That Runs Counter to Company Controls

The effect of informal group pressure on individual attitudes has been pointed out in Chapter 7. This social pressure applies to control as well as to other managerial action; as Roethlisberger points out:

> In any large business organization, there are at least two major evaluational systems in terms of which each contributor is being judged. In the case of one, he is evaluated in terms of certain measurable abstractions and standards relating to performance and efficiency. In the case of the other, he is being evaluated in terms of certain socially accepted codes and norms of conduct. The first evaluation tells him where he theoretically stands in the eyes of management; the second tells him where he stands in the eyes of his fellow associates. These two evaluations of a person may not coincide.[1]

[1] F. J. Roethlisberger, *Management and Morale* (Cambridge: Harvard University Press, 1941), p. 154.

Group attitudes are most serious when they directly oppose the standards set by management. The classic example is the group that has output standards significantly lower than those of management, and that puts severe pressure, even to the point of threatening violence, on any operator who joins in with management's "speed-up."

On the other hand, there are plenty of instances—especially in the executive ranks—when social pressures support the controls. The attitudes that really count are those of associates whose friendship and respect a man wants to keep. If these persons feel that a control standard and its measurement are fair and that cooperating with management is the right thing to do, they will constitute a social force supporting that standard. Thus there will probably be strong social support for a control over stealing money, whereas control over wasting money through unnecessary expenses will receive support only if employees feel that management administers the control reasonably and fairly. Actually these associates may not know the details of a particular control; if they believe that management is in general fair and reasonable in what it expects operators and executives to do, they will exert social pressure to support the system as a whole.

Between the two extremes of direct opposition and strong support, there are, of course, many shades of group attitude. Perhaps a group is indifferent to what management wants accomplished, but it may have certain goals of its own, such as group solidarity ("keeping the gang together"); even so, group pressure becomes significant only if it is difficult to meet both company and group objectives. Or a group may be neutral about the final results of a control system, but hold strong beliefs about particular points along the way, such as the tables of basic data used in setting output standards, the reliability of government statistics, or appraisals by persons who have never worked on the job under controls. The group is also likely to influence attitudes about who may "legitimately" take part in control work. In short, exactly how a group affects a man's feelings about control needs to be examined for each case.

One further point may be helpful in understanding group influence.

Fig. 26-2 Social pressure is a form of control. When the deviant is working effectively for the organization, social pressure may be a detrimental control; however, in other cases, social pressure may be beneficial.

Group attitudes toward control are neither unpredictable nor unchanging. They arise out of the past experiences of members of the group, especially the informal leaders. These individual experiences, in turn, are shaped by matters already discussed in this chapter—acceptance of objectives, reasonableness of par, confidence in measurements, adjustment to unfavorable reports, and attitudes about legitimacy of controls. A manager cannot dictate group attitudes, but by his behavior he *can* influence them.

ELICITING POSITIVE RESPONSES TO CONTROLS

Controls are essential whether anyone likes them or not. We simply cannot carry on purposeful endeavor efficiently if we fail to give regular attention to how well plans and results match up. Even though controls may be disliked, for any of the reasons already outlined, a manager cannot sidestep this phase of his job. Through the use of managerial pressure and "indirect" incentives (salary, bonus, and other off-the-job rewards), we can take corrective action and achieve results.

In fact, people learn to get along with many things they find unpleasant. Throughout history, man has had to accept the bitter with the sweet. Many of the great military and industrial achievements were accomplished by groups of men who were operating under the pressures of unpopular control. Work does get done that way, but at what cost?

Improved results are possible if a manager can reduce negative attitudes toward controls. Removing an irritation and replacing it with a positive desire increases the chances that company goals will be achieved. At the same time, the human cost has been reduced, because the balance of personal dissatisfactions and satisfactions has been altered.

What ways can we discover for getting positive responses to controls? Some obvious points suggest themselves from the mere identification of the reasons for disliking controls—for example, making objectives clear, not raising output standards without a recognized reason, and so on. But in addition, are there techniques that in practice have proved helpful in dealing with this general problem? What are some of the steps an intelligent manager should at least consider?

Important among the measures managers have found helpful in eliciting a positive response to controls are the following:

1) Maintaining a dispassionate view of control.
2) Encouraging subordinates' participation in setting standards.
3) Using "fact control" rather than executive, authoritarian control.
4) Introducing flexibility in the control system.
5) Being sensitive to personal needs and social pressures in the administration of controls.

Dispassionate View of Control

When a machine breaks down or a column of figures does not add up right, most of us do not become angry; we simply try to find what is wrong. But when a person does not do what is expected of him, we blame *him* and often get a little angry. As soon as two or more persons are involved in the control process—especially in the corrective-action phase— we tend to react emotionally, to think in terms of personalities and of what they are doing for or against us. This tendency is likely to be as true of the supervisor as of the supervised.

This common inclination toward emotional reactions suggests the first thing a manager should do to improve the human aspects of control. He must learn to take an *objective, unemotional approach to finding the causes and the cures* for difficulties uncovered by a control device. Deviations in human behavior have causes just as the breakdown of a machine does. In either case the causes may be easy or hard to fix. In a situation involving people, feelings and attitudes are facts to be reckoned with, just as a shortage of cash and a faulty spark plug are. Instead of passing moral judgment on how people ought to act and getting angry if they do not conform to his desired pattern, a successful executive learns to deal with control problems analytically and dispassionately.

Such an executive is not, however, cold and indifferent to personal feelings. On the contrary, he is sensitive and perceptive. But he keeps his mind on established objectives and thinks in terms of the actions that are necessary to achieve these goals. Controls, he realizes, are simply a means of spotting difficulties, and in using them he is looking for a cure, not for a person to blame.

The attitude of a boss toward controls tends to be reflected by his subordinates. This is by no means always so, but if a boss himself can maintain an objective, dispassionate view, the chance is good that sooner or later his subordinates will learn to adopt a similar approach.

Participation in Setting Standards

Participation can be a great help in securing acceptance of objectives, performance standards, and methods of measurement. When a person genuinely shares in drawing up a plan or standard he usually becomes psychologically involved.[2] Often he becomes committed, and at the least he has a fuller understanding. The following two examples indicate the possibilities.

The Tremco Manufacturing Company is a well-run firm that produces

[2]We are assuming that the persons asked to participate have a background and ability to deal with the subject. Quality control in a pharmaceutical plant, for instance, is too technical to provide much opportunity for participation by plant workers.

a variety of products used in the maintenance and construction of industrial buildings, schools, institutions, and commercial structures. It uses job descriptions, sales quotas, and many other of the usual management devices. Nevertheless, at one time its top management sensed a lack of clear understanding by each executive and supervisor of just what was expected of him. This lack made it difficult for individuals themselves to know whether their performance was good or bad, and many supervisors found it hard to tell them how they stood. Consequently, the president decided to try a new method for setting standards of executive performance.

Tremco's sales force of approximately one hundred men is supervised by a group of regional managers. These regional managers were among the first executives in the company to work out their own standards of performance. At a series of meetings, under the leadership of top management, the regional managers as a group took the following steps: First, the men identified the major functions of a regional manager's job; they established a list of sixty-one different "major" segments of responsibility. Next the group proceeded to define each of these items. This step was important in securing a clear understanding throughout the group. Overlapping was discovered, so that by the time the definitions were completed, the original list of segments was boiled down from sixty-one to thirty-two. The third step, and the most difficult one because so many intangibles were involved, was to set a standard for each listed segment. The group tried to put in writing a clear-cut statement of the conditions that would exist or the results that would be achieved before performance could be considered satisfactory. The group had to meet three different times before these steps were completed; the interval between the meetings was found to be beneficial because it gave all the participants an opportunity to think through what they were doing.

The president of Tremco emphasizes the following points in connection with this three-step process:

1) Most important, the standard should be set by the individual whose performance is going to be evaluated. We were careful not even to suggest a standard. The superior can safely rephrase or restate the ideas suggested, but he should refrain carefully from advancing his own ideas. (Do not be afraid that the standards set will not be high enough. More often, they will be too high, and you will have to scale them down.)

2) The standards must be considered fair and attainable by the individuals for whom they are being set.

3) The standards should be as specific as possible. Where actual data or statistical information is obtainable, it should be used.

4) Where the results are intangible, an effort should be made to arrive at as clear-cut and simple a statement and understanding as possible.

5) If in the process a lack of clear-cut authority and responsibility on the part of any person is discovered, confusions should be cleared up at once.

6) Theoretical ideas should be guarded against. Keep asking the question, "What do I hold you responsible for?" Draw out the individual until there is a meeting of minds and then write down the result. Do not worry about semantics. Get to the heart of the matter in simple words that everybody understands well.

The results with the regional managers were so successful that the company extended the process to cover all its managerial jobs. The benefits include a clear understanding by each executive and his boss of what constitutes satisfactory performance. In addition, rapport between each man and his boss became closer, work performance itself improved immediately, social pressure caused the group to set high standards, and self-appraisal and self-motivation were strengthened.[3]

A large frozen food company tried a similar approach with its salesmen. In this instance, the salesmen, in groups of twelve, were first asked to develop a picture of a first-class salesman in terms of his duties and his performance. Following a thorough and frank discussion of this ideal Mr. X, each man was asked to prepare for himself a statement of what he thought he would accomplish during the next year. The men were expected to cover all the functions that had been listed for Mr. X, but they were free to set whatever outputs they believed were reasonable. Management then used these statements as standards of performance for the following year. The only adjustments—and these were made with the concurrence of the salesmen involved—were to scale down some of the outputs where the men had set too high a standard for themselves. In this instance, as in the Tremco illustration, the participating process made the controls much more meaningful and acceptable.

The particular manner in which participation is sought, should, of course, be adapted to the circumstances peculiar to each company. In fact, several companies have found that an approach suitable for sales departments does not work well in plants. Some companies have been able to secure genuine participation in developing budgets, whereas other companies have felt that this practice leads to lax standards and that morale is weakened when management has to overrule proposals from subordinates.

The elapsed times used in preparing a PERT network are typically set by the men who perform each step; sometimes a weighted average of the best, normal, and slow time is used, but this array of estimates also comes from the participants.

Success really depends on management's ability to establish acceptable premises and ground rules and on its willingness to take the time and run the risks that are necessarily involved. But on the whole, there has

[3]For a more complete description of this case, see W. C. Treuhaft, "Experience with Executive Standards of Performance" (New York: American Management Association, General Management Series No. 183), pp. 3–11.

been sufficient success with the participation approach in setting control standards to commend it to any manager who is seeking to develop a more positive attitude among his subordinates toward controls.

Fact Control

A concept related to participation is fact control. The particular emphasis here is that the facts in a situation, rather than the pressure of a supervising executive, should call for any necessary corrective action. If a young lady with her arms full of books drops a piece of paper as she is walking down a hall, you think nothing of picking up the paper and handing it to her; but if a proctor in the hall requests you to pick up some paper on the floor and give it to him, you are likely to feel imposed upon.

A comparable situation arose in a company that manufactures complex processing equipment. Several months before the event in question an important customer had been told of a possible delivery date on a large order. When the order was finally placed half a year later, both the engineering department and the production department were crowded with work and looked forward to a two-week summer-vacation shutdown. Under these circumstances, the supervisors involved said that delivery before vacation was "impossible." Yet this customer had given the company a large amount of business in the past and would probably continue to do so in the future; and his need was clearly urgent. Consequently, after full discussion it was agreed to try to meet the new delivery date.

Management did not set a tight schedule, pound the table, and say that the schedule had to be met or heads would roll. Instead, they kept everyone who would take part in the job from its start to finish fully informed about the status of the work. When the customer's engineers visited the company, they met with people who were being asked to do "the impossible." Employees were also kept informed about the progress of related construction at the customer's plant. For several weeks, the general sentiment continued to be, "We sure can't make that one, but we'll try." Then the mood shifted to, "If everything goes right, we might make it."

Actually, the order was shipped one day before the plant shut down for vacation. The total time from the start of engineering to delivery had been cut to about half of the normal production period. Men had worked hard, they went out of their way to help one another, and they willingly shifted from their normal work to do what was most needed at the moment. In the final test before shipment, adjustments were fewer than ordinary; the machine worked right the first time. Production costs were higher than usual, of course, but the delivery date was met.

In this situation, detailed control charts and top-management pressure would have produced performance only a little better than normal, and that would not have been enough. But by letting the men know the full facts and respond to the demands of the situation, the work got done. By handling the job in this way, morale was higher than it would have been if pressure and rigid controls, which probably would have led to tension and ill-will, were used.

Fact control is not unusual when the need is obvious and the situation unique. When a heavy snowstorm, for instance, prevented about half of the employees of a large bank from getting to work, those who did arrive somehow managed to get the day's work done. But in more normal operations the aim of fact control is not that people should be expected to do herculean tasks; rather, control and pressure for work are dictated by the needs of the situation. Many adverse feelings about control can be avoided when this point of view prevails.

Flexibility in a Control System

"Flexibility" is a word, like "justice," that is used to rationalize both good and bad actions. There is a danger that flexibility will be used as an argument every time a person wants an excuse to evade sound management practice. Nevertheless, there are occasions when deviations from averages or theoretical principles are desirable, and we should not discard this principle just because there is a risk that it will be misused.

Flexibility has an important bearing on people's attitudes toward controls. If they feel that the standards of performance do not take adequate account of specific local factors, to them the standards become "unreasonable." The crux of the matter is how to introduce flexibility and still keep controls useful as a management tool.

One way of introducing flexibility into a control system while maintaining its integrity is to make the adjustments automatic. Both flexible budgets and standard costs, for example, provide a shifting standard for expenses as the volume of work goes up or down. A similar type of adjustment is in effect when sales quotas are tied to general business activity or to current activity in particular industries. In all such plans, the basis for shifting the control standard is built right into the system.

In other situations, variation in work is so great that no formal system for setting standards seems to be possible. At any rate, any formal system would probably be the cause of so many arguments that it would do more harm than good. But one consulting firm has developed a method for achieving some degree of control over output and scheduling in situations such as these. The method can be applied to office operations, storerooms, and maintenance work—in short to a wide variety of activity. Stripped of a lot of verbal trappings, which presumably make the consulting services more salable, the central idea is this: Each time a supervisor assigns a task to one of his men, he writes down an estimated time for completing the job. Preferably, he discusses the estimate briefly with

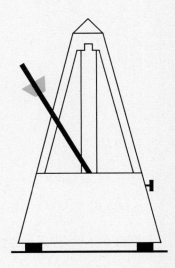

Fig. 26-3 In music a metronome provides a precise but adjustable gauge of tempo. Such a device is a good model for a manager who wants to introduce flexibility into a control system.

the man, and they both understand that it is merely a subjective guess based on past experience. Then the supervisor makes note of when the task is actually finished. If it takes longer than estimated, either the supervisor or the man himself simply jots down the reason for the extra time. Everybody recognizes that unexpected delays may occur, and so a man is not under pressure to make an excuse but is simply recording what the interference was. The reasons for delay are assembled in one place and analyzed carefully. When the same reason recurs, effort is made to remove this cause.

The mechanics of the plan are simple. A few special forms are needed to make it easy to record estimated times and actual times and to write up reasons for delay. The only really new job created is for the central analysis of the reports, and this task need not be elaborate.

Impressive results have been achieved where the plan has been properly installed. Both supervisors and operators become conscious of keeping busy, and so wasted time, especially before noon or closing, is greatly reduced. Identifying reasons for delay also leads to economies. After a few months' experience, the men and the supervisors become skillful in estimating time, and this background permits a closer control over the scheduling of work than formerly was possible. The essence of the idea seems to lie in these five factors: (1) systematic attention, (2) getting the facts before everyone concerned, (3) a high degree of self-control, (4) opportunity for constructive corrective action, and (5) control based on cooperation rather than on pressure. The last point is crucial because the use of estimates as pressure devices will inevitably lead to slowing down and shirking work in a way management will be unable to detect. Furthermore, if the cooperative spirit breaks down, the workers will probably feel only that they are confronted with yet another annoying needling device.

The chances that these particular methods of achieving flexibility can be applied precisely and without change by John Jones in the XYZ Corporation are, of course, very slim. Nevertheless, they do illustrate how, with a little ingenuity, it is possible to introduce flexibility into a control system. To the extent that such adjustments convince those being controlled that the system is "reasonable," the system's chances for success have been enhanced.

Sensitive Administration of Controls

Several different ways of obtaining favorable responses to controls have been discussed in the preceding pages. These suggestions have dealt principally with eliciting acceptance of objectives and output standards and with developing a constructive attitude toward control. But they have not been concerned with feelings about "legitimate" control action, nor directly with group responses to controls.

"Keep corrective action within the channel of command" is a widespread answer to the problem of legitimacy. There is a strong tradition that the line supervisor, and only the line supervisor, is the one who should criticize a person for poor performance, give him instructions for improvement, and impose penalties if necessary. On this premise, a staff man should be involved in control only in the evaluation stage, and corrective action remains the exclusive province of the line supervisor. Many companies have found that insistence on this basic concept avoids difficulties over illegitimate interference.

Unfortunately, this concept does not entirely resolve the problem. It is a sound beginning but several borderline issues may remain troublesome. These, for example: Should a staff man work on measurement only or extend his activity to the investigation of reasons for deviations from standard? After he has ferreted out reasons, is it acceptable for a staff man to explore possible remedies? Can the work of developing standards be done by someone other than a boss—for instance, is it legitimate for someone else to prepare budgets and demand that operating personnel justify modifications in these original proposals? Even within the lines of command, should a boss respect the skill of a craftsman as highly as he does the judgment of a medical director?

In some companies extensive use of staff in controlling would be regarded as quite legitimate. In other situations, such activity would be a source of great irritation. The extent to which any of the procedures just mentioned is put into effect depends on the traditional local pattern of behavior.

Unfortunately, no simple method has been found to modify traditional attitudes. But it is helpful if management is sensitive to employees' feelings about legitimacy. Once such feelings begin to interfere with the smooth working of a control system, management should at least let it be known that it considers staff activity necessary and legitimate. The management point of view can often be explained in terms of operating economy, the need for consistency of action, the concern of top management with a particular activity, benefit to the line supervisor, and by similar reasons. What operating people regard as legitimate may not be changed by these logical arguments, but at least the basis for a self-rationalization of a new point of view is provided.

Group feelings about control are more elusive. *Telling* a group that they *should* change their point of view rarely has any effect. Working with individual members of a group along the lines suggested above is likely to be the best approach. Particularly if these persons are the informal leaders within the group, an unconscious shift in group sentiment may take place. As we noted in Chapter 7, a person and, even more, a group may hold several inconsistent beliefs at the same time. For instance, the need for delivering good-quality products to customers may be accepted even though there is a feeling that the shop would be a much nicer place without inspectors around. Then, over a period of time, one view tends to become dominant. The job of a manager is to administer controls objectively and fairly—as we have been suggesting—with the hope that the supporting group feelings will emerge as the dominant ones.

CONCLUSION

The primary purpose of controls is to guide the behavior of executives and operators toward predetermined objectives and standards. Both the *anticipation* of control measurement and the *corrective action* that follows an unfavorable measurement tend to keep actual performance in line with plans. Much of this response depends on how workers feel about the control system itself. If workers feel that controls are inappropriate, unfair, or illegitimate, they will resist and resent them. Such resistance, especially when supported by social pressures, can go far toward nullifying the intended result of the controls. Consequently, we cannot disregard the human response to controls.

We probably should not expect controls to be popular. Occasionally they carry grim, unpleasant news, and frequently they are a stern reminder of work to be done. Nevertheless, we can take a variety of steps to make controls an acceptable feature of normal, purposeful endeavor: relating controls to recognized objectives; making measurements as accurately as possible, and quickly admitting inaccuracies when they do occur; getting acceptance of normal levels of performance, perhaps using participation in setting standards for each person; giving control information to the men being measured as soon as anyone else gets it; distinguishing between making measurements and taking corrective action; maintaining a dispassionate view when errors crop up; seeking a cure rather than a culprit when analyzing unfavorable results; and introducing flexibility into the control system.

In these, and perhaps in other ways, we can strive to have controls accepted as a valuable aid in getting a job done. Hopefully, the controls will be regarded much as we regard a gasoline gauge on an automobile or a periodic medical examination—as a source of useful information that helps us reach desired goals.

FOR CLASS DISCUSSION

Questions

1) List two controls that influence your actions in some significant ways. Make one of these a control that you accept as *necessary* and regard as a useful instrument to guiding your behavior. Make the other a control that you feel to be unnecessary and that you would circumvent if you could. (1) What accounts for the differences in your feelings about the two? (2) What, if anything, would you substitute for the second control?

2) "The fewer restrictions placed on *how* a job is to be done, the greater the obligation of the man who is assigned the job." Do you agree? Why? Why not? Even if true, what dangers should be watched for?

3) How may changes in personal needs, as discussed in Chapter 8, influence a man's acceptance of controls?

4) Does participation in the setting of standards guarantee acceptance of controls based on these standards? Discuss both sides of this point.

5) How may the trend away from manual labor to more "think-type" jobs influence the design of, and response of people to, controls?

6) How far should participation be used in setting control standards for students at a university? Consider standards for (1) social behavior on the campus, (2) behavior in class and when taking examinations, and (3) academic achievement.

7) In what ways does the use of "fact control" increase the risk for management that corrective action may not be along the same lines that would be deemed "best" from a company viewpoint?

8) This chapter presents several reasons why people resist controls and offers ideas on how to minimize this resistance. Some people, however, seem to thrive on controls and in fact seem uncomfortable without tight controls. What should management do in this latter case?

Cases

For cases involving issues covered in this chapter, see especially the following. Particularly relevant questions are listed after each case.

Western Office Equipment Manufacturing Company (p. 457), 16, 17
E.W. Ross, Inc. (p. 468), 17
Consolidated Instruments—A (p. 571), 19
Texas-Northern Pipeline Company (p. 665), 9

FOR FURTHER READING

Dalton, G.W., and P.E. Lawrence, eds., *Motivation and Control.* Homewood, Ill.: Richard D. Irwin, Inc., 1970. *Readings include several articles on personal responses to controls.*

Dubin, R., *Human Relations in Administration*, 3rd ed. Englewood Cliffs, N.J.: Prentice-Hall, Inc., 1968, Chap. 18. *Cogent description of workers' responses to controls.*

Hofstede, G.H., *The Game of Budget Control*. London: Tavistock Publications Limited, 1968 (U.S. distributor, Barnes & Noble, Inc., New York). *Actual operation and impact of budgets in six plants in the Netherlands; a thorough, unique, and very useful behavioral study.*

Tannenbaum, A.S., *Control in Organizations*. New York: McGraw-Hill Book Company, 1968. *Behavioral studies of the use of influence in organizations; includes some data on responses to formal controls.*

Chapter Twenty-seven

Integrating Controls

with Other Management Processes

MANAGEMENT SYNTHESIS

The intimate relationship of controls to other management processes has been indicated throughout the last three chapters. Objectives and other goals, for instance, are bases for control standards; programs find their financial expression in budgets; decentralization and participation have a marked influence on the acceptance of controls; and so on. Making controls a harmonious part of the whole management activity is perhaps as crucial as the design of the controls themselves

In this chapter, we have singled out several key challenges in integrating controls with other management processes. These challenges do not begin to cover all the interrelations. Rather, they are issues that arise time and again in actual practice, and resolving them wisely can be a great aid to effective management. These issues are: decentralizing without loss of control, harmonizing departmentation with controls, keeping the boss informed, using staff in control, enhancing controls by leadership action, designing a communication network that supports controls, balancing the control structure, and relating control to forward planning.

The concepts involved are already familiar, for we have explained them elsewhere in the book. In this chapter, we are concerned largely with reconciling, refining, and combining these ideas.

DECENTRALIZING WITHOUT LOSS OF CONTROL

Each time a manager delegates work (operating or managing) to a subordinate, he creates the problem of knowing whether the work is performed satisfactorily, and so delegating inevitably raises the question of control. In simple situations, a supervisor watches work while it is being done. But when the delegated work increases, control by direct observation no longer remains possible. Then, when a large part of planning as well as operating is delegated, new complications are added. For if a manager attempts to control the decisions of his subordinate, does he not repudiate his earlier delegation of planning?

This last question bothers many managers. They see the benefits that can come from a high degree of decentralization, and yet they are aware that they have a continuing obligation. Often they wish to go as far as full decentralization—if they can do so "without losing control."

How Control Shifts as Decentralization Increases

A manager need not lose control when he delegates a large measure of planning, but he should be prepared to change his controls. This alteration is illustrated in Table 27–1. First, the types of control standard

Table 27–1   Effect of decentralization on control

Degree of Decentralization	Nature of Control	
	Type of Standard	Frequency of Measurement
Centralization of all but routine decisions.	Detailed specifications on how work is to be done, and on output of each worker.	Daily for output; hourly to continuous for methods and for quality.
Action within policies, programs, standard methods; use of "exception principle."	Output at each stage of operations, expense ratios, efficiency rates, turnover, and the like.	Weekly to daily for output; monthly for ratios and for other operating data.
Profit decentralization.	Overall results, and a few key danger signals.	Monthly for main results and for signals; quarterly or annually for other results.

that are appropriate change. When decisions are centralized, the manager himself will establish rather detailed standards for the method and output of each phase of the work. But as he delegates increasing amounts of authority to plan and decide, the manager should shift his attention away from operating details to the results that are achieved. This is not a sudden shift from black to white, however. Just as varying degrees of planning authority are delegated for each of a wide range of subjects, so, too, standards cover more or less detail. As a general proposition, however, the manager does forego his personal control over detail and relies increasingly on the appraisal of results.

The frequency of appraisals also changes. Because the manager is no longer trying to keep an eye on detailed activities, most, if not all, daily reports can be dropped. As his attention shifts, with increasing decentralization, more and more toward overall results, the span of time covered by reports can typically be lengthened. For a division that operates on a profit-decentralization basis, monthly profit-and-loss statements and balance sheets come as frequently as most top managements want reports. Other factors, such as market position or product development, may be reported only quarterly.

Retained Safeguards

The shift from frequent, detailed control reports to periodic general-appraisal reports does not preclude the use of a few controls of the danger-signal type. In Chapter 24, we discussed the desirability of both attention-directing and scorecard controls. The manager who has delegated a large measure of authority may want some of these warning devices to come to his attention regularly. As decentralization of authority increases, however, it is common practice to expect a subordinate to keep his boss informed of impending difficulties rather than bother the manager with control data when conditions are satisfactory. A manager may ask to be notified when deviations from standard exceed a certain norm, thus applying the "exception principle" to control as well as to planning.

Moreover, it is common practice to use *pre-action* control for certain major moves, such as large capital expenditures or the appointment of key executives. Here again, the number of proposed actions that require confirmation will decrease as the degree of decentralization increases.

Still another kind of safeguard is to insist that lower levels of management use specific control devices even though an upper executive himself neither sets the standards nor receives reports on performance. A vice-president in charge of production, for example, may be vitally concerned that a reliable quality-inspection plan is in use, but he may take no personal part in its operation. He expects sufficient control data to be handy if the need for determining the cause of any particular problem arises.

Increased Importance of Self-control

As a manager delegates more authority to a subordinate and so shifts his control from the details of how work is done to an appraisal of overall results, the subordinate's responsibility for control increases. Details still have to be watched, but greater reliance is placed on the man down the line. He must control his own activities.

Control is partly a matter of attitude and habit. In a situation where centralized control has been the traditional practice, operating personnel naturally rely on senior executives or their staff to catch errors and initiate corrective action. If authority is then passed down to them, they need to formulate a new attitude. It may also be necessary to redirect the flow of information so that these people down the line have what they need in order to do their own controlling.

More Coaching, Less Ordering

Because the manager is no longer attempting to follow the details of daily operation and is not trying to solve a multitude of on-the-spot problems, he naturally issues fewer orders.

In place of ordering, he should cultivate a coaching relationship between himself and his subordinate. If standards have been set in terms of results, both the subordinate and the manager know what is expected. Hopefully, too, they fully agree on the desirability of achieving these results, and both men will interpret control information from the same viewpoint, especially if the subordinate has participated in setting standards and the method of measuring performance (as suggested in the preceding chapter). In these circumstances, the manager can easily become a coach. Instead of orders, he gives advice to the man on how to accomplish desired results. The control mechanism—standards, measurements, and reports—simply points to the need, and the boss's coaching tries to help the man fulfill it.

Ideally in this situation, the initiative for corrective action comes from the subordinate. To foster a relationship in which a subordinate is not reluctant to seek advice on tough problems, a manager should (1) avoid giving the impression that he feels an admission of difficulties is a sign of weakness, and (2) be careful not to make unilateral decisions that, in effect, take authority back from the subordinate.

Setting the Stage

The kinds of control and their associated relationships we are discussing grow only in a favorable climate. To create such an environment,

we must think out a clear set of objectives for a task that is being delegated and develop ways of measuring the achievement of these objectives.
Also necessary is a clear understanding about which policies, organization,
management methods, and other company rules *must* be followed and
which may be regarded only as recommended practice. Moreover, those
actions that require prior approval by a boss need to be so labeled. In
addition to the substantial amount of planning and organization clarification just outlined, high decentralization requires the right people. Subordinates able to perform the delegated duties must be selected, trained, and
properly motivated. An executive himself must be able and willing to
adjust his behavior, and the two particular personalities involved in each
delegation must be compatible and must trust each other. Remove or
significantly diminish any one of these aspects of an operating situation,
and there will be a corresponding reduction in the degree of decentralization that is possible without loss of control.

   To summarize: To decentralize without losing control we must really
know both what results we desire and how to measure the achievement
of those results. Then we should establish controls so that both supervising executives and men to whom tasks are delegated can keep track
of what is happening. These scorecard controls will typically be supplemented both by a few key measurements that give warning of impending
trouble and by insistence on pre-action approval. Such a control design will
function well only if it is accompanied by selecting, training, and motivating competent people; by developing means of self-control on the part
of subordinates over the many detailed operations for which freedom of
action has been granted; and by building a wholesome coaching relationship between managers and subordinates.

HARMONIZING DEPARTMENTATION WITH CONTROLS

   In the discussion of standards in Chapter 24, we emphasized the
need to relate controls directly to the work of specific managers or operators. In our discussions of budgets and of decentralization and at other
points, we have stressed the need to fit control mechanisms to company
organization. Actually, this kind of adjustment should work both ways.
Under some circumstances, the organization should be adjusted to facilitate control.

   In departmentation—that is, in the dividing up of managerial and
operating work into organizational units—two broad issues relate to control: (1) To what extent should control activities be separated from other
work, and (2) can operating units be created that are comparatively easy
to control? We shall take up the first of these issues later in this chapter
when we discuss the role of staff in control. Here our focus is on those
structures of operating work that lend themselves to control.

   The simplest suggestion for a way of departmentation that will facilitate control is to set the dividing line between departments or sections where work clearly passes from one stage to another. Thus a large steel company will have separate departments for mining ore, transporting ore, and making steel. On a smaller scale, a commercial laundry separates the contacting of customers from actually washing clothes and maintaining delivery equipment, because it is easy to make a *clean break* between these activities. But if the laundry attempted to departmentalize selling, delivery, and credit activities, it would run into difficulties because these activities are not clearly distinct. Control is easier when either the physical separation of operations or distinct stages of work make it simple for everyone to understand the organization structure.

A second suggestion is to create two or more operating units whose work is similar. A telephone company may set up a series of nearly identical divisions, or finance companies may organize each of many offices on the same general pattern. Control is enhanced because the results from any one office may be compared against the performance in the others. This deadly-parallel arrangement removes a great deal of personal opinion in setting standards. As we noted in the preceding chapter, it is important that employees accept standards as reasonable; and if one branch meets a given standard, an aura of reasonableness is created for that standard, and a wholesome attitude toward it tends to develop throughout all branches.

A proper grouping of activities can aid control in still another way, because by placing together activities that are closely interdependent, we can reduce the amount of "overhead" control that is required. When interrelated work is done in several different departments, we have to control with precision the quality and flow of work as it moves from one department to another. Even with the best of controls a mistake is likely to result in arguments and buck-passing. So a more satisfactory arrangement is to assign the interrelated work to a single department or "project team," or to an individual. Communication within the single unit is more direct and prompt and voluntary coordination is more likely to occur than when the work is fragmented. Members of the group become interested in

Fig. 27-1 *Establishing a series of virtually identical operating units introduces a deadly parallel and enhances control by making it easy to identify any unit that is out of line.*

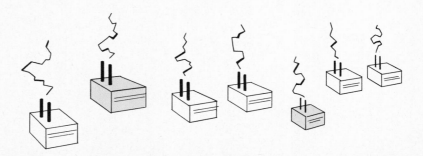

achieving good results, because their operation is no longer merely one little segment of a total process, and this increased interest leads to a substantial amount of self-control.

The product divisions of a decentralized company are perhaps the best example of this basic idea, which has already been discussed in earlier chapters. Each product division is in charge of its own production, selling, engineering, and other essential functions. Key people in the various departments know one another and exchange information freely and informally. If production falls behind schedule, the sales manager probably knows it almost as soon as the production manager, and so the former adjusts sales efforts and delivery promises accordingly. Or if price competition is very keen on a particular item, the engineering and production men find out about it and adapt their activities with an eye to cutting costs. In short, the division functions as a team. Elaborate controls are not imposed from someone several organizational levels higher; instead, control information is promptly available to the people best able to do something about it. The pressures for corrective action arise from the situation, not from the arbitrary requirements of some high official.

The same principle may be applied to smaller units of activity. The export department of a large food company, for instance, was experiencing long delays in processing orders and adjusting bills. Orders from twenty-five countries had to pass through separate units for translation, credit clearance, preparation of shipping documents, foreign exchange control, billing, and later collections. By changing to a series of small groups, each responsible for one or two countries, processing time was reduced from weeks to days. Each group identified with its customers, resolved questions by direct conversation, and volunteered help to avoid delays. The status of any order could be quickly determined. Self-control largely replaced the previously ineffective pressure from above.

In an organization where interdependent work is combined together in a single unit, supervisory control focuses on end results. Data on in-process activities do not pass through several layers of supervision, but are fed promptly to the appropriate operating team where they serve as a basis for self-regulation. Control is not only simplified, but there is also a much better chance for developing constructive attitudes toward control, as outlined in the preceding chapter.

KEEPING THE BOSS INFORMED

Our discussions both of delegating and of grouping interdependent activities together proposed reducing the number of control reports that go to higher-level executives. Relieving these managers of control over details gives them more time for other duties. But are we carrying this idea too far? Are we isolating the managers from actual operations so that they no longer have a feel for what is really happening?

A brief review of the kinds of information managers need will throw light on this question. The chief purpose of this rundown is to see whether higher-level executives need more control information than we have suggested. Generally speaking, our previous analyses have indicated that an executive needs information for the following purposes:

1) *Appraising results.* In the first place, an executive needs measurements of the results that have been accomplished compared with the objectives set up when duties were delegated to subordinate managers or operators. At high organization levels, the measurements may be broad and rather infrequent—hence, the fear of isolation mentioned earlier. Note, however, that such appraisals also include explanations of deviations from standard, and so they are likely to embrace a great deal of supplementary information on a nonrecurring basis.

2) *Warning of major troubles.* Even in a highly decentralized setup, few executives are content to discover that they are in major trouble only after it shows up in operating results. They may use any or all of the following means for avoiding such a predicament: (1) receiving regular reports about key barometers, (2) being notified when the barometers deviate outside a normal range, and (3) requiring subordinates to tell them of serious impending difficulties.

3) *Ensuring that policies and standard methods are being followed.* This step has particular reference to rules rather than to recommended practices. Such auditing of nonfinancial matters is usually done through sampling, often by staff people. An executive is sure to hear about it only when the rules are not being followed. But if the rules have been kept simple and few, as we have suggested, the amount of information an executive receives under this heading should be negligible.

4) *Data for dealing with exceptional problems.* When a manager uses the "exception principle"—that is, when he delegates authority to act only in normal cases and requires that exceptional problems be brought to his attention—he must, of course, also receive information about the circumstances in which the unusual problems arise. In dealing with these special cases, the manager will probably learn when operations are out of control. Extensive use of the exception principle, however, can be very time-consuming.

5) *Grounds for giving pre-action approvals.* Prudence dictates that at least certain major transactions be approved by a senior executive before a deal is closed. Such affairs may include large commitments for facilities or advertising, customer orders over a given size, the appointment of key personnel, the addition of a new product to the line, or any other single event that is of great consequence for the firm. Naturally, the executive involved will insist on having thorough background data before giving a judgment on such matters.

6) *Setting long-range plans, new policies, and the like.* How extensively an executive participates in these broad planning activities will vary according to his position. Still, all executives who free themselves of

detailed control will participate in broad planning to some degree. For this task they will need to have a sense of what is currently going on and what present problems are, in addition to a wealth of information on expected conditions in the future.

7) *Building up background for outside contacts.* All executives have at least occasional contact with customers, suppliers, bankers, legislators, competitors, or other outsiders who are important to the company. Top executives have many such contacts. Although no single executive is expected to know all the details of company operations, he cannot be naïve about them and still hope to make a favorable impression on these outsiders. It is good public relations if he just happens to be familiar with the current dealings between an outsider he is in contact with and the company. Consequently, executives are often given a "briefing" on relevant current information when it is known they will be seeing influential people.

8) *Coaching and umpiring.* If a manager is to coach his subordinates, to ask discerning questions, and to umpire disputes, he will need facts on each specific situation. He will have undoubtedly acquired a good bit of background in connection with the purposes we have already discussed. Nevertheless, from time to time, he will find it necessary to gather further facts in order to perform his supervisory functions effectively.

The preceding list does not paint a picture of a manager operating in isolation. Instead, from it we can sense how an executive moves from one important situation to another. He must regularly receive, then, only a few carefully selected reports; other reports may, of course, be sent to his office simply so that they will be easily available for reference. But he obtains the bulk of information as he needs it for dealing with each particular problem.

In passing, note that the notion that higher-level executives deal only with broad concepts is a mistake. The resolution of any problem requires dealing with specific, hard facts. The essential point is that an executive should not become bogged down with a lot of recurring detailed information, much of which will be of no use to him. Rather, information should be available someplace, and he should pick and choose from this reservoir as he needs it. An executive will not continue to need a certain type of information just because is was very important to him when he was wrestling with a particular problem. For if he does his work well, yesterday's problems will be set at rest and tomorrow's problems will be new ones.

USING STAFF IN CONTROL

Staff assists in performing managerial work. As we explained in Chapter 4, most staff assistance is concerned with planning, but it is not necessarily limited to this one phase of management. To what extent, then, should staff also be used in control?

A staff man becomes effective by giving useful advice. His specialized knowledge, judgment, discretion, and selfless dedication are all important in making him an influential person, and so the addition of control duties complicates the relationship of staff to the rest of an organization. People naturally dislike controls, for reasons we examined in the preceding chapter, and they are especially sensitive about who may legitimately exercise control. Consequently, as we think about assigning control duties to staff, we must be sure that the tasks are well suited to a person in an auxiliary position, and also that the control duties will not make it difficult for him to perform his other staff work.

Because the use of staff in control is a delicate arrangement, we shall consider different kinds of assignment, moving from clear-cut situations to those where the justification of a staff role is much more debatable.

Setting Standards

Staff is often used in setting control standards. Since the early days of Scientific Management, industrial engineers—by employing time and motion study—have set output standards, product engineers have set quality standards, and cost accountants have set detailed standards for product and process costs. Often a market-research man takes part in establishing sales quotas for individual salesmen, and in many government enterprises the budget director prepares tentative budget figures and has concurring authority on the final budget.

The reasons for using staff to help set standards are clear. Special skills, say, in engineering or research methodology, may be required. Besides, setting standards is often very time-consuming and an operating manager cannot give attention to all the necessary details. Of course, when we think of the whole range of control standards a company uses, it becomes evident that many standards are established without the aid of staff. When controls are formalized and detailed, however, staff men are likely to be active participants.

But the active participation of staff is also a major source of human problems with control. All too often the people being controlled feel that standards are unreasonable and that control pressure comes from illegitimate sources. The technical jargon of a staff man—say, an engineer—his preoccupation with certain aspects of a problem, the difference in his values, and his desire to make a good showing all contribute to a lack of confidence by workers and lower-level supervisors in the standards he sets. If, in addition, the staff man applies pressure to meet the standards and suggests corrective action, fuel is added to the flames. "Who does that slide-rule artist think he is?" is likely to be the response.

Further, if a staff man errs in being overzealous and "professional," a line manager often abdicates his duties. Frequently, the standards proposed by the staff man are accepted without question—provided the howl from those being controlled is not too loud. To be sure, in recent years lip service has been given to "selling the standards to the boys"; unfortunately, this effort often is unsupported by genuine desire and any deep understanding of what is involved in getting real acceptance. The remedy appears to lie in two directions: (1) Operating managers should be instructed to give more attention to the review of standards before they are put into effect and to discussion of these standards with people who will be exected to live up to them. (2) Staff men should be made to realize that their most constructive contribution lies in providing sound advice up and down the organizational hierarchy without usurping the functions that legitimately belong to the line managers.

Objective Appraisal

When control standards are expressed in terms of inches or dollars, the comparison of actual performance—as in auditing—is relatively simple. But measurements are often vague, and the allowances we must make— for illness, competition, and numerous other influences—are a matter

Fig. 27-2 Staff may take various roles in the control process. In these three examples, staff assumes the roles indicated by the color outline.

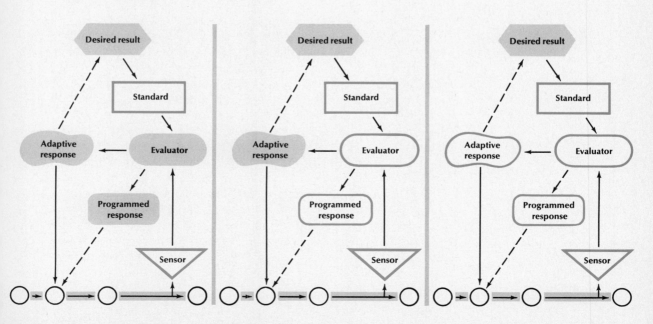

of subjective judgment. In this case, we must interpret available facts in order to arrive at an appraisal of performance. There is widespread debate about the value of staff participation in this kind of appraisal.

Operating managers, it is pointed out, often lack objectivity in making appraisals. They are committed to a program, and the drive they need to make the program succeed calls for optimism and a determination to "do the impossible." Besides, a manager must appraise the work of his personal friends, and he is sensitive to the effect of appraisal on their morale. On the other hand, it is argued that although a staff man has greater objectivity, he also has less intimate knowledge of the facts. He too may have a bias, especially if he is looking at a situation only from the point of view of, say, personnel, engineering, or public relations.

Management needs both kinds of appraisals. The objective views of staff men can be extremely valuable. But such appraisal finds its greatest use when we formulate *new* plans rather than when we attempt to control activities so that they conform to *existing* plans. Corrective action is predominantly a line activity, and inevitably, an operating manager will rely primarily on his own judgment. When formulating new plans, however, an operating manager normally has more time for contemplation, and in this activity both the appraisals and proposals of staff can make their greatest contribution.

Pre-action Control

In special circumstances, a staff unit, like an operating manager, may exercise pre-action control. The personnel department, for example, may have to give its approval before the sales manager can make a final commitment to hire a new salesman. Similarly, capital expenditures may require the approval of the controller, changes in organization the approval of the management-planning section, or property leases the approval of the legal staff. When pre-action control is exercised by a staff man, we say that he has "concurring authority."

Concurring authority has serious drawbacks, as we pointed out in Chapter 4. It is likely to slow down action, and it provides a means of stopping action without a corresponding push to get something done. It works best when the criteria on which a staff man can either concur on or reject a particular proposal are specified. For those transactions where a mistake would be very serious and where time is not critical, concurring authority may be desirable as a safety measure. The most serious difficulties with pre-action control by staff arise when a decision to turn down a proposal is based principally on subjective judgment. It is one thing for a controller to say that an advertising appropriation has been used up, and quite a different matter for him to turn down a proposal because he believes that advertising will not pay during a recession. An operating manager will be particularly annoyed by having his plans held up if he feels that a staff man lacks really distinctive technical competence in the area under judgment. An alternative arrangement is simply to have the staff man give advice; we may insist that a consultation take place, but we may provide that in the end the operating manager's judgment prevails. Clearly, discretion is needed in deciding when to grant pre-action control to staff.

Corrective Action

There are some control tasks where staff can be useful, as we have just seen. But experience also suggests a negative guide—keep staff out of corrective action. It is this phase of control that most clearly belongs to supervising executives. The prodding, the restraining, and the numerous adjustments to keep performance moving along according to plan are all functions of the boss. He has to judge which potential difficulties are most likely to cause serious difficulty, in what sequence these difficulties should be attacked, when additional pressure on his men will do more harm than good, and how several adjustments can be synchronized. A staff man has no place in this delicate part of a manager's activities. He may, of course, provide certain kinds of information; in fact, he may help design the control mechanism an operating executive uses. But he is likely to muddy the waters if he takes on himself the task of corrective action.

To summarize: Staff can make a unique contribution to control in auditing and in objective appraisal. In addition, under proper circumstances, staff may be very useful in handling clean-cut pre-action controls and in doing technical and detailed work in developing standards. But serious danger arises when staff goes beyond this. Actually setting standards, exercising concurring authority where personal judgment is paramount, and taking a lively part in corrective action push so far into what is generally regarded as the domain of legitimate line duties that resentment is apt to result; and deteriorations in human responses to control will probably more than offset the benefits. Moreover, the effectiveness of a staff man as a friendly advisor on other problems is likely to be undermined if he goes too far into control.

ENHANCING CONTROLS BY LEADERSHIP ACTION

Enforced standards communicate. Regardless of what a boss or a manual may say, those controls that are enforced are to the persons being controlled an unembellished guide to what they must do well and what they can do indifferently. They soon learn, for example, whether a "no smoking" rule means what it says or is merely a suggestion of desirable behavior. It is the action of the supervisor in disregarding or insisting that the standard be maintained that gives meaning to the control.

The permissive leader, discussed in Chapter 21, obviously faces a tough decision on which control standards he will seek to enforce. If he does not follow up on, say, established quotas, antipollution standards, or routine matters of attendance his subordinates will infer that he is indifferent to their actions in such areas. This kind of permissiveness results in no control. On the other hand, if he consistently checks up on deviations of actual performance from standard but then confines his response to mild suggestions for improvement, the amount of control will be a function of the motivation of the subordinate. Of course, even a permissive leader may single out a few subjects on which no permissiveness is tolerated; the key here is to pick these subjects carefully.

A wise senior executive who each month *does* review actual performance against the budget with each of his division managers has observed (1) that the men try to keep performance up to the budget standards so that they will not have to make an embarrassing explanation of why they failed to do so, and (2) that if there are unfavorable variances they try to start corrective action before each meeting so that they can explain what they are doing about the deviations from standard. These budgets, then, influence the behavior of the division managers, but the close attention of the president to the budgetary system is an important stimulus in bringing this about.

For a number of years, this same company prepared budgets on a three-year basis. When it was found that little use was made of the budget for the second and third year the president insisted that they be discontinued. In part, he was trying to save the expense of preparing the budgets for the second and third year, but principally he wanted to get rid of any nominal control devices that were not in fact used.

A match between leadership style and the number and nature of controls is essential to both the effectiveness of the controls and the success of the leader.[1]

DESIGNING A COMMUNICATION NETWORK THAT SUPPORTS CONTROLS

A flood of information flows throughout an organization by informal, face-to-face communication. To be assured of good control, however, we need a system of regular, formal reports. Every manager should give some attention to whether the report system in his department and

[1] Other connections between leadership action and controls have been discussed in the last part of the preceding chapter.

company provides the right kind of information, to the right people, and at the right time to enable his controls to work effectively.

Feedback Loops

The myriad of controls that exist within a company give rise to a diversity of arrangements for information feedback. As a general principle, it is desirable to have feedback loops as short and quick as possible. This principle is based partly on the idea that self-control—or, at least, control within relatively small operating units—is the best way to get corrective action. An elaborate, centrally administered flow of control information is not desirable. A second general reason for short, quick feedbacks is well illustrated in this quotation from J. W. Forrester:

> *The study of feedback systems deals with the way information is used for the purpose of control. It helps us understand how the amount of corrective action and the time delays in interconnected systems can lead to unstable fluctuation. Driving an automobile provides a good example:*
>
> *The information and control loop extends from steering wheel, to auto, to street, to eye, to hand, and back to steering wheel. Suppose the driver were blindfolded and drove only by instructions from his front seat companion. The resulting information delay and distortion would cause erratic driving. If the blindfolded driver could get instructions only on where he had been from a companion who could see only through the rear window, his driving would be even more erratic.*
>
> *Yet this is analogous to the situation in business. Top executives do not see the salesmen calling on customers, don't see the prospective buyers watching a TV commercial. They do not attend the board meetings of competitors. They do not have a clear view of the road ahead. The only thing they can tell with reasonable certainty (and*

Fig. 27-3 *Relying on control reports about what has already happened is as hazardous as trying to steer a ship through the night by shining a searchlight over the wake.*

*even here there is sometimes doubt) is what happened to wages,
sales, material costs, interest rates, and so on last year.*[2]

In Chapter 24 we suggested that, insofar as possible, controls should
be linked directly with a single manager or operator. Control data, then,
should normally go to this man first, or at least simultaneously with any
other distribution. In other words, we should not feed control data to a
boss or someone else in a position of authority so that he may put a
man on the spot unless we have also given the man the same facts. The
vast bulk of control data can simply stop with the person being controlled. Certain information, however, will also go to the supervising
executive, as we suggested in the earlier part of this chapter.

Periodic Review of Report Flow

From time to time the content, receipt, and timing of each control
report should be examined, for two reasons: (1) to ensure that the right
persons are getting the available information and (2) to try to discover
economies in the preparation and distribution of reports.

The inertia in report systems is by no means all bad. It takes people
some time to become familiar with the content and form of a given
report, and there is a great advantage in being able to refer quickly to
information. Besides, an executive often wants to know whether certain
data have, or have not, gone to his subordinates and to other executives
because this affects the need for him to pass on key control information. Consequently, some stability in the overall communication structure
is useful. Still, company operations change and the needs for data change,
and so periodic review of the report system is desirable.

BALANCING THE CONTROL STRUCTURE

Typically a manager deals with problems of control as separate,
specific issues. One time his attention may be focused, say, on the quality
of service to foreign customers; at another time, the issue may be the
investment in inventories; and so forth. At least occasionally, however,
he should consider all these separate controls in their totality. What is
the combined impact of all controls at work at the same time?

Danger of a Multiplicity of Controls

The effectiveness of any one control depends in part on how
many other controls are already in operation. For example, the manager
of a maintenance department had taken pride for years in keeping the

[2]"Industrial Dynamics," *Harvard Business Review* (July 1958), p. 40.

machinery in his plant in good operating condition. He watched closely the reports on production delays due to machine breakdowns. Then, when a new management set up budgetary control on expenses, asked for reports on scheduled time versus actual time spent on jobs, insisted on schedules of preventive maintenance by types of equipment, and installed a plan of semiannual performance ratings for each employee, the company experienced more trouble with machine breakdowns than formerly. The maintenance manager's explanation was that he now had so many different things to watch that he could not give his prime attention to keeping the machines running. This was partly just a negative reaction to additional controls, but it also suggests that we may run into "diminishing productivity" as we multiply the number of controls.

In extreme situations, an additional control may be "the straw that breaks the camel's back." Just as a tax on tea was the final irritation that led to the Boston Tea Party, one more control imposed by the home office on the way time is spent has caused many a salesman to quit.

There is no simple rule to alert us when there are too many controls. The point of superfluity depends on the nature of the job, the degree of delegation, the traditions of the company, the ways controls are administered, and other factors. Clearly, though, the entire control system should be taken into account when we think about any one control.

Direct and Indirect Effects

A control over one phase of operations may lead to less attention to other aspects. As every student knows from personal experience in writing reports, if the emphasis is on length, quality is likely to suffer, and vice versa. Similarly in an office or a hospital, when control puts pressure on employees to increase output, the quality of work, care of equipment, and prevention of spoilage of material are apt to be neglected. It is like squeezing a balloon—as one part is compressed, another part expands.

In designing controls, then, we should give attention to the indirect as well as the direct effects. If a particular control tends to produce indirect effects that are deleterious, complementary controls may be called for. One company, for instance, became concerned about delays in production caused by a lack of purchased parts. A special report was introduced that listed the reasons for every production delay, and this served as an effective control on the service the purchasing department provided the production department. Within a few months, the number of instances of "Materials not available" almost disappeared. Soon, however, the treasurer discovered that raw material inventories had gone up 25 percent. The purchasing agent, responding to the new control, was playing safe and ordering an ample stock of materials well in advance of needs. Therefore, still another control on the size of inventory was added. Only by instituting both controls and keeping them in balance was it practical to tighten up on this situation.

One of the greatest difficulties in keeping a balance among controls is that some things are much easier to measure than others. The actual orders salesmen receive or the expenses incurred in a particular department are quantitative figures that are relatively easy to compile; consequently, the tendency is natural to use such figures for control purposes. Intangible results, such as customer goodwill or cooperation with other departments, are more difficult to measure. This discrepancy in ease of measurement tends to result in an overemphasis on the tangible aspects of the work. Then, if controls are tightened on these observable elements, the result may be an even greater imbalance. Management must be ever alert to this danger. The greatest opportunities for substantial improvement in the control process lie in designing controls that will produce balanced results.

Matching Control Structure to Hierarchy of Plans

The concept of hierarchy of objectives, developed in Chapter 17, explains how the objectives of a company are narrowed in each successive delegation from president to low-level operator. Each person has his particular objectives that contribute to the broader objectives of his section or department, and the objectives of the department, in turn, contribute to the even broader objectives of the whole company. Scorecard controls should match up with these objectives. Theoretically a sound hierarchy of objectives, coupled with a control structure that measures the performance of each unit against its goals, provides an integrated mechanism for channeling the diverse activities of a firm toward a common set of objectives.

If the complete plans for the construction of a new building, for example, are properly integrated, and inspections are made of the work of the foundation subcontractor, the structural steel subcontractor, the electrical subcontractor, and everyone else who has a particular part to contribute to the total structure, the final results should be a building as conceived by the architect.

Unfortunately, this sort of matching of the control structure with company objectives is hard to achieve. One common source of difficulty stems from failure to readjust controls as objectives are changed. Take even the simple matter of a cutback in the sales of a particular line of products due to a change in competition or technology. It is entirely possible that although the overall income and expense objectives will be adjusted to the new conditions, the control standards for engineering and other service departments will remain unchanged. Or suppose the president of a company decides to increase the number of broadly trained young men in the organization as a reservoir for filling top management positions. If the job specifications that control the men who actually hire college students are not adjusted, the specific actions at the various recruiting centers will not be attuned to the new objective.

The several steps involved in translating the new company objective into revised subobjectives for different divisions of the company, securing understanding and acceptance of these revised objectives, adjusting the control standards and measurements accordingly, and using the control mechanism so that it actually influences behavior—all take time and effort. In extreme cases, the inertia is so great that inconsistency between company objectives and the controls that are really in effect continues indefinitely.

Another kind of discrepancy between a control structure and hierarchy of objectives concerns amount of detail. If the objectives of a particular division or department are stated in general terms, with the understanding that the handling of detail has been delegated to the manager of that unit, then the measurements should also be general. To use detailed controls in that situation would undermine the delegation and cause a great deal of confusion about who was responsible for what. On the other hand, if the objectives of a particular unit are stated in very specific terms, then there should be a corresponding specificity in the controls.

RELATING CONTROL TO NEW PLANNING

Two types of control standard were discussed in Chapter 24—signals to indicate whether work is proceeding satisfactorily while the operation is still in progress, and scorecards to evaluate results after the work is completed. Normally signals are used to adjust activities so that a predetermined objective will be achieved. A thermostat turns heat on or off, bacteria tests in a milk plant flash warnings to the processing units and to the whole collection system, and so forth. Corrective action may involve detailed planning, renewed motivation, and other managerial acts. In this sense, control may prompt action in any of the other managerial processes. Nevertheless, objectives usually remain the same, and the adjustments are like those of a ship's pilot who modifies his course with the winds and tide to reach home port. Only if there is a terrible storm or breakdown is the pilot likely to change (replan) his destination.

Controls of the scorecard variety almost always lead to planning. For example, if a sales campaign is only partially successful, both objectives and methods are likely to be modified; similarly, executive development activities planned for next year will be strongly influenced by an appraisal of results achieved this year. In situations such as these, control reports serve as a basis for an entirely new cycle of managerial activity—planning, perhaps organizing, leading, and controlling the new activities.

But this concept—that scorecard controls rather than signal controls are of principal use in planning—needs one important qualification. Often we must lay plans for new activities before a present cycle is completed. University budgets, for example, are often prepared in preliminary form in December and January for the following school year; this means that the results of the fall-semester activities are not yet known, and the spring semester has not even begun, when the first steps of planning for new courses and size of classes have to be taken. Automobile companies have an even greater lead time in planning for their new models; commitments on design and tooling, though not quantity, are often made with little or no measure of the popularity of the current year's model. When new plans must be made before the results of old ones are known, the results must be predicted. Control information of the signal type is naturally used in making these predictions. In some situations, then, we use information on how we are doing both as a guide to current operations and as part of the data on which the outcome of present and new plans are predicted.

With control data being used for planning, we see again the never-ending cycle of management—one round of planning, leading, and controlling, merging into a subsequent round. The service of control to planning, however, should not be exaggerated. If we want planning to be dynamic, we must consider new ways of performing work. Operating conditions change, and future opportunities may improve or diminish; consequently, more complete, or different, information is often needed for planning than control activities provide.

Occasionally confusion arises when the purpose of compiling data is not recognized. An executive may take information designed for planning purposes and try to use it for control. If such information is not easily related to established objectives or provided at a time and place when corrective action is feasible, the control effort may do more harm than good. An over-zealous vice-president of a furniture manufacturing company, for example, used some expense ratios projected for a new method of operation as a standard in appraising current activities; this discouraged and disgusted the men in the plant because they felt the new standards did not apply to their current operations. On the other hand, we may sacrifice accuracy for promptness in compiling control data, thereby limiting the value of our figures for planning. We can usually avoid such difficulties by clearly understanding the nature and purpose of a measurement, and when a report is to serve a dual purpose for planning and control, we need to take special care in its interpretation.

CONCLUSION

The issues discussed in this chapter clearly demonstrate how inextricably controlling affects, and is affected by, planning, organizing, and leading. A similar interdependence exists among all phases of management.

No great purpose is served by debating which phase of management is the most important. To be sure, advocates for different views can be found; for example, some stress control as the essential function of management, others contend that leadership is the essence, and recently we often hear people equate decision-making with managing. When pressed, such advocates recognize that management has many facets; usually they assume that if their specialty is properly performed, other phases will fall in line. Such one-sided views may be appropriate for specialized research or speech-making, but they are dangerous for a man actually engaged in managing.

When we are in an operating job we should be sensitive both to problems and to potential benefits of *all* phases of management—organizing, planning, leading, and controlling. Then we should adjust the emphasis on each depending upon the needs of the specific situation. As many examples throughout this book clearly indicate, the manager who sees the total configuration is in the best position to act wisely in any one area. An approach to effective *synthesis* of phases of management is examined in the next chapter.

FOR CLASS DISCUSSION

Questions

1) In what ways do approaches to organizing and planning like "management-by-objectives" affect the design and implementation of control systems?

2) Many department stores that have opened suburban branches consider each branch simply as an additional opportunity to contact customers; the buying, advertising, credit, accounting, and most other activities are performed at one location by centralized divisions. In contrast, Race Brothers has branches in separate communities up to 150 miles from the state capital where its main store is located. Because of this dispersion, each branch is a fully integrated unit with its own buying, credit, accounting, delivery, and so on. The main store provides a variety of services for all branches, but each branch is expected to operate as an independent unit. Discuss the differences in control systems you would recommend for a company with suburban branches and for Race Brothers.

3) How do recent trends towards wide diversification if not conglomeration affect the design and implementation of sound control systems?

4) A major reason for removing a particular group of activities from an operating unit and turning them over to an auxiliary divi-

sion is to ensure that these activities receive adequate attention. Would it not be as effective and less expensive to provide the operating unit with the incentive needed to ensure adequate attention by stressing that these activities will be subject to close scrutiny in the evaluation of the operating unit? Discuss the pros and cons of this viewpoint.

5) The use of staff experts in control may add considerable objectivity and expertise to the control process. What are the likely reactions to such staff work by the line managers whose performance is involved? How would you deal with these reactions?

6) Make a list, without referring to the text, of what you regard as key factors that must be considered in designing and using a sound control system. Ask yourself where else in the book, besides Part Six, each item has been discussed. You will probably find that virtually all of the items were considered in Parts One to Five. What does this tell you about the design and use of control systems?

7) "In their desire to make certain that their subordinates do not make unwise decisions, some managers create such extensive controls that no decisions at all are really made by the subordinates in question." What do you think of this statement? How does a manager estimate the losses from "over-control"?

8) In relating controls to the hierarchy of plans should one attempt to evaluate the results of programs that are "means" of achieving higher-order "ends," or should the controls be tied to the ends themselves?

Cases

For cases involving issues covered in this chapter, see especially the following. Particularly relevant questions are listed after each case.

General Machinery Corporation (p. 130), 18
Scott-Davis Corporation (p. 227), 18
Gerald Clark (p. 234), 18, 19
Harrogate Asphalt Products, Ltd.—AR (p. 557), 16
Texas-Northern Pipeline Company (p. 665), 10

FOR FURTHER READING

Ackoff, R.L., *A Concept of Corporate Planning*. New York: John Wiley & Sons, Inc., 1970, Chap. 6. *Observations on tying an information system to management needs for control data.*

Hill, W.A., and D. Egan, eds., *Readings in Organizational Theory*. Boston: Allyn & Bacon, Inc., 1966, Part VI. *Behavioral studies of evaluation and control in large organizations.*

Holden, P.E., C.A. Pederson, and G.E. Germane, *Top Management*. New York: McGraw-Hill Book Company, 1968, Chaps. 2, 5, and 6. *Central control in large enterprises; results are compared with those of a similar study twenty-five years ago.*

Jerome, W.T., *Executive Control*. New York: John Wiley & Sons, Inc., 1961. *Views control as dynamic catalyst in total management process. Part V describes du Pont, General Electric, and Koppers Company approaches to control.*

Prince, T.R., *Information Systems for Management Planning and Control*, rev. ed. Homewood, Ill.: Richard D. Irwin, Inc., 1970. *Focuses on designing the internal information flow for planning and control purposes.*

Schoderbek, P.P., ed., *Management Systems*. New York: John Wiley & Sons, Inc., 1967, Parts VII–XI. *Well-selected articles on management control systems, the use of computers in such systems, simulation, and measurement.*

Case Studies

 **TEXAS-NORTHERN PIPELINE COMPANY**

Texas-Northern Pipeline Company engages in transportation of liquid petroleum products (gasoline, jet fuel, other light oils) in interstate commerce from the oil fields and refineries in East Texas northward to the metropolitan districts of St. Louis, Minneapolis, St. Paul, and Milwaukee. This case reports on efforts by the top management of the company to control operations in each of six divisions, and to evaluate the performance of division managers. A division in this company consists of a geographic area defined by one section of the line. For example, the Central division covers a distance of four hundred miles along the pipe, together with narrow right-of-way on either side, in the states of Missouri and Iowa.

Briefly, a pipeline is operated from pumping stations at intervals along the line. The first pumping station is located at the output station of a refinery. There the product is drawn from specified storage tanks by pumpers, men who adjust the correct intake valves, draw off liquid periodically, perform chemical or color tests, and operate the pumps themselves. At each station along the line, pumpers perform the same duties. A pumping station is a complex set of machines that may cost several million dollars to construct. The pipeline itself is a costly capital investment, involving cost of pipe and construction, cost of land, and expensive maintenance. Line maintenance is important for two reasons. Break and spillage may cost several hundred thousand dollars, but shutdown and delay may be equally expensive. This is due to the extremely high cost of storage—so high that the storage tank farm at a refinery might have space for only two or three days' production. The storage capacity at the receiving terminal may equal only four or five days of consumption supply. Thus if the pipeline should be stopped for emergencies, the cost of idle storage tanks is great. If the emergencies should last for five days, much more money may be lost in shutting down refineries, lost sales to customers, or damage to customers' own operations. At the Milwaukee Terminal on Lake Michigan, for example, the storage tanks hold about six days' deliveries into Great Lakes tankers. Delay beyond this limit would cost heavily in idle capital investment in ships.

"It is for all of these reasons," states A.F. Coriano, Texas-Northern's president,

> that we must be extremely precise in our control of operations and costs. Essentially, the work of a pipeline is done in two categories: operations and maintenance. Reporting to the district manager are an operations manager and a maintenance manager. Each of these has reporting to him a pipeline supervisor and a pump and engine supervisor.
>
> Two years ago, our company spent about ten months in instituting a system of objectives for the purpose of evaluating division managers. It was our general plan that Mr. Harrison, the director of maintenance here in headquarters, would draw up a list of objectives that he thought every division manager should meet if his performance is to be considered satisfactory. Mr. Jackson [director of operations] would do the same. After checking these with me for approval, they would go out to the divisions and get the approval of the six division managers. I would also have Douglas Saunders, our management systems director in headquarters, advise the operations and maintenance directors, before they went to the regions. The theory here is that if district managers have agreed in advance to a set of objective criteria, there would be no personal ugliness attached when, at the end of the year, one of the standards may not be met. It would simply be a matter of saying, "Well, we both agreed at the beginning that total pipeline maintenance costs would be not more than $630 per mile of pipeline. If it averages $700 a mile in the Southern district, that's that." It is an objective fact to be dealt with. Not a personal blame by my staff put on the divisions.
>
> After all parties had agreed, we set up a set of sixty-two standards for all divisions, ranging all the way from the broad areas of personnel administration to public relations and operations. Here for example are thirteen of the standards, in this case applicable to the maintenance function [Exhibit 2]. Or, in the case of Public Relations, we would judge the manager on such items as how many times a year he visits with municipal officials in his area, how many presenta-

*tions he makes at local schools, and the number of favorable items
about our company that appear in local newspapers during the year.*

*The advantage of such a system of controls is that the top man-
agement of the company, such as myself and the financial vice-
president, can very quickly look across one sheet of paper to detect
where there is trouble in a division. On that sheet, the six divisions
are listed across the top. Down the left are listed the sixty-two control standards. Opposite each standard, in red, is the quantitative
level expected for that item. For example, in the newspaper publicity
area mentioned earlier, performance is considered satisfactory when
at least two articles about Texas-Northern appear in any one year.
Or, in the maintenance area [Exhibit 2] performance is satisfactory
when corrosion leaks in the line do not exceed thirty-five per one
hundred miles of pipeline operated.*

*Under each division's column are listed the actual performance of
that division. Performances rated satisfactory or above are listed in
black and those below satisfactory in red. As the eye scans down a
column, one can get a complete and quick picture of what went
wrong in that division. Or, if one scans across columns, he can see
instantly which Division is performing below satisfaction and which
above. This kind of document enables us to manage by exception.
We do not have to have our minds filled with thousands of details
and figures. The factors for success are already there. The figures are
all there. The exceptions are highlighted. We can evaluate the whole
company in a few hours and can have letters of inquiry going out
within a day, asking why something went wrong. This is a real help
to us and to the divisions.*

Setting Expense-Control Standards

During the process of setting standards, Richard Harrison included
two standards that dealt with the cost of maintenance. One of these
specified that the total cost of maintaining the pipeline should not exceed
$680 per mile, the other specified that the total cost of maintaining
pumps and engines should not exceed $720 for each pump maintained
in the district pumping stations. These standards were set by taking the
average costs throughout the company for the past year. Harrison also
obtained three man-months' time of one of the company's best maintenance engineers to adjust the averages slightly, based on good engineering (not historical) estimates. Both of the standards were subsequently
changed.

Before Harrison took these standards to the Division managers for
their agreement, he met with both Coriano and Saunders to obtain their
agreement. Saunders, a graduate of M.I.T. and a specialist in operations
research, had been with the company for seven years and had himself
spent much time out in the divisions solving operating problems. He raised
the point that the two figures—total cost of maintenance in the pipeline

category (3.3 in Exhibit 2) and the pump and engine category (3.6 in Exhibit 2)—were not sufficient for management control purposes.

> Maintenance [Saunders said] is a very complex matter. If we get a lump sum figure, it will be practically useless to top management. All we could say is "Your maintenance cost is too high on pumps (or the pipeline)." We ought to include at least the following four items:
>
> **1)** A standard for labor cost on line maintenance.
> **2)** A standard for materials costs on line maintenance.
> **3)** A standard for labor cost on pump and engine maintenance.
> **4)** A standard for materials costs on pump and engine maintenance.
>
> The total cost includes more than labor and materials, but these are the major elements.

After a rather long discussion, the president said, "Well, it just seems that you two cannot agree on this matter. My own inclination is that we in headquarters must be informed—we cannot really make sense when we speak if we aren't. I believe we should include these additional items." As Harrison said afterward, "That settled that." The items were included in the finally adopted set of standards (3.1, 3.2, 3.4, and 3.5 in Exhibit 2).

Saunders called attention to one other kind of discrepancy in the control standards.

> Take a look at the two standards we would have on maintenance labor [3.1 and 3.4 in Exhibit 2]. They specify that the total labor cost of maintaining a mile of line, or in maintaining a pump, shall be a certain amount. Again, we have no way to know why labor cost is either good or bad. One district manager may be very good at finding ways to pay his labor less (less overtime, utilizing the proper grades of laborer on lower priced work, and so on), but very bad at getting his labor to be productive while they work. So we need some standards to let us know if the division manager is using his workers effectively. In addition to the total money amount spent on labor, I propose that we add two other items:
>
> **1)** A standard for the actual man-hours, or people, used in pipeline work.
> **2)** A standard for the actual man-hours, or people, used in pump and engine work.

These two standards later were incorporated into the finally approved set of standards (3.7 and 3.8 in Exhibit 2).

Mr. Coriano had one other suggestion to make at the meeting. He believed that most of the standards set by Harrison and Saunders were technically accurate. That is, they represent the best that accountants and engineers can do to represent what can and ought to happen in operation and maintenance of the line. But there is another aspect to standards you have overlooked. They are intended to capture the attention and imagination of people whom we want to achieve them. No man will exceed an easy goal—a pushover. How have you set these in relation to a man's extra effort—the kind one has to stretch to achieve?

Harrison and Saunders agreed that they had set the standards as if a division manager and his men were working at a normal pace. "Just what 'normal' is," Harrison said, "is not too clear. But I think it means a man working with average energy at a job he hopes to accomplish."

Coriano said that eventually he got Harrison and Saunders to agree to raising the achievement levels on five items.

I told them that achievement just didn't occur without challenge. That I would be glad to spend two days of my time looking at all the standards, working out challenging levels item by item. We ended up, for example, by raising the level of performance on total cost of maintaining pipeline and engines. The acceptable cost for pipeline maintenance was lowered from $680 a mile to $630. Ditto for pumps and engines—from $720 per pump to $670.

Later, at a meeting of all division managers, I explained that the forces beyond our control are continuously setting standards for the whole company that are exacting—the market forces of supply and demand, as well as the Interstate Commerce Commission, will penalize the company unless we can keep our operations efficient and costs down. There was a certain amount of reaction against both the standards we put into the list and against the level we specified for each standard. However, in the end I told them that they could change them if they really wanted to. At that point, they all seemed to see both the necessity for checkpoints by headquarters and for not so easily attainable performance levels.

Problems in Evaluation of Performance

Coriano describes how the management-by-exception system has worked out:

We have now been operating under the standards using management by exception for three years. No system is perfect. I will give you some examples of things we have had to contend with. I'd also be interested in any suggestions for improving our system.

At the end of last year, Burton Jackson, our controller, sent out a routine inquiry to Paul Wheatley, division manager in the Central division. Under the procedures, the whole results tabulation is sent *in multiple copies to members of top management. Each of us had some set of items to watch. Jackson watches the expense items. As he scanned the control report, he noted that in the Central division, maintenance labor on the line was $325 per mile, entered in red. It was the only red figure in the row for line maintenance labor. All other divisions were in the black. So Jackson sent out the letter to Wheatley with a list of his exceptions. Harrison also sent his letter for exceptions in the operating section of the report, and our director of public relations sent out his letter on the public relations section.*

I thought Wheatley would split a vein. He called me on the telephone and said that the system was grossly unfair. That his total cost of maintenance was under $630 per mile and that that performance was well within our other standard [3.3 in Exhibit 2]. He said that they had had a flu epidemic in Missouri last year and that this caused him to pay the nonafflicted workers overtime. He also said, "The real need of the company is to have low total maintenance cost. I performed according to the spirit of that need by doing extra hard work myself to invent ways to save on the materials factor in maintenance. I even gave special engineering time myself to devise ways of repairing the line without ordering new sections of

Exhibit 1 *Organization Chart,
Texas-Northern Pipeline Company*

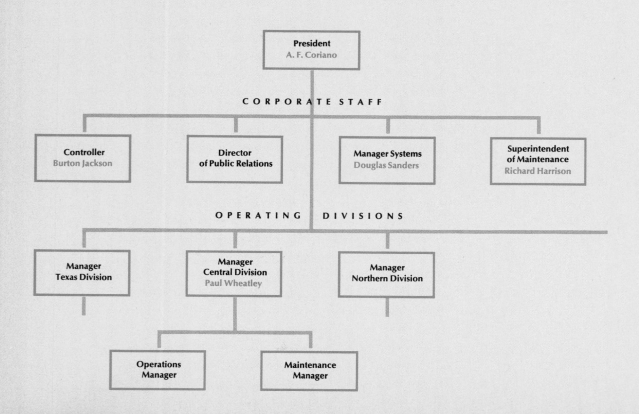

pipe, just to save money and show a low total maintenance figure. Look at my performance on the materials cost—$220 a mile of pipe. That's pretty good [see 3.2 in Exhibit 2]."

I assured Wheatley that we are understanding when he tells us what happened about the flu epidemic and congratulated him on the good performance in materials. That didn't seem to do a lot of good. He said that as the headquarters people like Jackson and Harrison scan the reports they form impressions without knowing the facts. That under the guise of "management by exception" or "management by objective" they look for the red figures in a report, send out their letters of inquiry, and get a negative picture of his operating abilities. Of course, I assured him that the letter was one of inquiry.

Wheatley suggested that the way to correct this situation is simply to remove the standards for materials and labor [3.1, 3.2, 3.4, and 3.5 in Exhibit 2] from the control standards and the evaluation report; and to leave only the total maintenance figure [3.3 and 3.6 in Exhibit 2]. Actually, I will have to give this some more thought. That would defeat the original arguments we settled when we included them. This is one alternative for overcoming this, but I'm hoping I can achieve both Wheatley's and Saunders' objectives.

Another problem is actually in Wheatley's favor. On that total maintenance standard, his was the only district that performed within the $630 per mile of pipe. All the others were in red. We circulate the whole evaluation report to all division managers, and I got two suggestions from different divisions that this target was too high. I must admit that I don't like to see a horizontal row of figures all in red. It looks like something is wrong with the company. And the two division managers complained that it looks like there's something wrong with them. On the other hand, my "stretch" theory worked with Wheatley. His back was against the wall and he devoted a lot of creativity and energy to savings on the use of materials, just to make a good showing on his total cost. Maybe the other division managers ought to do that.

These are typical examples of the most frequent complaints. Perhaps we should take a look at the system again, to see if it needs changing.

Exhibit 2 *Standards of Performance,* *
Texas-Northern Pipeline Company

3. MAINTENANCE STANDARDS

It is the general objective of Texas-Northern Pipeline Company to maintain both pipelines and pumping stations in such condition that

*The list contains standards that appear in the Maintenance section of the *Standards Manual.* Other sections are Safety, Personnel Administration, Operations, Public Relations, and Management Communication. Of the sixty-two standards in the entire division list, thirteen appear in the Maintenance section.

(1) our customers receive deliveries on time and with certainty, (2) our employees operate with safety to themselves and the public, and (3) our company achieves pipeline transportation with efficient use of resources and lack of waste. To implement these general objectives, each division manager is expected to accomplish the following standard objectives:

3.1 The labor cost for maintaining pipeline should be not more than $300 per year per mile of pipe maintained.

3.2 The materials used for maintaining pipeline should amount to not more than $280 per mile of pipe maintained.

3.3 The total cost of maintaining pipe should be not more than $630 per year per mile of pipe maintained.

3.4 The labor cost for maintaining pumps and engines should be not more than $250 per year per pump maintained.

3.5 The materials used for maintaining pumps and engines should be not more than $440 per pump unit maintained.

3.6 The total cost of maintaining pumps and engines should be not more than $670 per pump unit maintained.

3.7 Manpower used in line maintenance should be not more than 4.25 employees per 100 miles of pipeline.

3.8 Manpower used in pump and engine maintenance should be not more than 3.25 employees per 100 pump units maintained.

3.9 Materials consumed in maintenance of pumps and engines should not exceed $13,500 annually per employee.

3.10 Corrosion leaks should not exceed 35 per year per 100 miles of pipeline operated.

3.11 Accidental damage to pipelines should not exceed 4 incidents per 100 miles of pipe operated.

3.12 Unrecovered oil per leak should not exceed 75 percent of initial loss.

3.13 Warehouse turnover (except pipe) should be at least 200 percent per year.

FOR DISCUSSION AND REPORT-WRITING

Organizing: Structural Design

1) Study both the organization chart and Coriano's actions, and those of Saunders, Jackson, and Harrison. In what way is the corporate staff in Texas-Northern used? Can you see advantages? Disadvantages?

2) Study these same actions and try to deduce from them the "common-law" authority of operating division managers. What is this authority? How can you tell?

Human Factors in Organizing

3) What do you think of Coriano's theory of motivation? What basic human need or attribute might cause men to behave like that? Why didn't the Division managers like the standard set according to this theory?

4) Why did Wheatley "almost split a vein"? On the whole, in this specific situation, is it good or bad for the company for a division manager to act like this?

Planning: Elements of Decision-Making

5) From the facts in the case, diagnose why the Central district line maintenance labor expense was $325 per mile. What is the root cause? What are the higher-level goals? Explain how diagnosis is an inevitable part of every control problem.

Planning: Decision-Making in an Enterprise

6) Explain how the control standards in this case relate to "standing plans." Pick some specific standards to show the advantages of such standing plans.

Leading

7) If you were president of Texas-Northern, what steps might you take to achieve the voluntary cooperation of Wheatley in making the control standards work in practice?

Measuring and Controlling

8) What do you think of the "par" level that was set for various controls in this company? Can you think of some alternative way of stating the par that might overcome some of the problems the company is having with its system?

9) What do you think of Coriano's participation process in setting the control standards? Give examples of specific procedures or actions in the case. Could this be improved?

10) From Exhibit 2, draw a small diagram of the highest goals in the maintenance area, relating them in a means-end chain to the lower ones— particularly for items 3.1 through 3.9. You will see that these form a hierarchy of goals. What is meant by a hierarchy and how does this relate to the question of comprehensiveness (that is, "how many standards should be included" in a control system)?

11) Has the company used qualitative or quantitative standards, or both? Cite examples. What are the advantages of quantification (cite examples from the case to show these advantages)?

12) *Summary Report Question, Part Six:* Write a report that first comments on how Texas-Northern has accomplished the steps in the control process—the setting of standards (including characteristics, par levels, and selection of strategic points). On the basis of the description of these substeps in the text, show the advantages or disadvantages of the way this particular company is designing its control system.

Summary Question for Solution
of the Case as a Whole

13) If you were president of Texas-Northern, give recommendations with regard to: (1) what kind of authority you would assign to headquarters staff and division managers; (2) what kinds of procedures you would adopt for instituting and implementing the control system; and (3) how you would respond to Wheatley.

 CONSOLIDATED INSTRUMENTS—B

Consolidated Instruments (CI) began as a producer of precision control devices for the petroleum industry. During World War II its president, Homer Peake, successfully developed several important control devices used in aircraft and by 1970, through internal developments and acquisitions, Peake and his successor, David Myers, had broadened CI's market still further. With its most recent acquisition of the PCD (Pollution Control Devices) Company, CI found itself listed in *Fortune* magazine's list of the five hundred largest corporations in the United States. The company now designs and produces control devices and markets them not only to the oil and chemical industries, but also to the food processing, aircraft, space, and missile industries.

The newly acquired PCD Company differs from other parts of CI in that it is the only business that manufactures the end-products in which control devices are used. When acquired, there was considerable debate as to how PCD should be integrated into the existing organization, and it was finally decided to permit it to remain a separate division reporting directly to the president. Given its sales of only $28,000,000, PCD might more properly have been made a part of one of the three existing divisions (see Exhibit 1).

There was a double reason for maintaining PCD's separate identity. First, although PCD sold products in all the markets served by the other divisions, none of the existing divisional general managers wanted to take on the responsibility for the PCD business. Each argued that PCD fit better in another's division. Underlying this disinterest were the low margins and high risks associated with work in the pollution-control area. Many companies in recent years had sought to establish themselves in the pollution abatement market but despite growing concern by industry and government alike, very few companies were able to earn a profit in this market. When acquired, PCD had shown a $2,000,000 loss on $28,000,000 sales in its last fiscal year.

President Myers' second reason for keeping the PCD company intact as a separate division reporting to him was to facilitate its sale if in five years the division failed to satisfy him that it could meet at least minimum profit standards as well as contribute to technology in other divisions. "I'm eager to do my part to deal with our ecological problems," he told his Board, "and we will not expect any miracles from PCD, but within five years it will either be in the black or on the block."

He assigned several capable executives from other divisions of CI to key posts in PCD but kept Joseph MacAllister, PCD's founder and president, as president of the new division. Myers stated:

> *MacAllister knows the business. He is only fifty-one and although he may be a little too much of the Tom Swift inventor-type, he is an adequate coordinator. By backing him up with a new man in the top engineering post, a new controller, and two of our good marketing service men, I think we have the makings of a good team. Because MacAllister took most of his equity in PCD in the form of CI stock and options, I'm sure he is as anxious as we to see things work out.*
>
> *Finally, we have assigned one of our best personnel people, James Dickenson, as his new director of personnel. Jim will see to it that we bring their salary and benefit programs into line with ours as smoothly as possible, and more important, he will get them working with our management by objectives and related programs.*

The new division director of engineering is Paul Horn.[1] He is fifty-six years old and has been with CI for over twenty years. Before moving to the PCD division in Pittsburgh, Horn held several key posts in other parts of CI. Trained initially as a mechanical engineer, Horn gained both bachelor's and master's degrees in electrical engineering by attending night school for eleven years. After holding the second highest engineering post in first the oil and chemical and then the food processing divisions, he served as the director of engineering estimates and then divisional director of the government products division. A drop in govern-

[1]For additional background on Paul Horn, see Consolidated Instruments—A.

ment sales led to a reorganization of that division and for sixteen months Horn served as manager of the corporate engineering review department and reported to the corporate vice-president of engineering.

Horn at first resisted the move to PCD, but was eventually persuaded that he was needed there to put the new division on the road to profitable operations.

Myers himself spoke with Horn, telling him, "I would not ask this of you, Paul, if I didn't think it important. We need your experience, good business sense, and knowledge of our practices to help get them out of the red."

Myers informed the casewriter that

> Horn had some fool notion that we were unhappy with him for being a little hard-nosed in his corporate review job. Heck, that's why I wanted him in that post to help Shel Thayler [vice-president of engineering] sift through requests for new projects and get rid of the old ones that hadn't worked out. Paul Horn may not be the easiest man to work with, but technically he is first-rate and he's experienced enough and energetic enough to take on a tough assignment like this.

Horn accepted the new post, but he made it abundantly clear to Jim Dickenson, PCD's new personnel director, that he had a different understanding about the reasons behind his transfer.

> I know why I'm here, Jim, regardless of what Myers and Thayler say. They are all excited about your human relations ideas and these new organization development concepts. I've done a lot of tough jobs for this company over the years when we didn't have the time or resources to pussyfoot around. But times change; nowadays maybe the people-problems are more important than the technical ones. I've still got what I hope are eight to ten good years to go before retirement and I found when they sent me off to that six-week management course[2] that I adapted to, and handled, the new material and cases as well as men twenty years my junior.
>
> Although I was plenty upset about this transfer at first, I don't intend to go around sulking for the next ten years. Neither do I intend to make the same mistakes I've made before. If it's "develop people" and a "healthy climate" that they want, whatever that means, then I'll develop people and climate. But I'm going to need your help, Jim.

Dickenson explained to the casewriter that he had been pleasantly surprised by Horn's words. "I had expected that Paul would be something of a problem," Dickenson said. "I had heard that he was upset about the move and I had him down as a potential trouble spot in installing our

[2]Horn attended a six-week management seminar at a leading eastern university.

management-by-objectives program in PCD. But he seems genuinely interested in working with me and proving that he can be more than a hard-boiled engineering manager."

The management-by-objectives program that both Myers and Dickenson spoke of involved working with all key managers to develop new techniques for dealing with their subordinates in the planning, decision-making, and review phases of their work. Dickenson explained the program further:

> It is difficult to summarize the M.B.O. approach because it deals with intangibles like climate as well as specific procedures. In essence, a manager sits down with each of his key subordinates and they establish a few key objectives which then serve as targets. Most of the targets will be for a six- to twelve-month period but some will be longer-range. There are four main points to keep in mind during the target, or objective-setting, stage:
>
> **1)** Regardless of who initiates the objectives, the manager and the subordinate should discuss them until they are jointly satisfied that they can be reached.
> **2)** Wherever possible, objectives should be formulated in measurable terms.
> **3)** Where objectives might take a year or more to achieve, measurable checkpoints should be agreed to.
> **4)** The objectives, wherever possible, should be few and on the broad, integrated, end-result level. The department managers should not get into the numerous procedural steps to accomplish end-result objectives; these will be worked out by their subordinates. If managers interfere they will remove much of the challenge and commitment the subordinate should feel for the objective.
>
> Periodically, these objectives should be reviewed as results come in and are updated or revised as required. Unless significant failures to achieve key objectives take place, or appear imminent, the superior should not involve himself in the means by which his subordinates seek to accomplish their objectives.
> This approach involves an entire network of corollary systems. In order to make it work, you have to build recruiting, training, career development, and compensation programs that reinforce the M.B.O. approach. Communications, including management information systems, budgetary systems, and planning procedures have to fit too, and a climate of mutual respect and trust must be built. The total system, which is designed to more fully tap human resources by meshing individual and organizational goals, is often called O.D., or Organizational Development.

The casewriter asked Dickenson whether he felt Horn was sincere and if so, would be able to learn and use these concepts. Dickenson's response was:

*I think he is sincere, and despite his history of being a driver I
think he can learn. You know, the only time when you can't teach
an old dog new tricks is when the dog thinks he is too old to learn.
Paul can learn but is likely to be impatient with himself as well as
with the system. One thing that will help is that he will be managing
quite a few departments headed by people who are far more
knowledgeable than he is in the specific areas in which they work.
At least, I think this will help. His inability to plunge in with both
feet and show them a "better way" may force him to learn how to
manage a process rather than make a series of technical decisions.*

Horn, in fact, seemed anxious to get started when interviewed by
the casewriter just after his appointment was announced.

*There are some people in this company who think I can't adjust
to new management techniques. At first, I was angry about this
move but now I see it as a good opportunity to try something new.*

*Two years ago, when they first asked me to install the M.B.O.
program in my corporate engineering review department, I talked
Dickenson's former superior out of it. I explained that mine was an
unusual department with a very tough, dirty job to do at that time
and that it would be better to leave us alone for awhile. That was a
mistake on my part. I am sure that it is one of the reasons why I am
in Pittsburgh now. At that time, I was more interested in immediate
results than in trying to understand and institute what seemed like
the latest in an unending stream of management fads.*

*Furthermore, many of my friends at division level who were trying
to install M.B.O. didn't like it one bit. They complained that it often
left them with an uneasy feeling that they were losing control of the
work they supervised and that by focusing on results they were
overly dependent on their subordinates. Fred Biggs, whom I worked
with in Houston, said, "Paul, this is the gol-dangest approach I
ever saw. It's like playing poker. Only now my subordinates play all
the hands—with my money—and according to the rules they don't
even have to show me their cards. They just call me up twice a
month and tell me how much they won or we lost."*

*I guess my biggest objection, though, was that instituting a new
system like M.B.O. takes time and I wasn't prepared to invest it.
Judging by what happened I made a poor decision. I won't make the
same mistake twice, though!*

For the next six weeks Horn spent almost all of his time trying to
familiarize himself with the work done by the four departments under
his control and the men who managed them.

*I found [Horn said] that I was really in over my head on much
of the work they are doing. With all of my experience I know very
little about the technical aspects of their work. Only in production
estimating do I have a good feel, and this is based on my knowledge*

of good procedures and practices. This knowledge helps some in the technical service group but as far as the design and development departments, it would take me at least a year to feel qualified to make technical judgments in those areas. As I understand this M.B.O. approach, I shouldn't be terribly concerned about this.

At the end of the first six weeks, Horn requested that each of his department managers develop a plan for the next twelve months showing how they would increase their efficiency by at least 10 percent during that period. Horn did not give them any specifics on how this was to be accomplished but indicated that this efficiency must be achieved without deterioration of service or cutbacks in development of key personnel.

I told them that it was up to them to show the initiative and imagination required to give as good or better service for less money. I don't know enough about their work to know how they can do it, and I might interfere with their personal development if I did know enough to try. The one thing I do know, after more than twenty years' experience, is that there are almost always ways of improving efficiency. What you need are good men and a little pressure from above.

A month after making his request, Horn set up a meeting with each of his subordinates. He spent less than an hour alone with each man in the morning and then at a general meeting in the afternoon he allocated one hour for each man to present his plan to the others.

The tone of the meeting was described by one of the department managers as "firm but friendly." Andy Drechsel, manager of the technical service group, said:

I explained to Mr. Horn that it was difficult for me to forecast cost or efficiency, because so much of our work was tied to requests from the marketing people. We have several measures of productivity that we use but they are rough and involve a number of intangibles. I tried to explain some of these to Mr. Horn, but he indicated that he didn't feel he should get into them. He asked me to give him my honest estimates of how much I could do to meet his 10 percent increased efficiency goal.

Frankly, I came into the meeting prepared to hedge a bit and give him something a little more conservative, by way of targets, but he made me feel that he was counting on me and that I owed myself as well as him the best I could do. I ended up by giving him rather optimistic estimates and I am going to have to work like the devil to meet them. Judging from the afternoon meeting my overall target of 18 percent increase in efficiency is the highest, but we can make it if Mr. Horn helps when marketing puts too much pressure on.

Edward Deeb, manager of production estimating, agreed with Drechsel that his meeting with Horn had been friendly.

> Even though he understands my department better than the others [Deeb said], he made no attempt to get into the details I worked out to support our annual plan. All he wanted to know was could I do it? I came away feeling that he didn't really want to know how I would make my objectives. He didn't even keep a copy of my department plan; just a one-page summary of our overall budget. I promised him the 10 percent he wants and I think we can do it.

Sam Elster and Charles Graf, managers of the design and the development departments respectively, were more mixed in their reactions to the day's meeting.

> I spent a full month with my people [Elster said] working up a very detailed plan. It is very difficult to be precise about cost and efficiency in our design work but we tried. We made the best estimates we could of what kinds of things would come out of development and production and how we would tackle them. I developed several PERT diagrams to work out schedules and costs, but as near as I can tell, Mr. Horn never even looked at them.
> When I asked him this morning what he thought of our plans he said, "We're not here today to talk plans, Sam; we have to agree on targets—objectives. I'll leave the plans to you. All I want to know is what objectives we can set down now and count on you reaching by next year."
> When it became clear that he was not going to let me go into any detail on the many imponderables that I had to face in my plan, I was glad I had been a little cautious with my summary targets for departmental operations. If I thought he would be willing to dig in with me to understand why I may or may not succeed, then I might have revised my targets upward a little. Overall, I showed what amounts to a 7.5 percent improvement in efficiency. Mr. Horn went over the six key targets that will be the basis of this improvement and tried to get me to increase them to bring the total up to 10 percent, but I stood fast. I said, "Mr. Horn, if you want me to change the totals then you have to show me where we disagree in my plans." He laughed and said, "Sam, you know I don't know enough about the operation of your department to win a debate with you. I'm sure you can figure out how to get to 10 percent. Everybody else has."

Elster maintained, however, that he had given Horn the most accurate and aggressive objectives he could and Horn begrudgingly accepted them. On several occasions during the afternoon session, however, Horn made reference to the lower than 10 percent target for the design department.

Charles Graf, or "Doc" as he was known in his department, was a brilliant engineer himself and had built a very strong group of development people. His department was highly regarded for the quality and dependability of its work, but it also exceeded budget more frequently and by larger amounts than the other three. Graf gave his reaction to what had happened at the meeting.

I feel like the man who had a magician pull a tablecloth off the table without disturbing the food. I came in this morning with a plan that I felt supported my claim that it was impossible for our department to show any tangible evidence of improved efficiency and I left agreeing to a 15 percent improvement. The nature of development work and its heavy dependence on inputs from research and production makes planning virtually impossible. We must be able to do creative work under time pressure and do it well. If I get everyone overly budget conscious, I will lose more than I gain.

I told Horn this from the first day he arrived and I told him again this morning. I tried to show him why we should be evaluated in a different way. He had leafed through my plan but apparently only in search of budget or output summaries. When it became apparent that I wasn't getting anywhere I decided it would be wiser to go along with him. We went over the four major elements of cost in my department and for each of my targets he would ask, "How about it Doc, can't we tighten up a little here?" Before I knew it, we had "agreed" to objectives that show me improving overall efficiency by 15 percent.

It wasn't until this afternoon, when I had to present my "revised" plans to the others, that I realized what I had agreed to. Well, Mr. Horn made it clear that we would review our progress each month, and so now I have to figure out how I can gradually move his expectations back to a more realistic level.

Paul Horn was pleased with the meetings and told Jim Dickenson so the next day.

Jim, you have no idea how much I appreciate your help on this management-by-objectives approach. I have just gotten my people to agree on some good, ambitious objectives for the year and I think I can bring in a much better cost-effectiveness ratio as a result.

By staying away from details with them, Jim, I not only kept them from getting me to make the tough decisions for them, but I'm in a much better position to hold them fully accountable for results. The ones who deliver will be rewarded and if anyone doesn't, I'll have more time to help them out. I doubt that we will reach all our targets this year but it is healthy to try. Three of my men will probably come very close. There is only one about whom I am worried, but I will leave him alone for at least six months and give him a chance to prove me wrong.

Finally, Jim, by staying out of details, I will have time to work more closely with production, marketing, and research and better coordinate our overall efforts.

Dickenson was somewhat taken aback by Horn's comments and a little concerned.

I think Paul is sincere but I'm not sure he is fully aware of what it takes to make a management-by-objectives system work. I had no idea he would move this quickly, because I thought he would take a few more months to get a feel for operations. As a result, I haven't worked very closely with him on some of the wrinkles that have to be ironed out of this approach.

Exhibit 1 *Partial Organization Chart, Consolidated Instruments*

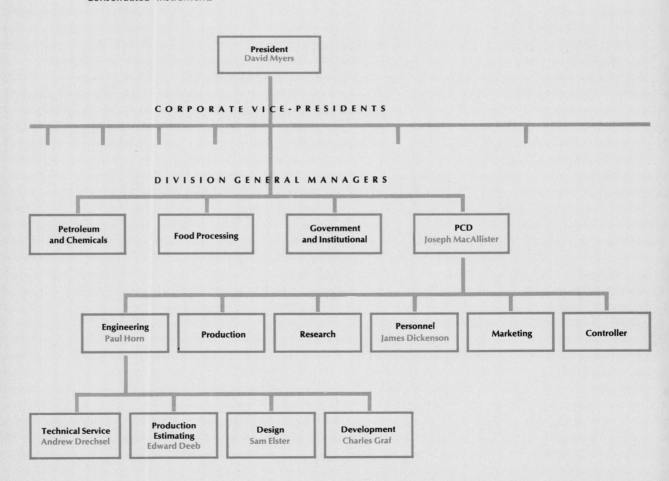

FOR DISCUSSION AND REPORT-WRITING

Organizing: Structural Design

1) What do you think of Myers' comments that he is eager to do his part to deal with ecological problems but that PCD in five years' time would either be "in the black or on the block"? How far should a business go in sacrificing profits for such things as contributing to major areas of social concern?

2) Did Myers make a wise decision in having the president of the PCD division report directly to him? What factors should he have considered in determining how to deal with the questions of basic departmentation and balance in the overall structure?

3) Discuss what else James Dickenson might do as a staff man to help Paul Horn develop a better grasp of management-by-objectives.

4) In what way may the attempt to use a management-by-objectives approach in the PCD division influence the relationship between the division and CI's corporate management? As part of your answer, consider the degree of decentralization CI should practice with regard to PCD.

How does the degree of decentralization you recommend affect the potential for CI to provide central service functions (legal, purchasing, and so on) for the PCD division?

Human Factors in Organizing

5) With which of Horn's subordinates (Drechsel, Deeb, Elster, or Graf) do you think he is most likely to become embroiled in serious conflict? In your opinion, what will cause this conflict?

6) Was Paul Horn a good man for the job assigned him? Does he appear to have the right technical and other qualifications?

7) How well do you feel this new job meets Paul Horn's needs at the present stage of his life?

Planning: Elements of Decision-Making

8) What effect on creativity, at the level of Horn's subordinates, is his approach to M.B.O. likely to have?

9) Comment on the process of reaching decisions on key goals. How rational was the choice process?

Planning: Decision-Making in an Enterprise

10) How do you feel Horn's approach with his subordinates will influence the nature and degree and level of uncertainty absorption that takes place in future planning sessions?

11) What effect is the M.B.O. approach taken by Horn likely to have on the long-range planning needs of the division?

12) What are the potential strengths and weaknesses of a *well-designed* and well-implemented management-by-objectives program?

Leading

13) How is Horn's approach to goal-setting likely to affect the probability of "voluntary cooperation" by his subordinates? Discuss each of his four subordinates separately.

14) How would you rate the communication between Horn and each of his subordinates? Discuss both strong and weak points of the direction he has given them.

Measuring and Controlling

15) How well will Horn be able to determine what constitutes appropriate corrective action if results in any of his four departments differ significantly from the objectives that he will use as control standards?

16) If a management-by-objectives system is well designed and implemented, what effect should controls growing out of it have on the motivation of each of Horn's four subordinates?

17) It is clear from the case that Myers expects to see the PCD division become profitable but realizes this may take several years. Because the basis for moving to a sound future profit will require many less tangible results in the short run, how should Myers determine whether the division is making satisfactory progress? What kinds of intermediate control points should he set and how should he measure and control them?

18) Now that the PCD division is a part of CI, some changes in strategy will be required to meet Myers' demand for profit within five years. In what ways may this shift affect the design for operating the PCD division? After you have read Chapter 28, relate your answers to appropriate issues raised in that chapter.

19) *Summary Report Question, Part Six:* How successful do you feel

Paul Horn will be in controlling the overall results of his department if he continues to follow the approach to management-by-objectives indicated in the case? Explain.

*Summary Question for Solution
of the Case as a Whole*

20) Based on your answer to question 19, what should Paul Horn do to improve the integration of a control system with other elements of the process of management? Who might be of help to Horn in seeking this integration?

PART SEVEN

Managing: An Adaptive Process

Thinking of management in terms of organizing, planning, leading, and controlling sharpens our analysis; it helps us sort out issues and then concentrate on a particular opportunity for improvement. But like any analytical device, it leaves us with parts. However much we refine these parts of the management process, they become operative only when we fit them back into the total management system. We may be especially pleased with a new scheme for motivating executives or with an operations-research model, but unless our new creation is compatible with the overall management design, it will be of little value. Achieving a *synthesis* of various management parts is the central theme in these concluding chapters.

In addition to achieving internal synthesis, the manager must keep his management design adjusted to external needs. In Chapter 16 we described master strategy as the evolving formulation of a company's plans for dealing with its environment. Now we shall give specific attention to the interrelations between that master strategy and the overall management design. In other words, as stressed in Chapter 1, full synthesis involves both internal and external integration.

Companies that are expanding their operations abroad face special problems of fitting their management design to their new environments. Local differences in culture may call for modifications in management systems that work well in the United States.

Complicating this entire meshing of overall management design with company strategy is unceasing change in the environment. A system that performs well today may well need revamping tomorrow. So a neatly integrated management design cannot remain static. Managers face over and over again the issues explored in the following chapters.

Chapter 28—Strategy and Management Design. Here we first identify key elements in a management design. Then we show how the design for a company can be matched to its strategy. Finally, this approach to strategy and management design is related to complex company structures.

Chapter 29—International Management. This chapter takes a different tack. We assume the reader has a good grasp of the array of concepts already covered in this book. With this background we ask the following question: When a company goes abroad, what aspects of the total system may require adjustment because of cultural differences? As we shall see, the premises on which United States management concepts are based may not be valid in another country.

Management is a great potential social resource in both our country and abroad. To be fully effective, however, the practice of management calls for great skill in fusing many elements into a total design suited to each specific opportunity.

Strategy and Management Design

MANAGEMENT SUITED TO THE MISSION

Two salient themes have permeated our analysis of management processes: (1) the interaction between the various parts of management and (2) the need to fit management systems to the particular tasks to be accomplished. Now, in this first of two concluding chapters, we are in a position to examine more fully these features of successful management.

Management designs differ. Every university is, and should be, managed in ways that are different from those used to manage the bus system that brings students to its doors. Likewise within the university, the managerial design best suited to research laboratories is inappropriate to the cafeteria. To be sure, several common processes—organizing, planning, leading, and controlling—are essential for each of these units, but as we adapt various concepts to the unique needs of each venture refinement is vital. Management sophistication is revealed in this adapting and refining of the design.

In suiting management to a particular mission the following issues require attention:

1) What constitutes a coherent, whole management design, and how are these parts interrelated?

689

2) How does a company's master strategy affect the kind of management design that the company should have?

3) Is the same management design suitable for all parts of a company?

4) What is involved in changing a familiar design to keep it in tune with new company strategy?

NEED FOR COHERENT MANAGEMENT DESIGN

In each particular situation the phases of management should be synergistic. That is, organization structure should facilitate control, control should generate useful data for planning, planning should be conducted in a way that assists in leading, and so forth. These mutually supporting effects are a vital feature of a good management design, as we have stressed repeatedly. Yet in practice a surprising number of instances arise where just the opposite pull occurs. Tensions mount instead of reinforcements.

Effect of Narrowly Conceived Change

A striking lack of synergy arose when one of the nation's leading railroads undertook a sweeping decentralization. According to the plan, regional managers were to replace a highly centralized headquarters as the focus for operating decisions, and these regional managers were given significantly increased authority. Unfortunately the control mechanisms did not change with the organization design. Detailed reports continued to flow to the vice-presidents at headquarters, and these men continued their previous practice of stepping into trouble spots and issuing orders. Confusion resulted. The fact that legal and technological reasons prevented regional managers from making their own plans regarding prices, train schedules, new equipment, wage rates, and other important matters merely aggravated the situation. So the actual planning mechanism did not line up with the announced organization. It soon became obvious that the total management design had not been thought through.

The chief executive of a computer company, to cite another example, decided that participative leadership would stimulate the engineers and other technical people in his firm. He arranged for all managers from vice-presidents to first-line supervisors to have T-group training so that everyone would understand the new leadership style. The results were not entirely happy. Competition forced the president himself to make several key decisions, specifications had to be frozen, pressure was placed on production people to meet tough deadlines, and budgetary-control limits were stipulated by headquarters. This top-down planning was a well-established pattern within the company. But to many managers who had just gotten the message about participative leadership, the former planning procedures suddenly became oppressive. Their morale was hurt rather than helped because their expectations, which had been raised by the leadership training, were soon undermined by use of the old planning mechanisms. Here again we see that a change in one phase of management was not matched by necessary adjustments in other phases.

The initial thrust for a modification in management design may arise in any sector. For instance, economy drives appear perennially in government offices, and they frequently take the form of reshuffling titles and divisions, but because neither the incentives nor the controls are usually altered, the net results are negligible. Plans for a new activity may also initiate the change. Thus a business school designed a fine M.B.A. program for junior executives, but failed to change its organization. The additional work of recruiting, scheduling, and teaching got secondary treatment by officials already busy with regular students, and so little happened until a separate organization unit was set up to concentrate on the new market. Again we see that a change in one sector requires a supporting management adjustment in other sectors if the initial move is to be effective.

Prominent Features of a Management Design

Recognition of need for a coherent management design raises a question of what is embraced in such a design. What features do we need to consider?

It is not very helpful to suggest that elements in the management design for a particular situation can be selected from the many concepts we have already discussed in this book, even though this statement is true. Such guidance is too broad. In order to narrow the focus a bit, let us concentrate on those managerial arrangements most likely to be affected by choice of strategy. In other words, which features probably will need adjustment when we fit a structure to new requirements?

Analysis of a wide variety of management designs points to the elements listed in the accompanying charts as distinguishing features. In any single design only a few of these features will dominate, and others may be insignificant. In addition, for unusual circumstances a feature not listed here may be critical. Nevertheless, careful consideration of the features listed will enable us to comprehend and to deal with the management designs of most enterprises.

1) *Distinguishing organizational features.* Organization is widely acknowledged as a prime vehicle for adapting a management design to new needs. In fact, organization often is overemphasized. Some managers make a change in their formal organization and then assume everything else will fall in place. To be fully effective, however, several compatible

Chart 1

**Organizational features that are likely
to vary with changes in strategy**

Centralization versus decentralization
Degree of division of labor
Size of self-sufficient operating units
Mechanisms for coordination
Nature and location of staff
Management information system
Characteristics of key personnel

changes in formal organization are frequently necessary. These changes
must be incorporated into informal behavior, and supporting adjustments
must be made in other facets of management.

Key personnel, the last feature listed in Chart 1, warrants special
emphasis. It is always involved in a change in management design, and
it may be as vital to the success of a change as any other feature. For
instance, when Corson Wholesale Drugs, Inc. (described in Chapter 5)
sought to meet local competition by increasing its degree of decentraliza-

Chart 2

**Planning features that are likely
to vary with changes in strategy**

Use of standing plans:

Comprehensiveness of coverage
Specificity

Use of single-use plans:

Comprehensiveness of coverage
Specificity

Planning horizon
Intermediate versus final objectives
"How" versus results

tion, a major training effort had to be undertaken. In any significant change in organization, men capable of functioning in the new jobs should be carefully selected and should be given time to learn new patterns of behavior.

2) *Distinguishing forms of plans.* The need to think carefully about forms of plans is illustrated sharply in any international airline. Preparation of tickets in Vienna that will be understood in Nairobi and Seattle, that can be reissued in Baghdad and canceled in Tahiti, and that provide the basis for allocating the fare collected among a dozen different airlines requires an impressive use of standing operating procedures. Nor can equipment maintenance be left to local ingenuity. On the other hand, companywide policies relating to sales promotion and pay-rates for baggage handlers must be cast in broad terms or shunned entirely. Then if the airline enters the local hotel business in several countries, the appropriateness of worldwide policies and procedures must be examined anew. For each subject, either too little or too much planning can lead to great confusion.

Questions about the kinds of plans suitable for a specific situation typically center around the topics listed in Chart 2.

Planning, in contrast to organizing, often receives scant attention during the preparation of a management design. This disregard of planning arises from two confusions. First, the substance of specific plans may be so engrossing that little thought is given to the more basic issue of the form in which guidance will be most useful. Second, the process of arriving at a decision is confused with the mechanisms introduced to guide decision-making activities throughout the enterprise. When shaping a management design, we are primarily concerned with these mechanisms (standing plans, project planning, intermediate objectives, and the like) because they help pull the entire managerial effort into a coherent thrust.[1]

3) *Distinguishing elements in leadership style.* The leadership features listed in Chart 3 are aspects of leading that should be adjusted to fit the total management design. As explained in Chapter 21, many other guides to good leadership practice that emerge from behavioral research apply to virtually all settings, and so they are not included in this particular list.

Leadership style is intimately tied to the temperament and beliefs of each manager. Consequently, this style is more difficult to change than, say, departmentation or control reports. Nevertheless, all of us can modify our behavior to some degree, especially when the environment in which we work reinforces our new behavior. If a manager cannot provide the kind of leadership needed in a given situation, replacing him is an alternative. So even though leadership style is not easy to change, it should be

---

[1] Good decisions on specific problems are vital, of course. But the elements of decision-making are similar in all sorts of situations, whereas the forms of plans and the organizational assignment of planning tasks differ widely. Consequently, it is the latter arrangements that deserve prime attention when we prepare a management design.

Chart 3

**Leadership features that are likely
to vary with changes in strategy**

Participation in planning
Permissiveness
Closeness of supervision
Sharing of information
Emphasis on on-the-job satisfactions

included in the total process of matching management design to strategy.

4) *Distinguishing features of the control process.* The design of controls all too often lags behind shifts in other aspects of management. The railroad reorganization and the government economy drives mentioned earlier, both revealed a failure to revise controls so that they would reinforce major moves in related areas. Over-reliance on short-run, quantitative measurements, discussed in Chapter 27, shows a similar tendency to pay too little attention to control structure. Yet controls can provide the synergy we seek in an effective management design.

The features of control most likely to need adjustment when changes are made in other phases of management are listed in Chart 4. Closely associated with changes in these features should be a refinement of the

Chart 4

**Control features that are likely
to vary with changes in strategy**

Performance criteria emphasized
Location of control points
Frequency of checks
Who initiates corrective action
Stress on reliability versus learning
Punitive versus reward motivation

management information system, which has already been listed under organization. Although the preparation of a total management design rarely starts with control, it would be well to remember the following maxim: "No plan is complete until provision is made for control."

Weaving the various features of organizing, planning, leading, and controlling that have been singled out in this section into a coherent management design calls for great skill. Each enterprise needs its own unique system. Fortunately, synergistic benefits are usually possible if we are ingenious enough to make reinforcing combinations, such as those suggested under "Nature of Technology" in Table 28–1 (p. 698). A company's design is effective, however, only when it fits neatly with the company strategy, and so we turn to the mating of strategy and management design in the next section.

INFLUENCE OF STRATEGY ON DESIGN

The idea of a management design is a useful concept because it turns our focus from analytical refinements to reinforcing integration. In the preceding section we identified an array of variable features that should be considered in building such an integrated design, and we indicated how some combinations of these features tend to be destructive whereas other combinations promote coherence.

We can now tackle the tougher task—relating management design and company strategy. We know from numerous examples in this book and from our direct dealing with actual enterprises that managerial design does have a profound effect on accomplishing a mission. But this general observation gives us little guidance. The deliberate linking of strategy and design is especially difficult because strategy takes a wide variety of forms as we saw in Chapter 16.

Technology: The Intervening Variable

The best bridge between strategy and design is "technology." Here we use technology in a very broad sense to include all sorts of methods for converting resource inputs into products and services for consumers. The inputs can be labor, knowledge, and capital as well as raw materials.[2]

[2]For an expansion of this concept of technology see C. Perrow, "A Framework for the Comparative Analysis of Organizations," *American Sociological Review*, April 1967. Other writers have explored the relation between technology and structure, but they have concentrated on the narrower concept of physical conversion of materials. See T. Burns and G.M. Stalker, *The Management of Innovation*, 2nd ed. (London: Tavistock Publications Limited, 1966); J. Woodward, *Industrial Organization* (Oxford: Oxford University Press, 1965); D.H. Hickson, D.S. Pugh, and D.C. Pheysey, "Operations Technology and Organization Structure: An Empirical Reappraisal," *Administrative Science Quarterly*, September 1969.

Thus an insurance company has its technology for converting money, ideas, and labor into insurance service just as an oil company has its technology for converting crude oil and other resources into petroleum products. By extending our thinking from strategy to the technology necessary to execute that strategy, we move to *work to be done*. Once we comprehend the work to be done—both managerial and operating work—we are on familiar ground. Most of our management concepts relate directly to getting work done, and so preparing a management design to fit a particular kind of work falls within the recognized "state of the art."

The use of technology as an intervening variable produces the arrangement shown in Fig. 28–1. To maintain perspective and to highlight key influences, strategy should focus on only a few basic ideas. Its formulation is by necessity in broad terms. We cannot jump directly from strategy to management design because we have not yet classified the array of actions that will be necessary to execute the strategy. Thinking of technology helps us to elaborate the work implications of the strategy and thereby provides us with the inputs for shaping an effective management design.

Types of Technology

Technology, especially in the broad sense in which we are using the term here, deals with all sorts of situations and methods. For purposes of relating technology to management, however, we can concentrate on only a few characteristics of the technology. For instance, the way a technology deals with change is very significant for our purpose.

In a company with a given strategy and technology, the need for change will fall somewhere along a continuum of infrequent to frequent. Similarly, the kinds of changes the company typically faces will somewhere along another continuum ranging from brand new, unprecedented problems to familiar, precedented problems; in the case of the familiar problems, the company will have a well-established pattern for resolving them.

Using these two characteristics of a firm's technology, we can set up the matrix shown in Fig. 28–2. Of course, many technologies will fit around the middle of one or both dimensions, but by thinking about technologies toward the ends of the scales we arrive at three well-known types of businesses.

Fig. 28-1   A simple flow diagram with technology as an intervening variable.

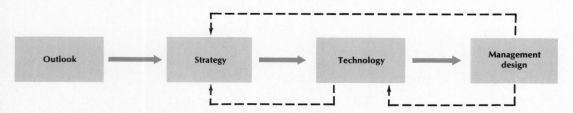

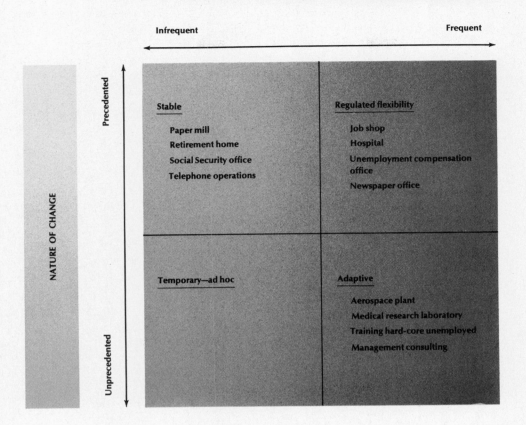

NEED FOR CHANGE

Infrequent   Frequent

NATURE OF CHANGE

Precedented

Stable

    Paper mill
    Retirement home
    Social Security office
    Telephone operations

Regulated flexibility

    Job shop
    Hospital
    Unemployment compensation office
    Newspaper office

Temporary—ad hoc

Adaptive

    Aerospace plant
    Medical research laboratory
    Training hard-core unemployed
    Management consulting

Unprecedented

Fig. 28-2 Types of businesses classified on the basis of need for, and nature of, change.

Enterprises confronted with familiar problems rather infrequently are basically *stable*. Paper mills and other firms processing large volumes of raw materials fall into this category. When the need for change moves from infrequent to frequent, and the problems remain precedented, we encounter businesses that display *regulated flexibility*. Job shops—used by management writers since Frederick Taylor to illustrate management concepts—fit this category. But when the need for change is frequent and the problems are unprecedented, as often occurs in the aerospace industry, we face a sharply different situation. Here technology requires an *adaptive* structure.

These three technology types—stable, regulated flexibility, and

Table 28–1 Typical features of management structures for three types of technology

Features That Distinguish Management Structures	Nature of Technology		
	Stable	Regulated Flexibility	Adaptive

Organizing

Features That Distinguish Management Structures	Stable	Regulated Flexibility	Adaptive
Centralization versus decentralization	Centralized	Mostly centralized	Decentralized
Degree of division of labor	Narrow specialization	Specialized, or crafts	Scope may vary
Size of self-sufficient operating units	Large	Medium	Small, if equipment permits
Mechanisms for coordination	Built-in, programmed	Separate planning unit	Face-to-face, within unit
Nature and location of staff	Narrow functions; headquarters	Narrow functions; headquarters and operating unit	Generalists at headquarters; specialists in operating units
Management information system	Heavy upward flow	Flow to headquarters and to operating unit	Flow mostly to, and within, operating unit
Characteristics of key personnel	Strong operators	Functional experts in line and staff	Analytical, adaptive

Planning

Features That Distinguish Management Structures	Stable	Regulated Flexibility	Adaptive
Use of standing plans: Comprehensiveness of coverage	Broad coverage	All main areas covered	Mostly "local," self-imposed
Specificity	Detail specified	Detail in interlocking activities	Main points only
Use of single-use plans: Comprehensiveness of coverage	Fully planned	Fully planned	Main steps covered
Specificity	Detail specified	Schedules and specs detailed	Adjusted to feedback
Planning horizon	Weekly to quarterly	Weekly to annually	Monthly to three years or more
Intermediate versus final objectives	Intermediate goals sharp	Intermediate goals sharp	Emphasis on objectives
"How" versus results	"How" is specified	Results at each step specified	End results stressed

Table 28–1 (cont.)

	Features That Distinguish Management Structures	Nature of Technology		
		Stable	Regulated Flexibility	Adaptive
Leading	Participation in planning	Very limited	Restricted to own tasks	High participation
	Permissiveness	Stick to instructions	Variation in own tasks only	High permissiveness, if results OK
	Closeness of supervision	Follow operations closely	Output and quality closely watched	General supervision
	Sharing of information	Circumspect	Job information shared	Full project information shared
	Emphasis on on-the-job satisfactions	Limited scope	Craftsmanship and professionalism encouraged	Opportunity for involvement
Controlling	Performance criteria emphasized	Efficiency, dependability	Quality, punctuality, efficiency	Results, within resource limits
	Location of control points	Within process; intermediate stages	Focus on each processing unit	Overall "milestones"
	Frequency of checks	Frequent	Frequent	Infrequent
	Who initiates corrective action	Often central managers	"Production control" and other staff	Men in operating unit
	Stress on reliability versus learning	Reliability stressed	Reliability stressed	Learning stressed
	Punitive versus reward motivation	Few mistakes tolerated	Few mistakes tolerated	High reward for success

adaptive—are found in many lines of endeavor. In the health field there are retirement homes, hospitals, and medical research labs. In government, offices for Social Security (old age pensions), for unemployment compensation, and for the training of hard-core unemployed illustrate the types. In the service industries examples are telephone operations, newspaper publications, and management consulting.

In contrast to the first three types, the fourth division in the change matrix does not point to a clear type of technology or management design. Unprecedented problems that arise only infrequently are handled by some temporary arrangement. This *ad hoc* setup does not exist long enough to modify the underlying structure.

From Technology to Management Design

An intriguing aspect of the three technology types just identified is that each leads to a well-known management design. The usual relationships between technology and design are presented in Table 28–1. For each of the distinguishing features of a management design, discussed at the beginning of this chapter, we can see the typical response to a stable technology, a regulated-flexibility technology, and an adaptive technology.

The primary features of each design remain substantially the same even though the companies come from different industries. For instance, when the work situation is stable as it usually is in a paper mill, retirement home, Social Security office, and telephone exchange, then planning tends to be comprehensive and detailed, intermediate goals are sharply defined, decision-making is centralized, and central staff is strong. In addition, we find limited participation and close supervision. Controls are focused on dependability and efficiency, checks are made frequently, and few mistakes are tolerated. These and other management features indicated in Table 28–1 enable an executive working in a stable situation to convert inputs of various resources into the maximum output of consumer services.

Actually in our modern world, regulated flexibility is much more common than the stable technology just described. A job shop, hospital, unemployment compensation office, and newspaper all face a continuing procession of new situations most of which can be handled by well-developed techniques for resolving such problems. For this kind of technology, the typical management design introduces flexibility by the use of craftsmen and professionals, by separate scheduling units, by careful programming of workloads, by close control of work passing from one stage to the next, by prompt information on the status of work at each stage, and so on. The kind of flexibility needed is anticipated, and provisions for dealing with it are built into the system. Each person understands the limits of his discretion, and other conditions are fully planned and controlled so that reliability of the total system is not lost.

Adaptive technology calls for quite a different management design. The research lab, consulting firm, and hard-core unemployed training project all face unprecedented problems frequently. Here operating units become smaller, greater reliance is placed on face-to-face contacts, authority is decentralized, planning tends to focus on objectives and broad programs, leaders use participation and expect high personal involvement, control checks are less frequent and concern results rather than methods. These and other features listed in Table 28–1 are often called "organic" or sometimes "democratic."

This adaptive type of situation is what many human relations advocates dream about. It provides ample opportunity for employee participation and self-actualization. However, the fact that only a small portion of all work involves frequent, unprecedented problems explains why a lot of human relations training has failed to find practical application.

Of course, no company will fit exactly into any one of the technology-management design types we have described. But the examples do suggest how thoughtful analysis of technology provides a basis for designing a suitable structure.

Related Influences on Design

Although the analysis of technology in terms of the frequency and uniqueness of the problems it faces is a fruitful first step, we should not overlook other influences. For instance, technology will also be affected by complexity and the need for speed. When several interrelated variables affect the work, as in building a communications satellite, more thorough planning and control will be necessary. The need for speedy action usually has an opposite effect. Here the urgency to get prompt action reduces the opportunity for thorough planning and control; quick results now may have a higher value than somewhat improved results that are available a month later.

Size and uncertainty should also be taken into account. A larger volume of work will support the expense of more division of labor, mechanization, and specialized staff, and greater size complicates communication and coordination. For both these reasons an increase in size tends to add to the planning and control.

Uncertainty permeates many activities. Because of an unknown environment or unpredictable responses to our own actions, we are confronted with uncertainty. If time permits we may try to reduce this uncertainty by further tests and experiments, and this will probably add staff to our organization and reduce the permissiveness in the structure. On the other hand, if such attempts to reduce uncertainty are impractical we may hire men with the best intuitive judgment we can find, get rid of our staff, and decentralize authority to the experts. This latter response to uncertainty, which is favored by the managers of some conglomerates, creates a simple, lean management design.

Management design, then, must be developed in light of a variety of influences. However, the added dimensions just cited still fit into our basic proposal of moving first from strategy to character of work, and then from work to management design.

COMPOUND DESIGN WITHIN A COMPANY

Thus far we have discussed the management design for a whole company. We have assumed that one technology and one design predominates, and for a single-function company this holds true. Most enterprises, however, are more complex. Within the corporate scope quite different activities may take place. So if we are correct in urging that management design reflect technology, the concepts should be applied to parts of a complex company as well as to the whole.

Diverse Technologies of Departments

Consider the Greenfield Company, which has a strategy of performing the complete job of providing new, low-cost housing, from land acquisition to planting shrubbery in the play yard. Separate departments deal with architecture, real estate and finance, component manufacture, and building. The architects are the planners who conceive of types of construction, space utilization, layouts, and specifications that will create good housing at low cost; their work ranges from the highly unique and creative to the painstaking preparation of specifications for actual construction. The real estate and finance people spend a lot of their time negotiating with government agencies and other outsiders; their problems are technical and often unique. In contrast, manufacture of components (standard wall-sections, bathroom and kitchen modules, and the like) is standardized, routinized, and mechanized as much as possible. Actual building construction necessarily is "job order" in character, and requires the synchronization of various craftsmen.

In this one company, two of the major departments, architecture and real estate and finance, come close to the adaptive type described in the preceding section. The building department clearly displays regulated flexibility, and the component manufacturing department is moving as close to the stable type as volume permits.

A university is as heterogeneous as the Greenfield Company. Although the suitability of the same technique for teaching biology, logic, and fine arts is debatable, everyone will agree that managing a controller's office and the buildings and grounds department is in a different category. Other enterprises may not have as much diversity as the Greenfield Company or a university, but mixed activities are very common.

This diversity has serious implications for management design. Many executives who have had successful careers in one type of design believe their style of managing should be extended to all parts of the company.

We often find that the managerial practices that are well suited to the dominant department of a company are automatically applied throughout. Such consistency in managerial methods does have benefits, but the astute manager will at least consider the possibility of using different administrative styles for diverse departments.

Composite Design

Generally, when a department is both large and important to the strategy of the company it should be managed with a design suited to its own activity. This means that companies embracing diverse technologies should use several different managerial styles. The justification for this mixture of managerial styles lies, of course, in the improved performance of the respective departments.

Such diversity has its costs:

1) *Cooperation between departments becomes increasingly difficult.* Voluntary cooperation between groups with different values, time orientations, and willingness to take risks is inevitably strained, as we saw in Chapter 9. Divergent management designs add to this "cultural barrier." Because the departments are so different, we may even separate them geographically—remove research labs from the plants, separate mills designed for long production runs from those for short runs, and so on.

When management designs of departments differ sharply, special liaison staff or other formal means for coordination is often needed. Having deliberately accentuated the difference between departments, we then add a "diplomatic corps" to serve as a communication link between them.

2) *Companywide services drop in value.* With a composite design, the rotation of key personnel is impeded, budgeting is complicated, training programs fit only parts of the company, capital allocation procedures have to be tailored to different inputs and criteria. In other words, synergy arising from pooled services and reinforcing features of a management design is lacking for the company as a whole.

3) *The task of central managers is complicated.* Understanding the subtleties of the several management designs and personally adjusting one's leadership style to each calls for unusual skill and sophistication. Most managers, often unconsciously, favor departments whose management design they find congenial.

Blended Designs

Because of the drawbacks of a composite design and because dissimilar departments may be too small to support their own distinct management structure, we often try to blend two or more systems.

Some types of designs are compatible. For instance, both the stable and the regulated-flexibility designs used as examples earlier call for a high degree of central planning, strong staff, limited permissiveness, and control at intermediate points. The chief difference lies in frequent adjustment by one system to variations in client requirements; nevertheless, these adjustments normally occur within anticipated limits and often follow rules. Consequently, a combined arrangement that accommodates both technologies (for example, the component manufacturer and building construction in the Greenfield Company) can be devised. The blended design is not just what each department would do for its own purposes, but the modification can be tolerated.

Another common arrangement is to build one strong structure and then recognize that exceptions must be made for some segments of the total operation. For instance, accounting usually gets special treatment in a research laboratory, just as members of the advertising group are accepted as "oddballs" in a manufacturing firm. If the people in the exception spots have enough missionary zeal for their specialty to withstand the normal pressure to conform with the majority, the mismatch can function reasonably well.[3]

The fact that many companies need a composite, or blended, management design does not detract from the major theme of this chapter. Coherence in each management design is vital whether the design be simple or complex. The springboard for shaping each design is the character of the work to be managed; the character of the work, in turn, is a function of the company strategy. Diversity of work and the resulting complexity of designs only multiply the components that we have to take into account. The combined result, of course, is a whole mosaic of planning instruments, organizational relationships, leadership influences, and control mechanisms.

A final check, after arranging the many parts, involves going back to the master strategy of the enterprise, identifying the elements that are keys to success, and then asking whether the management design promises to emphasize these elements. In thinking through the necessary refinements of a design we are always in danger of losing perspective on the major mission.

ADJUSTING DESIGN TO A NEW STRATEGY

The matching of strategy and management design involves more than rational choice. The configurations of plans, organization, leadership,

[3]A variation on making exceptions from the major pattern within the enterprise is to use outsiders for the deviant activity. Thus consultants may be called into a "stable" company to provide creative ideas. Brokerage firms subcontract janitorial and equipment-maintenance work. Dress manufacturers often obtain designs from free-lance designers. Although volume of work and flexibility are also factors in such subcontracting, simplification of the management design is a prime benefit.

and control that we have been discussing must be converted into social reality. This is a major, recurring task.

Inevitable Need for Change

Strategy cannot remain fixed. With the swirl of technical, political, social, and economic events a company's niche is sure to change. We see this clearly in a product's life cycle. When a product is new the key strategic variables are usually technical and educational. During expansion, market position is crucial; profits can be earned but initial capital investment is high. In maturity, the spotlight shifts to low cost; capital now flows in. Adjustment of strategy to these shifting key variables typically will move a company through all three types of structure that we discussed earlier in this chapter.

Success also breeds change. As the position of a company in its industry improves, its strategy has to be adjusted. Doubling from, say, 2 to 4 percent can be achieved with little external reaction, but doubling from 50 to 100 percent will precipitate price wars, antitrust suits, and vastly different social responsibilities. Here again the necessary shifts in strategy call for modification in management design. Also, success often means substantial change in size, and we have already noted that a larger scale of operations modifies the design that is optimum.

Few enterprises offer just the same service over a long period. Success prompts diversification. A decline in demand leads to a search for new opportunities. When the revised strategy pushes the firm into new lines of endeavor rarely will the old management design be best suited for the new venture. In fact, a very difficult design problem arises when a company is working with several lines in various stages of their development.

Every manager, then, should be prepared to assist in, and adapt himself to, changes in management design.

What Change in Design Involves

The process of changing to a new management design is more than an intellectual exercise. Both adjustment of the social structure and modification of personal values are required.

An enterprise is productive as a joint endeavor only when it has its own social structure. To work together effectively, people need to know what to expect of others, what their own role is, where they can get help, who has power, and what sources of information are available—as we have noted especially in Chapters 7 and 15. A revised management design upsets many of these established relationships.

Assume, for example, that you are a branch manager confronted with the following changes:

Bob Brown, whose actions after ten years in the treasurer's spot could be predicted, is now in Los Angeles; a young banker has the title of treasurer, but central budgeting work has been transferred to a new assistant controller. Meanwhile, all scheduling is to be done in regional offices, and data from the computer memory is available to everyone. The general manager has taken "personal charge" of the ailing mobile-home business. Your boss reports that the president has revived his campaign for management-by-results.

You will not know what these changes really mean until you and others have had actual experience with the new relationships, have observed carefully the behavior of new people, and have tested the strength of the central staff. The new social structure—the way of working together—takes time to form.

Values and behavior of individuals also have to change to fit the new design. When one of the most prestigious New York banks, for instance, changed its strategy to include active solicitation of small accounts, a host of modifications were made in procedures, branch office organization, lending authority, and the like. The basic problem, however, was to modify the attitudes of employees toward the blue-collar depositor. Genuine interest in such people had to replace crisp politeness.

Comparable adjustments in attitudes are usually necessary to achieve significant change in leadership style (see Chapter 21). So difficult are some of these value shifts that a new setup is ineffective until persons compatible with the new way of life are put in key posts. For example, federal programs for aid to local education have been significantly hampered because people administering them could not quickly adjust their personal values regarding local autonomy, desegregation, religious instruction, role of parent groups, importance of professional training, and similar issues.

Time to Absorb the Change

Conversion to a new management design takes time. Social structure and personal beliefs cannot be altered overnight. Managers can assist in the transition, however, by dealing with three psychological factors: learning, anxiety, and confidence (see Fig. 28–3).

Learning new relationships and attitudes—like other learning—is aided by clear explanations, opportunity to try the new way, further questions and explanations, more trials and adjustment, and then practice. If a manager can help everyone involved recognize that this kind of process may be tedious at first but will avoid confusion later, the total transformation will be expedited. But mature and successful people will not always willingly accept the need for learning.

Any change that alters a man's primary source of satisfaction for his security, social, and self-expression needs is sure to create anxiety. Just the uncertainty about how the new structure will affect him personally is unsettling. Such anxiety often causes odd behavior—irritability, resistance, lack of enthusiasm. A manager should do all he can to relieve anxiety during a transition period. Stating facts, explaining future plans, stressing future benefits, having people meet new associates, scotching rumors, showing awareness of a man's personal problems—all help allay anxiety. With rare exceptions, bad news faced promptly is better than extended worry. If answers to specific questions cannot be given, assurance of when and how the information will become available is helpful.[4]

Both learning and relief of anxiety help to rebuild confidence. In addition, a manager can bolster confidence by reinforcing desired behavior. Public recognition and reward to persons who successfully utilize the new design transfer attention from old ways to the new pattern, and continuing acknowledgment of success restores a sense of competence that had been placed in doubt when familiar behavior had to be altered.

The personal and social adjustments just described take time. Experience indicates that major reorganizations require at least a year to digest, even with strenuous efforts to speed the conversion. Because of this required investment in time and energy, we naturally hope that a new structure can be used for several years. Like research for a new medicine or tooling-up for a new airplane model, we want a period of stability when we can recoup our investment. Similarly, most people need

[4]*Participation* in the formulation of strategy and design of the new structure will speed up learning. On the other hand, participation may extend the period of anxiety, unless the participant sees clearly that he will fare well in any alternative being seriously considered.

Fig. 28-3 Psychological factors and change. Diagram shows how psychological factors are affected by change.

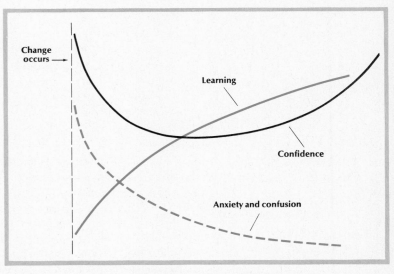

Fig. 28-4   *All phases of management are dynamically interrelated.*

a spell of stable productivity following a siege of readjustment. Although we anticipate recurring need for change in management design, the wise manager knows that there are personal and economic tolerance limits to the frequency of change.

CONCLUSION: NEED FOR SYNTHESIS

The study of any complex subject like management must be divided into parts and each must be examined carefully. We have followed this pattern by devoting separate parts of the book to organizing, planning, leading, and controlling. We considered the nature and importance of each of these processes, discussed the elements of each, covered problems in the field typically confronting a manager, and suggested possible ways of dealing with these problems. This analytical approach is more than a pedagogical device. It can be used directly by managers because they frequently encounter difficulties of the same scope as the subdivisions (chapters) of our discussion.

Nevertheless, the interdependence of the parts of the book has been frequently stressed. In the first chapter we singled out a manager's role in external and internal integration. The present chapter goes even further. Master strategy, which expresses a firm's attempt to integrate with its environment, has been related to management design, which expresses the firm's internal integration. We have focused especially on how a manager can design structures that are internally coherent and also suited to the company's strategy. Thus we have turned from analysis to synthesis.

A manager must be prepared either to redesign his management systems to support new developments in his strategy, or he must regard his existing management design as a limiting factor in selecting new strategy. Because shifts in the environment occur so rapidly, most managers set their strategy first and then undertake the difficult task of shaping a management design to match it. This kind of synthesis calls for a high order of sophistication and competence.

FOR CLASS DISCUSSION

Questions

1) The text emphasizes the importance of recognizing the potential impact of a change in one managerial process (for example, planning or organizing) on other elements of the process (for example, leadership or control). Who should be given the responsibility for considering these potential impacts and for seeking a coherent, whole management design?

2) Consider a company that has made extensive use of formal standing plans as part of a long-accepted strategy. Assume the company decides to make a major shift in strategy. In what ways may the network of standing plans, developed for the old strategy (1) *aid,* and/or (2) present problems, in shifting to the new strategy?

3) Many corporations are diversifying to the point where the differences in product/market mix within a single firm may be great. Would it be possible for one company to have some divisions that are in the stable category, while others are in the regulated flexibility and adaptive categories? When would such a situation prove most troublesome to central management?

4) Discuss what you see as the major job specifications and man specifications for liaison staff or "diplomatic corps" described on page 703.

5) One means of offering new challenges to managers besides those provided by promotion is through reassignment, on a horizontal basis, to a different part of the company. In what ways would the existence of substantially different designs in different divisions affect this horizontal movement?

6) To what extent may serious personnel problems arise as a company grows in size and finds it necessary to shift its strategy from skimming new products and markets to a strategy of profitability servicing more mature products and markets? How might these problems be dealt with?

7) In what ways might longer-range planning assist central management in dealing with design changes arising from changes in strategy?

8) From the enterprises you encounter in your daily life, pick an example of each of the technology types described in this chapter —stable, regulated flexibility, and adaptive. For each of these examples check what you know of their management design against Table 28–1. What reasons do you think explain any differences between the features listed in Table 28–1 and those in your examples?

Cases

For cases involving issues covered in this chapter, see especially the following. Particularly relevant questions are listed after each case.

FOR FURTHER READING

Burns, T., and G.M. Stalker, *The Management of Innovation,* 2nd ed. London: Tavistock Publications Limited, 1966 (U.S. distributor, Barnes & Noble, Inc., New York). *Perceptive sociological study of management response to change in strategy of British electronic firms.*

Chandler, A.D., *Strategy and Structure.* Cambridge, Mass.: M.I.T. Press, 1962. *Pioneering historical study.*

Katz, R.L., *Cases and Concepts in Corporate Strategy.* Englewood Cliffs, N.J.: Prentice-Hall, Inc., 1970, pp. 501–16. *Compares strategy and structure by stages of company growth.*

Morse, J.J., and J.W. Lorsch, "Beyond Theory Y." *Harvard Business Review,* May 1970. *Explains need to adjust management design to industry technology.*

Perrow, C., *Organizational Analysis: A Sociological View.* Belmont, Calif.: Wadsworth Publishing Company, 1970, Chap. 3. *A sociologist relates structure and technology; insightful, written in nontechnical language.*

Chapter Twenty-nine

International Management

CULTURE AND THE TRANSFER OF MANAGEMENT KNOW-HOW

A growing number of companies based in the United States are conducting operations abroad. Foreign-based companies, likewise, are opening branches in the United States or buying a controlling interest in an already established local company. Many more firms in all parts of the world exchange technical and management know-how. Day by day the pace of this internationalization is accelerating.

Joining the international movement immediately leads to questions about managing in different cultures.[1] Will the practices that work well here be equally effective where the customs, values, and patterns of life differ from ours? Are our management concepts "exportable"? Likewise, can we use ideas in the United States that work well in, say, Japan?

This chapter focuses on underlying problems of transferring United States management practice abroad. To get to the crux of the matter we ask: *What values and beliefs underlie normative United States management ideas?* We are especially interested in those assumed norms that differ significantly from values or beliefs prevailing in an "importing" country.

[1] This analysis of international management is adapted from "Is Management Exportable?" by William H. Newman, *Columbia Journal of World Business*, January-February 1970. Copyright 1970 by the Trustees of Columbia University in the City of New York. A further discussion of this topic can be found in *Management in an International Context*, eds. Joseph L. Massie and Jan Luytjes (New York: Harper & Row, 1972).

This concentration on cultural assumptions underlying management concepts in the United States has a second value here: it gives us a different perspective on the managerial concepts we have examined throughout the book.[2]

Perhaps the norms in a location where action is to occur will be close enough to those in the United States to create no problem of applicability. Occasionally the gap on one or two crucial points is large enough to play havoc with a beautiful managerial plan. Such difficulties need not lead us to abandon the attempt to utilize United States management know-how abroad or to transfer foreign ideas to the United States. Sophisticated and imaginative analysis can, and often does, lead to selective adaptation.

To conserve space, we have discussed only United States attitudes and values that differ from norms prevailing in one or more other countries and that consequently have direct relevance to studies of comparative management. Note that we are not trying to describe actual United States behavior or culture; instead we seek to state premises on which United States management concepts are based. Contrasting foreign attitudes and values will be indicated primarily to give perspective on the United States norm, but a full discussion of viewpoints that are held in other countries is far beyond the scope of a single chapter. Managerial concepts directly affected by the selected attitudes and values will be noted. These references also will be brief because the concepts have been examined in earlier chapters. Nevertheless, if this discussion is to have any operational value, it is important to relate cultural differences to specific facets of the managerial process.

For convenience in writing, ideas are presented under six general headings:

1) "Master of Destiny" Viewpoint.
2) Independent Enterprise—The Instrument for Social Action.
3) Personnel Selection on Merit.
4) Decisions Based on Objective Analysis.
5) Wide Sharing in Decision-Making.
6) Never-ending Quest for Improvement.

These are not mutually exclusive compartments, and the sequence is unimportant.

"MASTER OF DESTINY" VIEWPOINT

Underlying much of United States management thought is a belief that people can substantially influence the future. In fact, we are perhaps

[2]The special problems of central management in multinational companies are not discussed. Instead our concern here is with effective management within the respective countries. This is a broader issue of interest to locally managed firms as well as to multinational companies.

overly optimistic about our ability to control our own destiny. A familiar saying is, "Where there's a will, there's a way," and in a somewhat lighter vein, "Every day we do difficult things; the impossible just takes a little longer." This "master of destiny" viewpoint, however, involves more than mere cockiness; it is related to several other beliefs and values.

Confident belief in self-determination. The typical American believes that he exercises considerable choice in what he does and through this in what happens to him. To be sure, he may run into "bad luck," but even here he is inclined to place at least part of the blame on himself.

This belief in self-determination is in sharp contrast to a fatalistic viewpoint found in some Moslem countries. It also differs from a mystical view that holds that events are determined by perhaps the capricious influence of spirits that must be appeased. Whatever the explanation, the critical issue is whether a person believes that events will occur regardless of what he does, or whether he shares with the American the belief that he can help shape future events.

Realistic cost-benefit analysis of objectives. An important qualification in this self-determination concept is that an individual should be "realistic" in his aspirations. We scoff at the Peer Gynts and the Don Quixotes by saying that they engaged in flights of fancy. Of course, opinions may differ on what undertakings are reasonable, and in the business world we gather large quantities of data to assist us in predicting the feasibility of a proposal. In addition to making sure that a proposed action is possible, a balancing of costs versus benefits is considered to be a part of prudent behavior.

In other words, an American's belief in his mastery of his own destiny does not mean that he will endorse all sorts of idealistic schemes, such as are advanced in many reform movements throughout the world. Instead, a strong dose of pragmatic realism qualifies the objectives that are undertaken.

Results come from persistent hard work. Both our lore and our experience underscore the necessity for hard work if objectives are to be achieved. Even if one does not accept the Puritan ethic that hard work is a virtue in itself, there is a strong belief that persistent, purposeful effort

Fig. 29-1 A firm belief that good results will follow from hard work pervades American thought about management.

is necessary to achieve high goals. Hard work is not considered to be the only requisite for success; wisdom and luck also play their part. Nevertheless, the feeling is that without hard work a person is not only unlikely to achieve his objectives, but also that any expectation of achieving them under these circumstances is unjustified.

This belief in the efficacy of hard work is by no means worldwide. Sometimes a fatalistic viewpoint makes hard work seem futile. In other instances, one needs merely to curry the favor of the right man, and in still other situations hard work is unmanly.

Fulfilling commitments is an ethical obligation. The American manager believes he is master of his own destiny partly because he and those he works with feel that commitments should be honored. A commitment to deliver materials, to fix a machine, or to publicize a new product is not a mere statement of intention, it is a moral obligation. It is like honesty; a man "keeps his word." In fact, of course, a man may be prevented from fulfilling his contract by external forces, and adjustments are made. Nevertheless, the underlying social fabric contains a myriad of relationships in which it is presumed that men will do what they say they will.

In some parts of the world it is considered impolite to openly refuse to do something that has been requested by another person, and so the "yes" that a Westerner takes as a commitment may be in reality little more than friendly conversation. In other societies, it is understood that today's commitment may be superseded by a conflicting request received tomorrow, especially if that request comes from a highly influential person. In still other situations, agreements merely signify intention and have little relevance to capacity to carry out a promise; as long as the person tries to perform he feels no pangs of conscience or makes no special effort if he is unable to fulfill the agreement. Obviously, in these latter circumstances, uncertainty is greatly increased especially for new undertakings.

Time is a crucial aspect of performance. To an American *when* things occur is important. Effective use of one's own time and effective scheduling of independent activities requires a precise timing. This concern with precise time is reflected in our daily lives; for a television program to start three minutes later than announced is a national disgrace.

Virtually all studies of comparative management have noted the wide variation in attitude toward time in various cultures. Part of the charm of our Latin American friends arises from their relaxed view of the clock and the calendar. People in many other parts of the world fail to understand why the normal rhythms of life should be twisted to fit a schedule.

Influence of Beliefs on Management Processes

The preceding paragraphs have identified a cluster of attitudes and beliefs that, consciously or unconsciously, serve as underlying premises for United States management concepts. This first cluster relates to the confidence we Americans have about our ability to significantly affect the future. The feeling is not one of complete mastery over our own destiny; we believe that aspirations should be subjected to feasibility and cost-benefit analysis. Also we believe that hard work and respect for commitments and for time are vital components in shaping the future. Nevertheless, within these constraints the assumption is that managers can determine to a large degree the future fruits of their labors.

These beliefs have a profound effect on United States management concepts that are considered practical. Here are a few examples. *Planning*, and especially long-range planning, is worth a substantial investment of energy only because of a confidence that it will really make a difference in what happens. In addition, the degree of detailed scheduling and other specific arrangements that United States managers consider essential if plans are to become more than vague aspirations is justified only if a network of realistic, firm commitments can be established.

Similarly, our enthusiasm for *decentralization* rests on the assumption that men down the line share similar mores regarding self-determination, hard work, morality of commitments, and the significance of time. Further, if such mores prevail, then *supervision* can be general and consultative instead of close and disciplinarian. Also, *control* can become constructive feedback rather than suspicious verification.

As we shall see in the following pages, several conditions in addition to those already discussed contribute to the cultural background of United States management concepts. However, when we contemplate at least the more extreme forms of fatalism, unrealism, reliance on luck, vagueness of commitment, and preference for *mañana*, we easily recognize that the beliefs identified in this section have a substantial bearing on the viability of the American view of "good management practice."

INDEPENDENT ENTERPRISE: THE INSTRUMENT FOR SOCIAL ACTION

Most United States management concepts presume that joint action will be taken through an independent enterprise. In fact, a substantial part of our total business activity, both profit and nonprofit, is legally done by corporations. The well-recognized advantages of corporations include continuity of life, ability to assemble capital, limited liabilities for the owners, and the like. Less often mentioned is the managerial role of the corporation. Actually, the organization need not operate legally as a corporation; the crucial point for our discussion here is that it functions as an independent enterprise, whatever its legal status. Our strong, but usually unstated, belief is that enterprises having the characteristics outlined in the following paragraphs are the most effective instruments for the conduct of business.

Vitality of enterprises as separate social institutions. Faced with a task that requires the efforts of several people over a period of time, we "organize"—we set up an enterprise. The size and nature of the enterprise depends upon the mission. But regardless of scope, it will quickly take on an entity of its own. It will be viewed as an institution separate from its executives and other employees. Such enterprises are believed to have a vitality and a means for coordinative action that people acting merely as individuals cannot have.

This concept of a whole array of man-made distinct enterprises is not understood in all cultures. Frequently an undertaking is inseparable from the individual who initiates the action; in fact, one hundred years ago this was the prevailing attitude in our country. In other instances, major undertakings are usually associated with the church, the government, or perhaps a divine ruler. Here again, the feelings about the undertaking are intermingled with attitudes toward a personality, religion, or the state. History provides us with eloquent examples of what may be accomplished under a chauvinistic ruler or a powerful religion. United States management thought, in contrast, pins its faith on separate enterprises created to accomplish distinctive purposes.

Personal obligation to serve the enterprise. For the enterprise system to work well, all employees, and especially executives, must feel a strong obligation to do their respective parts in pursuing the mission. We assume, and in fact the mores of American society support the assumption, that acceptance of employment implies a willingness to be loyal to the company. Success of the enterprise takes priority over purely personal preferences and social obligations to friends. The practical manager realizes, of course, that there are extremes beyond which such loyalty cannot be stretched. Nevertheless, a primary commitment to the good of the enterprise is an underlying premise.

The concept of primary obligation to the enterprise runs into serious difficulty in societies in which each individual has an obligation to help his family, a "family" that often includes distant relatives. In a few cultures even doing favors for one's friends takes priority over what is effective for the enterprise. This question of first loyalty can affect a whole array of activities from employment to the extension of credit or use of company property. The issues may be quite subtle; for instance, many Latin Americans feel that they cannot rely upon a person unless they have a *simpatico* relationship with him. The result is that key transactions are likely to be influenced more by friendship than by economic analysis.

This association between the enterprise and an employee can be terminated by either party. Although Americans feel keenly about the obligation of an employee to his company, there is no stigma attached to terminating the relationship. Perhaps as a result of the American tradition of rugged individualism, we have a common saying, "If you don't like it, you can always quit," and people occasionally do quit. Contrariwise, the employer has an implied privilege of discharging an employee. Even though termination of employment is surrounded in practice by formal and informal constraints, the initial premise is that employment is a mutually acceptable contract. As long as the contract is in effect it carries with it the loyalty obligation discussed above. However, the system achieves flexibility by permitting honorable withdrawal.

This attitude toward terminating employment differs most noticeably from the Japanese concept of lifetime employment. In other countries switching employment is viewed at least with suspicion. In those countries where employment is closely tied in with personal friendship, changing jobs may have all the emotional aspects of breaking a personal friendship. The central issue is whether dependability, loyalty, and commitment can be a temporary and somewhat unemotional affair. The United States attitude is that it can be.

Respect for the total management system is expected. Americans expect an enterprise of any size to develop its own codes of behavior that are specifically designed to help achieve its mission. Objectives, policies, procedures, budgets, programs, organization structure, reports-flow, appraisal criteria, and a variety of other management tools are likely to be stated explicitly. People affected by such instruments often participate in their formulation and revision. Nevertheless, once they are established we assume they will be observed. Furthermore, changes in this management system that are designed to cope with new situations are considered a normal part of life. Basically, the assumption is that an effective enterprise will require a substantial managerial system and that executives and other employees will treat such system as a normal and necessary part of their corporate life.

In societies where both internal and external actions are often done as a favor to someone, company plans and regulations are inevitably pushed into a minor position. In fact, an attempt to superimpose a rationally designed system on top of an informal one based on personal favors will add to, rather than lessen, the confusion. Similarly, the Arab whose long traditions of hospitality require him to meet visitors personally whenever they appear, may find formalized work schedules and communication systems more trouble than they are worth.

Avoidance of divided interest. Because it is likely to be a source of potential trouble, special mention should be made of the American objection to divided interest. The feeling is that an executive should never permit himself to get in a situation where his sole consideration in any specific transaction is other than what is best for his company. Thus most executives work for only one company at a time, and if they should have financial or other interests in an outside company, they are expected to withdraw from any transaction involving their employer and the outside company. In this area Americans take very seriously the maxim that "A man cannot serve two masters well."

The receiving of gifts and what we would call "bribery" are customary in some countries. In fact, informal but nonetheless well-defined guides for the sharing of such contributions with other members of the organization often exist. We are familiar with paying sales commissions or finders' fees to *third* parties, but the idea of making personal contributions to individuals who represent an enterprise violates our sense of undivided loyalty and obligation. If corruption occurs and if individuals act on the basis of payoffs rather than in the best interests of their enterprise various results will follow: *planning* becomes difficult because unpredictable obstacles often arise; *organization* becomes difficult because one division cannot depend on the other, and the number of points at which a transaction can be held up or subverted must be minimized; managers must introduce frequent *controls* (perhaps even personal inspections) to get any reliable information of what actually transpires. United States management practice is simply not designed to deal with this kind of a situation.

The Enterprise Concept and Management Processes

In summary, the independent enterprise concept discussed in the preceding paragraphs provides an adaptable and effective mechanism for directing coordinated effort to specific missions. If the concept is to be workable, however, a strong sense of commitment and loyalty to the venture must exist. American management theory rests on the assumption that each member of an organization will give his primary efforts to performing his assigned tasks in the interests of that organization. A managerial system is recognized as necessary, and during his tenure as a member of the organization the individual expects to perform his role according to this system.

Implied in this concept is that helping one's family and friends will be subordinated. The belief is that such personal considerations should be given *no* weight in deciding on action for the enterprise (and family and friends recognize that these are the rules of the game). Moreover, in this scheme bribery of any sort is untenable.

With this unified and dependable effort presumed in the enterprise concept, *organization* can safely be elaborated. Duties can be divided up and delegated even though they are interdependent; decentralization can be extended without fear of personal, selfish abuse; sophisticated arrangements for staff advice become possible. Because both dependability and predictability are increased, managers in their planning can extend the time-span of their plans and can afford more detailed analysis of methods and schedules.

Leadership in the independent enterprise still requires inspiring associates, but the focus of leadership shifts from personality or family to the accomplishment of a mission. An individual works for a cause, not to do a favor for a close friend. The entire *control* process is affected by the assumption of loyalty and undivided interest. Aside from routine audits to verify that this assumption is being observed, control can be devoted to assessing progress, difficulties, and new opportunities; this information can be fed back to a variety of individuals who are already motivated to use such data for the good of the enterprise.

To avoid misunderstanding, let us keep the aim of this chapter in mind. We are not trying to describe universal American behavior. Instances of bribery and divided interest do occur in the United States; friendship may influence the placing of a big order. Nevertheless, the fact that bribery is headline news indicates that a social norm has been violated. In addition, the idea that a man owes first allegiance to his enterprise is so common that it is rarely stated.

The point here is that this concept of a deliberately designed, independent enterprise—an enterprise that receives loyalty and willingness to conform to its managerial system—is a major and underlying idea upon which many United States management concepts rest.

PERSONNEL SELECTION ON MERIT

A third cardinal belief on which United States management concepts are based is that individuals should be placed in jobs solely because they are the best-qualified person available. This idea is consistent with the tenet that decisions should be made objectively for the maximum good of the enterprise. Further analysis will enable us to catch some of the implications and difficulties in applying this concept.

Appoint the best man available for the specific job. The presumption is that we start with the needs of the enterprise. The mission, policies, and other plans call for a particular array of activities; these activities are then organized into jobs; man-specifications based on the duties of each job are prepared, and these specifications should be used in selecting a man to fill each post. Furthermore, executives who select men to fill positions are expected to make a diligent search of all likely sources of candidates; if well-qualified persons are not readily available this search should extend to all divisions of the enterprise as well as to outside sources.

Clearly implied in the preceding statement is the negative norm that family connections, friendship, and sponsorship by an influential person should not be considered. Only rarely is the belief carried to the point where relatives and friends are ineligible for consideration; typically they will be considered on their merits along with everyone else. In societies where each person has a moral responsibility for his immediate family and perhaps his extended family, or in other societies where the exchange of personal favors is an integral part of the social structure, these American beliefs about how appointments should be made generate serious difficulties.

Appointment on merit need not imply organizational inflexibility. For instance, if a particular position is being used for training purposes, the duties and the man-specifications will differ from those needed for performance of the short-run operations. In addition, if suitable candidates are unavailable for a position as conceived, the organization should be redesigned to match the kind of people that can be employed. But note that the flexibilities are introduced to promote the interests of the enterprise, not as a concession to personal indulgence.

Remove "second-raters." The belief just described extends beyond the initial appointment. The underlying assumption is that if a man is not continuing to perform his job well he should be replaced by someone who will. The cost to the enterprise of poor performance, especially of executives, is far greater than a man's salary; his poor performance complicates the task of people whose work interrelates with his and may undermine the effectiveness of the entire operation.

The need for continuing high performance is conspicuous in competitive team sports. One weak member can upset the effectiveness of his entire team. Because winning is more important than the feelings of the particular member, there is no question that he should be replaced if a better man is available.

In a number of countries the removal of a man from a recognized position involves so much loss of prestige that the action is rarely taken. This is particularly true when the appointment was made initially on the basis of family or friendship. United States business, also, is not indifferent to the pain that may result from the removal of a man from his job, especially if that man in the past has rendered distinctive service. However, the feeling is that such personal obligations to a man can be met by job transfer, early retirement, dismissal compensation, or the like. But such personal recompense simply makes easier the application of the idea that a man is not entitled to remain in a position where he blocks effective performance.

No limit to upward mobility. The American tradition that a man born in a log cabin has the opportunity to become President of his country has its counterpart in business where an office boy may rise to become company president. The stress is not so much on a classless

Fig. 29-2 American managers do not have much patience with second-raters. If a person is not contributing to the success of the organization, he will be replaced by someone who can get the job done.

society as on a mobile, open society. There may be a managerial elite (and an intellectual elite, artistic elite, and so on) but one achieves position in a group by personal merit rather than by birth.

Open access to all levels of management does, of course, run counter to ideas of social class that prevail in a number of countries. Fortunately, rigid class systems appear to be rapidly breaking down. Education has become the primary vehicle for achieving mobility. Even on this count, the American ethic stresses ability rather than formal education; we still have company presidents who are self-educated men.

An awkward issue for us is whether inherited ownership entitles a man to be a high executive in a company. If he is the sole owner, then our ideas about private property would permit him to indulge in self-aggrandizement. However, United States management thought has developed on the concept that an enterprise is independent of its owners, as we mentioned earlier. In fact, very rarely does a medium or a large-sized company have a sole owner. In addition, a medium or large enterprise cannot be capricious in dealing with its obligations to other interest groups, and so we quickly move over to concepts of professional management of independent enterprises. Part ownership may well affect a man's motivation and availability and these obviously should be included among the factors considered in appointing executives. In other words, the theory is that ownership does not entitle a man to a position in the company, but insofar as ownership stimulates his desire to contribute, it does receive indirect consideration.

Men should be free to move horizontally. This is simply an endorsement of the idea that horizontal movement is normal and not necessarily bad. It fits in with the idea that a man is not assured of life-tenure in a given position. The general belief is that movement, say, every three to five years, from one position to another—including the possibility of moving from line to staff and vice versa—is stimulating for the individual and encourages flexibility in company operations. We often think of these movements as progressions to increasing responsibility, but many moves are merely adjustments to changing conditions. In companies where horizontal transfers are common practice (IBM executives often say that the company's initials stand for "I've been moved"), removal of men who are in spots where they are no longer giving top performance involves less embarrassment.

Transfers of men to other companies is also acceptable if the new post a man takes is clearly more attractive than what his previous employer can offer. No one likes to lose a well-trained man and his present employer will probably point out the advantages of staying where he already knows the intricacies of company activity. On the other hand, the view that a man is entitled to move where his talents will be most productive has wide acceptance. Such tolerance of inter-company mobility is consistent with an attitude that executives perform a "professional" service. But note that the possibility or actuality of such transfers in no way diminishes the obligation of the executive to give highly loyal service to the enterprise for which he is currently working.

The kind of mobility just described does not readily fit into all cultures. Where appointments are based on highly personal relationships, such a movement from job to job is untenable. Also, where the holding of particular positions is essential to a man's status, horizontal movement is impeded. In countries like Japan, where for many years loyalty to a single company has been considered an important aspect of personal integrity, the idea of bettering oneself by transferring to another company is regarded by many as a deficiency in moral character.

Authority of position is compatible with egalitarian principles. In the American view, executive selection on the basis of merit bears directly on the acceptance and use of authority. Our egalitarian tradition holds that the next man is "no better than I am." Neither noble birth nor advanced age bestow on an individual the right to tell other people what they should do. Nevertheless, the need for authority in a complex, interdependent operation is clearly recognized. A way out of this dilemma is to attach such authority as the system may require to various positions and then to place people in those positions on the basis of their ability. Under these conditions, authority is not the personal prerogative of a particular individual (and this satisfies our egalitarian precept). Instead, it arises from the needs of an enterprise and is exercised by people objectively selected.[3]

Many foreign countries are not bothered by egalitarian principles and for them this last point is not important. Nevertheless, an analogous problem may exist. It is quite possible that the authority figures in a given society will not correspond with the authority allocation necessary for effective operation of independent enterprises. In such circumstances, some means of reconciling recognized authority and selection of executives will have to be worked out.

Selection on Merit and Management Processes

The preceding discussion of executive selection with its emphasis on picking the best-qualified men for vacancies, keeping them there only as long as they perform effectively, and encouraging vertical and horizontal mobility has stressed *executive competence*. More specific policies and

[3]The sociological observation that authority exists only to the extent that people are willing to recognize it is, of course, true, but is irrelevant to the point made above. Here our subject is the beliefs on which United States management concepts are based. As already pointed out, we make the assumption that in joining an organization (accepting employment) the individual accepts the necessity to become part of the enterprise system. He has a wide "zone of acceptance" and expects the enterprise to provide authoritative direction which is vital for coordinated action. The behavioral scientists may wish to make studies of when these assumptions do not hold. To date, the assumptions stated above have been sufficiently valid to make the management concepts viable.

techniques dealing with key personnel will, of course, be necessary. Nevertheless, such plans for key personnel will be strongly conditioned by the basic premises we have just outlined.

Another highly important consequence of this approach to personnel selection is its effect on *motivation*. The presumption is that attaining and holding a key position requires high performance; poor performance—regardless of one's birth or friends—leads to removal from "the first team."[4] This reward and penalty scheme is believed by Americans to be one of the strongest motivators of executives. Contrariwise, because the mores call for promotion on merit, serious damage to morale arises if attractive positions are filled on any other basis.

The attitudes and premises set forth in this section clearly imply that *organization* precedes personnel selection. The argument rests on a higher value attached to a viable, efficient enterprise than to personal friendship or to hereditary class. Organization structure is treated as the handmaiden of strategy, and personnel are selected on the basis of that structure. Obviously, the structure must be one for which staffing is possible, and if we already possess unique talent we may modify the organization so that the enterprise takes full advantage of its assets. But these are only qualifications, and they do not alter the value scale or the basic approach. If we did reverse the values and try to organize so as to provide maximum employment for friends and relatives, a vastly different structure would emerge.

Similarly, selection of personnel on merit has an impact on the types of *control* that are needed. With the stress laid on competent people who are motivated to carry out assigned tasks, control points shift from detailed checks of work-in-process to measurement of results. Furthermore, because evaluation of merit becomes a vital aspect of the entire management conception, attention is focused on making this evaluation as comprehensive, objective, and fair as possible.

DECISIONS BASED ON OBJECTIVE ANALYSIS

The high regard with which Americans view science is reflected in our approach to management. Although few managerial actions can be "scientific" in a strict sense of the word, we do have a strong cultural belief that decisions should be based on objective analysis of facts. This view significantly influences the nature of data obtained and the way these facts are communicated throughout the organization. Such attitudes

[4]High performance in one job does not necessarily qualify a man for promotion to a more responsible job; the qualities needed in the larger job may differ significantly from those needed in the subordinate position. Consequently, promotion cannot be purely a reward. Even so, sufficient overlap in job requirements is usually present to make first-class performance on past jobs a requisite for consideration for promotion.

about the handling of business information are by no means fully accepted throughout the world.

Factual, rational support for decisions. Most important business decisions involve substantial inputs of judgment, and often these judgments are based on intuitive feelings. The United States norm is that the entirely intuitive aspects of decision should be reduced to a minimum consistent with timely action. This implies that (1) considerable effort will be devoted to assembling all the relevant information and (2) that a rational explanation based on this information will be developed for each decision. The entire decision-making process need not be fully rational; creative ideas arise from many sources, and insights may be intuitive. Nevertheless, before becoming final each decision should be tested against tough, factual, rational analysis.

For many decisions the amount of raw data that is relevant far exceeds the capacity of a single individual to observe and appraise. Consequently, the executive who is making the decision must rely upon other people in his organization to provide an appropriate synthesis of batches of data. Sometimes this synthesis is expressed in terms of a policy or a planning premise; often it is a conclusion or an estimate prepared for the specific problem. Objective analysis, then, requires that the decision-maker, as a normal practice, consult all of the people who can contribute relevant, summarized information.

A factual, rational analysis of decisions is not made in some countries for one or more of the following reasons. First, personal judgment of a key executive may be the basis for a decision, and any attempt to explain it would be interpreted as a lack of confidence in the executive's judgment—by the executive himself and by others. Second, the use of "hard data" may not be customary; instead, decisions are expressions of wisdom and/or beauty that might become sullied by controversial detailed information. Third, it may be inappropriate for a senior executive to consult, at least personally, about matters on which he is already presumed to be wise. In such situations, an aura or mystique replaces objective analysis.

Integrity of data. If data are to play a key part in decision-making they must be reliable. Americans simply assume that basic data will be accurately and promptly recorded, and any dishonesty in reporting such information is considered adequate cause for the dismissal of the person doing so. In fact, we make such a fetish of having *the* correct figure that we may delay reports pending final verification, and the economist's concept that cost summaries will differ for various purposes is often viewed as a bit immoral. Of course, many estimates are used, but these should be scrupulously labeled as such. Clearly the provision of accurate data is considered a matter of personal integrity.

In other countries precise, accurate data may not be so highly valued. It is not uncommon to keep two or three sets of financial books so that reports submitted for tax purposes differ from those used to support a bank loan. This opens the way for juggling figures for other purposes. Also, the educational and cultural background of clerks may not have stressed accuracy. An added difficulty is that the tools for measuring market and economic phenomena may be rudimentary or nonexistent. The result is that for some decisions the kind of information the American executive takes for granted simply does not exist.

Open availability of data. The prevailing United States belief is that company information should be readily available to anyone who can use it to perform his work more effectively. The era of secrecy ended about fifty years ago. Today, a well-designed information system channels reports to all sorts of people on a regular basis. In addition, bureaucratic withholding of information to gain internal power is frowned upon. Instead, there is a general belief—often explicitly stated—that individuals needing information should go directly to its sources and are not required to go through hierarchical channels. The underlying belief is that benefits of ready availability of pertinent information far outweigh the embarrassment that occurs when a competitor occasionally learns a bit more than you wish he knew.

This idea of an open flow of data within a company contrasts sharply with the way information is handled in some foreign countries. Sometimes a tradition of secrecy demands that departmental information be revealed only to senior executives and always through hierarchical channels (in the absence of hard, objective data such a communication flow opens the way for considerable editing of the information that is passed along). In other circumstances where the internal relationships are on a highly personal, nonobjective basis communication is also personalized. An executive trusts the information only if he receives it from someone with whom he is *simpático* and with whom he has a continuing personal relationship. Even here there may be reluctance to pass along information that will hurt the other person. Finally, if a feeling prevails that most people in the organization are incompetent to handle any information except that which relates to their immediate task, availability of data is often considered wasteful, if not dangerous.

Frank expression of facts and judgments. Objective analysis in a complicated organization requires not only the availability of data; experts in various areas must be encouraged to present information and judgments that they believe are relevant. Each man is expected to form his own opinion, which may or may not agree with that of his associates and his bosses, and in the American view he has an obligation to present such views even though they may not support a popular plan of action. "Experts" in this connection include anyone who has an intimate understanding of a phase of a problem, such as salesmen, foremen, or purchasing agents as well as staff specialists. Pros and cons exist for any problem, and these can be properly assessed only when each person who has something to contribute speaks his mind freely. The American feeling is that to withhold or to distort information is a form of negligence or dishonesty.

This frank presentation of one's views is expected to take place prior to the time a decision is made. As stressed earlier (pp. 716–17), once an official course of action has been laid out, each person is expected to pursue it with vigor, even though from his particular vantage point the plan may appear undesirable.

The frankness of expression espoused by Americans does not easily fit some cultures. Great deference to people in positions of power has become a normal manner of behavior in some societies, and for a person in a subordinate position to present information and particularly judgments that might not support the ideas of senior executives is unthinkable. A similar obstacle arises in Far Eastern cultures where politeness is valued above naked truth. Above all, one must not say something that embarrasses or shames another person; and where this attitude prevails we cannot expect to get the outspoken exchange of ideas described earlier.

Bearing of Objective Analysis on Management Processes

In summary, United States culture places high value on factual, rational support for decisions. Whatever the origin of plan, the executive who makes it official is expected to gather facts and expert opinions on the proposal and submit it to hard, objective analysis. Such analysis requires dependable data, and we place high value on complete and accurate information. Moreover, the data should be freely communicated to many spots throughout the organization; the complexity of group decision-making requires the interweaving of diverse information at various subsidiary decision points. Also essential is a willingness to express judgments candidly, even though they may be unpopular.

Such a "laying all the cards on the table" approach has a profound effect upon the process of *planning* in an enterprise. Only in this manner can a wide dispersion of data-gathering and analysis be reconciled with wise central decisions. Long-range planning, which must involve many divisions of an enterprise if it is to be effective, is inconceivable without objective analysis as described in this section. Likewise, sophisticated techniques of discounted cash-flow and operations research become metaphysical exercises without an underpinning of objective data.

Less direct but still significant are the effects on *organization*. For instance, requisites for decentralization include confidence in the communication system and in the evaluation techniques, both of which are built on objective data. In addition, much of our staff work rests on the presumption of a free exchange of reliable data. Dependable facts are even more essential for *control*.

Clearly, then, our basic cultural assumptions about the desirability of, and manner of obtaining, objective analysis are crucial to the workability of many United States management concepts.

WIDE SHARING IN DECISION-MAKING

A modern United States enterprise is not run like a "New England town meeting" where presumably all citizens participate in all decisions of the local government. Nevertheless, much of our management practice does reflect a belief in wide participation in decision-making.

This participation in the planning process occurs both horizontally and vertically. Previous discussion has already implied that *horizontal consultation is desirable*. Here, the word "horizontal" is used loosely to include anyone outside the channel of command regardless of his title or echelon. Generally speaking, a decision-maker will be expected to consult with anyone who has information or judgment that can contribute to the quality of the decision and also with people within the company who will be significantly affected by the decision. Several of the points already noted tend to create a situation where such consultation can be effective. Obligation to serve the enterprise, respect for the total managerial system including company objectives, and avoidance of divided interests—all improve the chances of receiving constructive advice. Selection of personnel on the basis of merit has a similar effect. In addition, the emphasis on objective, reliable data—and its general availability—improves the chances that consultation will be fruitful.

Vertical sharing in decision-making moves beyond consultation into various degrees of decentralization. We Americans have a strong belief that localized—in contrast to centralized—decisions will be better suited to the actual operating situation and also will be executed with more enthusiasm. In practice, of course, decentralization is subject to a variety of restraints, such as need for consistency or allocation of scarce resources; nevertheless, the initial presumption is in favor of decentralization and the burden of proof is on the person who wishes to centralize. Several related beliefs and values should be noted in this connection.

Growth potential of men is high. The United States emphasis on pushing decision-making down the line stems in part from a belief in the high potential ability of men at all levels of the organization. The assumption is that able men can be found; with the requisite training they will respond to increased responsibility. More than mental capacity is involved. These men should also have enough self-confidence to make decisions, and they should be willing to accept the consequences of their decisions.

Our universal education system (which carries about a third of our young men into college work) reflects this same belief that high potential ability is widespread throughout the population. Our tradition that sons will achieve a better station in life than their fathers lends additional support to this belief in growth possibilities.

Not every man is a potential genius, of course. Intellectual and emotional energy, physical health, competing desires, and similar factors place limits on the capacity of each individual. But in the design of our managerial systems such differences in maximum capacity of individuals are not serious. The important consideration is that, broadly speaking, potential ability continues to run ahead of opportunities to delegate, and this unused capacity makes expansion of the sharing in decision-making both possible and desirable.

Cultures outside the United States often give less support to the premise that high potential is widespread. Opportunities for rigorous formal education may be limited, and social attitudes may discourage acceptance of responsibility. Especially in developing countries, capacity to comprehend a unique and changing managerial system of a specific enterprise calls for a very high degree of perception, and flexibility in accepting enterprise goals is hard to grasp. For these and for similar reasons the implicit American assumption about the capacity of people to participate in decision-making may require modification.

Ambition to "get ahead" is good. The desire to improve one's lot—to "get ahead"—is taken for granted in United States management concepts. We assume that a man will strive to increase his financial rewards and his status relative to associates. With the important proviso that success in these terms is based on merit, our social norm is that ambition is normal and healthy and that lack of ambition is a sign of weakness.

This idea of getting ahead increases the desire to share in decision-making because such participation is one of the symbols of status. The greater a man's participation in decision-making, the more important is his job. In fact, the kinds of decisions that a man makes and/or influences is a key factor in deciding the salary he should receive. Therefore, a part of the whole value pattern is that the ambitious individual will seek an enlarged share in decision-making.

The line of thought just outlined clearly implies that competition

Fig. 29-3 A person who has no ambition to get ahead will not get much support from his co-workers or his superiors. Americans in general and American managers in particular respect and encourage those who continually strive for personal improvement.

for status within the enterprise will exist. In general, we Americans feel that competition stimulates high performance (in sports, in the economy, and elsewhere), and we even introduce competition into many of our pastimes to add zest to the experience. Internal competition in a company, however, may interfere with cooperative effort. To deal with this incompatibility between individual ambition and cooperation, a whole set of ground rules inevitably arise within each company. The rules seek to define when cooperation will best serve the company and how individual ambition should be expressed. The subtleties of these ground rules may be difficult for an outsider to detect, but they serve an essential function of directing ambition into constructive channels.

In many countries, personal ambition is not given as much encouragement nor as free rein as in the United States. The structure of society may be sufficiently stable (or governed by other criteria) so that attempting to improve one's own status is frowned upon. In cultures that stress politeness and great respect for other persons, competitive attitudes can lead to trouble. In these circumstances, the motivational aspects implicit in United States management concepts must be carefully examined. Clearly, the aggressive American who in a foreign country follows practices encouraged in the United States may find himself *persona non grata*.

Dignity of all types of work. Another attitude that facilitates a high degree of decentralization is respect for all kinds of work. If a man is to be given considerable leeway in accomplishing a particular mission, he must interest himself in all activities necessary to achieve his assigned goal. For example, if the job requires personally standing in front of an open-hearth furnace then the man is expected to stand there. The common expression is that a man must be "willing to get his hands dirty." The point is that a man must have respect for his task and must be willing to do whatever is necessary to get the job done.

This apparently simple idea runs into difficulty in countries where various kinds of work are accorded high or low status. In some extreme instances, a man with a college degree will not concern himself directly with problems on the shop floor because he sought his degree in order to remove himself from such problems. In other instances a man may think it is below his dignity to drive a car, compute a set of averages, or visit retail shops to observe consumer buying. Perhaps more serious than physical behavior is a mental attitude that considers certain kinds of work as unworthy of careful analysis and firm supervision (this might be selling, record-keeping, or physical production). Clearly, United States management practices have not been designed to deal with such attitudes.

Impact on Management Processes

Attitudes about sharing in decision-making have already been related to decentralization at several points throughout this section. The beliefs and values discussed will also affect management processes in a variety of other ways. For instance, both the role assigned to staff and the design of management information systems will be influenced by beliefs about growth potential of personnel and about their eagerness to participate in decision-making. In its departmentation, *organization* may also have to recognize feelings about respectable versus "dirty" work.

Similarly, in *planning*, the amount of detailed procedure and the specificity of objectives will be affected by assumptions regarding the ambitions and growth potential of middle-management personnel. The manner and closeness of *supervision* likewise will be influenced by one's attitude about the people supervised. *Control* mechanisms will vary both in the points of measurement and their frequency if assumptions regarding the ambition, growth potential, and dignity of work differ.

NEVER-ENDING QUEST FOR IMPROVEMENT

Perhaps because the United States has been subject to rapid social change during its relatively short history, or perhaps because a large part of the population stems from immigrants who came to the country with the avowed purpose of making social change, a relentless urge for improvement is part of the American cultural fabric. This attitude expresses itself in various forms that affect our managerial concepts.

Change is normal and necessary. With technological and social change going on all around us, we naturally expect it in our business activities. In fact, many people feel that anything new is progress. As with fashions, change per se is good; a familiar greeting to a friend is, "What's new?" Of course, the social and psychological forces resisting change are also present, and, especially where results can be measured quantitatively, the innovator may have to demonstrate that change is in fact progress. Nevertheless, a presumption that change is desirable forms parts of the background of our management concepts.

Two beliefs are associated with the desirability of change: (1) Bringing about change requires hard work and substantial inputs of initiative, many man-hours of planning, and perhaps capital investment; often painful social readjustment is necessary. (2) Participating in the change process is personally rewarding. It typically is tied up with a sense of self-fulfillment, social contribution, and influence.

The attitudes toward change just described contrast sharply with a high reverence for tradition found in some societies. In these cultures the values associated with practices that are centuries old must be respected. Not infrequently the power of a ruling group rests on the continuation of a stable structure, and here change is viewed at least with suspicion. Even in developing countries where the idea of change has acceptance, the work involved to bring it about may be unrecognized.

Obviously, a managerial system based on the premise that change is normal and desirable will not easily fit a situation in which change is frowned upon or not considered worth the effort needed to bring it about.

Any aspect of business is a legitimate target for improvement. One of Frederick Taylor's basic contributions to American management thought was that traditional management, in any part of a company, should be subjected to rigorous analysis. Change should not be limited to production methods and product design. Marketing, finance, the board of directors, and every other segment of a company should be examined periodically for the purpose of improving its effectiveness and reducing its cost. The presumption is that new ideas, changing environment, and internal development of the company itself will create opportunities for improvement. Consequently, a challenge of past arrangements should be encouraged.

This expectation of change and improvement does not mean that a company should be in a continuous state of ferment. A workable plan, just like a successful product, has to be used long enough to reap some benefits from its design. A military commander does not change his organization structure in the midst of a battle. The point merely is that no part of the business is exempt from reexamination from time to time.

This attitude that the desirability of change applies everywhere runs into snags in some countries. For instance, until recently the aura surrounding a British board of directors virtually precluded an analysis of its operation by an outsider. In other countries, where divisions of a company become, in effect, the private domain of their respective managers, change can be thwarted for long periods of time. An even more general difficulty in some societies is caused by the belief that the need for change reflects failure on somebody's part; consequently pride and dignity are at stake. This is in sharp contrast to the American practice of attributing changes to the foresight of "an alert and aggressive executive."

Results are what count. Accompanying the endorsement of change, United States management practices also reflect a strong pragmatic emphasis on results. We may endorse face-to-face communications, rational explanations, willingness to listen to suggestions, and the like, but in the end we are impressed with what produces the most effective results. Policies, procedures, budgets, and other management techniques are similarly regarded as means. Their value lies in the results they produce.

This emphasis on what really works in terms of results achieved is a pervasive social norm. It does not say that a manager is concerned only with profits at the end of the year. He may, and does, consider social costs. The point being made here is that whatever the goals may be, managerial processes should be designed for their achievement. The underlying doctrine is that a beautiful scheme should always be tested against the hard reality of how well it works in practice.

Such pragmatic emphasis is by no means universal. Some societies place much greater stress on symbols of office and flourish in execution than on final results. Some Latin American executives, for example, are highly skilled in logical and dialectic discussions—so much so that they may lose sight of the object around which an argument is centered. In the United States, the beauty of the argument will be measured in terms of the results it produces.

Evaluation is constructive. In the United States we have evaluations of many sorts—evaluation of school systems, of annual reports to stockholders, and the like. The idea that results should be evaluated is, of course, a corollary of the importance attached to results noted in the preceding paragraphs. It also fits closely with the stress on objective analysis discussed earlier (pp. 723–26) because an important source of information for future decisions is an accurate appraisal of past results.

Although we have the usual array of audits and cross-checks to ensure accuracy, the basic premise in management thought is that evaluation plays a constructive role. It provides a basis for special rewards and, more important, it provides feedback on progress being made to the people doing the work and to their supervisors. At a ball game we expect somebody to "keep score"—it's as simple as that.

Actually, in other cultures evaluation as we conceive of it proves to be difficult. To cite a specific instance, an American executive working in the Iranian government created considerable consternation when he asked for what he thought would be a routine report on work that he had assigned to a subordinate. Apparently the presumption was that having delegated the task he would not check up on it unless he had received a complaint about the work. Regular check-ups on progress clearly were not customary; the life of the executive was made easier when he simply assumed that the assignment would be accomplished. In some Far Eastern countries, evaluation is done in ways that avoid embarrassing specific individuals. Thus a sales contest involving the posting of individual results would be in bad taste because of the embarrassment to the people low on the list.

Impact of Quest for Change on Management Processes

This last group of beliefs underlying United States management concepts, like some of the others already discussed, are typically unstated in our management literature. A continuing quest for improvement is part of the American heritage. We regard change as normal and believe that there should be no sacred preserves exempt from the search for a better way. The viewpoint is pragmatic; we are interested in results, and we strongly endorse evaluations that assess progress toward such improvement.

The high value attached to improvement permeates much of our management thinking. Some writers, for instance, say that the major function of a manager is to be "an agent of change." Clearly, a primary reason for long-range *planning* is to ensure that the requisites for improvement and growth will be available when needed. In *organizing*, we establish special staff units to seek out opportunities for improvement (for example, research and development, industrial engineering, market research, operations research, corporate planning, and the like). Decentralization is espoused because it aids more rapid adjustment to new opportunities.

Similarly, *control* systems are designed not to maintain the *status quo* but to measure progress, to detect opportunities and obstacles that call for replanning, and to focus attention on moving ahead. Several United States firms operating in Europe, for instance, have grown not because their initial plans were wise, but because their control systems (and attitude toward change) enabled them to learn quickly from experience and to adjust to new inputs of observation.

In contrast, where change is greeted with great reluctance, where key aspects of a total system are beyond reproach, where the flourish of the effort is valued more than the end result, where control is confined to auditing for accuracy—or where any combination of these attitudes prevail—then United States management concepts should be used with caution.

CONCLUSION

The chief aim of this chapter has been to make explicit a variety of cultural premises upon which normative United States management concepts are based. Hopefully a quick review of headings and subheadings will highlight the picture that has been painted. In conclusion, a few general observations will help put the whole piece in perspective.

1) Attitudes and values affect managerial practices, as we have seen in the numerous examples cited. Consequently, when we wish to transfer an effective device from one culture to another, careful attention should be given to the underlying premises on which the managerial practice is based.

2) The preceding analysis, however, tends to exaggerate the difficulties of transfer. It compares United States premises with attitudes in many different countries, whereas in practice we typically are concerned with cultural differences between only two specific countries—the exporter and the importer.

3) Several approaches are available when cultural differences are significant: (1) Nontypical individuals may be sought in the importing country, persons who already have, or can acquire, the values necessary to make the imported technique work. This approach has been used by petroleum refineries located in nonindustrialized countries. (2) The imported technique can be modified to fit local conditions—for example, full communication and participation may be restricted to special groups, "slack" may be added to production schedules, control points may be added, novel incentives may be related to attendance or output, and the like. (3) Hybrids may be created. The imported technique may be applied only to part of an operation while the remaining activities are "subcontracted" to local *maestros* who follow local customs. (4) New, creative adaptations can be made. For example, American business budgeting is a substantial modification of British government budgets, and American staff concepts are adaptations of German military staff.

4) Perhaps most impressive is the very substantial body of managerial concepts that can be transferred. The deliberate emphasis in this chapter on differences should not overshadow (1) the universality of basic management processes in purposeful, cooperative endeavors, nor (2) the frequent—but not universal—usefulness of many managerial concepts in connection with these processes.

FOR CLASS DISCUSSION

Questions

1) Explain how the custom of giving gifts to people involved in a business relationship can interfere with the use of United States management concepts. How do you reconcile the practice of tipping with your answer? How do you distinguish between tipping and graft?

2) To what extent may changes in the United States during the last twenty to thirty years alter the general attitude toward the "master of destiny" viewpoint that has characterized United States management thought?

3) In some foreign countries workers feel a stronger obligation to their families than to the organization for which they work. What effect does this attitude toward obligation have on managerial practice? In the United States, Ralph Nader, the strong advocate of consumer interests, urges that "professional" obligation requires a person to report to public officials or to Mr. Nader's organization any action by one's employer that transgresses consumer interests. How would acceptance of this concept of obligation affect management practice?

4) In what ways may increased affluence and growth of consumer-goods industries in foreign countries lead these countries toward values and beliefs that are more like those prevailing in the United States? Which of the six categories listed on page 712 are most likely to be affected?

5) What attitudes and beliefs about the future underlie extensive use of long-range planning? Would you expect to find these attitudes and beliefs in Russia? Do you think that long-range planning will be more difficult in the future in Russia or in the United States?

6) In Chapter 6 we discussed the growing interest in the concept of "matrix management." Review this material and consider how the success of this practice may be influenced by the historical tendency of American managers to avoid divided interest.

7) List all the reasons mentioned in this chapter that lead toward centralization in foreign countries. Now assume that you manage the international operations of a pharmaceutical company and that you want to decentralize as much as possible. How would you try to overcome, or otherwise deal with, each of the reasons for centralizing contained in your list?

8) Do you see any current forces at work that may make United States attitudes toward "selection on merit" more difficult to follow than in the past? How may these forces affect companies in countries that typically have not shared American values on selection based on merit?

Cases

For cases involving issues covered in this chapter, see especially the following. Particularly relevant questions are listed after each case.

Trans-World Mutual Funds, Ltd. (p. 121), 8
Harrogate Asphalt Products, Ltd.—AR (p. 557), 13
Consolidated Instruments—A (p. 571), 5

FOR FURTHER READING

Boddewyn, J., *Comparative Management and Marketing.* Glenview, Ill.: Scott, Foresman & Company, 1969. *Scope and methods for comparative research in management.*

Granick, D., *The European Executive.* New York: Doubleday & Company, Inc., 1964. *Origins, education, and practices of European managers.*

Grosset, S., *Management: European and American Styles.* Belmont, Calif.: Wadsworth Publishing Company, 1970. *Clear summary of numerous studies relating to management on two continents.*

Haire, M., E.E. Ghiselli, and L.W. Porter, *Managerial Thinking: An International Study.* New York: John Wiley & Sons, Inc., 1966.

Comparisons of attitudes of managers in fourteen countries, based on unique questionnaire survey.

Harbison, F., and C.A. Myers, *Management in the Industrial World*. New York: McGraw-Hill Book Company, 1959. *Pioneering study comparing management as an economic resource, a system of authority, and a social class in twenty-three countries.*

Richman, B.M., *Soviet Management: With Significant American Comparisons*. Englewood Cliffs, N.J.: Prentice-Hall, Inc., 1964. *Focus is on work of Russian industry executives.*

Webber, R.A., *Culture and Management*. Homewood, Ill.: Richard D. Irwin, Inc., 1969. *Text and readings in comparative management.*

Yoshino, M., *Japan's Managerial System*. Cambridge, Mass.: M.I.T. Press, 1968. *Insightful analysis of external and internal elements in Japanese managerial practice.*

Index